Using Crises and Disasters as Opportunities for Innovation and Improvement

Saeed Siyal
School of Economics and Management, Beijing University of Chemical Technology, China

IGI Global
PUBLISHER of TIMELY KNOWLEDGE

A volume in the Advances in Public Policy and Administration (APPA) Book Series

Published in the United States of America by
IGI Global
Information Science Reference (an imprint of IGI Global)
701 E. Chocolate Avenue
Hershey PA, USA 17033
Tel: 717-533-8845
Fax: 717-533-8661
E-mail: cust@igi-global.com
Web site: http://www.igi-global.com

Library of Congress Cataloging-in-Publication Data

Names: Siyal, Saeed, 1989- editor.
Title: Using crises and disasters as opportunities for innovation and improvement / edited by: Saeed Siyal.
Description: Hershey, PA : Information Science Reference, [2023] | Includes bibliographical references and index. | Summary: "The objective of this Book Edit is to highlight the pandemic as a promise in terms of behaviors, challenges and opportunities which assist in the smooth operationalization as well as prove useful in promotion, growth, and development of the society and organizations. In this regard, this Book Edit invites novel research work of the scholars and researchers around the globe with focus on the pandemic as a promise and its role in society and organizations. Thus, the selected topic is very important in business, industry, management, academic, and economic value of the practitioners and academic institutions of all levels and those having their country-wide and international offices. This Book Edit will contribute through novel approaches and will provide implications for the managers and leaders of corporate sectors, MNCs and SMEs, academicians, academic institutions, social scientists, students, policy makers, government and non-government agencies and other related stakeholders to learn adapting and finding new solutions to the problems occurring from nature and circumstances"-- Provided by publisher.
Identifiers: LCCN 2023014954 (print) | LCCN 2023014955 (ebook) | ISBN 9781668495223 (hardcover) | ISBN 9781668495261 (paperback) | ISBN 9781668495230 (ebook)
Subjects: LCSH: Crisis management. | Emergency management. | Communication in crisis management. | Organizational change.
Classification: LCC HD49 .U56 2023 (print) | LCC HD49 (ebook) | DDC 658.4/77--dc23/eng/20230502
LC record available at https://lccn.loc.gov/2023014954
LC ebook record available at https://lccn.loc.gov/2023014955

This book is published in the IGI Global book series Advances in Public Policy and Administration (APPA) (ISSN: 2475-6644; eISSN: 2475-6652)

British Cataloguing in Publication Data
A Cataloguing in Publication record for this book is available from the British Library.

For electronic access to this publication, please contact: eresources@igi-global.com.

Advances in Public Policy and Administration (APPA) Book Series

ISSN:2475-6644
EISSN:2475-6652

Mission

Proper management of the public sphere is necessary in order to maintain order in modern society. Research developments in the field of public policy and administration can assist in uncovering the latest tools, practices, and methodologies for governing societies around the world.

The **Advances in Public Policy and Administration (APPA) Book Series** aims to publish scholarly publications focused on topics pertaining to the governance of the public domain. APPA's focus on timely topics relating to government, public funding, politics, public safety, policy, and law enforcement is particularly relevant to academicians, government officials, and upper-level students seeking the most up-to-date research in their field.

Coverage

- Government
- Law Enforcement
- Political Economy
- Politics
- Public Administration
- Public Funding
- Public Policy
- Resource allocation
- Urban Planning

IGI Global is currently accepting manuscripts for publication within this series. To submit a proposal for a volume in this series, please contact our Acquisition Editors at Acquisitions@igi-global.com or visit: http://www.igi-global.com/publish/.

The Advances in Public Policy and Administration (APPA) Book Series (ISSN 2475-6644) is published by IGI Global, 701 E. Chocolate Avenue, Hershey, PA 17033-1240, USA, www.igi-global.com. This series is composed of titles available for purchase individually; each title is edited to be contextually exclusive from any other title within the series. For pricing and ordering information please visit http://www.igi-global.com/book-series/advances-public-policy-administration/97862. Postmaster: Send all address changes to above address.

Titles in this Series

For a list of additional titles in this series, please visit: www.igi-global.com/book-series

Financial Evaluation and Risk Management of Infrastructure Projects
Kleopatra Petroutsatou (Aristotle University of Thessaloniki, Greece) and Constantin Zopounidis (Technical University of Crete, Greece & Audencia Business School, France)
Information Science Reference • copyright 2024 • 248pp • H/C (ISBN: 9781668477861) • US $225.00 (our price)

Cognitive Governance and the Historical Distortion of the Norm of Modern Development A Theory of Political Asymmetry
Renny Rueda (American University in the Emirates, United Arab Emirates)
Information Science Reference • copyright 2024 • 310pp • H/C (ISBN: 9781668497944) • US $215.00 (our price)

Policies, Practices, and Protocols for International Commercial Arbitration
Basheer Ahmed Mohammed Khan (Supreme Court of India Bar Association, India) and Kaushal Kishore (Supreme Court of India Bar Association, New Delhi, India)
Information Science Reference • copyright 2023 • 271pp • H/C (ISBN: 9781668440407) • US $225.00 (our price)

Governmental Power Market-Ing in the VU-CHAOS World
Kittisak Jermsittiparsert (University of City Island, Cyprus) Srirath Gohwong (Universitas Muhammadiyah Sidenreng Rappang, Indonesia) Shayut Pavapanunkul (Universitas Muhammadiyah Sidenreng Rappang, Indonesia) and Nasaran Mahittichatkul (Universitas Muhammadiyah Sidenreng Rappang, Indonesia)
Information Science Reference • copyright 2023 • 296pp • H/C (ISBN: 9781668472804) • US $205.00 (our price)

Historical and Political Analysis on Power Balances and Deglobalization
Emily Brynn Stacey (Rose State College, USA)
Information Science Reference • copyright 2023 • 253pp • H/C (ISBN: 9781668456330) • US $205.00 (our price)

Juvenile Justice in African and Western Criminal Justice Systems
Simeon Peter Sungi (United States International University-Africa, Kenya) George Rugaimukamu Kakoti (Tennessee State University, USA) and Deneil D. Christian (Tennessee State University, USA)
Information Science Reference • copyright 2024 • 300pp • H/C (ISBN: 9781668493434) • US $215.00 (our price)

Public Policy's Role in Achieving Sustainable Development Goals
Mahani Hamdan (Universiti Brunei Darussalam, Brunei) Muhammad Anshari (Universiti Brunei Darussalam, Brunei) Norainie Ahmad (Universiti Brunei Darussalam, Brunei) and Emil Ali (Universiti Brunei Darussalam, Brunei)
Information Science Reference • copyright 2023 • 370pp • H/C (ISBN: 9781668489031) • US $235.00 (our price)

IGI Global
PUBLISHER of TIMELY KNOWLEDGE

701 East Chocolate Avenue, Hershey, PA 17033, USA
Tel: 717-533-8845 x100 • Fax: 717-533-8661
E-Mail: cust@igi-global.com • www.igi-global.com

Editorial Advisory Board

Table of Contents

Detailed Table of Contents

The United States is facing a growing crisis in the form of increasing medical care costs for both the insured and uninsured. One innovative strategy to address increasing costs is the use of medical tourism. Medical tourism is defined by the OECD as "the practice of travelling to another country to obtain medical treatment." It has become an increasingly popular option as it offers patients the ability to access treatment outside of their home country, often at a lower cost. This chapter will provide a brief overview of medical tourism, its current and potential applications, and potential challenges and benefits associated with it as an innovative approach to address the healthcare crisis of high medical costs in some specific areas of treatment.

The study focuses on ethical, cultural, and research into the public health sector. The content analysis of research identifies disproportionate knowledge of implications affecting the misappropriated, disenfranchised, and institutionalized minority segments of the general population affected by COVID-19 cases. Historic mistreatment of minority individuals, inmates, and the military has left a lasting negative impression of clinical research on minority groups. In 1932, the United States Public Health Service (USPHS) began a public health research study on the lethality of syphilis using African American men from Macon County, Alabama as research subjects. Referred to as the Tuskegee Syphilis Studies (or Tuskegee Experiments), researchers monitored 600 subjects, 399 of which were previously infected with

An increasing number of reports of sexual harassment in the workplace and medical education is challenging the current state of medical education and healthcare. The trauma and long-term consequences of sexual harassment are well documented, yet the issue of sexual harassment has been overlooked mainly in healthcare, leading to a culture of silence and a lack of meaningful and practical solutions. These dynamics represent a significant crisis. This chapter examines the prevalence of sexual harassment in the healthcare and medical education workplace and explores the need for innovative solutions and prevention strategies. The chapter concludes by discussing potential innovative solutions and prevention strategies developed by a management consulting group at Sunshine Health Regional Hospital and Medical Education Training Center, which has experienced a sexual harassment crisis. The intent is to find innovative solutions to influence the world of practice.

Many firms are unaware of which patent is comparatively more important in their patent portfolio. A firm needs to prioritize patents in terms of effective management of its patent portfolio and efficient allocation of resources. The COVID-19 pandemic was one of the most impactful disasters affecting daily human life in the last century. It is critical to evaluate and prioritize technologies developed to reduce the impact of this pandemic. To this end, patents related to COVID-19 are prioritized with the CRITIC-based TOPSIS approach in this study. 935 patents-related data were obtained from the USPTO (United States Patent and Trademark Office) patent database. To the best of the authors' knowledge, there is no study in the literature that uses the CRITIC-based TOPSIS approach to prioritize patents for the COVID-19 pandemic. The results of this study showed decision-makers and investors can consider technologies related to anti-infectives, medicinal preparations containing organic active substances, and medicinal preparations with a special physical form as investment options.

This book chapter assesses the process of restoring archives materials in South Africa. South Africa experience the disaster of loss of archives materials as results of human factors and natural disasters. This led to loss of institutional memory. The researcher utilized literature review to assess archives materials created or received by an organisation. To address the issue of loss of institution, the country has developed and worked towards implementing several policies, strategies, action plans, and projects aimed at responding to and addressing climate change mitigation. Those interventions include raising awareness, training, conferences, publications, and the development of disaster control plans.

The purpose of this book chapter is to understand and analyze the impact of logistics companies' contributions to humanitarian logistics on company marketing. The analysis of logistics processes tells us what kind of results will emerge in the stages of humanitarian aid logistics. The humanitarian aid logistics and corporate social responsibility contribution to logistics companies is analyzed. It is important for the research to be conducted to investigate the logistics performance criteria and to emphasize their importance especially through trying times such as COVID-19 epidemic. These operations enable companies to truly utilize crises and unfortunately disasters as tools and opportunity for improvement and growth. Evaluating the performance criteria of the company and its employees and measuring their contribution to the brand image of the company is very important in this book chapter which enables companies to improve their brand image.

In recent years, advances in digital health have enabled researchers and clinicians to develop innovative solutions to address health disparities in urban areas, particularly in underserved communities. Digital health technologies have been leveraged to improve access to health services, reduce health disparities, and promote urban sustainability. Digital health interventions can improve access to health care, provide education and information about health, and support self-management of health conditions. Digital health interventions are also increasingly used to improve health literacy and reduce health disparities. This chapter explores the utility of these new technologies to address health disparities, promote health innovation, improve health outcomes, and improve urban sustainability.

Preface

In times of crises and disasters, our collective resilience is put to the test. The onset of pandemics, in particular, presents a challenging dichotomy—an affliction that disrupts life's normalcy while also serving as a catalyst for innovation and evolution. In *Using Crises and Disasters as Opportunities for Innovation and Improvement*, Saeed Siyal eloquently navigates this paradox, shedding light on the pandemic's dual nature as a curse and a promise.

Pandemics, throughout history, have indiscriminately impacted societies, economies, and lives. The COVID-19 pandemic, an unprecedented global event, exemplified the devastating reach of such crises. However, amid adversity, it unveiled unforeseen opportunities for growth and transformation across various spheres.

Siyal artfully delineates how the pandemic acted as a harbinger of change, catalyzing progress in critical domains:

- Healthcare emerged at the forefront, accentuating the need for robust systems and accelerated technological integration. Telemedicine and remote patient monitoring became pivotal, revolutionizing access to healthcare.
- Remote work witnessed a seismic shift, enabling operational continuity for businesses while fostering improved work-life balance.
- Education underwent rapid digitization, democratizing learning and paving the way for personalized educational experiences.
- Environmental benefits emerged from reduced human mobility, showcasing sustainable alternatives and prompting a reevaluation of our impact on the planet.
- Social connections, albeit physically distanced, thrived through innovative digital platforms, nurturing communities and volunteerism.

This edited reference book serves as an invitation to scholars and researchers worldwide to explore and dissect the pandemic's promise—its role in shaping societies and organizations. The collection aims to underline the behavioral, challenging, and opportunistic facets, crucial for the seamless functionality, growth, and advancement of societies and institutions.

By delving into topics ranging from climate change and energy conservation to advancements in healthcare systems and remote work, this compendium envisages offering novel approaches and insights. It aspires to empower corporate leaders, academicians, policymakers, and stakeholders with innovative solutions to navigate challenges stemming from unforeseen circumstances.

The targeted audience spans industries, academia, and governance—a comprehensive spectrum encompassing managers, leaders, corporations, academics, and policy influencers. This endeavor envisions becoming a cornerstone for adopting novel methodologies, thereby elevating standards and fostering societal progress.

Siyal's compilation dives into multifaceted aspects, exploring the silver linings within crises and disasters. Through empirical research, this compendium aims to inspire, inform, and equip stakeholders across sectors with tools to thrive in an ever-evolving landscape.

In essence, "Using Crises and Disasters as Opportunities for Innovation and Improvement" stands as a testament to our adaptability, resilience, and capacity to forge a path toward a more promising future, despite the challenges presented by nature and circumstance.

CHAPTER OVERVIEW

Chapter 1: The Crisis and Connection Between Organizational Culture and Performance in Law Enforcement

The first chapter, by Quatavia McLester and Darrell Burrell, delves into the crisis of law enforcement cultures failing to address police misconduct and its implications on community trust. It explores the impact of organizational culture on employee performance and emphasizes the need for change management processes within police departments to restore trust through cultural change and meaningful community engagement.

Chapter 2: Healthcare Treatment Innovation, Medical Tourism, and Hospital Business Strategy for Global Markets

Authored by a multidisciplinary team, the second chapter explores the crisis of rising healthcare costs in the United States. It outlines the concept of medical tourism as an innovative approach to mitigate high medical costs, analyzing its current and potential applications, benefits, and challenges in specific areas of treatment.

Chapter 3: A Study of the Impact of COVID-19 on Education and Teachers' Resilience

Written by Usha Malayankandy and Saeed Siyal, Chapter 3 investigates the adverse effects of the pandemic on education, focusing on barriers to access, opportunities, and learning outcomes perceived by teachers. It analyzes survey data from Tamil Nadu, India, highlighting the pandemic's disruptive impact and the role of technology in education.

Chapter 4: The Complexities of Conducting Public Health Research on Minority Populations

Authored by Allison Huff, Darrell Burrell, and a team, this chapter examines ethical and cultural complexities in public health research, particularly concerning minority groups historically subjected to mistreatment. It scrutinizes the historical context of such mistreatment and its lingering influence on participation in clinical trials and vaccination programs among African Americans, addressing the crisis of trust and bioethics.

Chapter 5: Post-Traumatic Stress Disorder (PTSD) Among Police Officers Is a Public Health and Safety Crisis

Authored by Grace McGrath and Darrell Burrell, Chapter 5 highlights the prevalence of PTSD among police officers, identifying it as a crisis impacting public health and safety. The chapter discusses interventions and support mechanisms crucial for mitigating the disorder's effects within law enforcement.

Chapter 6: Telehealth Technology, Business, and Marketing Strategy Approaches for Mental Health Practices as a Result of COVID-19

Written by Darrell Burrell and collaborators, this chapter explores the exacerbation of mental health issues during the pandemic, analyzing its impact on vulnerable populations. It investigates telemedicine's potential in providing mental health care to underserved communities affected by the crisis.

Chapter 7: Management Consulting in Healthcare as an Innovative Means of Addressing an Organizational Cultural Crisis

Maria Baez, Allison Huff, and others examine sexual harassment in healthcare settings, underscoring its overlooked nature and the need for innovative solutions. The chapter explores strategies developed by a management consulting group to tackle this crisis.

Chapter 8: Portfolio Analysis of COVID-19-Related Patents Using CRITIC-Based TOPSIS Approach

In Chapter 8, Fatma Altuntas, focuses on patent prioritization amidst the COVID-19 pandemic. The chapter introduces a novel approach, CRITIC-based TOPSIS, to evaluate and prioritize patents related to COVID-19, aiding decision-makers and investors in identifying critical technologies for investment and resource allocation.

Chapter 9: Restoring Archival Materials Through Digitalization South Africa

Authored by Nkholedzeni Sidney Netshakhuma, Chapter 9 addresses the crisis of lost archival materials in South Africa due to human and natural disasters. The chapter assesses restoration efforts and policy interventions aimed at preserving institutional memory through digitalization, emphasizing the importance of disaster control plans and awareness initiatives.

Chapter 10: The Effect of Humanitarian Aid on Logistics Companies' Marketing

Chapter 10, authored by Nazlı Gülfem Gidener, Damla Kartal, and colleagues, examines the impact of logistics companies' contributions to humanitarian aid on their marketing strategies. It analyzes the performance criteria and their influence on brand image, emphasizing the role of corporate social responsibility during crises like the COVID-19 epidemic.

Chapter 11: Exploring the Intersection and Crisis of Urban Sustainability, Policy, and Digital Health

Written by Kevin Richardson and Darrell Burrell, this chapter explores how digital health advancements address health disparities in urban areas. Focusing on technology's role in improving access to healthcare and reducing disparities, the chapter discusses interventions enhancing health innovation and urban sustainability.

Chapter 12: Developments in the Remote Work and Learning: Perspectives From Industry and Academia

Chapter 12, authored by Kiran Thakur, Badr-un-nisa Chand, and Shivani Dhand, examines the exponential growth of remote work and learning post-pandemic. It delves into technological advancements, the emphasis on digital literacy, and the evolution of work and learning paradigms.

Chapter 13: From Crisis to Opportunity: How VGI Is Transforming Disaster Response and Recovery Efforts

Written by Munir Ahmad, this chapter focuses on Volunteered Geographic Information (VGI) and its role in disaster management. The chapter explores the use of VGI in disaster response, emphasizing its significance, challenges, and future directions for improving data quality and inclusivity.

Chapter 14: Managing a Breast Cancer Crisis Through Innovation, Community Engagement, and the Expansion of Fisheries Management Education Programs

Chapter 14, by Darrell Burrell, discusses breast cancer as a global crisis and its impact on survivors' mental health. It proposes community education programs, like a fly-fishing support group, to aid breast cancer survivors, promoting psychological well-being.

Chapter 15: Need to Increase Awareness of NCDs in MICs on the Edge of the Syrian Refugee Crisis

Authored by Songul Cinaroglu and Busra Saylan, the last chapter focuses on increasing awareness of noncommunicable diseases (NCDs), particularly breast cancer, in Middle-Income Countries (MICs) like Turkey. The chapter highlights the rising incidence and costs of breast cancer in MICs, emphasizing the need for public awareness and preparedness in the context of refugee influxes.

Each chapter within this edited reference book offers comprehensive insights into various crises, their implications, and innovative approaches aimed at addressing and leveraging these challenges for positive change and growth across different domains.

IN SUMMARY

As we reach the culmination of this edited reference book, *Using Crises and Disasters as Opportunities for Innovation and Improvement*, the depth and breadth of exploration into multifaceted crises across diverse spheres become vividly apparent. Each chapter illuminates the intricate dynamics, presenting a mosaic of challenges and innovative solutions arising from crises—transforming adversity into opportunity.

From the critical examination of law enforcement cultures and the crisis of trust within marginalized communities to the innovative strategies like medical tourism to address escalating healthcare costs, this compendium traverses complex terrains.

The impact of COVID-19 on education, mental health, and research methodologies unveils the profound implications of global crises on various facets of human life. It underscores the imperative for innovative adaptations in education, healthcare, and research practices.

Ethical considerations in public health research, the prevalence of PTSD among police officers, and the role of technology in disaster response exemplify the intricate interplay between societal crises, healthcare, and technological advancements.

Furthermore, discussions on archive restoration, humanitarian aid's impact on logistics, and breast cancer management highlight the importance of preserving heritage, corporate social responsibility, and holistic healthcare approaches in crisis mitigation.

The chapters resonate with a common thread—the essence of crisis as a catalyst for innovation, prompting new strategies, policies, and mindsets that transcend adversity. They underscore the resilience and adaptability of human endeavors in the face of daunting challenges.

As editors, it's our privilege to curate these insights, fostering a compendium that not only identifies crises but also illuminates pathways for progress. Each contribution serves as a beacon of hope, advocating for change, and presenting opportunities amid adversity.

We hope this book serves as a compass for policymakers, practitioners, academics, and stakeholders navigating the tumultuous waters of crises. May the innovative approaches and lessons gleaned from these chapters inspire transformative actions, fostering a future where crises are not only managed but leveraged as catalysts for positive change and societal advancement.

In closing, we extend our gratitude to the contributing authors for their profound insights, dedication, and commitment to shedding light on the transformative potential inherent within crises. May their contributions sow seeds of innovation, resilience, and progress, guiding us toward a future where crises are met with unwavering resolve and collective ingenuity.

Warmest regards,

Saeed Siyal
School of Economics and Management, Beijing University of Chemical Technology, China

Acknowledgement

I would like to express my heartfelt gratitude to all those who have supported and encouraged me throughout the process of Editing this book. I am truly thankful for the prayers of my Late Parents, unwavering support of my family, friends, and colleagues. Their belief in me has been a constant source of inspiration. I would also like to extend my appreciation to the experts and professionals who have generously shared their knowledge and expertise, helping me to shape this book into its final form. Lastly, I am grateful to the readers who will soon embark on this journey with me. Thank you for your interest and support.

I would like to express a special thank you to my little son, Qalb E Momin, whose boundless energy and innocent curiosity have brought joy and inspiration to my life.

Chapter 1
The Crisis and Connection Between Organizational Culture and Performance in Law Enforcement

Quatavia McLester
https://orcid.org/0000-0003-1596-0517
Capitol Technology University, USA

Darrell Norman Burrell
https://orcid.org/0000-0002-4675-9544
Marymount University, USA

ABSTRACT

This chapter examines the crisis of law enforcement cultures that fail to address police brutality and misconduct, and the resulting lack of trust in police by marginalized communities. Through a review of the literature, this article examines the impact of law enforcement organizational cultures on employee performance. Finally, the article suggests that police departments must develop change management processes that incorporate an accountability system that holds officers accountable for their actions and provides a mechanism for addressing misconduct. Ultimately, this article argues that only by changing police cultures and engaging with communities meaningfully can trust between police and communities be restored.

INTRODUCTION

The crisis surrounding public protests and growing concerns about police misconduct and unethical behavior has ignited a profound focus on change and innovation within law enforcement agencies and the broader criminal justice system. The emergence of these concerns has shed light on longstanding systemic issues, highlighting the need for transformative solutions and a fundamental reevaluation of

DOI: 10.4018/978-1-6684-9522-3.ch001

policing practices (Burrell et al., 2023). In this context, the crisis has catalyzed a powerful impetus for change and innovation, driven by an urgent recognition of the imperative to rebuild trust, promote transparency, and ensure accountability in law enforcement (Burrell et al., 2023).

One of the most notable outcomes of this crisis has been the widespread adoption of innovative technologies and practices aimed at enhancing accountability and transparency. Body-worn cameras, for instance, have become a pivotal tool in documenting police interactions with the public, providing an objective record that can be crucial for investigations and legal proceedings (Burrell et al., 2023). Moreover, data analytics and artificial intelligence are being employed to scrutinize and identify patterns of misconduct, allowing agencies to proactively address issues and implement preventative measures (Burrell et al., 2023).

In addition to technological innovations, the crisis has spurred a reevaluation of traditional policing models and tactics. Community-oriented policing, for example, has gained renewed prominence as a strategy that prioritizes engagement, collaboration, and problem-solving within communities (Burrell et al., 2023). This shift underscores the importance of building positive relationships between law enforcement officers and the communities they serve, ultimately fostering a safer and more equitable environment for all. The crisis has also propelled efforts to diversify police forces and promote cultural competence, recognizing that a diverse and inclusive workforce is essential for building trust and understanding within diverse communities (Burrell et al., 2023).

Furthermore, the crisis has prompted a reexamination of the role of law enforcement in society, leading to calls for reallocating resources from traditional law enforcement functions to social services, mental health support, and community development. This shift in resource allocation reflects a growing consensus that many of the issues traditionally handled by law enforcement, such as mental health crises and substance abuse, may be better addressed through alternative, community-based approaches (Burrell et al., 2023).

Police misconduct, stress management, and unethical conduct on the part of police officers have been essential topics of discussion and debate in recent years (Burrell et al., 2023; Von Robertson & Chaney, 2019). Incidents of police brutality, excessive force, and racial profiling have heightened scrutiny of police departments and their practices (Burrell et al., 2023; Von Robertson & Chaney, 2019). The public has become increasingly aware of the extent of police misconduct, job stress behaviors, and the consequences of these actions have become more serious (Burrell et al., 2023; Von Robertson & Chaney, 2019). Police misconduct is defined as any form of behavior that violates the law, public policy, or ethical standards of a police officer (Burrell et al., 2023). It may include violations of civil rights, excessive use of force, corruption, dishonesty, or any other form of unethical behavior (Burrell et al., 2023). The term is also used to describe any action taken by a police officer that is deemed to be inappropriate or illegal (Burrell et al., 2023). This conduct can often be influenced by organizational culture.

A culture of impunity is another potential cause of police misconduct. This refers to a culture in which misconduct is tolerated or even encouraged by the police department (Burrell et al., 2023). This can create an environment where officers can get away with misconduct or unethical behavior (Burrell et al., 2023). "Culture" is a stable set of values, beliefs, and behaviors commonly held by society (Lim, 1995). Even though the term is "derived from social anthropology as a framework for understanding primitive societies," the idea has currently been utilized in the framework of organizations. Organizational culture refers to an arrangement of shared meaning held by members that differentiate the organization from other organizations (Robbins & Judge, 2015). Seven principal characteristics capture the core of an organization's culture. Those characteristics are innovation and risk-taking, attention to detail, outcome orientation, people orientation, team orientation, aggressiveness, and stability (Robbins & Judge, 2015). There are roles that culture performs. Culture is a boundary-defining role (Robbins & Judge, 2015). In regards to the organization, culture delivers a sense of identity for members, enables the generation of commitment, improves the solidity of the social system, and serves as a control mechanism to shape employees' attitudes and behavior (Robbins & Judge, 2015).

The relationship between the police and their community is one of the most essential aspects of effective and responsible law enforcement. Unfortunately, this relationship has been strained in recent years due to several high-profile incidents of police brutality and excessive force (Burrell et al., 2023; Von Robertson & Chaney, 2019). In order to improve community relations and enhance public trust in law enforcement, police departments must make an effort to change their organizational culture to promote de-escalation, ethics, and professionalism (Burrell et al., 2023; Von Robertson & Chaney, 2019). Organizational culture can affect organizational outcomes, specifically how the organization performs. Prior research supports a link between organizational culture and performance.

RESEARCH PROBLEM STATEMENT AND SIGNIFICANCE

In order to understand the prevalence of police misconduct and unethical conduct, it is necessary to look at the statistics and research available on the topic. Racial disparities in police misconduct are well documented (Burrell et al., 2023; Von Robertson & Chaney, 2019; Peoples, 2020). Numerous studies have found that people of color are more likely to experience police misconduct than their white counterparts (Burrell et al., 2023; Brookings Institution, 2020). This is especially true for African Americans, who are disproportionately represented among those who experience police misconduct (U.S. Department of Justice, 2020). Further, research has found that police officers are more likely to use force against people of color, even when the resistance level is the same (Burrell et al., 2023). This idea suggests that there is a bias among police officers that leads them to treat people of color differently than white people. This perspective is further evidenced by the fact that African Americans are more likely to be stopped and searched by the police than white people, even when they are not engaged in criminal activity (Brookings Institution, 2020).

According to a recent report from the Department of Justice, approximately 10,000 complaints of police misconduct are filed each year (U.S. Department of Justice, 2020). This number has remained relatively steady over the past decade. The report also found that approximately 25% of these complaints are substantiated, meaning the misconduct allegations are true. The report also found that the most common types of police misconduct reported include excessive use of force, false arrest and imprisonment, and racial profiling (U.S. Department of Justice, 2020). For example, a recent survey found that one in five people reported experiencing some form of police misconduct in the past year (Brookings Institution, 2020). While it is difficult to measure the exact prevalence of these types of misconduct, research suggests that they can be influenced by organizational culture. This paper looks to explore this topic through previous and emerging research.

METHOD

An examination of recent, historical, and ongoing research from the literature was the approach taken. The literature review procedure consisted of conducting an in-depth analysis of the collected sources. Depending on the nature of the study being reviewed, the framework of the review's organization might be thematic or chronological. The procedure consisted of thoroughly analyzing earlier studies' methodologies, findings, and implications, intending to identify specific areas that require additional research. To maintain rigor, a thorough and varied collection of sources was used. This approach of searching critical literature studies helped ensure that various perspectives and essential contributions were considered. Making links between different research and conclusions is an effective way to help show some of the voids this article intends to address. This technique demonstrated the article's unique contribution by situating the study's significance within the more extensive academic debate. It also highlighted the potential consequences of the article for theory, practice, or policy. The keywords used included: police misconduct, police ethics, police brutality, and police harassment. Databases used include National Institutes of Health, ProQuest Dissertations, IGI Global Publishing, Research Gate, Google Scholar, ProQuest, and SCOPUS.

THE CRISIS AND IMPACT OF CULTURES OF MISCONDUCT

The causes of police brutality and misconduct are multi-faceted and complex, but they can generally be attributed to a combination of institutional, organizational, and individual factors (Peeples, 2020; Burrell et al., 2023). On the institutional level, there is evidence that particular law enforcement cultures, such as those emphasizing militarization over community-based policing, can foster an environment where police brutality and misconduct are more likely to occur (Peeples, 2020; Burrell et al., 2023). On the organizational level, there is evidence that specific police departments are more likely to experience police brutality and misconduct due to inadequate training and supervision, oversight and accountability, and policies and procedures (Burrell et al., 2023; Burrell et al., 2018). On the individual level, numerous studies suggest police officers are more likely to engage in brutality and misconduct if they function in cultures that are unhealthy, toxic, and improper (Burrell et al., 2023; Burrell et al., 2018).

Law enforcement cultures rampant with police brutality and misconduct in community relations are significant (Peeples, 2020; Burrell et al., 2023). Studies have shown that police brutality and misconduct lead to distrust and alienation among public members, increasing crime levels, decreased cooperation with law enforcement, and a general sense of fear and insecurity in the community (Peeples, 2020; Burrell et al., 2023). This, in turn, can lead to a deterioration of community relations as public members become less likely to trust and cooperate with police officers and more likely to view them with suspicion and resentment (Peeples, 2020; Burrell et al., 2023).

CULTURE AND PERFORMANCE

Organizational culture can have a significant influence on the behavior and ethical conduct of police officers. Research has found that organizational culture affects police officers' attitudes toward ethical conduct (Burrell et al., 2018). Police officers in departments with a stronger sense of organizational justice were likelier to report unethical behavior by fellow officers (Burrell et al., 2018). Additionally, research has found that organizations with a strong sense of ethics and professionalism are likelier to have higher ethical behavior among police officers (Burrell et al., 2023; Burrell et al., 2018). The values, norms, and artifacts of an organization's culture can also shape the behavior of police officers.

Organizational values can shape the behavior of police officers. Research has found that organizations with a strong sense of values are more likely to have higher levels of ethical behavior among police officers (Burrell et al., 2023; Burrell et al., 2018). Values such as integrity, fairness, and respect for human rights can guide police officers and help shape their behavior. Additionally, research has found that organizations with strong values are likelier to have higher public trust in their police departments (Peeples, 2020; Burrell et al., 2023).

Organizational norms can also shape the behavior of police officers. Research has found that organizations with strong norms of organizational justice are more likely to have higher levels of ethical behavior among police officers (Burrell et al., 2023; Burrell et al., 2018). Norms such as transparency, accountability, and respect for human rights can help to create a culture of ethical behavior and can help to shape the behavior of police officers. Additionally, research has found that organizations with explicit norms of behavior are more likely to have higher public trust in their police departments (Burrell et al., 2023; Burrell et al., 2018).

Organizational artifacts can also shape the behavior of police officers. Artifacts such as logos, symbols, and rituals can serve as visual reminders of the values and norms of an organization and can help to shape the behavior of police officers. Additionally, research has found that organizations with solid organizational artifacts are likelier to have higher public trust in their police departments (Burrell et al., 2023; Burrell et al., 2018).

Organizational culture can also have a significant impact on police ethical conduct. Research has found that organizations with a strong sense of values and norms are more likely to have higher levels of ethical behavior among police officers (Burrell et al., 2023; Burrell et al., 2018). Additionally, research has found that organizations with a strong sense of organizational justice are more likely to have higher levels of ethical behavior among police officers (Burrell et al., 2023; Burrell et al., 2018). An organization's culture's values, norms, and artifacts can guide police officers and help shape their ethical conduct.

Jacobs, Mannion, Davies, Harrison, Konteh, and Walshe (2013) investigated the relationship between senior management team culture and organizational performance in English acute hospitals between 2001/2002 and 2007/2008. The authors used a validated culture rating instrument, the Competing Values Framework, to measure senior management team culture (Jacobs et al., 2013). Various routinely collected indicators are used to access organizational culture (Jacobs et al., 2013). The authors used ordered probit and multinomial logit models to investigate the relationships between organizational culture and performance (Jacobs et al., 2013). The researchers found that organizational culture varies across organizations and over time. This discrepancy is, in part, linked in predictable and consistent ways with various organizational traits and repetitive performance measures. The study provided evidence that there is a relationship between culture and performance.

Similar to the O'Reilly et al. (2014) and Jacobs et al. (2013) study, Allard (2011) mentioned the influence of senior management on organizational culture, specifically managers. Allard (2011) discusses the pressure on managers to solve organizational challenges. According to Allard (2011), a quantitative study is needed to explore the relationship between the employee-organization culture gap and performance. 247 of 369 employees from three technical institutes in South Dakota partook in the study (Allard, 2011). Allard (2011) utilized the Organizational Culture Profile (OCP) to measure organizational culture. Correlation and regression analysis was used to analyze the survey data. The study's outcome indicated a significant negative relationship between the employee-organization culture gap and organizational performance, $r = -.52$, $p < .001$ (Allard, 2011). The results also indicated that employee longevity moderated the relationship between the employee-organization culture gap and organizational performance, $p = -.15$, $p = .012$ (Allard, 2011). The findings in the Allard (2011) study added to the literature on the associations between organizational culture and performance.

Analogous to Allard's (2011) belief that there is a need for more exploration regarding the relationship between organizational culture and performance, there are researchers that believe organizational culture is an important aspect to be considered in order to develop a competitive advantage to ensure enhanced organizational performance (Khan & Afzal, 2011). Khan and Afzal (2011) sought to "elaborate the dimensions of cultural construct in the organization of diversified sectors and their implications in Pakistan." The authors selected ten organizations for the study, and four hundred and seventy-eight questionnaires were received from these ten organizations (Khan & Afzal, 2011). The questionnaires had three parts. The first part had nine elements related to the respondents' organization and personal profile (Khan & Afzal, 2011). The second part had 60 cultural construct elements: mission, adaptability, consistency, and involvement (Khan & Afzal, 2011). Within the third part of the questionnaire, the dependent variable appears as organization performance, and this was evaluated by asking eight questions (Khan & Afzal, 2011). The results indicate that organizational performance increases from negative 56% to positive 92% due to organizational culture concerning education. The results indicate that organizational culture is an essential part of organizational success. The questionnaire Khan and Afzal (2011) used highlights the different kinds of established cultures.

Some previous research has conceptualized culture into four different kinds based on competing standards (Robbins & Judge, 2015). The four types include (1) The collaborative and cohesive clan, (2) the innovative and adaptable adhocracy, (3) the controlled and consistent hierarchy, and (4) the competitive and customer-focused market (Robbins & Judge, 2015).

Several studies have used these types to investigate the relationship between culture and performance in various industries. Kotrba, Gillespie, Schmidt, Smerek, Ritchie, and Denison (2012) examined the notion that the influence of cultural consistency on organizational performance may vary contingent on the levels of other cultural traits. Using the Dension Organizational Culture Survey, the authors utilized data from 88,879 individuals in 137 public organizations (Kotrba et al., 2012). The data was then paired with three objective organizational performance measures to investigate the collaboration effects of adaptability, involvement, and consistency with the mission (Kotrba et al., 2012). The study showed that consistency significantly interacted with all three traits in predicting market-to-book ratios and sales growth (Kotrba et al., 2012). For example, consistent and adaptable firms are high performers (Kotrba et al., 2012).

The traits the authors investigated in the study are a part of the conceptualized culture that has been put into different types based on competing values. As stated, the study results showed that consistency substantially interacts with all three traits in predicting market-to-book ratios and sales growth. In other words, consistency has a substantial positive interaction with all three traits in predicting performance. Furthermore, firms that are both consistent and adaptable are high performers. The study shows that firms with an organizational culture with adaptable adhocracy and consistent hierarchy may be higher performers. Firms that perform higher most likely contain high-performing employees.

Research by Carroll (2009) on the role of organizational culture in strategic human resource management research in Canada. Two simultaneous studies were conducted using a complex analysis with multiple-level respondents. The first study involved a sample of manager respondents. The second study involved two field studies that included rank-and-file employees and managerial employees as respondents. The HR horizontal alignment and the association between HRM and firm performance were tested in both studies. The findings were consistent with past research, suggesting the legitimacy of the measures. Carroll (2009) utilized Cameron and Quinn's (2006) Competing Values (CVF) to measure organizational culture. Cameron and Quinn (2006) defined four culture types which are referred to as adhocracy (i.e., entrepreneurial), clan (i.e., social), market (i.e., competitive), and hierarchy (i.e., bureaucratic) (Carroll, 2009).

The outcomes of the studies presented that clan and adhocracy were positively related to firm performance (Carroll, 2009). Market and hierarchy were negatively associated with firm performance. Organizational culture types were found to have both direct and indirect associations with effective organizational performance, resulting from superior employee performance. While hierarchy and adhocracy cultures were significantly associated with the organizational performance in Study 1, clan and market were not significant with the organizational performance in Study 1 or Study 2. The study's findings suggest that culture is directly linked with organizational performance with two culture types and indirectly linked with organizational performance by the relationship of clan and market cultures with employee performance and operational performance (Carroll, 2009).

In many previous studies, the research regarding the relationship between organizational culture and performance has not been limited to the United States. There have been several research studies on the topic outside of the United States. One author took their investigation to Nigeria. Using data from merged banks in Nigeria, Okoro (2011) investigated whether a relationship existed between organizational culture and performance. According to Okoro (2011), most merged banks in Nigeria are suffering and have yet to succeed in increasing organizational performance. Organizational leaders face obstacles involving assimilating two or more merged cultures to preserve job satisfaction, employee commitment, and employee retention. In order to determine if a relationship existed between organizational culture and performance, Okoro (2011) utilized a "quantitative correlational and regression study" and collected data connected to a merged bank in Abuja, Federal Capital Territory (FCT) of Nigeria.

The results of the Okoro (2011) study showed that a measure of the grouping of cultural traits (mission, involvement, consistency, and adaptability) had a significant relationship with each of the organizational performance measures (employee commitment, job satisfaction, and employee retention). Results of the study uncovered that an absence of cultural assimilation during merger and acquisition was linked to merger failure and a decrease in organizational performance (Okoro, 2011). This study adds to the existing literature regarding the relationship between organizational culture and performance and shows that cultural differences may hinder organizational performance. There is further affirmation that a significant relationship exists between organizational culture and performance. Furthermore, this study utilizes the different cultural traits mentioned previously.

Lee and Yu (2004) examined the possible relationships between corporate culture and organizational performance among Singaporean companies. The study's objectives are twofold (Lee & Yu, 2004). First, the study aims to examine the validity of the culture construct (Lee & Yu, 2004). The study seeks to discover whether or not culture construct can be operationalized along distinct, repeatable dimensions (Lee & Yu, 2004). Secondly, the study assesses how culture affects organizational performance (Lee & Yu, 2004). The organizational culture profile was utilized as the principal research instrument. The study found that culture impacted various organizational processes and performance (Lee & Yu, 2004). The study has established the influence of culture in manipulating organizational performance.

Petty et al. (1995) investigated the association between organizational culture and performance. A survey designed to assess employee acceptance of the values described in the organization's "vision statement" was completed by 832 employees in 12 organizations of a firm in the electric utility industry (Petty et al., 1995). One year later, the survey was administered to 884 employees in these 12 service organizations. The outcomes showed that measures of organizational culture were significantly linked to objective measures of performance (Petty et al., 1995).

CHANGE MANAGEMENT MODELS AND THEORIES

In order to improve police-community relations requires creating and promoting organizational cultures of trust and respect. Police departments must prioritize de-escalation, ethics, and professionalism. De-escalation refers to using strategies and tactics that help to reduce the potential for violence in a given situation. Officers need to be trained in de-escalation techniques to reduce the potential for violence without resorting to force. Professionalism, on the other hand, refers to the conduct and behavior of officers on the job. Professionalism involves treating the public with respect and courtesy, as well as adhering to the laws, regulations, and policies of the police department. Professionalism is essential for building public trust and developing positive relationships with the community.

There are a variety of change management models and theories that can be used to effect positive change in law enforcement cultures. One such model is the Lewin Change Model, which was developed by Kurt Lewin in the 1950s (Higgs & Rowland, 2008). According to this model, change can be broken down into three stages: unfreezing, changing, and refreezing (Higgs & Rowland, 2008). The unfreezing stage creates a sense of urgency and a desire for change (Higgs & Rowland, 2008). The actual change occurs in the changing stage (Higgs & Rowland, 2008). Finally, the refreezing stage is where the new changes become entrenched in the organization's culture (Higgs & Rowland, 2008).

Another change management model that can effect positive change in law enforcement cultures is the Kotter Change Model, developed by John Kotter in the 1990s (Kotter, 1996). According to this model, change is a process that involves eight steps: creating a sense of urgency, forming a powerful coalition, creating a vision for change, communicating the vision, empowering others to act on the vision, planning for and creating short-term wins, consolidating gains and producing more change, and institutionalizing new approaches (Kotter, 1996). This model emphasizes the importance of creating a sense of urgency and a shared vision for change, empowering people to take action and celebrating short-term successes (Kotter, 1996).

In addition to these models, several change management theories can be applied to law enforcement cultures. One such theory is the Social Learning Theory, which posits that people learn through observing the behavior of others and can be motivated to change through modeling, reinforcement, and self-regulation (Bandura, 1977). Another theory is the diffusion of innovation theory, which suggests that change is most likely to spread when it is introduced promptly and when it is seen as beneficial to the organization (Rogers, 1995). Finally, the Organizational Development Theory suggests that change is most successful when it is focused on the whole organization rather than individual departments or teams (Beckhard & Harris, 1987).

Implementing change in law enforcement cultures can be a difficult and complex task. One of the primary challenges is resistance to change. Police officers may be reluctant to embrace new ideas and practices and resist change due to fear of the unknown or a lack of understanding of how the change will

It may be beneficial for organizations to examine the characteristics of their own organization. There may be more than one size fit for organizational culture. However, it is beneficial for organizations to consider integrating the organizational culture traits that are most successful, such as adaptable adhocracy and consistent hierarchy. Organizations can utilize some of the surveys and questionnaires mentioned in the studies. Using climate surveys would help organizations get a sense of what their existing culture is and where improvement needs to be made.

Organizations have training programs that teach employees how to execute their jobs effectively. There are training programs that teach ethical standards, work etiquette, discourage sexual harassment, and respect for diversity. Training applications/programs that discuss the organization's culture would be beneficial. These applications could be integrated into the onboarding process and orientation. Enough studies support the need for more emphasis on organizational culture and remarkable strides to establish a solid organizational culture where all employees engage in professional, respectful, and ethical behavior.

The contexts explored underscore the pivotal role that organizational culture plays in influencing the behavior and ethical conduct of police officers, and it offers valuable insights into potential improvements and innovations concerning disasters and areas of crisis related to police brutality, toxic community relations, and police miscount in the following critical areas:

Cultural Influence on Behavior: The research underscores that an organization's culture significantly shapes the behavior of its police officers. This observation suggests that police departments can actively work towards modifying their organizational cultures to foster better behavior and ethical conduct among their personnel. By acknowledging the impact of culture, law enforcement agencies can identify areas for improvement and innovation.

Encouraging Ethical Behavior: The study advocates creating a culture within police organizations that explicitly promotes ethical behavior. This suggests that agencies should articulate a commitment to ethics and embed it deeply within their cultural fabric. This shift towards a values-driven culture can serve as an innovation by redefining the priorities and expectations placed on police officers.

Justice, Transparency, and Accountability Culture: The research emphasizes the importance of cultivating a culture of justice, transparency, and accountability within law enforcement organizations. This cultural shift can be viewed as an innovation in response to the crisis of police misconduct and brutality. It implies a commitment to fairness, openness, and responsibility in all aspects of policing, which can help rebuild trust between communities and the police.

Ethical Culture for Ethical Action: The core assertion of the research is that a culture that encourages ethical behavior can lead to more ethical actions by police officers. This implies that by addressing cultural shortcomings and nurturing a culture of ethics, police organizations can proactively tackle the issues of misconduct and brutality. This forward-thinking approach recognizes the root causes of these problems and seeks to address them systematically.

In sum, the research suggests that organizational culture is not a static entity but a dynamic force that can be intentionally molded to promote ethical behavior and address the crisis of police misconduct and brutality. By instigating cultural shifts towards values, transparency, justice, and accountability, police departments can proactively contribute to positive change. These proposed cultural innovations hold the potential to reshape the behavior and ethical conduct of police officers, ultimately working towards a more just and accountable law enforcement system. The crisis sparked by public protests and concerns about police misconduct and unethical behavior has served as a catalyst for innovation and change within the realm of law enforcement. From the adoption of advanced technologies to the transformation of policing philosophies, the crisis has driven a renewed commitment to rebuilding trust, fostering transparency, and promoting accountability within law enforcement agencies. The ongoing pursuit of these transformative initiatives reflects a collective determination to address systemic issues and create a more just and equitable criminal justice system for all citizens.

RECOMMENDATIONS FOR FUTURE RESEARCH

While the existing literature provides valuable insights into the relationship between organizational culture and ethical behavior, professionalism, and upstanding conduct among police officers, several avenues for future research can enrich our understanding and address current gaps in knowledge. These recommendations explore novel research approaches beyond traditional literature reviews and offer a deeper understanding of this critical crisis issue. These potential options include:

- Longitudinal Studies: Conducting longitudinal studies can help establish causality and identify the long-term impact of organizational culture on ethical behavior and professionalism among police officers. By following the same group of officers over an extended period, researchers can track changes in their conduct as the organizational culture evolves.
- Mixed-Methods Research: A mixed-methods approach can provide a comprehensive understanding of the complex relationship between organizational culture and ethical behavior. Combining qualitative methods, such as interviews or focus groups, with quantitative data can offer a more nuanced perspective and help identify underlying mechanisms that can create areas of crisis.
- Experimental Research: Experimental designs, such as randomized controlled trials, allow researchers to manipulate specific aspects of organizational culture and measure their effects on ethical behavior and professionalism among police officers. This approach can help establish causal relationships and inform potential interventions that can advert disasters and areas of crisis in organizations.
- Ethnographic Studies: Ethnographic research involves immersing researchers within police departments to observe and understand the daily interactions, practices, and dynamics that shape ethical conduct. This approach can capture the contextual nuances that quantitative data might miss.
- Comparative Analysis: Conducting cross-cultural or cross-organizational comparisons can provide insights into how different organizational cultures influence ethical behavior and professionalism. Comparing police departments with varying cultural norms and management styles can reveal patterns and differences that shed light on effective practices.
- Social Network Analysis: Exploring the social networks within police departments can uncover influential individuals or groups that impact ethical behavior and professionalism. Analyzing communication patterns and relationships can highlight informal structures contributing to organizational culture.
- Technology and Ethical Conduct: Investigating the role of technology in shaping ethical behavior and professionalism among police officers is an emerging area of interest. Research could explore how digital communication, surveillance tools, and AI technologies interact with organizational culture to influence conduct.
- Multi-Stakeholder Perspectives: Engaging not only police officers but also their supervisors, community members, and external oversight bodies can provide a holistic view of the dynamics be-

tween organizational culture and ethical behavior. Incorporating diverse perspectives can lead to more comprehensive insights.

- Intervention and Change Management Studies: Research focusing on the implementation and effectiveness of interventions designed to reshape organizational culture for improved ethical behavior can provide actionable insights. Understanding how change efforts unfold and their impact is crucial for practical applications.
- Narrative Analysis: Exploring narratives, stories, and personal experiences of police officers can provide rich qualitative data to understand the subjective aspects of ethical conduct. Analyzing officers' own accounts can reveal the complexities of navigating organizational cultures that can lead to areas of crisis.
- Incorporating Psychological Factors: Integrating psychological theories and assessments can provide deeper insights into individual motivations, decision-making processes, and moral reasoning within organizational culture.
- Intersectional Analysis: Investigating how race, gender, and socioeconomic background intersect with organizational culture and influence ethical behavior can lead to a more inclusive understanding of the dynamics at play.

By pursuing these alternative research approaches, scholars can contribute to a more comprehensive and nuanced understanding of the relationship between organizational culture and ethical behavior, professionalism, and upstanding conduct for police officers. These recommendations encourage innovative methodologies that offer fresh insights and contribute to the ongoing discourse surrounding law enforcement ethics and conduct.

REFERENCES

Allard, I. N. (2011). Examining the relationship between organizational culture and performance: Moderators of the culture gap. *Dissertation Abstracts International Section A*, *71*, 3329.

Bandura, A. (1977). *Social learning theory*. Prentice-Hall.

Beckhard, R., & Harris, R. T. (1987). *Organizational transitions: Managing complex change*. Addison-Wesley.

Brookings Institution. (2020). *Police use of force: What the data say*. Brookings Institution. https://www.brookings.edu/research/police-use-of-force-what-the-data-say/

Burrell, D. N., Bhargava, N., Kemp, R. E., & Vemuganti, D. (2018). Public health and safety leadership challenges around law enforcement ethics and whistleblowing in the age of the# Black Lives Matter movement. *International Journal of Latest Research in Humanities and Social Science*, *2*, 1–12.

Burrell, D. N., Burton, S. L., & McGrath, G. E. (2023). Racially Motivated Police Brutality Is a Community Public Health Issue in the United States. [IJHSTM]. *International Journal of Health Systems and Translational Medicine*, *3*(1), 1–15. doi:10.4018/IJHSTM.315296

Carroll, W. R. (2009). Organizational culture, HRM and firm performance: Examining relationships using the competing values framework in call centres. *Dissertation Abstracts International Section A*, *70*, 932.

Higgs, M., & Rowland, D. (2008). *The change handbook: The definitive resource on today's best methods for engaging whole systems*. Berrett-Koehler.

Jacobs, R., Mannion, R., Davies, H. O., Harrison, S., Konteh, F., & Walshe, K. (2013). The relationship between organizational culture and performance in acute hospitals. *Social Science & Medicine, 76*, 76115–76125. doi:10.1016/j.socscimed.2012.10.014 PMID:23159305

Khan, M. A., & Afzal, H. (2011). High level of education builds up a strong relationship between organizational culture and organizational performance in Pakistan. *International Journal of Human Resource Management, 22*(7), 1387–1400. doi:10.1080/09585192.2011.561955

Kotrba, L. M., Gillespie, M. A., Schmidt, A. M., Smerek, R. E., Ritchie, S. A., & Denison, D. R. (2012). Do consistent corporate cultures have better business performance? Exploring the interaction effects. *Human Relations, 65*(2), 241–262. doi:10.1177/0018726711426352

Kotter, J. (1996). *Leading change*. Harvard Business School Press.

Lee, S. J., & Yu, K. (2004). Corporate culture and organizational performance. *Journal of Managerial Psychology, 19*(4), 340–359. doi:10.1108/02683940410537927

Lim, B. (1995). Examining the organizational culture and organizational performance link. *Leadership and Organization Development Journal, 16*(5), 16–21. doi:10.1108/01437739510088491

O'Reilly, C. I. III, Caldwell, D. F., Chatman, J. A., & Doerr, B. (2014). The promise and problems of organizational culture: CEO personality, culture, and firm performance. *Group & Organization Management, 39*(6), 595–625. doi:10.1177/1059601114550713

Okoro, H. M. (2011). The relationship between organizational culture and performance: Merger in the Nigerian banking industry. [Dissertation, University of Phoenix].

Peeples, L. (2020). *What the data say about police brutality and racial bias—and which reforms might work*.

Petty, M. M., Beadles, N. A., Lowery, C. M., Chapman, D. F., & Connell, D. W. (1995). Relationship between organizational culture and organizational performance. *Psychological Reports, 76*(2), 483–492. doi:10.2466/pr0.1995.76.2.483 PMID:8559874

Robbins, S. P., & Judge, T. A. (2015). *Organizational Behavior*. Pearson Education, Inc.

Rogers, E. M. (1995). *Diffusion of innovations* (4th ed.). Free Press.

U.S. Department of Justice. (2017). Police-community relations. US DoJ. https://www.justice.gov/ag/page/file/906896/download

U.S. Department of Justice. (2020). Report to the nation on police use of force. US DoJ. https://www.justice.gov/opa/report-nation-police-use-force

Von Robertson, R., & Chaney, C. D. (2019). *Police use of excessive force against African Americans: Historical antecedents and community perceptions*. Rowman & Littlefield.

Chapter 2
A Study of the Impact of COVID-19 on Education and Teachers' Resilience

Usha Ajithkumar Malayankandy
https://orcid.org/0000-0001-8555-8406
SASTRA University, India

Saeed Siyal
https://orcid.org/0000-0003-0982-157X
School of Economics and Management, Beijing University of Chemical Technology, China

ABSTRACT

This study investigated teachers' perception of the impact of COVID-19 on education. Their perceptions were analyzed in three aspects: barrier to access, opportunities, and learning outcomes. This study employed a descriptive design with a mixed approach. A self-developed survey questionnaire was used to elicit the responses of 119 school teachers from eights schools in Tamil Nadu, India. This study's findings revealed that the pandemic had impacted adversely the access, opportunities, and outcomes of education. The independent variables like age, years of experience, and subject taught did not influence perceptions of teachers. The findings show no correlation among perception of barrier to access, opportunities, and outcomes. Though more than half of the teachers didn't agree on the effectiveness of online education, they could show the right attitude toward using technology to teach online. The current crisis, COVID-19, highlighted the role of the internet and technology in education.

INTRODUCTION

Today, the world is taking a fresh start by leaving behind the tragedy of COVID-19 and moving forward to the era of technology and trade. When looking behind, we see that the increased urbanization, growing population and ample business and social activities between the countries and geographical areas had played a very important role in the spread of COVID-19 disease (Owen Jarus, 2020). Right

DOI: 10.4018/978-1-6684-9522-3.ch002

now, no matter the world has progressed so much but still some anomalies in human civilization exist. Fortunately, as time is progressing, this COVID-19 pandemic has started becoming a part of the history books (Walsh, 2020).

Severe acute respiratory syndrome, also known as COVID-19, is a contagious respiratory disease caused by the SARS-CoV-2 virus, which was first identified in a seafood market in Wuhan in late December 2019 (Huang, 2020). The disease is airborne and mainly spreads through physical proximity with infected people. Broadly speaking, there are two modes of transmission— direct and indirect. The direct mode involves droplet and air transmission, while indirect transmission may occur via contaminated surfaces (Karia, 2020). Due to its highly contagious nature, the COVID-19 virus swept the globe in the matter of weeks. Between December 2019 and October 2020, more than 45 million cases of COVID-19 were reported, including over a million deaths. (European Centre for Disease Prevention and Control, 2020). By March 2020, the epidemic was declared a pandemic by the World Health Organization. It prompted counties around the world to adopt a sequence of emergency response systems (Zhang et al., 2020). Authorities worldwide issued stay-at-home orders, imposing prolonged periods of lockdown. In many parts of the world, this meant a temporary shutdown of educational institutions. These nationwide closures impacted millions of students and their families, particularly those from underprivileged communities (UNESCO, 2020). Some of the educational institutions that faced closure progressively re-opened and started operating under online learning models in order to continue the academic progress of students, while simultaneously observing measures to reduce the impact of the current health crisis. Educational institutions have been compelled to make an immediate transition to remote methods of learning that rely heavily on technology. The immediate transition to online learning has not made it possible for many to be adequately prepared for the challenges ahead (Hodges et al., 2020). This migration to remote learning had to be implemented as quickly as possible, and for many learning institutions, it happened several months into the academic year, leaving both staff and students with little time to plan, adjust and adapt.

In response to COVID-19, a lot of countries were faced with pressure to contain the spread of this highly contagious disease. To many educational institutions, this meant either partial or complete closure. Others transitioned to technology-based distance learning. A systematic review was conducted by Viner et al. (2020) examines existing knowledge to identify the effects of school closures and other social distancing measures during outbreaks on infection rates and virus transmission. It suggested that school closures played a relatively small role in the control of disease transmission, and that the insignificant benefits such closures bring to transmission reduction could be easily outweighed by their profound negative economic and social consequences (Viner et al., 2020). There is no strong evidence to support the effectiveness of full closure in controlling the pandemic. If anything, there are significant economic downfalls to such a response, not to mention the academic delay incurred by students. That is why a lot of academic institutions opted for the less drastic measure of transitioning to online distance education (ODE).

Due to the COVID-19 pandemic, India's poor educational records have been exacerbated, with schools being closed since March 2020. Schools in India have been closed for the largest number of weeks, the longest duration that schools have been closed worldwide. (UNESCO), As a result of this, 1.5 million schools were shut and 247 million primary and secondary students have been out of school since the lockdown of March 2020 (UNICEF). Since most primary school students have not gone to school in more than a year, schools have been trying to replace in-person classes with online learning. Teachers and schools have been trying various ways to reach out to their students, using television, radio, WhatsApp groups, group tutoring, Zoom and Skype.

Teachers had to play a role not conventionally tailored for them. Consequently, the COVID-19 pandemic threw teachers into an unescorted precarious teaching arena. The teaching mode suddenly became virtual teaching all over the globe. However, everything comes with a cost, and COVID-19 juxtaposed with virtual teaching had a penetrating inescapable influence on access, opportunities and learning outcomes as well. The pandemic had a quivering impact on the access to education in term of availability of on line devices, uninterrupted bandwidth, lack of technical support and so. The teachers had adjustment issues while transiting to online mode of teaching. The COVID-19 pandemic has negatively impacted the well-being of children in many ways: isolation, fear, lack of socialization, lack of physical activity, curtailment of lab work, long screen time, and others have had a significant impact on their mental health. The pandemic threw children into an unescorted precarious teaching arena. The teaching mode suddenly became virtual teaching all over the globe. It impacted the learning outcomes. The study aims to understand the perception of teachers who have been doing virtual teaching to children during a period of uncertainty due to COVID-19, on the access, opportunities and learning outcomes and how they coped with online teaching. The teachers' perceptions were analyzed on the basis of variables like age, years of teaching experience and subject taught.

BACKGROUND

India is the second largest education system in the world, and it has significant history. The first case of COVID-19 in India was reported on 30 January 2020. A 14-hour voluntary public curfew was called by the Indian Prime Minister on March 22, 2020. The first nationwide lockdown was declared by the Government of India on 24 March 2020 affecting a population of 1.3 billion. On 14 April, the Prime Minister extended the ongoing nationwide lockdown further till 3 May 2020. On 1 May 2020 lockdown across the country was further extended by two more weeks till 17 May. On 17 May, NDMA further extended the nationwide lockdown till 31 May. On 16 March, the Union government declared a countrywide lockdown of schools and colleges (https://en.wikipedia.org/wiki/COVID-19_pandemic_lockdown_in_India). Thus, the coronavirus lockdown measures fully closed all the educational institution in India and more than 32 crore students have been affected by the various restrictions. The pandemic acted as a barrier to access to education, opportunities and learning outcomes.

Barrier to Access to Education

Teachers from urban and rural schools had limited access to smartphones and online internet services. Even if the resources were available, unsteady bandwidth, electricity supply, lack of technology skills, inadequate training for online classes acted as barriers to conducting online education for school teachers. Most teachers did not have sufficient resources to deal with the given situation of the pandemic.

Barrier to Opportunities in Education

There has been a decrease in academic learning activities, and children are more inclined toward digital media (Robinson et al., 2017) Many children spend their time playing video games and watching TV. This has brought concern to the overall physical and cognitive development of the children and is also leading to a sedentary lifestyle for children [Dunton et al.,)

Owing to the online mode of education there is reduced interaction of the children with teachers and their friends as they cannot see, meet, or play with them [Brown et al.,) This has also reduced the extracurricular activities like dancing, singing, and participating in competitions. This has affected the peer interaction and social and cognitive development of the children.

The school closure and online education, impacted the learning opportunities for students and teachers.

Barrier to Learning Outcomes

On account of the pandemic, students missed out the interaction with teachers and peer. It affected their physical, cognitive, social and emotional growth. The attendance for the online classes was thin. Students did not take the assignments and online evaluation seriously. Some even felt they could not concentrate as much in online classes. As expected, students faced problems in various numerical subjects.

Anderson's Online Learning Model

Anderson considered a number of theories and models but focused on the well-respected work of Bransford, Brown, and Cocking (1999) who posited that effective learning environments are framed within the convergence of four overlapping lenses: community-centeredness, knowledge-centeredness, learner-centeredness, and assessment centeredness. These lenses provided the foundational framework for Anderson's approach to building an online education theory, as he examined in detail the characteristics and facilities that the Internet provides with regards to each of the four lenses. Second, he noted that the Internet had evolved from a text-based environment to one in which all forms of media are supported and readily available. He also accurately commented that the Internet's hyperlink capacity is most compatible with the way human knowledge is stored and accessed. In this regard, he referred to the work of Jonassen (1992) and Shank (1993) who associated hyperlinking with constructivism. Finally, Anderson extensively examined the importance of interaction in all forms of learning and referred to a number of mostly distance education theorists such as Holmberg (1989), Moore (1989), Moore and Kearsley (1996), and Garrison and Shale (1990). The essence of interaction among students, teachers, and content is well understood and is referenced in many theories of education, especially constructivism.

Anderson's evaluation of interaction concludes that interactions are critical components of a theory. With these three elements in mind (the Bransford, Brown, and Cocking lenses, the affordances and facilities of the Internet, and interaction), Anderson then proceeded to construct a model **(see Figure 1)**. Anderson (2011) emphasized the four overlapping lenses: learner, knowledge, assessment, and community that contribute to interactive online learning. The typologies of interactions, namely student-student, student teacher, student-content, teacher-content, content-content, teacher-teacher interactions, serve as the basis of the instructional process of online learning. Within this learning community, teachers organize and initiate cooperative activities, promote dialogues among learners, and provide learning guidance, thus engaging community members in the meaningful learning process and accomplishing academic goals. Learners can of course interact directly with content that they find in multiple formats, and especially on the Web; however, many choose to have their learning sequenced, directed, and evaluated with the assistance of a teacher. This interaction can take place within a community of inquiry, using a variety of net-based synchronous and asynchronous activities. These environments are particularly rich, and allow for the learning of social skills, the collaborative learning of content, and the development of personal relationships among participants. However, the community binds learners in time, forcing regular sessions or at least group-paced learning. The second model of learning (on the right) illustrates the structured learning tools associated with independent learning. Common tools used in this mode include computer-assisted tutorials, drills, and simulations (Anderson, 2011, p. 61-62). Figure 1 demonstrates the instructional flow within the two sides and represents the beginnings of a theory or model from the distance education perspective. Anderson concluded that his model "will help us to deepen our understanding of this complex educational context" (Anderson, 2011, p. 68), which he noted needs to measure more fully the direction and magnitude of each input variable on relevant outcome variables. Anderson also commented about the potential of the Internet for education delivery, and that an online learning-based theory or model could subsume all other modes with the exception of the "rich face-to-face interaction in formal classrooms" (Anderson, 2011, p. 67). This becomes a quandary for Anderson in trying to develop a common theory of online education in that it does not provide for in-person, face-to-face activity and is problematic for those who see online education as a subset of education in general.

Figure 1. Anderson's online learning model

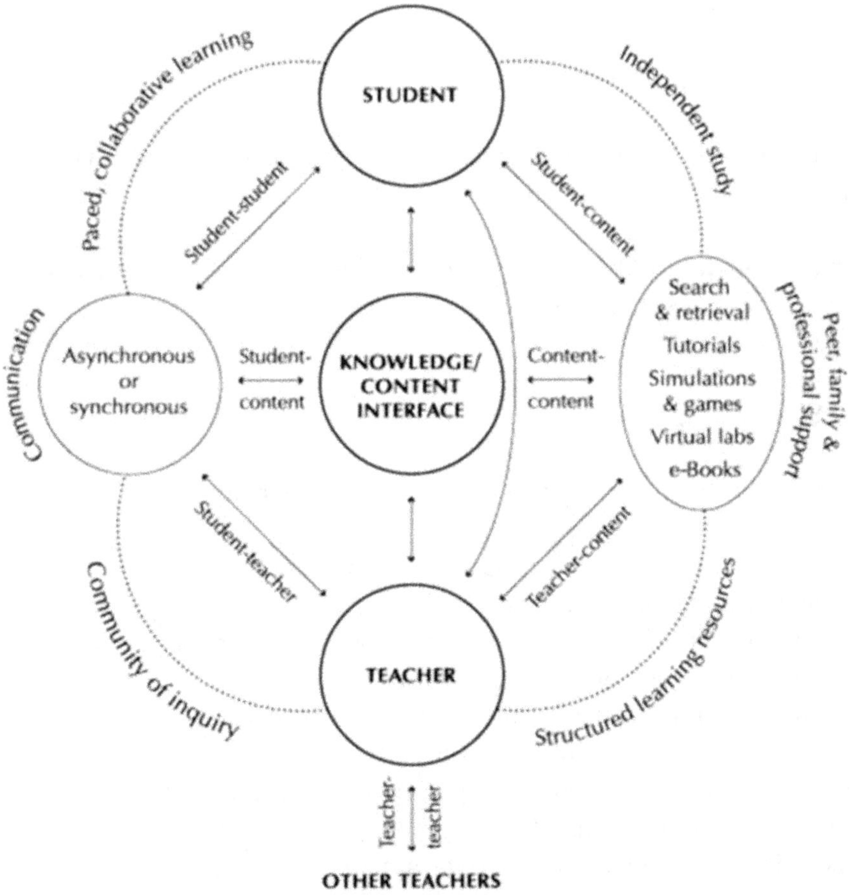

Emergency Remote Teaching (ERT)

It is a temporary alternative to an online instructional mode due to crisis and differs from previous typical online courses (Hodges et al., 2020). For regular online teaching, besides delivering instructional content to students, teachers also address the significance of building a learning community for learners to engage and thus get social supports. The teaching materials, content, and activities used in ERT are primarily designed for physical learning environments but utilized in a virtual learning setting (Adedoyin & Soykan, 2020; Bozkurt & Sharma, 2020; Ferri et al., 2020; Mohmmed et al., 2020). Bozkurt et al. (2020) distinguished online learning and ERT by indicating that online learning is planned activities based on teachers' practical knowledge and grounded in educational theories, while ERT is for keeping education survival during a crisis by providing students with offline and online resources. Unlike in typical online classes where instructors are trained for teaching in the distance, in ERT classes, both students and their instructors had little or no experience with online education (Jeffery & Bauer, 2020).

PURPOSE OF THE STUDY

Notably, the four main objectives that drive this study are

1. To find out the impact of COVID-19 on barrier to access to education as perceived by teachers
2. To find out the impact of COVID-19 on barrier to opportunities in education as perceived by teachers
3. To find out the impact of COVID-19 on barrier to learning outcomes as perceived by teachers
4. To find out how teachers coped with the online classes

HYPOTHESES OF THE STUDY

The researcher developed the following null hypotheses for the study.

1. There is no significant difference in the perception of teachers on the impact of COVID-19 on barrier to education on basis of age
2. There is no significant difference in the perception of teachers on the impact of COVID-19 on barrier to education on basis of teaching experience
3. There is no significant difference in the perception of teachers on the impact of COVID-19 on barrier to education on the basis of subject taught
4. There is no significant correlation in the perception of teachers on the impact of COVID-19 on barrier to access, opportunities and learning outcomes of education
5. There is no relationship among the variables access, opportunities and learning outcomes of education

RESEARCH QUESTION

1] How did the teachers cope with the online classes during the pandemic?

RESEARCH METHODOLOGY

This study adopted a survey research design. The current study used a mixed approach to answer the objectives of the study. The quantitative analysis like percentage, ANOVA, Pearson's correlation, multiple regression method was used in this investigation to answer objectives 1,2 and 3. For answering objective 4, data analysis was done using thematic analysis. This included reading and re-reading transcription, coding and collating, coding themes, and then finalizing themes.

Participants

Data for this paper came from 119 secondary school teachers from eight schools of Tamil Nadu.

Table 1. Demographic profile of the sample

Demographic factors N		
Gender	female	90 (75.6%)
	male	29 (24.4%)
	total	119 (100%)
Age	below 25 years	23 (19.3%)
	25-35 years	46 (38.7%)
	36-45 years	34 (28.6%)
	above 45 years	16 (13.4%)
	total	119 (100%)
Years of experience	less than 2 years	28 (23.5%)
	2-5 years	35 (29.4%)
	6-15 years	39 (32.8%)
	above 15 years	17 (14.3%)
	total	119 (100%)
Subject taught	Language	44 (40%)
	Mathematics	41 (34.5%)
	Science	23 (19.3%)
	Social Sciences	11 (9.2%)
	total	119 (100%)

Research Instruments

The researcher developed a questionnaire for collecting quantitative data from the teachers. The questionnaire contained 66 items distributed into 3 parts. Part A, is a checklist consisting of 17 items, to assess the teachers' perception of the impact of COVID-19 on access to education. Part B, is a Likert five-level rating scale containing 21 items to assess the teachers' perception of the impact of COVID-19 on opportunities in education. Part C, is a Likert five-level rating scale containing 28 items to assess

Table 2. Reliability of the tool

Section	Cronbach's Albha	No of Items
PART-A	0.719	17
PART-B	0.862	21
PART-C	0.867	28

the teachers' perception of the impact of COVID-19 on learning outcomes. The Likert five-level scale ranges from 5= Strongly Agree, 4= Agree, 3= Neutral, 2= Disagree and 1=Strongly Disagree

The reliability of the tool is given in Table 2

As evident in **Table 2**, the reliability of Part-A (barrier to access to education), Part-B (barrier to opportunities in education), Part-C (barrier to learning outcomes), is high and the constructed tool is highly reliable.

The qualitative data about teacher resilience during the pandemic, was collected by interviewing 20 teachers.

DATA ANALYSIS PROCESS

All the data collected from the respondents were gathered together to be analyzed using Statistical Package for the Social Sciences (SPSS) version 20. The analysis included descriptive and inferential analysis. The researchers used descriptive analysis percentage, mean and standard deviation to identify the teachers' perception about COVID -19 barrier to access, opportunities and outcomes. To answer posed hypotheses ANOVA, Pearson's correlation and multivariate analysis techniques were employed.

Findings

The descriptive findings are presented under three headings for the sake of clarity.

Section-A: Barrier to Access to Education

Objective-1: To find out the impact of COVID-19 on access to education as perceived by teachers.

The descriptive findings are presented in the table below.

As evident in **Table 3** teachers faced serious challenges during COVID-19, like unsteady internet facility and electricity supply, during COVID -19. 5% did not have an online device. Teachers encountered serious challenges like lack of awareness of online platforms, insufficient technological skills to manage online teaching, lack of support from family, colleagues nor proper training from school for handling online classes. Teachers mostly muted the students and even kept the camera off during the online classes. Though most of the classes were in synchronous mode, asynchronous mode was also adopted. Majority of the teachers faced challenges in operating the online devices and were not competent in the use of online devices.

Table 3. Descriptive statistics of the impact of COVID-19 on barrier to access to education

S.NO	ITEMS	YES		NO	
		F	P	F	P
1	I had a device for online teaching during COVID -19	113	95%	6	5%
2	I had steady internet facility during COVID -19	93	78.20%	26	21.80%
3	I had uninterrupted electricity facility during COVID -19	72	60.50%	47	39.50%
4	I had sufficient technological skills to manage my online teaching	86	72.30%	33	27.70%
5	I had awareness of online platforms introduced by the government	61	51.30%	58	48.70%
6	I kept my audio on for the students to interact in the online classes during COVID-19	77	64.70%	42	35.30%
7	I kept my camera on for the online classes during COVID-19	45	37.80%	74	62.20%
8	I felt confident while using online teaching devices during COVID-19	101	84.90%	18	15.10%
9	I felt confident while using online- teaching content during COVID -19	86	72.30%	33	27.70%
10	I received support from my family for online teaching during COVID-19	57	47.90%	62	52.10%
11	I received training from my school for online teaching during COVID-19	50	42.00%	69	58.00%
12	I received support from my colleague for online teaching during COVID-19	80	67.20%	39	32.80%
13	I could easily operate online teaching devices during COVID-19	68	57.10%	51	42.90%
14	I could easily find necessary information when using e- learning platforms during COVID-19	94	79.00%	25	21.00%
15	I was competent in the use of the online devices during COVID-19	68	57.10%	51	42.90%
16	I had synchronous online classes (live virtual classes) during COVID-19	105	82.20%	14	11.80%
17	I had asynchronous online classes (recording video/audio) lessons during COVID -19	89	74.80%	30	25.20%

Section-B: Barrier to Opportunities in Education

Objective-2: To find out the impact of COVID-19 on barrier to opportunities in education as perceived by teachers

The descriptive findings on the impact of COVID-19 on opportunities in education as perceived by teachers are presented in the table below-

Looking at **Table 4**, it can be stated that when it came to barrier to opportunities during online classes, teachers perceived the online classes as serious barrier for students' participation and interaction with teachers and peer. According to them online classes were not effective in developing drawing skills, mathematical skills, scientific temper, reading skill, speaking skills, writing skills and listening skills. Majority of the teachers reported challenges in theory and practical classes due to lack of teacher- student interaction. Teachers reported prominent barriers in enhancing teaching skills and difficulties in using innovative teaching strategies.

Section-C: Barrier to Outcomes in Learning

Objective-3: To find out the impact of COVID-19 on barrier to learning outcomes as perceived by teachers.

Table 4. Descriptive statistics of impact of COVID-19 on barrier to opportunities in education

S.NO	ITEMS	SA	A	N	D	SD
1	COVID-19 online classes students participation was as good as face to face mode	19.3%(23)	37%(44)	17.6%(21)	16.8%(20)	9.2%(11)
2	COVID-19 online classes students had adequate discussions with peers	21.8%(26)	30.3%(36)	16.8%(20)	15.1%(18)	16%(19)
3	COVID-19 online classes could cater to individuals differences	16%(19)	27.7%(33)	37%(44)	16.8%(20)	2.5%(3)
4	COVID-19 online classes there was lack of teacher- student interaction	5.9%(7)	5.9%(7)	20.2%(24)	44.5%(53)	23.5%(28)
5	COVID-19 online classes it was difficult to control group interaction	7.6%(9)	15.1%(18)	8.4%(10)	33.6%(40)	35.3%(42)
6	COVID-19 online classes helped me to use innovative teaching strategies	3.4%(4)	27.7%(33)	15.1%(18)	27.7%(33)	26.1%(31)
7	COVID-19 online classes accommodated different types of learning styles	25.2%(30)	36.1%(43)	13.4%(16)	19.3%(23)	5.9%(7)
8	COVID-19 theory classes could be taught without real interaction between tutors and students	4.2%(5)	17.6%(21)	29.4%(35)	27.7%(33)	21%(25)
9	COVID-19 practical classes could be taught without real interaction between tutors and their students	11.8%(14)	31.1%(37)	17.6%(21)	25.2%(30)	14.3%(17)
10	COVID-19 online classes were effective for developing drawing skills	16.8%(20)	31.9%(38)	19.3%(23)	16.8%(20)	15.1%(18)
11	COVID-19 online classes were effective for developing mathematical skills	28.6%(34)	37%(44)	11.8%(14)	19.3%(23)	3.4%(4)
12	COVID-19 online classes were effective for developing scientific temper	14.3%(17)	25.2%(30)	28.6%(34)	21%(25)	10.9%(13)
13	COVID-19 online classes were effective for developing reading skills	30.3%(36)	19.3%(23)	17.6%(21)	18.5%(22)	14.3%(17)
14	COVID-19 online classes were effective for developing speaking skills	15.1%(18)	35.3%(42)	19.3%(23)	17.6%(21)	12.6%(15)
15	COVID-19 online classes were effective for developing writing skills	4.2%(5)	16.8%(20)	35.3%(42)	22.7%(27)	21%(25)
16	COVID-19 online classes were effective for developing listening skills	6.7%(8)	25.2%(30)	26.1%(31)	28.6%(34)	13.4%(16)
17	COVID-19 online classes allowed quick share of reading material	14.3%(17)	23.5%(28)	22.7%(27)	28.6%(34)	10.9%(13)
18	COVID-19 online classes provided flexibility in time and space	8.4%(10)	21.8%(26)	27.7%(33)	21.8%(26)	20.2%(24)
19	COVID-19 online platforms had tools to facilitate online classes	10.9%(13)	26.1%(31)	23.5%(28)	28.6%(34)	10.9%(13)
20	COVID-19 online teaching enhanced my teaching skills	14.3%(17)	20.2%(24)	26.1%(31)	28.6%(34)	10.9%(13)
21	COVID-19 developed my technological skill	8.4%(10)	18.5%(22)	16%(19)	37%(44)	20.2%(24)

Table 5. Descriptive statistics of the impact of COVID-19 on barrier to learning outcomes

S.NO	ITEMS	SA	A	N	D	SD
1	Online classes can replace offline classes in the future.	17.6%(21)	47.1%(56)	18.5%(22)	12.6%(15)	4.2%(5)
2	Online classes are more effective than face to face classroom mode.	21.8%(26)	38.7%(46)	19.3%(23)	19.3%(23)	8%(1)
3	Online classes made me conscious about my teaching skills.	21%(25)	27.7%(33)	35.3%(42)	11.8%(14)	4.2%(5)
4	Online classes triggered anxiety in me.	2.5%(3)	24.4%(29)	34.5%(41)	22.7%(27)	13.4%(16)
5	Online classes has resulted in learning gaps	19.3%(23)	40.3%(48)	19.3%(23)	20.2%(24)	8%(1)
6	Online teaching has boosted my confidence as a teacher	21.8%(26)	40.3%(48)	17.6%(21)	14.3%(17)	5.9%(7)
7	COVID-19 online classes, I had to alter the medium of instruction .	28.6%(34)	27.7%(33)	21.8%(26)	17.6%(21)	4.2%(5)
8	COVID-19 online classes, I had to alter the method of teaching.	24.4%(29)	32.8%(39)	26.1%(31)	8.4%(10)	8.4%(10)
9	COVID-19 online classes, I had to alter the content of classes.	19.3%(23)	27.7%(33)	38.7%(46)	10.9%(13)	3.4%(4)
10	COVID-19 online classes, I had to alter the grading scheme.	16%(19)	40.3%(48)	23.5%(28)	16%(19)	4.2%(5)
11	COVID-19 online classes, I had to alter the examination pattern.	31.9%(38)	28.6%(34)	16%(19)	16.8%(20)	6.7%(8)
12	COVID-19 adversely impacted my students' physical development	11.8%(14)	38.7%(46)	21%(25)	23.5%(28)	5%(6)
13	COVID-19 adversely impacted my students' emotional development	23.5%(28)	28.6%(34)	27.7%(33)	14.3%(17)	5.9%(7)
14	COVID-19 impacted my students' social development	27.7%(33)	44.5%(53)	16.8%(20)	6.7%(8)	4.2%(5)
15	COVID-19 adversely impacted my students' cognitive development	22.7%(27)	40.3%(48)	20.2%(24)	15.1%(18)	1.7%(2)
16	COVID -19 adversely impacted academics interaction between teachers and students	26.9%(32)	32.8%(39)	29.4%(35)	9.2%(11)	1.7%(2)
17	I found it difficult to adapt to the online teaching mode during the online classes.	12.6%(15)	34.5%(41)	42%(50)	10.1%(12)	8%(1)
18	I feel students had not coped well with remote learning during the online classes.	15.1%(18)	46.2%(55)	23.5%(28)	11.8%(14)	3.4%(4)
19	I feel students had responded positively to my remote teaching during the online classes.	22.7%(27)	26.9%(32)	34.5%(41)	12.6%(15)	3.4%(4)
20	I feel students with face to face learning outperform students with online learning	20.2%(24)	21%(25)	16%(19)	25.2%(30)	17.6%(21)
21	I feel students had trouble with concentration and staying focused during the online classes.	30.3%(36)	32.8%(39)	18.5%(22)	11.8%(14)	6.7%(8)
22	I feel teacher- students disconnect was high in online classes	28%(28)	27.7%(33)	14.3%(17)	26.1%(31)	8.4%(10)
23	I found it difficult to evaluate students activity during online classes.	12.6%(15)	22.7%(27)	28.6%(34)	21.8%(26)	14.3%(17)
24	I got easily distracted during online classes	19.3%(23)	39.5%(47)	26.1%(31)	13.4%(16)	1.7%(2)
25	I feel that some students cheated in their online assignments/exams	26.9%(32)	28.6%(34)	22.7%(27)	16.8%(20)	5%(6)
26	I felt lack of motivation to take online classes	25.2%(30)	42%(50)	22.7%(27)	7.6%(9)	2.5%(3)
27	I felt my skills as a teacher has improved through online teaching method.	22.7%(27)	34.5%(41)	18.5%(22)	19.3%(23)	5%(6)
28	COVID-19 online teaching helped in saving resources like time and money	16.8%(20)	34.5%(41)	26.1%(31)	14.3%(17)	8.4%(10)

The descriptive findings on the impact of COVID-19 on learning outcomes as perceived by teachers are presented in the table below

The result shown in **Table 5** confirms that teachers reported that they had to alter medium of instruction, content, method of teaching, examination pattern, and grading scheme. According to the teachers, online classes have adversely impacted students' physical development, emotional development, social development and cognitive development and resulted in learning gaps. Teachers perceived online classes negatively in terms of students' coping, students' response and interaction, focus and concentration in the class, students' cheating in the assignment and exams. Teachers reported that they felt demotivated, got easily distracted, and a feeling of disconnect with the students.

Inferential Analysis

Null Hypothesis -1 Testing:

1. There is no significant difference in the perception of teachers on the impact of COVID-19 on education on basis of age

To test the above null hypothesis, ANOVA is computed and presented in the following tables.

TEST OF ANOVA

Looking at **Table 6** and **Table 7**, we conclude, the null hypothesis is accepted and there is no significant difference found about the perception of teachers on the impact of COVID-19 on education on basis of age, $(p>.05)$

Null Hypothesis-2 Testing:

2. There is no significant difference in the perception of teachers on the impact of COVID-19 on education on the basis of years of teaching experience

To test the above null hypothesis, ANOVA is computed and presented in the following tables.

TEST OF ANOVA

Looking at **Table 8 and Table 9**, the null hypothesis is accepted and there is no significant difference found about the perception of teachers on the impact of COVID-19 on education on basis of years of teaching experience $(p>.05)$.

Null Hypothesis-3 Testing:

3. There is no significant difference in the perception of teachers on the impact of COVID-19 on education on the basis of subject taught

To test the above null hypothesis, ANOVA is computed and presented in the following tables.

TEST OF ANOVA

The results shown in **Table 10** and **Table 11** confirm that the null hypothesis is to be accepted ($(p>.05)$). No significant difference found about the perception of teachers on the impact of COVID-19 on education on basis of subject taught.

Null Hypothesis-4 Testing:

Table 6. Descriptive statistics for the perception of teachers on the impact of COVID-19 on education on basis of age

Tool	Age	N	Mean	Std Deviation	Std Error	95% Confidence Interval of the Difference(Lower)	95% Confidence Interval of the Difference(Upper)
Part-A	Below 25 years	23	11.26	2.22	0.463	10.3	12.22
	25-35 Years	46	11.11	2.931	0.432	10.24	11.98
	36-45 Years	34	11.5	2.82	0.484	10.52	12.48
	Above 45 Years	16	12.69	3.24	0.81	10.96	14.41
	Total	119	11.46	2.831	0.259	10.95	11.98
Part-B	Below 25 years	23	68.04	8.407	1.753	64.41	71.68
	25-35 Years	46	61.2	13.732	2.025	57.12	65.27
	36-45 Years	34	61.06	14.42	2.473	56.03	66.09
	Above 45 Years	16	61.56	14.236	3.559	53.98	69.15
	Total	119	62.53	13.28	1.217	60.12	64.94
Part-C	Below 25 years	23	69.83	11.629	2.425	64.8	74.85
	25-35 Years	46	66.39	16.776	2.474	61.41	71.37
	36-45 Years	34	71.24	13.623	2.336	66.48	75.99
	Above 45 Years	16	72.13	14.375	3.594	64.46	79.79
	Total	119	69.21	14.704	1.348	66.54	71.88

Table 7. Test of ANOVA results for the impact of COVID-19 on education on basis of age

		Sum of Squares	df	Mean Square	F	Sig. (p)
Part A	Between Groups	30.751	3	10.25	1.289	0.282
	Within Groups	914.829	115	7.955		
	Total	945.58	118			
Part B	Between Groups	869.632	3	289.877	1.672	0.177
	Within Groups	19942.016	115	173.409		
	Total	20811.647	118			
Part C	Between Groups	649.619	3	216.54	1.002	0.395
	Within Groups	24864.129	115	216.21		
	Total	25513.748	118			

Table 8. Descriptive statistics for the perception of teachers on the impact of COVID-19 on education on basis of years of teaching experience

Tool	Years of teaching experience	N	Mean	Std Deviation	Std Error	95% Confidence Interval of the Difference(Lower)	95% Confidence Interval of the Difference(Upper)
Part A	Less than 2 years	28	11.39	2.699	0.51	10.35	12.44
	2 to 5 years	35	10.8	2.564	0.433	9.92	11.68
	6-15 years	39	12	2.782	0.445	11.1	12.9
	above 15 years	17	11.71	3.567	0.865	9.87	13.54
	Total	119	11.46	2.831	0.259	10.95	11.98
Part B	Less than 2 years	28	66.11	12.363	2.336	61.31	70.9
	2 to 5 years	35	60.6	11.983	2.026	56.48	64.72
	6-15 years	39	62.26	14.293	2.289	57.62	66.89
	above 15 years	17	61.24	14.83	3.597	53.61	68.86
	Total	119	62.53	13.28	1.217	60.12	64.94
Part C	Less than 2 years	28	70.21	12.856	2.43	65.23	75.2
	2 to 5 years	35	68.97	16.718	2.826	63.23	74.71
	6-15 years	39	67.21	14.633	2.343	62.46	71.95
	above 15 years	17	72.65	13.747	3.334	65.58	79.72
	Total	119	69.21	14.704	1.348	66.54	71.88

4. There is no significant correlation in the perception of teachers on the impact of COVID-19 on

Table 9. Test of ANOVA results for the impact of COVID-19 on education on basis of years of teaching experience

Section		Sum of Squares	Df	Mean Square	F	Sig. (p)
Part A	Between Groups	27.772	3	9.257	1.16	0.328
	Within Groups	917.808	115	7.981		
	Total	945.58	118			
Part B	Between Groups	520.074	3	173.358	0.982	0.404
	Within Groups	20291.573	115	176.448		
	Total	20811.647	118			
Part C	Between Groups	387.821	3	129.274	0.592	0.622
	Within Groups	25125.927	115	218.486		
	Total	25513.748	118			

Table 10. Descriptive statistics for the perception of teachers on the impact of COVID-19 on education on basis of subject taught

Section	Years	N	Mean	Std Deviation	Std Error	95% Confidence Interval of the Difference(Lower)	95% Confidence Interval of the Difference(Upper)
Part A	Language	44	11.86	3.107	0.468	10.92	12.81
	Mathematics	41	10.98	2.688	0.42	10.13	11.82
	Science	23	11.48	2.538	0.529	10.38	12.58
	Social Science	11	11.64	2.873	0.866	9.71	13.57
	Total	119	11.46	2.831	0.259	10.95	11.98
Part B	Language	44	62.61	12.931	1.949	58.68	66.55
	Mathematics	41	63.95	15.03	2.347	59.21	68.7
	Science	23	59.09	11.623	2.423	54.06	64.11
	Social Science	11	64.09	11.095	3.345	56.64	71.54
	Total	119	62.53	13.28	1.217	60.12	64.94
Part C	Language	44	68.27	14.06	2.12	64	72.55
	Mathematics	41	69.71	16.279	2.542	64.57	74.85
	Science	23	71.13	15.286	3.187	64.52	77.74
	Social Science	11	67.09	10.435	3.146	60.08	74.1
	Total	119	69.21	14.704	1.348	66.54	71.88

barrier to access, opportunities and learning outcomes of education

Table 11. Test of ANOVA results for the impact of COVID-19 on Education on basis of subject taught

Section		Sum of Squares	df	Mean Square	F	Sig.(p)
PartA	Between Groups	17.138	3	5.713	0.708	0.549
	Within Groups	928.442	115	8.073		
	Total	945.58	118			
PartB	Between Groups	382.578	3	127.526	0.718	0.543
	Within Groups	20429.069	115	177.644		
	Total	20811.647	118			
PartC	Between Groups	183.015	3	61.005	0.277	0.842
	Within Groups	25330.733	115	220.267		
	Total	25513.748	118			

To test the above null hypothesis, correlation is computed and presented in the following table.

TEST OF CORRELATION

The result shown in **Table 12**, confirms no significant correlation at 0.05 level therefore, we infer no significant association among the variables, barrier to access, opportunities and learning outcomes.

Null Hypothesis-5 Testing:

5. There is no effect of the constant variables, access and opportunities on the dependent variable, learning outcomes

To test the above null hypothesis, multiple regression is computed and presented in the following table.

TEST OF MULTIPLE REGRESSION

a. **Dependent variable Part C, b. Predictors: (Constant), Part B, Part A**

Table 12. Test of correlation results for the variables access, opportunities and learning outcomes

Section		TotalPart A	TotalPart B	TotalPart C
Part-A	Pearson Correlation	1	0.063	-0.131
	Sig. (2-tailed)		0.495	0.156
	N	119	119	119
Part-B	Pearson Correlation	0.063	1	0.052
	Sig. (2-tailed)	0.495		0.573
	N	119	119	119
Part-C	Pearson Correlation	-0.131	0.052	1
	Sig. (2-tailed)	0.156	0.573	
	N	119	119	119

Table 13. Test of multiple regression for effect of constant variables on independent variable

	Model	Sum of Squares	df	Mean Square	F	Sig.
1	Regression	530.378	2	265.189	1.231	.296b
	Residual	24983.37	116	215.374		
	Total	25513.748	118			

The results shown in **Table 13** confirms (p >.05), the independent variables perception of barrier to access to education and opportunities have not influenced the dependent variable the perception of barrier to learning outcomes.

Research Question

1] How did the teachers cope with the online classes during the pandemic?

Although teachers acknowledged that conducting classes remotely during the COVID-19 pandemic was challenging since they did not have the experience, they perceived resilience as the ability to be patient, act immediately, and adapt to the changing landscape in education during a health crisis. Such perceptions allowed them to design their teaching and learning environment that is relevant and according to the needs of the COVID-19 situation. For instance,

At first, I was not sure of what I was going to do. But, I was very patient with the sudden change of the teaching and learning policies of the government during this time. I accepted the fact that online class is, our new normal. So, I thought the best way to deal with this is to be patient and adapt to this new normal in education (T1,6,10,12,18)

As can be reflected, teachers equated resilience to mental resistance to difficulties and stresses.

I realized things won't work if I continue to contemplate on the negatives, so I used my resources, took help of my family, friends, colleagues and did my best to facilitate quality teaching learning (T2,6,9,17).

Teacher participant 10 supported the above response highlighting that rigorous planning was done weekly, to survive the challenges of virtual classes.

During the interview, teacher-participants also recognized some challenges in their teaching design. One of these challenges is developing teaching materials suitable for remote and online teaching.

I had to put in extra work when developing the content of educational materials because I had to consider how students would comprehend, and learn from them. I spend hours preparing power point slides, online quizzes, games and assignments. (T 1,6,14,18,20).

Teacher participants also revealed that though their schools conducted periodic training for conducting online classes, they were also committed to self-learning. This is evident from the following excerpt-

I was very committed to equipping myself with the knowledge and skills needed to use online platforms, so I watched you tube videos, took help of anybody who was willing to help me, my family, colleagues, neighbors, relatives and co-workers(T2,7,9,11,12,14,19).

The above findings reflect that even in the most difficult times the pursuit for a learner-centered approach can still be sustained. This characteristic of teaching and learning processes has to be promoted as always, since the core concern of education is the learners. Reinventing strategies and approaches may help teachers to cope with any calamity.

DISCUSSION AND CONCLUSION

The result of this study indicates that face- to- face learning was perceived more positively than online learning in term of access, opportunities and learning outcome by the teachers. Teachers perceived it to be less effective and structured when compared to classroom mode of learning. Technical support was found to be an important factor critical to determining satisfaction with online classes. Yang and Cornelius (2003) in their study had reported similar findings. Thus, these findings from previous studies are in tandem with the current survey results where technical issues were found to be the most influential factor when it came to satisfaction with online classes to lack quality.

As far as barrier to access to education was concerned teachers perceived interrupted electricity and internet connection, broadband issue, poor audio and video quality, problems with the app, getting disconnected in between the classes. Many of them even reported that having lack of supportive home environment and family issues makes it harder for them to fully involve themselves during online classes. Also, the need for providing adequate technological training to teachers about method of conducting online classes should have been prioritized as it is found to be a pre-requisite for successful online class implementation. The asynchronous online classes were very useful as students could view them when free.

As far as barrier to opportunities to education was concerned things such as lack of structure, disturbance in the flow of classes, problems in clarifying doubts, lack of interest and motivations to attend the classes were some prominent factors reducing the effectiveness of online classes, Thus, the online classes teachers felt were less lively, lacked friendly atmosphere and social interaction. Significant number of teachers disagreed with changing the traditional teaching method with e-learning.

As far as impact of COVID-19 on barrier to learning outcome is concerned, our findings reveal that the educational process was teacher-centred rather than student-centred.

Surprisingly, it was demonstrated in this study that there was no significant difference in faculty's perception in terms of age, subject taught, years of teaching, this is in contrast with the findings of studies done prior to the pandemic.

The finding of this research suggests that problems and challenges associated with online education must be addressed, and online courses must be carefully planned and regulated. The undesirable preconceived notions about online education commonly held by faculty must be modified or corrected to improve the views of faculty about teaching online. It is recommended that faculty must be provided with robust resources and more technology infrastructure to support online education. There is still a need to improve and enhance the level of competency of teachers on certain skills like using complex Information, Communication and Technology (ICT) tools. Additionally, faculty must learn to embrace the educational challenges brought by the COVID-19 pandemic and view online teaching and learning as an inviting challenge.

However, considering the short period of time in which teachers had to adapt to the new teaching conditions, most of them managed to cope successfully with the challenges, teachers used diverse tools while delivering courses online in order to make the course more attractive, but sometimes feedback from students was delayed, tasks were not concise, and teachers often failed to express clearly their expectations. The reason why the online educational process encountered so many issues is represented by the fact that the traditional way in which teachers used to deliver the practical part of the course was no longer suitable for the online environment. In spite, of all odds teachers demonstrated resilience during the pandemic virtual teaching.

ACKNOWLEDGMENT

This study is part of a larger study, and the author gratefully acknowledges the funding by Indian Council of Social Science Research (ICSSR), under its minor research funding.

REFERENCES

Adedoyin, O. B., & Soykan, E. (2020). COVID-19 pandemic and online learning: The challenges and opportunities. *Interactive Learning Environments*, 1–13. doi:10.1080/10494820.2020

Anderson, T. (2011). *The theory and practice of online learning* (2nd ed.). AU Press.

Attard, C., & Holmes, K. (2020). "It gives you that sense of hope": An exploration of technology use to mediate student engagement with mathematics. *Heliyon*, *6*(1), e02945. doi:10.1016/j.heliyon.2019.e02945 PMID:31922039

Bozkurt, A., & Sharma, R. C. (2020). Emergency remote teaching in a time of global crisis due to Coronavirus pandemic. *Asian Journal of Distance Education*, *15*(1), 1–6.

Bransford, J., Brown, A., & Cocking, R. (1999). *How people learn: Brain, mind experience and school.* National Academy Press/National Research Council., Retrieved from https://www.colorado.edu/MCDB/LearningBiology/readings/Howpeople-learn.pdf

Brown, N. T., Snethen, J. A., & Greenberg, C. S. (2021). When pandemics collide: the impact of COVID-19 on childhood obesity. *J Pediatr Nursing, 56*, 90–98. [PMC free article] [PubMed] [Google Scholar]

Dunton, G. F., Do, B., & Wang, S. D. (2020). Early effects of the COVID-19 pandemic on physical activity and sedentary behavior in children living in the U.S. *BMC Public Health, 20*, 1351.

Ferri, F., Grifoni, P., & Guzzo, T. (2020). Online learning and emergency remote teaching: Opportunities and challenges in emergency situations. *Societies (Basel, Switzerland)*, *10*(4), 1–18. doi:10.3390oc10040086

Garrison, D. R., & Shale, D. (1990). *Education at a distance: From issues to practice.* Robert E. Krieger.

Hodges, C., Moore, S., Lockee, B., Trust, T., & Bond, A. (2020). The difference between emergency remote teaching and online learning. *EDUCAUSE Review.* https://er.educause.edu/articles/2020/3/the-difference-between-emergency-remote-teaching-and-online-learning

Holmberg, B. (1989). *Theory and practice of distance education.* Routledge.

Huang, J. (2020). Successes and Challenges: Online Teaching and Learning of Chemistry in Higher Education in China in the Time of COVID-19. *Journal of Chemical Education*, *97*(9), 2810–2814. doi:10.1021/acs.jchemed.0c00671

Jeffery, K. A., & Bauer, C. F. (2020). Students' responses to emergency remote online teaching reveal critical factors for all teaching. *Journal of Chemical Education*, *97*(9), 2472–2485. doi:10.1021/acs.jchemed.0c00736

Jonassen, D. (1992). Designing hypertext for learning. In E. Scanlon & T. O'Shea (Eds.), *New directions in educational technology* (pp. 123–130). Springer-Verlag. doi:10.1007/978-3-642-77750-9_10

Karia, R. (2020). *COVID-19 and its modes of transmission.* NIH.

Mohmmed, A. O., Khidhir, B. A., Nazeer, A., & Vijayan, V. J. (2020). Emergency remote teaching during Coronavirus pandemic: The current trend and future directive at Middle East College Oman. *Innovative Infrastructure Solutions*, *5*(3), 1–11. doi:10.100741062-020-00326-7

Moore, M. (1989). Three types of interaction. *American Journal of Distance Education*, *3*(2), 1–6. doi:10.1080/08923648909526659

Moore, M., & Kearsley, G. (1996). *Distance education: A systems view*. Wadsworth Publishing Company.

Owen Jarus. (2020, March 20). *20 of the worst epidemics and pandemics in history*. Live Science. https://www.livescience.com/worst-epidemics-and-pandemics-in-history.html

Robinson, T. N., Banda, J. A., Hale, L., Lu, A. S., Fleming-Milici, F., & Calvert, S. L. (2017). Screen media exposure and obesity in children and adolescents. *Pediatrics.*

Shank, G. (1993). Abductive multiloguing: The semiotic dynamics of navigating the Net. *The Arachnet Electronic Journal of Virtual Culture, 1*(1). http://serials.infomotions.com/aejvc/aejvc-v1n01-shank-abductive.txt

UNESCO. (2020). *Education: From disruption to recovery*. UNESCO. https://en.unesco.org/covid19/educationresponse

UNESCO. (2021). *Education: From disruption to recovery*. UNESCO. https://en.unesco.org/covid19/educationresponse #durationschoolclosures.

Viner, R. M., Russell, S. J., Croker, H., Packer, J., Ward, J., Stansfeld, C., Mytton, O., Bonell, C., & Booy, R. (2020). Review School closure and management practices during coronavirus outbreaks including COVID-19: A rapid systematic review. *The Lancet. Child & Adolescent Health, 2019*(20), 1–8. doi:10.1016/S2352-4642(20)30095-X PMID:32272089

Walsh, B. (2020). COVID-19: The history of pandemics. *BBC Future*. https://www.bbc.com/future/article/20200325-COVID-19-the-history-of-pandemics

Yang, Y., & Cornelious, L. (2003, November). *Ensuring the quality of online education instruction.* Paper presented at Mid-South Educational Research Association Conference, Biloxi, MS.

Zhang, W., Wang, Y., Yang, L., & Wang, C. (2020). Suspending classes without stopping learning: China's education emergency management policy in the COVID-19 outbreak. *Journal of Risk and Financial Management*, *13*(3), 55. doi:10.3390/jrfm13030055

Chapter 3
Healthcare Treatment Innovation, Medical Tourism, and Hospital Business Strategy for Global Markets

Marlena Daryousef
https://orcid.org/0000-0001-9513-501X
Colorado Technical University, USA

Darrell Norman Burrell
https://orcid.org/0000-0002-4675-9544
Pellegrino Center for Clinical Bioethics, Georgetown University Medical Center, USA

Allison J. Huff
https://orcid.org/0000-0001-6102-8013
College of Medicine, University of Arizona, USA

Quatavia McLester
https://orcid.org/0000-0003-1596-0517
The Chicago School of Professional Psychology, USA

Kevin Richardson
https://orcid.org/0009-0002-3212-8669
Capitol Technology University, USA

Kiana S. Zanganeh
Florida Institute of Technology, USA

Delores Springs
https://orcid.org/0000-0003-0940-1225
Regent University, USA

William Quisenberry
Purdue University Global, USA

Elizabeth I. Omotoye
University of the Cumberlands, USA

ABSTRACT

The United States is facing a growing crisis in the form of increasing medical care costs for both the insured and uninsured. One innovative strategy to address increasing costs is the use of medical tourism. Medical tourism is defined by the OECD as "the practice of travelling to another country to obtain medical treatment." It has become an increasingly popular option as it offers patients the ability to access treatment outside of their home country, often at a lower cost. This chapter will provide a brief overview of medical tourism, its current and potential applications, and potential challenges and benefits associated with it as an innovative approach to address the healthcare crisis of high medical costs in some specific areas of treatment.

DOI: 10.4018/978-1-6684-9522-3.ch003

INTRODUCTION

The high cost of medical care in the United States has become a crisis for many individuals and households. In recent years, medical costs have risen dramatically. From 2008 to 2018, the average cost of employer-sponsored family health insurance increased by 55%, from $12,298 to $19,004 (Kaiser Family Foundation, 2018). This increase in medical costs has profoundly affected individuals and households, who often cannot afford health care coverage and services. In addition, the survey found that the average annual deductible for single coverage increased from $826 to $1,505 over the same period (Kaiser Family Foundation, 2018).

The high cost of medical care in the United States has profoundly impacted individuals and households (Centers for Disease Control and Prevention, 2015). The dramatic increase in the cost of employer-sponsored health insurance over the past decade has been particularly burdensome for many families (Centers for Disease Control and Prevention, 2015). The increase in out-of-pocket spending on healthcare services has also affected many households, particularly those with lower incomes (Centers for Medicare and Medicaid Services, 2018). Low-income individuals and households have been particularly hard-hit, with an increasing number of individuals reporting that they have skipped or delayed getting medical care due to cost (Centers for Disease Control and Prevention, 2015).

Medical Tourism is a rapidly growing segment of the healthcare industry. It represents an innovation that creates an alternative to the medical cost crisis in the U.S. It is projected to grow from $13.98 billion in 2021 to $53.51 billion in 2028, with an estimated 14 million people globally traveling to various countries to seek medical services (Fortune Business Insights, 2020). Patient care, safety, quality, affordability, and Very Important Person (VIP) services are just a few reasons why many American patients seek medical treatment abroad, particularly in Bangkok, Thailand (Health Tourism, n.d.). The comfort of a five-star hotel, lattes and Americanos from Starbucks, and exceptional customer service are what awaits tourists and why Thailand is one of the top destinations to seek medical treatment. Bangkok, Thailand, clinical quality and affordability are advancing 15%-20% faster than in most countries, including the United States (OECD, 2017). Thailand in the global medical tourism market (Finch, 2014). Medical tourism in Thailand has been steadily increasing since the early 2000s and has resulted in being placed at the top of the global medical tourism market (Health Tourism, n.d.). Thailand has over 1,000 hospitals, of which over 470 are private facilities, and of those, 37 have been accredited by the Joint Commission International (JCI) (Health Tourism, n.d.).

This new facility is the #2 ranked hospital in the country and performs the following procedures at 5% of what they would cost in the United States:

- Cosmetic surgery (breast, face, liposuction)
- Dentistry (cosmetic and reconstruction)
- Cardiology/cardiac surgery (bypass, valve replacement)
- Orthopedic surgery (hip replacement, resurfacing, knee replacement, joint surgery)
- Bariatric surgery (gastric bypass, gastric banding)
- Fertility/reproductive system (IVF, gender reassignment)

Hence, the increase in American tourism for medical procedures and treatments has affected the American Medical Industry because Americans have lost trust in the quality and high cost of performing these medical procedures and treatments sought after.

PROBLEM STATEMENT

American hospitals and clinics are affected by the increased popularity of American tourists seeking medical procedures and treatments overseas. According to a survey conducted by the World Tourism Organization (WTO) in 2017, the number of medical tourists worldwide was estimated to be around 11 million, with an estimated annual growth rate of 20-25% (WTO, 2017). Most medical tourists come from the United States and Europe, although there is a growing trend of medical tourists from Asia and the Middle East (WTO, 2017). This increasing popularity of medical tourism suggests that the industry will continue to grow in the coming years.

According to a survey by the International Healthcare Research Center (IHRC) in 2017, most medical tourists are now looking for healthcare services that provide superior quality of care rather than simply the lowest cost (IHRC, 2017). This suggests that medical tourism providers must focus on providing high-quality services to remain competitive in the global market.

Finally, medical tourism is becoming increasingly accessible to more patients. According to a survey by the National Center for Biotechnology Information (NCBI) in 2017, most medical tourists are now seeking treatment for conditions such as cancer, fertility, and plastic surgery, previously only available to those with higher incomes (NCBI, 2017). This indicates that the industry is becoming more equitable, allowing more people to access healthcare services that were once out of reach.

The most popular destination for medical tourists is India, estimated to have accounted for around 60% of all medical tourists in 2017 (WTO, 2017). This is primarily due to India's reputation for providing high-quality healthcare services at relatively low costs. India is followed by Thailand, Mexico, and Turkey, which account for around 20% of all medical tourists (WTO, 2017).

The ascendancy of medical tourism in Thailand presents a prospective panacea for mitigating the persistent crisis of the medical expenditure crisis in the United States, concomitantly proffering a salutary antidote to the quandary of accessibility to superlative healthcare.

The general business problem of our organization is that 90% of the patients currently using Thailand hospital's medical tourism services are traveling from the Middle East. The specific business problem is that there needs to be a clear understanding of organizational strategy and marketplace assessment to position a hospital in Thailand to recruit patients from America.

SIGNIFICANCE OF THE PROJECT

The United States is facing a growing crisis in the form of increasing medical care costs for insured and uninsured. The percentage of Americans without health insurance has risen sharply since the beginning of the 21st century, and the financial burden of medical care is becoming increasingly difficult to bear for the uninsured or underinsured.

According to the Centers for Disease Control and Prevention (CDC), the average per capita healthcare spending in the United States was $10,224 in 2017, the highest in the world (CDC, 2019). This is more than double the average of other wealthy countries, such as Japan, France, and the United Kingdom, which spent approximately $4,300 per capita in 2017 (CDC, 2019). This high cost of health care has been attributed to various factors, such as a fee-for-service system, high administrative costs, pricing of drugs and treatments, and a lack of competition between providers (Frakt & Pizer, 2018).

The financial implications of medical care for uninsured or underinsured are a significant crisis. People without health insurance are more likely to forgo needed medical care due to the high cost of treatment, which can lead to more severe health problems down the line (Sommers et al., 2012). Uninsured individuals are also more likely to experience financial hardship due to medical bills, as the cost of care can be significantly more than what insurance covers (Sommers et al., 2012). This can lead to a cycle of debt and financial insecurity for those who cannot afford to pay for medical care.

This research focuses on the increase of Americans traveling to Thailand to receive quality medical procedures and treatments at a lower cost than in the United States. Thailand attracts medical tourists because it offers high-quality and readily accessible medical services at affordable rates while enabling patients to combine treatment with vacationing (Cohen, 2014). This paper explores the nature of a hospital business strategy focused on exploiting the crisis of high medical costs in America through medical tourism.

METHODOLOGY

The method used was intervention action research. Intervention Action Research (IAR) is a research methodology that enables practitioners to identify and address issues related to their work environment and make changes to improve their practice (Cousins, 2011; Chambers & Boulton, 2011). IAR is a cyclical and iterative process of problem-solving, evaluation, and reflection involving stakeholders in designing, implementing, and evaluating interventions (Cousins, 2011; Chambers & Boulton, 2011). It is a powerful tool for learning, problem-solving, and improvement, and it has been used in healthcare, education, community development, public policy, and other fields (Cousins, 2011; Chambers & Boulton, 2011).

The value of IAR lies in its ability to provide practitioners with an understanding of the complexities of their work settings and the information needed to develop effective interventions (Cousins, 2011; Chambers & Boulton, 2011). IAR can help practitioners make evidence-based decisions about addressing their practice-related challenges best and evaluate the interventions' effectiveness (Cousins, 2011; Chambers & Boulton, 2011). It can also provide insight into how interventions can be adapted and improved over time (Cousins, 2011; Chambers & Boulton, 2011). Additionally, IAR can provide a platform for practitioners to collaborate and share best practices (Cousins, 2011; Chambers & Boulton, 2011).

Overall, IAR is a powerful tool for practitioners to use in order to understand and improve their practice (Cousins, 2011; Chambers & Boulton, 2011). It can provide insight into the complexities of their work environment, help practitioners develop evidence-based interventions, and provide a platform for collaboration and sharing of best practices (Cousins, 2011; Chambers & Boulton, 2011).

LITERATURE REVIEW

Marketing in the medical field is unique as it has concepts and intricacies not found in other types of industries (Purcarea, 2019). It is imperative, however, because global spending on healthcare has increased by 9.8% over the past year and is up to $8.5 trillion of the global Gross Domestic Product (GDP) (World Health Organization, 2021). Market research should be the first step when developing a marketing strategy in the healthcare industry. This market research defines the four P's: product, price, place, and promotion (Berkowitz, 2022, p. 7). A marketing team can use these variables to develop a marketing strategy. Healthcare is marketing to a demographic split between needs and wants. This can be a problem because the patient may only sometimes want what they need, and vice versa; they may not need what they want. Marketers can strategically curtail their strategies towards this population by identifying the target customer (in our case, this is the U.S. population who wants cosmetic surgery). Once the customer is identified, proper marketing must be applied. Mass-marketing strategies can be utilized when marketing to the most significant number of people possible; however, this decreases competitiveness because the market consumers feel the organization needs to be marketing directly to them. By utilizing market segmentation, diverse population groups can be reached with a marketing strategy tailored to their needs (Berkowitz, 2022, p. 282).

The current healthcare consumer has so many options that the best way for a company to distinguish itself is by creating memorable and unique marketing strategies and services. In 2005, Chan Kim used the terms blue ocean and red ocean to describe the marketplace. Red oceans are what we are used to seeing. They are competitive markets where companies try to perform better than their counterparts. As more of the same companies enter this market, profits reduce (Berkowitz, 2022). On the other hand, blue oceans are new markets where growth and opportunity are endless (Berkowitz, 2022). A company must find its blue ocean strategy to differentiate itself.

Developing customer loyalty is essential in healthcare, especially in a market such as cosmetic surgery, as these are voluntary surgeries. By creating loyal customers, the organization increases its chances of repeat customers and free marketing through word of mouth. Developing professional relationships to help market our services in the United States will also be necessary.

Digital marketing expenses have increased, with healthcare companies spending about 4 billion dollars in 2020 (Purcarea, 2019). Marketing costs for mobile and digital platforms make up 4%, while T.V. advertising costs have dropped 33% (Purcarea, 2019; Finch, 2014). Seeing these trends, marketing in the digital world is necessary for healthcare companies. Utilizing social media, healthcare companies can reach many individuals as the number of adults using social media has increased to 79% (Sweeney, 2022, p. 189).

Our marketing plan, developed through an extensive SWOT analysis, will target consumers using the above research. We will create a user-friendly landing page to simplify the process for our customers. We will also utilize digital marketing to reach as many consumers as possible.

SWOT ANALYSIS

One of the main strengths that we identified in our organization is the costs. Thailand has positioned itself as a country with the lowest costs in medical tourism in Southeast Asia (Finch, 2014). Likewise, our organization offers services at 5% of the costs of the United States. The services offered include cosmetic surgeries, dentistry, orthopedic surgery, and bariatric surgery. As part of the strategy to attract American consumers, we can develop financial packages around these services and promote their lower costs. This can be financially attractive to many Americans with high out-of-pocket expenses for elective procedures.

For example, some of the most common cosmetic surgeries in the United States are nose reshaping (nose jobs), liposuction, facelift, eyelid surgery, and breast augmentation (American Society of Plastic Surgeons, 2020). At the top of the list are rhinoplasties, or nose jobs, with a national average cost of $5,483 (American Society of Plastic Surgeons, 2020). This could be done at our facility for as little as

$500. Similarly, the national average for breast augmentation in the U.S. is $4,516, which can be done in Thailand for at least half the costs.

The next strength we identified is the organization's second-best in the country. This provides a competitive advantage amongst other organizations in Thailand and brings visibility to its offerings. By being ranked second, it has a strategic positioning as a leader in the healthcare market of Thailand and can promote itself better to other markets. This also results in attraction to Americans who place a high value on the rankings and ratings the organizations receive. It can leverage this positioning to gain visibility in other markets by utilizing paid media in medical journals, newspapers, and professional organizations, in the U.S.

Weaknesses

Currently, the organization has no customers from America, while 90% are from the Middle East. This is a challenge because the organization needs to pave its way into the U.S. healthcare market and gain the trust of its consumer base. This can be a weakness because the healthcare market in the U.S. is highly competitive, and many other organizations are promoting medical tourism and fighting for consumer attention. As such, it is crucial to have a historical presence with American consumers that can share their experience receiving services at their organization or gaining proof in the wisdom of the crowds (Sweeney, 2022, p. 120). One way to overcome this would be by partnering with more than 60 companies in the U.S. dedicated to medical tourism, as we will elaborate further elsewhere in this paper (Dalen & Alpert, 2018).

The perception of Americans' quality of care in other countries, such as Thailand, is a primary reason to go to Thailand for medical procedures and treatments. However, many Americans believe that U.S. healthcare has the highest standard of care than other countries and needs to follow Western standards regarding medical quality, safety issues, and cost. This perception can create hesitancy amongst Americans to wait and analyze which medical direction is best, maintaining the quality of care and lower cost for them. According to the Joint Commission International (JCI), the comparison between American Medical Services and Thailand is evaluated according to data and information that American tourists read for increased travel to Thailand. Although there has been an increase in Thailand for medical reasons, a challenge they face is the need to receive more accreditation from the Joint Commission International (JCI), which 60 organizations in Thailand have received (Collingwood, 2022). This validates that processes and protocols follow strict standards of care as in the U.S. medical facilities.

Opportunities

Thailand is a leading destination in medical tourism, representing 40% of the market share in global medical tourism (Finch, 2014). This is an opportunity for our organization to leverage the country's position, capture the attention of people looking into having a procedure done in Thailand and attract its consumer base. In addition, Thailand attracts more than 1 million American tourists to its majestic destinations. This is an opportunity to attract customers staying in the country for other purposes and can take advantage of their visit by having an elective procedure done.

Some estimates state that enrollment in high-deductible plans has grown to 45% among workers (U.S. Bureau of Labor Statistics, 2020). This type of policy has a minimum deductible of $1,500 per year and can be as high as $4,000. Individuals enrolled in these plans pay a lot out-of-pocket, even for services that may be covered by health insurance. This represents an opportunity for the organization to develop targeted marketing promoting its low costs services to this segment of the population in the U.S.

Threats

The worldwide COVID-19 pandemic created havoc across the world. While Thailand was deemed successful in its response to COVID-19 and had one of the lowest death rates in Southeast Asia, this decreased the influx of tourists to the country (Nguyen et al., 2022). The country is devoting many efforts to attracting tourism to pre-pandemic levels. This can be a threat to the organization as it may hinder the efficacy of its efforts to attract American customers. It is crucial that the organization develops strong communication channels with government officials and local authorities and is conscious of potential changes in public health restrictions.

Lastly, at least 60 healthcare organizations that the Joint Commission International accredits, and more than half are in Bangkok's capital (Collingwood, 2022). Assuming that our organization is also in the capital, this can be considered a threat to our organization since consumers have many options to choose from. To address this threat, it is essential to emphasize its differential advantage and bring visibility to the organization. One way is to leverage its ranking as a leader in the country. It is also essential to have the organization listed in several online directories and platforms that are easy to access or search for, and that highlight this ranking. Another way that the organization can gain visibility is by gaining expert proof or celebrity proof, which can serve as marketing tools.

EXPLORING THE CULTURE

The culture of the Thailand hospital is innovative and open to growth to be successful in marketing and strategic planning. It is important to note that this facility is open to process improvement and tackling the areas of opportunities presented to them. To attract the target American audience, this facility is willing to learn from others in the industry and incorporate any strategies or marketing tactics that effectively bring in this audience. Employees are encouraged to bring their ideas to management, which will cascade to various organizational leadership as necessary. Every employee is willing to work together and make appropriate changes to meet the organizational goals the Thailand hospital leadership has set out to accomplish.

This Thailand hospital will be OK with implementing new procedures or policies through hands-off leadership that empowers employees to bring their ideas to the table and work as change leaders throughout the organization. Everyone involved understands there will be a necessary change, and working towards increasing the number of American patients who use the services is the goal. Working in a psychologically safe environment will allow this organization to take risks together to achieve success. This is one organization that marketing consultants dream of working with, as they are open to all ideas and even bring helpful suggestions and ideas to the table.

We recommend introducing and utilizing the Purnell Model for Cultural Competence to continue fostering this environment as the practice grows. "The Purnell Model of Cultural Competence is proposed as an organizing framework to guide cultural competence among multidisciplinary healthcare team members in various primary, secondary, and tertiary settings" (Purnell, 2005). As healthcare providers, the Thailand organization adds a new and different dimension to the complexity of providing culturally competent care. Within all cultures, there are subcultures, ethnic groups, or ethnocultural populations (Purnell, 2005). Purnell writes about how cultural competence has several characteristics and includes knowledge and skills as well as "developing an awareness of one's own culture, existence, sensations, thoughts, and environment without letting them have an undue influence on those from other backgrounds" (Purnell, 2005).

Accepting and integrating a model for cultural competence will help set this Thailand hospital apart from others. Not only will we be appealing to patients in the United States, but we could also start providing services to other nations by becoming culturally competent in their ways of living. Providing care authentically and realistically will help spread the name of this practice and facility to many prospective clients. This facility will excel in patient treatment and care by creating a culture and environment that accepts all.

MARKETING MODEL(S)

Numerous marketing models are available to create a marketing strategy that addresses our organization's stated problem. After conducting research, our team has chosen to focus on the following concepts:

- Decision-making model
- Blue Ocean Strategy
- Customer relationship management

Decision-making power in the healthcare industry has grown enormously and is led by various drivers. There are increasingly more variables, which affect marketing initiatives, and therefore challenge marketing managers to find the suitable methodology to place significant investments and resources in the correct market segments (Oztekin, 2017). Many healthcare consumers are concerned with the economic and financial burdens that may arise from certain services or procedures. The need to make choices between competing claims on resources has focused consumer attention on economic evaluation, "ranging from evaluation of individual pharmaceuticals to evaluation of appropriate forms of healthcare financing and service delivery, all of which require a valuation of healthcare and health outcomes" (Lancsar & Louviere, 2008). Our organization must communicate our service prices transparently and openly to assist our target market in choosing us from our competitors. As stated earlier, our cosmetic procedures cost 5% of what they would cost in the United States. These financial differences will be critical to informing our consumers and potential patients as we market to them.

Blue Ocean Strategy offers users a framework for creating an uncontested marketplace and a chance to change the concentration from the current competition to a new creation of innovative value and demand (Alam, 2017). The idea is that the "blue ocean" represents all the industries that do not exist today, also known as the unknown market space untainted by competition (Kim & Mauborgne, 2005). This marketing strategy creates demand, and there is plenty of room for profitable and rapid growth (Kim & Mauborgne, 2005). The way we would utilize the Blue Ocean Strategy for our Thailand hospital would be to incorporate the VIP benefits and 5-star resort facility into the middle-class American market. Since these services in America only exist for highly wealthy individuals, our organization would open this market to middle-class individuals and create an affordable experience for our consumers – just traveling to Thailand. This is not something that has been done before and is a significant risk to take. It will take the help of other marketing concepts to ensure this strategy is successful.

Customer relationship management (CRM) is another concept we would utilize as consultants to impact the Thailand marketplace and target market. To meet customers' ever-changing needs, this organization must capitalize on technology and innovative service strategies, such as CRM (Al-Gasawneh et al., 2022). The emphasis on meeting customers' needs via innovation and technology is critical in gaining a sustainable competitive advantage in the marketplace (Al-Gasawneh et al., 2022). As stated before, service quality is among the key factors this organization prides itself on and is an aspect that can be utilized to gain the confidence of the customers in a competitive marketplace. Currently, Americans need to utilize our services more than Middle Easterners. In this cosmetic surgery industry, service quality is deemed a vital core concept and a critical success factor. "Service quality is measurable, and several general scales are available for measurement" (Al-Gasawneh et al., 2022). In this regard, it will be necessary to emphasize the quality available at our facility to be marketed appropriately to customers.

PROJECT THEORIES

Thailand offers cost-effective services, which, in many cases, patients can save up to 80%, making it very affordable. Shorter waiting times and healthcare quality for various procedures and treatments depend on the patient's needs. Thailand's patients are easily accessible to some of the best doctors and specialists, and the patient does not need to wait months for an appointment. Thailand is known to be on the cutting edge of technology; therefore, the patient receives the latest procedures and treatments from a world-class staff of healthcare professionals. These approaches often incorporate Very Important Person (VIP) and excellent accommodation for patients' medical stay.

RECOMMENDATIONS, SOLUTIONS, AND CONCLUSION

Medical tourism is a rapidly growing industry in the healthcare arena, and many people are electing to receive care in other countries besides their native countries. This is most evident by the continued increase in individuals traveling, an estimated 14 million, and the projected market size growth of medical tourism, from $13.98 billion in 2021 to $53.51 billion in 2028. The American population is no different, and an estimated 1.4 million Americans sought medical care in various countries, including Thailand, as is in the top 10 (Dalen & Alpert, 2018). Services include dentistry, cosmetic surgery, cardiac conditions, in vitro fertility, weight loss, dermatology, liver and kidney transplants, spine surgery, and the most frequent conditions treated (AJM).

Our team of marketing and strategy consultants was hired and challenged with the task of creating a strategic marketing approach in which to draw the American market to a new hospital in Thailand, which is the #2 ranked hospital in the country and performs the following procedures at 5% of what they would have cost in the United States.

- Cosmetic surgery (breast, face, liposuction)
- Dentistry (cosmetic and reconstruction)
- Cardiology/cardiac surgery (bypass, valve replacement)

- Orthopedic surgery (hip replacement, resurfacing, knee replacement, joint surgery)
- Bariatric surgery (gastric bypass, gastric banding)
- Fertility/reproductive system (IVF, gender reassignment)

Based on market research at the foundation, a strategic marketing approach is created through the Ps of product, price, place, and promotion. Through a SWOT analysis, the organization can leverage our strengths and opportunities identified to differentiate our hospital and services as the world's most sought-after. VIP treatment, clinical quality, and affordability will further highlight and strengthen our ability to promote through mass-marketing strategies, such as social media platforms, key partnerships with award-winning travel agencies, innovative and user-friendly landing pages, and patient testimonials that engage and highlight all that Thailand has to offer both in tourism and medical care.

Medical tourism in Thailand has emerged as a potential solution to address the ongoing medical cost crisis in the United States while simultaneously offering a remedy to the issue of access to high-quality healthcare. Thailand's burgeoning medical tourism industry is predicated on offering world-class medical treatments at a fraction of the cost found in the U.S. This economic advantage is a beacon of hope for countless Americans grappling with exorbitant healthcare expenses. By seeking medical care in Thailand, American patients can access a wide spectrum of treatments, including elective surgeries, specialized procedures, and even complex treatments such as organ transplants, without the crippling financial burden associated with healthcare in the U.S.

Moreover, Thailand's healthcare infrastructure boasts an impressive pedigree. Many of its medical facilities are accredited by international organizations and staffed by highly trained professionals. This stellar reputation for delivering quality healthcare services positions Thailand as a prime destination for those in search of high-quality care. It addresses a critical challenge faced by many Americans who confront barriers to accessing timely and specialized healthcare within the U.S. system. By opting for medical tourism in Thailand, patients can bypass the long waiting times and scarce specialist crisis often experienced in the U.S., thus ensuring rapid access to superior medical expertise.

Nonetheless, the role of medical tourism in Thailand in mitigating the healthcare access and cost crisis in the U.S. does come with considerations. Ensuring the seamless integration of post-treatment care and maintaining rigorous standards for medical tourism facilities are essential to make this solution sustainable. Nevertheless, it is evident that Thailand's medical tourism sector has the potential to not only provide cost-effective alternatives for Americans but also to redefine the discourse on healthcare accessibility and affordability, contributing to more equitable healthcare outcomes globally through innovation.

RECOMMENDATION FOR FUTURE RESEARCH

- **PEST analysis** – assessing the Political, Economic, Sociological, and Technological (PEST) factors that affect the business could be another approach to explore this topic. Current geopolitical events are shifting the political relationships of many countries or regions. As mentioned elsewhere, there is also the threat of the COVID-19 pandemic that has limited the flow of tourists into Thailand and has caused a policy shift on international traveling. Utilizing the PEST analysis could be an excellent way to explore all these factors further.
- **Analysis of the policy implications from care received abroad** – the care received abroad is generally paid out-of-pocket and not covered by healthcare insurance in the U.S. A critical piece

of the research includes assessing the risks associated with care. While we identified that the JCI accredits most healthcare facilities engaged in medical tourism in Thailand, there is always a risk for complications and adverse outcomes. What would happen if there were a complication, such as an infection or a need to repeat the procedure? Would insurance cover this in the U.S.? (In my experience with some insurance companies, complications of a cosmetic procedure abroad are not a covered benefit) Could the patient go back to the same facility at no cost? What are accountability measures in place that give some peace of mind to American consumers? Further research should explore these issues.

- **Qualitative data** – to increase the effectiveness of the marketing strategy, there should be additional research that explores the perceptions, acceptability, and appeal of medical tourism to Americans. This could be done by conducting research with focus groups across market segments and geographic locations. This could further assist in identifying potential market segments and opportunities.
- **Case studies and testimonials** – we identified no availability of patient testimonials about receiving care abroad. Those patient narratives are essential to gain an understanding of the experiences and journeys of receiving care abroad and have a potential impact on capturing other consumers. A qualitative study of patient narratives can also bring visibility to potential barriers and additional opportunities to improve offerings. It can also provide insights into consumers' motivations.
- Finally, there needs to be a study on the **travel agencies available in the U.S. that are focused on medical tourism.** One of the limitations of our research is that the available information on these agencies was published more than ten years ago. There is a need to update this data to reflect the currently available list of agencies. It would also be helpful to explore this further by regions or areas of the U.S. where they offer services and to profile these in some online directories.

REFERENCES

Al-Gasawneh, J. A., AlZubi, K. N., Anuar, M. M., & Padlee, S. F. ul-Haque, A., & Saputra, J. (2022, January 12). *Marketing Performance Sustainability in the Jordanian Hospitality Industry: The Roles of Customer Relationship Management and Service Quality.* ProQuest. https://www.proquest.com/central/docview/2621383917/fulltextPDF/33C795C2AD3243F7PQ/2?accountid=14244

AlamS. (2017, January). Impact of Blue Ocean Strategy on Organizational Performance: A Literature Review Toward Implementation Logic. SSRN. doi:10.9790/487X-1901030119

American Society of Plastic Surgeons. (2020). *Plastic Surgery Statistics Report 2020.* ASPS National Clearinghouse of Plastic Surgery Procedural Statistics. https://www.plasticsurgery.org/documents/News/Statistics/2020/plastic-surgery-statistics-full-report-2020.pdf

Berkowitz, E. N. (2022). *Essentials of Health Care Marketing* (5th ed.). Jones & Bartlett Learning.

Bumrungrad International Hospital. (2022). *Bumrungrad International Hospital.* Bumrungrad International Hospital. https://www.bumrungrad.com/en/medical-travel

Centers for Disease Control and Prevention. (2015). *Health care access disparities: Delaying or skipping care due to cost.* CDC. https://www.cdc.gov/health disparities/health careaccess/delaying-skipping-care-due-cost.htm

Centers for Disease Control and Prevention. (2019). *Health, United States, 2018: With Special Feature on Aging*. CDC. https://www.cdc.gov/nchs/data/hus/hus18.pdf

Centers for Medicare and Medicaid Services. (2018). *National health expenditure projections 2017-2026*. CMS. https://www.cms.gov/research-statistics-data-and-systems/statistics-trends-and-reports/nationalhealthexpenddata/nhe-projections.html

Chambers, E., & Boulton, M. (2011). Intervention action research as a knowledge practice. *Educational Action Research, 19*(3), 371–387.

Cloud Hospital. (2022, May 13). *Plastic surgery market real facts you need to know.* ICloudHospital. https://icloudhospital.com/articles/inside-thailand%27s-plastic-surgery-market-real-facts-you-need-to-know

Cohen, E. (2014). Medical Tourism in Thailand. *AU-GSB e-JOURNAL, 1*(1). Retrieved from Medical Tourism in Thailand: http://www.assumptionjournal.au.edu/index.php/AU-GSB/article/view/381

Collingwood, J. (2022, January 4). *ITIJ*. Retrieved from Quality Healthcare with easy access in Thailand: https://www.itij.com/latest/long-read/quality-healthcare-easy-access-thailand

Cooper, N. (2022). *World's Best Hospitals.* Newsweek. https://www.newsweek.com/best-hospitals-2021/thailand

Cousins, J. B. (2011). Intervention action research: A methodology for developing, enacting, and evaluating interventions. *New Directions for Evaluation, 2011*(130), 7–20.

Dalen, J. E., & Alpert, J. S. (2018, July 15). Medical Tourists: Incoming and Outgoing. *The American Journal of Medicine, 132*(1), 9–10. doi:10.1016/j.amjmed.2018.06.022 PMID:30016635

Dean, B. (2021, October 10). *Social Network Usage & Growth Statistics: How Many People Use Social Media in 2022?* Bancklinko. https://backlinko.com/social-media-users

Express Healthcare. (2010). *Healthcare and Marketing or Healthcare Marketing?: Consumerism driving a change to result in healthcare marketing*. ProQuest. https://www.proquest.com/docview/217541725/fulltext/8C6DE098C0A74B1DPQ/1?accountid=14244

Fairfield, J. (2021, October 17). Thailand's healthcare system ranked among best in the world. *Asean Now*. https://aseannow.com/topic/1235740-thailands-healthcare-system-ranked-among-best-in-the-world/

Finch, S. (2014). Thailand top destination for medical tourists. *Canadian Medical Association Journal, 186*(1), E1–E2. doi:10.1503/cmaj.109-4655 PMID:24246587

Fortune Business Insights. (2020). *Medical Tourism Market Size, Share & COVID-19 Impact Analysis, By Service (Medical et al., and Alternative Treatment), By Service Providers (Public and Private), and Regional Forecasts, 2021-2028*. Fortune Business Insights.

Frakt, A., & Pizer, S. (2018). The U.S. healthcare cost crisis: What might be done? *The New England Journal of Medicine*, *378*(2), 159–162. doi:10.1056/NEJMp1714269

Health Tourism. (n.d.). Medical Tourism in the USA. *Health Tourism.* https://www.health-tourism.com/medical-tourism/usa-research/#:~:text=Reasons%20Why%20American%20Patients%20are%20Traveling%20Abroad%20for,6%20Researching%20medical%20tourism%20for%20USA%20patients%20

Health Tourism. (n.d.). *Medical Tourism to Thailand.* Health Tourism. https://www.health-tourism.com/medical-tourism-thailand/

International Healthcare Research Center (IHRC). (2017). *Medical Tourism: Global Trends & Statistics.* IHRC. https://ihrc.org/medical-tourism-global-trends-statistics/

Kaiser Family Foundation. (2018). *2018 employer health benefits survey.* KFF. https://www.kff.org/report-section/ehbs-2018-section-two-trends-in-employer-sponsored-insurance/

Kim, W. C., & Mauborgne, R. (2005). *Blue Ocean Strategy.* Arthur McKeown. https://arthurmckeown.typepad.com/files/blue-ocean-strategy---wikipedia.pdf

Lancsar, E., & Louviere, J. (2008). *Conducting Discrete Choice Experiments to Inform Health-care Decision Making.* SpringerLink. https://link-springer-com.libproxy.lib.unc.edu/article/10.2165/00019053-200826080-00004

Mathew, B. (2021, February 12). *Healthcare Report.* Retrieved from Impact of Social Media on Health-care Marketing: https://healthcare.report/articles/impact-of-social-media-on-healthcare-marketing

National Center for Biotechnology Information (NCBI). (2017). *Medical Tourism: An Overview.* NCBI. https://www.ncbi.nlm.nih.gov/pmc/articles/PMC5546406/

Nguyen, A., & Yuvejwattana, S. (2022, May 19). *Thailand to Promote Medical Tourism in Post-Covid Era, PM Says.* Bloomberg. https://www.bloomberg.com/news/articles/2022-05-19/thailand-to-promote-medical-tourism-in-post-covid-era-pm-says

Noree, T., Hanefeld, J., & Smith, R. (2015). Medical tourism in Thailand: A cross-sectional study. *Bulletin of the World Health Organization*, *94*(1), 30–36. doi:10.2471/BLT.14.152165 PMID:26769994

OECD. (2017). *Medical tourism: A global overview.* OECD. https://www.oecd-ilibrary.org/docserver/9789264270770-en.pdf?expires=1594850587&id=id&accname=guest&checksum=9C9F4DD4DE2C2A4E4F4BD3266D86F10F

Oztekin, A. (2017, May 2). *Creating a marketing strategy in the healthcare industry: a holistic data analytic approach.* ProQuest. https://www-proquest-com.libproxy.lib.unc.edu/docview/2112472733?pq-origsite=summon

Polkowski, T., & Cho, J. (n.d.). *Medical Tourism in Thailand: A Multi-Billion-Dollar Blue Ocean.* Blue Ocean Strategy. https://www.blueoceanstrategy.com/blog/medical-tourism-in-thailand-multi-billion-dollar-blue-ocean/

Purcarea, V. L. (2019). The impact of marketing strategies in healthcare systems. *Journal of Medicine and Life*, *12*(2), 93–96. doi:10.25122/jml-2019-1003 PMID:31406509

Purnell, L. (2005). *The Purnell Model for Cultural Competence.* ProQuest. https://www.proquest.com/docview/220301419?pq-origsite=gscholar&fromopenview=true

Sommers, B., Collins, S., Gunja, M., & Beutel, S. (2012). Rising insured rates, but persistent uninsurance among working-age adults in a weakened economy: Evidence from the Commonwealth Fund Biennial Health Insurance Survey, 2010. *Health Affairs, 31*(6), 1188–1198. 10.1377/hlthaff.2011.1176

Sweeney, B. (2022). *Digital Marketing; Quickstart Guide*. ClydeBank Media.

U.S. Bureau of Labor Statistics. (2020, September 3). *High deductible health plans and health savings account*. U.S. Bureau of Labor Statistics. https://www.bls.gov/ncs/ebs/factsheet/high-deductible-health-plans-and-health-savings-accounts.htm

World Health Organization. (2021). *Global expenditure on health: Public spending on the rise?* World Health Organization.

World Tourism Organization (WTO). (2017). *Medical Tourism: Trends and Implications*. WTO. https://www.e-unwto.org/doi/pdf/10.18111/9789284419133

Chapter 4
The Complexities of Conducting Public Health Research on Minority Populations

Allison J. Huff
https://orcid.org/0000-0001-6102-8013
College of Medicine, University of Arizona, USA

Darrell Norman Burrell
https://orcid.org/0000-0002-4675-9544
Pellegrino Center for Clinical Bioethics, Georgetown University Medical Center, USA

Quatavia McLester
https://orcid.org/0000-0003-1596-0517
The Chicago School of Professional Psychology, USA

Margaret J. Crowe
https://orcid.org/0000-0002-9862-5265
Liberty University, USA

Delores Springs
https://orcid.org/0000-0003-0940-1225
Regent University, USA

Aleha M. Ingle
Nebraska Methodist College, USA

Kiana S. Zanganeh
Florida Institute of Technology, USA

Kevin Richardson
https://orcid.org/0009-0002-3212-8669
Capitol Technology University, USA

Laura Ann Jones
https://orcid.org/0000-0002-0299-370X
Capitol Technology University, USA

Elizabeth I. Omotoye
The University of the Cumberlands, USA

ABSTRACT

The study focuses on ethical, cultural, and research into the public health sector. The content analysis of research identifies disproportionate knowledge of implications affecting the misappropriated, disenfranchised, and institutionalized minority segments of the general population affected by COVID-19 cases. Historic mistreatment of minority individuals, inmates, and the military has left a lasting negative impression of clinical research on minority groups. In 1932, the United States Public Health Service (USPHS) began a public health research study on the lethality of syphilis using African American men from Macon County, Alabama as research subjects. Referred to as the Tuskegee Syphilis Studies (or

DOI: 10.4018/978-1-6684-9522-3.ch004

Tuskegee Experiments), researchers monitored 600 subjects, 399 of which were previously infected with the syphilis bacteria. This paper looks at the historical contexts of the lack of bioethics during Tuskegee Experiments and how it currently influences African-Americans reluctance early on to get the COVID-19 vaccines and reluctance to participate in clinical trials research.

INTRODUCTION

The pressing issue of health disparities, especially concerning the underrepresentation of African-Americans in clinical trials, serves as a crisis due to its significant implications for equitable healthcare access and outcomes (Webber-Ritchey & Lane-Cordova, 2021). However, within this crisis lies the potential for transformative innovations and solutions. Addressing this disparity demands creative and inclusive strategies to engage underrepresented populations in clinical research (Webber-Ritchey & Lane-Cordova, 2021). Innovations such as community-based participatory research, culturally sensitive recruitment approaches, and enhanced education and outreach efforts can bridge the gap in representation. By recognizing this crisis as an opportunity to develop more inclusive and equitable healthcare practices, the healthcare community has the chance to pioneer new approaches that not only address the current disparities but also contribute to more equitable healthcare systems and improved public health outcomes for all.

The ongoing pursuit of equitable healthcare access and outcomes requires vigilant attention to the multifaceted dimensions of health disparities. A particularly critical facet pertains to the pervasive underrepresentation of African-Americans within clinical trials, and new vaccine introductions across the United States represent a potential health disparities crisis (Webber-Ritchey & Lane-Cordova, 2021). This critical crisis is a consequence of this inadequacy, illuminating how the lack of African-American participation undermines the integrity of medical research, impedes the development of targeted interventions, and perpetuates a crisis of health inequities (Webber-Ritchey & Lane-Cordova, 2021). This crisis includes:

Diminished External Validity: The underrepresentation of African-Americans in clinical trials engenders a glaring deficiency in the generalizability of research findings. As medical interventions and treatments are designed and calibrated based predominantly on non-diverse populations, the potential effectiveness and safety of these interventions among African-American patients remain inadequately understood.

Biased Inferences: The absence of a representative sample hampers the capacity to extrapolate conclusive inferences about the unique physiological responses, side effects, and therapeutic efficacies relevant to African-Americans. Consequently, clinical decision-making becomes skewed, potentially exposing this demographic to suboptimal treatment outcomes and avoidable health risks.

Perpetuating Health Inequities: The absence of comprehensive data from African-American participants perpetuates a cycle of health inequities, compounding the pre-existing disparities. This exacerbation is observable across many medical conditions, where interventions predicated on non-diverse trials fail to address African-American populations' nuanced health challenges.

Delayed Diagnosis and Substandard Care: The lack of tailored insights derived from representative clinical trials culminates in diagnostic delays and substandard care for African-Americans. Misdiagnoses, inappropriate treatments, and the oversight of specific health needs become prevalent, contributing to the persistence of health disparities that disproportionately affect this community.

Ethical Imperative: The underrepresentation of African-Americans in clinical trials accentuates disparities and underscores ethical concerns. The ethical imperative of ensuring inclusivity in research arises from the necessity to uphold principles of justice and equity in medical investigation, aligning with foundational ethical guidelines.

Cultural Competence and Trust: Distrust within African-American communities, stemming from historical mistreatment and the Tuskegee Syphilis Study, further contribute to low participation rates. Culturing cultural competence and establishing trust are pivotal in fostering greater engagement and participation in clinical trials among African-Americans (Webber-Ritchey & Lane-Cordova, 2021).

Some Black Americans were more hesitant to sign up for COVID-19 vaccines and even actively participate in clinical trials due to an enduring suspicion of the U.S. medical care system (Elliott, 2021). The wariness is entrenched in history, including the notorious U.S. study of Syphilis that violated the rights of some African-American men to suffer from the disease for the sake of medical research (Elliott, 2021). The vaccine rollout has sparked conversation among African-Americans familiar with the syphilis study (Elliott, 2021). The coronavirus pandemic and its disparate impact on people of color have exposed the shortcomings of the U.S. healthcare delivery system (Elliott, 2021). For instance, no hospital serves the general public in Tuskegee, and coronavirus testing was hard to come by early on (Elliott, 2021). There is also a lingering result of African-Americans' reluctance to participate in clinical trials (Durant et al., 2014; Swanson & Ward,1995).

There is also literature that suggests that physician bias, false perceptions, and prejudices surrounding medical decision-making dictate the lower number of minority participants in trials (Smedley et al., 2003). Research has shown that physicians are less likely to prescribe specific treatments to their minority patients (Smedley et al., 2003). According to Smedley, Stith, and Nelson (2003), physicians are fewer physicians operate on a cognitive heuristic learned in medical school and residency that brings prior expectations to each encounter with their patients.

Concepts of race and ethnicity in research can potentially improve public health, health care, clinical care, and medical science (Bhopal, 2008; Quinn, 2021). Nevertheless, researchers and practitioners must be sensitive to the broader events of health improvement needed, especially among African Americans (Bhopal, 2008; Wedge, 2020; Ndugga et al., 2022). Healthcare professionals must be mindful of healthcare risks amongst the minority segments in public health as there is a lingering mistrust within the medical system (Bhopal, 2008; Quinn, 2021). An emphasis on "doing good" should be the intention regardless of the ethnic make-up of the individual (Bhopal, 2008). Beneficence towards minority ethnic groups is not universal across time or demographics (Bhopal, 2008; Quinn, 2021). According to Bhopal (2008), doing good implies improving health and care amongst ethnic groups should be imperative, not requiring special attention or a sense of fairness (Bhopal, 2008). In several minority communities, people of color and homelessness were disproportionately impacted by COVID-19 during the initial outbreak (Wedge, 2020). The Boston Medical Center (BMC) study reviewed by 2,729 laboratories confirmed that COVID-19 adult patients treated were minorities. Research suggests that an awareness of the primary goal of health improvements concerning potential adverse outcomes is still an ethical and cultural issue (Bhopal, 2008). Many individuals are differentiated by age, race (ethnicity), underlying medical issues, and homelessness in the public health sector. These findings demonstrate a deep inequity in the impact of COVID-19 on subverted environments (Wedge, 2020). Statistics found that 44% of hospitalized COVID-19 patients were Black, 30% Hispanic, and 16% homeless. A higher proportion of Hispanic patients, 46.5%, were hospitalized compared to Black 39.5% and White 34.4%, respectively. Most of the patients from the study were older than 60, according to the data (Quinn, 2021; Ndugga et al., 2022).

The proclivity to such data has seen many African Americans reluctant to take the COVID-19 vaccine. It has played out in data that show a disparity in who is getting shots in this country – 60% going to white people and less than 6% to African Americans (Quinn, 2021; Ndugga et al., 2022). The medical mistrust is rooted in the history of the U.S. Study of Syphilis that left Black men in Tuskegee, Alabama, to suffer and die from the deadly disease (Quinn, 2021). The most critical ethical pillar in the ethnicity and health field is the concept of the magnitude of ethnic drawbacks and differences (Bhopal, 2008). These differences are a mere act of rigorous attention to ethical codes related to equality, justice, tolerance, and sensitivity to people of color (Bhopal, 2008). Although, some fear the root cause of COVID-19 is miseducation and ethical behavior by health professionals (Ndugga et al., 2022). The Boston Medical Center (BMC) study analyzes the clinical observation statistically. However, it does not provide an assessment of the cognitive response to a behavioral issue due to the circumstances surrounding the observations from the study.

In the United States of America, providing citizens with a fair and equitable healthcare system with access for all is a topic at the forefront of many high-visibility political debates. Historically, minority groups have not been appropriately represented in test subject populations. This is due to a long-standing record of unethical practices in early American medical experiments such as the Tuskegee Syphilis Experiment (Elliott, 2021). The Tuskegee Experiment continues to be one of the most notorious examples of African Americans being used as subjects in medical experiments built upon the attempt to establish a race-based classification system among humans (Elliott, 2021). Those who imposed this study lacked moral sensitivity and regard for the concentration of effect. Under the guise of treatment for "bad blood," the study was not only misrepresentative of its true intent but in its failure to provide medical treatment by subjecting its participants to placebos, unnecessary procedures, or other non-therapeutic treatments, which often resulted in excruciating and unnecessary death (Alsan & Wanamaker, 2018).

Furthermore, in addition to the deaths of the original test subjects, many of their wives and children had been infected, proving that the degree of deception was severely underestimated and with widespread damage (Alsan & Wanamaker, 2018). The Tuskegee syphilis study highly represents the extent and duration of deception and mistreatment that often proves rooted in racism and cognitive dissonance. The history of medical experimentation and abuse within medical research and the healthcare infrastructure has continued systemically over more than four centuries to exploit African Americans, leading to a legacy of medical mistrust from minority communities (Alsan & Wanamaker, 2018). Implementing strict and enforceable ethical guidelines would have allowed the practitioners to review the outcomes of their actions and reflect upon the value of the study to compare it to the damage it inflicted upon the subjects.

PROBLEM STATEMENT

Statistics demonstrate a disparity between those getting the COVID-19 shots. It played out in data in early 2021, which showed a stark disparity in who gets shots in this country, with more than 60% going to White people and less than 6% to African Americans (Elliott, 2021). Increasingly, researchers grapple with meaningful efforts to involve communities in research that are not fully protected, recognizing that communities are distinct from individuals (Quinn, 2004; Ndugga et al., 2022). Researchers and scholars must conduct investigative studies on developing strategies to improve clinical trial participation and patient outcomes and alleviate public health safety challenges (Wedge, 2020). This study looks to provide insight into why African-Americans were initially reluctant to get the COVID-19 vaccine and only participate in small numbers in clinical trials through a historical exploration of what occurred with Tuskegee experiments and looks to make those that are focused on engaging African-American communities to become more knowledgeable and self-aware as they develop strategies to treat African-Americans or to get them to participate in clinical trials.

THE GAP IN THE RESEARCH

Ndugga et al. (2022) postulated from federal data from the Center for Disease Control and Prevention (CDC) 78% of the total population in the United States have received at least one dose of a COVID-19 vaccine. Nonetheless, across the 36 states for which a total vaccination rate could be calculated by race/ethnicity as of July 11, 2022, 87% of Asian, 67% of Hispanic, and 64% of White people had received at least one COVID-19 vaccine dose, higher than the rate for Black people (59%) (Ndugga et al., 2022). The gap in research consists of statistics still exhibiting that Black people and Hispanic people are still less likely than their white counterparts to have received a vaccine throughout the vaccination rollout (Ndugga et al., 2022). This study seeks to evaluate further the long-standing potential ethical and cultural leadership implications affecting public health challenges amongst minority populations.

METHOD

The approach is a content analysis of strategies developed from the literature. The aim is to combine dispersed approaches into one comprehensive and relevant discussion based on current insights and dynamics. Keywords used in the search include Tuskegee syphilis experiments, medical ethics, bio-ethics, informed consent, African-Americans and COVID-19 vaccines, and African-Americans and clinical trials.

SOCIAL AND COMMUNITY ASPECTS OF RESEARCH

In the United States of America, providing citizens with a fair and equitable healthcare system with access for all is a topic at the forefront of current political debates (Yearby, 2018). Access to healthcare in the United States can vary based on race, ethnicity, age, sex, socioeconomic status, disability status, sexual orientation, gender identity, and residential location (Agency for Healthcare Research and Quality, 2018). Providing a culturally diverse healthcare system improves healthcare access, satisfies unmet health needs, reduces preventable disease, and minimizes financial burdens on our underserved citizens (Agency for Healthcare Research and Quality, 2018). Culturally competent healthcare is required, with culturally inclusive healthcare research, to ensure that all ethnic groups receive individualized healthcare (Dawes, 2019). This care must focus on effective medical treatments and unique disease prevention (Dawes, 2019). Therefore, healthcare for all is only possible if a diverse mix of research candidates is used at all healthcare research stages. Specifically, clinical research trials must keep pace with population diversity changes to provide scientific evidence that healthcare treatments work across ethnic groups.

Historically, minority individuals have been shown to hesitate to enroll in clinical trials or opt-out (Durant et al., 2014). Research recruitment strategies have been implemented to improve minority participation in healthcare and pharmaceutical research (Hamel et al., 2016). Even with these implementations, minimal improvement in minority recruitment has occurred (Oh et al., 2015). This lack of diversity in clinical trial participation results in huge minority groups of U.S. citizens receiving inadequately tested medical treatment or being at risk for healthcare complications from ineffective medications and treatments.

Clinical trials in the United States have statistically enrolled a disproportionately dwindling number of minority study participants compared to white research participants. Minority population rates in the U.S. are increasing, yet minorities account for less than 10 percent of patients enrolled in clinical trials (Clark et al., 2019). Ramamoorthy et al. (2015) studied 167 new molecular compounds approved by the FDA in the five years from 2008-2013 and estimated that one in five of these drugs has different response rates across ethnic and racial groups. Therefore, a continued need for minorities in clinical trials remains.

Fear of ill-treatment, mistreatment, the unknown, and large pharmaceutical conglomerates, physicians, and healthcare institutions have been widely studied as barriers to minorities participating in clinical trials (Blume, 2016; Clark et al., 2019). For example, the fear of being a "guinea pig" or a subject in an experimental study has been studied as a significant reason for minorities not participating in clinical trials (Clark et al., 2019). Historic mistreatment of minority individuals, inmates, and the military has left a lasting negative impression on clinical research on ethnic groups (Farr et al., 2015). Conversely, research suggests that these potential minority research candidates would consider research participation if asked by their physicians (Hamel et al., 2016).

Promoting diversity in clinical trials through a broad ethnic mix of study participants improves disease research and care for all and decreases racial and ethnic disparities (Polite et al., 2017). Research has historically identified that minorities are not enrolling in clinical trials (Martin et al., 2011). Recently, the U.S. population is becoming increasingly minority-centric, and by 2045 will be a "Caucasian minority" (Colby & Ortman, 2015). Researchers identify that this shift in minority groups furthers the acute need for improving minority rates in clinical trials (Haley et al., 2017). Americans generally believe research is essential to advance disease treatment and prevention. Americans expect to receive the best, most scientifically valid preventative treatment and therapy for disease (Saultz et al., 2015). Research shows that most Americans would be willing to participate in studies if asked. However, most do not consider clinical trials as a form of health care that is appropriate to consider personally. Others do not believe their participation in clinical trials would impact medical treatments (Garza et al., 2017).

Munro and Ward (2005) state, "Although researchers, policymakers, and local authorities may all work to enhance the well-being of vulnerable groups, they may well have different perspectives which frequently affect and occasionally undermine the research process" (p. 1025). This is a critical issue, particularly concerning the gatekeeping of information related to identifying research participants and the level of participation the agency or the professional deems adequate. Additionally, interpretations of the boundaries of confidentiality and informed consent often conflict with the elements and importance of the research project (Munro **et al.,** 2005).

Vulnerable populations could include minorities, low-income, and limited education populations. Past research with vulnerable populations highlights that many participants considered participation in research as a positive experience and linked this with being able to tell their stories (Sutton et al., 2003). Research has also shown that those participants feel that by agreeing to participate in the research, their story may benefit others but are fearful based on a history of mistreatment towards specific populations (Cooper, 1999).

One of the critical issues in planning this study was balancing the risk of participation with the potential benefits of the study both to society and the study participants. Reference was made to the

Belmont Report (NCPHS, 1979). One of the fundamental human rights outlined in the Belmont Report is the right of participants to decide whether to participate in a study.

TUSKEGEE EXPERIMENT ETHICAL CASE STUDY

The Tuskegee Syphilis Study (TSS) marked a turning point in developing research ethics in the United States. In 1932, the historical syphilis study of Tuskegee involved the enrollment of six hundred African American men into a medical treatment program for "bad blood." Of these six hundred individuals, close to four hundred were previously infected with Syphilis but remained uninformed of what was taking place (Mandal et al., 2011).

Using endowment funds from the Julius Rosenwald Foundation, the United States Public Health Service (USPHS) began a research study on the lethality of Syphilis using African American men from Macon County, Alabama, as public research human subjects. The research, referred to as the "Tuskegee Study of Untreated Syphilis in the Negro Male" (Tuskegee University National Center for Bioethics in Research and Health Care, n.d.), occurred on the campus of the Tuskegee Institute in Alabama.

While medical examinations were provided to all subjects involved in the study, the disclosure as to the purpose or aims of the study was never offered (Nichols, 2011). Fifteen years into the study, penicillin became widely available and was found to be a satisfactory cure for Syphilis; however, Tuskegee participants were not offered this treatment in any fashion (Nichols, 2011). To add further insult, the subjects' physicians who suspected these individuals had contracted Syphilis were not permitted to intervene in any nature by the very researchers who developed the study (Mandal et al., 2011). The gross infractions associated with this study demonstrated the long-term effects that racial profiling in medical science could exert on a population. It is conceivable that if the study population had not been African American males in a time of racial dissension in the U.S., this study might never have grown in the exponential fashion in which it did. The Tuskegee Syphilis Study transpired from 1932 until the study was shut down in 1972. The study was conducted in Macon County, Alabama, which had a predominately Black population (84.5%) with high low-income and illiteracy rates (TSS Ad Hoc Advisory Panel, 1973). The study recruited 399 Black men with late latent Syphilis and a control group of 201 men without Syphilis to "follow and study the disease over a long period of time (1973)." To recruit and keep them in the study, men were told they were being treated for "bad blood," a colloquial term for Syphilis and other maladies (Brandt, 1978). Spinal taps were conducted for diagnostic purposes but promoted to the men as a "special free treatment" (Brandt, 1978). Although penicillin became available as an effective treatment for Syphilis in the early 1950s, men were not treated with it. Instead, they were given placebos or other non-therapeutic treatments. In one or more instances, treatment was withheld from infected men so that the study could continue (TSS Ad Hoc Advisory Panel, 1973). Furthermore, to assure access to the men's bodies for autopsy, the USPHS offered to pay for burial expenses but avoided disclosing their intent behind the offer (Brandt, 1978).

Although study reports were published every few years beginning in 1936, it was in July 1972 that newspaper reports made the story public. In August 1972, the Department of Health, Education, and Welfare established an Ad Hoc Committee that concluded that the study was not ethically justified and must be stopped immediately. Survivors and anyone potentially affected were to be treated at once, and a national body to oversee human subjects' research was to be set up (1973). The Tuskegee Health Benefit Program was established in 1973 following a class action lawsuit to provide lifetime medical care and burial services for the study participants. Benefits were extended to the families of the participants in 1975 (CDC, 2011).

The National Commission for the Protection of Human Subjects of Biomedical and Behavioral Research, established in 1974, published "The Belmont Report – Ethical Principles and Guidelines for the Protection of Human Subjects of Research" in 1979 (NIH, 2008). On May 16, 1997, President Clinton, following the recommendation of the Tuskegee Syphilis Study Legacy Committee (1996), publicly apologized to Tuskegee study survivors and their families and set in motion the establishment of the Tuskegee University National Center for Bioethics in Research and Health Care and the President's Council on Bioethics (CDC, 2011).

ETHICAL VIOLATIONS

The ethical violations associated with the Tuskegee Syphilis Study span 40 years and affected a sizable portion of the population (Mandal et al., 2011). The principle of beneficence, or the duty of healthcare practitioners to provide a possible benefit to patients, is a foundational ethical principle not evident in the Tuskegee study (Nichols & Leonard, 2011). The Tuskegee researchers imparted long-term harm to the participants, their families, and the population. Even though a public health law enacted in 1943 (Henderson Act) mandated testing and treatment for venereal diseases, TSS researchers withheld the newly discovered syphilis treatment of penicillin in 1943 (Stebbing & Bower, 2004). Researchers supplied a list of study participants to local physicians, unethically requesting these TSE men not be given penicillin for Syphilis; the local physicians wrongly complied (Devettere, 2010). In response to the unethical atrocities inflicted on humans in World War II, the international Nuremberg Code was established in 1947; this code noted fundamental principles that require consideration for satisfying "moral, ethical, and legal concepts in the conduct of human subject research" (National Institutes of Health, 2008, p. 5). Even following the Nuremberg code, the unethical practices in TSS continued. Although the World Health Organization's Declaration of Helsinki in 1964 mandated informed consent for human experiments, no informed consent was given to participants in TSS (Stebbing & Bower, 2004; Torke et al., 2004).

Another violation stemming from the study was the lack of participant autonomy. This principle stipulates that the decision-making process in healthcare stems from the ability of the patient to make an informed decision voluntarily (Nichols & Leonard, 2011). In the case of the Tuskegee study, the researchers did not consider this principle as they exerted their own autonomy and desires in caring for patients who willingly assumed they were receiving excellent and honest medical services (Nichols, 2011; Nichols & Leonard, 2011).

Non-malfeasance, the principle of not harming patients or subjects, was significantly neglected in the Tuskegee study. The researchers knowingly withheld a safe and effective treatment from the study participants. This violation dovetails with a similar principle that reflects the necessity for researchers to be forthright in their treatment of all study participants. Justice, as a method of implementing fair practices among all individuals, was indiscriminately violated in the Tuskegee study from when a viable treatment for Syphilis was discovered and available (Nichols & Leonard, 2011).

Veracity, the ethical principle of truthfulness, was debased during the Tuskegee study through the evident lack of full disclosure from the researchers to the participants as to the expectations of the study. The researchers did not offer full disclosure of intent or treatment once available at any point in time during the study's evolution. Additionally, the researchers did not consider the principles of individual respect and a person's right to know relative to informed consent (Nichols & Leonard, 2011).

Respect for Persons-The TSS participants was not viewed as autonomous with the right to self-determination. Instead, the men were considered not intelligent enough to seek treatment for their illness or to understand what was being done, or not done, to them in the study. Not only were the participants not afforded clear explanations about tests and treatments, but they were also expressly coerced and deceived into participating in the study (Brandt, 1978).

Justice: The uneducated, low-income men coerced into the TSS were chosen because of their race and social status. It was unjust to refuse treatment to the study participants once effective treatment for Syphilis was available. Because the men were not treated, the health of the larger community was endangered (Brandt, 1978).

Professional Issues-Violations of human subjects' rights that occurred before the publication of the Belmont Report are now becoming known, involving medical professionals, the U.S. Public Health Service, and the NIH. In October 2010, the U.S. apologized to Guatemala for intentionally infecting prisoners with Syphilis (McNeil, 2010). Rebecca Skloot detailed the use of tissue taken from a poor Black woman in the early 1950s without her knowledge or consent (2010). In the 1960s, 22 patients of Brooklyn's Jewish Chronic Disease Hospital received injections of cancer cells without their knowledge (Lerner, 2004). It is inconceivable today to imagine how the professionals involved in these situations could have rationalized their actions.

In 1966, Harvard professor Henry Beecher published his exposé on 22 cases that showed clear violations of ethical research (Lerner, 2004). In his essay, he provided guidelines and recommendations to scientists and physicians to be more mindful in their research. However, it appears that, despite public outrage resulting from Beecher's evidence, the formal accusation of physicians and administrators at the War Crimes Tribunal at Nuremburg, and the subsequent development of the Nuremburg Code in 1947, research ethics were not well developed until after the TSS ended. It was not until 1974 that the National Research Act was signed into law and not until 1980 that the American Medical Association included a provision for protecting human subjects in its Code of Ethics (American Medical Association, n.d.). Allan Brandt posits that Eunice Rivers, the nurse involved in the study, did not understand the potential health effects on the participants (1978). While the current Code of Ethics of the American Nurses Association cites principles of respect for human dignity and patient right of self-determination (2001), it is doubtful that those principles were communicated in the years of the TSS.

BREACH OF ETHICAL CODES AMONG HEALTHCARE PROFESSIONALS

According to the American Medical Association (AMA) (2011), the code of ethics for physicians and the medical workforce has a defined clause relative to patients' treatment, care, and involvement in the medical relationship. The AMA (2011) stipulates that any proposed experiment must be subject to an ethical review by a human studies board. The historical tenets of bioethics demonstrate medical science's recognition of atrocities such as the Tuskegee study and define a commitment to progress from a paternalistic model to a patient-centered individualized decision-making process grounded in informed consent. The period in which the Tuskegee study occurred demonstrates this nation's historical struggles with racism, sexism, and recognition of the intrinsic worth of all populations (Slavicek & Forsdahi, 2009). As a result of the Tuskegee study and other human atrocities, institutional review board development and global mandates that dictate the parameters of human studies now attest to a necessary correction in medical research.

ETHICAL DECISION MODELS

While the devastation of the Tuskegee study can never be rescinded, it is essential to understand why it occurred. Making decisions when an ethical dilemma presents itself may be difficult and stressful for healthcare practitioners or researchers. An ethical decision-making model that defines a specific sequence of steps assists in thoroughly analyzing all aspects of the situation before making decisions (Swisher & Davis, 2005). Various authors have proposed decision-making models (Gabard & Martin, 2003; Greenfield & Jensen, 2010; Swisher & Davis, 2005). Regardless of the framework selected to guide decision-making, it must be remembered that limitations may exist in any model. For example, ethical dilemmas may involve relational or emotional aspects that are not easily factored into decision-making models (Swisher & Davis, 2005). Therefore, it is vital to ensure that any hidden values, biases, and implications be uncovered during the reasoning and decision-making process (Greenfield & Jensen, 2010; Swisher & Davis, 2005).

Had an ethical decision-making model been used to analyze the design and potential implications of the Tuskegee Experiment prior to implementation, the mistreatment of human subjects could have been avoided (Stone, 2002). Suppose the decision models associated with patient-centered care and quality improvement initiatives had been present during the Tuskegee study. In that case, the events may have been prevented or mitigated. The tenets of such models dictate that research must shift from a utilitarian approach to a humanistic approach, considering a subject's right to consent, justice, and veracity through full disclosure (Miles & Mezzich, 2011). The global society has come to expect that healthcare providers will treat all patients in a dignified, moral manner that prioritizes the needs of the individual seeking medical assistance.

In reviewing this case and its presiding ethical concepts, an established model is necessary to assist with decision-making. The Kantianism theory provides the conceptual framework to guide the justification for problem-solving in this dilemma. The premise of the Kantian theory states that an individual must act per obligation but in a morally required manner (Hemmings, 2006). The Tuskegee researchers blatantly disregarded the requirements of Kantian bioethical decision-making by negating the principles of informed consent and right-to-know of the individuals involved in the study. Patient self-determination, informed consent, and an infusion of quality care throughout all human studies offer credibility to the research design (Hemmings, 2006).

The field of bioethics is based on the principles of moral obligation upholding the rights to autonomy, beneficence, justice (the three precepts of the Belmont Report), and non-malfeasance (Devettere, 2010). The Nuremberg Code, an international standard for research on human subjects, outlines ten directives that reflect these principles and certainly could have been applied to the TSS as early as the 1950s (National Institutes of Health, 2008).

Several models could have been utilized by the investigators and staff of the TSS as guidelines for future research. The first is the four-component model for moral reasoning. The steps within this model are: 1) Moral sensitivity, which helps to identify conflicts, looks at all interested parties, the consequences of the study, and any obligations to the subjects; 2) Moral judgment, which includes the justification process for conducting the study, 3) Moral commitment, which looks at the researcher's responsibility to the subjects, and 4) Moral action, which identifies the best action to be taken. (Rest, 1979).

Another model is the reflective equilibrium approach which could have been used as an ethical decision-making model by testing beliefs in 1) The Liberty principle – making sure all participants have an equal right to fundamental liberties (Rawls, 1999) and 2) The Difference principle – Making sure that all social and economic inequalities give the most significant advantage to the least advantaged (Daniels, 1996).

The Four-Boxes method looks at the medical indications, quality of life, patient preferences, and contextual features of the study (Jonsen et al., 2002). It is essential to consider all these topics in clinical research settings. A newer model might have been effective as an ethical decision-making model. The Medical Ethical Reasoning Model combines the models of ethics and reasoning into one process. It identifies the problem encountered, looks at the possible diagnosis or decision in the process, recognizes commonality, seeks information and data, plans, manages the project, identifies the outcome indicator, and establishes a foundation for justification (Tsai & Harasym, 2010).

Beemsterboer (2010) outlined a Six-Step Model, which includes:

1. Identify the Ethical Dilemma or Problem- This is the process's first and most critical step. Once a problem has been recognized, the decision maker must clearly and succinctly state the ethical question, but only after considering all pertinent aspects of the problem. Step two is unnecessary if a precise determination of right or wrong has been made.
2. Collect Information- The decision maker must gather information for an informed decision. This may include facts about the situation as they are developed, which may come from multiple sources. Information regarding the parties' values, including the patient and the healthcare provider, is needed. This step often takes time since the information may be limited.
3. State the Options- This step involves brainstorming to identify as many possible alternatives (or options). There is also a tendency to think a question has only one answer. This step forces decision-makers to view the situation from all angles to identify what stakeholders might see as alternative answers to the problem.
4. Apply Ethical Principles to the Options- This step views the situation with a focus on ethical principles (autonomy, beneficence, non-malfeasance, and justice) and ethical concepts (paternalism, confidentiality, and informed consent).
5. Come to a Decision- When each alternative has been clearly outlined in terms of pros and cons, having a reasonable framework to reference to make a decision.
6. Implement the Decision - The last step involves acting on the decision. Unfortunately, appropriate decisions sometimes need to be implemented. Taking no action represents tacit approval of a situation.

PROFESSIONAL CODES OF ETHICS

Scholl (1981) outlines that another necessary ethical standard is using codes, rules, guidelines, and other systems to identify unethical behaviors or means. These culturally designed and promulgated codes of conduct or ethical systems provide lists of what things one should and should not do. They also function to balance power and protect the powerless. From a social-psychological perspective, these ethical codes operate like other process-based control systems, such as state laws, company rules, policies, or social norms enforced through external and internal mechanisms. In the case of the Tuskegee experiments, physicians, researchers, and public health professionals, who knew about the study, all breached professional codes of ethics. They deliberately and wrongly withheld penicillin, a treatment known to cure the disease. The purpose of this was to retain research integrity. Knowingly waiting for the symptoms of Syphilis to manifest is the same as intentionally harming the patient (Devettere, 2010).

Furthermore, the researchers purposely did not tell the patients about their condition and the research protocol. Instead of telling them they were studying Syphilis, they told them they were studying and treating "bad blood." Other physicians that not directly involved in the study but knew about the research and the misleading information given to patients did not provide treatment to the participants either (Kampmeier, 1972). Using Decision-Making Capacity models can help determine patients' capacity to make certain decisions. Three general steps must be present to accurately measure the patient's decision-making capacity. The three recommended steps are Understanding, Evaluations, and Reasoning (Devettere, 2010). In the understanding step, the researchers should have told the patients about Syphilis and sought physician recommendations. Physicians or medical professionals should have been present and available to give these TSS participants recommendations. This would allow the patient to be fully informed of the risks and benefits of the study and enter the evaluation phase. Then the patient can make the best healthcare decision for themselves and produce the best course of action. However, some situations warrant that providers make the decisions for a participant.

An example would be giving a mentally ill patient medication to stabilize them. Another course of action used to make ethical decisions (such as involving the mentally ill patient) involves the Reasonable Treatment Standard. The Reasonable Treatment Standard neither uses substituted judgment nor the best interest standard. Physicians in the TSS at some point in the duration of the study would have needed to treat the patient beyond a certain baseline of Syphilis symptoms.

IMPACTS

Ethics is sometimes referred to as *"the study of values and moral behavior"* and "*Ethical behavior is acting in ways consistent with one's personal values and the commonly held values of the organization and society"* (Nelson and Quick, 2008, p, 107). This means using personal and social variables as criteria in organizational decision-making and behavioral choice decisions. These ethical definitions refer to a decision's effect on others. This stakeholder-based approach is based on the belief that organizational decisions that bring harm to one or more stakeholders are unethical. This is especially true if the relevant stakeholders are powerless or feel "at the decision makers' mercy" (Nelson & Quick, 2008). A more rigid standard in this category holds that individuals should avoid harming others and work to help others.

One unanswered question is whether the TSS contributed to the current mistrust of medical research evidenced in the African American community. Brandon, Isaac & LaVeist make a compelling argument that African Americans' greater likelihood to decline to participate in medical research and donate organs does not stem from the TSS but from "broader historical and personal experiences" (2005). Because our country lacks a health care system that provides equal access for all, vulnerable populations suffer more from disease than those with higher incomes (World Health Organization, 2000), leading to mistrust and lack of participation in studies that could benefit those populations. While Institutional Review Boards protect the rights of individuals, broader issues have been identified relating to the rights of communities in conducting research (Shore et al., 2010).

CONCLUSION

The content analysis of the literature outlines some key aspects to can be effective in helping more African-Americans become more active in clinical trials and less reluctant when new vaccines come out. These recommendations include:

1. A potential approach could include partnering with minority primary care physicians with solid relationships with minority patients. Trust and access to minority participants are significant barriers to participation. Having someone who is culturally congruent on the team makes them more trusting. These partnerships should include training and education programs for minority physicians to address the center's clinical trial work, how to have patients participate, and the benefits of advocating for clinical trial participation by minority patients. Physicians are more likely to refer people to clinical trials if they have a working relationship with the hospital/university conducting the clinical trial.
2. Communication and community outreach are essential. Communicating in a transparent, culturally relevant manner also helps build trust. Rather than trying to convince minority participants to participate, engage them in ways that welcome them so they want to participate.
3. Address barriers that would limit participation or include support to make it easier for those to participate. These barriers could include the need for transportation, the need for childcare, or a long commitment to participate. Other steps include communicating with potential participants by phone and meeting them before their clinical appointments. Having staff available to help with health literacy and to answer questions when the research nurse explains the trial, and they help patients fill out consent forms.

In a rapidly changing healthcare environment, clinical healthcare professionals face difficult choices concerning what is best for their patients. In some cases, these choices become enmeshed in ethical dilemmas; additionally, what patients choose for themselves may differ from what the family or physicians believe should be done. Even between similar individuals, value systems may prove to be radically different. As clinical research continues to be an essential facet of medicine, healthcare professionals face more challenges. Commercial and federal entities that fund research projects require results, and this pressure often translates into unethically managed or falsified studies. Participants who are unfortunate enough to be enrolled in these studies are at greater risk of receiving inadequate or no treatment at all. Exploring the Tuskegee Experiments in this context provides public health research professionals with a framework for understanding the predominant ethical theories and principles used in health care, determining any legal and regulatory implications, and in collaboration with their colleagues and patients/clients, making effective decisions that determine the appropriate course of treatment or refusal of such, for and with those for whom they care. The Tuskegee syphilis experiment remains one of the most outrageous examples of disregard and maligned ethical principles. The principle for respect of human dignity was violated when patients did not receive the available penicillin. The apparent lack of respect for study participants was evident in a statement by the Public Health Service Director of the Venereal Disease Unit, John Heller, when he stated, "The men's status did not warrant ethical debate. They were subjects, not patients, clinical material, not sick people," (Jones, 1993).

The results of the outcry against the Tuskegee Syphilis study are still felt today. The requirement of the Institution Review Board (IRB) in approving human subject research has helped to stem unethical research projects, and researchers are more aware of the importance of ethical decision-making models when setting up new research. Protocols and informed consent documents must be created in adherence to the IRB's guidelines and approved by the Board prior to distribution to the participants. Rules for protecting human subjects in research should help prevent projects such as the Tuskegee Syphilis project and protect people from being exploited in the name of scientific inquiry.

Using an ethical decision-making model helped the researchers to make more ethical, legal, and moral decisions in this case. Framing the experiments within a principles-based approach, the researchers would have discovered that the study conflicted with the fundamental ethical principles of beneficence, non-malfeasance, justice, and autonomy. A rights-based approach could also have prevented or shortened the 40-year study. Fundamental human rights like the right to choose freely, the right to human dignity, the right to truth, the right to what is agreed, the right not to be injured, and the right to privacy were all neglected in the Tuskegee experiments (Velasquez et al., n.d.). A care-based model could have helped the nurse to decide to refuse to participate in the study of the men. A caring model frames decision analysis and facilities decision-making in terms of empathy, compassion, caring, and love (American College of Obstetricians and Gynecologists Committee on Ethics, 2007).

Although the Tuskegee Syphilis experiment took place a century ago, the consequences of the study are still very pertinent. The flaws and errors in the conduct of the study have served as the foundation for much-needed change in the research community. As the United States government has passed a result, laws and regulations to prevent further exploitation of vulnerable populations, ethics models and approaches have been created and developed to aid researchers in their studies. Institutional Review Boards have been established to monitor and oversee human research. Implementing these models and guidelines allows research to be conducted ethically and constructively (Biasetti & Mori, 2021). Researchers must utilize the lessons learned from failed experiments like the TSS to ensure research integrity.

The crisis posed by the dearth of African-American representation in clinical trials is both substantial and multifaceted. The potential health disparities crisis that ensues not only impedes the advancement of medical science but also perpetuates a cycle of health inequities that disproportionately affects this marginalized demographic. Addressing this crisis demands concerted efforts to rectify historical wrongs, cultivate cultural competence, and engender a comprehensive and equitable participation of African-Americans in clinical trials. Through such endeavors, the United States can engender a more inclusive and just healthcare landscape that resonates with the principles of equitable healthcare access and outcomes.

REFERENCES

Agency for Healthcare Research and Quality. (2018, June). *Access and Disparities in Access to Health Care.* AHRQ. https://www.ahrq.gov/research/findings/nhqrdr/nhqdr15/access.html

Alsan, M., & Wanamaker, M. (2018). Tuskegee and the Health of Black Men. *The Quarterly Journal of Economics, 133*(1), 407–455. doi:10.1093/qje/qjx029 PMID:30505005

American College of Obstetricians and Gynecologists Committee on Ethics. (2007). *Ethical Decision Making in Obstetrics and Gynecology.* (ACOG Committee Opinion Number 390). ACOG. https://www.acog.org/from_home/publications/ethics/co390.pdf

American Medical Association. (2011). Opinion 2.30 – Information from Unethical Experiments. *Code of Medical Ethics.* AMA. https://www.ama-assn.org/ama/pub/physician-resources/medical-ethics/code-medical-ethics/opinion230.page?

American Medical Association. (n.d.). *Ethics Timeline: 1941 to 1980.* AMA. https://www.ama-assn.org/ama/pub/physician-resources/medical-ethics/code-medical-ethics/history-ama-ethics/ethics-timeline-1941-1980.page?

American Nurses Association. (2001). *Code of Ethics for Nurses.* ANA. http://nursingworld.org/MainMenuCategories/EthicsStandards/CodeofEthicsforNurses.aspx

Baker, R., Caplan, A., Emanuel, L. L., & Latham, S. R. (1997). Crisis, Ethics, and the American Medical Association 1847 and 1997. *JAMA*, *278*(2), 163-164. doi:10.1001/jama.278.2.163

Beemsterboer, P. (2010). *Ethics and Law in Dental Hygiene* (2nd ed.). Saunders Elsevier.

Bhopal, R. (2008). Ethical issues in health research on ethnic minority populations: Focusing on inclusion and exclusion. The Association of Research Ethics Committees. *Research Ethics*, *4*(1), 15–19. https://journals.sagepub.com/doi/pdf/10.1177/174701610800400104. doi:10.1177/174701610800400104

Biasetti, P., & de Mori, B. (2021). The Ethical Matrix as a Tool for Decision-Making Process in Conservation. *Frontiers in Environmental Science*, *9*, 584636. doi:10.3389/fenvs.2021.584636

Blume, A. W. (2016). Advances in Substance Abuse Prevention and Treatment Interventions Among Racial, Ethnic, and Sexual Minority Populations. *Alcohol Research : Current Reviews*, *38*(1), 47–54. PMID:27159811

Brandon, D., Isaac, L., & LaVeist, T. (2005). The Legacy of Tuskegee and Trust in Medical Care: Is Tuskegee Responsible for Race Differences in Mistrust of Medical Care? - Research - Hopkins Center for Health Disparities Solutions. *Journal of the National Medical Association*, *97*(7). https://www.jhsph.edu/healthdisparities/Research/the_legacy_of_tuskegee_and_trust_in_medical_care_is_tuskegee_responsible_for_race_differences_in_mistrust_of_medical_care.html PMID:16080664

Brandt, A. (1978). Racism and Research: The Case of the Tuskegee Syphilis Study. *The Hastings Center Report*, *8*(6), 21–29. doi:10.2307/3561468 PMID:721302

CDC. (2011, June 15). The Tuskegee Timeline. *U.S. Public Health Service Syphilis Study at Tuskegee.* CDC. https://www.cdc.gov/tuskegee/timeline.htm

Clark, L. T., Watkins, L., Piña, I. L., Elmer, M., Akinboboye, O., Gorham, M., & Regnante, J. M. (2019). Increasing Diversity in Clinical Trials: Overcoming Critical Barriers. *Current Problems in Cardiology*, *44*(5), 148–172. doi:10.1016/j.cpcardiol.2018.11.002 PMID:30545650

Colby, S. L., & Ortman, J. M. (2015, March). *Projections of the Size and Composition of the U.S. Population: 2014 to 2060 Population Estimates and Projections.* Census. https://www.census.gov/content/dam/Census/library/publications/2015/demo/p25-1143.pdf

Cooper, J. (1999). Ethical Issues and Their Practical Application in a Psychological Autopsy Study of Suicide. *Journal of Clinical Nursing*, *8*(4), 467–475. doi:10.1046/j.1365-2702.1999.00276.x PMID:10624264

Daniels, N. (1996). *Justice and Justification. Reflective Equilibrium in Theory and Practice*. Cambridge University Press. doi:10.1017/CBO9780511624988

Dawes, D. E. (2019). The Future of Health Equity in America: Addressing the Multiple, Intersecting Determinants of Health. *Ethnicity & Disease*, *29*(Suppl 2), 343–344. doi:10.18865/ed.29.S2.343 PMID:31308602

Devettere, R. (2010). *Practical Decision Making in Health Care Ethics: Cases and Concepts* (3rd ed.). Georgetown University Press.

Downs, J. (2012). *Sick From Freedom: African-American Illness and Suffering During the Civil War and Reconstruction*. Oxford University Press. doi:10.1093/acprof:osobl/9780199758722.001.0001

Durant, R. W., Wenzel, J. A., Scarinci, I. C., Paterniti, D. A., Fouad, M. N., Hurd, T. C., & Martin, M. Y. (2014). Perspectives on Barriers and Facilitators to Minority Recruitment for Clinical Trials Among Cancer Center Leaders, Investigators, Research Staff, and Referring Clinicians: Enhancing Minority Participation in Clinical Trials (EMPaCT). *Cancer, 120 Suppl 7*(0 7), 1097–1105. doi:10.1002/cncr.28574

Elliott, D. (16 Feb 2021). *In Tuskegee, Painful History Shadows Efforts to Vaccinate African Americans*. NPR. https://www.npr.org/2021/02/16/967011614/in-tuskegee-painful-history-shadows-efforts-to-vaccinate-african-americans

Farr, D. E., Brandt, H. M., Comer, K. D., Jackson, D. D., Pandya, K., Friedman, D. B., Ureda, J. R., Williams, D. G., Scott, D. B., Green, W., & Hébert, J. R. (2015). Cancer Research Participation Beliefs and Behaviors of a Southern Black Population: A Quantitative Analysis of the Role of Structural Factors in Cancer Research Participation. *Journal of Cancer Education*, *30*(3), 522–529. doi:10.100713187-014-0749-0 PMID:25385692

Gabard, D. L., & Martin, M. W. (2011). *Physical Therapy Ethics*. F.A. Davis Company.

Garza, M. A., Quinn, S. C., Li, Y., Assini-Meytin, L., Casper, E. T., Fryer, C. S., & Thomas, S. B. (2017). The influence of race and ethnicity on becoming a human subject: Factors associated with participation in research. Contemporary clinical trials communications, 7, 57–63. doi:10.1016/j.conctc.2017.05.009

Greenfield, B., & Jensen, G. M. (2010). Beyond a code of ethics: Phenomenological ethics for everyday practice. *Physiotherapy Research International*, *15*(2), 88–95. doi:10.1002/pri.481 PMID:20564757

Haley, S. J., Southwick, L. E., Parikh, N. S., Rivera, J., Farrar-Edwards, D., & Boden-Albala, B. (2017). Barriers and strategies for recruiting racial and ethnic minorities: Perspectives from neurological clinical research coordinators. *Journal of Racial and Ethnic Health Disparities*, *4*(6), 1225–1236. doi:10.100740615-016-0332-y PMID:28176157

Hamel, L. M., Penner, L. A., Albrecht, T. L., Heath, E., Gwede, C. K., & Eggly, S. (2016). Barriers to clinical trial enrollment in racial and ethnic minority patients with cancer. *Cancer control. Cancer Control*, *23*(4), 327–337. doi:10.1177/107327481602300404 PMID:27842322

Heintzelman, C. (2003). The Tuskegee Syphilis Study and Its Implications for the 21st Century. *The New Social Worker*. https://www.socialworker.com/tuskegee.htm

Hemmings, A. (2006). *Great ethical divides: Bridging the gap between institutional review boards and researchers*. Ethical Researcher.

Johnson, C. E. (2022). *Organizational ethics: a practical approach* (5th ed.). SAGE.

Jones, J. H. (1993). *Bad blood: The Tuskegee syphilis experiment*. The Free Press.

Jonsen, A., Siegler, M., & Winslade, W. (2002). Clinical ethics: a practice approach to ethical decisions in clinical medicine, (5th ed.) Columbus, OH: McGraw-Hill/ Appleton & Lange.

Kampmeier, R. H. (1972). The Tuskegee study of untreated Syphilis. *Southern Medical Journal*, *65*(10), 1247–1251. doi:10.1097/00007611-197210000-00016 PMID:5074095

Kampmeier, R. H. (1974). Final report on the Tuskegee syphilis study. *Southern Medical Journal*, *67*(11), 1349–1353. doi:10.1097/00007611-197411000-00019 PMID:4610772

Lerner, B. H. (2004). Sins of omission—Cancer research without informed consent. *The New England Journal of Medicine*, *351*(7), 628–630. doi:10.1056/NEJMp048108 PMID:15306661

Mandal, J., Acharya, S., & Parija, S. C. (2011). Ethics in human research. *Tropical Parasitology*, *1*(1), 2–3. doi:10.4103/2229-5070.129140 PMID:23509672

Martin, M. A., Swider, S. M., Olinger, T., Avery, E., Lynas, C. M., Carlson, K., & Rothschild, S. K. (2011). Recruitment of Mexican American adults for an intensive diabetes intervention trial. *Ethnicity & Disease*, *21*(1), 7–12. PMID:21462723

McNeil, D. (2010, October 1). U.S. Apologizes for Syphilis Tests in Guatemala. *New York Times*. https://www.nytimes.com/2010/10/02/health/research/02infect.html

Miles, A., & Mezzich, J. E. (2011). Advancing global communication and research for personalized healthcare. *International Journal of Person Centered Medicine*, *1*(1), 1–5. doi:10.5750/ijpcm.v1i1.10

Moon, M. R., & Khin-Maung-Gyi, F. (2009). The history and role of institutional review boards. *The Virtual Mentor*, *11*(4), 311–321. PMID:23195065

Munro, E., Holmes, L., & Ward, H. (2005). Researching vulnerable groups: Ethical issues and the effective conduct of research in local authorities. *British Journal of Social Work*, *35*(7), 1023–1024. doi:10.1093/bjsw/bch220

National Commission for the Protection of Human Subjects of Biomedical and Behavioural Research. (1979). *The Belmont report*. NCPHSBBR.

National Institutes of Health. (2008). Protecting Human Research Participants. Retrieved from http://phrp.nihtraining.com/index.php

Ndugga, N., Hill, L., Artiga, S., & Haldar, S. (14 July 2022). *Latest Data on COVID-19 Vaccinations by Race/Ethnicity*. KFF. https://www.kff.org/coronavirus-covid-19/issue-brief/latest-data-on-covid-19-vaccinations-by-race-ethnicity/

Nelson, D. L., & Quick, J. C. (2008). Understanding Organizational Behavior. Mason, OH: Centage Learning.

Nichols, M. (2011). Ethical decision making. *CME Resource, 3707*, 1–40.

Nichols, M., & Leonard, J. M. (2011). Medical ethics for physicians. *CME Resource, 4717*, 1–26.

Oh, S. S., Galanter, J., Thakur, N., Pino-Yanes, M., Barcelo, N. E., White, M. J., de Bruin, D. M., Greenblatt, R. M., Bibbins-Domingo, K., Wu, A. H. B., Borrell, L. N., Gunter, C., Powe, N. R., & Burchard, E. G. (2015). Diversity in clinical and biomedical research: A promise yet to be fulfilled. *PLoS Medicine, 12*(12), e1001918. doi:10.1371/journal.pmed.1001918 PMID:26671224

Polite, B. N., Adams-Campbell, L. L., Brawley, O. W., Bickell, N., Carethers, J. M., Flowers, C. R., Foti, M., Gomez, S. L., Griggs, J. J., Lathan, C. S., Li, C. I., Lichtenfeld, J. L., McCaskill-Stevens, W., & Paskett, E. D. (2017). Charting the future of cancer health disparities research: A position statement from the American Association for Cancer Research, the American Cancer Society, the American Society of Clinical Oncology, and the National Cancer Institute. *CA: a Cancer Journal for Clinicians, 67*(5), 353–361. doi:10.3322/caac.21404 PMID:28738442

Quinn, S. C. (2004). Ethics in Public Health Research. *American Journal of Public Health, 94*(6), 918–922. doi:10.2105/AJPH.94.6.918 PMID:15249289

Ramamoorthy, A., Pacanowski, M. A., Bull, J., & Zhang, L. (2015). Racial/ethnic differences in drug disposition and response: A review of recently approved drugs. *Clinical Pharmacology and Therapeutics, 97*(3), 263–273. doi:10.1002/cpt.61 PMID:25669658

Rawls, J. (1999). *A theory of justice* (revised ed.). Harvard University. doi:10.4159/9780674042582

Rest, J. (1979). *Development in judging moral issues.* University of Minnesota Press.

Saultz, J. W., Jones, S. M., McDaniel, S. H., Bagley, B., McCormally, T., Marker, J. E., Weida, J. A., & Green, L. A. (2015). A new foundation for the delivery and financing of American health care. *Family Medicine, 47*(8), 612–619. PMID:26382119

Scharff, D. P., Mathews, K. J., Jackson, P., Hoffsuemmer, J., Martin, E., & Edwards, D. (2010). More than Tuskegee: Understanding mistrust about research participation. *Journal of Health Care for the Poor and Underserved, 21*(3), 879–897. doi:10.1353/hpu.0.0323 PMID:20693733

Scholl, R. W. (1981). An analysis of macro models of organizations: The goal and political models. *Administration & Society, 13*(3), 271–298. doi:10.1177/009539978101300303

Shore, N., Brazauskas, R., Drew, E., Wong, K. A., Moy, L., Corage Baden, A., & Seifer, S.D. (2010). Understanding Community-Based Processes for Research Ethics Review: A National Study. *Am J Public Health*, AJPH.2010.194340. doi:<p> doi:10.2105/AJPH.2010.194340</p>

Skloot, R. (2010). *The Immortal Life of Henrietta Lacks.* Crown Publishers.

Slavicek, G., & Forsdahl, G. (2009). Ethics and regulatory aspects in medical research. *International Journal of Stomatology & Occlusion Medicine, 2*(1), 45–49. doi:10.100712548-009-0007-y

Smedley, B. D., Stith, A. Y., & Nelson, A. R. (2003). *Unequal Treatment: Confronting Racial and Ethnic Disparities in Health Care.* National Academy of Sciences.

Stebbing, J., & Bower, M. (2004). Lessons for HIV from Tuskegee. *Journal of HIV Therapy*, *9*(3), 50–52. PMID:15534560

Stone, J. (2002). Race and healthcare disparities: Overcoming vulnerability. *Theoretical Medicine and Bioethics*, *23*(6), 499–518. doi:10.1023/A:1021524431845 PMID:12546167

Sutton, L. B., Erlen, J. A., Glad, J. M., & Siminoff, L. A. (2003). Recruiting vulnerable populations for research: Revisiting the ethical issues. *Journal of Professional Nursing*, *19*(2), 106–112. doi:10.1053/jpnu.2003.16 PMID:12748936

Swanson, G. M., & Ward, A. J. (1995). Recruiting minorities into clinical trials toward a participant-friendly system. *Journal of the National Cancer Institute*, *87*(23), 1747–1759. doi:10.1093/jnci/87.23.1747 PMID:7473831

Swisher, L. L., & Davis, C. M. (2005). The realm-individual-process-situation (RIPS) model of ethical decision-making. *HPA Resource*, *5*(3), 1–8.

Torke, A. M., Corbie-Smith, G. M., & Branch, W. T. (2004). African American patients ' perspectives on medical decision-making. *Archives of Internal Medicine*, *164*(5), 525–530. doi:10.1001/archinte.164.5.525 PMID:15006829

Tsai, T., & Harasym, P. (2010). A medical ethical reasoning model and its contribution to medical education. *Medical Education*, *44*(9), 864–873. doi:10.1111/j.1365-2923.2010.03722.x PMID:20716096

TSS Ad Hoc Advisory Panel. (1973). *Final Report of the Tuskegee Syphilis Study Ad Hoc Advisory Panel*. USF. https://www.research.usf.edu/cs/library/docs/finalreport-tuskegeestudyadvisorypanel.pdf

Tuskegee Syphilis Study Legacy Committee. (1996). Final Report of the Tuskegee Syphilis Study Legacy Committee | www.hsl.virginia.edu. *University of Virginia Health Systems, Claude Moore Health Sciences Library*. US Able Net. http://transcoder.usablenet.com/tt/www.hsl.virginia.edu/historical/medical_history/bad_blood/report.cfm

Tuskegee University National Center for Bioethics in Research and Health Care. (n.d.). *About the USPHS Syphilis Study*. Tuskegee University. https://www.tuskegee.edu/about_us/centers_of_excellence/bioethics_center/about_the_usphs_syphilis_study.aspx

Tymchuk, A. (1981). Ethical decision making and psychological treatment. *Journal of Psychiatric Treatment and Evaluation*, *3*(6), 507–513. PMID:11651663

Velasquez, M., Andre, C., Shanks, T., & Meyer, M. (n.d.). *Thinking ethically: A framework for moral decision-making*. SCU. https://www.scu.edu/ethics/publications/iie/v7n1/thinking.html

Washington, H. (2006). *Medical Apartheid: The Dark History of Medical Experimentation on Black Americans from Colonial Times to the Present*. First Anchor Books.

Webber-Ritchey, K. J., & Lane-Cordova, A. D. (2021). Health disparities and COVID-19 pandemic: Increasing clinical research participation among African Americans. *Journal of Health Disparities Research and Practice*, *14*(2), 5.

Wedge, D. (July 9, 2020). *Strategies Based on COVID-19 Patient Characteristics could improve outcomes, reduce hospital strain, research suggests - hospital data confirming the higher disease burden on patients who face social adversities also under possible care strategies*. Health City. https://healthcity.bmc.org/research/covid-19-patient-characteristics-could-inform-tailored-strategies

World Health Organization. (2000). [*Health Systems: Improving Performance*. Geneva.]. *World Health Report*, 2000.

Yearby, R. (2018). Racial disparities in health status and access to healthcare: The continuation of inequality in the United States due to structural racism. *American Journal of Economics and Sociology*, *77*(3-4), 1113–1152. doi:10.1111/ajes.12230

Chapter 5
Post-Traumatic Stress Disorder (PTSD) Among Police Officers is a Public Health and Safety Crisis

Grace McGrath
Marymount University, USA

Darrell Norman Burrell
https://orcid.org/0000-0002-4675-9544
Marymount University, USA

ABSTRACT

This chapter discusses how post-traumatic stress disorder (PTSD) among police officers is a public health and safety crisis. Given the prevalence of PTSD among police officers and its potential impact on their lives, police organizations and supervisors must implement measures to support officers struggling with the disorder. It is also essential for supervisors and co-workers to be aware of the signs and symptoms of PTSD, as this can help them to identify officers who are at risk and provide them with the necessary support and resources. This chapter explores emerging and proven interventions to help those in law enforcement facing PTSD.

INTRODUCTION

Post-Traumatic Stress Disorder (PTSD) has emerged as a significant public health crisis, particularly among police officers who daily navigate the complex landscapes of crime, violence, and trauma. The well-being of law enforcement personnel is not only a matter of individual health but also a critical societal crisis. Post-Traumatic Stress Disorder (PTSD) among police officers represents a crisis that demands renewed attention, engagement, and active interventions. The nature of policing exposes officers to traumatic events and high-stress situations, often resulting in long-lasting psychological consequences. However, within this crisis lies the potential for innovations and new approaches to address the mental health and well-being of those who serve and protect our communities.

DOI: 10.4018/978-1-6684-9522-3.ch005

Police officers are frequently exposed to traumatic incidents such as violent crimes, accidents, and life-threatening situations. These experiences can lead to the development of PTSD, a debilitating condition characterized by intrusive memories, hyperarousal, and emotional numbing. The toll of trauma on officers extends beyond their well-being, as their mental health directly affects their decision-making, performance, and interactions with the public. Therefore, understanding PTSD among police officers as a public health crisis necessitates a broader perspective that accounts for its implications.

The well-being of police officers directly influences the safety and trust of the communities they serve. Officers grappling with untreated or unrecognized PTSD may experience impaired judgment, decreased situational awareness, and an elevated risk of use of force incidents. Moreover, unaddressed mental health challenges can lead to strained relationships between law enforcement and the public, exacerbating tensions and diminishing community cooperation. The societal implications of this crisis are further underscored by potential increases in absenteeism, early retirements, and the loss of experienced officers who leave the force due to mental health issues. The ensuing gaps in expertise could jeopardize public safety and hinder law enforcement agencies ability to respond to emergencies effectively.

Law enforcement personnel face many unique stressors in the workplace. The very nature of the job can create an atmosphere of stress and pressure, leading to various physical and psychological health issues. Law enforcement personnel are tasked with the difficult job of protecting and serving the public. This often requires making decisions in dangerous and uncertain situations (Rosemond, 2018; Pickens, 2011; Parker, 2016; Gersons, 1989; Lees et al., 2019). Decisions must be made quickly and often with limited information, leading to heightened stress and pressure (Rosemond, 2018; Pickens, 2011; Parker, 2016; Gersons, 1989; Lees et al., 2019).

The job's physical demands can also contribute to the stress and pressure law enforcement personnel face (Rosemond, 2018; Pickens, 2011; Parker, 2016; Gersons, 1989; Lees et al., 2019). Law enforcement personnel are often required to engage in physical activity or confront dangerous situations, leading to physical fatigue and further stress (Rosemond, 2018; Pickens, 2011; Parker, 2016; Gersons, 1989; Lees et al., 2019). Furthermore, officers may be required to work long hours, leading to exhaustion and further stress (Rosemond, 2018; Pickens, 2011; Parker, 2016; Gersons, 1989; Lees et al., 2019).

The emotional demands of law enforcement can also contribute to stress and pressure (Rosemond, 2018; Pickens, 2011; Parker, 2016; Gersons, 1989; Lees et al., 2019). Law enforcement personnel often face difficult situations that can lead to emotional distress (Rosemond, 2018; Pickens, 2011; Parker, 2016; Gersons, 1989; Lees et al., 2019). Additionally, officers may be exposed to traumatic events, leading to psychological trauma (Rosemond, 2018; Pickens, 2011; Parker, 2016; Gersons, 1989; Lees et al., 2019).

Excessive stress and pressure can lead to various physical and psychological health issues for law enforcement personnel (Rosemond, 2018; Pickens, 2011). Physical health issues may include an increased risk of heart attack, stroke, and other diseases (Gersons, 1989; Lees et al., 2019). Additionally, excessive stress can decrease job performance and satisfaction (Gersons, 1989; Lees et al., 2019). Psychological health issues may include depression, anxiety, and post-traumatic stress disorder (PTSD) v These issues can lead to decreased job performance, decreased job satisfaction, and increased absenteeism (Gersons, 1989; Lees et al., 2019). These psychological issues can also lead to decreased quality of life, increased suicide risk, and increased risk of substance abuse (Pickens, 2011; Parker, 2016). Post-traumatic Stress Disorder (PTSD) is an anxiety disorder that can develop after exposure to a traumatic event or workplace stress. It is characterized by intrusive memories, flashbacks, and avoidance of situations that may trigger the trauma. Symptoms of PTSD include nightmares, flashbacks, avoidance of reminders of the traumatic event, hyperarousal, negative thoughts and feelings, and dissociation (American Psychiatric

Association, 2013). PTSD can significantly affect an individual's functioning and quality of life and is associated with various physical and mental health problems, including depression, substance use, and suicidality (Green, 2004; Rosemond, 2018; Parker, 2016).

Post-traumatic stress disorder (PTSD) is a severe issue in the law enforcement community with police officers' suicidality (Green, 2004; Rosemond, 2018; Parker, 2016).

PTSD can have a profound and long-lasting impact on the lives of those who experience it, and it is especially prevalent among police officers, who are exposed to a high degree of traumatic events during their duties suicidality (Green, 2004; Rosemond, 2018; Parker, 2016). Police officers face traumatic events, such as responding to domestic violence calls, investigating homicides, or witnessing fatalities (Green, 2004; Rosemond, 2018; Parker, 2016).

They also face the daily risk of death or severe injury, leading to chronic stress and anxiety (Green, 2004; Rosemond, 2018; Parker, 2016). In addition, police officers often experience guilt, shame, and helplessness when they witness traumatic events and cannot intervene (Green, 2004; Rosemond, 2018; Parker, 2016).

All of these factors can contribute to the development of PTSD in police officers.

The symptoms of PTSD can vary from person to person, but they typically include intrusive thoughts and memories, avoidance of situations that remind the person of the trauma, emotional numbing, and hyperarousal (APA, 2013). These symptoms can significantly impact an individual's day-to-day functioning, leading to difficulties with relationships, work, and other areas of life (Green, 2004; Rosemond, 2018; Parker, 2016). For police officers, these symptoms can lead to decreased job performance, increased sick leave, and difficulty functioning in their daily duties (Green, 2004; Rosemond, 2018; Parker, 2016).

PROBLEM STATEMENT AND SIGNIFICANCE

Police officers and other law enforcement personnel are essential members of our society, yet they are exposed to countless stressful situations that can damage their mental health. It is estimated that police officers have post-traumatic stress disorder at over six times more than the prevalence rates for the community (Green, 2004; Rosemond, 2018).

The high-stress levels associated with police work have been linked to the development of PTSD. Various environmental and personal factors have been identified as potential risk factors for PTSD among police officers (Green, 2004; Rosemond, 2018). Environmental risk factors include exposure to traumatic events, long hours, and inadequate resources (Green, 2004; Rosemond, 2018). Personal risk factors include poor coping skills, lack of social support, and pre-existing mental health issues (Green, 2004; Rosemond, 2018).

Research has also found that police officers are more likely to develop PTSD if they have experienced a traumatic event or a series of traumatic events (Faust & Ven, 2014).

In one study, researchers found that police officers who experienced multiple traumatic events were three times more likely to develop PTSD than those who experienced a single event (Faust & Ven, 2014). Furthermore, research has revealed that police officers who experience high levels of job-related stress are more likely to develop PTSD (Faust & Ven, 2014).

Neglecting to address PTSD as a public health crisis within the law enforcement community can lead to a cascade of adverse societal consequences. A comprehensive approach that encompasses early identification, de-stigmatization, effective treatment, and ongoing support is paramount. By prioritizing officers' mental well-being, agencies can mitigate the risk of PTSD-related impairments and foster an environment where officers feel valued, empowered, and capable of serving their communities with resilience and professionalism. Recognizing the symbiotic relationship between the mental health of police officers and the safety of the public underscores the urgency of addressing this crisis on both an individual and societal level.

The prevalence of PTSD among police officers has severe implications for both the individual and police departments. Police officers with PTSD are likelier to experience mood disturbances, impaired cognitive functioning, and physical health issues (Nievas, 2015). Furthermore, PTSD can lead to lower job performance, increased absenteeism, and an increased risk of suicide (Nievas, 2015). For police departments, this can lead to higher costs, decreased morale, and increased turnover (Nievas, 2015). This paper seeks to find solutions from current and emerging research to address this complex public health crisis.

METHOD

The method employed was a review of current, previous, and emerging research. The literature review process involved a systematic analysis of the gathered sources. Organizing the review can follow thematic or chronological structures, depending on the nature of the research. The process involved critically evaluating previous studies' methodology, findings, and implications, highlighting areas where further investigation is warranted. A comprehensive and diverse selection of sources was employed to maintain rigor, ensuring that different perspectives and critical contributions were addressed. Drawing connections between various studies and findings helps reveal some gaps the article aims to fill. By contextualizing the study's significance within the broader academic discourse, the approach established the unique contribution of the article, highlighting its potential implications for theory, practice, or policy. The keywords used included: law enforcement stress, PTSD in law enforcement, public safety job stress, police stress management, police culture, stigma, treatment, workplace stress, and occupational stress. Databases used include National Institutes of Health, ProQuest Dissertations, IGI Global Publishing, Research Gate, Google Scholar, ProQuest, and SCOPUS.

THEORIES OF OCCUPATIONAL AND WORKPLACE STRESS

One of the most commonly accepted occupational and workplace stress theories is the Demand-Control-Support (DCS) model (De Jonge & Kompier, 1997; Macklin et al., 2006; Gilbert-Ouimet et al., 2014). This model suggests that stress results from an imbalance between the demands placed on an individual and their ability to control their work environment (De Jonge & Kompier, 1997; Macklin et al., 2006; Gilbert-Ouimet et al., 2014). Stress can be reduced through increased control, increased support from colleagues and supervisors, employer resources, and reduced job demands (De Jonge & Kompier, 1997; Macklin et al., 2006; Gilbert-Ouimet et al., 2014).

Another commonly cited occupational and workplace stress theory is the Job Demands-Resources (JD-R) model (Schaufeli, 2017; Bauer et al., 2014; Demerouti et al., 2001). This model suggests that job demands (such as workload, time pressure, and role ambiguity) can lead to stress but that these demands can be managed through the presence of job resources (such as autonomy, feedback, and support), which looks at job demands and resources in detail (Schaufeli, 2017; Bauer et al., 2014; Demerouti et al., 2001).

Workplace stress is a significant factor in developing PTSD for public safety employees (Queirós et al., 2020; Lucas et al., 2012; Trivellas et al., 2013). Workplace stress can manifest in various forms, including long hours, excessive workloads, and tight deadlines. These factors can cause an employee to become overwhelmed and feel hopeless and helpless (Queirós et al., 2020; Lucas et al., 2012; Trivellas et al., 2013). Furthermore, workplace stress and pressure can lead to cognitive impairment in employees (Queirós et al., 2020; Lucas et al., 2012; Trivellas et al., 2013). These difficulties can lead to further anxiety and stress, which can interfere with an employee's ability to perform their job duties (Queirós et al., 2020; Lucas et al., 2012; Trivellas et al., 2013). Additionally, cognitive impairment can lead to an increased risk of accidents or errors in the workplace, which can have severe consequences for the employee and their employer (Queirós et al., 2020; Lucas et al., 2012; Trivellas et al., 2013).

Finally, workplace stress and pressure can lead to social isolation among employees (Sahai et al., 2020). This can lead to loneliness and alienation, preventing employees from forming meaningful relationships with their colleagues (Sahai et al., 2020). Additionally, social isolation can lead to feelings of guilt and shame, which can further exacerbate the symptoms of PTSD (Sahai et al., 2020).

PTSD HISTORICAL BACKGROUND

PTSD is a debilitating psychiatric disorder that may develop after exposure to traumatic events (Lees et al., 2019). Officers with the disorder will experience frequent re-livings of the event in their minds (Lees et al., 2019). This will lead them to avoid stimuli associated with the trauma (Lees et al., 2019). Overall this has adverse outcomes for the officer and leads them to have affected cognition and mood (Lees et al., 2019). Officers are more likely to have high incidences of trauma and PTSD than everyday citizens (Lees et al., 2019). The reasons for this trauma stem from "occupational stressors and organizational stressors" (Soomro & Yanos, 2019). Occupational stressors include officer-involved shootings and traffic stops (Soomro & Yanos, 2019). In contrast, organizational stressors include shifts and police leadership (Soomro & Yanos, 2019). Other factors can add to this burden as well. If officers had past trauma and unhappy home situations, that can add to the PTSD experienced (Parker, 2016).

PTSD as a diagnosis has been around since the *Diagnostic and Statistical Manual of Mental Disorders* version three. At first, the diagnosis was used on veterans because of the trauma they experience in war, but later the professionals saw how police could have PTSD as well. However, getting officers to buy into the concept had its challenges, with the stigma of mental illness and police officers not wanting to appear weak. This led to using "avoidant coping strategies" like drugs, betting, and not seeing friends and family (Soomro & Yanos, 2019). However, this only creates more problems in "long-term consequences that further exacerbate the underlying causes of the problem" (Soomro & Yanos, 2019).

Untreated PTSD can have scary consequences that can lead to officer suicide. Officers are more likely to die by their own hands than that of a suspect, and PTSD can play a role. This is especially true if they have not received treatment and use negative coping strategies. "Numerous studies indicate that protective service workers (police officers included) are susceptible to a relatively higher rate of suicidal thoughts and behaviors" (Soomro & Yanos, 2019).

EMPLOYER TOOLS

Employers can use tools to assess employees with PTSD in a structured interview. Structured interviews are designed to provide a consistent and standardized approach to assessing psychological symptoms. Structured interviews are beneficial for assessing PTSD, as they are designed to accurately capture the severity of PTSD symptoms and provide a basis for developing an individualized treatment plan. For example, the Clinician-Administered PTSD Scale (CAPS) is a widely used structured interview for assessing PTSD symptom severity and is used to assess prevalence (van der Meer, Bakker, Smit, van Buschbach, den Dekker, Westerveld, & Olff, 2017; Weathers et al., 2004).

In addition to structured interviews, employers can also use self-report questionnaires to assess PTSD in their employees. Self-report questionnaires are a popular tool for assessing mental health disorders, including PTSD. One of the most widely used self-report questionnaires for assessing PTSD is the Post-traumatic Stress Disorder Checklist (PCL-5), which is designed to measure the severity of PTSD symptoms (van der Meer, Bakker, Smit, van Buschbach, den Dekker, Westerveld, & Olff, 2017; Weathers et al., 2004).

Self-report questionnaires can be used to quickly and easily assess an employee's PTSD symptoms and can provide employers with valuable insight into their employees' PTSD.

Employers can also use functional assessments to assess employees with PTSD. Functional assessments are a type of assessment that focuses on the impact of PTSD on an individual's functioning in everyday life. This type of assessment can provide employers with a comprehensive picture of how PTSD is affecting their employees' ability to perform their job duties (van der Meer, Bakker, Smit, van Buschbach, den Dekker, Westerveld, & Olff, 2017; Weathers et al., 2004). These tools can measure an employee's ability to perform job-related tasks and assess the need for workplace accommodations or modifications (van der Meer, Bakker, Smit, van Buschbach, den Dekker, Westerveld, & Olff, 2017; Weathers et al., 2004). Finally, employers can use psychometric tests to assess employees with PTSD. Psychometric tests assess various psychological factors, including cognitive and emotional functioning (Shea & De Cieri, 2011).

Police Culture/Training. In most cases, the culture of police departments is one of not seeking help. Things are not openly discussed (Soomro & Yanos, 2019). Employees are more likely to get help if they have a physical injury because that is something people can see. PTSD is something internal and mental that everyone experiences differently. If officers get outside help, they may be seen as weak and cannot be trusted by their fellow officers (Soomro & Yanos, 2019). This would especially be the case if there were a dangerous call. Officers can compare police officers' values to warrior values, which include "resilience, personal sacrifice, courage, and strength" (Soomro & Yanos, 2019). In the training officers go through, it is taught that they must always be clear-eyed in their actions and cannot let their emotions take over, as that could lead to death or career loss (Soomro & Yanos, 2019). When training happens, the goal is to form the individuals into the mold of the department. Officers often want to break down the self and what was thought before regarding the warrior mentality (Soomro & Yanos, 2019). So when someone starts experiencing PTSD, that is unwelcome and breaks the norm. Police are held to a different standard, and those who may be seen putting their mental health first may be deemed selfish and not looking out for the team.

SOLUTIONS DEVELOPED FROM THE LITERATURE

Neuroimaging Techniques: Advanced neuroimaging technologies, such as functional MRI and PET scans, offer insights into the neural circuitry underlying PTSD. Integrating neural markers with clinical assessments enhances diagnostic accuracy, aiding early intervention (Akiki et al., 2017).

Biomarker Research: Research into PTSD biomarkers, encompassing genetic, epigenetic, and neurochemical indicators, holds promise for objective diagnosis. Biomarker panels could facilitate personalized treatment plans tailored to individual responders (Al et al., 2023).

Machine Learning and AI: Applying machine learning algorithms to diverse data sources, including physiological, behavioral, and textual data, enables predictive modeling of PTSD risk. This aids in timely intervention and tailored support strategies (Mentis et al., 2023; McDonald et al., 2019).

Resilience Training: Equipping law enforcement personnel with psychological tools, coping strategies, and stress management skills fosters resilience and prevents escalating trauma symptoms (Fernandez & Short, 2014; Phillips, 2020).

Peer Support Networks: Establishing peer support programs within organizations creates a culture of mutual assistance, enabling officers to share experiences, seek advice, and build emotional bonds, thereby reducing the stigma around seeking help (Fernandez & Short, 2014; Phillips, 2020).

Virtual Reality Exposure Therapy (VRET): VRET leverages immersive environments to recreate traumatic scenarios, providing a controlled context for officers to confront and process trauma. This innovative therapy complements traditional methods, aiding desensitization (Eshuis et al., 2021; Kothgassner et al., 2019).

Holistic Wellness Programs: Organizations can adopt wellness programs encompassing physical fitness, mental health, nutrition, and sleep hygiene. A holistic approach enhances officers' overall well-being and resilience (PTSD et al., 2014; Phillips, 2020).

Trauma-Informed Leadership: Training supervisors and leadership in recognizing trauma, supporting open communication, and reducing stigma create a supportive organizational culture (Fernandez & Short, 2014; Phillips, 2020).

Educational Resources: Educational resources are also an essential tool employers can provide to help employees suffering from PTSD. This includes providing information on the symptoms of PTSD, the treatments available, and how to access those treatments (Anders et al., 2022; Burchell et al., 2023; Violanti et al., 2018). Employers can also provide access to resources such as books, videos, or websites that provide information on PTSD and how to manage it (Anders et al., 2022; Burchell et al., 2023; Violanti et al., 2018).

Reducing Stigma. In talking about police culture earlier, it was mentioned that an officer would be deemed weak if they sought help. This is a mentality that has to change. That is up to the police officer's colleague and those in leadership to create a culture where people feel open to getting help and admitting that they may have PTSD (Anders et al., 2022; Burchell et al., 2023; Violanti et al., 2018). This could lead to others reflecting on their experiences and seeing that they may not be okay as well. It would be helpful if it were mandatory to seek help after a traumatic event so officers can at least see what good can happen from seeking help. A caveat to that is there needs to be culturally competent care meaning that the provider has to be able to handle whatever was said. It is up to the department leadership to make sure they find the right people. It would be good if the provider could follow the police for some days to understand the culture better. There should be encouragement from higher-ups to check in on people and see how officers are doing. It would also be good if environments were created to have police share their stories of PTSD and how they were affected. After particular traumatic calls, leadership should sit down with those involved and ask how they are doing because everyone can be affected differently. It is also suitable for verbiage to exist that is used not to demonize those who get help (Anders et al., 2022; Burchell et al., 2023; Violanti et al., 2018). For example, police should not refer to each other as crazy because that can be stigmatizing. Each officer should reduce their internal stigma because that is something people can see.

Working Conditions. Liking where an officer works matters when they are dealing with PTSD. Police fared much better when they felt they had the support of their colleagues, could do a good job day to day, and felt what they were doing mattered (Anders et al., 2022; Burchell et al., 2023; Violanti et al., 2018). This is primarily up to the leadership and the environment they want to create. Ensuring "work intensity" is also considered (Anders et al., 2022; Burchell et al., 2023; Violanti et al., 2018).

Police supervisors and police departments do not want to push the police too hard, especially when they are already unwell. That is why it is vital to ensure that police departments have the proper staffing and are not just having one person on a shift and getting rid of resources. To ensure the conditions are meeting the needs of the officers, there need to be open lines of communication with leadership. Officers should not be penalized for speaking up. Policing done right can be meaningful, so police supervisors must ensure they provide officers with the right environment to do that.

Mindfulness and Medication. According to Flannery and Greenhalgh (2018), "the physical symptoms of heightened arousal" in PTSD "respond to aerobic exercise, relaxation exercises, mindfulness, and short-term anti-anxiety medications." Compared to the "intrusive symptoms" that respond to "anti-depressant medications" (Flannery & Greenhalgh, 2018). Learning about mindfulness should be done in a wellness or employee assistance program. Officers should be required to have it mandatory for the first session and then encouraged for the rest. Doing it this way should help all officers see the benefits. For the medication, officers have to make sure that it is okay with leadership to take it since the officers have guns. It would often be on a short-term basis so police could get out in the field faster once they felt better. Both have benefits and should be used as much as needed to make the officer whole.

Workplace Accommodations. Employers can provide workplace accommodations to help employees suffering from PTSD. These accommodations may include changing the physical environment, such as providing a more private workspace, allowing employees to work flexible hours, and providing noise reduction measures (Edgelow et al., 2023; Shields et al., 2020). Employers can also provide ergonomic adjustments to the employee's workspace to make it more comfortable and suitable for their needs (Edgelow et al., 2023; Shields et al., 2020). Additionally, employers can provide access to regular breaks as a way of helping employees cope with their symptoms (Edgelow et al., 2023; Shields et al., 2020).

Mental Health Support. Mental health support is another crucial tool employers can provide to help employees suffering from PTSD (Vig et al., 2020; Stelnicki et al., 2021). This includes providing access to mental health professionals such as counselors or therapists who can provide evidence-based treatment for PTSD, such as cognitive behavioral therapy, eye movement desensitization, reprocessing, or interpersonal psychotherapy. Additionally, employers can provide access to support groups, either in-person or online, so that employees can connect with others in similar circumstances (Vig et al., 2020; Stelnicki et al., 2021). There is a growing interest in this type of treatment by officers. Previous use of this type of treatment has not been great to date, but when educating people on its benefits, many officers wanted to opt in, especially those with PTSD (Vig et al., 2020; Stelnicki et al., 2021). Another type of treatment that should be considered is cognitive behavior therapy. This is a growing form of popular therapy where one works on changing their thinking. It has been used on coroners with PTSD and is effective (Flannery & Greenhalgh, 2018). It is excellent for "intrusive symptoms" (Flannery & Greenhalgh, 2018). For someone who has become more avoidant in their symptoms, this can be helped by "discussions and re-experiencing the event in small, gradual steps" (Flannery & Greenhalgh, 2018). Training on PTSD should also be required for those not affected to learn more about spotting the signs in others (Vig et al., 2020; Stelnicki et al., 2021).

Innovation in diagnosing and supporting law enforcement personnel with PTSD holds immense promise in enhancing mental health outcomes and sustaining job performance. Advanced diagnostic techniques, early intervention strategies, and comprehensive support frameworks collectively form a paradigm shift in addressing PTSD among law enforcement, promoting resilience, and improving overall well-being. Future research should continue to explore these innovative approaches, refining and adapting them to the evolving needs of law enforcement personnel.

The demanding nature of law enforcement exposes personnel to traumatic incidents, potentially leading to the development of PTSD. Law enforcement personnel can use various strategies to mitigate the stress and pressure of the job (Pickens, 2011; Rosemond, 2018). Proper training and education can help law enforcement personnel develop the necessary skills to cope with the stress and pressure of the job (Pickens, 2011; Rosemond, 2018). Additionally, providing officers with support systems, such as peer support groups and counseling, can help them cope with the stress and pressure of the job (Pickens, 2011; Rosemond, 2018).

Organizations can also develop policies and procedures to help reduce stress and pressure in the workplace (Pickens, 2011; Rosemond, 2018). These policies may include stress management training, flexible scheduling, and additional measures to ensure the safety of officers (Pickens, 2011; Rosemond, 2018). Additionally, organizations can provide officers with access to mental health services, such as counseling and therapy, to help them cope with the stress and pressure of the job (Pickens, 2011; Rosemond, 2018).

In conclusion, the research provides a comprehensive framework for addressing the crisis of PTSD among police officers. It emphasizes a proactive and supportive approach that includes awareness, early identification, and intervention, as well as the exploration of new treatments. These innovations have the potential to not only improve the mental health and well-being of police officers but also enhance their overall effectiveness and the safety of the communities they serve. By implementing these strategies, police organizations can take significant steps towards mitigating the impact of PTSD on their personnel and the public they protect.

In essence, addressing PTSD among police officers is not just a crisis; it is an opportunity to reshape the way we support those who uphold the law while safeguarding their own mental well-being. Through commitment, research, and innovation, we can pave the way for a brighter future where police officers receive the care and support they need to heal from trauma and continue their vital roles in our communities.

RECOMMENDATIONS FOR FUTURE RESEARCH

In considering future avenues for research on the intersection of PTSD and occupational workplace stress crisis among police officers, it is imperative to expand the methodological toolkit beyond traditional literature reviews to gain deeper insights and generate a comprehensive understanding of the issue. While this inquiry has effectively synthesized existing knowledge, further investigation can be enriched by incorporating alternative research approaches that offer diverse perspectives and enhance the validity of findings.

Longitudinal Studies: Future research could benefit from longitudinal studies that track police officers over an extended period, allowing for the examination of the long-term effects of workplace stress on the development of PTSD. By collecting data at multiple time points, researchers can identify potential causal relationships, explore the trajectory of symptoms, and ascertain the factors that contribute to resilience or vulnerability. This approach would provide a more nuanced understanding of how workplace stressors impact officers' mental health over time to crisis levels.

Mixed-Methods Designs: Integrating quantitative and qualitative methods would provide a more comprehensive view of the experiences of police officers facing occupational stress and PTSD. Quantitative data can offer statistical insights into prevalence rates and correlations, while qualitative data through interviews or focus groups can capture officers' lived experiences, perceptions, coping mechanisms, and contextual nuances that quantitative measures might miss. This combined approach would yield a richer understanding of the complex interplay between stressors, individual coping strategies, and the development of PTSD.

Physiological and Neurobiological Studies: Exploring the physiological and neurobiological underpinnings of PTSD and workplace stress in police officers can contribute a new dimension to the research landscape. Techniques like functional neuroimaging, cortisol level monitoring, and heart rate variability analysis can offer objective measures of stress and potential biomarkers associated with the development of PTSD. This biological perspective can offer insights into the underlying mechanisms and guide the development of targeted crisis aversion interventions.

Intervention Studies: Future research could focus on evaluating the effectiveness of interventions to prevent or mitigate PTSD among police officers exposed to occupational stressors. Implementing randomized controlled trials to assess the impact of mindfulness programs, resilience training, peer support networks, or organizational policy changes would provide evidence-based insights into practical crisis management strategies that could enhance officers' mental well-being and resilience.

In conclusion, while literature reviews provide valuable insights, embracing alternative research approaches can expand the depth and breadth of knowledge surrounding PTSD and the occupational workplace stress crisis among police officers. Longitudinal studies, mixed-methods designs, physiological and neurobiological investigations, and intervention studies can collectively contribute to a more holistic and actionable understanding of this critical issue, ultimately supporting the development of evidence-based interventions and policies that promote the mental health and well-being of police officers.

REFERENCES

Akiki, T. J., Averill, C. L., & Abdallah, C. G. (2017). A network-based neurobiological model of PTSD: Evidence from structural and functional neuroimaging studies. *Current Psychiatry Reports*, *19*(11), 1–10. doi:10.100711920-017-0840-4 PMID:28924828

Al Jowf, G. I., Ahmed, Z. T., Reijnders, R. A., de Nijs, L., & Eijssen, L. M. (2023). To Predict, Prevent, and Manage Post-Traumatic Stress Disorder (PTSD): A Review of Pathophysiology, Treatment, and Biomarkers. *International Journal of Molecular Sciences*, *24*(6), 5238. doi:10.3390/ijms24065238 PMID:36982313

American Psychiatric Association. (2013). *Diagnostic and statistical manual of mental disorders* (5th ed.). APA.

Anders, R., Willemin-Petignat, L., Rolli Salathé, C., Samson, A. C., & Putois, B. (2022). Profiling police forces against stress: Risk and protective factors for post-traumatic stress disorder and burnout in police officers. *International Journal of Environmental Research and Public Health, 19*(15), 9218. doi:10.3390/ijerph19159218 PMID:35954576

Bauer, G. F., Hämmig, O., Schaufeli, W. B., & Taris, T. W. (2014). A critical review of the job demands-resources model: Implications for improving work and health. *Bridging occupational, organizational and public health: A transdisciplinary approach*, 43-68.

Burchell, B., Miller, J., Brewin, C., Soffia, M., & Wang, S. (2023). The association between job quality and the incidence of PTSD amongst police personnel. *Policing. Journal of Policy Practice*, 17.

De Jonge, J., & Kompier, M. A. (1997). A critical examination of the demand-control-support model from a work psychological perspective. *International Journal of Stress Management, 4*(4), 235–258. doi:10.1023/B:IJSM.0000008152.85798.90

Demerouti, E., Bakker, A. B., Nachreiner, F., & Schaufeli, W. B. (2001). The job demands-resources model of burnout. *The Journal of Applied Psychology, 86*(3), 499–512. doi:10.1037/0021-9010.86.3.499 PMID:11419809

Edgelow, M., Legassick, K., Novecosky, J., & Fecica, A. (2023). Return to work experiences of Ontario public safety personnel with work-related psychological injuries. *Journal of Occupational Rehabilitation*, 1–12. doi:10.100710926-023-10114-6 PMID:37022655

Eshuis, L. V., van Gelderen, M. J., van Zuiden, M., Nijdam, M. J., Vermetten, E., Olff, M., & Bakker, A. (2021). Efficacy of immersive PTSD treatments: A systematic review of virtual and augmented reality exposure therapy and a meta-analysis of virtual reality exposure therapy. *Journal of Psychiatric Research, 143*, 516–527. doi:10.1016/j.jpsychires.2020.11.030 PMID:33248674

Faust, K. L., & Ven, T. V. (2014). Policing disaster: An analytical review of the literature on policing, disaster, and post-traumatic stress disorder. *Sociology Compass, 8*(6), 614–626. doi:10.1111oc4.12160

Fernandez, M. A., & Short, M. (2014). Wounded Warriors with PTSD: A compilation of best practices and technology in treatment. *The Professional Counselor, 4*(2), 114–121. doi:10.15241/maf.4.2.114

Flannery, R. B. Jr, & Greenhalgh, T. (2018). Coroners and PTSD: Treatment Implications. *The Psychiatric Quarterly, 89*(4), 765–770. doi:10.100711126-018-9580-9 PMID:29651735

Gersons, B. P. (1989). Patterns of PTSD among police officers following shooting incidents: A two-dimensional model and treatment implications. *Journal of Traumatic Stress, 2*, 247–257.

Gilbert-Ouimet, M., Trudel, X., Brisson, C., Milot, A., & Vézina, M. (2014). Adverse effects of psychosocial work factors on blood pressure: Systematic review of studies on demand-control-support and effort-reward imbalance models. *Scandinavian Journal of Work, Environment & Health, 40*(2), 109–132. doi:10.5271jweh.3390 PMID:24108310

Green, B. (2004). Post-traumatic stress disorder in UK police officers. *Current Medical Research and Opinion*, *20*(1), 101–105. doi:10.1185/030079903125002748 PMID:14741078

Kothgassner, O. D., Goreis, A., Kafka, J. X., Van Eickels, R. L., Plener, P. L., & Felnhofer, A. (2019). Virtual reality exposure therapy for post-traumatic stress disorder (PTSD): A meta-analysis. *European Journal of Psychotraumatology*, *10*(1), 1654782. doi:10.1080/20008198.2019.1654782 PMID:31489138

Lees, T., Elliott, J. L., Gunning, S., Newton, P. J., Rai, T., & Lal, S. (2019). A systematic review of the current evidence regarding interventions for anxiety, PTSD, sleepiness, and fatigue in the law enforcement workplace. *Industrial Health*, *57*(6), 655–667. doi:10.2486/indhealth.2018-0088 PMID:30760652

Lucas, T., Weidner, N., & Janisse, J. (2012). Where does work stress come from? A generalizability analysis of stress in police officers. *Psychology & Health*, *27*(12), 1426–1447. doi:10.1080/08870446.2012.687738 PMID:22612444

Macklin, D. S., Smith, L. A., & Dollard, M. F. (2006). Public and private sector work stress: Workers compensation, levels of distress and job satisfaction, and the demand-control-support model. *Australian Journal of Psychology*, *58*(3), 130–143. doi:10.1080/00049530600940190

McDonald, A. D., Sasangohar, F., Jatav, A., & Rao, A. H. (2019). Continuous monitoring and detection of post-traumatic stress disorder (PTSD) triggers among veterans: A supervised machine learning approach. *IISE Transactions on Healthcare Systems Engineering*, *9*(3), 201–211. doi:10.1080/24725579.2019.1583703

Mentis, A. F. A., Lee, D., & Roussos, P. (2023). Applications of artificial intelligence– machine learning for detection of stress: A critical overview. *Molecular Psychiatry*, 1–13. doi:10.103841380-023-02047-6 PMID:37020048

Nievas, V. (2015). Post-traumatic stress disorder and police officers. *Australian Police Journal*, *69*(4).

Parker, K. A. (2016). *A paradigm of police stress from the lens of retired police officers: A phenomenological study. (Order No. 3718153)*. Available from ProQuest Dissertations & Theses Global.

Phillips, M. D., & Naval War College. (2020). *The Ethics of Emerging Technologies in the Diagnosis and Treatment of PTSD among Service Members*. Naval War College.

Pickens, W. J. (2011). *Critical incidents in law enforcement: A phenomenological analysis of coping with traumatic stress. (Order No. 3448468)*. Available from ProQuest Dissertations & Theses Global.

Queirós, C., Passos, F., Bártolo, A., Marques, A. J., Da Silva, C. F., & Pereira, A. (2020). Burnout and stress measurement in police officers: Literature review and a study with the operational police stress questionnaire. *Frontiers in Psychology*, *11*, 587. doi:10.3389/fpsyg.2020.00587 PMID:32457673

Rosemond, K. V. (2018). *Post-traumatic stress disorder in public safety workers: Cultural aspects and implications for effective treatment. (Order No. 10285161)*. Available from ProQuest Dissertations & Theses Global.

Sahai, S., Ciby, M. A., & Kahwaji, A. T. (2020). Workplace isolation: A systematic review and synthesis. [IJM]. *International Journal of Management*, *11*(12), 2745–2758.

Schaufeli, W. B. (2017). Applying the job demands-resources model: A 'how to' guide to measuring and tackling work engagement and burnout. *Organizational Dynamics*, *46*(2), 120–132. doi:10.1016/j.orgdyn.2017.04.008

Shea, T., & De Cieri, H. (2011). *Workplace stress evaluation tools: A snapshot review*. ISCRR & Monash University.

Shields, J., Pechek, A. A., Brinck, E. A., & Sprong, M. E. (2020). Strategies for improving employment outcomes of veterans diagnosed with post-traumatic stress disorder (PTSD). *Rehabil Prof*, *28*, 225–244.

Soomro, & Yanos, P. T. (2019). Predictors of Mental Health Stigma among Police Officers: the Role of Trauma and PTSD. *Journal of Police and Criminal Psychology, 34*(2), 175–183. https://doi.org/doi:10.1007/s11896-018-9285-x

Stelnicki, A. M., Jamshidi, L., Fletcher, A. J., & Carleton, R. N. (2021). Evaluation of before operational stress: A program to support mental health and proactive psychological protection in public safety personnel. *Frontiers in Psychology*, *12*, 3218. doi:10.3389/fpsyg.2021.511755 PMID:34484013

Trivellas, P., Reklitis, P., & Platis, C. (2013). The effect of job-related stress on employees' satisfaction: A survey in health care. *Procedia: Social and Behavioral Sciences*, *73*, 718–726. doi:10.1016/j.sbspro.2013.02.110

van der Meer, C. A., Bakker, A., Smit, A. S., van Buschbach, S., den Dekker, M., Westerveld, G. J., & Olff, M. (2017). Gender and age differences in trauma and PTSD among Dutch treatment-seeking police officers. *The Journal of Nervous and Mental Disease*, *205*(2), 87–92. doi:10.1097/NMD.0000000000000562 PMID:27434192

Vig, K. D., Mason, J. E., Carleton, R. N., Asmundson, G. J. G., Anderson, G. S., & Groll, D. (2020). Mental health and social support among public safety personnel. *Occupational Medicine*, *70*(6), 427–433. doi:10.1093/occmed/kqaa129 PMID:32705138

Violanti, J. M., Ma, C. C., Mnatsakanova, A., Fekedulegn, D., Hartley, T. A., Gu, J. K., & Andrew, M. E. (2018). Associations between police work stressors and post-traumatic stress disorder symptoms: Examining the moderating effects of coping. *Journal of Police and criminal psychology, 33*, 271–282.

Weathers, F. W., Newman, E., Blake, D. D., Nagy, L. M., Schnurr, P. P., Kaloupek, D. G., & Keane, T. M. (2004). *Clinician-administered PTSD scale:(CAPS)*. Western Psychological Services.

Chapter 6
Telehealth Technology, Business, and Marketing Strategy Approaches for Mental Health Practices as a Result of COVID-19

Darrell Norman Burrell
https://orcid.org/0000-0002-4675-9544
Pellegrino Center for Clinical Bioethics, Georgetown University Medical Center, USA

Allison J. Huff
https://orcid.org/0000-0001-6102-8013
College of Medicine, University of Arizona, USA

Quatavia McLester
https://orcid.org/0000-0003-1596-0517
The Chicago School of Professional Psychology, USA

Delores Springs
https://orcid.org/0000-0003-0940-1225
Regent University, USA

Judith-Jolie Mairs-Levy
A.T. Still University, USA

Margaret J. Crowe
https://orcid.org/0000-0002-9862-5265
Liberty University, USA

Kevin Richardson
https://orcid.org/0009-0002-3212-8669
Capitol Technology University, USA

Kiana S. Zanganeh
Florida Institute of Technology, USA

Elizabeth I. Omotoye
The University of the Cumberlands, USA

Laura A. Jones
https://orcid.org/0000-0002-0299-370X
Capitol Technology University, USA

ABSTRACT

The pandemic exacerbated pre-existing mental health issues. These people are more likely to develop anxiety, sadness, and PTSD. The pandemic may also harm at-risk mental health patients. Pandemic-related financial difficulty increases the risk of mental health issues like sadness and anxiety. The COVID-19 pandemic has exacerbated anxiety, depression, and PTSD, according to the literature. Social separation

DOI: 10.4018/978-1-6684-9522-3.ch006

also makes accessing mental health care harder. Given the pandemic's increasing mental health service demand, this is worrying. Pre-existing and at-risk mental health issues are more likely to be affected by the epidemic. This research examines the potential of telemedicine to provide care to underserved communities and those needing increased mental health care due to COVID-19.

INTRODUCTION

This chapter explores the complex nature of a real organization attempting to adapt is business and marketing strategy due to the crisis of COVID-19. The COVID-19 pandemic has caused a significant increase in mental health stressors, with individuals facing an increased risk of anxiety, depression, and PTSD (Liu et al., 2020). Social distancing has limited access to health services, decreasing the number of individuals seeking mental health services (Hoffman et al., 2020). This is particularly concerning given the increased demand for mental health services during the pandemic (Hoffman et al., 2020). Social distancing has made it more difficult for individuals to access medical care, as many healthcare providers have shifted to telehealth services (Hoffman et al., 2020). This has made it more difficult for individuals to receive the mental health care they need.

The COVID pandemic revealed and spotlighted the deep racial disparities in African Americans' access to behavioral health care. African Americans have lower access to mental health and substance-use treatment services than their white counterparts (SAMHSA, n.d.). Such disparities, coupled with the stigmatization of mental health in the African American community, have exacerbated the mental health crises, thus amplifying the calls for change. As a result, there are now more national conversations around this topic and a gradual acceptance and de-stigmatization of mental health in Black communities. A positive perception may lead to more African Americans seeking mental health services than ever before. However, as we will uncover in this paper, the mental health field lacks enough African American practitioners to effectively support this potential increase in demand for mental health services from the Black community. As telehealth and telemedicine solutions emerge, there are also opportunities for technology to be adapted to support the increase in demand to reach the most significant number of customers. As a result, this research aims to analyze the current business operations of an African American female-led mental health practice to create a marketing strategy to grow its customer base and incorporate telemedicine in its service offerings.

PROBLEM STATEMENT

The pandemic inadvertently created a shift in mental health services. Telehealth services have helped bridge the gap in rural and urban areas considered care deserts. However, a significant gap exists in psychological practitioners joining telehealth as they navigate technology and patient utilization once implemented (Langarizadeh et al., 2017). Many people turned to telehealth therapists, but studies show that the psychology workforce is 85% white and 2% Black leaving a disproportionate amount of Black people searching for therapists that could relate to their life experiences (Lindsey et al., 2017). The general problem is that African Americans seeking mental health services have more difficulty finding mental health practitioners who look like them. As a result, they often decide not to receive care leaving their mental health issues untreated (Lindsey et al., 2017, p. 138).

There is also the specific problem of the lack of mental health services in Black communities, making it difficult for Black Americans to access care when they need it, inadvertently leading to a delay in care or no care. With this, we will explore ways that our practice can take advantage of this gap in mental health services for Black Americans by positioning themselves as a viable option to serve this population with telehealth offerings to increase their market share and grow their customer base.

Notably, the COVID-19 pandemic illumined an existing disparity regarding the lack of access experienced by African Americans. The Pew Research Center found that 43% of Black adults did not have access to computing devices such as desktops or laptops, compared to 27% of their White adult counterparts. Further, 37% of Black adults did not have internet access in their homes, compared to 22% of White adults (Perrin & Anderson, 2021). This lack of access carried significant risks for African Americans during the pandemic and beyond. It restricted the ability to work virtually, obtain telehealth services, and engage in online learning opportunities (Ahmed et al., 2020), further increasing the digital divide. The digital divide also exacerbates existing health disparities, as African Americans are more likely to have chronic health conditions and have been disproportionately affected by COVID-19 (Yancy, 2020). Addressing the digital divide is crucial for ensuring access to requisite telehealth services. This intervention explores a management consulting organizational intervention due to the COVID-19 crisis.

METHOD

The method that was employed was Intervention action research (IAR). IAR is an effective method for organizational development research, including its ability to provide a comprehensive understanding of complex organizational issues, its capacity to produce actionable results, and its potential to foster collaboration between researchers and organizational stakeholders (Argyris, 1983). Organizational development (OD) research focuses on understanding and improving organizational practices, processes, and outcomes (Anderson, 2019). It is critical for improving organizational effectiveness and efficiency (Anderson, 2019).

Intervention action research (IAR) is a participatory, action-oriented approach to OD research that involves a collaborative effort between researchers and organizational stakeholders to identify and address organizational problems (Argyris, 1983). IAR differs from traditional research methods in that it is more comprehensive and participatory, allowing for a more in-depth exploration of complex organizational issues (Argyris, 1983). Additionally, IAR has the potential to produce actionable results that can be used to improve organizational practices, processes, and outcomes (Argyris, 1983).

CLINICAL BACKGROUND OF THE PRACTICE AND CASE STUDY ASSUMPTIONS

The practice has chosen to focus on treating and assessing five of the population's most prevalent mental health/psychological problems, which include depression, bipolar disorder, anxiety, ADHD, and autism. The practice focuses on identifying these disorders and their treatment using a combination of counseling and pharmacologic interventions offered through the practice. As a result, we will summarize the disease processes focused on as part of the clinical practice we are looking to expand.

Depression is a mood disorder that insistently triggers sadness and loss of interest. This mood disorder affects how individuals feel, think, and behave and can lead to various emotional and physical problems. In its most severe manifestations, this disorder can affect an individual's ability to perform day-to-day activities and make them feel like life is not worth living (Karrouri et al., 2021). The treatment of this disorder is a combination of counseling and pharmacologic interventions.

Bipolar disorder is a mood disorder characterized by extreme mood swings that include emotional highs (mania or hypomania) and lows (depression). There are several distinct types of bipolar disorder that represent the many different clinical manifestations this disease can present. In addition to the highs and lows that define this disorder, individuals affected by this disease can also have other features such as anxiety, melancholy, or psychosis. Just like depression, bipolar disorder is treated with a combination of pharmacologic therapy and psychological counseling. (Mayo Foundation for Medical Education and Research, 2021)

Generalized anxiety disorder is another psychiatric disorder that the clinic will target. This disorder involves excessive, ongoing anxiety and worry that is difficult to control and interferes with day-to-day activities. Symptoms include persistent worry not in line with the consequence of the events, overthinking plans and corrective actions to possible worst-case results, difficulty handling uncertainty, and indecisiveness and fear of making the wrong decision. This disorder can also be physical manifestations such as fatigue, trouble sleeping, muscle tension, and sweating. As with most mood disorders, treating anxiety includes a combination of psychological counseling and pharmacologic therapy, but after ruling out other possible medical causes of anxiety. (Mayo Foundation for Medical Education and Research, 2017)

Attention deficit/hyperactivity disorder (ADHD) is a mood disorder characterized by difficulty paying attention, hyperactivity, and impulsivity. Diagnosis for this disorder usually occurs in childhood; however, its symptoms may go untreated into adulthood. The clinic focuses on diagnosing and treating this disorder in its patients and offering ADHD screening will be part of our marketing plan. Treatments focus on counseling and pharmacologic interventions as with the previously described mental health disorders. (Mayo Foundation for Medical Education and Research, 2019)

Attention deficit/hyperactivity disorder (ADHD) is a mood disorder characterized by difficulty paying attention, hyperactivity, and impulsivity. Diagnosis for this disorder usually occurs in childhood; however, its symptoms may go untreated into adulthood. The clinic focuses on diagnosing and treating this disorder in its patients and offering ADHD screening will be part of our marketing plan. Treatments focus on counseling and pharmacologic interventions as with the previously described mental health disorders. (Mayo Foundation for Medical Education and Research, 2019)

The final area of specialty for the clinic is autism, specifically autism screening. Autism spectrum disorder is a condition related to brain development that effects how a person distinguishes and engages with others, interfering with social interaction and communication. The term "spectrum" in autism spectrum disorder refers to the wide range of symptoms and severity that can be present with this disease. Manifestations of this disorder usually become visible in a child's life, some showing signs as early as 18-24 months. While there is no cure for this disorder, early recognition and intervention can make an enormous difference in the child's life and ability to function in society. (Mayo Foundation for Medical Education and Research, 2018) Offering screening for this disorder will be one of the services that we highlight as part of our marketing plan.

The need for mental health services cannot be overstated, with an estimated one in five Americans suffering from some sort of mental health disorder. There was already a disparity in the availability of care for minorities, but the COVID-19 pandemic worsened this (Centers for Disease Control and Prevention, 2022). The campaign that we will lay out for this clinic will highlight different strategies that will be employed to fight this in the community that the clinic serves. To this end, we make the following assumptions about the clinic/practice in this case study:

- The practice is only marketing to patients. "Direct to consumer" (not contracting with organizations).
- The customer base of the practice is overwhelmingly African American and female.
- There is a high demand for the therapy services the practice provides. However, they have yet to gain a significant market share of this demand.
- The practice's customer base has remained steady over the last year, with no increase in new customers in that time.
- The practice revenue grew by 2% in 2021.
- The practice conducts business entirely in person with no online/telehealth offerings.
- Exceptional customer service and earned media have helped the practice to grow its customer base in the past.
- There is a growing demand and interest from corporate entities and organizations to contract with external mental health providers to offer mental health benefits to their employees.

LITERATURE REVIEW

In our literature review, we will explore the different marketing theories, models, and tools applied to develop an effective marketing strategy for the practice.

Strategic Marketing for Tele-Mental Health

The London School of Business and Finance defines strategic marketing as a business technique to provide value and superior service to customers (Zebley, 2022). Strategic marketing integrates the business with a marketing plan to dictate the organization's direction. Strategic marketing must be sensitive to stakeholders, the environment, and society (Berkowitz, 2022). In this study, we will use the stakeholder-society-environment framework to evaluate telehealth for behavioral and mental healthcare services, or "tele-mental health," for brevity. "Telehealth, sometimes called telemedicine, is the use of electronic information and telecommunications technologies to extend care when the provider and patient are not in the same place at the same time" (U.S. Department of Health and Human Services, 2021).

Stakeholders

Stakeholder identification is critical in healthcare because of its complex and dynamic nature. Stakeholders are any individual or group that can impact or is impacted by the attainment of the entity's objectives (Marks& Augenstein, 2022). Including all stakeholders help to ensure proper communication and coordination for a successful strategic marketing strategy. Otherwise, a resistant or forgotten stakeholder can undermine progress.

Stakeholders typically encompass two groups: primary and secondary. Primary stakeholders interact with the organization and are essential for organizational success. In contrast, secondary stakeholders provide the infrastructure but do not directly participate in the organization (Marks & Augenstein,

2022). The Essentials of Healthcare Marketing provides a framework for stakeholder analysis that we will implement. Enabling stakeholders are those that have control or authority over an organization. Examples of enabling stakeholders that are critical to the success of a telehealth offering for the practice, in this case, the study includes:

- Centers for Medicare and Medicaid Services (CMS) - CMS controls the services eligible for reimbursement and rates for its beneficiaries. In doing so, CMS influences coverage provided by other health plans.
- Congress – The House of Representatives and Senate controls the introduction of bills and passage of laws that govern the use and criteria of telehealth services.

Furthermore, functional stakeholders are those stakeholders that provide the input and output functions of the organization (Berkowitz, 2022). Examples, in this case, the study includes:

- Clinicians – The four therapists are functional stakeholders because they provide counseling services to patients.
- Clinic Staff – The clinic staff supports the providers with intake and follow-up care.
- Telehealth Technology Companies – Telehealth companies provide the technology to conduct video visits.
- Technical Support Team – A team must provide technical support to patients and providers. This support can be a part of the clinic staff or outsourced to a third party.
- Patients – Patients receive care and make up the practice's customer base.
- Pharma Organizations – Pharma companies provide the medications prescribed to patients by clinicians.
- Payors are essential to the input function to support the reimbursement of psychological and behavioral visits.

Additionally, normative stakeholders describe linkages to groups in which there is a common interest (Berkowitz, 2022). This includes:

- American Telemedicine Association (ATA) - The American Telemedicine Association (ATA) is a non-profit association of over 400 organizations focused on advancing telehealth (ATA About Us, 2022). The ATA is working with the Centers for Medicare and Medicaid (CMS) and Congress on behalf of these organizations and applying significant lobbying pressure for permanent change.
- Other stakeholders include other counseling and behavioral health clinics that provide similar tele-mental health services.
- On-Demand Mental Health & Therapy Companies – This group of stakeholders includes companies that provide telehealth video technology and provide support infrastructure. The expansion of these companies continues to increase awareness of the benefits of tele-mental health care. These platforms' advertising and promotion also help reduce the stigma associated with mental health. However, these companies are direct competitors to small behavioral health clinics such as the one in this study. The most influential players in this space include BetterHelp, Sesame, Talkspace, Amwell, MDLive, and Pride Counseling (Treichler, 2022). Each competitor has pros and cons in the space. For example, BetterHelp has an extensive provider network of over 14,000

licensed therapists and can match an individual to a therapist with a brief questionnaire. However, BetterHelp does not accept insurance. AmWell accepts insurance from many major providers. In addition, some companies allow for chat messages with a provider, while others do not support such services.

The last type of stakeholder is diffused stakeholders, who infrequently interact with the organization (Berkowitz, 2022). These include:

- Community Organizations – Maintaining a good relationship with and showing commitment to the community they serve is essential.
- Media – The media may cover events related to clinical practice, which can sway public opinion about the business.

Society

Marketing strategy develops within a broader societal context that is constantly evolving. Brands must have a clear purpose that moves the needle on social good. There are three ways to affect real change in communities: "commit to the purpose and social good, prioritize authenticity, and create collective accountability" (Christian, 2020). The Essentials of Healthcare Marketing encourages organizations to be ethically responsible and consider the impact of their products and services on society at large (Berkowitz, 2022).

In this context, how is tele-mental health affecting society at large? Lockdowns during COVID-19 forced people to adopt teleconferencing alternatives to in-person work. This shift has made society more comfortable interacting with their provider over video. As already discussed, some patients prefer telehealth over in-person for routine care. However, we should keep patient preference paramount and provide a choice to patients to receive their care virtually or in person. Overall, according to a report by the U.S. Department of Health and Human Services, telehealth is moving the needle on social good by increasing continuity of care, helping with physician shortages, making care more accessible for some patient populations, and preventing the spread of infectious disease (U.S. Department of Health and Human Services, 2021).

As we continue to collect more data on the outcomes of telehealth visits, we should develop better guidelines that show when telehealth is an appropriate form of care. Counseling and behavioral health are widely considered appropriate telehealth use. Some behavioral health providers have found it preferable because of the opportunity to observe the patient's home setting to aid in diagnosis and treatment (MacMillan, 2021). Finally, technology companies should continue to improve the ease and accessibility of their telehealth solutions. To make telehealth for all, technology organizations should listen and assist patients with connectivity challenges and simplify the technology for ease of use (U.S. Department of Health and Human Services, 2021).

PEST Analysis

We will utilize the PEST analysis to evaluate the environmental aspect of the stakeholder-society-environment framework. PEST analysis assists organizations with understanding the changes and effects of the environment on their competitive position (Sammut-Bonnici, 2015). The acronym PEST stands for four sources of change: Political, Economic, Social, and Technological (Sammut-Bonnici, 2015). An organization should deeply understand the external influences on its market segment and prepare the business plan accordingly. A PEST analysis is an effective tool with a SWOT analysis for further analysis of a potential new venture, partnership, or product (Sammut-Bonnici, 2015). It examines all facets of the "O.T.," opportunities, and threats for a more in-depth analysis. Here, we will perform a PEST analysis on tele-mental health care to understand further the complex environment facing clinics interested in launching a new telemedicine arm of their business.

Political

The "P" stands for political change. Consideration of the political climate and the likelihood of policy intervention are critical components of the strategic planning process (Sammut-Bonnici, 2015). Global, national, and local-level politics can influence the success of an organization. In March 2022, President Biden signed the Consolidated Appropriations Act of 2022. This omnibus funding bill included telehealth policies that extended flexibility to Medicare beneficiaries for 151 days post the Public Health Emergency (PHE) (Marks & Augenstein, 2022). The most significant part of the legislation that impacts patients seeking tele-mental health services stipulates, *"Any site in the United States, including a patient's home, will be considered an eligible originating site for the delivery of telehealth services. Federally qualified health centers and rural health clinics may serve as originating or distant sites for the delivery of telehealth services. Eligible telehealth practitioners will continue to include qualified occupational therapists, physical therapists, speech-language therapists, and audiologists. Providers will not be required to meet in-person visit requirements to deliver mental health services via video or audio-only visits. This applies to all sites of care, including Federally Qualified Health Centers and Rural Health Clinics (except in the case of hospice patients)"* (Marks & Augenstein, 2022).

In summary, reimbursement for tele-mental health services received a temporary extension for a 90-day extension on October 13, 2022. The extension can end at any time with a sixty-day notice. The temporary extension introduces uncertainty into the healthcare system, motivating affected parties, including providers, payors, and technology companies, to call for the permanent extension of these flexibilities. As of November 2022, the ATA is tracking over two thousand telehealth-related bills and is actively involved in forty states through testimony and written comments (Zebley, 2022). Twenty-six positive telehealth bills have passed into law. One of the most notable bills already passed in the House and currently under review in the Senate is H.R.4040 - Advancing Telehealth Beyond COVID-19 Act of 2021. The bill stipulates the following, *"Beneficiaries to continue to receive telehealth services at any site, regardless of type or location (e.g., the beneficiary's home); Occupational therapists, physical therapists, speech-language pathologists, and audiologists to continue to furnish telehealth services; Federally qualified health centers and rural health clinics to continue to serve as the distant site (i.e., the location of the health care practitioner); Evaluation and management and behavioral health services to continue to be provided via audio-only technology; and hospice physicians and nurse practitioners to continue to complete certain requirements relating to patient recertifications via telehealth"*. These provisions are allowed by law until December 31, 2024 (H.R.4040 - 117th Congress, 2021-2022).

The Senate also introduced Tele-mental Health Care Access Act (s. 2061, H.R. 4058). It eliminates certain restrictions on Medicare coverage of mental health services provided through telehealth. This bill also tackles the in-person restrictions mentioned (S.2061) - 117th Congress (2021-2022). The bill also delays some in-person evaluation requirements for mental health until January 1, 2021 (H.R.4040

- 117th Congress, 2021-2022). The Telehealth Response for E-prescribing Addiction Therapy Services Act or TREATS Act (S.340, H.R. 11647) has also been introduced in the House, allowing the prescribing of certain controlled substances via telehealth and allowing audio-only technology if the provider has already conducted a video or in-person visit. If these bills become law, tele-mental health services will have fertile ground for expansion and further development. There have been stakeholder letters urging the Senate to act on this front, as the temporary nature of the current laws makes it difficult for organizations, and small clinics, to invest in infrastructure and processes to support and scale telemedicine (2022). It also introduces uncertainty and stress for patients who implement telehealth services in their care plan. Returning to an in-person environment for patients with long distances, immunocompromised, or ongoing care management may experience insurmountable barriers to continuing their level of care if Congress does not pass these bills into law (Phinney, 2022).

Economic

Economic factors have apparent implications on an organization's profitability and, thus, strategic marketing. The political factors previously discussed have a sweeping impact on reimbursement rates and, thus, the feasibility of expanding telehealth services. Here we will consider the economic environment for both providers and patients. Since the start of the COVID-19 pandemic, providers in North Carolina have received an average of $150 per video visit and $70 per phone visit in professional payments (Phinney, 2022). During high-infection seasons and social distancing mandates, the conversion of in-person to virtual care was essential. Now, providers can use virtual care to scale and grow their in-person clinic operations (Phinney, 2022). Virtual visits do not require a brick-and-mortar facility, allowing clinics to improve access to care. Most organizations have also improved efficiency in virtual visits. At Duke Health, patients arrive on time for their virtual appointments 93% of the time, having completed their forms and co-payments before arrival (Phinney, 2022). During critical staff shortages, efficiency directly translates to bottom-line savings. Finally, providers can convert their clinics to virtual in case of infection or inclement weather, preventing appointment cancellations and missed revenue (Phinney, 2022).

From the patient's perspective, telehealth prevents travel, saving time and associated travel costs. Duke Health has calculated 1.5 million miles saved for patients across an average of 22,000 visits each month (Phinney, 2022). Virtual appointments equate to forty-seven million miles saved since the start of the COVID-19 pandemic. Concerning patient out-of-pocket costs, COVID-19 introduced new insurance coverage for tele-mental health services. Uninsured patients can face a range of $65-250 per one-hour traditional therapy session (Good Therapy, 2020). Co-pays for some plans could be as little as $20 per visit (Good Therapy, 2020). Uncertainty around a pending recession may further dissuade patients from pursuing mental health services.

Social

The perception of telehealth has transformed in the wake of the pandemic. The social factors include demographics, lifestyle trends, consumer preferences, buying behavior, public relations, influencers, and role models. The J.D. Power 2022 U.S. Telehealth Satisfaction Study shows that 67% of respondents have accessed video telehealth during the past year, up two-fold from 2019 (J.D. Power, 2022). Another National Center for Health Statistics study found that only 37% of all respondents have used telemedicine in the past year (Lucas & Villarroel, 2021). Respondents to the J.D. Power study also indicated telehealth to be the preferred channel for specific routine care: 81% prefer telehealth for prescription refills, 72% prefer telehealth for renewing medication options, 71% prefer it for discussing test results, and 57% prefer it for regular mental health visits (J.D. Power, 2022). Patients prefer telehealth for the convenience, speed, and ease of accessing health information (J.D. Power, 2022). Notably, 94% of telehealth users indicate they would use technology to receive medical services in the future (J.D. Power, 2022). Telehealth also strengthens continuity of care, allowing for more frequent touchpoints with a patient's care team between in-person encounters (Phinney, 2022). In addition, telehealth bridges care for patients in rural communities who lack services in proximity, which can benefit many underserved communities in healthcare deserts (Zebley, 2022). Coupled with an increased willingness to pursue mental health services, the social climate for tele-mental health is ripe for expansion.

The National Center for Health Statistics conducted a population-based study on the use of telemedicine in 2021. The study found that women are more likely than men to use telemedicine (42.0% compared to 32.7%) (Lucas & Villarroel, 2021). The percentage of adults who used telemedicine also increased with age, 29.4% in adults aged 18-29 and 43.3% in adults aged 65 and over (Lucas & Villarroel, 2021). Non-Hispanic White adults (39.2%) were more prone than Hispanic (32.8%), non-Hispanic Black (33.1%), and non-Hispanic Asian (33.0%) adults to have used telemedicine (Lucas & Villarroel, 2021). Telehealth use is also highest among those living in the Northeast and West (40.0% and 42.4%, respectively), compared to those in the Midwest and South (33.3% and 34.3%, respectively) (Lucas & Villarroel, 2021). Telemedicine use also decreased with declining urbanization. Additionally, adults with increased education levels are more apt to use telemedicine (28.7% with less than a high school diploma or GED and 43.2% among adults with a college degree or higher) (Lucas & Villarroel, 2021). Finally, adults with higher income are more likely to use telemedicine (40.7% for families at 400% or greater FPL compared to 33.1% less than 100% FPL (Lucas & Villarroel, 2021).

Technological

Innovations in technology are increasingly influential in strategic marketing. The pandemic accelerated advances in telehealth and overall digital infrastructure. The most prominent video visit vendors are Zoom, Doximity, AmericanWell, Microsoft Teams, Teladoc, and Epic's native video client (Phinney, 2022). Some companies offer a provider group for primary or surge telehealth staffing. Surge staffing would include peak times for video visit demands, such as disaster response, inclement weather, or COVID infection (Phinney, 2022). In addition, companies differ in their technical support model for patients and providers.

The list of features and functionality of telehealth solutions is extensive. Some telehealth providers have restrictions on the type of services and capabilities they can provide. Consequently, the practice in this case study will use an RFP process to outline their criteria and specific video visit technology requirements when selecting a vendor partner for telehealth services and solutions (Phinney, 2022). Additional criteria include advanced data and analytic capabilities about usage and connectivity. While data through an embedded EMR integration is preferred, API (application programming interface) or SFTP (secure file transfer process) for video visit data is considered sufficient (Phinney, 2022).

SWOT ANALYSIS

To kickstart the strategic planning process, we conducted a situational assessment of the practice to gain an in-depth understanding of the current business environment. Berkowitz (2022) explained that a situational assessment analyzes an organization's internal and external environment. To conduct this analysis, we utilized a SWOT analysis. This business tool enables us to identify and analyze the practice's strengths, weaknesses, opportunities, and threats. This tool is best suited for this analysis as it helps to uncover and examine the various aspects of the business while providing a full view of the internal and external factors affecting the practice. With such in-depth knowledge of the practice, we can develop a long-term strategic plan well-tailored to meet the practice's business needs and enable the growth of its customer base. Our findings from the SWOT analysis are summarized below:

Strengths

- The firm is Black owned, which positions the practice well to garner a large share of the current demand for mental health services from Black clients.
- The firm is Female-owned, which gives the practice a strategic advantage to obtain a share of those female clients that prefer female mental health practitioners.
- The firm has specific areas of specialization which speak to its expertise in those specific practice areas. Specialization can help them become the best in that area.
- Loyal customer base.
- The firm excels in customer service and customer satisfaction.

Weaknesses

- The area of specialization is limited, impacting the market opportunity and growth of the firm.
- Marketing efforts and outreach have mainly focused on African American females, with little to no outreach to other demographic groups.
- Lack of investment in telehealth.
- Presence and social media engagement are little to none.
- No online patient portal.

Opportunities

- Growing demand for psychological and counseling services.
- They are growing demand and market for telehealth services. Fifty-seven percent of patients prefer telehealth for regular mental health visits
- Opportunity to partner with corporations or educational institutions to provide mental health services to their organizations.
- Digital expansion.
- Expand marketing through channels, including social media, podcasts, and blogs.
- Leverage customer testimonials.

Threats

- Commercial telehealth companies are moving into the mental health space.
- Reimbursement for telehealth may go away in the future – the uncertain political landscape.
- African Americans are less likely to seek psychological and counseling services.
- The social stigma to mental health may prevent potential clients from seeking mental health services.
- Slow responders to telehealth
- Lack of availability of broadband access may prevent potential telehealth clients from accessing telehealth services.
- Increased competition in the space.

The SWOT analysis enabled us to identify these internal and external factors impacting the practice's business and led to the development of our marketing strategy and recommendations for implementing telehealth and growing the practice's customer base.

RECOMMENDATIONS

Expand Target Market

At the core of strategic marketing is the identification of a target market. Pappas (2021) found that therapy provided to Black women by Black women therapists is significant because they tend to have a deeper understanding of the societal challenges that Black women face. The Essentials of Healthcare Marketing defines the target market as the group of customers the organization wishes to attract with its offerings (Berkowitz, 2022). The Digital Marketing QuickStart Guide defines the target market as the portion of the serviceable available market in which the product or service is directly aimed (Sweeney, 2022). The target market includes the people most likely to buy and should be the focus of any marketing efforts. To grow the practice, it must expand the target market. Expansion should occur in two dimensions: geographically and in additional market segments.

First, the target market can be expanded geographically through telehealth. Telehealth expands the target market because patients can conveniently receive care from home rather than requiring onsite service; however, state licensing limits expansion. The providers' licenses will allow them to provide telehealth services to patients within state borders. Expanding to other states will require physicians to be certified to practice in each state. Some exceptions to this expansion exist through state agreements (i.e., North Carolina and South Carolina), so the practice must investigate state-to-state regulatory relationships. Out-of-state licensure may be advisable in states with a large SAM (serviceable available market). Factors that may influence the size of the SAM include access to counseling and psychological services in the respective state, the mental health of the population, and other telehealth competitors.

Second, the practice can expand the target market by introducing organizations as a new market segment. Currently, direct-to-consumer, or patients, is the only market segment the practice is considering. The most opportunity for growth is in corporations and universities. Large corporations have deep pockets and financial incentives to keep their employees healthy. Companies can also advertise the benefit of free or reduced-cost counseling and behavioral health visits to attract and retain talent within the organization. In addition, many companies are including Diversity, Equity & Inclusion in their mission statements and commitments to employees and customers. Therefore, partnering with a black, female-owned clinic could align with the organization's strategic mission. We have also seen the COVID-19 issue in a greater need for mental health services in schools. College campuses, like West Virginia University, found remarkable success in providing free tele-mental health services to their students both on and off campus (Carrasco, 2021). Universities are more interested than ever in providing services to support their students with the stress and anxiety of pursuing a degree. Contracts with these organizations could generate a recurring revenue stream that supports the clinic's expansion. Given the competition from large telemedicine providers like Teladoc and AmericanWell, we recommend targeting local companies and universities. Local organizations could offer in-person or virtual care and may be incentivized to support local businesses.

Finally, the clinic can expand its market share by creating referral pathways with primary care and emergency medicine providers. Marketing to these local hospitals and clinics will create awareness about the services offered by the clinic, encouraging providers to place referral orders for patients in need of counseling or behavioral healthcare.

Shift to Become a Market-Orientated Organization

After the expansion to different market segments, marketing efforts should target these markets. *The Essentials of Healthcare Marketing* suggests becoming a market-oriented organization when different customers have unique needs and buying or purchasing requirements (Berkowitz, 2022). Messaging should center on the problem the clinic is solving for the customer. Market-oriented organizations tend to be more customer-focused, aware of deeply understanding their customers' situations and providing a unique solution that differentiates from the competition. Market-oriented organizations also seek to build long-term relationships with customers. The market-oriented segments include patients, corporations, educational institutions, and Primary Care and Emergency Medicine providers.

Launch Telehealth Embedded in a Digital Patient Experience

In addition to offering tele-mental health visits, we recommend that the clinic invests in an end-to-end digital patient experience for its patients. An app offers an easy-to-navigate experience and can connect users with the practice's available therapists. The digital experience should include an online patient portal on the web or mobile application (iOS and Android). At a minimum, the platform should have embedded capability to launch the telemedicine visits between the patient and provider. Users will be encouraged to utilize available self-scheduling directly from the app to schedule their first or next telehealth visit. In addition, an enhanced digital experience would include virtual check-in, payment, and form completion for a seamless digital visit workflow. The enhanced capability could also include messaging one's Care Team with specific questions or medication refill requests. This type of interaction with a provider would be classified as an "E-Visit" and is billable for about $20 per encounter through most payors (Phinney, 2022).

Today, many patients use Google searches to understand more about their health (Berkowitz, 2022). Another enhanced feature includes digital patient education and resources about their disease condition, including information about disease management and patient success stories. These digital resources would provide relevant, trustworthy information for patients vetted by their Care Team. The app would also include a designated area where users can find a variety of exercises that to reduce symptoms of anxiety, bipolar disorder, depression, and ADHD.

Since developing a digital patient portal is a significant investment, we recommend sourcing feedback and requirements for a remarkable digital experience from current patients. Patient focus groups or 1:1 interviews with patients is essential for requirements gathering. Launching the platform's first beta version should involve these patients upon scaling.

Content Marketing and Social Media

Another strategy is to utilize the development of new channels and content marketing. The Digital Marketing QuickStart Guide describes content marketing as one of the most effective inbound marketing concepts of all time and defines it as "the practice of creating, publishing, and distributing content of potential interest to targeted audiences" (Sweeney, 2022). To this end, using social media platforms is strongly encouraged to market and expand the practice's services. Through social media content marketing, the practice can develop a user following and reputation based on their distributed content. Social media will provide an opportunity to inform and educate the public on the advantages of therapy for anxiety, bipolar disorder, depression, ADHD diagnosis, and Autism assessments. Distributing content of potential interests can also include sharing daily information with their followers to develop patient encouragement to begin seeking counseling. The practice can focus on using social media platforms to appear more personable by sharing images and background information on available psychologists within the practice. Offering this content allows prospective patients to relate to their prospective psychologist on an individual level.

The practice is encouraged to share their available connection services through telemedicine to broadcast the elimination of location barriers for patients. Studies show that individual practices need to focus on the experience and that practice's own brand and individualized touch. More diverse platforms that offer thousands of choices for practices will have to compete on the breadth of offering. Individual practices must focus on their niche to provide helpful and specific content to patients and offer a better experience (Wicklund, 2020). The practice will benefit from offering helpful services to online users and their targeted audiences. Offering these resources without a patient binding will enhance the patient experience for their targeted audience. Content marketing will provide the practice with the platform to illuminate their benefits and available services.

Incorporate Podcasts/Blogs

As an African American female in counseling and psychological practice, there is room to educate their target audience on the advantages of counseling. Through podcasts, the practice can target a new market that does not utilize social media platforms and prefers to listen to content while completing other tasks. Podcasts can be advantageous in sharing news about mental health or raising awareness about mental health. Podcasts and blogs provide a space to address the stigma around mental health. Podcasts are available through social media, music streaming services, YouTube, or Google searches. As the podcast increase in traction, this is a great option to help listeners broadcast to new audiences.

Blogging is another proven method to accelerate the practice's growth while providing helpful information to customers. Several businesses use blogging to drive organic traffic to their website, which helps to increase customer engagement and online visibility. As a result, we recommend that the practice incorporate blogging as part of its online strategy to drive patient engagement and improve chances of gaining new customers.

Customer Testimonial Marketing

As a small practice operating in a large and competitive telehealth market, we would like to introduce customer testimonial marketing as an additional expansion method. Customer testimonial marketing is one of the few forms of "social proof that establishes value and encourages recent subscribers to buy" (Sweeney, 2022). Introducing customer testimonial marketing opens the practice up to developing a customer or patient-based reputation. Since the practice has experienced success in patient satisfaction and earned media, it can leverage these strengths and incorporate them into customer testimonials. Such testimonials are comments or experiences consumers leave based on their experience(s) with the practice. Customer Testimonial Marketing is a designated area future patients can refer to normalize conversations around counseling and psychological experiences. The practice can further improve by using patient feedback and testimonies to make improvements as they identify what is working versus what is not.

The African American community faces mental health disparities caused by systemic racism and long-term health inequalities exposed by COVID-19. In seeking opportunities to normalize psychological and counseling services, we are encouraging partnerships with local and community celebrities. These partnerships allow well-known individuals to share their experiences with mental health and encourage others to start talking about it. These actions will help de-stigmatize the disease among the African American community, potentially generating new business from this demographic to the practice.

Measure Success

Recommended is the creating a scorecard with Key Performance Indicators (KPIs) to track the success of our recommendations. Recommended KPIs include the percentage growth of unique patients, the percentage growth of visits, the count of virtual visits, the count of in-person visits, the percentage of virtual visits out of total visits, the count of patients that self-schedule using the patient portal, percentage of patients that schedule online, percentage of patients that are representative of each demographic segment (race, ethnicity, payor, sex, zip code). A scorecard should be published each month to summarize measures and trends. In tracking KPIs, due diligence and due care must be exercised throughout the process to comply with healthcare laws such as HIPPA to protect patient data appropriately and to reduce the risk of unauthorized access or misuse.

CONCLUSION

The advent of the COVID-19 pandemic heralded a seismic shift in the delivery of mental health services, with telehealth emerging as a pivotal innovation in disaster management strategies. As the virus spread and lockdowns ensued, the traditional in-person delivery of mental health care became fraught with challenges, from infection risks to logistical hurdles. Telehealth, encompassing virtual therapy sessions, counseling, and psychiatric consultations via video conferencing platforms, has emerged as a transformative response to these exigencies.

One of the foremost advantages of telehealth in the context of the COVID-19 pandemic is its capacity to bridge the gap between mental health professionals and those in need of care, circumventing the physical barriers imposed by social distancing and quarantine measures. This innovation has been instrumental in ensuring the continuity of mental health services, allowing individuals grappling with anxiety, depression, and other mental health issues to access timely support and intervention. Furthermore, it has extended the reach of mental health practitioners, transcending geographical constraints and addressing the surge in demand for mental health services triggered by the pandemic.

Telehealth's role as a disaster management strategy in the COVID-19 crisis extends beyond accessibility. It has also facilitated the real-time monitoring of patients' mental well-being. With the ability to conduct regular virtual check-ins, mental health professionals can assess the evolving needs of their patients, track their progress, and make necessary adjustments to treatment plans. This proactive approach is especially critical during times of crisis, where the psychological impact of the pandemic is multifaceted and dynamic. Additionally, telehealth has played a pivotal role in disseminating psychoeducation and coping strategies to individuals and communities at large, thereby promoting resilience and emotional well-being in the face of unprecedented challenges. In sum, the integration of telehealth in mental health practices during the COVID-19 pandemic has exemplified how innovative solutions can serve as a linchpin in disaster management, ensuring the provision of vital mental health services when they are needed most.

REFERENCES

About Us. (2022). American Telemedicine Association. https://www.americantelemed.org/about-us/

Ahmed, S. M., Ahmed, S., & Mayo, R. (2020). African American's perceptions of COVID-19 exposure risks, testing, and willingness to participate in biomedical research: A United States cross-sectional survey. *Journal of Health Disparities Research and Practice*, *13*(5), 1–12.

Anderson, D. L. (2019). *Organization development: The process of leading organizational change*. Sage Publications.

Argyris, C. (1983). Action science and intervention. *The Journal of Applied Behavioral Science*, *19*(2), 115–135. doi:10.1177/002188638301900204

B., M. (2020, July 24). *Why is it so hard to find a black therapist?* TODAY.com. https://www.today.com/tmrw/why-it-so-hard-find-black-therapist-t187608

Berkowitz, E. N. (2022). *Essentials of Health Care Marketing* (5th ed.). Jones & Bartlett Learning.

Carrasco, M. (2021, September 1). *Colleges Seek Virtual Mental Health Services.* Inside Higher Ed. https://www.insidehighered.com/news/2021/09/20/colleges-expand-mental-health-services-students

Centers for Disease Control and Prevention. (2022, July 12). *Prioritizing Minority Mental Health.* Centers for Disease Control and Prevention. https://www.cdc.gov/healthequity/features/minority-mental-health/index.html

Christian, L. (2020). 3 ways to build a more equitable industry with purpose-driven marketing. Future of Marketing. *Think with Google.* https://www.thinkwithgoogle.com/future-of-marketing/management-and-culture/diversity-and-inclusion/social-impact/

Hoffman, K., Burroughs, E., Brown, C., & Smith, M. (2020). Telehealth: A solution to the mental health crisis caused by COVID-19. *Journal of Mental Health (Abingdon, England)*, *4*(3), 119–124.

H.R. 1647 - 117th Congress (2021-2022): TREATS Act. (2021, May 18). https://www.congress.gov/bill/117th-congress/house-bill/1647

H.R. 4040 - 117th Congress (2021-2022): Advancing Telehealth Beyond COVID–19 Act of 2021. (2022, July 28). https://www.congress.gov/bill/117th-congress/house-bill/4040

Karrouri, R., Hammani, Z., Benjelloun, R., & Otheman, Y. (2021). Major depressive disorder: Validated treatments and future challenges. *World Journal of Clinical Cases*, *9*(31), 9350–9367. doi:10.12998/wjcc.v9.i31.9350 PMID:34877271

Kirsch, L. (2004). Action research: A participatory approach for organizational development. *Human Resource Development International*, *7*(3), 383–395.

Langarizadeh, M., Tabatabaei, M. S., Tavakol, K., Naghipour, M., Rostami, A., & Moghbeli, F. (2017). Telemental Health Care, an Effective Alternative to Conventional Mental Care: A Systematic Review. *Acta Informatica Medica*, *25*(4), 240–246. doi:10.5455/aim.2017.25.240-246 PMID:29284913

Lindsey, M. A., Joe, S., Nebbitt, V., & Thurlow, M. L. (2017). Help-Seeking Behaviors and Mental Health Service Utilization Among African American College Students. *Journal of College Student Development*, *58*(2), 133–149. doi:10.1353/csd.2017.0013

Liu, P., Zhang, Y., Wang, Y., & Zou, X. (2020). Mental health and psychological distress among the general population during the COVID-19 pandemic: A systematic review. *International Journal of Environmental Research and Public Health*, *17*(13), 4813. PMID:32635450

Lucas, J. W., & Villarroel, M. A. (2021). Telemedicine use among adults: United States. NCHS Data Brief, no 445. Hyattsville, MD: National Center for Health Statistics. https://dx.doi.org/ doi:10.15620/cdc:121435

MacMillan, C. (2021). *Why Telehealth for Mental Health Care is Working*. Yale Medicine. https://www.yalemedicine.org/news/telehealth-for-mental-health

Marks, J. D., & Augenstein, J. (2022). *Health Highlights: Telehealth Policies in the Omnibus FY 2022 Spending Bill*. Manatt Health. https://www.manatt.com/insights/newsletters/health-highlights/telehealth-policies-in-the-omnibus-fy-2022spendin#:~:text=Providers%20will%20not%20be%20required,the%20case%20of%20hospice%20patients

Mayo Foundation for Medical Education and Research. (2017, October 13). *Generalized anxiety disorder*. Mayo Clinic. https://www.mayoclinic.org/diseases-conditions/generalized-anxiety-disorder/symptoms-causes/syc-20360803

Mayo Foundation for Medical Education and Research. (2018, January 6). *Autism spectrum disorder*. Mayo Clinic. https://www.mayoclinic.org/diseases-conditions/autism-spectrum-disorder/symptoms-causes/syc-20352928

Mayo Foundation for Medical Education and Research. (2019, June 22). *Adult attention-deficit/hyperactivity disorder (ADHD)*. Mayo Clinic. https://www.mayoclinic.org/diseases-conditions/adult-adhd/symptoms-causes/syc-20350878

Mayo Foundation for Medical Education and Research. (2021, February 16). *Bipolar disorder*. Mayo Clinic. https://www.mayoclinic.org/diseases-conditions/bipolar-disorder/symptoms-causes/syc-20355955

Mayo Foundation for Medical Education and Research. (2022, October 14). *Depression (major depressive disorder)*. Mayo Clinic. https://www.mayoclinic.org/diseases-conditions/depression/symptoms-causes/syc-20356007

Pappas, S. (2021, November 1). *Effective therapy with black women*. Monitor on Psychology. https://www.apa.org/monitor/2021/11/ce-therapy-black-women

Perrin, A., & Anderson, M. (2021). *Digital divide persists even as Americans with lower incomes make gains in tech adoption*. Pew Research Center. https://www.pewresearch.org/fact-tank/2021/01/28/digital-divide-persists-even-as-americans-with-lower-incomes-make-gains-in-tech-adoption/

Phinney, D. (2022). *Duke Health Telehealth Past, Present, and Future*. Duke Health.

S.2061 - 117th Congress (2021-2022): Telemental Health Care Access Act of 2021. (2021, June 15). https://www.congress.gov/bill/117th-congress/senate-bill/2061

SAMHSA. (n.d.). Double jeopardy: Covid-19 and behavioral health disparities for black and Latino Communities in the U.S. *SAMHSA.gov*. https://www.samhsa.gov/sites/default/files/covid19-behavioral-health-disparities-black-latino-communities.pdf

Sammut-Bonnici, T., & Galea, D. (2015). Pest analysis. Wiley Encyclopedia of Management, 1–1. https://doi.org/ doi:10.1002/9781118785317.weom120113

Stakeholder Letter Urging Senate to Take Action This Fall on Telehealth. (2022). American Telemedicine Association. https://www.americantelemed.org/wp-content/uploads/2022/09/Telehealth-Stakeholder-Letter-to-Senate-FINAL.pdf

Sweeney, B. (2022). *Digital Marketing Quickstart Guide*. ClydeBank Media, LLC.

JD Power. (2022). *J.D. Power 2022 U.S. Telehealth Satisfaction Study*. J.D. Power. https://www.jdpower.com/sites/default/files/file/2022-09/2022132%20U.S.%20Telehealth.pdf

Treichler, C. (2022). The Top 6 Online Mental Health & Therapy On-Demand Services of 2022. *Online Doctor*. https://www.onlinedoctor.com/best-online-mental-health-therapy-on-demand-services/

U.S. Department of Health and Human Services. (2021). *Telehealth for Providers: What You Need to Know*. CMS. https://www.cms.gov/files/document/telehealth-toolkit-providers.pdf

Wicklund, E. (2020, November 25). *Guidelines for marketing a practice's new telehealth platform*. Mental Health Intelligence. https://mhealthintelligence.com/news/guidelines-for-marketing-a-practices-new-telehealth-platform

Wicklund, E. (2020). *Guidelines for Marketing a Practice's New Telehealth Platform*. mHealth Intelligence. https://mhealthintelligence.com/news/guidelines-for-marketing-a-practices-new-telehealth-platform

Yancy, C. W. (2020). COVID-19 and African Americans. *Journal of the American Medical Association, 323*(19), 1891–1892. doi:10.1001/jama.2020.6548 PMID:32293639

Zebley, K. (2022). *Comments on the CY2023 Physician Fee Schedule proposed rule (CMS-1700-P)*. American Telemedicine Association. https://www.americantelemed.org/wp-content/uploads/2022/08/CY23-PFS-Comments_ATA_FINAL.pdf

Zebley, K. (2022). *Updates on the ATA and ATA Action's Policy and Advocacy Work*. American Telemedicine Association.

Chapter 7
Management Consulting in Healthcare as an Innovative Means of Addressing an Organizational Cultural Crisis

Maria D. Baez
https://orcid.org/0000-0002-5693-3825
Capitol Technology University, USA

Allison J. Huff
https://orcid.org/0000-0001-6102-8013
College of Medicine, University of Arizona, USA

Darrell Norman Burrell
https://orcid.org/0000-0002-4675-9544
Marymount University, USA

Quatavia McLester
https://orcid.org/0000-0003-1596-0517
The Chicago School of Professional Psychology, USA

Delores Springs
https://orcid.org/0000-0003-0940-1225
Regent University, USA

William Quisenberry
Purdue University Global, USA

Elizabeth I. Omotoye
University of the Cumberlands, USA

Marlena Daryousef
https://orcid.org/0000-0001-9513-501X
Colorado Technical University, USA

Kiana S. Zanganeh
Florida Institute of Technology, USA

Kevin Richardson
https://orcid.org/0009-0002-3212-8669
Capitol Technology University, USA

Laura Jones
https://orcid.org/0000-0002-0299-370X
Capitol Technology University, USA

ABSTRACT

An increasing number of reports of sexual harassment in the workplace and medical education is challenging the current state of medical education and healthcare. The trauma and long-term consequences of sexual harassment are well documented, yet the issue of sexual harassment has been overlooked mainly in healthcare, leading to a culture of silence and a lack of meaningful and practical solutions. These dynamics represent a significant crisis. This chapter examines the prevalence of sexual harassment in

DOI: 10.4018/978-1-6684-9522-3.ch007

the healthcare and medical education workplace and explores the need for innovative solutions and prevention strategies. The chapter concludes by discussing potential innovative solutions and prevention strategies developed by a management consulting group at Sunshine Health Regional Hospital and Medical Education Training Center, which has experienced a sexual harassment crisis. The intent is to find innovative solutions to influence the world of practice.

INTRODUCTION

The Sunshine Health Regional is a hospital and medical education training center in crisis due to a recent class action multimillion-dollar class settlement for sexual harassment against female doctors, staff, and medical.

Consequently, consultants of Management consulting solutions have assisted this organization in enhancing the working environment for female doctors who have experienced sexual assault and harassment and healthcare quality. Sexual harassment against women in the medical education and healthcare workplace is a problem that has been gaining more attention in recent years. With increased attention to the issue, more data about its prevalence and adverse effects on women in the medical field has been revealed.

Sexual harassment within the healthcare sector represents a deeply concerning crisis that demands immediate attention, urgency, and innovative solutions. This issue not only threatens the well-being and dignity of healthcare professionals but also undermines patient care and the trust that the healthcare system relies upon. To address this crisis effectively, it is imperative to approach it with a profound commitment to equity, inclusion, and diversity. Innovative solutions can emerge from a comprehensive understanding of the problem and a willingness to challenge systemic biases and power imbalances. These solutions may encompass culturally sensitive education and training programs, the establishment of clear reporting mechanisms, and the promotion of a culture that prioritizes respect and accountability. By tackling sexual harassment with a sense of urgency and a dedication to innovative approaches, the healthcare community has the potential to not only rectify this crisis but also foster an environment of safety, respect, and equality for all its members, ultimately enhancing the quality of patient care and the overall integrity of the profession.

What Is Sexual Harassment?

The Equal Employment Opportunity Commission (E.E.O.C.) defines *sexual harassment* as unwanted sexual advances, requests for sexual favors, and other verbal or physical conduct of a sexual nature (Jamieson & Milbrandt, 2018; Robinson et al., 2005).

Sexual assault is a sexual act committed against a person's will or without their consent and involves physical force, intimidation, coercion, or physical contact (Phillips & Schneider, 1993; Robinson et al., 2005). It is important to note that organizational development work is crucial for combating sexual harassment and assault in the workplace. Understanding and enhancing any substantive processes an organization may develop for performing tasks and pursuing objectives is part of organizational development work (Jamieson & Milbrandt, 2018).

Sexual harassment is an issue that has been pervasive in medical education and healthcare workplaces for decades, and the consequences of such behavior can be devastating for the victims. Women are particularly vulnerable to sexual harassment in these settings and are more likely than men to be exposed to various forms of gender-based discrimination and harassment (Ansari, 2020).

Studies have consistently found that the prevalence of sexual harassment against women in medical education and healthcare workplaces is frequent and concerning (Collins, 2020). Women in these settings report higher levels of sexual harassment and are more likely to experience hostile work environments than men (Ansari, 2020). For example, a recent survey of medical students in the United States found that over a quarter of female respondents reported experiencing sexual harassment or gender-based discrimination in the past year (Collins, 2020). The prevalence of sexual harassment in medical education and healthcare workplaces is even higher in some other countries. For example, a recent survey of medical students in India found that nearly half of female respondents reported experiencing sexual harassment or gender-based discrimination in the past year (Ansari, 2020).

The statistics and trends of sexual harassment against women in medical education and the healthcare workplace demonstrate that it is a pervasive problem. In recent years, there has been an increase in awareness of the issue, but more needs to be done to address it. Sexual harassment and assault of doctors in the medical field begin prior to their employment. In medical schools, where sexual harassment and assault typically begin, half of the student population consists of women (Jagsi et al., 2016; Jamieson & Milbrandt, 2018). Sexual assault and harassment in medical schools likely began long before the MeToo movement gained traction; a 1995 cross-sectional survey found that 52% of U.S. academic medical faculty women reported harassment in their careers, compared to 5% of men (Jagsi et al., 2016). In addition, not only in the workplace but also in academic settings, there has been an increase in instances of sexual harassment against women (Jagsi et al., 2016). This concept raises several concerns regarding the impact of this behavior on the affected women and the patients they serve (Jagsi et al., 2016). According to an online survey of practitioners, 30% of respondents reported sexual harassment or assault from patients directly impacting burnout (Notaro et al., 2021).

Background

Sunshine Health System consists of three hospitals, all located within 40 miles of each other. Sunshine Health Metro is in the heart of Metro City, a medium-sized city in a southern state. It operates with about 1,000 employees and has a significant, high-traffic Emergency Department. It is ranked the number one trauma center in the state and specializes in oncology and complex surgery, including transplant, cardiothoracic, and orthopedic. People travel from all over the country, sometimes the world, to receive transplants or oncology care from Metro Hospital. Sunshine Health Metro is affiliated with the local University, Metro City University, a teaching hospital accepting interns; among all the care services, it provides speech-language pathology, physical therapy, radiology, dietetics, and other services related to the health care field. The center also provides medical training and education for nurses, doctors, physician assistants, audiologists, and speech pathologists. In addition, many attending physicians are adjunct professors at Metro City University, which has a robust resident physician program.

Sunshine Health Riverside sits about 35 miles outside of Metro City limits. This hospital is the smallest of the three, with only 600 employees. Its specialties include geriatrics and nephrology, and while it is not quite as prestigious in trauma and surgery as Metro, it does have a high-functioning cardiac I.C.U. In addition, due to its many geriatric patients, this hospital usually serves as a stepping stone to a long-term care facility for its patients. Thus, its average L.O.S. is double Metro's.

Sunshine Health Regional sits 25 miles from Metro in a highly populated suburb of Metro City. Compared to Metro and Riverside, it has 750 employees as a midsize hospital. This hospital is known for and specializes in neurology, obstetrics, and pediatrics. Its pediatric unit is one of the best in the state, and the hospital has both a Pediatric I.C.U. and a Neonatal I.C.U. One of this hospital's missions is to reduce the rate of maternal and fetal death in the region, particularly among black and indigenous women.

Problem Statement

Over the past three decades, sexual harassment has remained consistent across industries, including healthcare (Binder et al., 2018). According to the 2017 medical school graduation questionnaire of the Association of American Medical Colleges, only 21% of students who had experienced harassment or other offensive behaviors reported these incidents to faculty or medical school administrators (Albert-Henry, 2018; Binder et al., 2018).

A survey conducted by the American Medical Association (A.M.A.) in 2018 reported that more than half of female physicians (56%) reported experiencing sexual harassment in the workplace (American Medical Association, 2018). This includes both subtle and overt sexual harassment. The report also found that 41% of female physicians reported receiving inappropriate comments, 28% reported experiencing unwanted sexual attention, and 13% reported experiencing sexual coercion (American Medical Association, 2018).

This paper explores the development of best practices and innovative approaches developed by a management consulting intervention at a regional hospital. The intent is to find innovative solutions to influence the world of practice.

Purpose/Significance Statement

The client, Sunshine Health, has enlisted the services of a management consultant to provide a comprehensive approach for the human resources department to curb the high incidences of sexual harassment experienced by women physicians. Sunshine Health has seen an increase in the number (150%) of sexual harassment claims from female clinical staff, especially those on the front. In addition, per reports, insurance utilization shows increases in the number of sick days for female employees (32%), the number of female employees leaving (45%), and the increased use of employee mental health services by female employees (65%). Sunshine Health cares about its employees and understands that sexist microaggressions, unwanted sexual attention, and even sexual battery occur across its three regional hospitals. Management consulting solutions will provide several deliverables for Sunshine Health, including an overview of the problem (background information and literature review), recommended change management models to incite behavior change, and a list of activities that can be implemented to eliminate this crisis effectively.

METHODOLOGY AND THEORIES FROM THE LITERATURE REVIEW

The purpose of this study is to conduct a comprehensive, systematic literature review on sexual harassment towards female doctors and to identify solutions to the problem. Some valuable databases used to search for articles, journals, and books included Google Scholar, U.N.C. Online Library, J.S.T.O.R., and ResearchGate. The study also employed inclusion and exclusion criteria to select relevant articles. The review findings will contribute to the existing knowledge on sexual harassment in the medical profession, medical education, and healthcare and inform policy development. A broad range of search terms related to (and including) "sexual harassment against females in healthcare, " sexual harassment against females in medical education," and "sexual harassment against female doctors" were used in searches across these databases.

After compiling all search results into one document, duplicates were removed, and all articles published more than 20 years ago were excluded. The remaining articles were screened based on their titles and abstracts, and those not meeting the inclusion criteria were excluded. The full text of the remaining articles was then assessed to determine their eligibility for inclusion in the systematic review. In the next screening stage, article relevance was assessed using the title and abstract combined. After screening articles by title and abstract using the exclusion criteria, 126 articles were narrowed to 29 sources included in the final review stage.

Lewin's Change Theories

To understand how to apply recommendations effectively at Sunshine Health, one must understand the implications change has on an organization. As shown in Figure 1, Three-step

Model of Change, also known as Lewin's Change theory, outline the steps and processes that lead to effective organizational change (Burke, 2018; Cheung-Judge & Holbeche, 2021). First, it is essential to note that the organization must establish sexual harassment and assault as intolerable acts. Mobilizing the organization and establishing this expectation is only the beginning, though, as there need to be actionable items that follow the unfreezing stage (Burke, 2018; Cheung-Judge & Holbeche, 2021). Figure 1 Lewin's Change Theories shows the recommendations align with freezing, moving, and refreezing.

Figure 1. Lewin's change theories

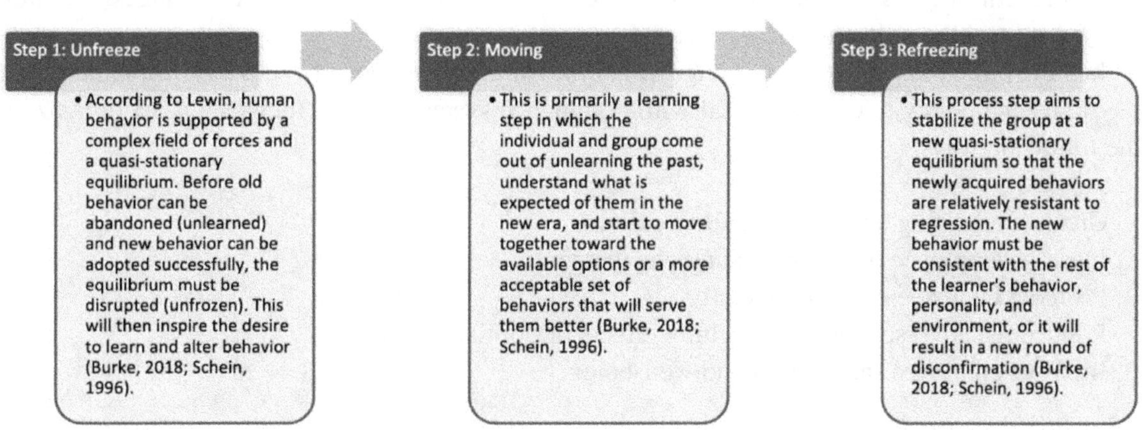

Lewin's Change Theory Principles in Action

Figure 2 shows how Lewin's model can be used to implement organizational changes like bystander empowerment interventions in the workforce during the unfreezing phase, the implementation of a reporting

Figure 2. Lewin's change theory principles in action

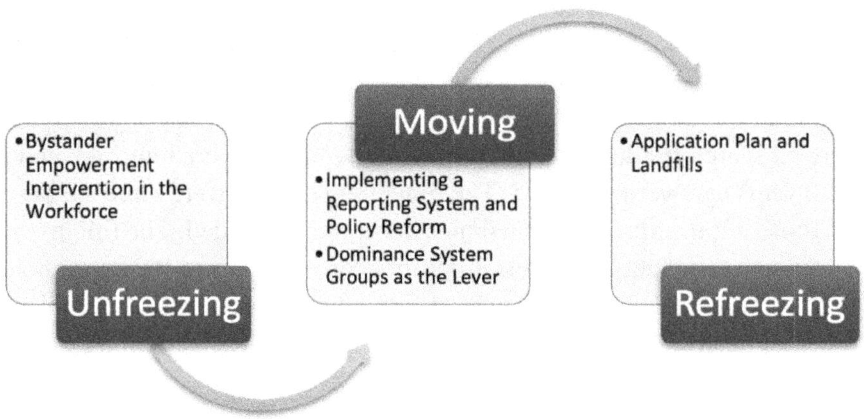

system and policy reform, and the use of dominance system groups as the lever during the moving phase, which leads to the application plan and landfills during the refreezing phase. Bystander empowerment interventions in the workforce (unfreezing) will contribute to creating awareness and comprehension of the need for change. Also, by educating employees about the advantages of bystander empowerment, reporting systems, and policy reform, it is more likely that they will accept the alterations.

Planning and executing the changes is required to implement a reporting system and policy reform, with dominance system groups as the lever (moving). Organizations can improve their chances of successful implementation by developing a detailed plan and involving employees.

The application plan and landfills (refreezing) involve institutionalizing and reinforcing the changes. Creating a clear and comprehensive implementation plan, providing employees with training and support throughout the process, identifying key stakeholders and change champions, conducting a needs assessment and identifying areas for improvement, developing programs to support the changes, monitoring progress, and making adjustments necessary.

When the principles of Lewin's Change Theory are used to empower bystanders, implement reporting systems and policy reform, and deal with dominance system groups, they can assist organizations in the following ways:

- Create a reporting and accountability culture.
- Increase employee participation and engagement.
- Promote inclusiveness and diversity.
- Reduce the adverse workplace culture effects of dominance systems.
- Improve employee satisfaction and well-being.

Bystander Empowerment Intervention in the Workforce_

One of our recommendations to help combat the issue of sexual harassment and assault of physicians in the workforce is to help change organizational culture by targeting those who are witnesses, defenders, and upstanders of sexual harassment and assault. However, this bystander training must be comprehensive and empower companies and employees to prevent harassment. The Equal Employment Opportunity

Commission's Select Task Force on the Study of Harassment in the Workplace issued a report in 2016 finding that some sexual harassment training caused men to be more likely to blame both the harasser and the victim involved in a sexual harassment scenario (James, 2021). The E.E.O.C.'s study says training often focuses too much on legal standards and avoids legal liability (James, 2021).

Bystander role consciousness is meant to help employees and others intercede when they witness a person being subjected to inappropriate behavior, typically sexual harassment or discriminatory comments (James, 2021). There are several standard components of bystander intervention as denoted by the U.S. Department of Justice Office on Violence Against Women; those components are:

Awareness. A critical first step is to heighten awareness, so individuals and groups can better identify instances of sexual violence (James, 2021).

Responsibility. A sense of responsibility gives the bystander motivation to step in and act. Bystanders are much more likely to help friends than strangers and to help strangers if they see them as part of a group they identify with, like supporting the same sports team (James, 2021).

Perceptions of Norms. Perceptions of peer norms and perceptions of authorities' attitudes influence bystander attitudes (James, 2021). People often mistakenly think others are less supportive of doing something to address sexual violence than they are. However, studies show links between perceptions of helping, trust, and commitment among community members, reliance on campus authorities, and their willingness to act as a bystander (James, 2021).

Weighing the Pros and Cons:

People weigh the costs and benefits of getting involved in a risky situation, and these include threats to their safety, negative consequences for their relationships with others, and the potential to change the outcome of a risky situation or to help a victim (James, 2021).

Confidence:

People who feel more confident in their ability to help are more likely to act. A consistent research finding is that prevention programs, particularly in-person educational and skill workshops, increase individuals' sense that they can take effective action (James, 2021).

Building Skills:

According to James (2021), many people need help with specific ways to help, and data from population surveys shows that many people need assistance in this area. Additionally, abuse survivors often report that friends and family do not always provide helpful or supportive responses, making coping with and recovering from abuse much more difficult. Bystander intervention training promises to give motivated community members the skills they need to intervene in ways that protect their safety and truly support victims.

Context:

Bystanders also need safety nets, resources, and community policies supporting intervention (James, 2021).

Bystander Intervention Necessity

Some wonder why the victim does not speak up if harassed or no one else steps in. Victims do not speak up for various reasons (James, 2021). Physicians may be concerned about their jobs, unsure how to respond, and some victims may be embarrassed (James, 2021). This embarrassment may be why they do not report sexual assault (James, 2021). Not only does the victim struggle to respond to sexual harassment, but bystanders face numerous challenges in reporting and intervening (James, 2021). Bystanders

Figure 3. Kindall James bystander training

Note 1: According to Kindall James (2021), author of Bystander Training, bystander intervention can be broken down into five steps. This approach is vital to create a workplace free of sexual violence.

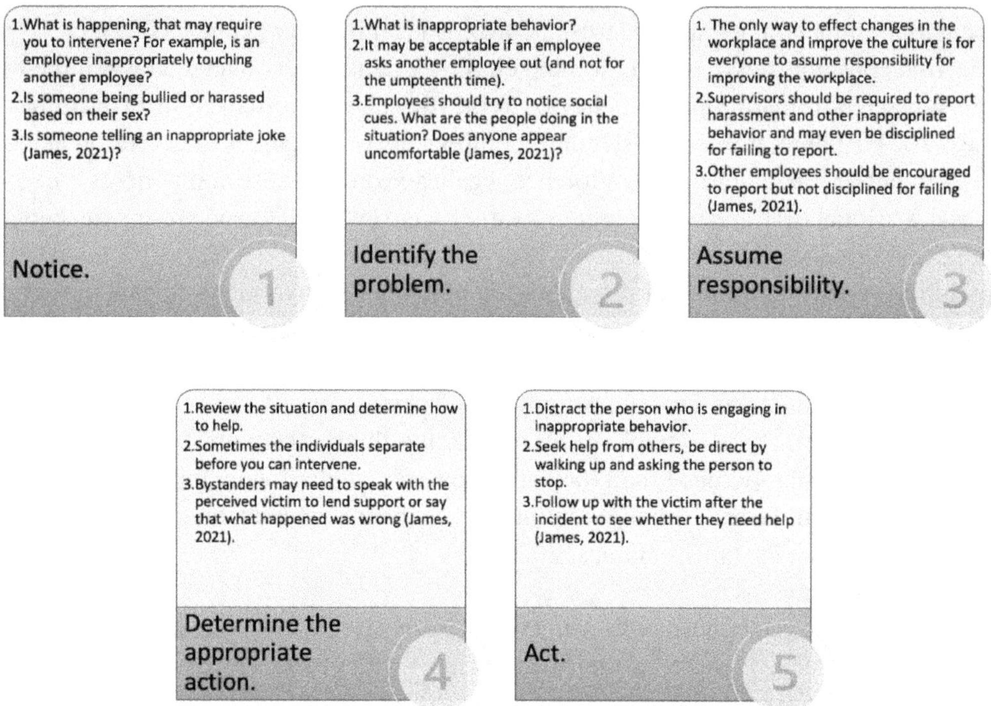

face psychological barriers such as the belief that someone else will intervene to solve the problem and that the issues do not affect them, so it is not their problem (James, 2021). These are some of the reasons why the bystander effect, in which multiple people witness an emergency or wrongdoing but do nothing, is such a common phenomenon (James, 2021).

The Human Resources department at Sunshine Health will ensure that appropriate bystander training is provided to all staff throughout the healthcare organization and refresher training throughout each employee's stay at the company. Chris White's Ted Talk discussing three ways to create a work culture that brings out the best in employees highlights the importance of communication in the workplace (White, 2019). He talked about unblocking communication, being responsive when people share, and inviting people to bring their whole selves to work (White, 2019). Bystander intervention training is designed to help individuals recognize potentially harmful situations and take action to prevent or reduce harm. Figure 3 shows the Kindall James' bystander intervention training outlining the steps for noticing, interpreting, assuming personal responsibility, taking action, and following up.

By following these steps, bystander intervention training can help individuals become more aware of potentially harmful situations and take action to prevent or reduce harm. If a bystander does report an incident, organizational leaders must carefully investigate it and ensure there is an appropriate intervention. Thus, ensure that harassers, patients, and colleagues know that the organization does not tolerate this behavior.

In conclusion, this recommendation will help change the organizational culture to a safer, more inclusive space where people can work without fearing harassment. This change management process will take time and require multiple teams to work together to combat the issue. Organizational practitioners will ensure the organization is where it needs to be to react to outside stimuli. If employees do not feel safe, the reaction time to any strategy will be slow. Thus, we recommend ensuring employees feel safe and are cared for so that they, in turn, care for their patients.

Implementing a Reporting System and Policy Reform

Strategies to minimize sexual harassment in a healthcare organization include clear and consistent protocols and procedures for reporting, addressing, and mitigating incidents in which harassment has occurred (Fenwick et al., 2022). Not only can this help to eliminate harassment, but well-designed reporting systems can improve organizational culture and the perception around this type of harassment, provide a framework for implementing anti-harassment programs, and create a system that can track these incidents (Fenwick et al., 2022). Authors of a study that sought to identify expert recommendations for creating systems within healthcare settings that effectively help staff and patients report patient-perpetrated sexual harassment conducted qualitative interviews with sexual harassment prevention experts. Though this study is focused on harassment by patients, the authors of this research paper believe the recommendations can be transferable to staff-staff harassment.

Results from these interviews included the following recommendations:

- Promote a culture and environment that has zero tolerance for harassment.
- Take appropriate and remedial action on all reports.
- Consequences and barriers for those reporting incidences.
- Create easy-to-use and simple reporting processes.
- Hold the reporting system accountable.

These recommendations aim to promote trust among employees and patients, which will encourage victims of this harassment to report them and, of course, eliminate incidences of harassment (Fenwick et al., 2022). Strategies to support these recommendations include anti-harassment training and teachings for all employees to create a zero-tolerance climate and create proportional and timely action steps in response to reports, including warnings, education, etc. (Fenwick et al., 2022). To mitigate fear for victims, organizations should provide a system with anonymous reporting that supports and validates reporters and allows the reporting party to have some control in the process (Fenwick et al., 2022). To allow for an easy-to-use system, organizations should provide various options for reporting, such as personal (in-person, telephone, others) and impersonal (email, app, others), and policies/procedures should be accessible (Fenwick et al., 2022). Since healthcare providers are overworked, a quick and straightforward reporting process is imperative to ensure that reports are made (Headley, 2020). Strategies to hold the reporting system accountable include monitoring these reporting systems, the interventions, and their effectiveness in reducing and mitigating incidences (Fenwick et al., 2022).

Since sexual harassment has been present and tolerated in healthcare organizations for many years, eliminating it from the culture can be a difficult task. A survey conducted by Medscape revealed that only 45% of physicians, nurses, and Advanced Practice Providers (APPs) who experienced sexual harassment in the workplace reported it (Headley, 2020). An impactful way to change the environment and perception of sexual harassment in the healthcare workplace is to, as noted above, provide consistent sexual harassment training to all staff from top to bottom (Headley, 2020). Equally impactful is to remove all barriers to safe reporting, which includes a culture change to one that is supportive and safe (Headley, 2020). Aside from ensuring employees will not be punished or retaliated against if they come forward, they must create a feedback loop that includes reporting back the findings of an investigation to the person who reported it (Headley, 2020). The system's speed is also essential since this situation can expose victims to vulnerability (Headley, 2020). Further, executive leadership must be involved in encouraging such programs and policies and committed to improving them (Headley, 2020).

Gardner & Johnson (2001), authors of the article *Sexual Harassment in Healthcare: Strategies for Employers,* provide further details on how organizations can create policies to help prevent sexual harassment. This report includes frequently distributing a copy of the policy and reporting procedures to all employees and placing both within employee handbooks and ensuring understanding; each employee should sign this policy, their direct supervisor, and executives (Gardner & Johnson, 2001). Similarly, regarding policies they cited, they should include key elements described above but also protection from retaliation, an easy-to-use reporting system, quick and proportionate corrective action, and continuous follow-up (Gardner & Johnson, 2001). Other elements cited in this article include training sessions to educate employees on their rights and responsibilities, covering *the dos and don'ts* (Gardner & Johnson, 2001).

Further, this training should be consistently provided to all staff at least once every year, where sessions should be interactive to sensitize the employees, and trainers should continue to measure the effectiveness of the training through comprehension tests (Gardner & Johnson, 2001). An element not covered previously is the idea that managers and supervisors must set an example for employees to follow (Gardner & Johnson, 2001). This includes ensuring that advocates for eliminating sexual harassment are not engaging in sexual harassment among employees (Gardner & Johnson, 2001), for example, in the case of Smith Vs. St. Louis University Hospital and Medical Center, the court found that the person responsible for preventing sexual harassment (the head of anesthesiology) had sexually harassed many female residents (Gardner & Johnson, 2001; Stone et al., 2019).

Additional recommendations for keeping female providers safe from harassment were discovered in a study where researchers provided female resident doctors with questionnaires to garner their experience with sexual harassment (Stone et al., 2019; Ulusoy et al., 2011). A unique finding from this questionnaire was that many female residents felt the need for protection at work (Stone et al., 2019; Ulusoy et al., 2011). This includes security personnel, surveillance cameras, and establishing provisions so that female providers do not have to be alone with male patients (Stone et al., 2019; Ulusoy et al., 2011). Further, many of these female providers were taking variance precautions against sexual harassment, such as dressing conservatively and minimizing eye contact. This provided a different perspective for the researchers that female providers may feel harassment stems from their behaviors (Stone et al., 2019; Ulusoy et al., 2011).

Dominance System Groups as the Lever

Dobbin (2019) postulates that sexual harassment is a women's experience but a men's issue; men often do not believe women who complain of harassment, thinking they have overreacted or have extortion in mind. On the other hand, one research shows that men's influence on other men's behavior is significantly more substantial. Therefore, it may improve outcomes if groups within the system, e.g., *men,* take a more

Table 1. Levels of men's allyship

Level	Action	Rationale
Interpersonal	By deterring and supporting victims, male bystanders can act as allies when they witness sexual harassment incidents in workplaces.	Male bystanders can be powerful allies in the fight against sexual harassment in the workplace by deterring and supporting victims, creating a more inclusive and respectful work environment, encouraging male coworkers to become aware of their role as bystanders, advocating for policy change, and using their voice and privilege to amplify women's stories and experiences to create positive change.
Community	Influential community members' involvement in prevention efforts can help take countermeasures to sexual harassment issues.	The involvement of influential community members in prevention efforts can make a significant difference in the fight against sexual harassment. By leveraging their power and influence, they can help raise awareness, shift cultural norms, advocate for policy changes, support victims, and create safe spaces for all community members and society.
Influential figures	Influential figures, such as the C.E.O. of the healthcare facility, are the key components of programs against sexual harassment.	The presence of influential people, such as the C.E.O. of the healthcare facility, is essential for successful anti-sexual harassment initiatives. This is because they can bring attention and legitimacy to the issue, which can help raise awareness and provide a platform for discussion. Furthermore, influential people can serve as role models for the community, inspiring change in attitudes toward sexual harassment. Additionally, they can support victims and ensure existing policies are adequately enforced.
Societal	To help those in power (men) make the right decisions, defaults can be set within the organization. This may include mandatory female representation in decision-making processes or devotion from the annual budget to the programs against sexual harassment. By educating themselves, speaking up, supporting victims, holding others accountable, advocating for change, and leading by example, men can help create a culture prioritizing respect, safety, and equality.	Defaults can be a powerful tool in assisting those in power in making sound decisions. Organizations, for example, can establish a default that requires female representation in decision-making processes or allocate a portion of their budget to social causes. This default type communicates to all members that the organization values diversity and is dedicated to making positive changes. Defaults can also be used to encourage people to live healthier lifestyles, such as imposing a calorie limit on restaurant meals or requiring employees to opt out of unhealthy eating options at work. People are likelier to stick with it and make decisions that benefit their overall well-being if a default is established. Furthermore, defaults can help reduce decision fatigue by eliminating the need for people to evaluate every single decision they make. This is especially useful for large purchases or long-term investments where numerous factors must be considered.

significant role in addressing sexual harassment issues and use *men as allies* (Fabiano et al., 2019). Given this information, one of our recommendations is to involve men as allies to eliminate sexual harassment incidents in healthcare settings. To drive systemic improvement to the workplace culture, gender fairness and equity can be promoted through supportive and collaborative personal relationships and public acts of sponsorship and advocacy (Reinicke, 2022). Resources are required for reform implementation, and men often control resource access (Reinicke, 2022). Therefore, men's involvement in active programs against sexual harassment can change the life situations of both men and women (Reinicke, 2022). Table 1 explains how the four levels of men's allyship can act and spread through different spheres (Dai et al., 2014; Reinicke, 2022):

On the other hand, Smith (2017) argued that male allies tend to have three things in common to create institutional changes. First, as mentioned above, men are the main stakeholders and possess more excellent knowledge of the organization (Smith, 2017). Second, they genuinely understand the cost of inequality for everyone. Finally, they demonstrate an honest commitment to what is fair (Smith, 2017). However, the same research revealed that many men identify as allies in the fight against harassment in private but become uncomfortable expressing their support or intervening in public settings (Smith, 2017). One of the reasons for this is the bystander effect when people expect that someone else will act;

the second reason is what psychologists call psychological standing, a sense of having skin in the game (Smith, 2017). As explained above, bystander intervention training can help overcome these factors (Smith, 2017). Moreover, by creating a culture where men can be allies, gender equality can be reframed as a leadership issue instead of a women's issue (Smith, 2017).

Application Plan and Landfills

Our recommendations are set to action through the implementation of our intervention called Combating Assault and Sexual Harassment (C.A.S.H.) Program. This application plan outlines the necessary steps for successfully implementing our C.A.S.H. Program at landfills across the three hospitals of Sunshine Health System. The program is intended to provide education, resources, and support to employees at these sites to prevent instances of sexual harassment and assault from occurring in the workplace.

Objective. Our consultancy mission is to provide Sunshine Health System with a robust program such as the C.A.S.H. and help create a safe, inclusive workplace free from harassment and assault. By providing a comprehensive plan involving documented steps, needed resources, a budget, and a timeline, the program will help implement policies and procedures to protect employees from the harmful effects of sexual harassment and assault.

The program has several objectives, including:

1. To provide Bystander Training and Men as Allies training at three hospitals of Sunshine Health System.
2. To involve key community stakeholders and patient advocacy groups to prevent sexual harassment and assault.
3. To update Sunshine Health's Human Resource policy on identification, tracking, and responding to sexual harassment issues against female providers.
4. To establish a systemwide reporting system.
5. The Sunshine Health System will implement these strategic goals from November 2022 until December 2027.

Scope. The phases of this project will be planning, active training, marketing, and completion of the reporting system. 'Bystander' training and 'Men as Allies' training will equip employees at all levels to transform culture by (1) preventing all forms of harassment and (2) increasing supportive, positive interactions with the end goal of increasing safety, productivity, and retention of a diverse and talented workforce. In addition, the systemwide reporting system will enhance the ability to provide comprehensive and standardized victim case management.

Methodology. The team will focus on completing the project by choosing the proper time and resources that Sunshine Health utilizes. In addition, the project administrator will ensure that the tools and materials comply with Sunshine Health's mission, vision, and values. The team will also brainstorm ideas and stick to a schedule to complete all tasks.

Success Criteria. The team needs to communicate with project stakeholders and agree upon success criteria. These include cost, timeline, scope, deliverables, resource capacity, project goals, and stakeholders' satisfaction.

Timeline. Table 2 shows the program's development, application, and landfill over time. It includes a description of each phase, a completion date, and the tracking system that will be used to track progress.

Table 2. C.A.S.H. Program development timetable

Phase	Description	End date
Planning	Finalizing the project's papers, schedule, action plan, and budget.	March 2023
Active training	Getting the staff involved in structured activities, training, and events that support the learning process.	March 2024-2026
Marketing	Selection of target audience: key community stakeholders and patient advocacy groups and involvement in the project.	December 2027
Completion of reporting system	Establishing the systemwide application program and inspecting the finished work	December 2027

Budget. To successfully implement the C.A.S.H. program, we need two types of training: bystander training for clinicians, support staff, and administrators, and "men as allies" training for the same groups. The next budget outlines a 5-year budget request to train 2,350 staff in one year and provide refresher training for potential staff and new staff entering the Sun Health system. The suggested goal of 35 people per training session results in 67 training sessions in one year at $66 per employee. Across the entire Sunshine Health system (three hospitals), we require 22 training sessions per hospital. Each hospital will add three trainers to its facility-level human resources department to help conduct training sessions, collect materials, and work closely with nursing staff to minimize workflow disruptions. Each year, marketing materials are produced for the Bystander Training and Men as Allies programs. Key community stakeholders and patient advocacy groups will be invited to attend training sessions using the same marketing materials. Posters and booklets will be printed and provided to all clinical floors in the three hospitals, and posters will be displayed inwards and in common areas. Figure 4 shows the allocation of costs for two training, policy reform, and others. 74% of the total cost of the C.A.S.H. program is allocated to Bystander Training and Men as Allies training; policy reform represents 13% of the total cost, followed by 13% of indirect operating costs and contingency.

Figure 4. Budget composition C.A.S.H. program

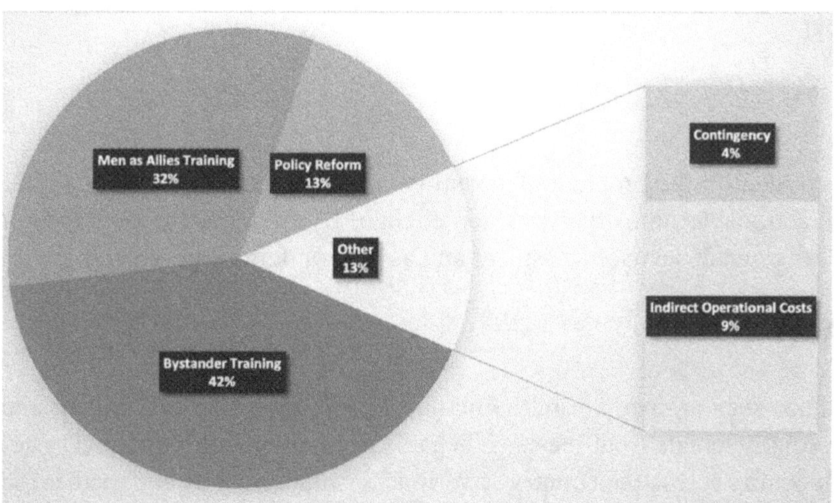

Table 3. C.A.S.H. Program budget for sunshine health

Programme Resources	Years (U.S. Dollars)					Total
	1	2	3	4	5	
Bystander Training	$ 87,600	$ 35,325	$ 35,325	$ 35,325	$ 35,300	$228,875
Men as Allies Training	$ 67,700	$ 48,700	$ 48,700	$ 48,700	$ 48,700	$262,500
Policy Reform	$ 28,200	$ 22,050	$ 14,625	$ 14,625	$ 12,600	$ 92,100
Contingency	$ 9,175	$ 5,304	$ 4,933	$ 4,933	$ 4,730	$ 29,075
Indirect Operational Costs	$ 18,350	$ 10,608	$ 9,865	$ 9,865	$ 9,460	$ 58,148
Total	$ 211,025	$ 121,987	$ 113,448	$ 113,448	$ 110,790	
Project Total	$ 670,698					

It is essential to note that the money spent on training and marketing will decrease after the first year, as we reduce the number of training sessions and required materials. The same trainers who conduct the "Bystander Training" will also conduct the "Men as Allies" training, which will save Sunshine Health money. The total cost of the two training sessions over the next five years is $491,375 (Table 3). In addition to suggested training and marketing materials, we will update Sunshine Health's human resources policies to help identify, track, and respond to sexual harassment of clinicians and patients within the healthcare system. The revamp will include meetings at each facility to review current policies, identify gaps, interview employees, research industry standards, and determine appropriate sexual assault and harassment tracking systems. Table 3 displays that the total cost of policy reform is $92,100 over five years, with costs declining after the first year, as well the contingency budget is 5 percent of the total budget of $29,075 over five years. These funds will help cover any unexpected costs that may arise. We also included 10% overhead operating costs over five years, or $58,148 (Table 3). These funds will help pay for space, utilities, back-office staff, and other activities that contribute to the overall success of our programs. As disclosed in Table 3, the total amount for the entire project is about $670,698 across a five-year implementation and execution period.

CONCLUSION

The Crisis

It is not enough to identify the problem of sexual harassment and assault among female providers but rather to impose actionable items that produce change. By utilizing the organizational development perspective, we can combat sexual harassment and assault on female providers.

Our Call to Action

Sunshine Health has seen an increase in the number (23%) of sexual harassment claims from female clinical staff, especially female frontline staff. What is happening at this hospital system is likely a mirror of what is happening across the country at various hospital systems and medical schools which is a public health and safety crisis.

Our Solution

Combating Assault and Sexual Harassment (C.A.S.H.) Program Implementation and Execution:

- Bystander Empowerment Training in the Workforce is about training bystanders to address situations where they witness harassment.
- Men as Allies Training in the Workforce is about training men to support women in the workplace.
- A reporting system for anonymous complaints:
- One of the most effective solutions to combat workplace sexual harassment is the implementation of comprehensive workplace policies (Bosman et al., 2019). These policies should include definitions of what constitutes sexual harassment, examples of prohibited conduct, and clear instructions on how to report incidents. Additionally, the policy should clearly explain how complaints will be investigated and how perpetrators will be held accountable (Cook et al., 2019). Employers must also provide ongoing training and education on sexual harassment and resources for employees who experience it (Cook et al., 2019).
- In addition to comprehensive policies, the organization should create a workplace culture of respect and inclusion (Cook et al., 2019). This can be accomplished through various tactics, such as creating an environment where everyone is respected, discouraging jokes and other inappropriate behavior, and providing leadership role models who promote a culture of respect (Cook et al., 2019). Additionally, the organization should ensure that women's voices are heard and their contributions are recognized.
- The organization should also ensure that any complaints of sexual harassment are taken seriously and acted upon promptly (Cook et al., 2019). This includes providing a safe and confidential way for employees to report incidents and establishing procedures for investigating and addressing complaints. Employers must also protect victims from retaliation by not punishing or penalizing them for reporting incidents (Cook et al., 2019).
- The organization should consider implementing anonymous surveys to assess the prevalence of sexual harassment in the workplace (Cook et al., 2019). This can help employers identify the specific types of behavior that are most prevalent, as well as the areas in which they need to take steps to reduce or eliminate it. It can also help employers identify areas to improve their policies and procedures.

By changing the organizational policies, procedures, structure, and culture, hospitals like Sunshine Health can eliminate sexual harassment and assault by creating an environment that will not tolerate the behavior and encourages victims *and* bystanders to act.

In light of an escalating number of reports documenting sexual harassment within the domains of healthcare and medical education, this article cogently addresses a pressing crisis that has long remained inadequately acknowledged. Sexual harassment's traumatic repercussions, comprehensively substantiated within the literature, are particularly disconcerting when transposed onto the healthcare and medical education landscape. Yet, it is this very setting where this issue has been predominantly obscured, cultivating an environment shrouded in silence and bereft of efficacious remedies. The cumulative impact of these dynamics represents a formidable challenge to the status quo, demanding decisive and innovative interventions.

This article embarks on an insightful exploration of the pervasiveness of sexual harassment within the healthcare and medical education arenas. It underscores the urgency of devising innovative solutions and preventive strategies to address this distressing concern. Through a meticulous review of existing literature, the article meticulously dissects the multifaceted manifestations of sexual harassment in these contexts, illuminates the extensive ramifications borne by the victims, and critiques the conspicuous dearth of effective preventative measures.

The culmination of this scholarly endeavor lies in a thought-provoking discussion of innovative solutions and prevention strategies. Drawing inspiration from the pioneering initiatives undertaken by a management consulting group at Sunshine Health Regional Hospital and Medical Education Training Center, a healthcare institution that has grappled with its own sexual harassment crisis, this article strives to illuminate a path forward. The intent, undeniably noble, is to effectuate transformative change within the realm of practice.

In closing, this article stands as a potent testament to the crisis of addressing sexual harassment in healthcare and medical education. Its rigorous analysis of the issue's scope, consequences, and dearth of solutions makes a compelling case for action. By delving into innovative interventions, it beckons practitioners and stakeholders to confront this crisis with purpose and determination, ultimately striving to engender a safer, more equitable environment for all within the healthcare and medical education domains.

REFERENCES

Albert-Henry, T. (2018, August 2). *3 significant ethical issues medical school does not prepare you for. American Medical Association.* AMA. https://www.ama-assn.org/education/accelerating-change-medical-education/3-big-ethical-issues-medical-school-doesn-t-prepare

American Medical Association. (2018). Sexual harassment in medicine: An analysis of surveys, A.M.A. policies, and best practices. AMA. https://www.ama-assn.org/system/files/2019-03/sexual-harassment-medicine.pdf

Ansari, A. (2020). Prevalence of sexual harassment in medical education: A systematic review. *Journal of Medical Education and Curricular Development*, *7*(1), 1–7.

Binder, R. (2018). *Sexual harassment in medical schools: The challenge of covert retaliation as a barrier to reporting.* L.W.W. https://journals.lww.com/academicmedicine/Fulltext/2018/12000/Sexual_Harassment_in_Medical_Schools__The.17.aspx

Burke, W. W. (2018). Organization change: Theory & practice. *Sage (Atlanta, Ga.).*

Cheung-Judge, M., & Holbeche, L. (2021). *Organization development: A practitioner's guide for O.D. and H.R* (3rd ed.). Kogan Page.

Collins, K. (2020). Sexual harassment in medical education and healthcare workplaces. *Nursing Forum*, *55*(4), 573–580.

Dai, H., Milkman, K. L., & Riis, J. (2014). The fresh start effect: Temporal landmarks motivate aspirational behavior. *Management Science*, *60*(10), 2563–2582. doi:10.1287/mnsc.2014.1901

Dobbin, F., & Kalev, A. (2019). The promise and peril of sexual harassment programs. *Proceedings of the National Academy of Sciences, 116*(25), 12255–12260. 10.1073/pnas.1818477116

Fabiano, P. M., Perkins, H. W., Berkowitz, A., Linkenbach, J., & Stark, C. (2003). Engaging men as social justice allies in ending violence against women: Evidence for a social norms approach. *Journal of American College Health, 52*(3), 105–112. doi:10.1080/07448480309595732 PMID:14992295

Fenwick, K. M., Dyer, K. E., Klap, R., Oishi, K., Moreau, J. L., Yano, E. M., Bean-Mayberry, B., Sadler, A. G., & Hamilton, A. B. (2022). Expert recommendations for designing reporting systems to address patient-perpetrated sexual harassment in healthcare settings. *Journal of General Internal Medicine, 37*(14), 3723–3730. doi:10.100711606-022-07467-8 PMID:35266124

Gardiner, P. (2016). Sexual harassment in healthcare: Prevalence, prevention, and response. *Nursing Standard, 30*(31), 8–13.

Gardner, S., & Johnson, P. R. (2001). Sexual harassment in healthcare: Strategies for employers. *Hospital Topics, 79*(4), 5–11. http://libproxy.lib.unc.edu/login?url=https://www.proquest.com/scholarly-journals/sexual-harassment-healthcare-strategies-employers/docview/214588405/se-2. doi:10.1080/00185860109597912 PMID:11942090

Headley, M. (2020). Creating a culture that puts an end to sexual harassment in healthcare. *Medical Environment Update, 30*(3), 6–8. http://libproxy.lib.unc.edu/login?url=https://www.proquest.com/trade-journals/creating-culture-that-puts-end-sexual-harassment/docview/2355327831/se-2

Jagsi, R., Griffith, K. A., Jones, R., Perumalswami, C. R., Ubel, P., & Stewart, A. (2016). Sexual Harassment and Discrimination Experiences of Academic Medical Faculty. *Journal of the American Medical Association, 315*(19), 2120. doi:10.1001/jama.2016.2188 PMID:27187307

James, K. (2021, April 8). Bystander training: The best defense against sexual harassment. *The Energy Law Blog*. https://www.theenergylawblog.com/2021/04/articles/business/employment-law/bystander-training-the-best-defense-against-sexual-harassment/ doi:10.7326/M18-2047

Jamieson, D. W., & Milbrandt, J. M. (2018). Peter B. Vaill: A life in the art of managing and leading change. The Palgrave Handbook of Organizational Change Thinkers, 1, 26. doi:10.1007/978-3-319-49820-1_60-2

Lilia, M. C. & Reshma, J. (2018). What Can Medicine Learn From Social Science Studies of Sexual Harassment? *Ann Intern Med., 169*, 716-717. doi:10.7326/M18-2047

Mikulak, A. (Ed.). (2022, February 22). *Women's experiences of sexual assault and harassment linked with high blood pressure*. National Institute of Mental Health. https://www.nimh.nih.gov/news/science-news/2022/womens-experiences-of-sexual-assault-and-harassment-linked-with-high-blood-pressure

Nadeau, K. (2021, February). *New data show that the majority of U.S. medical students are women.* MLO. https://www.mlo-online.com/21206907.

Nguyen, T. H., Bui, T. T. T., Nguyen, A. T. T., Pham, T. H., Ngo, T. H., Bui, T. T., & Hong, N. X. (2019). Prevalence of sexual harassment among medical students in Vietnam: A cross-sectional survey. *BMC Medical Education, 19*(1), 1–9. PMID:30606170

Notaro, E., Pascoe, V. L., Hippe, D. S., Lachance, K., Shinohara, M. M., & DeNiro, K. L. (2021). Prevalence of sexual harassment and sexual assault from patient to provider among women in dermatology and across specialties. *International Journal of Women's Dermatology*, *7*(3), 270–275. doi:10.1016/j.ijwd.2020.10.006 PMID:34222582

Phillips, S. P., & Schneider, M. S. (1993). Sexual harassment of female doctors by patients. *The New England Journal of Medicine*, *329*(26), 1936–1939. doi:10.1056/NEJM199312233292607 PMID:8247058

Reinicke, K. (2022). *Men after #MeToo: Being an ally in the fight against sexual harassment.* Springer Nature Switzerland.

Robinson, R. K., Geralyn, M. F., Tinney, C. H., Crow, S. M., & Hartman, S. J. (2005). Sexual harassment in the workplace: Guidelines for educating healthcare managers. *Journal of health and human services administration.* https://pubmed.ncbi.nlm.nih.gov/16318016/

SAMHSA. (2020). *National Guidelines for Behavioral Health Crisis Care.* SAMHSA. https://www.samhsa.gov/sites/default/files/national-guidelines-for-behavioral-health-crisis-care-02242020.pdf

Smith, D.G., Johnson W.B. (2017). Lots of men are gender-equality allies in private. Why not in public? *Harward Business Review.*

Stone, L., Phillips, C., & Douglas, K. A. (2019). Sexual assault and harassment of doctors, by doctors: A qualitative study. *Medical Education*, *53*(8), 833–843. doi:10.1111/medu.13912 PMID:31144346

Ulusoy, H., Swigart, V., & Erdemir, F. (2011). Think globally, act locally: Understanding sexual harassment from a cross-cultural perspective. *Medical Education*, *45*(6), 603–612. doi:10.1111/j.1365-2923.2010.03918.x PMID:21501219

White, C. (2019). *Three ways to create a work culture that brings out the best in employees.* T.E.D. Talk. https://www.ted.com/talks/chris_white_3_ways_to_create_a_work_culture_that_brings_out_the_best_in_employees

Chapter 8
Portfolio Analysis of COVID-19-Related Patents Using CRITIC-Based TOPSIS Approach

Fatma Altuntas
https://orcid.org/0000-0001-8644-5876
Department of Management, Istanbul Topkapi University, Turkey

ABSTRACT

Many firms are unaware of which patent is comparatively more important in their patent portfolio. A firm needs to prioritize patents in terms of effective management of its patent portfolio and efficient allocation of resources. The COVID-19 pandemic was one of the most impactful disasters affecting daily human life in the last century. It is critical to evaluate and prioritize technologies developed to reduce the impact of this pandemic. To this end, patents related to COVID-19 are prioritized with the CRITIC-based TOPSIS approach in this study. 935 patents-related data were obtained from the USPTO (United States Patent and Trademark Office) patent database. To the best of the authors' knowledge, there is no study in the literature that uses the CRITIC-based TOPSIS approach to prioritize patents for the COVID-19 pandemic. The results of this study showed decision-makers and investors can consider technologies related to anti-infectives, medicinal preparations containing organic active substances, and medicinal preparations with a special physical form as investment options.

1. INTRODUCTION

A country's technological competitive advantage has a great impact on its economic development. Competitive advantage will be achieved not only with material and monetary resources but also with the right management of intellectuality (Haykır, 2011). Patents are important indicators of technological development and are one of the most important intellectual capital information guiding technological development. They are used to following the industry or technology under concern. On the other hand, today's knowledge economies are largely based on the production, effective use of resources, and dissemination of knowledge (Alper, 2011). Patents must be used to track value-creating activities. A similar

DOI: 10.4018/978-1-6684-9522-3.ch008

situation exists in enterprises. The competition that exists among business institutions in the market place is heating up with the great harmony of the world economy (Yuan and Song, 2022). Some enterprises invest significantly in training human resources to properly manage their patent portfolios (Grimaldi et al., 2015). The position of countries in the macro area may develop depending on the setting of micro-enterprises. The reason for this is that when a business owns a patent, it first uses it to get ahead of the competition, but as time passes, it may provide financial benefits in practice due to methods such as licensing, technology transfer, and tax reductions (Yavuz and Baki, 2019).

Economic globalization highlights the need for science and technology businesses to improve their research, intellectual capability, and intellectual property strategies (Lei et al., 2021). Hence, the company-level patent portfolio provides useful information for evaluating overall R&D plans (Huang, 2016). It is emphasized that patent portfolio is very significant tool because this portfolio can be used to develop implications for R&D in companies (Ernst, 1998). Mouritsen and Koleva (2015) claim that the value of a company's stock on the capital market is strongly positively connected with information regarding patents. In determining the economic value of knowledge-intensive companies, the correct evaluation of patents depends on the right patent management system (Grimaldi et al., 2015). Barbazza et al. (2015) highlight that regarding intellectual property, ranking and selecting patents is crucial. Both the financial and non-financial criteria set can be considered in patent prioritization (Collan et al., 2013).

Businesses and nations need to examine the pandemic not only as a biological condition but also from a technological perspective. To overcome the COVID-19 pandemic, new technologies have been developed and demand for these technologies has arisen (WIPO, 2022).

Patent documents are good indicators for evaluating related technologies. In this study, the prioritization of the patents related to the COVID-19 pandemic is conducted using multi-criteria decision-making (MCDM) techniques. Among the methods, the CRITIC (The CRiteria Importance Through Intercriteria Correlation)-based TOPSIS (The Technique for Order of Preference by Similarity to Ideal Solution) method is applied to the patent selection process. The CRITIC method is used to find out the criteria's weight, which refers to the importance of the criteria. The TOPSIS method is extensively performed for the solution of selection and prioritization problems in real life.

The research question (RQ) of this study is stated as follows:

RQ: How should the patent selection be for an investor who wants to invest in developing technologies related to the COVID-19 pandemic?

The contribution of this study to literature is presented as follows.

i. No study prioritizes the COVID-19 pandemic-related patents in the literature.

ii. While ranking the patents with MCDM techniques in the literature, different criteria are used in almost every study, the criteria used in this study can be used in the evaluation of all patents granted in practice.

iii. This study is carried out with CPC (Corporate Patent Classification) codes. CPC codes were developed in 2013 for use as a universal patent classification tool (Jotisakulratana et al., 2013). Because CPC codes are crucial in establishing the technology covered by patents (Altuntas et al., 2020). CPC codes are also used to indicate technical areas where patents can be applied. (Erdogan et al., 2022). All existing studies in the literature are using the IPC (International Patent Classification) codes. Since CPC codes are the most up-to-date and broader classification tools, they are used in this study. Section descriptions of 9 CPC codes are given in Table 1.

Alshrari et al. (2022) reviewed the patent literature of COVID-19 vaccines using Patentscope and Espacenet databases. In another study, Keestra et al. (2022) researched university patenting and licensing practices in the United Kingdom during the first year of the COVID-19 pandemic. Bachmann and Frutos-Bencze (2022) examined the role of universities with respect to R&D and innovation efforts during the COVID-19 pandemic. de Araujo Andrade et al. (2021) conducted a patent analysis for patents related to the protective mask for technology evaluation. Durmusoglu and Durmusoglu (2022) focused respiratory technologies which are quite important technologies during the COVID pandemic such as medical ventilators and masks and conducted the topic modeling technique for analysis of patents granted in the field of medical respiratory technologies. Falciola and Barbieri (2022) researched and analyzed patent-relevant COVID-19 information. In addition, the use of patent information for the management of innovation is quite significant to better respond the cirses (Guderian et al., 2021). Patent documents are the documents that companies must effectively manage in their innovation management processes. Firms' innovation management and decision making process are highly affected by crises such as the COVID-19 pandemic (Guderian et al., 2021). In times of crisis and disaster, companies should determine which patents to invest in order to turn the current competitive environment into an opportunity. They can reduce the negative impacts of crises and disasters on the company by effectively managing their patent portfolios. Additionally, since patent documents are used to identify trends in technological developments, monitoring and prioritizing patents related to a specific crisis or disaster during those times will also enable the firm to explore technological opportunities.

An open system is one that can provide material, energy, and information transfers from its working environment (Yenisu et al., 2019). As open systems, businesses are always interacting with their environment (Akkuş and İzci 2018). Since businesses are in the structured of open system theory, they are adversely affected by major health crises such as pandemic. "Pandemics are periods of crisis and disaster during which companies prioritize and evaluate their investments and seek new opportunities. In this period, companies strive to seize every crisis as an opportunity, and therefore patent data is one of the most effective sources of information that can be utilized to capture these opportunities.

During the pandemic period, people stay away from social life with quarantine applications. With quarantine applications, isolated from social life, intensification of R&D studies and intense brain training, technologies can develop rapidly. Development evolutions of past patent researches should be examined in case of possible health crisis in future periods. The patent prioritization discussed in this study is also expected to provide insight into future research. In addition, patent searches can be a good strategy tool for investors who see investment as an opportunity in times of crisis and expect good timing. In this study, a multi-criteria decision-making-based application is implemented to enable companies to achieve effective distribution of investments during crisis periods by prioritizing their investment alternatives. This application is based on identifying and prioritizing patents in the field related to the crisis and disaster that have occurred.

There is a big time difference between the 1918 pandemic and the Covid-19 pandemic. This long time can put distances in terms of technology development. Due to long distances, the technologies used for the pandemic are out of date. It's impossible to know when the next pandemic might happen, but policymakers can plan first actions when faced with a major outbreak. Governments, on the other hand, can first predict the investments to be made and the direction of technological opportunities in the measures to be taken. Patent research is the basis of these predictions. The health crisis has the feature of spreading extremely fast. For this reason, all manual and technology-supported measures must be carried out in an agile manner. The right decision, the right plan, the right timing, the right strategies

Table 1. Section descriptions of CPC codes (www.epo.org)

A	Human necessities
B	Performing operations, transporting
C	Chemistry, metallurgy
D	Textiles, paper
E	Fixed constructions
F	Mechanical engineering, lighting, heating, weapons, blasting engines or pumps
G	Physics
H	Electricity
Y	General tagging of new technological developments; general tagging of cross-sectional technologies spanning over several sections of the IPC, technical subjects covered by former USPC cross-reference art collections and digests

should be supported by the right investments. All the right investments to be made are possible within the framework of patent research.

Early warning, early intervention, early technological initiatives add value to people's lives when there is a health crisis. Early technological initiatives can be initiated as a result of patent searches. However, it can be effective in deciding where to start early intervention practices. While struggling with the health crisis, governments will definitely have a foresight, but it is thought that patent research should be based on accurate predictions. In the health crisis, technological advances add value to society and human life as it provides welfare in society However, these technological advances are very difficult to realize at the time of the health crisis. Continuous monitoring of patent analyzes will shed light on technological advances before a crisis occur.

The remaining parts of this study were organized as follows: Within the scope of the study, the literature about our keywords was searched and included in Section 1. The method is explained in Section 3. Prioritization of patent documents is provided in Section 4. Results are evaluated and suggestions are made for future researchers in Section 5.

2. LITERATURE REVIEW

Literature on the application of MCDM techniques to patent documents is presented in this section. Table 2 lists the criteria that were applied in the literature. Patents are one of the important milestones in increasing the competitiveness of businesses, and some companies use patents to protect their intellectual property over the long term (Lei et al. 2021). The use of MCDM techniques is utilized to manage the patent portfolio of companies in literature. Among these studies, the TOPSIS method is employed because it is a widely used in-group comprehensive evaluation method that can fully benefit from the original data (Lei et al. 2021). Collan et al. (2013) developed a decision support system to rank patent documents based on experts' opinions using TOPSIS and AHP (Analytic Hierarchy Process) framework. Luukka and Collan (2016) used a similarity based TOPSIS for patent selection. In another study, Luukka (2020) proposed a new TOPSIS approach based on n-ary norm operators and applied it to the patent selection problem. Huang and Liu (2018) evaluated patent quality using the entropy weight method and improved TOPSIS. Additionally, Weiling and Hao (2018) assessed patent portfolios using the TOPSIS-

Entropy method. Ernst (1998) explained how to manage patent portfolios that serve to make research and development decisions for high-level important applications. Yuan and Song (2022) used a patent document in the field of solar cells and used an entropy-based TOPSIS approach to evaluate companies' technological innovation capabilities. Huang (2016) used the TOPSIS method for patent portfolio analysis. Mukundan et al. (2019) performed AHP–TOPSIS to rank a firm's patents. In addition, Yavuz and Baki (2019) used entropy, TOPSIS, and VIKOR (VlseKriterijumska Optimizacija I Kompromisno Resenje) methods to rank a firm's patents. Deniz (2020) utilized MOORA VE ARAS methods for the prioritization of patent data obtained from the study of Yavuz and Baki (2019). Zhao et al. (2022) found out core patents using entropy based TOPSIS method. Additionally, Wang and Hsieh (2015) and Fan et al. (2023) used several criteria for patent evaluation.

The COVID-19 pandemic has affected people's habits (nutrition, shopping, cleaning, education, sports, in almost every area of our active working life) to a surprising extent. Major pandemics and epidemics impacted humanity, including the plague, cholera, flu, severe acute respiratory syndrome coronavirus (SARS-CoV), and Middle East respiratory syndrome coronavirus (MERS-CoV) (Piret and Boivin, 2021). The Pandemic has a long history and the pandemic affected many area in daily life negatively, such as health, economies, and even national security in the World (Qui et al., 2017). Details on pandemic throughout history can be found in Piret and Boivin (2021), Saunders-Hastings and Krewski (2016).

Bloom et al. (2021) highlight that the number of patent applications with technology content that supports working from home increased due to the COVID-19 pandemic. These situations created an opportunity to turn the crisis into an opportunity (Do et al., 2021). It is predicted that the COVID-19 pandemic's effects will continue for years (Imran et al., 2021). Due to this influence, our relations with technology have gained a different direction. According to our old information, while the harms of spending too much time in front of the screen and with electronic devices are emphasized, it is thought that we have started to live with technologies that make our lives easier today. Some patent researches are available in the literature which is among the studies evaluated in the field of technology presented by Lee et al., (2009), and Kim and Bae (2017).

It is emphasized that data-driven patent analytics should be relied on instead of ad hoc decisions to overcome crises such as the COVID-19 pandemic (Guderian et al., 2021). It is noteworthy that the patent research conducted in the literature on the COVID-19 pandemic is generally related to the vaccine structure, vaccine development, and clinical research (e.g., Imran et al. (2021); Alshrari et al. (2022); Zhuang et al. (2020); Storz, 2022), Rogosnitzky et al. (2020), Jaber et al. (2022).

In addition, studies applying MCDM techniques to various COVID-19 pandemic-related issues have also been examined in the literature. Among these studies, the selection of a COVID-19 diagnostic model (Mohammed et al., (2020), the evaluation of asymptomatic COVID-19 carriers (Albahri et al., 2021), prioritizing Covid-19 patients (Albahri et al., 2021), evaluation of quarantine decisions during the Covid-19 pandemic (Altuntas and Gok, 2021), evaluation of critical decisions for the government during the Covid-19 pandemic (Alkan and Kahraman, 2021), and determination of risk factors (Majumder et al., 2020) were examined in the literature.

Literature on the use of CRITIC and TOPSIS method is given in Table 3. As it can be seen from Table 3, integrating CRITIC and TOPSIS method has been performed frequently in the literature for evaluation, assessment, and selection problems.

As can be seen from the above literature review, the patent selection problem is extensively researched in detail. However, COVID-19 pandemic-related patent documents are not examined in detail. In this study, citation score, legal score, technology score, claim count, priority count, number of coopera-

Table 2. Criteria used in literature

Author(s) (Year)	Criteria
Yuan and Song (2022)	Total Number of Patents, Total Number of Core Patents, Patent Growth Rate, The average number of family patents, The average number of inventors, The average number of IPC, The average number of citing patents, The average number of patents cited, The average number of articles cited, The average patent age
Deniz (2020); Yavuz, and Baki (2019)	Number of claims, Remaining life of the patent, Patent family size, IPC code, Product life cycle, Potential market share, Difficulty of violation detection method, Technological level, Objection status, Number of backward citation, Time until registration, Number of competitors
Weiling and Hao (2018)	Total Number of Patents, Patent Growth Rate, Total Number of Core Patents, Average Number of Patents Cited, Average Number of Examiner Citations, Average Number of Citation Instances, Average Scope of Technology Coverage, Current Impact Index, Average Number of Inventors, Average Patent Maintenance Time, Average Number of Claims, Average Number of Patents in the Same Family, Average Time Interval from Patent, Application to Being Made Public
Huang and Liu (2018)	The number of backward citations, The number of forward citations, The number of non-patent literature citations, The number of IPC, The number of USPC, Priority period, The number of claims, The number of patent family members, The number of inventors, Legal Status
Huang(2016)	Patent activity, Patent quality

tive patent classification codes, reverse cites, and forward cites criteria are considered to rank patent documents related to the COVID-19 pandemic of a firm. These criteria were employed to perform the CRITIC-based TOPSIS approach.

3. METHOD AND METHODOLOGY

In this research application, the CRITIC method is used to determine criterion weights. Then, the patent portfolio is evaluated with the TOPSIS approach.

Table 3. Literature on the use of CRITIC and TOPSIS method

Author(s) (Year)	Method	Problem
Yuan et al. (2023)	CRITIC-TOPSIS	Evaluating English media analytics
Onocak (2023)	CRITIC-TOPSIS	Financial performance assessment
Lin et al. (2023)	CRITIC-TOPSIS	Evaluation of an activity in online health interventions
Wang et al. (2023)	CRITIC-TOPSIS	Evaluation of Smart Community Safety
Yu et al. (2023)	CRITIC-TOPSIS	Component detection in transmission media/lines
Gaur et al. (2023)	CRITIC-TOPSIS	Stakeholder assessment in construction projects
Yin et al. (2023)	CRITIC-TOPSIS	Evaluation of smart community governance
Ertemel et al. (2023)	Pythagorean Fuzzy CRITIC-TOPSIS	Smartphone addiction assessment
Liu and Yang (2023)	CRITIC-TOPSIS	Evaluation of innovation capacity of high-tech industries
Li et al. (2023)	CRITIC-TOPSIS	Evaluating human-computer interaction education
Thakkar et al. (2022)	CRITIC-TOPSIS	Selection of power generation technology
Gurrala et al. (2022)	CRITIC-TOPSIS	Edible packaging selection
Bhadra et al. (2022)	AHP-TOPSIS and CRITIC-TOPSIS	Selection of the natural fiber
Saxena et al. (2022)	CRITIC-TOPSIS	Selection of software reliability growth model
Dhara et al. (2022)	CRITIC-TOPSIS	Selection of very light business jet
Li et al. (2022)	AHP-CRITIC-TOPSIS	Evaluation of the effectiveness of VOC-contaminated soil preparation
Kalvakolanu et al. (2022)	Entropy, CRITIC and TOPSIS	Measuring job satisfaction level
Saravanakumar et al. (2022)	CRITIC-TOPSIS	Selection of oil and best bio-diesel blend
Akandere and Zerenler (2022)	CRITIC-TOPSIS	Evaluation of the environmental and economic performance of countries
Tandon et al. (2022)	CRITIC-TOPSIS	Evaluation of the source code of the sixteen versions of the open-source software
Zhang et al. (2022)	CRITIC-TOPSIS	Spare parts importance evaluation
Aydın (2021)	CRITIC-TOPSIS	Evaluation of regional health services in Türkiye
Erkılıç (2021)	CRITIC-TOPSIS	Evaluating the financial performance of hospital services
Gupta et al. (2021)	CRITIC-TOPSIS	Assessment of stress level in urban area's during COVID-19 outbreak
Mohamadghasemi et al. (2020)	Multiobjective stochastic CRITIC–TOPSIS	The shipboard crane selection
Xu et al. (2020)	CRITIC-TOPSIS	Dynamic radiator threat assessment
Wu et al. (2020)	CRITIC-TOPSIS	Construction safety risk assessment of bridges
Yang et al. (2019)	CRITIC-TOPSIS	Evaluation of distributed energy generation projects
Slebi-Acevedo et al. (2019)	CRITIC-TOPSIS	Multi-Response Optimization of Porous Asphalt Mixtures Reinforced with Aramid and Polyolefin Fibers
Işıl (2019)	CRITIC, TOPSIS, MULTIMOORA	Financial performance assessment
Babatunde and Ighravwe (2019)	CRITIC-TOPSIS	Hybrid renewable energy systems evaluation
Ighravwe et al. (2018)	CRITIC, TOPSIS, and WASPAS with interval type-2 fuzzy sets	Selection of a mini-grid business model
Rostamzadeh et al. (2018)	Fuzzy TOPSIS- CRITIC	Evaluation of sustainable supply chain risk management
Stanojković and Radovanović (2017)	CRITIC-TOPSIS	Selection of the best end mil
Kazan and Ozdemir (2014)	CRITIC-TOPSIS	Financial performance assessment

3.1 The TOPSIS Method

The TOPSIS technique is recognized as the proper method for rating the alternatives since it is founded on the idea of selecting the alternative that is the shortest distance from the positive ideal solution and the farthest distance from the negative ideal solution (Yavuz and Baki, 2019). In the literature, the TOPSIS approach is commonly employed to address prioritization problems. The TOPSIS method is given as Figure 1 in a stepwise manner based on Li et al. (2011):

3.2 The CRITIC Method

It is considered a weighting method in which the relative importance of the criteria is calculated objectively (Bulğurcu, 2019). The CRITIC approach is used to quantify the degree of conflict between two compared objectives based on the correlation coefficient *(Fan* et al. *(2021).* Akbulut (2019) presented the CRITIC method step by step as Figure 2:

4. ANALYSIS OF RESULTS

4.1. Data Acquisition and Data Preprocessing

Data acquisition and preprocessing are presented in this section. Figure 3 depicts the implementation details of this study. In Step 1, an extensive literature review on the COVID-19 pandemic was conducted. In Step 2, the keywords used for obtaining patent documents related to the COVID-19 pandemic were decided. These keywords are taken from the study of Falciola and Barbieri (2022) used for the research query which is given in Table 4.

In Step 3, patent documents are obtained by Acclaim IP software which is a patent search & analysis software. The USPTO (United States Patent and Trademark Office) database frequently used in the literature was employed to obtain patent data. In Step 4, the patents with a matching percentage of 80 and above with the query used in Table 4 are taken into account in this study. The reason and aim are to use patents that have a high relationship with the COVID-19 pandemic for the analysis. Accordingly, 12 alternative patents have been selected for analysis. A total of 8 criteria were determined for the application of MCDM approaches. In Step 5, the CRITIC method is used for the weighting process, which shows the importance level of the criteria. Then, the patents are prioritized by applying the TOPSIS method.

A total of 935 patents related to the COVID 19 pandemic are obtained from the USPTO database through the use of Acclaim IP software. The top 20 most frequently used CPC codes of these patents are shown in Figure 4. Accordingly, the top three most common CPC codes are A61P31, A61K31, and A61K9, respectively. Figure [4-6] is created using Acclaim IP software. The A61P31 CPC code relates to anti-infectives, ie antibiotics, antiseptics, and chemotherapeutics. A61K31 CPC code refers to medicinal preparations containing organic active substances. A61K9 relates to medicinal preparations with a special physical form.

Patent portfolio evaluation by CPC codes is illustrated in Figure 5. It shows the distribution of patents according to the density of CPC codes. As seen in Figure 5, between 2017 and 2019, there are no studies about COVID-19. It can be emphasized that the studies on COVID-19-related technologies started in 2020. The reason for this may be that World Health Organization announced the COVID-19 pandemic

Figure 1. The TOPSIS method steps

Step 1: Decision matrix is created. Decision matrix is denoted by A_{ij}. The basic structure of a m x n dimensional decision matrix is depicted in matrix (1).

i= alternative; i= 1, 2, . . . , m.

j= criterion; j=1, 2, . . . , n.

$$A_{ij}=\begin{bmatrix} a_{11} & \cdots & a_{1n} \\ \vdots & \ddots & \vdots \\ a_{m1} & \cdots & a_{mn} \end{bmatrix} \quad (1)$$

Step 2: Obtaining the normalized decision matrix. The normalized decision matrix is denoted by N_{ij} and calculated using Equation (2).

$$N_{ij} = \frac{a_{ij}}{\sqrt{\sum_{i=1}^{m} a_{ij}^2}} \quad (2)$$

The normalized decision matrix is denoted by N_{ij} and should be like a matrix depicted in Equation (3).

$$N_{ij} = \begin{bmatrix} n_{11} & \cdots & n_{1p} \\ \vdots & \ddots & \vdots \\ n_{m1} & \cdots & n_{mp} \end{bmatrix} \quad (3)$$

Step 3: Calculation of weighted normalized matrix. Each value of the normalized matrix is weighted with a value such as w_j; (j: 1, 2,..n). Herein, these weights are obtained from the CRITIC method. Calculation of weighted normalized matrix is calculated by Equation (4)

$$V_{ij}= (w_j{*}N_{ij}) \quad (4)$$

The weighted normalized matrix should be like a matrix depicted in Equation (5).

$$V_{ij} = \begin{bmatrix} w_{11}n_{11} & \cdots & w_{1p}n_{1p} \\ \vdots & \ddots & \vdots \\ w_{m1}n_{m1} & \cdots & w_{mp}n_{mp} \end{bmatrix} \quad (5)$$

Step 4: Calculating the positive ideal (A^+) and negative ideal (A^-) solution. The positive ideal (A^+) and negative ideal (A^-) solution are calculated using Equation (6) and (7), respectively.

$$A^+ = \{(max\ i\,V_{ij} | j \in J), (min\ i\,V_{ij} | j \in J')\}, \quad A^+ = \{v_1^+, \dots, v_n^+\} \quad (6)$$

$$A^- = \{(min\ i\,V_{ij} | j \in J), (max\ i\,V_{ij} | j \in J')\}, \quad A^- = \{v_1^-, \dots, v_n^-\} \quad (7)$$

Step 5: Determining the distances to the positive ideal (A^+) and negative ideal (A^-) points. The distance of each alternative from the positive ideal solution (Si^*) and the distance from the negative ideal solution (Si^-) are calculated based on Equation (8) and (9), respectively.

$$S_i^+ = \sqrt{\sum_{j=1}^{n} (v_{ij} - v_j^+)^2} \quad (8)$$

$$S_i^- = \sqrt{\sum_{j=1}^{n} (v_j - v_j^-)^2} \quad (9)$$

Step 6: Calculation of relative closeness to the ideal solution (Ci^*). Relative closeness to the ideal solution is calculated using Equation (10). The alternatives are sorted according to relative closeness to the ideal solution from the largest to the smallest.

$$C_i^+ = \frac{S_i^-}{S_i^- + S_i^+} \qquad 0 \leq C_i^+ \leq 1 \quad (10)$$

Figure 2. The CRITIC method steps

Step 1: The decision matrix is created. Decision matrix is denoted by X. Basic structure of a m x n dimensional decision matrix is depicted in Equation (11).

m = alternative; i= 1, 2, . . . , m.

n = criterion; j=1, 2, . . . , n.

$$X = \begin{bmatrix} x_{11} & \cdots & x_{1n} \\ \vdots & \ddots & \vdots \\ x_{1m} & \cdots & x_{mn} \end{bmatrix} \quad (11)$$

Step 2: Obtaining the normalized decision matrix. This matrix is calculated using Equations (12) and (13). It should be noted that benefit and cost oriented criteria are normalized using Equations (12) and (13), respectively.

$$r_{ij} = \frac{x_{ij} - x_j^{min}}{x_j^{max} - x_j^{min}} \quad (12)$$

$$r_{ij} = \frac{x_j^{max} - x_{ij}}{x_j^{max} - x_j^{min}} \quad (13)$$

where,

x_j^{min} : the lowest value of the j criterion

x_j^{max} : the highest value of the j criterion

Step 3: Creating the correlation coefficient matrix. After the criteria are normalized, the correlation matrix is designed in Step 3, the strength of the relations between the criteria was calculated (Akbulut, 2019: 253). The formula used to calculate the correlation matrix of the criteria is shown in Equation (14).

ρ_{jk} : correlation coefficient between criteria

$$\rho_{jk} = \frac{\sum_{i=1}^{m}(r_{ij} - r_j)(r_{ik} - r_k)}{\sqrt{\sum_{i=1}^{m}(r_{ij} - r_j)^2 \sum_{i=1}^{m}(r_{ik} - r_k)^2}} \quad j,k=1,2,3....n \quad (14)$$

Step 4: Calculation of C_j value. Equation (16) is used to determine the C_j value, which shows the total amount of information in the j criterion. Standard deviation of the criteria in the normalized matrix is calculated using Equation (15).

$$\sigma_j = \sqrt{\sum_1^m \frac{(r_{ij} - r_j)^2}{m}} \quad (15)$$

$$C_j = \sigma_j \sum_{k=1}^{n}(1 - t_{jk}), j = 1,2,3 \ldots n \quad (16)$$

where,

C_j : The total amount of information in the criteria,

σ_j : Standard deviation of the criteria in the normalized matrix.

t_{jk} : Correlation coefficient values of the criteria

Step 5: Calculation of Criterion Weights which are calculated using Equation (17).

$$W_j = \frac{C_j}{\sum_{k=1}^{n} C_k}, \ j,k = 1,2,3 \ldots\ldots, n \quad (17)$$

Wj: the weight of j-th criterion

Table 4. Research query

Research query	Patent Database
(covid-19 OR ("covid 19" OR (covid19 AND (SARS-CoV-2 OR (SARS-CoV2 OR (sarscov2 AND ("2019 ncov" OR (2019-n CoV OR (2019nCoV OR (covid-2019 OR ("covid 2019" OR (COVID2019 OR ("severe acute respiratory syndrome coronavirus 2" OR ("2019 novel coronavirus" OR ("coronavirus disease 2019" OR ("novel corona virus" OR ("novel coronavirus" OR ("new corona virus" OR "new coronavirus")))))))))))))))))	USPTO

Figure 3. Application steps

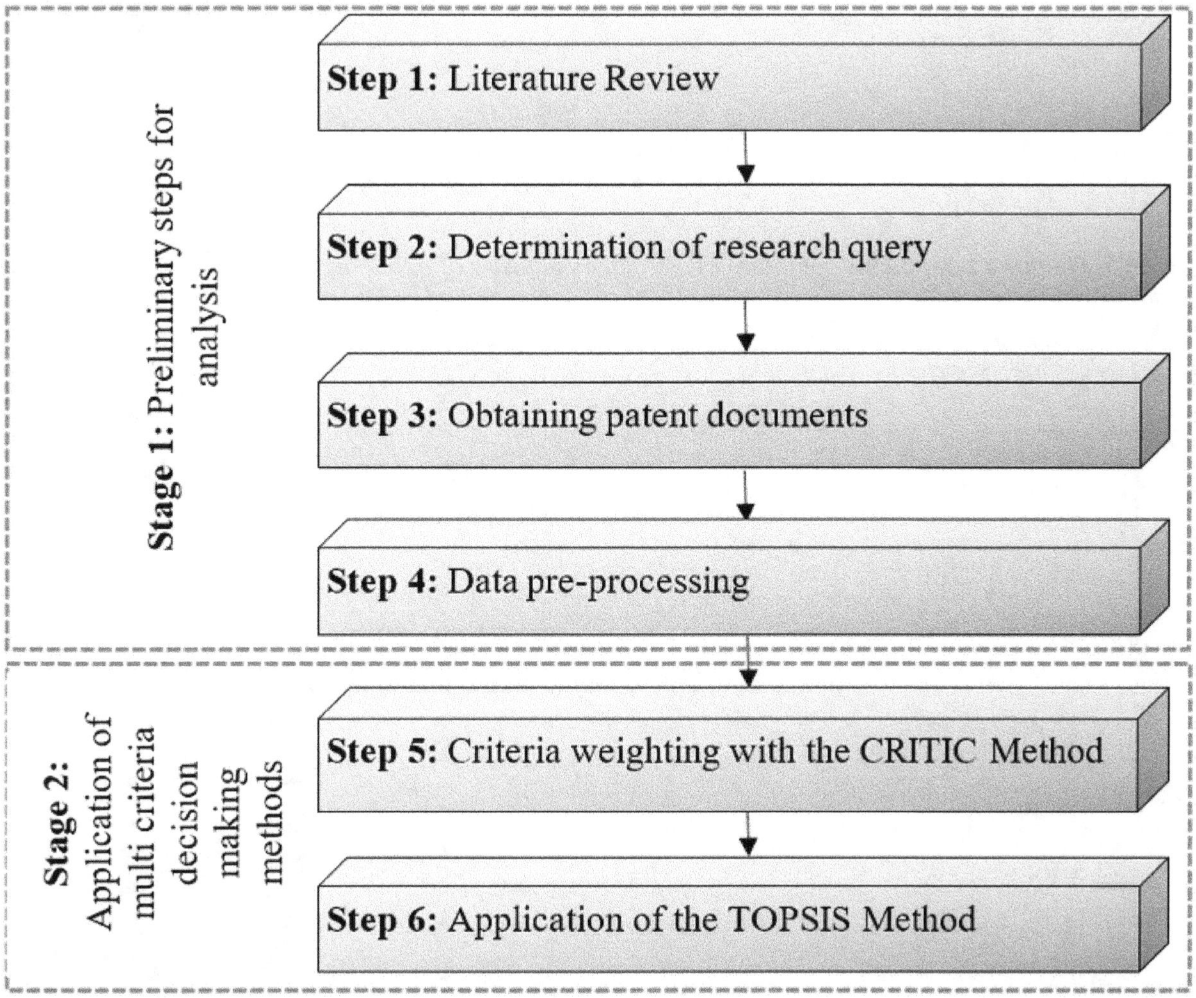

Figure 4. The top twenty most frequent CPC codes (AcclaimIP.com)

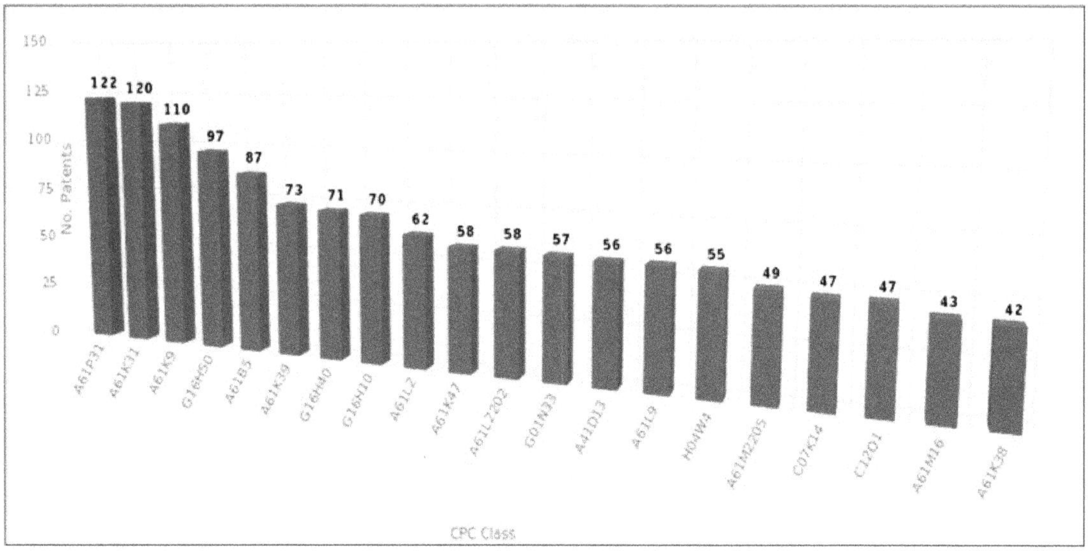

Figure 5. Quantities of patents containing CPC codes in years of publication (AcclaimIP.com)

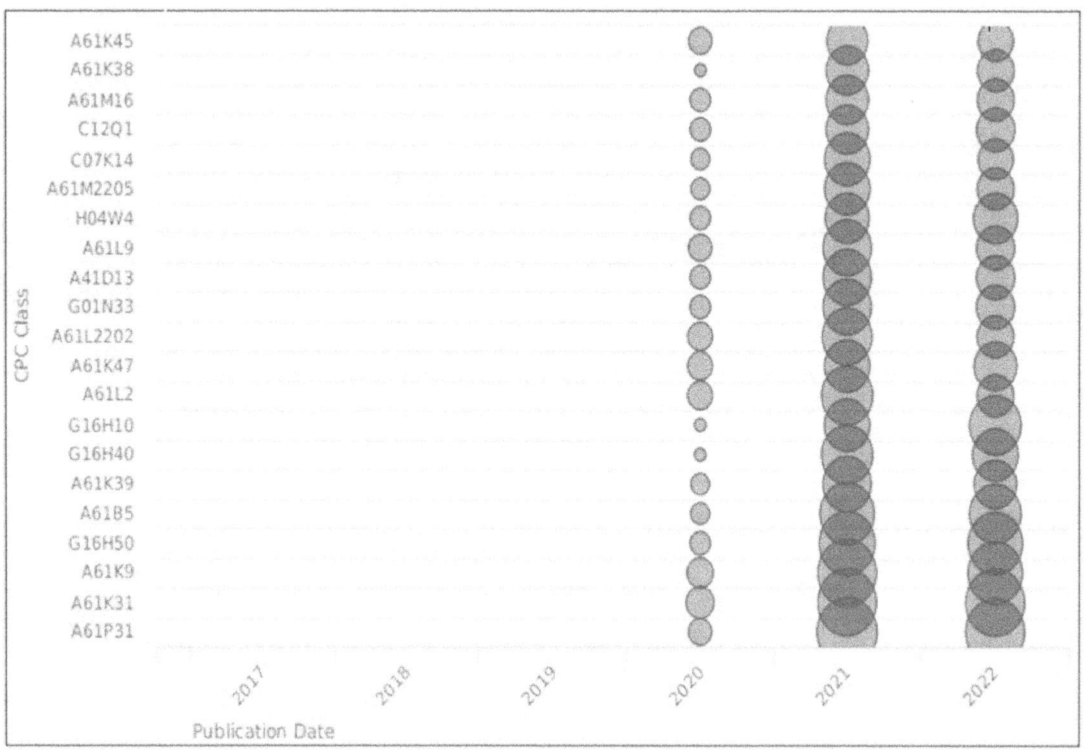

Figure 6. Word cloud of top 100 most relevant patents
(AcclaimIP.com)

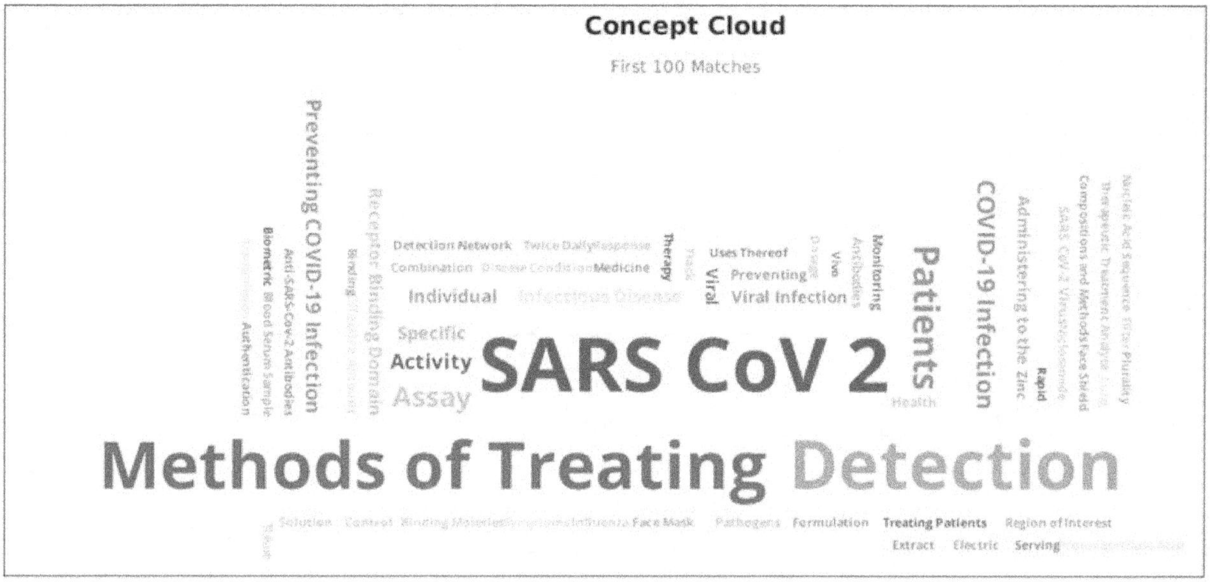

as a pandemic in 2020. The circles shown in Figure 5 represent the relative number of patents granted. Herein, among the patents received by the inventors in 2020, the patents granted related to the A61K31 code are more than the patents granted related to the A61P31 code. Another point that draws attention in Figure 5 is that G16H10, G16H40, and A61K38 CPC codes have the lowest number of patent documents, while the number of patent documents for these codes increased considerably in 2021. Quantities of patents containing CPC codes are based on the 2020, 2021, and 2022 years.

The word cloud of the data obtained for this study is given in Figure 6. The words with the most important among the words expressed in the top 100 most relevant patent documents are shown in Figure 6. As seen in Figure 6, the most important word is "SARS Cov 2".

4.2. Application of MCDM Methods

Application MCDM methods, namely TOPSIS and CRITIC methods, are reported in this section. The applications are presented below in a stepwise manner.

- **Step 1.** Creating the Decision Matrix: In the first step, the alternatives, and criteria to be used in the analysis were determined. The criteria used in the analysis are given in Table 5. The sample decision matrix is provided in Table 6. As seen in Table 6, alternative patents have numbers starting with the USXPQ code. The criteria are expressed with the abbreviations $C^{rtk.}$ 1, $C^{rtk.}$ 2, $C^{rtk.}$ 3, $C^{rtk.}$ 4, $C^{rtk.}$ 5, $C^{rtk.}$ 6, $C^{rtk.}$ 7, and $C^{rtk.}$ 8, given in Table 5. This table forms input data for analysis and A_{ij} is a decision matrix which is provided in Table 6. In the creation of the decision matrix, the values of the patents in the USPTO in terms of criteria to evaluate the patent portfolio were used.

Table 5. Criteria to evaluate the patent portfolio

No	Criteria	Abbreviation
1	C Score	$C^{rtk.}1$
2	L Score	$C^{rtk.}2$
3	T Score	$C^{rtk.}3$
4	Claim Count	$C^{rtk.}4$
5	Priority Count	$C^{rtk.}5$
6	Number of CPC Codes	$C^{rtk.}6$
7	Reverse Citations	$C^{rtk.}7$
8	Forward Citations	$C^{rtk.}8$

Table 6. Sample decision matrix

Alternatives	Criteria							
	$C^{rtk.}1$	$C^{rtk.}2$	...	...	...	...	$C^{rtk.}7$	$C^{rtk.}8$
USXPQ 1	**16**	**24**	**16**	**21**	**3**	**10**	**30**	**0**
...	...	...	...	...	...	...	...	...
...	...	...	...	...	...	...	...	...
...	...	...	...	...	...	...	...	...
USXPQ 12	**16**	**4**	**89**	**3**	**3**	**9**	**8**	**0**

Explanations of the criteria are given as follows:

✓ **C Score (Citation Score):** Highly cited patents have a calculation that includes auditor citations, pending citations, citations that result from the forward 102 arguments (preventing direct use of someone else's claims), citations that result from the forward 103 argument, age-weighted citation rate, and citations to the main application (https://www.acclaimip.com).

✓ **L Score (Legal Score):** "*The legal score is composed of several metrics that are indicative of a patent's strength including the following measurements, namely pendency (time between file date and grant date), length of independent claims, number of claims, degree to which claims were modified during prosecution, number of office actions, family size, and remaining life*" (https://www.acclaimip.com).

✓ **T Score (Technology Score):** This criterion is based on statistical calculations, which determine which classes are strong and which are relatively weak, depending on the hierarchical structure of the CPC class system, in the background of the software from which the data is received. (https://www.acclaimip.com). *The score is shown as numerical values, which are the power indicators of the patented* *technology branches. (*Altuntas et al., 2020). It is stated that the higher the T score, the more powerful it reflects in technology.

✓ **Claim Count:** A patent document's claim count is indicated by the number of claims it contains.

✓ **Priority Count:** The number of times a patent has been granted in different patent offices. Patents can be granted repeatedly in different countries.

✓ **Number of CPC Codes:** This criterion shows the number of CPC codes assigned to a patent.

✓ **Reverse Cites: It** is the number of citations given by the patent owner in the text of the patent document.

✓ **Forward Cites:** It is the number of citations to that patent.

- **Step 2.** Creating the Normalized Decision Matrix: Normalized decision matrix is calculated using Equation (2) and provided in Table 7.

Table 7. Normalized decision matrix

Alternatives	Criteria							
	$C^{rtk.}1$	$C^{rtk.}2$	$C^{rtk.}3$	$C^{rtk.}4$	$C^{rtk.}5$	$C^{rtk.}6$	$C^{rtk.}7$	$C^{rtk.}8$
USXPQ 1	0.0844	0.2607	0.0677	0.3299	0.3000	0.2672	0.0243	0.0000
USXPQ 2	0.3061	0.1303	0.3850	0.2042	0.3000	0.2672	0.0243	0.1290
USXPQ 3	0.0844	0.4019	0.3681	0.3142	0.1000	0.4008	0.0364	0.0000
USXPQ 4	0.4486	0.4888	0.3893	0.3142	0.2000	0.2939	0.0267	0.5163
USXPQ 5	0.3747	0.2824	0.3850	0.3299	0.3000	0.2939	0.0243	0.2581
USXPQ 6	0.4750	0.3258	0.3639	0.2670	0.1000	0.4276	0.9900	0.7745
USXPQ 7	0.2111	0.1738	0.0550	0.2670	0.4000	0.3207	0.0243	0.1290
USXPQ 8	0.3061	0.4127	0.2877	0.0628	0.4000	0.2405	0.1182	0.0000
USXPQ 9	0.2797	0.1520	0.0634	0.2513	0.4000	0.2405	0.0243	0.1290
USXPQ 10	0.3061	0.2824	0.0677	0.3299	0.3000	0.2405	0.0243	0.1290
USXPQ 11	0.0844	0.1520	0.2073	0.4713	0.1000	0.0801	0.0097	0.0000
USXPQ 12	0.0844	0.0434	0.3766	0.0471	0.3000	0.2405	0.0064	0.0000

- Step 3. Determination of importance weights of criteria by the CRITIC method

In Step 3, the CRITIC method is used to determine the importance levels of the criteria. The importance weights of the criteria can be calculated impartially by taking into account the standard deviations of the criteria and the relationships of the criteria (Özcan, 2019: 547).

The decision matrix is first used for the CRITIC approach. This matrix is given in Table 6. In the decision matrix, all criteria are taken as maximized-based criteria. The normalized matrix for the CRITIC method is then calculated using Equations (9) and (10). The normalized matrix for the CRITIC method is given in Table 8. The correlation matrix is given in Table 9. Finally, σ_j, C_j, and W_{jk} values are calculated and reported in Table 10. The value indicating the importance level of each criterion is given in the last row of Table 10.

Table 8. Normalized matrix for the CRITIC approach

Alternatives	Criteria							
	$C^{rtk.}1$	$C^{rtk.}2$	$C^{rtk.}3$	$C^{rtk.}4$	$C^{rtk.}5$	$C^{rtk.}6$	$C^{rtk.}7$	$C^{rtk.}8$
USXPQ 1	0.0000	0.4878	0.0379	0.6666	0.6666	0.5384	0.0181	0.0000
USXPQ 2	0.5675	0.1951	0.9873	0.3703	0.6666	0.5384	0.0181	0.1666
USXPQ 3	0.0000	0.8048	0.9367	0.6296	0.0000	0.9230	0.0304	0.0000
USXPQ 4	0.9324	1	1	0.6296	0.3333	0.6153	0.0205	0.6666
USXPQ 5	0.7432	0.5365	0.9873	0.6666	0.6666	0.6153	0.0181	0.3333
USXPQ 6	1	0.6341	0.9240	0.5185	0.0000	1	1	1
USXPQ 7	0.3243	0.2926	0.0000	0.5185	1	0.6923	0.0181	0.1666
USXPQ 8	0.5675	0.8292	0.6962	0.0370	1	0.4615	0.1136	0.0000
USXPQ 9	0.500	0.2439	0.0253	0.4814	1	0.4615	0.0181	0.1666
USXPQ 10	0.5675	0.5365	0.0379	0.6666	0.6666	0.4615	0.0181	0.1666
USXPQ 11	0.0000	0.2439	0.4556	1	0.0000	0.0000	0.0032	0.0000
USXPQ 12	0.0000	0.0000	0.9620	0.0000	0.6666	0.4615	0.0000	0.0000

Table 9. Correlation matrix

Alternatives	Criteria								
	$C^{rtk.}1$	$C^{rtk.}2$	$C^{rtk.}3$	$C^{rtk.}4$	$C^{rtk.}5$	$C^{rtk.}6$	$C^{rtk.}7$	$C^{rtk.}8$	
$C^{rtk.}1$	1	0.4552	0.2918	-0.055	0.0414	0.3729	0.5060	0.8225	
$C^{rtk.}2$	0.4552	1	0.2639	0.1422	-0.280	0.4344	0.2127	0.3897	
$C^{rtk.}3$	0.2918	0.2639	1	-0.271	-0.455	0.3094	0.2474	0.3467	
$C^{rtk.}4$	-0.055	0.1422	-0.271	1	-0.518	-0.165	-0.044	0.1316	
$C^{rtk.}5$	0.0414	-0.280	-0.455	-0.518	1	-0.183	-0.420	-0.363	
$C^{rtk.}6$	0.3729	0.4344	0.3094	-0.165	-0.183	1	0.5506	0.5413	
$C^{rtk.}7$	0.5060	0.2127	0.2474	-0.044	-0.420	0.5506	1	0.7693	
$C^{rtk.}8$	0.8225	0.3897	0.3467	0.1316	-0.363	0.5413	0.7693	1	

Table 10. σ_j, C_j and W_{jk} values

	Criteria							
	$C^{rtk.}1$	$C^{rtk.}2$	$C^{rtk.}3$	$C^{rtk.}4$	$C^{rtk.}5$	$C^{rtk.}6$	$C^{rtk.}7$	$C^{rtk.}8$
σ_j	0.3677	0.2994	0.4431	0.2773	0.3849	0.2526	0.2829	0.3124
C_j	1.6788	1.6113	2.7770	2.1584	3.5337	1.2986	1.4653	1.3632
W_j	0.1056	0.1014	0.1748	0.1358	0.2224	0.0817	0.0922	0.0858

The most important criterion among the criteria is “Priority Count” coded with $C^{rtk.}$ 5. Other criteria are listed as follows: $C^{rtk.}$ 3, $C^{rtk.}$ 4, $C^{rtk.}$ 1, $C^{rtk.}$ 2, $C^{rtk.}$ 7, $C^{rtk.}$ 8, and $C^{rtk.}$ 6, respectively.

- **Step 4.** Build the weighted matrix for the TOPSIS method: The weighted decision matrix for the TOPSIS method is given in Table 11.

Table 11. Weighted matrix for the TOPSIS method

Alternatives	Criteria							
	$C^{rtk.}1$	$C^{rtk.}2$	$C^{rtk.}3$	$C^{rtk.}4$	$C^{rtk.}5$	$C^{rtk.}6$	$C^{rtk.}7$	$C^{rtk.}8$
USXPQ 1	0.0089	0.0264	0.0118	0.0448	0.0667	0.0218	0.0022	0.0000
USXPQ 2	0.0323	0.0132	0.0673	0.0277	0.0667	0.0218	0.0022	0.0110
USXPQ 3	0.0089	0.0407	0.0643	0.0426	0.0222	0.0327	0.0033	0.0000
USXPQ 4	0.0474	0.0495	0.0680	0.0426	0.0444	0.0240	0.0024	0.0443
USXPQ 5	0.0396	0.0286	0.0673	0.0448	0.0667	0.0240	0.0022	0.0221
USXPQ 6	0.0502	0.0330	0.0636	0.0362	0.0222	0.0349	0.0913	0.0664
USXPQ 7	0.0223	0.0176	0.0096	0.0362	0.0889	0.0262	0.0022	0.0110
USXPQ 8	0.0323	0.0418	0.0503	0.0085	0.0889	0.0196	0.0109	0.0000
USXPQ 9	0.0295	0.0154	0.0110	0.0341	0.0889	0.0196	0.0022	0.0110
USXPQ 10	0.0323	0.0286	0.0118	0.0448	0.0667	0.0196	0.0022	0.0110
USXPQ 11	0.0089	0.0154	0.0362	0.0640	0.0222	0.0065	0.0008	0.0000
USXPQ 12	0.0089	0.0044	0.0658	0.0064	0.0667	0.0196	0.0005	0.0000

- **Step 5.** Closeness coefficient values: First, the distances to the positive ideal and negative ideal points are calculated using Equation (6), and then the closeness coefficient values are calculated by Equation (7). Table 12 shows the ranking of alternatives.

Table 12. Ranking of alternatives

Alternatives	S^*_i	S^-_i	C_i^*	Ranking
USXPQ 1	0.1370	0.0646	0.3205	11
USXPQ 2	0.1209	0.0821	0.4045	5
USXPQ 3	0.1373	0.0795	0.3668	8
USXPQ 4	0.1046	0.1049	0.5008	2
USXPQ 5	0.1069	0.0954	0.4716	3
USXPQ 6	0.0742	0.1406	0.6544	1
USXPQ 7	0.1306	0.0788	0.3763	6
USXPQ 8	0.1220	0.0913	0.4280	4
USXPQ 9	0.1302	0.0779	0.3742	7
USXPQ 10	0.1265	0.0699	0.3559	9
USXPQ 11	0.1474	0.0644	0.3041	12
USXPQ 12	0.1430	0.0728	0.3375	10

As seen in Table 12, the top three patents are USX 6, USX 4, and USX 5, respectively. These patents are to be considered first while making the selection. However, the USX 11 patent, on the other hand, takes the last place in the ranking.

5. DISCUSSION AND CONTRIBUTIONS

5.1. Implications of the Study

Scientific studies in the field of health have increased both practically and theoretically because of the COVID-19 pandemic in recent years.

This study contributes to the literature by providing insights into research related to the COVID-19 pandemic. The focus of this study is on prioritizing COVID-19-related patents. This study is based on patents, which serve as indicators of technological advancements related to the COVID-19 pandemic. Multi-criteria decision-making techniques were employed to prioritize COVID-19 patent documents. In the analysis, the weights of the criteria were determined, and the levels of importance for the criteria were calculated. Subsequently, the patents were prioritized based on their importance, taking into account the weights assigned to the criteria.

In this study, prioritization of patents for the COVID-19 pandemic was conducted to sort them concerning their importance for a firm. Among the 935 patents, 12 patents belonging to a company with a correlation level of 80% or more related to the COVID-19 pandemic were selected for this study. The CRITIC-based TOPSIS application was conducted to rank patent documents. The importance weights of the criteria were determined using the CRITIC method. The most important criterion was determined as "Priority Count" coded with $C^{rtk.}5$. Then, patents related to COVID-19 were prioritized with the TOPSIS method.

The results of this study show that the most common CPC code sections were A, G, and H sections, respectively. The general titles of A, G, and H sections are human needs, physical, and electricity, respectively. It was also found that the most relevant CPC codes were A61P31, A61K31, and A61K9, respectively. A61P31 CPC code relates to anti-infectives, ie antibiotics, antiseptics, and chemotherapeutics. A61K31 CPC code refers to medicinal preparations containing organic active substances. A61K9 relates to medicinal preparations with a special physical form.

The patent that ranks first in this analysis should be closely monitored for a long period. In future periods, the technology trend should be tracked based on the citations received by this top-ranked patent among the patents acquired. It is recommended that the company owning the patents regularly prioritize and evaluate their patents. The relevant company should monitor the citations received by the top-ranked patent, which also provides an opportunity to track their competitors. To make the correct decision on which stage to start the work in case of a future pandemic, patent portfolios should be well-managed. The sudden and abnormally rapid spread of an epidemic creates a crisis. The relevant patents should be monitored within the framework of patent research, covering preventive measures against similar diseases, disease detection, disease treatment, and post-disease developments, in order to control and manage this crisis effectively.

The findings of the study are important both for the firm and public health. On the firm side, it contributes to strategic planning and firm valuation by evaluating patents. Additionally, it can serve as valuable input for guiding R&D activities. On the other hand, priority patents that stand out through the prioritization process should be supported by government assistance to facilitate their industrialization by the inventors. Hence, the diagnostic, treatment, and preventive efforts provided to the public will be beneficial during crisis moments.

There is a lack of study related to the use of contemporary systematic methods although there is a large body of research on patent analysis in the literature (Kalıp et al. 2022). This book chapter enhances the current literature using CRITIC-based TOPSIS approach.

5.2. Limitation and Future Research

This study focuses on the analysis and prioritization of patents acquired by a single company only. The analysis was conducted considering 8 criteria for 12 patents. The primary limitation of this study is that it was conducted for a single company only. In future studies, a holistic approach can be taken by evaluating patents acquired by different companies separately to enable decision-makers to make more accurate decisions. Hence, this approach would facilitate a comprehensive understanding by considering the parts as well as the whole.

In the future, the search for solutions for vaccines or treatments in the past can be revealed by examining the patents. Patents related to COVID-19 research can be evaluated by cluster analysis. In addition, citation analysis of these patents can be conducted with data mining methods. Companies can prioritize the patents obtained by their competitors on the same subject, by comparing the patents in the ranking and generating research and development strategies.

Moreover, the patent value related to COVID-19 should be examined at specific intervals. Finally, there are available data/information/sources/documents/live witnesses/cases of pandemics experienced at different times worldwide. These data can be collected and used to create a realistic pandemic using augmented reality technologies. By creating simulations of disasters and crisis periods through augmented reality, practical recommendations regarding everyday life can be derived.

REFERENCES

Akandere, G., & Zerenler, M. (2022). Doğu Avrupa ülkelerinin çevresel ve ekonomik performansının bütünleşik CRITIC-TOPSIS yöntemiyle değerlendirilmesi. *Selçuk Üniversitesi Sosyal Bilimler Meslek Yüksekokulu Dergisi, 25*(Özel Sayı), 524-535. doi:10.29249/selcuksbmyd.1156615

Akbulut, O. Y. (2019). CRITIC ve EDAS yöntemleri ile İş Bankası'nın 2009-2018 yılları arasındaki performansının analizi. *Ekonomi Politika ve Finans Araştırmaları Dergisi, 4*(2), 249–263. doi:10.30784/epfad.594762

Akkuş, B., & İzci, N. A. (2018). Sistem yaklaşımı, kavramları ve yönetim. *Recep Tayyip Erdoğan University Journal of Social Sciences, 4*(7), 223-237. https://dergipark.org.tr/en/pub/rteusbe/issue/34053/370196

Albahri, A. S., Hamid, R. A., Albahri, O. S., & Zaidan, A. A. (2021). Detection-based prioritisation: Framework of multi-laboratory characteristics for asymptomatic COVID-19 carriers based on integrated Entropy–TOPSIS methods. *Artificial Intelligence in Medicine, 111*, 101983. doi:10.1016/j.artmed.2020.101983 PMID:33461683

Albahri, A. S., Hamid, R. A., Albahri, O. S., & Zaidan, A. A. (2021). Detection-based prioritisation: Framework of multi-laboratory characteristics for asymptomatic COVID-19 carriers based on integrated Entropy–TOPSIS methods. *Artificial Intelligence in Medicine, 111*, 101983. doi:10.1016/j.artmed.2020.101983 PMID:33461683

Alkan, N., & Kahraman, C. (2021). Evaluation of government strategies against COVID-19 pandemic using q-rung orthopair fuzzy TOPSIS method. *Applied Soft Computing, 110*, 107653. doi:10.1016/j.asoc.2021.107653 PMID:34226821

Alper, D. (2011). Patent Degerlemesi ve Reel Opsiyonlar/Patent Valuation and Real Options. *Business and Economics Research Journal, 2*(1), 153.

Alshrari, A. S., Hudu, S. A., Imran, M., Asdaq, S. M. B., Ali, A. M., & Rabbani, S. I. (2022). Innovations and development of COVID-19 vaccines: A patent review. *Journal of Infection and Public Health, 15*(1), 123–131. doi:10.1016/j.jiph.2021.10.021 PMID:34742639

Alshrari, A. S., Hudu, S. A., Imran, M., Asdaq, S. M. B., Ali, A. M., & Rabbani, S. I. (2022). Innovations and development of COVID-19 vaccines: A patent review. *Journal of Infection and Public Health, 15*(1), 123–131. doi:10.1016/j.jiph.2021.10.021 PMID:34742639

Altuntas, F., & Gok, M. S. (2021). The effect of COVID-19 pandemic on domestic tourism: A DEMATEL method analysis on quarantine decisions. *International Journal of Hospitality Management, 92*, 102719. doi:10.1016/j.ijhm.2020.102719 PMID:33519015

Altuntas, S., Erdogan, Z., & Dereli, T. (2020). A clustering-based approach for the evaluation of candidate emerging technologies. *Scientometrics, 124*(2), 1157–1177. doi:10.100711192-020-03535-0

Aydın, G. Z. (2021). Evaluation of regional health services in Turkey using CRITIC based TOPSIS methods. *Uluslararası Sağlık Yönetimi ve Stratejileri Araştırma Dergisi, 7*(2), 412-433. https://dergipark.org.tr/en/pub/usaysad/issue/64697/988692

Babatunde, M., & Ighravwe, D. (2019). A CRITIC-TOPSIS framework for hybrid renewable energy systems evaluation under techno-economic requirements. *Journal of Project Management, 4*(2), 109–126. doi:10.5267/j.jpm.2018.12.001

Bachmann, P., & Frutos-Bencze, D. (2022). R&D and innovation efforts during the COVID-19 pandemic: The role of universities. *Journal of Innovation & Knowledge, 7*(4), 100238. doi:10.1016/j.jik.2022.100238

Barbazza, A., Collan, M., Fedrizzi, M., & Luukka, P. (2014). Consensus modeling in multiple criteria multi-expert real options-based valuation of patents. *In Intelligent Systems' 2014: Proceedings of the 7th IEEE International Conference Intelligent Systems IS'2014*. Springer International Publishing.10.1007/978-3-319-11313-5_25

Bhadra, D., Dhar, N. R., & Salam, M. A. (2022). Sensitivity analysis of the integrated AHP-TOPSIS and CRITIC-TOPSIS method for selection of the natural fiber. *Materials Today: Proceedings, 56*, 2618–2629. doi:10.1016/j.matpr.2021.09.178

Bloom, N., Davis, S. J., & Zhestkova, Y. (2021, May). Covid-19 shifted patent applications toward technologies that support working from home. *AEA Papers and Proceedings. American Economic Association, 111*, 263–266. doi:10.1257/pandp.20211057

Bulğurcu, B. (2019). Çok nitelikli fayda teorisi ile CRITIC yöntem entegrasyonu: Akıllı teknoloji tercih örneği. *OPUS Journal of Society Research, 13*(19), 1930–1957. doi:10.26466/opus.584123

Collan, M., Fedrizzi, M., & Luukka, P. (2013). A multi-expert system for ranking patents: An approach based on fuzzy pay-off distributions and a TOPSIS–AHP framework. *Expert Systems with Applications, 40*(12), 4749–4759. doi:10.1016/j.eswa.2013.02.012

de Araujo Andrade, T., Nascimento, J. A. C. Junior, Santos, A. M., Borges, L. P., Quintans-Junior, L. J., Walker, C. I. B., Frank, L. A., & Serafini, M. R. (2021). Technological scenario for masks in patent database during Covid-19 pandemic. *AAPS PharmSciTech, 22*(2), 1–22. doi:10.120812249-021-01918-x PMID:33575845

Deniz, N. (2020). Teknoloji yönetiminde MOORA ve ARAS çok ölçütlü karar verme teknikleri ile patent değerleme. *Dumlupınar Üniversitesi Sosyal Bilimler Dergisi*, (64), 191-207. https://dergipark.org.tr/tr/pub/dpusbe/issue/53850/684050>

Dhara, A., Kaur, G., Kishan, P. M., Majumder, A., & Yadav, R. (2022). An efficient decision support system for selecting very light business jet using CRITIC-TOPSIS method. *Aircraft Engineering and Aerospace Technology, 94*(3), 458–472. doi:10.1108/AEAT-04-2021-0135

Do, Q. N., Mishra, N., Wulandhari, N. B. I., Ramudhin, A., Sivarajah, U., & Milligan, G. (2021). Supply chain agility responding to unprecedented changes: Empirical evidence from the UK food supply chain during COVID-19 crisis. *Supply Chain Management, 26*(6), 737–752. doi:10.1108/SCM-09-2020-0470

Durmuşoğlu, A., & Durmuşoğlu, Z. D. U. (2022). Remembering medical ventilators and masks in the days of covıd-19: Patenting in the last decade in respiratory technologies. *IEEE Transactions on Engineering Management*, 1–15. doi:10.1109/TEM.2022.3151636

Erdogan, Z., Altuntas, S., & Dereli, T. (2022). Predicting patent quality based on machine learning approach. *IEEE Transactions on Engineering Management*, 1–14. doi:10.1109/TEM.2022.3207376

Erkılıç, C. E. (2021). Hastane hizmetleri sektörünün CRITIC temelli TOPSIS yöntemi ile finansal performansının değerlendirilmesi, *Pamukkale Üniversitesi Sosyal Bilimler Enstitüsü Dergisi. Sayı, 46*, 63–84. doi:10.30794/pausbed.865686

Ernst, H. (1998). Patent portfolios for strategic R&D planning. *Journal of Engineering and Technology Management, 15*(4), 279–308. doi:10.1016/S0923-4748(98)00018-6

Ertemel, A. V., Menekse, A., & Camgoz Akdag, H. (2023). Smartphone addiction assessment using pythagorean Fuzzy CRITIC-TOPSIS. *Sustainability (Basel), 15*(5), 3955. doi:10.3390u15053955

Falciola, L., & Barbieri, M. (2022). Searching and analyzing patent-relevant Covid-19 information. *World Patent Information, 68*, 102094. doi:10.1016/j.wpi.2022.102094

Fan, S., Liu, G., Tu, Y., Zhu, J., Zhang, P., & Tian, Z. (2023). Improved multi-criteria decision making method integrating machine learning for patent competitive potential Evaluation: A case study in water pollution abatement technology. *Journal of Cleaner Production*, *403*, 136896. doi:10.1016/j.jclepro.2023.136896

Fan, W., Xu, Z., Wu, B., He, Y., & Zhang, Z. (2022). Structural multi-objective topology optimization and application based on the criteria importance through intercriteria correlation method. *Engineering Optimization*, *54*(5), 830–846. doi:10.1080/0305215X.2021.1901087

Gaur, S., Dosapati, S., & Tawalare, A. (2023). Stakeholder assessment in construction projects using a CRITIC-TOPSIS approach. *Built Environment Project and Asset Management*, *13*(2), 217–237. doi:10.1108/BEPAM-10-2021-0122

Grimaldi, M., Cricelli, L., Di Giovanni, M., & Rogo, F. (2015). The patent portfolio value analysis: A new framework to leverage patent information for strategic technology planning. *Technological Forecasting and Social Change*, *94*, 286–302. doi:10.1016/j.techfore.2014.10.013

Guderian, C. C., Bican, P. M., Riar, F. J., & Chattopadhyay, S. (2021). Innovation management in crisis: Patent analytics as a response to the COVID-19 pandemic. *R & D Management*, *51*(2), 223–239. doi:10.1111/radm.12447

Gupta, S., Vijayvargy, L., & Gupta, K. (2021). Assessment of stress level in urban area's during COVID-19 outbreak using CRİTİC and TOPSIS: A case of Indian cities. *Journal of Statistics and Management Systems*, *24*(2), 411–433. doi:10.1080/09720510.2021.1879470

Gurrala, K. R., Helmy, M., & Ndiaye, M. (2022, March). *Edible packaging selection employing Hybrid CRITIC and TOPSIS Method.* 2022 International Conference on Decision Aid Sciences and Applications (DASA), Chiangrai, Thailand. 10.1109/DASA54658.2022.9765061

Haykır, E. (2011). Entelektüel sermayenin önemi. sınıflandırılması ve ölçme yöntemleri: kuramsal bir çerçeve, *Sosyal bilimler dergisi*. (1) 86-99. https://dergipark.org.tr/tr/pub/iusosbil/issue/9498/118670

Huang, J. Y. (2016). Patent portfolio analysis of the cloud computing industry. *Journal of Engineering and Technology Management*, *39*, 45–64. doi:10.1016/j.jengtecman.2016.01.002

Huang, L. C., & Lıu, C. W. (2018). Patent quality evaluation with entropy weight method and improved TOPSIS: The case of geriatric technology. *2018 International Conference on Management Science and Engineering (ICMSE),* (pp. 156-164). IEEE. 10.1109/ICMSE.2018.8745300

Ighravwe, D., & Babatunde, M. (2018). Selection of a mini-grid business model for developing countries using CRITIC-TOPSIS with interval type-2 fuzzy sets. *Decision Science Letters*, *7*(4), 427–442. doi:10.5267/j.dsl.2018.1.004

Imran, M., Kumar Arora, M., Asdaq, S. M. B., Khan, S. A., Alaqel, S. I., Alshammari, M. K., Alshehri, M. M., Alshrari, A. S., Ali, A. M., Al-shammeri, A. M., Alhazmi, B. D., Harshan, A. A., & Alam, M. T. (2021). Discovery, development, and patent trends on molnupiravir: A prospective oral treatment for COVID-19. *Molecules (Basel, Switzerland)*, *26*(19), 5795. doi:10.3390/molecules26195795 PMID:34641339

Işık, Ö. (2019). Türkiye'de hayat dışı sigorta sektörünün finansal performansının CRITIC tabanlı TOPSIS ve MULTIMOORA yöntemiyle değerlendirilmesi. *Business & Management Studies: An International Journal, 7*(1), 542–562. doi:10.15295/bmij.v7i1.1090

Jaber, N., Al-Remawi, M., Al-Akayleh, F., Al-Muhtaseb, N., Al-Adham, I. S., & Collier, P. J. (2022). A review of the antiviral activity of Chitosan, including patented applications and its potential use against COVID-19. *Journal of Applied Microbiology, 132*(1), 41–58. https://dergipark.org.tr/tr/pub/dpusbe/issue/53850/684050. doi:10.1111/jam.15202 PMID:34218488

Jotisakulratana, M., Koomgun, N., Virojrid, R., & Udomsaph, B. (2013). Applying International Patent Classification (IPC) to strategic planning processes of an R&D organization: The case of NECTEC, Thailand. *In 2013 Proceedings of PICMET'13: Technology Management in the IT-Driven Services (PICMET*). IEEE.

Kalıp, N. G., Erzurumlu, Y. Ö., & Gün, N. A. (2022). Qualitative and quantitative patent valuation methods: A systematic literature review. *World Patent Information, 69*, 102111. doi:10.1016/j.wpi.2022.102111

Kalvakolanu, S., Sama, H. R., Mathew, M., & Somasekhar, D. (2022). Measuring job satisfaction levels of airport employees using entropy, critic and TOPSIS methods. *International Journal of Business Excellence, 27*(1), 1–22. doi:10.1504/IJBEX.2022.123031

Kazan, H., & Ozdemir, O. (2014). Financial performance assessment of large scale conglomerates via TOPSIS and CRITIC methods. *International Journal of Management and Sustainability, 3*(4), 203–224. doi:10.18488/journal.11/2014.3.4/11.4.203.224

Keestra, S., Rodgers, F., Osborne, R., & Wimmer, S. (2022). University patenting and licensing practices in the United Kingdom during the first year of the COVID-19 pandemic. *Global Public Health: An International Journal for Research, Policy and Practice, 17*(5), 641–651. doi:10.1080/17441692.2022.2049842 PMID:35298347

Kim, G., & Bae, J. (2017). A novel approach to forecast promising technology through patent analysis. *Technological Forecasting and Social Change, 117*, 228–237. doi:10.1016/j.techfore.2016.11.023

Lee, S., Yoon, B., Lee, C., & Park, J. (2009). Business planning based on technological capabilities: Patent analysis for technology-driven roadmapping. *Technological Forecasting and Social Change, 76*(6), 769–786. doi:10.1016/j.techfore.2009.01.003

Lei, Q., Liu, C., Xie, W., & Bao, X. (2021). A TOPSIS-Based Model for Evaluating the Performance of the Intellectual Property Value Strategies of Science and Technology Enterprises. *Discrete Dynamics in Nature and Society, 2021*, 1–6. doi:10.1155/2021/4745702

LiQ.YinX.YinW.DongX.LiQ. (2023). Evaluating human-computer interaction education based on active learning methods using the CRITIC and TOPSIS approach. Research Square, DOI: doi:10.21203/rs.3.rs-2490226/v1

Li, X., Wang, K., Liu, L., Xin, J., Yang, H., & Gao, C. (2011). Application of the entropy weight and TOPSIS method in safety evaluation of coal mines. *Procedia Engineering, 26*, 2085–2091. doi:10.1016/j.proeng.2011.11.2410

Li, Y., Wei, M., Liu, L., Yu, B., Dong, Z., & Xue, Q. (2021). Evaluation of the effectiveness of VOC-contaminated soil preparation based on AHP-CRITIC-TOPSIS model. *Chemosphere*, *271*, 129571. doi:10.1016/j.chemosphere.2021.129571 PMID:33460903

Lin, Y., Alshehri, Y., Alnazzawi, N., Abid, M., Khan, S. A., Jabeen, F., & Elwarfalli, I. (2023). Social media analytics and their applications to evaluate an activity in online health interventions using CRITIC and TOPSIS techniques. *Soft Computing*, 1–13. doi:10.100700500-023-08004-3 PMID:37362268

Liu, Y., & Yang, R. (2023). Independent innovation capacity of chinese high-tech ındustries Using CRITIC and TOPSIS Methods. *Journal of Engineering Science & Technology Review*, *16*(1), 18–25. doi:10.25103/jestr.161.03

Luukka, P. (2020). N—ary norm operators and TOPSIS. In *2020 IEEE International Conference on Fuzzy Systems (FUZZ-IEEE)*. IEEE. 10.1109/FUZZ48607.2020.9177580

Luukka, P., & Collan, M. (2016). Histogram ranking with generalised similarity-based TOPSIS applied to patent ranking. *Journal of Engineering and Technology Management*, *25*(4), 437–448. doi:10.1504/IJOR.2016.075290

Majumder, P., Biswas, P., & Majumder, S. (2020). Application of new TOPSIS approach to identify the most significant risk factor and continuous monitoring of death of COVID-19. *Electronic Journal of General Medicine*, *17*(6), em234. doi:10.29333/ejgm/7904

Mohamadghasemi, A., Hadi-Vencheh, A., & Hosseinzadeh Lotfi, F. (2020). The multiobjective stochastic CRITIC–TOPSIS approach for solving the shipboard crane selection problem. *International Journal of Intelligent Systems*, *35*(10), 1570–1598. doi:10.1002/int.22265

Mohammed, M. A., Abdulkareem, K. H., Al-Waisy, A. S., Mostafa, S. A., Al-Fahdawi, S., Dinar, A. M., Alhakami, W., Baz, A., Al-Mhiqani, M. N., Alhakami, H., Arbaiy, N., Maashi, M. S., Mutlag, A. A., García-Zapirain, B., & Torre Díez, I. D. L. T. D. L. (2020). Benchmarking methodology for selection of optimal COVID-19 diagnostic model based on entropy and TOPSIS methods. *IEEE Access : Practical Innovations, Open Solutions*, *8*, 99115–99131. doi:10.1109/ACCESS.2020.2995597

Mouritsen, J., & Koleva, G. (2005). Packing and unpacking knowledge: Patents and intellectual capital. *Journal of Intellectual Capital*, *6*(3), 308–321. doi:10.1108/14691930510611076

Mukundan, R., Jain, K., & Pathari, V. (2019). A model for measuring and ranking a firm's patent portfolio. *Technology Analysis and Strategic Management*, *31*(9), 1029–1047. doi:10.1080/09537325.2019.1583327

Onocak, D. (2023). BİST'te İşlem gören konaklama işletmelerinin finansal performanslarının CRITIC ağırlıklandırmalı TOPSIS yöntemine göre değerlendirilmesi. *Muhasebe ve Finansman Dergisi*, (97), 79–98. doi:10.25095/mufad.1177612

Piret, J., & Boivin, G. (2021). Pandemics throughout history. *Frontiers in Microbiology*, *11*, 631736. doi:10.3389/fmicb.2020.631736 PMID:33584597

Qiu, W., Rutherford, S., Mao, A., & Chu, C. (2017). The pandemic and its impacts. *Health, Culture and Society (Pittsburgh, Pa.)*, *9*, 1–11. doi:10.5195/HCS.2017.221

Rogosnitzky, M., Berkowitz, E. & Jadad, A. R. (2020). Delivering benefits at speed through real-world repurposing of off-patent drugs: the COVID-19 pandemic as a case in point. *JMIR Public Health and Surveillance*, *6*(2) e19199. doi:10.2196/19199

Rostamzadeh, R., Ghorabaee, M. K., Govindan, K., Esmaeili, A., & Nobar, H. B. K. (2018). Evaluation of sustainable supply chain risk management using an integrated fuzzy TOPSIS-CRITIC approach. *Journal of Cleaner Production*, *175*, 651–669. doi:10.1016/j.jclepro.2017.12.071

Saravanakumar, K., Robinson, Y., Madhu, P., & Manoj, M. (2022). Selection of oil and best bio-diesel blend based on performance and emission characteristics of IC engine: An integrated CRITIC-TOPSIS Approac. *Journal of Scientific and Industrial Research*, *81*(12), 1342–1352. doi:10.56042/jsir.v81i12.47120

Saunders-Hastings, P. R., & Krewski, D. (2016). Reviewing the history of pandemic influenza: Understanding patterns of emergence and transmission. *Pathogens (Basel, Switzerland)*, *5*(4), 66. doi:10.3390/pathogens5040066 PMID:27929449

Saxena, P., Kumar, V., & Ram, M. (2022). A novel CRITIC-TOPSIS approach for optimal selection of software reliability growth model (SRGM). *Quality and Reliability Engineering International, 38*(5), 2501-2520. doi:10.1002/qre.3087

Slebi-Acevedo, C. J., Pascual-Muñoz, P., Lastra-González, P., & Castro-Fresno, D. (2019). Multi-response optimization of porous asphalt mixtures reinforced with aramid and polyolefin fibers employing the CRITIC-TOPSIS based on Taguchi methodology. *Materials (Basel)*, *12*(22), 3789. doi:10.3390/ma12223789 PMID:31752227

Stanojković, J., & Radovanović, M. (2017). Selection of solid carbide end mill for machining aluminum 6082-T6 using CRITIC and TOPSIS methods. *Journal of Production Engineering*, *20*(1), 133–136. doi:10.24867/JPE-2017-01-133

Storz, U. (2022). The COVID-19 vaccine patent race. *Nature Biotechnology*, *40*(7), 1001–1004. doi:10.103841587-022-01376-1 PMID:35831656

Tandon, S., Kumar, V., & Singh, V. B. (2022). *An empirical analysis of code smells using CRITIC-TOPSIS method.* 2022 12th International Conference on Cloud Computing, Data Science & Engineering (Confluence), Noida, India. 10.1109/Confluence52989.2022.9734202

Thakkar, P. & Paliwal, M. S. (2021). *Ghole, selection of power generation technology using a combination of CRITIC and TOPSIS.* 2021 IEEE 2nd International Conference On Electrical Power and Energy Systems (ICEPES), Bhopal, India. . doi:10.1109/ICEPES52894.2021.9699756

Wang, B., & Hsieh, C. H. (2015). Measuring the value of patents with fuzzy multiple criteria decision making: Insight into the practices of the Industrial Technology Research Institute. *Technological Forecasting and Social Change*, *92*, 263–275. doi:10.1016/j.techfore.2014.09.015

Wang, C., Wang, L., Gu, T., Yin, J., & Hao, E. (2023). CRITIC-TOPSIS-Based evaluation of smart community safety: A case study of Shenzhen, China. *Buildings*, *13*(2), 476. doi:10.3390/buildings13020476

Weiling, S., & Hao, Y. X. Z. (2018). The Patent portfolios value evaluation based on the TOPSIS-Entropy method. *In 2018 Portland International Conference on Management of Engineering and Technology (PICMET).* IEEE. 10.23919/PICMET.2018.8481868

WIPO. (2022), *World Intellectual Property Report 2022*. WIPO. https://www.wipo.int/edocs/pubdocs/en/wipo-pub-944-2022-en-world-intellectual-property-report-2022-the-direction-of-innovation.pdf (accessed 27 January 2023)

Wu, H., Liu, S., Wang, J., & Yang, T. (2020). Construction safety risk assessment of bridges in the marine environment based on CRITIC and TOPSIS models. *Journal of Coastal Research, 108*(SI), 206-210. doi:10.2112/JCR-SI108-040.1

Xu, Y., Siyi, C., & Mengyang, P. (2020). Dynamic radiator threat assessment based on CRITIC-TOPSIS. [in Chinese]. *Journal of Beijing University of Aeronautics and Astronautics*, *46*(11), 2168–2175. doi:10.13700/j.bh.1001-5965.2019.0585

Yang, Y., Li, C., Xue, W., & Kang, S. (2019, April). Economic benefit evaluation analysis for distributed energy generation projects based on CRITIC-TOPSIS model. In IOP Conference Series: Earth and Environmental Science, 252(3), 032059, IOP Publishing. doi:10.1088/1755-1315/252/3/032059

Yavuz, N., & Baki, B. (2019). Patent değerlerinin çok kriterli karar verme yöntemleri ile sıralanması: Otomotiv sektöründe bir uygulama, *Karadeniz Teknik Üniversitesi Sosyal Bilimler Enstitüsü Sosyal Bilimler Dergisi*, *9*(17) 27-52. <https://dergipark.org.tr/tr/pub/sbed/issue/46469/448470>

Yenisu, E., Şahin, F., & Öztekkeli, H. (2019). Yönetim düşüncesinin evriminde sistem kuramının etkileri: Kavramsal bir çözümleme. *Akademi Sosyal Bilimler Dergisi, 6*(18), 514-527. https://dergipark.org.tr/en/pub/asbider/issue/48571/616909

Yin, J., Wang, J., Wang, C., Wang, L., & Chang, Z. (2023). CRITIC-TOPSIS based evaluation of smart community governance: A case study in China. *Sustainability (Basel)*, *15*(3), 1923. doi:10.3390u15031923

Yu, H., Gao, Y., Yang, L., Liu, F., Gao, X., & Tan, Q. (2023). Knowledge reasoning of transmission line component detection using CRITIC and TOPSIS approaches. *Soft Computing*, *27*(2), 991–1004. doi:10.100700500-022-07540-8

Yuan, X., & Song, W. (2022). Evaluating technology innovation capabilities of companies based on Entropy-TOPSIS: The case of solar cell companies. *Information Technology and Management*, *23*(2), 65–76. doi:10.100710799-021-00344-6

Yuan, Y. (2023). Decision support system for evaluating English media analytics and the role of visualization in online business development using CRITIC and TOPSIS approaches. *Soft Computing*, 1–15. doi:10.100700500-023-08094-z

Zhang, W., Bo, Z. H. A. O., Yashuo, L. I., Liming, Z. H. O. U., Kang, N. I. U., Jıang, H., & Guangrui, L. I. (2022). Construction of spare parts importance evaluation for cross-region harvester based on CRITIC and TOPSIS method. *INMATEH - Agricultural Engineering*, *68*(3), 798–808. doi:10.35633/inmateh-68-79

Zhao, X., Zhang, X., & Emmanuel, A. (2022). Research and demonstration of technology opportunity identification model based on text classification and core patents. *Computers & Industrial Engineering*, *171*, 108403. doi:10.1016/j.cie.2022.108403

Zhuang, W., Fan, Z., Chu, Y., Wang, H., Yang,Y., Wu, L., Sun, N., Sun, G., Shen, Y., Lin, X., Guo, G., & Xi, S. (2020). Chinese patent medicines in the treatment of coronavirus disease 2019 (COVID-19) in China. *Frontiers in Pharmacology*, *11*(2020). doi:10.3389/fphar.2020.01066

Zulqarnain, R. M., Siddique, I., Jarad, F., Ali, R., & Abdeljawad, T. (2021). Development of TOPSIS technique under pythagorean fuzzy hypersoft environment based on correlation coefficient and its application towards the selection of antivirus mask in COVID-19 pandemic. *Complexity*, *2021*, 1–27. doi:10.1155/2021/6634991

Chapter 9
Restoring Archival Materials Through Digitalization South Africa

Nkholedzeni Sidney Netshakhuma
https://orcid.org/0000-0003-0673-7137
University of Cape Town, South Africa

ABSTRACT

This book chapter assesses the process of restoring archives materials in South Africa. South Africa experience the disaster of loss of archives materials as results of human factors and natural disasters. This led to loss of institutional memory. The researcher utilized literature review to assess archives materials created or received by an organisation. To address the issue of loss of institution, the country has developed and worked towards implementing several policies, strategies, action plans, and projects aimed at responding to and addressing climate change mitigation. Those interventions include raising awareness, training, conferences, publications, and the development of disaster control plans.

INTRODUCTION

This chapter discusses the restoration of archives material through digitization in South Africa. The initiatives to preserve archives materials on digital platforms expanded throughout the world. Restored archives materials and digitized them and ensured that such archives materials were accessible online to empower both local and international audiences. During digitization, consideration of legislative framework, Coordination of government programs, risk assessments, executive Management support, allocation of funds to support the digitization process, training of staff on the management of records in preparation for digitalization processes, providing access to archives materials, and privacy are concepts to be considered. The management of archives materials in South Africa suffers from ineffective implementation of the archives management framework, and inadequate capabilities of the archives management systems to manage archives materials (Ngulube & Tafor 2006). The complexity is raised significantly during the digitization of archives materials. Against this background, I conducted a literature review to assess the framework for restoring archives materials through digitalization.

DOI: 10.4018/978-1-6684-9522-3.ch009

BACKGROUND INFORMATION

Africa is projected to be vulnerable to climate change which led to flooding and natural fires that destroy both infrastructure and archives materials (Dube, and Nhamo 2020). In recent years: South Africa has experienced natural disasters caused by climate change which contributed to wildfires in areas such as the Cape Peninsula and flooding (Dube, Nhamo, and Chikodzi, 2021). This study is supported by Ogbomo, Ejedafiru & Olukotun (2023) who found that human factors and natural disasters affect the management of archives materials. Valuable African literature was threatened when the University of Cape Town suffered from fire during the fire disasters (Hoffman, Rick Rohde, Gillso 2019). A joint initiative was established to recover archives materials lost caused by a fire disaster. The case of the University Cape Town library demonstrates another aspect of ensuring continuity after the loss of archives materials (Jethro 2021). The remaining archives materials preserved in the archives repository need to be digitized to ensure the accessibility of such rich archive materials. Despite natural disasters causing loss of property and people, they also led to the loss of archival materials with historical, cultural, and scientific significance (Kirkwood 2021). As the urgency of climate change has risen to the political agenda, there has been equal recognition of the need to strive towards restoring archival materials caused by natural disasters.

A similar story unfolded at the parliament of the Republic of South Africa where records were historical, cultural records were destroyed because of fire. It seems that archivists were powerless as they watched those images of the loss of archives materials in parliament. This is because most of the archive's materials lost and preserved in the parliament were irreplaceable. Organizations are to be ready to deal with disasters neither caused by natural disasters nor fire.

To begin with, apart from highlighting the cultural importance of the archive's materials, restoring damaged archive materials is essential. Archives institutions have a role in preserving records with historical, cultural, and social significance (Delaney & De Jong 2015).

The rationale to conduct this research is the loss of archives of materials in South Africa and in other countries such as Nigeria through human factors or natural disasters (Ogbomo, Ejedafiru, and Olukotun 2023). It is significant to assess whether the organization developed policies, procedures, and processes to mitigate the loss of archives materials. Organizations without neither policies, procedures, procedures, and processes may not afford to deal with the challenge of losing archives materials.

The review of the literature shows that some archival materials destroyed because of fire cannot be replaced or repaired (Chance, 2015). It is the responsibility of the archivist to ensure that records survive after the disaster (Humphreys, McCarthy, Dowling, Kertesz, & Tropea 2014). Restoring archives materials can be done by ensuring that a preservation and disaster recovery plan is in place. The reason for ensuring that archives materials are restored is because such archives materials are irreplaceable. Response to such disasters is to be handled in compliance with the Disaster Management Act to minimize disaster. The review of the literature shows that some of the African State is lagging in implementing disaster recovery management systems. Despite these challenges, there is a need for archives professionals to embark on the digitization project. Other mechanisms which need to be employed by the government to minimize the risk include fire detectors should be included in the system.

RESEARCH PROBLEM

Most archives materials preserved by South African institutions are not digitized (Balogun, Kalusopa 2021). Most of organization's records are preserved in paper-based format. These records preserved in this form pose a challenge when a disaster happens because when such disaster such as happens such as fire such records are lost forever and cannot be replaced. This shows that the implementation of electronic records management systems in South Africa is a challenge in the public sector (Marutha & Ngulube 2012). To prevent this, organizations must embark on digitization projects to ensure that such records are digitized for permanent preservation. Archivists are concerned with the type of records that need to be kept and preserved for the long term by the organization (Reine 2019).

METHODOLOGY

The researcher applied a literature review to assess factors that influence restore of archival materials through digitalization in South Africa. The review of the literature shows that developed countries experience more information losses as opposed to human deaths and injuries due to high levels of preparedness to counter such calamities (Odongo 2018). This is because most countries have systems to counter any challenge caused by a disaster. Records are created for no apparent reason and are kept unexploited in cabinets and stands where they gather dust for years without anybody referring to them (Odongo 2018 p. 15).

South Africa recognized that climate change which causes floods and fires caused damage to archive materials (Ngulube, and Tafor 2006). To address this issue, the South African governments through various departments developed several policies, strategies, action plans, and projects aimed to respond to and address climate change mitigation. Those interventions include raising awareness, training, conferences, publications, and the development of disaster control plans.

The South African digitization framework was initiated to ensure that the government promotes the use of electronic systems to improve service delivery (Nel, & Masilela, 2020),. And commit the country to achieving the vision of the digital world. The digitization framework recognizes that decision-making about cultural records is complex and requires careful deliberation. One area that needs to be considered and analyzed is the use of climate change projections and hazard, vulnerability, and risk assessments to provide an evidence base for decision-making related to climate change adaptation. This means that the South African government needs to adopt a comprehensive strategy to ensure the management of information within an organization. Significantly, policies, procedures, and processes are developed to mitigate the occurrence of potential disasters (Ayoung, Boatbil, & Baard 2016 p.1297). This implies organizations develop a strategic plan to ensure that archived materials are organized in their systems. A critical assessment at most South African institutions shows that organizations lack strategies to mitigate any disaster in their environment.

LEGISLATIVE FRAMEWORK

This section provides insight into the legal framework that impacted the management of archives management in South Africa. The government applied a legislative framework to ensure archives are managed and preserved (Mnjama' 2005 Makwae; 2021,). There are various legislations in South Africa as stipulated at the end of this paragraph. In South Africa, legislation was enacted to promote the management of archives management systems (Wamukoya & Mutula 2009). For example, the National Archives and Records Service Act 43 of 1996 guides the management of records of the Public Sector in South Africa. It gives the framework that enables the National Archives of South Africa and its provincial archives institutions to operate with authority in its dealing with various government departments and municipalities. The Protection of Personal Information Act (Act No. 4 of 2013) ensures the protection of personal information (Mullon & Ngoepe 2019). The Promotion of Access to Information Act (PAIA) is legislation providing access to information (Katuu & Van Der Walt 2016).

The review of the literature shows that some African countries' legislations were not up to date (Khumalo, 2017). The researcher recommended countries update their national archives legislation and other legislations impacting the management of archives and records management.

The roles of archives are the combination of records management and access the theoretical recognition (Ceeney, 2008). Legislations provide guidelines on the type of records which need to be managed. Though an important area, a lot of non -compliance with national legislation is evidenced by several research conducted on records and archives management systems in South Africa. It can be concluded that the management of institutional memory in South Africa is guided by the legislative framework.

COORDINATION OF GOVERNMENT PROGRAM

In South Africa, there are three spheres of government namely national, provincial, and local levels (Malan 2005). There is a need for the spheres of government to cooperate to deliver service to various stakeholders (Ebi, 2021, P 26). Coordination of national, provincial, and local government is conducted in compliance with the Public Service Charter of South Africa. Sharing and preservation of archives materials is necessary to coordinate archives management. This shows that the organization's mandate is to promote and support the preservation of archives materials (Bowker and Villamizar, 2017). It is essential for national, provincial, and local government (Municipality) records to be managed in terms of the National Archives and Records Service Act 43 of 1996 (Matlala, Ncube, & Parbanath, 2022). The National Archives of South Africa oversees all records created by governmental bodies neither national, provincial, or local government. Government records transfer of records to the Public Archives has been done in small quantities because of a lack of space to preserve such records (Muchefa, & Chigodora, 2016). Archives management is an energetic integral of good governance in a planned civilization (Dikopoulou, 2012). This shows that public services turn to archives management professionals (Dikopoulou & Mihiotis 2012). This charter is linked to restoring archives materials to improve service delivery. Government departments or ministries support each other and promote one another in sharing information or archives materials. Service delivery is a socio-economic right that must be afforded the full protection of the law (Ebi, 2021, p. 107). Intergovernmental structure raises questions about the management of archives (Baker, 1997: 243). Archives institutions collect, store, and disseminate information to their users (Wangutusi, 2013 p.5) through the National Archives and Records Service Act 43 of 1996. The

National Archives of South Africa and provincial archives provide advice to governmental bodies on all issues related to the creation, control, and general management of public records on the acquisition, processing, and preservation of public records and archives. The Department of Arts and Culture, which is the custodian of the National Archives and Records Service Act 43 of 1996 selects, collect, process, and preserves archival materials transferred by various governmental departmental bodies and ministries. Intergovernmental play a role in the coordination of records management. In South Africa, government departments both at national and local government exchange data and information to execute their duties and responsibilities. However, the bulk of records created during post-apartheid is digital records (Balogun and Kalusopa 2021). Therefore, government departments are required to develop strategies aligned with the intergovernmental relation framework. The government ensures that there are coordination mechanisms to consider national policies and legislative instruments for emergency preparedness. The National Archives of South Africa leads in terms of coordination of archives management programs. Archivists are responsible for the management of archives materials, accessibility of archives materials, and preservation of archives materials. This is because the National Archives and its provincial archives are responsible for receiving archives materials transferred from various governmental bodies. There is a need for an integrated approach to dealing with cultural heritage. Partnerships and collaboration increase the sharing of expertise across sectors to better address the loss of archives materials and determine shared objectives rather than struggling as standalone authorities.

The government needs to develop systems to enhance the management of digital records. This is done to improve the service delivery of government.

EXECUTIVE MANAGEMENT SUPPORT

Executive management provides leadership of the organization by developing a strategy for archives management, privacy, approval of records and archives management policies, and overseeing and monitoring of archives management system (Swartz, Da Veiga, & Martins, 2021). Executive management has to be convinced about cost reduction and effective implementation of the archives management system (Dikopoulou, 2012). The executive management officer designated to oversee the organization's archives management system is well-informed about archives management policies. Records are one of the organization's most valuable assets within an organization. Executive management should play an essential role in the management and approval of policies.

RISK ASSESSMENTS

South African organizations focus on either conducting risk assessment with the issue of managing records or compliance with applicable legislation to ensure the preservation of archives materials through digitization (Ngulube, and Tafor2006). Digitization became a solution to preserve cultural, historical, and archives materials (Abdeen, Fernando, Kulatunga, Hettige, & Ranasinghe 2021). Legislations are important when organizations conduct the organizational assessment. Risk assessment continues conducted to ensure risk continuous assessment by the government. Information management for surveillance and early warning as well as access to emergency diagnostic services should be conducted by the government.

The evaluation of the key management and compensating controls implemented to address the associated organization risks shows the significance of implementing archives and related management policies.

ALLOCATION OF FUNDS

Nothing would be possible without finance. Financial challenges are hindrance to establishing digitization systems for most African governments (Mudzaki 2017, Fabunmi, Paris, & Fabunmi 2006). Lack of financial resources limit most countries to implement the restoration of archives materials. This means that some countries may not update their archive's legislations, policies, and procedures to manage archives management. Organizations need resources such as finance for the operations of a society or business enterprise to ensure archives recovery (Wangutusi 2013, p.70). Allocation for funding for emergency readiness and contingency response to restore archives materials should be prioritized. Resource enlistment will be a game changer for the government's records management strategy. Resources will provide the capacity and experience needed within the national archives management systems. The organizations faced the challenge of inadequate resources to improve facilities and infrastructure that would enhance archives management systems.

The budgetary allocation enhanced good governance. This statement is alluded to by (Matlala, Ncube, & Parbanath 2022) who stated that funding should be provided to advance archives management programs. The review of the literature shows that government-run archival institutions in South Africa are so underfunded that they cannot currently care for the influx of archives materials transferred by governmental bodies. Therefore, there is a need to allocate a budget to ensure the sustainability of archives management within an organization. Even though South Africa has several legislative frameworks governing records and archives management in South Africa, there is a limited budget allocated to government departments to implement digitalization (Mullon & Ngoepe 2019).

TRAINING

Governmental bodies have policies and procedures, but these will be ineffective unless there is an obligation to instrument such policies (Wangutusi 2013). Organizations need to embark on awareness of records management (Asogwa, Ezeani, & Asogwa 2021 p 525). This ensures that people understand the significance of archives management. Organizations should ensure that elements such as filing, classification, appraisal of records, and disposal are significant during records management. The training was critical to mitigate disaster management. Purposeful engagement requires the development of capacity within an organization (Page- Reeves, Marin, Bleecker, Moffett, DeerInWater, EchoHawk, & Medin 2017) The low level of training and awareness on archives management is a major challenge experienced by most organizations. This statement is alluded to by Khumalo & Baloyi (2017), and Makwae (2021) who stated that the lack of policy shows ineffective accountability and awareness of the personnel records management standards. Furthermore, the study conducted by Venson, Ngoepe, & Ngulube, (2014) shows a limited understanding of archives management. This shows that staff may not be aware of the importance or significance of archives management. Training on disaster management is mostly offered by national and international organizations. After employees and organizations are trained in disaster management, organizations are assisted in monitoring their progress continuously.

The distributed nature of climate change planning within South Africa introduces challenges to the selection of appropriate digitization technology. It became clear that South African communities had already established archives institutions. During the past several years, scholars in several disciplines have examined archives materials which led to the loss of archives materials. Those working with international disasters should work with international organizations and national emergency organizations to restore whatever was lost. to restore archives materials lost. The international organizations include the International Council on Archives (ICA), The International Council of Museums (ICOM), and the International Federation of Library Associations and Institutions (IFLA). What purpose does an archives institution serve if not to both collect and share its holdings with the international community? South African archivists understand their role in disseminating information to various communities. Moving forward requires the government to invest a lot of funds in the digitization of archives materials to ensure that such records are available online.

PROVIDING ACCESS TO ARCHIVES MATERIALS

In this study, access is defined as the availability of records to various stakeholders. People exercise their democratic rights by ensuring that archives are accessible to stakeholders (Taylor & Gibson 2017). Organizations comply with the Promotion of Access to Information. This means that organizations are to develop a Promotion of access to information manual to provide access to information. Organizations documented the right to access information by ensuring such records were prevented from any loss (Khan & Akhter 2017). In South Africa, the Promotion of Access to Information Act No. 2000 was enacted in 2000 to promote access to information. South Africa is supposed to be concerned about public opinion in their environment. The act established access rights to public and non-public records of the Republic of South Africa. The National Archives of South Africa preserves archival heritage and makes it accessible to the public (Nengomasha & Nyanga 2012). Organizations are responsible for ensuring that active records preserved in their records center are stored in their archive's repositories. This implies that both public and non-public institutions develop systems and processes to promote access to information. PAIA is dependent on the implementation of an archives management system within an organization. The lack of archives management systems posed a challenge to the organization. Access to archives materials is influenced by access policy. This statement is alluded to by (Mudzaki 2017) who indicated that the development, organization, availability, and preservation of archival materials depend on access management policy (Mudzaki 2017). Access to information is influenced by effective records and information management systems, which guarantee the management of records throughout their life cycle (Khumalo & Baloyi 2017). Effective archives management systems enable organizations to provide access to information. Despite that organizations collect some archival materials in different areas, there is a need for institutions to preserve archives materials collected and preserved by organizations. Therefore, organizations are required to develop classification to ensure records with archival records are preserved and made accessible within the archive's repository (Muchefa & Chigodora 2016). Access management policy is necessary because it ensures that the organization can keep track of its records and have a plan for its retention and disposal. Access to archives materials is the most neglected aspects in Africa. The promotion of Access to Information Act was enacted in South Africa to provide access to information. This enables various stakeholders to access various information. Accessibility of archives materials is dependent on effective archives management programs. Organizations are to ensure that access to records is controlled continuously and kept secret.

Privacy

The literature demonstrates that organizations have a degree of privacy concern, and Information Technology can enable individual abilities to safeguard information (Earp & Payton 2001). During the digitization of archives materials, the privacy of personal information should be considered and protected. This is because some of the archive's materials include personal information. The preservation of the right to personal data protection is, without doubt, a significant right in the law of right in the modern information society (Addulrauf & Fombard 2017). The Protection of Personal information (POPIA) ensures the protection of personal information (Mullon & Ngoepe 2019). The review of the literature shows inadequate controls to ensure the records and data collected from data subjects, third parties, and within the divisions were completed, accurate, and monitored regularly as outlined in Condition 5 of the Protection of Personal Information Act (POPIA). Data subjects in this study are referred to as stakeholders who create records. While third parties are referred to as the second person who preserves records. POPIA came into effect in July 2020. Organizations are required to develop policies, procedures, and procedures to comply with the legislation. Organizations are required to ensure that personal information is protected in line with the Act. There are eight conditions to which organizations need to adhere to. Namely: accountability, purpose specification collection, data quality and integrity, storage, retention and destruction of records, and security safeguarding. The purpose of the Act is to give effect to the constitutional rights to privacy by safeguarding personal information created or received by an organization. There is a need to balance the right to privacy against other rights, particularly the right to access personal information. This implies that personal information generated by internal and external organizations needs to be regulated. Regulation of personal information contributed to the protection of organizations. There is a need to protect the significant interests of organizations. This includes the free flow of information within the Republic of South Africa. Personal information should be regulated regularly., by establishing conditions, in harmony with international standards that prescribe the minimum threshold requirements for the lawful processing of personal information. This means that organizations should ensure that the following is implemented about records management. This means that the following should be undertaken by organizations:

- Organisations should start verifications on records security and monitor compliance with records management procedures ‘
- Measure the outcomes of any records security forms or compliance monitoring against key performance indicators to provide strategic oversight to those with overall responsibility.
- Organisations should ensure the classification of records in place.
- Organisations should conduct an information audit or records survey to identify records and personal information sets held by the organization.
- Create a central log or record of which organization functions create convinced records, which records are vital to the functioning of the organization, where they are kept, how long they are kept for about applicable laws or internal policies, and who needs to use them now and in the future.

- Ensure that all service providers who are either hosting or managing business applications with critical information or any personal information on behalf of the organization guarantee the protection of personal information.
- Ensure that the security around the office is enhanced and old equipment and storage cabinets are replaced with fireproof, waterproof, and lockable filing cabinets including steel bars on counters to encourage limited access to the storage areas. Implement a vibrant screen and pure desk policy culture with regular forms to provide pledges in compliance with the protection of personal information.
- Organisations are to implement secure records disposal practices for all record types.
- Regularly review the retention/ disposal schedule to ensure it continues to meet group essential and statutory requirements.
- Organizations are required to implement a formal periodic process for verifying the completeness and accuracy of personal information collected, processed, and stored by the organization. Furthermore, there is a need to modernize file plan arrangements to ensure archives' accessibility. There is a need for organizations to develop a clear screen and clear desk policy culture with regular checks to provide assurances in compliance with the protection of personal information. This requires the organization to develop a retention and disposal schedule.

Organizations embarked on data protection impact assessment. Risk assessment procedures must be in place to assess, identify, and management of risk (Swartz, Da Veiga, and Martins 2021, p.766) The objective of the assessment is to evaluate the extent to which the organization complies with the protection of Personal Information. It seems that personal information Impact Assessments (PIIA) are not conducted at the development, testing, and delivery stages such as pre-, and post-implementation of systems and processes. This implies that the organization should ensure that impact assessment is conducted throughout the system implementation stages/ phases for any project and initiative that entails treating personal information to ensure compliance. Personal Information Impact assessment safeguards organization in identifying and mitigating data protection risks, planning for the application of explanations to those risks, and assessing the treating activities of the organization Personal impact assessment should outline the description of the nature, scope, context, and purposes of the processing, Assess necessity, proportionality and compliance measures. This will also ensure the identity and assessment of risk to data subjects and identify any additional measures to mitigate risk within an organization. Therefore, management should ensure that data privacy is identified as the risk in the institutional Risk register.

Organizations are to ensure that the personal information impact assessment plan should be documented. It is also the accountability of the organization to inform the institutional Risk register to include data privacy as a risk.

Organizations are to ensure that personal information collected is completed, accurate, not misleading, and updated where necessary. A responsible party must take reasonable practice. A responsible party must take reasonably practicable steps to ensure that the personal information is complete, accurate, not misleading, and updated where necessary.

Organizations ensure the lawful processing of personal information. Organizations are required that the processing of personal information must be done lawfully in a manner that does not infringe upon a data subject's privacy. Management should ensure that there is documentation of policies such as personal information policy, Records and Archives policy, Information Communication Technology Cybersecurity strategy, and Information Classification policy. This will ensure the classification of information that will be collected, and the plan for the documentation of policy is in place. The protection of personal information compliance framework assists in outlining the processing of the personal information cycle. The organizational policies identified should be developed and approved by management. Organizations are also required to define and implement the Protection of Personal Information Act project charter.

Any digitization information, personal is to ensure consent, justification, and objections. POPIA indicated that there is a limitation in the implementation of the act. Although organizations have developed an inventory of personal information and outlined the different types of Personal Information collected/ required by the different divisions within the organization, management should ensure the information provided is complete and true. The inventory developed by the organization should list all the personal information required by the departments. The 'inventory developed should include methods of collection, method of transfer, consent required, format the information is stored, the storage location of the personal information collected, and the method of destruction if any furthermore. Management should ensure that all the onboarding forms include a consent disclaimer and the purpose for requesting such information is outlined. This implied that the organization is to finalize the inventory list with the above-mentioned recommendation. All organizations should update the type of personal information collected. All integrated organizations should secure written consent for personnel from organizations for whatever purpose and/ or function that such information is being collected. The request for consent should be included in onboarding forms and online forms developed for collecting information.

Security and safety of personal information are significant for the continuation of the organization. This implies that organizations are to develop contractual conditions for the management of third-party contracts. Organizations are to develop a data privacy policy to ensure the management of information. There is a need to develop and regularly monitor security controls around paper-based records and electronic records management systems.

Organizations ensure that backup management and retention and destruction of personal information are conducted regularly. Section 14 of the Personal Information Act states that an organization must destroy or delete a record of personal information or de-identify it as soon as reasonably practicable after the responsible party is no longer authorized to retain the record in terms of subsection (1) or (2). The review of the literature shows that most organizations lack or are absent of Backup management processes and procedures for electronic and paper-based data (Asogwa, Ezeani, & Asogwa 2021). The destruction of records raised questions about the integrity of records (Luker 2017). There is a need for organizations to develop a preservation strategy to ensure the continuous back of archives materials (Adu & Ngulube 2016). However, the development of a backup strategy does not imply the sustainability of archives materials (Corrado & Moulaison 2014). The sustainability of organizational records requires organizations to update their electronic records management systems. This implies that organizations are to buy information and communication technologies systems to ensure that data within the electronic records management system is maintained. Therefore, organizations need to develop a Backup policy and monitor procedures to ensure data is adequately retained destroyed and safeguarded. There is a need for scheduling of records neither on daily, nor weekly backup job schedules should be maintained, approved, and reviewed to ensure data is adequately retained. Management should ensure that the destruction of previously backed-up data is outlined in the policies procedures and procedures in place. This means that organizations are required to develop a Data Backup and Recovery Policy, develop a Disaster recovery plan, Develop a Back- Up schedule and monitoring process, and ensure paper-based records are backed up.

Organizations are to ensure that internal and external audits are conducted to monitor compliance with privacy legislation by limiting the destruction of records (Swartz, Da Veiga, & Martins 2021). Organizations are to ensure security audit logging and breach incidents are monitored regularly. Section 22 Notification of security compromises sets out that security compromises data breaches. It happens anytime there are reasonable grounds to believe that the personal information of a data subject has been accessed or acquired by any unauthorized person. Most organizations lack a documentation baseline level of logging and auditing on all systems, and a higher baseline level on all critical and normal behaviors of networks, systems, and applications. It is therefore recommended that organizations develop security incident plans or update the incident management policy to ensure mechanisms for outside parties to report incidents. There should be a baseline level of logging and auditing on all systems and a higher baseline level on all critical systems. There is a need for normal and abnormal behaviors of networks, systems, and applications. There is also a need for a clear requirement for forensic disk images to be made to sanitize write–protectable or write-one media. Furthermore, there is a need for a process for lessons-learned meetings after major incidents happen to organizations.

In South Africa, a formal and legal process of requesting personal information gave rise to legal disputes about archival records disclosure and destruction. These disputes show the significance of ensuring the management of personal information created and preserved by organizations. It further shows the significance of legal power as a way of keeping records in line with government requirements. Security measures on integrity and confidentiality of personal information should be maintained. Section 19 of the Personal Information Act outlines that a responsible party must secure the integrity and confidentiality of personal information in its possession or under its control by taking appropriate, reasonable, technical, and organizational measures. This is done to prevent loss, damage, or unauthorized destruction of personal information and unlawful access to or processing of personal information. Organizations should ensure that the following security safeguards and control procedures as stipulated in condition 7 of POPIA are not adequately implemented for example:

- Absence of data encryption
- Maintenance of the records stored, and regular monitoring were not outlined in the data retention policy and procedure.
- Absence of personal information data classification grades
- Inadequate personal information inventory plan
- Absence of paper-based records Back - up
- Absence of User access/ role matrixes for systems
- Absence of Network and System access form
- Absence of consent clauses on websites
- Absence of 3rd party contracts that process personal information
- Absence of Data Privacy and POPIA compliance.

Custodial and environmental security measures are of significance for organizations (Nengomasha & Nyanga 2012). Management should ensure that security safeguards and control procedures are reviewed to control access to areas where personal information is stored. Organizations consider encrypting organizations' laptops, computers, and external devices to protect data stored on these devices from being intercepted by malicious users. Furthermore, organizations need to develop security incident plans to cover mechanisms for outside parties to report incidents. The organization must ensure normal and abnormal behaviors of networks, systems, and applications. The process for lessons learned meetings after major incidents should be initiated by organizations. Organizations should ensure the inventory plan is updated as outlined above and includes security measures to safeguard the information. Management should ensure that all the existing Information technology security policies and procedures are regularly updated to include the disposal of personal information stored on computers and other electronic devices. Security measures should be put in place when collecting personal information for integrity and confidentiality. So, the following actions should be implemented by organizations to ensure effective management of information of the organization. This includes the implementation of encryption across all organization's devices. There is a need to maintain, develop, and control third-party contracts involved in processing personal information. Organizations need to develop a data privacy policy. There is a need to develop and regularly monitor security controls around paper–based records and electronic records. There is also a need to develop a Backup plan procedure, furthermore, there is a need to define user access/ role matrix access for systems. Archivists are to ensure data classification grades such as confidential, restricted, public, or private records are documented. Document security measures for personal information collected for all organizations should be maintained. There is a need to ensure access forms outline security measures for sensitive/ confidential information. There is also a need for further development and implementation of the Information Technology Asset Register policy.

There should be the quality of information preserved and made accessible to various stakeholders. Individual privacy needs to be protected to ensure that access to information is available to various stakeholders. Some organizations ensure that the privacy of information is also included in the organization. There is a need to guarantee the privacy of information created by an organization.

CONCLUSION

Archive materials are significant because they ensure accountability of government actions and decisions. While the government transition to the digital environment expands and information provisions in digital environment expand to grow, the question of whether records management has kept up with the rapid pace of digital information flow to ensure that records are permanent preservation. The study concluded that lack of implementation of the legislative framework, lack of coordination of archives management, limited resources allocated to government ministries to implement archives management programs, and lack of coordination of archives management is the main pillar for the loss of archive materials. Therefore, the study recommended that government bodies implement a legislative framework to implement preservation of archives materials. Government should invest resources in the development and implementation of digitisation projects. This chapter adds value to archivists to analyze pre–disaster public spending, promote better understanding and coordination of the archival sector, identify a critical area that needs to be analyzed and gaps, isolate inefficient disaster mitigation expenditure, and promote efficiency and transparency in disaster financing. Furthermore, the study will enable the disaster mitigation finance literature in Southern Africa.

AREAS OF FURTHER STUDIES

A study can be conducted on the process of building a digital library system in South Africa

ACKNOWLEDGEMENT

This study is funded and supported by the National Institute for the Humanities and Social Sciences

REFERENCES

Abdeen, F. N., Fernando, T., Kulatunga, U., Hettige, S., & Ranasinghe, A. (2021). Challenges in Multi-agency collaboration in disaster management: A Sri Lankan perspective. *International Journal of Disaster Risk Reduction, 62*, 102399. doi:10.1016/j.ijdrr.2021.102399

Adbulrauf, A. L., & Fombad, M. C. (2017). Personal Data Protection in Nigeria: Reflections on Opportunities, Options and Challenges to Legal Reforms. *The Liverpool Law Review, 38*(2), 105–135. doi:10.100710991-016-9189-8

Adu, K., & Ngulube, P. (2016). Preserving the digital heritage of public institutions in Ghana in the wake of electronic government. *Library Hi Tech, 34*(4), 748–763. doi:10.1108/LHT-07-2016-0077

Asogwa, E. B., Ezeani, N. C., & Asogwa, N. M. (2021). Status of electronic records management (e-RM) in African university libraries: Experience from Nigerian universities. Status of e-RM in African university libraries. *Library Management, 42*(8/9), 515–530. doi:10.1108/LM-04-2021-0036

Ayoung, D. A., Boatbil, S. C., & Baada, N. F. (2016). Disaster preparedness libraries Insights from polytechnic librarians in Ghana. *Information Development, 32*(5), 1296–1305. doi:10.1177/0266666915588794

Balogun, T., & Kalusopa, T. (2021). A framework for digital preservation of Indigenous knowledge system (IKS) in repositories in South Africa. *Records Management Journal, 31*(2), 176–196. doi:10.1108/RMJ-12-2020-0042

Barker, K. H. (1997). The Business of Government and the Future of Government *Archives. The American Archivist, 60*(2), 234–252. doi:10.17723/aarc.60.2.p728118660482531

Bowker, L., & Villamizar, C. (2017). Embedding a records manager as a strategy for helping to positively influence an organization's records management culture. Embedding a records manager. *Records Management Journal, 27*(1), 57–68. doi:10.1108/RMJ-02-2016-0005

Ceeney, N. (2008). The Role of a 21st-Century National Archive- The Relevance of the Jenkinsonian Tradition, and a Redefinition for the Information Society. *Journal of the Society of Archivists, 29*(1), 57–71. doi:10.1080/00379810802499868

Corrado, E. M., & Moulaison, H. L. (2014). *Digital preservation for libraries, Archives and Museums.* Rowman & Littlefield.

Delaney, B., & De Jong, A. (2015). Media Archives and Digital Preservation Overcoming Cultural Barriers. *New Review of Information Networking, 20*(1-2), 73–89. doi:10.1080/13614576.2015.1112626

Dikopoulou, A., & Mihiotis, A. (2012). The contribution of records management to good governance. *The TQM Journal, 24*(2), 123–141. doi:10.1108/17542731211215071

Dube, K., & Nhamo, G. (2020). Evidence and impact of climate change on South African national parks. [Elsevier]. *Environmental Development*, 33.

Dube, K., Nhamo, G., & Chikodzi, D. (2021). Rising Sea level and its implications on coastal tourism development in Cape Town, South Africa. *Journal of Outdoor Recreation and Tourism, 33*, 33. doi:10.1016/j.jort.2020.100346

Earp, B. J., & Payton, C. F. (2001). Data Protection in the University Setting: Employee Perceptions of Student Privacy. *Proceedings of the 34th Hawaii International Conference on System Sciences*. IEEE 10.1109/HICSS.2001.927152

Ebi, O. A. (2021). *Post–1996 Service delivery in South Africa: Constitutional and Social Contract perspectives.* [PhD Thesis, University of the Western Cape].

Fabunmi, A.; Paris, M & Fabunmi, M (2006). Digitization of Library Resources: Challenges and Implications for Policy and Planning. *International Journal of African & African American Studies, 5*(2) 23 – 36.

Hoffman, M. T., Rick, F., Rohde, R. F., & Gillso, L. (2019). *Rethinking Catastrophe? Historical trajectories and modeled future vegetation change in Southern Africa.* Anthropocene.

Humphreys, C., McCarthy, G., Dowling, M., Kertesz, M., & Tropea, R. (2014). Improving the Archiving of Records in the Out-of-Home Care Sector. *Australian Social Work, 67*(4), 509–524. doi:10.1080/0312407X.2013.856453

Jethro, D. (2021). Ash: Memorializing the 2021 University of Cape Town Library Fire. *The Journal of Objects. Art and Belief., 17*(5), 671–677.

Katuu, S., & Van der Walt, T. (2016). Assessing the legislative and regulatory framework supporting the management of records in South Africa's public health sectors. *South African Journal of Information Management, 18*(1), a686. doi:10.4102ajim.v18i1.686

Khan, U. N., & Akhter, S. (2017). Right to Information as an Instrumental Force of Good Governance in South Asia. *A Research Journal of South Asian Studies. South Asian Studies, 32*(1), 151–160.

Khumalo, B. N., & Baloyi, C. (2017). The possible benefits of Freedom of Information laws to the records management landscape in the ESARBICA region. *Information Development*, 1–15.

Kirkwood, C. (2021). *The Fire Disaster in the University of Cape Town's Jagger Library, and its consequences.* HDL. https://hdl.handle.net/10520/ejc-cabo_v2021_n1_a5

Luker, T. (2017). Decolonising Archives: Indigenous Challenges to Records Keeping in 'Reconciling' Settler Colonial State. *Australian Feminist Studies, 32*(91-92), 91–92. doi:10.1080/08164649.2017.1357011

Makwae, N. E. (2021). Legal frameworks for personnel records management in support of accountability in devolved governments: A case of Garissa County Government. Personnel records management. *Records Management Journal, 31*(2), 109–133. doi:10.1108/RMJ-05-2019-0024

Malan, L. (2005). Intergovernmental relations and co-operative government in South Africa: the ten–year review. *Politeia, 41*(2).

Marutha, S. N., & Ngulube, P. (2012). Electronic records management in the public health sector of the Limpopo province in South Africa. *Journal of the South African Society of Archivists, 45*, 39–67.

Matlala, E. M., Ncubem, R. T., & Parbanath, S. (2022). The State of digital records preservation in South Africa's public sector in the 21st Century: A literature review. *Records Management Journal, 32*(2), 198–212. doi:10.1108/RMJ-02-2021-0004

Mnjama, N. (2005). Archival landscape in Eastern and Southern Africa. *Library Management, 26*(8/9), 457–470. doi:10.1108/01435120510631747

Muchefa, L., & Chigodora, T. (2016). A historical account of backlog challenges at National Archives of Zimbabwe and the Access Implications. *ESARBICA Journal, 35*, 112–119.

Mudzaki, F. (2017). Establishing a lasting solution to collection development policy: Challenges for audiovisual archives to enhance access in Zimbabwe. *ESARBICA Journal, 36*, 94–107.

Mullon, A. P., & Ngoepe, M. (2019). An integrated framework to elevate information governance to a national level in South Africa. *Records Management Journal, 29*(1/2), 103–116. doi:10.1108/RMJ-09-2018-0030

Nel, D. & Masilela, L., (2020), Open Governance for Improved Service Delivery Innovation in South Africa. *International Journal of eBusiness and eGovernment Studies, 12*(1), 33-47. Doi: doi:10.34111/ijebeg.20201210333

Nengomasha, T. C., & Nyanga, H. E. (2012). Managing semi-current records: A case for records centers for the public service of Namibia. *Journal for Studies in Humanities and Social Sciences, 1*(2).

Ngulube, P., & Tafor, V. F. (2006). The Management of Public records and archives in the member countries of ESARBICA. *Journal of the Society of Archivists, 27*(1), 57–58. doi:10.1080/00039810600691288

Odongo, O. J. (2018). Achieving information safety in a disaster environment: The way forward for Africa. *Regional Journal of Information and Knowledge Management, 3*(1), 15–29.

Ogbomo, O. B., Ejedafiru, F. E., & Olukotun, V. (2023). Human Factors Affecting the Preservation of Series Materials: A Case Study of Federal University Libraries in North Central Nigeria. *Management, 8*(1), 1–10.

Ogbomo, O.M, Ejedafiru, F.E & Olukotun, V (2023). Human Factors affecting the preservation of serial materials: A case study of Federal university libraries in north-central Nigeria. *Regional Journal of Information and Knowledge Management, 8*(1)

Page-Reeves, J., Marin, A., Bleecker, M., Moffett, M. L., DeerInWater, K., EchoHawk, S., & Medin, D. (2017). From Community Data to Research Archive. *Gateways : International Journal of Community Research & Engagement, 10*, 282–297. doi:10.5130/ijcre.v10i1.4947

Reine, R. (2019). Archivists and Time: Conceptions of Time and Long-Term Information Preservation among Archivists. *Journal of Contemporary Archival Studies, 6*(6).

Ryan Chance, R. K. (2015). Where there is fire, there is politics: Ungovernability and Material Life in Urban South Africa. *Cultural Anthropology, 30*(3), 394–423. doi:10.14506/ca30.3.03

Swartz, P., Da Veiga, A., & Martins, N. (2021). Validating an information privacy governance questionnaire to measure the perceptions of employees. *Information and Computer Security, 29*(5), 761–789. doi:10.1108/ICS-08-2020-0135

Taylor, J., & Gibson, K. L. (2017). Digitization, digital interaction, and social media: Embedded barriers to democratic heritage. *International Journal of Heritage Studies, 23*(5), 408–420. doi:10.1080/13527258.2016.1171245

Venson, L. S., Ngoepe, M., & Ngulube, P. (2014). The role of public archives in national development in selected countries in the East and Southern Africa Regional Branch of the International Council on Archives region. *Innovation, 48*, 43–63.

Wamukoya, J., & Mutula, S. (2009). Public Sector Information management in East and Southern Africa: Implications for FOI, democracy, and integrity in government. *International Journal of Information Management, 29*(5), 331–341.

Wangutusi, J. (2009). *Assessing the Impact of Institutional E-Readiness for Provision of Archival Information to Researchers: The Case of Kenya National Archives and Documentation Service.*

KEY TERMS AND DEFINITIONS

Archives Materials: These are records with historical, and cultural, significance that need to be permanently preserved by neither national nor provincial archives.

Digitalization: This is a process of changing records from analog to digital form.

National Archives and Records Service Act 43 of 1996: This is a piece of legislation in South Africa that provides a guideline on the management and care of the records of governmental bodies and the preservation and use of a national archives' heritage.

POPIA: This is a piece of legislation enacted in South Africa to protect privacy and personal information.

Restoration: This is a process of ensuring that records are repaired to their original format.

Chapter 10
The Effect of Humanitarian Aid on Logistics Companies' Marketing

Nazlı Gülfem Gidener
https://orcid.org/0000-0002-2626-1597
Dokuz Eylül University, Turkey

Damla Kartal
Dokuz Eylül University, Turkey

Burak Koca
https://orcid.org/0009-0008-8938-531X
Dokuz Eylül University, Turkey

Aleyna Çevir
Dokuz Eylül University, Turkey

ABSTRACT

The purpose of this book chapter is to understand and analyze the impact of logistics companies' contributions to humanitarian logistics on company marketing. The analysis of logistics processes tells us what kind of results will emerge in the stages of humanitarian aid logistics. The humanitarian aid logistics and corporate social responsibility contribution to logistics companies is analyzed. It is important for the research to be conducted to investigate the logistics performance criteria and to emphasize their importance especially through trying times such as COVID-19 epidemic. These operations enable companies to truly utilize crises and unfortunately disasters as tools and opportunity for improvement and growth. Evaluating the performance criteria of the company and its employees and measuring their contribution to the brand image of the company is very important in this book chapter which enables companies to improve their brand image.

DOI: 10.4018/978-1-6684-9522-3.ch010

HUMANITARIAN AID LOGISTICS

Humanitarian logistics is fundamentally different from standard logistics in that its goal is to give medical, water, food, and shelter to people in need. Even though these operations are always hampered by logistical problems, difficulties in humanitarian logistics management, disaster-management policy, and an overabundance of financial resources, humanitarian logistics focuses on response at search and rescue, sustaining or saving life, and restoring self-sufficiency (Thevenaz et.al., 2010). This type of logistics activities are essential during times of crises or disasters.

The following processes are necessary during humanitarian logistics: delivering adequate supplies in good condition; coordinating and prioritizing the use of restricted and shared transportation; storing, staging, and moving bulk goods; and transferring people. Specific delivery from outside the impacted area (Van Wassenhove, L. N. 2006).

The concept of humanitarian aid, which has existed since the early days of history, is a sector of billions of dollars in budgets. Millions of different types of organizations such as non-profit organizations, foundations, associations, charities and profit-making organizations have emerged for this purpose. Emerging as a third sector, humanitarian organizations have always attracted attention with their budgets and activities in the world (Humanitarian Effectiveness, 2017

Humanitarian Logistics

Humanitarian aid logistics, especially in the implementation phase, has some difficulties in itself and with the effects of environmental factors. The fact that the demands are uncertain at first, that they appear suddenly, that large deliveries need to be delivered as soon as possible, that the resources are not available or that they are insufficient are among the factors that make the operation difficult (Balcik et.al., 2008).

Figure 1. Humanitarian aid logistics confusion
(Overstreet et.al., 2011)

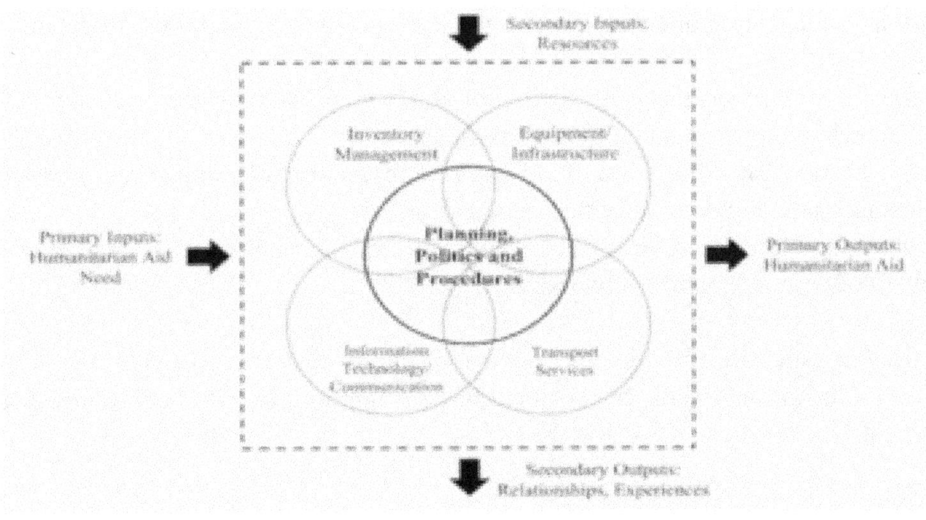

Security issues in the area where the aid will go also create a great challenge for that region. For example: Famine, thirst or any natural disaster that occurs in that region due to war in a country affects inventory management (Kovacs et.al., 2009).

Due to the different characteristics of disaster types, humanitarian aid operations emerge in different forms each time. For example, if there is an earthquake or war in a region, the physical infrastructure of that region is affected. Due to these effects, special routes have to be found. Another important logistics issue is designing the destination point transport. First aid supplies, food, equipment, and rescue personnel need to be delivered from the supply point to a large number of destinations geographically dispersed in the disaster area. In addition, disaster-affected people need to be transported to health centers quickly and safely (Barbarosoğlu et.al., 2002). Preparations for such activities should be provided by good training programmes, simulations and the ability to predict. Disasters have a different impact in each of the different sub-regions, depending on geography, demographics and socio-economic situation. It is predicted that the situation will get worse due to the change in the global situation in the future (Kovacs et.al., 2009).

Humanitarian Aid Operation

The world has faced many humanitarian crises all over the world, has been exposed to natural disasters such as earthquakes, floods and tsunamis, and has suffered great difficulties due to social displacement as a result of wars. Humanitarian aid, which acts to solve the problems, is one of the important elements of the international community for political, economic and military purposes for places in need for reasons such as security, hunger, thirst, famine, shelter, epidemic disease due to natural disasters, war, drought and social conflicts. It is defined as assistance or assistance such as independent search and rescue situations, emergency health services, nutrition and shelter (T.C.Başbakanlık Afet ve Acil Durum Yönetimi Başkanlığı, 2014).

Humanitarian aid is the aid provided to people in need. Generally, these aids can be aid, food, shelter or medical aid. These donations can also be made in cash. The primary purpose of humanitarian aid is to save lives and protect human dignity in times of crisis. Secondary purposes are to provide for people's livelihoods and to protect other life-saving purposes (Maxwell, 2009).

Types of Humanitarian Aid Operations: The three possible categories of humanitarian aid are shown below, according to the degree of contact between the people helping and those affected:

1. Direct assistance: It covers face-to-face distribution of goods and services such as food distribution, first aid, search and rescue, and family assistance.
2. Indirect assistance: Transportation of aid goods, construction of refugee camps, water treatment, mine clearance, etc. includes activities such as
3. Infrastructure support: Represents general engineering work such as road repair, power generation or recovery of communication networks (OCHA, 2007).

Humanitarian logistics are activities that involve efficient, cost-effective planning, implementation and control of goods and materials, from source to consumption, to help people in distress (Thomas and Kopczak, 2007).

Humanitarian logistics is an activity that tries to deal with the occurrence of events such as earthquakes, tsunamis, hurricanes, epidemics, droughts, famines, terrorist attacks and war situations (Kovacs et.al., 2009).

The humanitarian logistics system boundary is the line that separates the humanitarian logistics components from the general external environment. The border indicates the control area of the logistician (Overstreet et.al., 2011). Hutarian aid efforts are characterized by significant uncertainty and complexity, which presents a number of challenges. Therefore, they must be properly managed in order to give a good response. The humanitarian aid operation is an important point for the successful execution of this process and it starts with the process design (Tomasini et.al., 2009).

Logistics accounts for 80% of rescue efforts and is an important factor in humanitarian operations (Trunick, 2005).

Table 1. Characteristics of humanitarian aid logistics (Kovacs et.al., 2007)

Main Purpose	Helping people affected by disaster
Actor Structure	There is a focus on stakeholders who do not have clear links with each other, and the dominance of ngos and government actors.
Three Stage Organization	Preparedness, emergency response, rebuilding
Key Features	Supply and supplier diversity, large-scale activities, erratic demand, and unusual constraints in large-scale emergencies.
Supply Chain Philosophy	The 'pushed' philosophy is the philosophy applied to the emergency response phase of the consumables while they are going to the disaster area. The 'pull' philosophy is applied during the restructuring phase.
Transportation And Infrastructure	Infrastructure is unclear. Assurance of food and medical supplies quality is uncertain.
Time Effects	Time delays can cause loss of lives.
Limited Knowledge Activities	Supply chains need to be designed and implemented all at once because most disasters require immediate response.
Supplier Structure	The choice is limited, in some cases undesirable suppliers may be employed.
Control Status	Due to the urgency of the situation, there is a lack of control over the transactions.

Fundamental of Humanitarian Logistics Process

The process of deploying people, resources, skills, and expertise to assist disaster victims is known as humanitarian logistics. Logistics is at the heart of all humanitarian mobilization activities, serving as a link between catastrophe preparedness and response, procurement and distribution, and headquarters and the field. It can also be one of the most expensive components of a relief effort, and the performance of the operation is constantly assessed in order to optimize the operation and reduce operating costs while maximizing the operation's results (Tomasini et.al., 2009).

The term "reaction" refers to the different actions taken as soon as a tragedy strikes. The major goals of this stage are to respond quickly by activating the "silent network" or "temporary networks," and to restore basic services and commodities delivery to the greatest number of beneficiaries in the shortest time possible. In the aftermath of a disaster, the reconstruction stage refers to many operations. It entails rehabilitation, with the goal of resolving the issue in the long run. For example, transportation businesses may experience a modal shift from road to rail soon following a tragedy that lasts long after the crisis has occurred (Kovács et.al., 2007).

Humanitarian Logistician

A humanitarian aid logistician, unlike other logistics operations, aims to deliver aid (Kovacs et.al., 2007). They are logistics personnel working in humanitarian aid logistics, who want different characteristics from other commercial logistics, and who need to be professional in humanitarian aid and who work in natural disaster operations (Allen et.al., 2013).

The employee who can be assigned to humanitarian aid logistics needs to have many skill criteria and this skill is very important. These skill criteria are factors that affect the success of the task, and this should be criteria that enable different actors to work in harmony and increase efficiency. Supply chain management is a profession that involves the management of inventory, information, and financial flows over a network of customers, distributors, manufacturers, and suppliers. The integration of each part of the chain with other institutions ensures the successful progress of this system (Yurdakul et.al., 2015).

Managing the supply chain effectively is a challenging task as a result of increases in product diversity, short product life cycles, increase in outsourcing, globalization of businesses and continuous developments in technology (Lee, 2002).

Top managers in logistics and supply chains play an important role in the continuation of competitiveness and success. These managers should not only have knowledge, they should also be people who manage business relations well (Mangan et.al., 2005). Many studies are being conducted to measure these competencies (Murphy et.al., 2007). The data revealed by the study in terms of determining the mid-level logisticians are as follows: management skills, business skills, logistics skills (Bisogni, 2008).

The skills that a modern supply chain manager should have are as follows: Communication, Research and Planning, Human Relations, Organization, Management and Leadership, Work Sustainability and Global Perspective. The skills that a humanitarian aid logistician should have are listed as follows: general management skills, functional logistics skills, interpersonal characteristics, problem solving skills, humanitarian skills (Kovács et.al., 2012).

General Management Skills: General management skills are tools that managers use to achieve the organization's goals (Ermasova et.al., 2018). In order to manage an organization successfully, manpower, inspiring dedication, ability to change management, establishing and fulfilling the job, facilitating the psychological and social contexts of the job, using business connections to serve a purpose, managing decision-making processes, managing strategy and innovations, and It is defined as concepts that include the management of logistics and technological developments (Robbins et.al., 2012). General management skills are the set of features required for a manager to be successful in a job, regardless of their level (Draganidis et.al, 2006).

Functional Logistics Skills: These skills are related to the field of logistics. It contains all professional information (Lin 2018). Logistics professionals are required to be highly skilled in a range of management skills, have logistics knowledge and skills, and have both general and specialist knowledge (Thai, 2012).

Interpersonal Features: Personal skills are goal-oriented behaviors that can be used in face-to-face interactions. With these skills, it is aimed to achieve the success of the task performed (Hayes, 2002). Interpersonal skills encompass a wide variety of techniques and approaches, and employees have a common denominator. Everything that people say and do has effects on the result. The impression that the person creates on other people and the organization is very important (Stainsby et.al., 2007).

Problem Solving Skills: Identifying complex problems, reviewing and evaluating options, and reviewing information about solutions is the required competency to determine a solution to a problem using information about the problem (Kyllonen, 2018).

CORPORATE SOCIAL RESPONSIBILITY

The concept of corporate social responsibility means that businesses determine their goals and objectives by taking into account the benefit of the society, and make strategies and plans in this direction without making profit (S.L. Wartick et.al., 1985).

Corporate Social Responsibility Dimensions: According to Carroll, corporate social responsibility can be examined in four dimensions: economic, legal, moral and voluntary responsibilities. Carroll has developed a social responsibility pyramid consisting of these four dimensions (Carroll, 1991).

Economic Responsibilities: The purpose required for commercial companies to be sustainable is to create a profitable business cycle. This is important in order to encourage its stakeholders to invest. When companies add value to their services, they create profits, and in doing so they benefit all of the company's stakeholders. Therefore, economic responsibility is a basic requirement that must be met in a competitive business world.

Legal Responsibilities: Society has not only viewed businesses as economic entities, but has also established the ground rules by which businesses are expected to operate and operate. This includes ground rules, laws and regulations. Businesses are expected and obligated to comply with these laws and regulations as a condition of operation.

Ethical Responsibilities: The expectations of most societies recognize that laws are necessary but not sufficient. Society expects businesses to operate and conduct business in an ethical manner. The purpose of these expectations is to require businesses, consumers, employees, owners and society to be consistent with regard to protection.

Philanthropic Responsibilities: Corporate philanthropy includes all forms of business giving. Corporate philanthropy embraces business's voluntary or discretionary activities.

Corporate social responsibility has many contributions to companies. Some of these benefits are:

Benefits to the Business; Increase in company shares and brand value, easy financial access, increase in corporate image, increase in sales volume, educated employees and retention, ease of entering new markets, increasing customer loyalty, competition.

Benefits provided to stakeholders; Increased investment in commercial activities, higher appeal of the stock to investors, increased reputation of the stock.

Employee benefits; Safe working environment for employees, better working conditions, reduction of employment costs, equal opportunity.

Benefits to Customers; To present the brand image of the product at the right price and quality.

Benefits Compared to Competitors; Clearly provide necessary information and understanding of ethical advertising. The benefits of this; Demonstrating honesty towards the product in the product or service.

Benefits to Society; To be educated for human rights, to contribute to the fields of health and culture, education, employees and sustainability.

Environmental Benefits; Sustainability, use of vegetation in the protection of our culture, use of animal generations, recycling, benefiting from production, being environmentally friendly, energy, use for use (Aktan, 2006).

Brand Image: Brand image leads consumers to prioritize their purchasing behavior. Brand image, strengths and weaknesses, positive and positive control perceptions all come together. These perceptions consist of direct or one-day experiences with the brand (Perry et.al., 2003).

Prioritizing the brand image allows the company to increase its brand value without advertising to be preferred. Creating a socially beneficial brand image is less expensive than targeted promotional and advertising campaigns (Frost, 2005).

METHODOLOGY

In this book chapter The effect of humanitarian aid on logistics companies' marketing was investigated. The research method used in this research is interview. This interview was conducted with Key Account Manager working at X Company. The reason for preferring to meet with X Company is that the company contributes to many social responsibility projects. These are the company opening its warehouses free of charge in case of fires in Turkey, the aid vehicles contract with the Red Crescent, and their contribution to humanitarian aid logistics for Ukraine, which is currently at war. The interview with X Company was conducted over the Zoom application and lasted 60 minutes.

The reason for meeting with Key Account Manager is that the manager leads these logistics operations and it is thought that the most reliable answers can be given about this issue. Additionally, the reason for choosing the interview as the research method is to obtain reliable information from the interviewed company and it was tried not to restrict the interviewer with the unstructured structure type and to get more open source information. An unstructured interview is one in which the interviewer is not given precise instructions, restrictions, predefined questions, or possibilities. The interviewer presents several broad questions to get a clear, informal and spontaneous response from the respondent. To gain additional in-depth knowledge of the topic, the interviewer explores with additional questions and/or contradictions. When there is limited information on a topic, unstructured interviews are very useful for understanding the underlying narrative of participants' experiences (M. Easwaramoorthy, et.al., 2006).

Company: It was established in Europe in 70s and is a 3PL logistics company with companies in many countries, including Turkey. Company X is an active and global company, providing logistics services by land, sea, and air. X Company is a company that attaches importance to corporate social responsibility values.

Interview: An interview is a conversation in which information is gathered. An interviewer and a participant participate in a research interview. The interviewer moderates the session and asks questions, and the participant answers the questions. Interviews can be done face-to-face or over the phone. The internet is also becoming more popular as a tool for conducting interviews. (M. Easwaramoorthy, et.al., 2006)

Interview

1. What are your thoughts on humanitarian logistics as a company?

As a company, this is an issue that we attach great importance to. We have various aids, including social assistance projects, logistical support in case of disasters, and non-profit organizations. As a company, we have budgets for these projects. From the company's point of view, it is also emotionally satisfying to have helped people professionally in situations such as disasters first. This also gives the employees an emotional satisfaction. Secondly, if we look at the actual professional part of the job; it's not like we should do this for advertising and marketing, but it gives us serious benefits when we look at advertising and marketing in Turkey, whether we want to or not. In short, our point of view is mainly the humanitarian part, but also the commercial part.

2. What do you think are the factors that make humanitarian logistics difficult for your company?

In fact, you have touched on the most correct difficulties. As you said, these difficulties are the ones we have experienced the most. In particular, insufficient equipment and time constraints are a challenge that we experience quite often. For example, in the Ukraine –Russia war, various aid is sent to Ukraine from both Turkey and other countries. In particular, the United Nations conducts the most extensive of its activities through Turkey. For this purpose, X Company was also asked for help, as we are a company that can provide large and more convenient support in Turkey. Under normal circumstances, the entire Sales Operation Procedure of the work is removed, but there is no such thing in the logistics of war and disaster. We are experiencing these difficulties when the United Nations says that we will come and deliver 2,000 vehicles of aid directly within 3 months. Equipment may be insufficient or time constraints such as 3 months may occur. These are things that are far beyond capacity, but ultimately we are sending help to people. As such, various solutions are being tried to be produced. For example, the transport model is like diversification. At the moment it is quite difficult to get to Ukraine only by road it is not clear what will happen to your trucks, they can get stuck at the border. We decided to use Ro-ro in our transport model. We transported it by ship from Istanbul to the port of Constanta in Romania. After transporting them, we planned to go to Ukraine with the tow truck organization from the opposite side. We have also received funding support from the United Nations, as we must have a very large fleet of vehicles. For these solutions, all the planning inside had to go right. In addition, October the network part of our company is quite wide, we do not have problems with the lack of information. We attach great importance to our information flow.

3. Can you tell us about what you are doing in the preparation, response, reduction processes, which are the stages of humanitarian logistics?

Since we are a Logistics company here, we are actually only involved in the intervention part. For example, we have opened a logistics center consisting of 60m2 to the public to collect all the assistance at the request of various aid organizations and certain people in case of forest fires, which was one of the disasters we experienced last year, at the request of us. In addition, we sent our X Company trucks to various parks in Istanbul and Izmir, and from there we collected the help that people wanted and took it to the center. These were purely non-profit benefits. We have also joined with different logistics companies and provided various assistance. That's how we got involved in the intervention part. The other stages hardly cover the company.

4. What kind of logistics skills do you want your employees to have for these issues in your company?

Under each transport model, we have colleagues who specialize in various topics depending on the company's capacity. We have friends who specialize in road transport, for example, in certain regions. We have various teams specializing in pricing separately and certification separately. All of them actually serve for sales marketing. Sales and marketing brings together and reports your entire business. Here we usually look at if we want to get these skills working in the operations part. For example, the flow of information; it is important that the employee has a good dialogue with the opposing agencies, is in constant communication. He/she must have good relations with the drivers for the highway. The most important skill in every operations department is good information flow. Secondly, in the sales and marketing department, he/she must be on good terms with the customers and is expected to provide accurate information.

5. Do you provide your employees with values such as education, motivation in this regard?

Considering all the projects on the social responsibility side, we have a social assistance team under the sales marketing team. We have social responsibility projects where anyone can participate, from the blue collar to our social worker. Everyone can also come up with their own projects. This is not how we train all our employees, but we hold monthly meetings with our friends who are volunteers and exchange ideas about what we can do. In the professional part, training is a process that is continuous globally because we do logistics.

6. Performance management is an important dimension in humanitarian aid logistics. Are you making talent acquisitions related to your company? What do you do?

Yes, we do. As I mentioned earlier, the basis of this issue is situations such as time constraints, operations management, planning. For these, we have a performance analysis called KPI (key performance indicator) that we keep for each employee. It is an analysis that is carried out every 3 months, starting from the individual and ending with the company as a whole. It is a process that usually proceeds through human resources. It consists of assessments that go from the manager to the lowest employee. It actually includes what we need to improve on and how. If there is any training that can be given through this, interviews are conducted. Sometimes there are trainings within the company itself, sometimes from other companies. We have an education called cross-education. These are processes such as training each other in-house. It is a system that we use in the general flow of work, not through humanitarian aid. As a result, we see increased performance.

7. What kind of aid do you provide more than the types of humanitarian operations?

Transportation and storage aids are mainly the aids we provide. We are also able to provide financial assistance in different situations. On the other hand, we are unable to provide professional assistance in other matters. For example, book equipment assistance to village schools, financial assistance to animal shelters. In these, it provides good returns as an emotional plus marketing.

8. What is your definition of corporate social responsibility as a company?

I can tell you my personal point of view, the priority in this regard is the people. Not as a financial or moral gain. It is neither right from the point of view of the company nor from the personal point of view to try to extract benefits from any social assistance. Helping living things is a priority. But as a result, of course, we all see his contribution to marketing, no matter what we do.

9. What are the effects of corporate social responsibility on the company's marketing? What effects do you think it has on your marketing? For example, customer acquisition, employment growth, increase in brand value, corporate image provision...

There are always implications. In fact, it is not a targeted thing. As X Company, we are a business to business company. We are a company that caters to companies, not to the end user. But for example, as an example of the most serious benefits we have received, we opened our warehouse for use during the fire period. The purpose was definitely not advertising. Because we are very wide as a network, it has developed fast and we have announced that we will help other companies. So I got a lot of help and a lot of thank-you emails. We have not been able to measure its direct effect, and it is also not accurate to measure it. It has developed as a completely positive result. It has also increased the global recognition that comes with doing business with the United Nations. It has greatly improved the marketing within the company. But as a company, we didn't turn it into advertising material.

10. What is your opinion about the brand image that corporate social responsibility brings to your company?

It brings the brand image to a good point. It has a positive effect both as awareness and as an image.

11. How much do you think the humanitarian aid you have done has affected your marketing?

In fact, both of the agreements we have made are for-profit agreements, let me say this first. Of course, there is, of course, the social assistance part of these agreements. Since these are professional agreements, we cannot consider them as just an outreach agreement for both X Company and its partners. As an example, where you are going to make the same amount of money to a X Company, you are making half of it to the Red Crescent or the UN. In other words, these jobs cannot be done for free, only agreements involving cooperation. In any case, there are few companies in the world that can handle this job. The aim is to contribute to ourselves both in the commercial dimension of the business and to provide an advantage in brand awareness and marketing. And besides all this, it is important to make the cooperation that affects us emotionally. For example, tomorrow the next day, when the need for X aid logistics arises again, one of the first companies that people can think of is X Company ensures that our contributions to this humanitarian aid logistics. Organizations such as the Red Crescent and the UN are organizations that everyone knows and follows in the world, and it is always a serious advantage for your company that these companies make agreements with you.

12. Do you see the contribution of these humanitarian aids to your global recognition as well?

The fact is that when we consider Ukraine, now that it is a war zone, the UN is running the organization because it is a risky process depending on the region and requires special permits, which is why the X Company is running this business together. There are necessarily organizations other than the UN, but since this is a special process, you cannot cooperate with very different organizations.

13. Do you have any humanitarian projects that you plan to do in the future as a company, can you tell us if there are any?

These help ideas become instant events that develop. Of course, there is a planning process going on, but it cannot be determined in advance. Especially in natural disasters, etc. there are events that develop in 1-2 hours in events. When we say we don't have a plan, we always have a budget that we allocate for social assistance in sales marketing in a serious sense. We plan and manage this budget together with our employees. For example, we are thinking about whether we can help a village school in the east and how to plan it. A month or two ago, we, as a company, took over the 6-month food assistance of an animal shelter in Bursa. We are ready to help with the budget we have allocated for any kind of assistance needs that may occur outside of this.

DISCUSSION

Company X has many social responsibility projects. A few of these are for-profit and a few are non-profit projects. In these social responsibility projects, Company X takes part in the intervention section, which is one of the stages of humanitarian aid logistics in our thesis.

In our interview, Key Account Manager explained that Company X provides a good flow of information in all projects and that the reason for their smooth progress in their projects is to establish a good connection in each department. The fact that they create a well-functioning information flow with this information system is one of the keys to the smooth realization of their humanitarian aid logistics.

There are also benefits provided by CSR projects for employees. Employees at Company X participate in these projects voluntarily. In addition, only those who want to participate are given training and assignments for these projects. It was explained in the interview that the employees working in these projects did not earn any income from them, but only participated in these projects for an emotionally positive effect. As explained in the interview, the fact that these projects are the result of an emotional impact supports the definitions of humanitarian aid mentioned in our thesis.

The positive reception of companies working on corporate social responsibility projects and sustainability by their customers is an indication that companies create value in this regard.

In our interview, when we asked Key Account Manager whether the aforementioned social responsibility projects had any contribution to company marketing, we learned that these projects did not keep any

Table 2. Company X financial reports

X COMPANY	2019	2020	2021
CURRENT RATIO	0,96	1,049	1,10
DEBT RATIO	0,49	0,50	0,53
REVENUE	$94,701	$115,932	$182,306
VOLUME	1,907,126 (TEU)	2,204,902(TEU)	2,493,951 (TEU)

data on their contributions and they did not find it ethical to measure it. It was revealed during the interview that they only received thank you e-mails as a response and did not make any other measurements.

But when we analyzed Company X's financial reports, we got the following results:

Despite the pandemic period, the current ratio increases from 2019 to 2021 are quite high. We can think that being a global company and the signing of an agreement with the Red Crescent affects their current ratios.When we look at the debt ratio, it can be said that it is a very low ratio. It is seen in the table that revenue increases and TEU-based sales increased in parallel.

These corporate social responsibility values and awareness raising have contributed to global recognition and positive impact on their marketing.

It can be said that for-profit agreements are multi-lot and high-budget agreements also affect their volume and revenues. It can also be seen that these projects facilitate the company's entry into new markets.

CONCLUSION

Today, the concept of corporate social responsibility is gaining more and more importance. Companies support humanitarian aid as a moral value, without making a profit. For this reason, many companies even create a department for these investments. When we look at the logistics sector, the importance of the supply chain in humanitarian aid emerges and as a result, humanitarian aid logistics is born. Logistics companies play an important role in ensuring that aid reaches its destination faster, even in disaster situations. In our interview with Key Account Manager from X Company, one of the companies that make these aids, we evaluated the impact of X Company's humanitarian aid logistics on the marketing of their own companies. As a result, it was emphasized that the first priority of companies is to help, which is a moral value. As a result of these aids, it has been seen that although the companies do not use it as advertising material, it contributes to the brand image of the company. It has been emphasized that no data is kept regarding the effect of X Company's aids on company marketing and that this is unethical. It is of great importance for X Company to provide logistic support for firefighting in 2021 and to open its warehouses free of charge in order to set an example for companies in the future. The fact that Ukraine cooperates with the UN for logistical support due to the situation it shows that X Company is a company that attaches importance to humanitarian aid logistics. The increase in the recognition of the company as a result of these collaborations may bring the company forward in future partnerships. For this reason, humanitarian aid logistics is primarily carried out for a sustainable world, but it also plays an important role in the marketing of companies with its contribution to the brand image of the company.

In today's world, sustainability is very important in every market. This shows that companies should contribute not only to their products or services, but also to the environment and society. Other companies, such as X Company, which we have seen in the research, also need to contribute to corporate social responsibility and contribute to the environment and people as well as their products or services.

While X COMPANY has undertaken some projects for profit, some natural disasters have been undertaken without profit. They have done most of these with the budget they have collected within their own structure.

Logistics is a sector that is most needed in situations such as war and disasters. We think that logistics companies should be more at the forefront of such disasters. If all companies created a budget for such projects, in the event of a disaster, we could intervene more quickly with a good flow of information and deliver better aid both to our own country and to other countries in the world.

The interviewed X company do not keep the marketing situation that these projects add to their companies as data. They do not see this situation as ethical. However, we think that if they can turn these aids into data, it may be easier to involve other companies in these projects.

REFERENCES

Aktan, C. C., & Börü, D. (2006). Corporate Social Responsibility, Corporate Culture, Organizations, Rules and Institutions (Editor; Coşkun Can Aktan). CMB Publication No: 195. CMB.

Balcik, B., & Beamon,, B. (2008). *Facility Location In Humanitarian Relief.*

Barbarosoğlu, G., Özdamar, L., & Çevik, A. (2002). An Interactive Approach For Hierarchical Analysis Of Helicopter Logistics In Disaster Relief Operations. *European Journal of Operational Research, 140*(1), 118–133. doi:10.1016/S0377-2217(01)00222-3

Carroll, A. B. (1991). *The Corporate Social Responsibility Pyramid: Towards the Moral Governance of Organizational Stakeholders.* Business Horizons. http: www.cbe.wwu.edu/dunn/ Reprint.pyramidofcsr.pdf

Easwaramoorthy, M., & Zarinpoush, F. (2006). *Interviewing For Research.* Imagine Canada.

Frost, R. (2005). *Corporate Social Responsibility and Globalization: Re-evaluation.* A World connected. http://www.aworldconnected.org/article.php/524

Kovács, G., & Spens, K. M. (2007). Humanitarian Logistics in Disaster Relief Operations. *International Journal of Physical Distribution & Logistics Management, 37*(2), 99–114.

Kovács, G., & Spens, K. M. (2009). Identifying Challenges in Humanitarian Logistics. *International Journal of Physical Distribution & Logistics Management, 39*(6), 506–528. doi:10.1108/09600030910985848

Perry, A., & Wisnom, D. III. (2004). *The DNA of Brands The Rules for Creating Unique and Durable Brands* (Z. Yılmaz, Trans.). MediaCat Books.

Thomas, A., & Kopczak, L. R. (2007). Life-saving supply chains: Challenges and the path forward. In *Building supply chain excellence in emerging economies* (pp. 93–111). Springer US. doi:10.1007/978-0-387-38429-0_4

Tomasini, R., & Van Wassenhove, L. N. (2009). From preparedness to partnerships: Case study research on humanitarian logistics. *International Transactions in Operational Research, 16*(5), 549–559. doi:10.1111/j.1475-3995.2009.00697.x

Van Wassenhove, L. N. (2006). Blackett Memorial Lecture. Humanitarian Aid Logistics: Supply Chain Management in Hih Gear. *The Journal of the Operational Research Society*, *57*(5), 475–489. doi:10.1057/palgrave.jors.2602125

Wartick, S.L. & ve Cochran, P.L. (2013). The Evolution of the Corporate Social Performance Model. *The Academy of Management Review, 10*.

Chapter 11
Exploring the Intersection and Crisis of Urban Sustainability, Policy, and Digital Health

Kevin Richardson
https://orcid.org/0009-0002-3212-8669
Capitol Technology University, USA

Darrell Norman Burrell
https://orcid.org/0000-0002-4675-9544
Capitol Technology University, USA

ABSTRACT

In recent years, advances in digital health have enabled researchers and clinicians to develop innovative solutions to address health disparities in urban areas, particularly in underserved communities. Digital health technologies have been leveraged to improve access to health services, reduce health disparities, and promote urban sustainability. Digital health interventions can improve access to health care, provide education and information about health, and support self-management of health conditions. Digital health interventions are also increasingly used to improve health literacy and reduce health disparities. This chapter explores the utility of these new technologies to address health disparities, promote health innovation, improve health outcomes, and improve urban sustainability.

INTRODUCTION

Health disparities, inadequate digital health literacy, and limited access to digital health technologies pose a significant crisis to urban minority communities, exacerbating existing inequalities in health-care access, outcomes, and overall well-being. In recent years, advances in digital health have enabled researchers and clinicians to develop innovative solutions to address health disparities in urban areas, particularly in underserved communities (Kumar & Kumar,2020; Liu & Liu, 2019; Maharjan & Bhandari, 2020). Digital health technologies have been leveraged to improve access to health services, reduce

DOI: 10.4018/978-1-6684-9522-3.ch011

health disparities, and promote urban sustainability (Kumar & Kumar,2020; Liu & Liu, 2019; Maharjan & Bhandari, 2020). Digital health is "using technology to deliver health care services, promote health, and manage health data" (Wang et al., 2018, p. 1). Digital health interventions can improve access to health care, provide education and information about health, and support self-management of health conditions (Wang et al., 2018). Digital health interventions are also increasingly used to improve health literacy and reduce health disparities. For example, digital health interventions can provide culturally and linguistically appropriate health information, facilitate communication between patients and providers, improve access to care, and track health outcomes (Longenecker et al., 2017).

A health disparity crisis is defined as "avoidable differences in the burden of disease, injury, violence, or opportunities to achieve optimal health experienced by socially disadvantaged populations," exist in many urban areas and disproportionately affect underserved populations (CDC, 2020). These disparities create a significant crisis and are often the result of limited access to healthcare services, inadequate social services, and limited resources in the communities in which these populations reside (CDC, 2020). Urban minority communities frequently face lower income levels, limited access to quality education, and inadequate healthcare facilities. These factors contribute to reduced health awareness, delayed treatment, and a higher burden of chronic diseases and ultimately a community-based crisis. Digital health technologies offer an innovative approach to address these disparities, as they can provide a more equitable delivery of healthcare services and support to underserved populations.

Digital health technologies can also improve access to health services for underserved populations. For example, telehealth services, such as remote patient monitoring, can provide access to healthcare services that would otherwise be inaccessible due to distance or cost (CDC, 2020). Additionally, digital health technologies, such as mobile health applications, can provide individuals access to health information, resources, and support services (CDC, 2020). These technologies can help bridge the gap between healthcare providers and underserved populations and enable the delivery of healthcare services more equitably and cost-effectively.

Research has shown that digital health interventions can positively impact health outcomes, particularly for underserved populations (Longenecker et al., 2017; Wang et al., 2018). For example, a systematic review of digital health interventions by Longenecker et al. (2017) found that digital health interventions significantly improved health outcomes, including health-related quality of life, health behaviors, and health literacy. Furthermore, digital health interventions effectively improve access to care and health services for underserved populations, including those with limited access to traditional healthcare services (Longenecker et al., 2017).

The world's population is rapidly urbanizing, with over 50% of the global population now residing in urban areas (Nieuwenhuijsen, 2020). This trend is expected to continue, with projections indicating that by 2050, up to 70% of the world's population will live in cities (United Nations, 2018; Tripathi et al., 2019). As a result, there is a growing need for urban sustainability initiatives to ensure that cities can accommodate and support the needs of their inhabitants. This should occur without compromising the environment's health (Elmqvist et al., 2019). Urban sustainability aims to create livable and healthy cities that meet residents' current and future needs. At the same time, urban sustainability should minimize negative impacts on the environment.

As a result of the world's growing urbanization, urban sustainability measures are urgently needed to assure urban populations' well-being without jeopardizing the ability of future generations to meet their demands (Al Ridhawi et al., 2020). Digital health technologies in urban sustainability efforts have emerged as one of the best and most workable solutions to address healthcare access. Digital health is also praised for promoting healthy behaviors and enhancing disease surveillance (Yigitcanlar et al., 2020; Dinh-Le et al., 2019). According to Dinh-Le et al. (2019), digital health technologies, such as mobile health applications, wearable devices, and telemedicine, can provide innovative solutions to address the health challenges faced by urban populations.

While the benefits associated with digital health and urban growth are tremendous, incorporating digital health technologies into urban sustainability, initiatives pose challenges related to infrastructure, cost, and data privacy and security (Ismagilova et al., 2020; Tan & Taeihagh, 2020). The use of digital health technologies requires robust and reliable infrastructure. Modern infrastructure may be lacking in many urban areas, particularly in low- and middle-income countries (Attaran, 2022; Olu et al., 2019). The cost of digital health technologies is also a significant barrier to their widespread adoption. This is particularly so in resource-constrained settings such as developing nations or within marginalized communities such as black-dominated areas. While using digital health technology, data privacy and security are essential issues to consider, especially when sensitive health information is involved (Whitelaw et al., 2021).

Using digital health interventions to reduce health disparities can improve population health outcomes and reduce costs. Digital health interventions can reduce the burden of non-communicable diseases, such as diabetes and hypertension, disproportionately seen in underserved populations (Wang et al., 2018). Furthermore, digital health interventions can be used to reduce healthcare costs by reducing the need for costly hospitalizations, emergency room visits, and other hospital services (Longenecker et al., 2017).

Despite the potential of digital health to reduce health disparities and improve health outcomes, several challenges must be addressed. These include the need for reliable and secure health information systems, improved patient engagement, and research to evaluate the effectiveness of digital health interventions (Wang et al., 2018). Furthermore, there is a need for improved digital health literacy to ensure that digital health interventions are used effectively and that digital health interventions reach their intended populations (Longenecker et al., 2017).

Problem Statement

Urban sustainability programs that can encourage healthy living and meet the demands of urban populations are urgently needed. This is a result of the increase in the rate of urbanization globally (Al Ridhawi et al., 2020). These programs should also be in a position to minimize negative impacts on the environment. Digital health technologies have emerged as a promising solution for addressing healthcare access, promoting healthy behaviors, and enhancing disease surveillance in urban settings (Biggs et al., 2019; Fleming et al., 2020). However, integrating digital health technologies into urban sustainability initiatives poses significant challenges related to infrastructure, cost, and data privacy and security (Ismagilova et al., 2020; Tan & Taeihagh, 2020). These challenges present the problem of integrating digital health into urban sustainability strategies, making the process slow and difficult, especially for developing nations.

The digital divide has unveiled a new facet of health disparities, revealing how unequal access to digital health technologies perpetuates a crisis in underserved communities. To mitigate this crisis and promote equitable health outcomes, concerted efforts are needed to bridge the digital divide through infrastructure development, digital literacy programs, and inclusive telehealth strategies. Addressing the digital divide and employing digital health technologies is an imperative step towards achieving health equity for all populations.

This study aims to identify the potential benefits and challenges of incorporating digital health technologies into urban sustainability strategies and to propose solutions to improve health disparities and health outcomes. By addressing these challenges, the study aims to develop sustainable and healthy cities that meet residents' needs while preserving the environment's health.

Purpose of the Study

This study explores the potential benefits and crisis of integrating digital health technologies into urban sustainability through an exploration of current and emerging literature in the field. The benefit of this approach is the ability to take dispersed research and explorations on this topic and conform them into one highly focused discussion. This integration is necessitated by the need to promote healthy living and support the needs of urban populations while minimizing negative impacts on the environment. The study aims to identify solutions to address infrastructure, cost, and data privacy and security challenges. The challenges are alarming because of their potential to hinder the widespread adoption of digital health technologies in urban sustainability initiatives. By providing insights into the intersection of urban sustainability and digital health, this study seeks to contribute to developing sustainable and healthy cities. Sustainable and healthy cities are cities that can meet the needs of their residents while conserving the environment.

Significance of the Study

The significance of this study lies in its potential to inform policymakers, urban planners, and healthcare professionals about the benefits, crisis, and challenges of incorporating digital health technologies into urban sustainability strategies (Kutty et al., 2020). By identifying solutions to address infrastructure, cost, and data privacy and security challenges, this study can help promote the widespread adoption of digital health technologies in urban sustainability initiatives, particularly in low- and middle-income countries. Furthermore, this study can contribute to developing sustainable and healthy cities that meet their residents' current and future needs while minimizing negative environmental impacts. Ultimately, this study can improve healthcare access, promote healthy behaviors, and enhance disease surveillance in urban settings, thereby improving the health and well-being of urban populations worldwide.

LITERATURE REVIEW

Urban Sustainability and Digital Health

Digital health and urban sustainability are two ideas that could be very helpful to urban people. Urban sustainability, on the other hand, attempts to satisfy the requirements of existing city dwellers without compromising the capacity of future generations to meet their own needs (Abd et al., 2021). A multidisciplinary strategy considering environmental, social, and economic aspects is necessary to accomplish urban sustainability goals. Conversely, digital health refers to using digital tools and devices to better disease surveillance, encourage healthy behaviors, and improve healthcare services (Mathews et al., 2019). To increase the sustainability and equity of urban settings, digital health technologies should be incorporated into urban sustainability strategies.

Integrating digital health technologies into urban sustainability strategies can enhance access to health-care services (Scott et al., 2020). For example, telemedicine can improve access to healthcare services in remote and under-served areas, reducing the need for patients to travel long distances to see a doctor (Haleem et al., 2021). Digital health technologies can also improve the quality of healthcare services by enabling real-time monitoring of patients, facilitating communication between healthcare providers, and supporting the collection and analysis of health data (Rubbio et al., 2020; Olu et al., 2019)). Using digital health technologies in urban sustainability initiatives can improve access to healthcare services and encourage healthy lives (Shan et al., 2019). Digital health tools can track physical activity, monitor diet, and give feedback to users, motivating them to adopt healthier behaviors. Examples include mobile health applications and wearables. Digital health technologies can assist in preventing chronic diseases and lowering healthcare expenditures by promoting healthy lives.

Digital health has the potential to improve urban sustainability in a variety of ways. One of the most common ways digital health can help with sustainability is by helping to reduce healthcare costs and improve outcomes (Kumar & Kumar,2020; Liu & Liu, 2019; Maharjan & Bhandari, 2020). By providing telehealth services, digital health can reduce the need for in-person care, freeing up time and resources devoted to other urban sustainability initiatives (Kumar & Kumar,2020; Liu & Liu, 2019; Maharjan & Bhandari, 2020). Additionally, digital health can help connect people to health resources, allowing them to make better lifestyle choices that reduce their carbon footprint and improve their overall health (Kumar & Kumar,2020; Liu & Liu, 2019; Maharjan & Bhandari, 2020).

Digital health can also help to improve urban sustainability by providing data-driven insights. By leveraging data from digital health technologies, cities can better understand the health needs of their citizens and the environmental impact of various urban sustainability initiatives (Kumar & Kumar,2020; Liu & Liu, 2019; Maharjan & Bhandari, 2020). This data can then inform decisions that maximize the efficiency and effectiveness of urban sustainability projects.

Disease surveillance can be enhanced by incorporating digital health technologies into urban sustainability plans. Digital health tools, by allowing early detection and response, can support real-time monitoring of disease outbreaks (Benis et al., 2021; Tseng & Shih, 2020). Urban regions, where high population densities and widespread travel patterns can contribute to the rapid spread of infectious diseases, especially need this. Digital health technologies can safeguard the health of urban populations by enhancing disease surveillance and assisting in the prevention of epidemics and pandemics (Scott et al., 2020).

Smart Cities

With the rise of smart cities, using digital health technologies in urban sustainability efforts has become increasingly important (Allam & Jones, 2021). Smart cities leverage digital technologies and data analytics to improve the efficiency and sustainability of urban environments (Rohmah et al., 2023). In particular, intelligent digital health technologies have the potential to play a critical role in improving healthcare access and outcomes in smart cities. According to Deloitte (2022), building a smart city with smart digital health requires a comprehensive and integrated approach considering each city's unique needs and challenges. With this strategy, data analytics and digital tools are used to analyze urban populations' health needs and behaviors, create targeted treatments to meet those needs, and then track and assess the effectiveness of those interventions over time. One example of this approach is using data analytics to identify and address health disparities within urban populations (Chen et al., 2019). By analyzing health data from diverse sources, including electronic health records, mobile health apps, and wearable devices, policymakers and healthcare providers can identify patterns and trends in health outcomes. They can also note behaviors and develop targeted interventions to address disparities and promote health equity.

In addition to addressing health disparities, smart digital health technologies can improve healthcare access and outcomes. This can be done by leveraging mobile and telehealth technologies to provide remote consultations, telemedicine services, and home-based monitoring for chronic diseases (Craig et al., 2021). These technologies can improve access to care for under-served populations and reduce healthcare costs by preventing unnecessary hospitalizations and emergency department visits (Fan & Zhao, 2022). Overall, the integration of digital health technologies into urban sustainability strategies has the potential to create more sustainable and equitable urban environments. This can happen while improving healthcare access and outcomes for all (Sieck et al., 2021). However, it requires careful planning and collaboration among policymakers, healthcare providers, technology experts, and urban communities to ensure these technologies are accessible, affordable, and respectful of individual rights and freedoms.

Challenges of Incorporating Digital Health Into Urban Sustainability Strategies

Integrating digital health technologies into urban sustainability strategies presents several challenges that must be addressed to achieve effective and equitable outcomes (Praharaj, 2021). One of the main hurdles is infrastructure. While developed urban areas may have adequate digital infrastructure to support digital health technologies, low-income communities often need reliable internet connections and other essential digital tools (Gasser et al., 2020). As a result, digital health solutions may not be accessible to the people who need them most, exacerbating existing health disparities and inequalities.

The cost of digital health technologies is another challenge that must be overcome to ensure widespread adoption and integration into urban sustainability strategies (Mardani et al., 2020). While developed countries may have the financial resources to invest in expensive technologies, developing countries may need help to afford them. This poses a significant barrier to achieving global health equity and highlights the need for affordable and accessible digital health solutions that can be scaled to meet the needs of diverse populations.

To address these challenges, Al-Sharif and Pokharel (2022) note that data privacy and security concerns must be addressed to protect personal health information and maintain public trust in digital health solutions. The collection and use of health data raise complex ethical and legal issues that must be carefully considered and addressed to ensure that data is collected, stored, and used in an ethical, secure, and respectful of individual rights and freedoms (Rao & Deebak, 2022). These challenges must be tackled collaboratively by policymakers, health professionals, and technology experts to achieve the full potential of digital health in advancing urban sustainability and improving health outcomes for all.

Case Studies

Case studies from India, Kenya, and the United States demonstrate the potential impact of digital health technologies on urban sustainability efforts. In India, using digital tools in maternal and child health programs improved access to healthcare services and increased patient engagement. In Kenya, mobile phone-based technologies improved disease surveillance and control. Integrating digital tools in chronic disease management enhanced patient outcomes and reduced healthcare costs in the United States.

METHODOLOGY

To find pertinent research on the intersection of urban sustainability and digital health, this paper's authors systematically searched the literature to take dispersed research and strategies and create one cohesive conversation, which is the essence of a sound research approach. The following keywords were used in a thorough search of electronic databases, including PubMed, Scopus, and Web of Science: "digital health," "urban sustainability," "mHealth," "telemedicine," "health disparities & technology," and "wearables." The search was limited to articles published in English, focusing on articles published in the last 5-10 years. The inclusion criteria included studies that (1) examine the use of digital health technologies in urban sustainability initiatives, (2) report on the benefits and challenges of incorporating digital health technologies into urban sustainability efforts, and (3) include case studies from India, Kenya, and the United States. The exclusion criteria included studies that focus on something other than urban sustainability or digital health or are unavailable in full text. Data extraction involved summarizing key findings, including the benefits and challenges of integrating digital health technologies into urban sustainability strategies. The study included case studies from India, Kenya, and the United States to demonstrate the potential impact of digital health technologies on urban sustainability efforts.

DISCUSSION

The literature review and additional sources highlight the potential benefits of integrating digital health technologies into urban sustainability strategies. Integrating digital health technologies can enhance access to healthcare services, improve the quality of healthcare services, promote healthy lifestyles, and improve disease surveillance (Mathews et al., 2019; Shan et al., 2019). However, infrastructure, cost, data privacy, and security concerns must be addressed to achieve effective and equitable outcomes (Praharaj, 2021). In addition to these challenges, there is a need to address the issue of data interoperability. Data interoperability refers to the ability of different digital health systems to share data and communicate (Jeong et al., 2020). With data interoperability, it can be easier to integrate digital health technologies into urban sustainability strategies and to create a seamless and efficient healthcare system (Jeong et al., 2020). Therefore, policymakers and technology experts must work to ensure that digital health systems are designed with interoperability in mind.

Furthermore, it is vital to consider the role of community engagement in integrating digital health technologies into urban sustainability strategies (Irvine et al., 2022). Community engagement can ensure that digital health solutions are tailored to the needs and preferences of local communities. They can also ensure that the benefits of these solutions are distributed equitably. In addition, community engagement can help to build trust and promote acceptance of digital health solutions.

Another important consideration is the need for a solid regulatory framework to guide the development and implementation of digital health technologies (Yigitcanlar et al., 2020). The regulatory framework should ensure that digital health solutions meet high safety, efficacy, and privacy protection standards. Additionally, the regulatory framework should facilitate innovation and the development of new digital health solutions that address unmet healthcare needs. It is also essential to consider the potential impact of digital health technologies on healthcare jobs and workforce development. As digital health technologies become more prevalent, there may be a shift in the types of jobs and skills required in the healthcare industry. Therefore, policymakers and healthcare providers must work to ensure that healthcare workers are equipped with the necessary skills and training to effectively use and maintain digital health technologies (Kutty et al., 2020). The potential impact of digital health technologies on healthcare costs must be considered. While digital health technologies have the potential to reduce healthcare costs by improving disease surveillance and promoting healthy behaviors, the initial costs of implementing these technologies may be high (Scott et al., 2020). Therefore, policymakers and healthcare providers must carefully consider the cost-effectiveness of digital health solutions and ensure that they are implemented to maximize their benefits while minimizing costs (Kumar & Kumar,2020; Liu & Liu, 2019; Maharjan & Bhandari, 2020).

CONCLUSION AND RECOMMENDATIONS

The digital divide has shed light on a hidden crisis of health inequities, namely the unequal access to digital health technologies that contributes to the maintenance of a crisis in communities that are underserved. It is imperative that concentrated efforts be made to bridge the digital gap through the construction of infrastructure, the implementation of digital literacy initiatives, and the implementation of inclusive telehealth and biotechnology strategies in order to alleviate this crisis and promote equitable health outcomes. In order to achieve health equity for all populations, bridging the digital divide is an essential step that must be taken.

Digital health can help to improve urban sustainability by connecting citizens to resources (Kumar & Kumar,2020; Liu & Liu, 2019; Maharjan & Bhandari, 2020). For example, digital health can provide access to health-related information and services, such as access to healthy food, exercise resources, and mental health services. By providing access to such resources, digital health can help to improve the overall health of citizens, which in turn helps to improve the sustainability of cities. Digital health has the potential to play an essential role in urban sustainability. By providing access to health resources, improving outcomes and reducing costs, and leveraging data to inform decisions, digital health can help cities become more efficient and sustainable (Kumar & Kumar,2020; Liu & Liu, 2019; Maharjan & Bhandari, 2020)

Integrating digital health technologies into urban sustainability strategies has significant implications for policy and practice (Gasser et al., 2020). Policymakers can promote digital health initiatives in a variety of ways. One approach is to create policies that incentivize the use of digital health technologies by providing financial incentives for providers and patients who use digital health tools (Troxel et al., 2017). For example, policymakers can create tax incentives for providers who use digital health technologies or provide subsidies for patients who use digital health tools (Troxel et al., 2017). Additionally, policymakers can create policies that promote the adoption of digital health technologies by providers and patients by providing technical assistance, promoting public awareness campaigns, and developing educational programs (Troxel et al., 2017). Policymakers can create policies that ensure the safety and effectiveness of digital health technologies by establishing safety protocols, requiring quality assurance measures, and developing standards for data security (Troxel et al., 2017).

One of the critical challenges for digital health technologies is the need for investment in infrastructure. There is a need for investments in broadband internet, connectivity, and digital health platforms (Lane & Skirboll, 2020; Becker & Knoop, 2019; Liang & Escobar, 2020).

To this end, governments should provide targeted funding to support the development of digital health systems and infrastructure. Additionally, governments should incentivize private sector organizations to invest in digital health technologies. These incentives could include tax incentives and grants to support developing and deploying digital health technologies (Lane & Skirboll, 2020; Becker & Knoop, 2019; Liang & Escobar, 2020).

Another key crisis for digital health is ensuring access and engagement. To this end, governments should incentivize healthcare providers and patients to use digital health technologies (Lane & Skirboll, 2020; Becker & Knoop, 2019; Liang & Escobar, 2020). These incentives could include providing subsidies or tax credits to providers and patients for using digital health technologies (Lane & Skirboll, 2020; Becker & Knoop, 2019; Liang & Escobar, 2020). Additionally, governments should incentivize healthcare providers to integrate digital health into their practice. This could include providing grants to providers to develop and implement digital health systems in their practice.

Governments should also provide incentives to promote the development of digital health applications and services tailored to meet underserved populations' needs (Lane & Skirboll, 2020; Becker & Knoop, 2019; Liang & Escobar, 2020). These incentives could include providing grants to developers to create digital health applications and services tailored to meet underserved populations' needs (Lane & Skirboll, 2020; Becker & Knoop, 2019; Liang & Escobar, 2020). Additionally, governments should incentivize healthcare providers to use digital health applications and services tailored to meet the needs of underserved populations.

Governments should provide incentives to promote the adoption of digital health technologies in urban settings (Lane & Skirboll, 2020; Becker & Knoop, 2019; Liang & Escobar, 2020). These incentives include providing subsidies or tax credits to organizations and individuals that deploy digital health technologies in urban settings. Additionally, governments should provide incentives to promote the development of digital health technologies tailored to urban environments. This could include providing grants to developers to create digital health applications and services tailored to urban settings (Lane & Skirboll, 2020; Becker & Knoop, 2019; Liang & Escobar, 2020).

Additionally, cost-effective digital health solutions need to be developed and implemented to ensure the affordability of digital technologies in low-income communities. Data privacy and security concerns must be addressed to protect personal health information (Praharaj, 2021). Integrating digital health technologies into urban sustainability initiatives can improve access to healthcare services, promote healthy behaviors, and enhance disease surveillance. Further research is necessary to explore digital health technologies' potential benefits and crisis in urban sustainability efforts.

This literature review has examined the intersection of urban sustainability and digital health. Integrating digital health technologies into urban sustainability strategies can enhance access to healthcare services, promote healthy lifestyles, and improve disease surveillance (Mathews et al., 2019; Shan et al., 2019). However, several challenges must be overcome to achieve effective and equitable outcomes, including infrastructure, cost, and data privacy and security concerns. The case studies from India, Kenya, and the United States demonstrate the potential impact of digital health technologies on urban sustainability efforts (Gathara et al., 2016). These case studies provide valuable insights into how digital health technologies can be used to address complex health crisis in urban areas. By leveraging digital health solutions, urban sustainability efforts can be more sustainable, equitable, and effective.

Moving forward, policymakers, health professionals, and technology experts must work collaboratively to address the crisis of integrating digital health technologies into urban sustainability strategies. Efforts must be made to ensure that digital health solutions are accessible, affordable, and scalable for implementation in diverse urban settings (Kamruzzaman et al., 2022). Data privacy and security concerns must be carefully addressed to protect personal health information and maintain public trust in digital health solutions (Praharaj, 2021). This literature review suggests that integrating digital health technologies into urban sustainability strategies can create more sustainable and equitable urban environments, promoting health and well-being for all. As cities continue to grow and face complex health crisis, digital health solutions can be essential in advancing urban sustainability efforts and improving health outcomes.

REFERENCES

Abd Elrahman, A. S., & Asaad, M. (2021). Urban design & urban planning: A critical analysis to the theoretical relationship gap. *Ain Shams Engineering Journal, 12*(1), 1163–1173. doi:10.1016/j.asej.2020.04.020

Al Ridhawi, I., Otoum, S., Aloqaily, M., Jararweh, Y., & Baker, T. (2020). Providing secure and reliable communication for next-generation networks in smart cities. *Sustainable Cities and Society, 56*, 102080. doi:10.1016/j.scs.2020.102080

Al-Sharif, R., & Pokharel, S. (2022). Smart city dimensions and associated risks: Review of the literature. *Sustainable Cities and Society, 77*, 103542. doi:10.1016/j.scs.2021.103542

Allam, Z., & Jones, D. S. (2021). Future (post-COVID) digital, smart, and sustainable cities in the wake of 6G: Digital twins, immersive realities, and new urban economies. *Land use policy, 101*, 105201. American Diabetes Association (ADA) Diabetes Technology Working Group. *Diabetes Care, 43*(1), 250–260.

Attaran, M. (2022). Blockchain technology in healthcare: Challenges and opportunities. *International Journal of Healthcare Management, 15*(1), 70–83. doi:10.1080/20479700.2020.1843887

Becker, A. M., & Knoop, A. A. (2019). Digital Health Technologies: An Overview and Considerations for Policymakers. *Journal of Medical Internet Research, 21*(3), e11453. doi:10.2196/11453

Benis, A., Tamburis, O., Chronaki, C., & Moen, A. (2021). One digital health: A unified framework for future health ecosystems. *Journal of Medical Internet Research, 23*(2), e22189. doi:10.2196/22189 PMID:33492240

Biggs, J. S., Willcocks, A., Burger, M., & Makeham, M. A. (2019). Digital health benefits evaluation frameworks: building the evidence to support Australia's National Digital Health Strategy. *Medical Journal of Australia, 210*, S9-S11.

Centers for Disease Control and Prevention. (2020). Health disparities and inequalities. CDC. https://www.cdc.gov/minorityhealth/healthdisparities/index.html

Chen, X., Orom, H., Hay, J. L., Waters, E. A., Schofield, E., Li, Y., & Kiviniemi, M. T. (2019). Differences in rural and urban health information access and use. *The Journal of Rural Health, 35*(3), 405–417. doi:10.1111/jrh.12335 PMID:30444935

Craig, K. J. T., Fusco, N., Gunnarsdottir, T., Chamberland, L., Snowdon, J. L., & Kassler, W. J. (2021). Leveraging Data and Digital Health Technologies to Assess and Impact Social Determinants of Health (SDoH): A State-of-the-Art Literature Review. *Online Journal of Public Health Informatics, 13*(3). doi:10.5210/ojphi.v13i3.11081 PMID:35082976

Dinh-Le, C., Chuang, R., Chokshi, S., & Mann, D. (2019). Wearable health technology and electronic health record integration: A scoping review and future directions. *JMIR mHealth and uHealth*, *7*(9), e12861. doi:10.2196/12861 PMID:31512582

Elmqvist, T., Andersson, E., Frantzeskaki, N., McPhearson, T., Olsson, P., Gaffney, O., Takeuchi, K., & Folke, C. (2019). Sustainability and resilience for transformation in the urban century. *Nature Sustainability*, *2*(4), 267–273. doi:10.103841893-019-0250-1

Fan, K., & Zhao, Y. (2022). Mobile health technology: A novel tool in chronic disease management. *Intelligent Medicine*, *2*(1), 41–47. doi:10.1016/j.imed.2021.06.003

Gasser, U., Ienca, M., Scheibner, J., Sleigh, J., & Vayena, E. (2020). Digital tools against COVID-19: taxonomy, ethical challenges, and navigation aid. *The Lancet. Digital Health*, *2*(8), e425–e434. PMID:32835200

Gathara, D., Serrem, K., Kigen, S., Nyandigisi, A., & Snow, R. W. (2016). Mobile phone-based infectious disease surveillance system, Kenya. *Emerging Infectious Diseases*, *22*(4), 715–721. doi:10.3201/eid2204.150842

Haleem, A., Javaid, M., Singh, R. P., & Suman, R. (2021). Telemedicine for healthcare: Capabilities, features, barriers, and applications. *Sensors International*.

Ismagilova, E., Hughes, L., Rana, N. P., & Dwivedi, Y. K. (2020). Security, privacy, and risks within smart cities: Literature review and development of a smart city interaction framework. *Information Systems Frontiers*, 1–22. PMID:32837262

Jeong, S., Kim, S., & Kim, J. (2020). City data hub: Implementation of standard-based smart city data platform for interoperability. *Sensors (Basel)*, *20*(23), 7000. doi:10.339020237000 PMID:33297506

Kamruzzaman, M. M., Yan, B., Sarker, M. N. I., Alruwaili, O., Wu, M., & Alrashdi, I. (2022). Blockchain and fog computing in IoT-driven healthcare services for smart cities. *Journal of Healthcare Engineering*, *2022*, 2022. doi:10.1155/2022/9957888 PMID:35126961

Kumar, A., & Kumar, K. (2020). Digital health and urban sustainability: The emerging trends and opportunities. *Sustainability*, *12*(18), 7520.

Kutty, A. A., Abdella, G. M., Kucukvar, M., Onat, N. C., & Bulu, M. (2020). A system thinking approach for harmonizing smart and sustainable city initiatives with United Nations sustainable development goals. *Sustainable Development (Bradford)*, *28*(5), 1347–1365. doi:10.1002d.2088

Lane, A. J., & Skirboll, S. (2020). Digital Health Incentives: An Analysis of Current Federal and State Policies. *Health Affairs*, *39*(3), 472–479. doi:10.1377/hlthaff.2019.00633

Liang, S. Y., & Escobar, M. J. (2020). Digital Health in Urban Settings: Opportunities and Challenges. *Journal of Medical Internet Research*, *22*(4), e16356. doi:10.2196/16356 PMID:32347802

Liu, Y., & Liu, J. (2019). Digital health and urban sustainability: A review of recent trends. *Telemedicine Journal and e-Health*, *25*(2), 145–151.

Longenecker, J. T., Gebregziabher, M., Park, E. R., Shih, T., & Karter, A. J. (2017). Digital health interventions for chronic disease management: A systematic review. *Journal of Medical Internet Research, 19*(7). Advance online publication. doi:10.2196/jmir.7153

Maharjan, B., & Bhandari, S. (2020). Role of digital health in urban sustainability: A systematic review. *International Journal of Environmental Research and Public Health, 17*(5), 1486. PMID:32106591

Mardani, A., Saraji, M. K., Mishra, A. R., & Rani, P. (2020). A novel extended approach under hesitant fuzzy sets to design a framework for assessing the key challenges of digital health interventions adoption during the COVID-19 outbreak. *Applied Soft Computing, 96*, 106613. doi:10.1016/j.asoc.2020.106613 PMID:32834799

Nieuwenhuijsen, M. J. (2020). Urban and transport planning pathways to carbon neutral, liveable and healthy cities; A review of the current evidence. *Environment International, 140*, 105661. doi:10.1016/j.envint.2020.105661 PMID:32307209

Olu, O., Muneene, D., Bataringaya, J. E., Nahimana, M. R., Ba, H., Turgeon, Y., Karamagi, H. C., & Dovlo, D. (2019). How can digital health technologies contribute to the sustainable attainment of universal health coverage in Africa? A perspective. *Frontiers in Public Health, 7*, 341. doi:10.3389/fpubh.2019.00341 PMID:31803706

Praharaj, S. (2021). Area-based urban renewal approach for smart cities development in India: Challenges of inclusion and sustainability. *Urban Planning, 6*(4), 202–215. doi:10.17645/up.v6i4.4484

Rao, P. M., & Deebak, B. D. (2022). Security and privacy issues in smart cities/industries: Technologies, applications, and challenges. *Journal of Ambient Intelligence and Humanized Computing*, 1–37.

Rohmah, A. A., Rachmawati, R., & Mei, E. T. W. (2023). Smart City Achievement Through Implementation of Digital Health Services in Handling COVID-19 Indonesia. *Smart Cities, 6*(1), 639–651. doi:10.3390martcities6010030

Rubbio, I., Bruccoleri, M., Pietrosi, A., & Ragonese, B. (2020). Digital health technology enhances resilient behaviour: Evidence from the ward. *International Journal of Operations & Production Management, 40*(1), 34–67. doi:10.1108/IJOPM-02-2018-0057

Scott, B. K., Miller, G. T., Fonda, S. J., Yeaw, R. E., Gaudaen, J. C., Pavliscsak, H. H., Quinn, M. T., & Pamplin, J. C. (2020). Advanced digital health technologies for COVID-19 and future emergencies. *Telemedicine Journal and e-Health, 26*(10), 1226–1233. doi:10.1089/tmj.2020.0140 PMID:32456560

Shan, R., Sarkar, S., & Martin, S. S. (2019). Digital health technology and mobile devices for the management of diabetes mellitus: State of the art. *Diabetologia, 62*(6), 877–887. doi:10.100700125-019-4864-7 PMID:30963188

Sieck, C. J., Sheon, A., Ancker, J. S., Castek, J., Callahan, B., & Siefer, A. (2021). Digital inclusion as a social determinant of health. *NPJ Digital Medicine, 4*(1), 52. doi:10.103841746-021-00413-8 PMID:33731887

Tan, S. Y., & Taeihagh, A. (2020). Smart city governance in developing countries: A systematic literature review. *sustainability, 12*(3), 899.

Tripathi, A. D., Mishra, R., Maurya, K. K., Singh, R. B., & Wilson, D. W. (2019). Estimates for world population and global food availability for global health. In *The role of functional food security in global health* (pp. 3–24). Academic Press. doi:10.1016/B978-0-12-813148-0.00001-3

Troxel, A. B., Asch, D. A., Vijayaraghavan, M., & Burdick, T. E. (2017). Policy approaches to promote digital health: A review. *Health Affairs*, *36*(7), 1201–1208. PMID:28679806

Tseng, Y. J., & Shih, Y. L. (2020). Developing epidemic forecasting models to assist disease surveillance for influenza with electronic health records. *International Journal of Computers and Applications*, *42*(6), 616–621. doi:10.1080/1206212X.2019.1633762

Wang, S. J., Edelman, E. J., & Park, E. R. (2018). Digital health interventions: A review of the literature. *Journal of the American Medical Informatics Association : JAMIA*, *25*(1), 1–10. doi:10.1093/jamia/ocy003

Whitelaw, S., Pellegrini, D. M., Mamas, M. A., Cowie, M., & Van Spall, H. G. (2021). Barriers and facilitators of the uptake of digital health technology in cardiovascular care: A systematic scoping review. *European Heart Journal. Digital Health*, *2*(1), 62–74. doi:10.1093/ehjdh/ztab005 PMID:34048508

Yigitcanlar, T., Kankanamge, N., Regona, M., Ruiz Maldonado, A., Rowan, B., Ryu, A., Desouza, K. C., Corchado, J. M., Mehmood, R., & Li, R. Y. M. (2020). Artificial intelligence technologies and related urban planning and development concepts: How are they perceived and utilized in Australia? *Journal of Open Innovation*, *6*(4), 187. doi:10.3390/joitmc6040187

Chapter 12
Developments in the Remote Work and Learning:
Perspectives From Industry and Academia

Kiran Thakur
University Canada West, Canada

Badr-un-nisa Chand
University Canada West, Canada

Shivani Dhand
Lovely Professional University, India

ABSTRACT

Post-pandemic, there has been an exponential growth in the adoption of remote work and remote learning. Recent years have marked a significant growth in technologies to assist humanity in integrating effortlessly into the virtual world. Communication tools such as Zoom, Teams, and Slack have become essential tools everybody must be comfortable working on. Digital literacy has become a vital skill any worker requires to sustain their job. For remote work and learning, there is an increased emphasis on soft skills such as time management, collaboration, communication, and perseverance. One must be self-directed and disciplined to succeed in a less supervised environment. Overall, technologies have transformed how we work and learn, and it will be interesting to witness how they will continue evolving in the coming years.

INTRODUCTION

While remote working is not a novel concept, in recent times, it has witnessed immense growth and recognition as an effective tool for redesigning traditional office-based jobs (Butler, 2023). As remote work is rapidly being institutionalized across industries (MacRae & Sawatzky, 2020), it is receiving greater attention from researchers. There is a consensus among the authors that remote work no longer

DOI: 10.4018/978-1-6684-9522-3.ch012

represents the future direction of the workplace, as it has already become the present-day reality for many organizations (Dávila Morán, 2023; Evans, 2022). The existing studies have defined remote work in a similar manner, where the difference has been mostly limited to the scope of activity. We provide a few definitions of the term remote work below to understand the varying ways in which authors have attempted to describe it.

According to Grant et al. (2013), remote work (also referred to as work from home [WFH] or telecommuting) is a flexible alternative work setting facilitated by technology that enables an employee to perform organizational work from anywhere and not just from the office space. Sullivan's work (2003) defines remote working as an option provided to employees to work in a remote setting with clearly outlined arrangements for providing employees with technological equipment to perform their work and maintain interaction with the organization. Buira (2012) has a similar but slightly extended definition. Buira describes it as a paid work setting, where employees are not bound to work from a designated office space, and the communication patterns between employers and employees are established beforehand. A more comprehensive definition of the term remote work, from a legal perspective, is given by the International Labour Organization – ILO (2020), which describes remote work as a legal contract where an employee willingly and thoughtfully chooses to work away from the office for an agreed upon pay, job duties, working hours, and the ways of monitoring job progress and work outcome.

It is noticeable from the definitions since remote work requires employees to work outside of their designated office space, it can be facilitated only by solid technological innovation and supporting tools, including mobile devices, laptops, desktops, and internet connectivity (Sullivan, 2003; Dávila Morán, 2023). Hence, the adoption of remote work is contingent upon a sound technological infrastructure that includes investment from the employers in ICT technologies such as digital communication platforms and applications that will facilitate communication between the employers and employees in a remote setting, the availability of speedy internet connection without interruptions, the digital literacy of the employees being offered the remote working options, and most importantly the willingness of employees to accept this digital change (Pasquel, 2023). If the employees lack digital skills and are uncomfortable using technologies independently (without technical support), they will resist technological change, including remote work (Gifford, 2022).

Regardless, the demand for the availability of remote working choices has escalated in recent times, making it a widely used practice in many other industries, including accounting, finance (Felstead, 2022), and IT (Chalishazar, 2022), to name a few. According to a 2019 UK report, 49% of employees now seek alternative work arrangements instead of traditional office-based jobs (Wheatley & Gifford, 2019). Albeit being viewed as a favourable work policy by a majority of employees, many challenges can impede the institutionalization of remote work at a large scale globally. The challenges surrounding the remote work policy for various industries include cyber security risks (Nickson & Siddons, 2004), communication and connectivity issues (Yang, 2019), the concentration level of employees (AL-rfou, 2021), conflicts in roles, and control and supervision issues (Karunarathne, 2021).

This chapter highlights the pressing issues that necessitate careful consideration with the rise of remote work trends across industries. These difficulties go beyond logistical obstacles and involve complex problems with technological infrastructure, an organization's ability to adjust to this new way of working and staff digital literacy (Sullivan, 2003; Dick et al., 2020; Pasquel, 2023). Understanding the varied nature of remote work, technology requirements, and underlying legal framework is the first aspect of the problem (International Labour Organization - ILO, 2020). The second aspect entails dealing with the enormous difficulties brought on by the broad use of remote work, including cybersecurity concerns, communication hurdles, employee concentration levels, role conflicts, and control and supervision issues (Nickson & Siddons, 2004; Yang, 2019; AL-rfou, 2021; Gong et al., 2023). The third and most crucial aspect includes bridging the knowledge gap and exploring these challenges comprehensively to pave the way for practical solutions (Gifford, 2022). The digital divide that emerges when employees need more skills to navigate digital tools independently can lead to resistance and hinder the smooth adoption of remote work practices (Buira, 2012). This study aims to conduct a thorough investigation into these issues and examine the implications for businesses and workers across a range of industries, along with future directions that will contribute to creating plans and solutions that will help remote work practices be successfully incorporated into the workplace of the future.

LITERATURE REVIEW

The introduction of remote working options within industrial settings is widely attributed to two organizations: NASA and IBM. In NASA, working from distance practice can be traced back to as early as 1973, when a NASA engineer, Jack Niles, first used the term 'telecommuting' (Butler, 2023). Niles developed a communication system for NASA's team to be able to work without interruption caused by the 1970s oil crisis when vehicles could not operate due to fuel shortages (MacRae & Sawatzky, 2020). He collaborated with the 'University of Southern California… to replace transportation with telecommunications', which later became known as the first-ever effort to develop a 'remote work' arrangement (Dávila Morán, 2023, p. 03). IBM was also one of the pioneer organizations to adopt remote work (Butler, 2023). IBM, in 1979, at its Silicon Valley location, experimented with a newer form of work setting where they installed home computers for its five employees and let them work from home to reduce the burden on its office's mainframe computers (Useem, 2017). WFH concept became such a popular work arrangement at IBM that by 1983, the size of team telecommuting increased to 2000 employees, and by 2009, the company reported that 40% of its workforce in 170 different countries had successfully shifted to the WFH option. The company saved approximately 2 billion dollars by cutting office space expenses (Useem, 2017).

In recent times, although the widespread use of remote working practices is associated mainly with COVID-19 (Hamingson, 2023; Battisti et al., 2022), alternative work practices, including working from home, teleworking, flexible schedules, compressed work hours/weeks, and virtual teams, existed way before the pandemic (Butler, 2023). According to Gifford (2022), in the 1980s, the scope of remote working was limited to manufacturing and craft work/trade done at a small scale from home. On the contrary, many authors claim that before the Industrial Revolution forced people to come together and work from designated places – factories and offices – people used to work in isolation, mostly from their houses (Butler, 2023). Hence, WFH preceded the concept of commuting to a designated place every day to work together. However, the concept of a collective workplace became institutionalized globally due to mass manufacturing and factory production work that could be only facilitated at a specific location (because of resource availability). While the work from designated places offered many advantages to the industrialists, it also rendered visible problems, including the rigidity of workers' collective and mandatory presence at the workplace, no matter what. A safe assumption here would be that despite their unequal proportions, work-from-home and work-from-office practices have co-existed since the beginning in one way or another.

In literature, authors have presented varying viewpoints about remote work. On the one hand, remote work has been criticized by scholars for creating social isolation, limiting the interaction of employees with anyone apart from their immediate family (Kraut, 1989; Venkatesh & Vitalari, 1992; Cooper & Kurland, 2002; Gilson et al., 2015), setting up the trap of constant connectivity resulting in longer than usual working hours, burnout, and mental health issues (Ng & Feldman, 2008; Virtanen et al., 2011). On the other hand, proponents of remote work highlight its various advantages for employees and employers. For the workforce, it offers work-family balance (Raghuram et al., 2010), eliminates the need for travel, provides cost-efficiency (Raghuram et al., 2010), enhances freedom (Gilson et al., 2015), offers flexible work hours, reduces diversions due to socialization between workers at the office (Maznevski & Chudoba, 2000); and does not trap employees in 9-5 office presence policy (Kraut, 1989). At the organizational level, it brings cost efficiency by reducing energy wastage, overhead charges, carbon footprint (Church, 2015), sick leaves, and employee turnover, boosting work efficiency (Bloom et al., 2015; Dick et al., 2020) and access to global talent pool located anywhere (Horwitz et al., 2006) to fill complex, skill shortage job positions (Raghuram et al., 2001; Gajendran & Harrison, 2006). We discuss and address these challenges and opportunities in detail in the later section of this chapter. In the following section, the authors discuss the key drivers responsible for the evolution of remote work over the years

PANDEMIC AND REMOTE WORKING

A crisis is an inevitable part of operating businesses – big or small. Within a business setting, crisis management is an organization's ability to navigate through challenges, think out of the box, and propose solutions that can turn the crisis into new avenues for expansion and growth (Colquitt & George, 2011). While global crises present critical situations, if managed properly, these situations can provide opportunities for societies and organizations (Eisenhardt et al., 2016). Businesses around the globe have suffered due to many crises, including the crash of financial markets in 2008 to the outbreak of various diseases, including Spanish FLU, Ebola, and most recently, COVID-19. Since these challenges are non-programmed in nature, organizations tend to respond differently to these crises based on their preparedness. We have seen this in practice after the outbreak of COVID-19 in December 2019. According to a Yelp data survey, almost 60% of the active businesses across the USA went out of business within six months of the Pandemic (Sundaram, 2020). While some organizations and businesses went bankrupt and closed permanently, others responded to these challenges by reshaping their strategies and practices to emerge as clear winners (Pecujlija et al., 2019). For instance, while the pandemic adversely impacted many businesses, we saw Jeff Bezos's company – Amazon – increasing its profit by 220% during the first quarter of the pandemic due to customer's shifting shopping patterns and Amazon's agility to respond to the rapidly changing business landscape (Weise, 2021). COVID–19 was perhaps the biggest challenge that businesses had to face in recent times. A significant shift in organizational practices during the pandemic has been exploring remote working options for businesses to keep their core business activities intact by allowing employees to work from home. In COVID-19, organizations faced a situation where they could not force employees to work from their offices (Hoeritzauer 2022). As a result, exploring alternative working choices was deemed appropriate to ensure the health and safety of the workforce and the public (Hamingson, 2023). Although remote working has been in place even before COVID-19, it was never practiced at such a large scale (Delfino & van der Kolk, 2021). The pre-covid teleworking numbers, as provided by a study, indicate that only 19.29% of employees in the USA and 2% in Europe had experienced remote working before the pandemic (Wang et al., 2021). These numbers also provide an understanding that traditionally, employers have been reluctant to offer teleworking opportunities to their employees due to a fear of losing productivity. However, one thing that organizations have learned from the pandemic is the employees' ability to work independently, even without supervision. According to Businesswire - Prodoscore report of 2020, 'employees' productivity increased 47 percent during the lockdown in March and April 2020, …. communication activities such as emailing up by 57 percent, telephoning up by 230 percent, and chat messaging up by 9 percent' (As cited in Hamingson, 2023).

Although organizations have started acclimatizing to the pandemic, it is safe to assume that remote working practice is the future in a post-pandemic world. This is a big transition for employers that adopted it as an enforced choice to work from home during the pandemic, becoming a norm in the modern workplace. Employees who have now worked remotely and seen the first-hand benefits of it, including work-life balance and flexibility, are less likely to accept five days of work from their offices. Many employees now prefer at least one day of work from home and connect it to higher job satisfaction (Hamingson, 2023). As per Gartner's 2020 report, 74% of employers consider remote work choices for their workers as their post-COVID strategy.

GLOBALIZATION AS A KEY DRIVER FOR REMOTE WORK

While the concept of WFH existed before Industry 3.0, the rise of digitalization and computerization in the 1980s has facilitated synchronous and asynchronous business activity via concepts such as virtual teams, outsourcing, and digital nomads (people working from anywhere in the world) (Butler, 2023). Such movements in Industry 3.0 redefined the concept and scope of remote working in ways not considered possible before. Globalization has provided seamless connectivity to people and organizations worldwide by removing cultural and geographic barriers that typically exist in economies (Talent'd Newsletter, 2023). The concept of the world as a global village has been further strengthened by improved modes of transportation and information communication technologies that have enabled people and organizations to work remotely together to share resources and provide goods and services from anywhere in the world. Two main advantages of globalization and remote working have been the organization's ability to recruit talent from anywhere in the world (Horwitz et al. 2006) and shift manufacturing activities to countries with lower production costs. Over the years, we have seen developed economies utilizing economies of scale by shifting manufacturing activities remotely to markets like China, which has mastered the low-cost mass production model (Bajpai, 2022).

Similarly, most IT sector jobs have been shifted to regions such as Asia and Africa due to the availability of a highly skilled workforce to perform these specialized jobs (Chalishazar, 2022). The benefits of recruiting global talents via remote working options are twofold: 1. It lets organizations respond to local skill shortages effectively, and 2. It helps businesses financially by hiring low-income people from developing markets (Chalishazar, 2022). Figure 1 outlines the hourly rate for IT professionals in different parts of the world. It can be observed from the figure that Asia, Africa, and South American regions have a much lower hourly rate for IT jobs as compared to North America, Europe, and Australia.

Figure 1. Hourly pay rate for IT talent outsourcing globally
Note. Global outsourcing hourly rate for the year 2020. Chalishazar, T. (n.d.). Remote Work In IT Industry: Stats, Perks & Best Practices. Peerbits. https://www.peerbits.com/blog/ultimate-guide-to-remote-work.html#:~:text=Remote%20working%20was%20in%20practice,compared%20to%20the%20office%20working.

TECHNOLOGY DEVELOPMENT AND REMOTE WORKING

Globalization and Remote working concepts would not be widespread without the help of technology. Technological advancements such as the internet, video conferencing applications, and social media platforms provide a more face-to-face communication experience to the otherwise globally dispersed workforce to coordinate their work activities and communicate with co-workers effectively (Butler, 2023). Creating virtual teams has also helped solve widespread organizations' challenges of working in varying time zones. It also helps with the reduction of commute times to and from work. With new advancements, the technologies' ability to embed multiple functions under one platform has made it easier for people to work remotely. According to Gifford, 2022 'due to advances in videoconferencing, file sharing, cloud-based systems …… and in the last two years due to lockdown …. more people have been using these technologies daily (P.03). Although videoconferencing applications such as Zoom, Skype, and TEAMS existed before the pandemic, their user base increased manifold during and post-pandemic setting. Nonetheless, using technology to perform work from home has a security risk for the workers whose information can be hacked and misused, leading to cyber and physical risks (Nickson & Siddons, 2004).

While working remotely, Communication and collaboration issues lead to inconsistencies and productivity gaps (Ilag, 2021). To achieve practical cooperation, communication and information-sharing must run without disruption so everyone can participate in innovative brainstorming sessions, feedback loops, and cross-functional decision-making (Deshpande et al., 2016). Because an IT infrastructure and team-sharing tools are required to establish connectivity using a top-down strategy swiftly, organizations must have a sizable IT infrastructure to adopt remote work. High-quality digitization and communication technologies can improve connections inside and outside the organization (Min & Kim, 2020). Mature IT systems can boost the effectiveness of technical investments, resulting in higher company performance and ensuring that enterprises are on the correct route (Li, 2020).

Business machines frequently come with sophisticated antivirus software, specialized firewalls, and automatic online backup solutions that are not always present on personal devices. As a result, there is a higher chance that malware will access personal devices and steal information about the user and their employment (Reuters, 2021). The best strategy is to force remote workers to utilize devices that the employer has provided and configured for work-related purposes to prevent them from sharing or retaining sensitive information on their devices. Employers can use mobile application management (MAM) and mobile device management (MDM) software if they allow employees to use their laptops or smartphones for work-related purposes (Bixenstine, 2023). According to a digital.com poll from September 2021, 60% of businesses with remote workers use monitoring tools to measure employee activity and productivity. Of the monitored employees, 53% spend three or more hours daily engaged in things unrelated to their jobs. After implementing surveillance software, 88% of employers fired employees, and 81% of those businesses reported increased worker productivity. Although these tools help monitor remote employees, managing employee privacy is always a concern for employers. Employee privacy is only to a certain extent protected by federal law. State or municipal statutory law may provide additional restrictions on some employer monitoring (Finkin, 2017). The Electronic Communications Privacy Act (ECPA), which includes the Stored Communications Act and the Computer Fraud and Abuse Act (CFAA), are the primary federal statutes that safeguard employee privacy. Anyone who "intentionally accesses a computer without authorization" is subject to civil and criminal sanctions under the Computer Fraud and Abuse Act (CFAA) (Bixenstine, 2023).

According to a recent Tenable study, 74% of firms believe that recent business-impacting hacks resulted from tech vulnerabilities related to remote labor (Tenable, 2021). The traditional approach to setting up secure remote access is VPN and multifactor authentication; other, more secure options include zero trust via a software-defined perimeter (SDP) (also known as "zero-trust network access" (ZTNA), SD-WAN, Remote desktop software, Virtual Remote Software, and other cloud services such as 'Software as a Service' (SaaS) and 'Infrastructure as a Service' (IaaS) (Bixenstine, 2023). The alternative secure technique can comprise Web Application and API protection (WAAP), URL filtering antivirus and antimalware software, firewall, encryption, multifactor authentication, and Web Application and API protection (WAAP) (Bixenstine, 2023).

LEGAL ASPECTS OF REMOTE WORK

With large firms like 3M, SAP, and Spotify pledging to make their remote work policies permanent, research reveals that remote work could save businesses up to $10,600 per employee year (Chávarro, 2023). Employers no longer have the same level of control over the security and stability of their workers' working conditions as they formerly did due to the improved flexibility and cost savings that come with remote employment. Employees may also find it more challenging to separate their personal lives from their work life. These problems have sparked the creation of new regulations to guarantee that teleworkers, home workers, and remote workers are covered by current environmental, health, and safety rules and regulations and that companies are not violating labor laws (Chávarro, 2023). The majority of businesses (82 percent), according to the most recent KPMG survey (2022), regard tax and legal compliance as their top hurdle when implementing remote working. Organizations actively develop policy restrictions and conduct case-by-case evaluations to identify and manage the related compliance risks or automated solutions (Donnelly & Johns, 2021).

The level of security provided by a home office should be comparable to that of the employee's designated work site (CCOHS, 2023). Directive 2003/88/EC – Outlines particular elements of working time, such as rest periods and maximum working hours – in Europe. It applies to remote workers to protect employees' health and safety and establishes limitations on working hours and rest times (OPOCE, 2003). The goal of Directive 2019/1152/EU on predictable and transparent working conditions is to enhance working conditions for all employees, including those who work remotely. It establishes guidelines for fundamental employment rights, including a minimum salary and information on working conditions (The European Parliament and The Council of the European Union, 2019). Most EU nations have some legislation governing remote employment, although few are comprehensive. Some consider enacting amendments, extensions, or conventions to overcome these issues. In nations like Germany, France, Italy, Spain, and Belgium, workers' "right to disconnect" was largely embraced, enabling employees to disregard work-related issues outside of regular working hours (Rae, 2022). Portugal goes a step further by placing the responsibility on businesses, stating that they must avoid contacting their employees after hours. For each violation, the employer could face fines of up to EUR 10,000 (Rae, 2022). These new laws prohibit employers from monitoring their workers' online work, mandate that they give employees the tools they need to execute their tasks and forbid them from getting in touch with their staff outside of the agreed-upon working hours unless an emergency arises. For employees who work from home, employers must contribute to their utility expenditures, including power and Internet (Rae, 2022). Working parents with kids under eight can also work remotely without prior approval from their employers. If a parent's job allows for remote work, businesses cannot turn down their request. On the other hand, employees can decline remote work if they want (Rae, 2022).

The US Department of Labor (2021) provides recommendations to clarify that employers must pay workers for all hours worked, including unpaid but permissible overtime and work from home. The time must be recorded as hours worked if the employer knows or has cause to suspect that an employee is working. The Canada Labour Code states you can seek a flexible work schedule as an employee. Changes that make it easier to balance work and home life are examples of flexible work arrangements. However, only those employees who have been employed continuously for six months are eligible to request flexible work arrangements under the Code, including requests for adjustments to the employee's number of hours worked, work schedule, and place of employment (ESDC, 2023). Organizations must collaborate cross-functionally with key stakeholders and subject matter experts to develop a comprehensive framework for addressing the risks related to remote work. Representatives from human resources, cyber and IT security, legal, immigration, tax, and risk management can work together to address various issues and create a more robust framework for addressing risks related to remote work (Chang & Ong, 2023).

Employers' Attitude: A Shift from Workplace Presence to Flexible Work Arrangements

Although remote working or virtual teams is not an alien concept for organizations, traditionally (except in a few industries), organizations have avoided the work-from-home setting in favour of a physical office setup. This includes the previous IT giant Yahoo, which in 2013, under the leadership of Marissa Mayer (CEO of Yahoo), discontinued remote working options and forced the employees to work from offices (Smith, 2013)—the year 2020, forced employers to shift their business activity remotely if they wanted to survive the pandemic. As a result, the remote working norm saw a significant boost globally. The remote work fraction in the USA increased from 5% to 50% during COVID-19 (Barrero, Bloom, & Davis 2021). A UK report affirms this change in leadership/organizational behaviour towards remote working, where 40% of employers are flexible in offering work-from-home options to their employees as opposed to 15% before COVID-19 (Brinkley et al. 2020). Another UK report finding of 2020 highlights that the pandemic had a positive impact on employees and employers: '6 in 10 UK employees working remotely indicated they would be more likely to request WFH in the future, whereas only 5% thought they would be less likely to do so' (Gifford and Green 2020 as cited in Gifford, 2022, P.02). Similarly, Gartner's 2020 survey outline that Telecommuting practice has increased by 115% in the past ten years and is expected to grow steadily in the coming years. With remote working practice yielding better than expected results, employers are now willing to allocate a budget to support the work-from-home ar-

Figure 2. Future projections for employees shifting permanently to remote work setting
Note. Projection of workforce shifting to permanent remote work. Shifting some employees to remote work permanently | Gartner. (2020, April 3). Gartner. https://www.gartner.com/en/newsroom/press-releases/2020-04-03-gartner-cfo-surey-reveals-74-percent-of-organizations-to-shift-some-employees-to-remote-work-permanently2

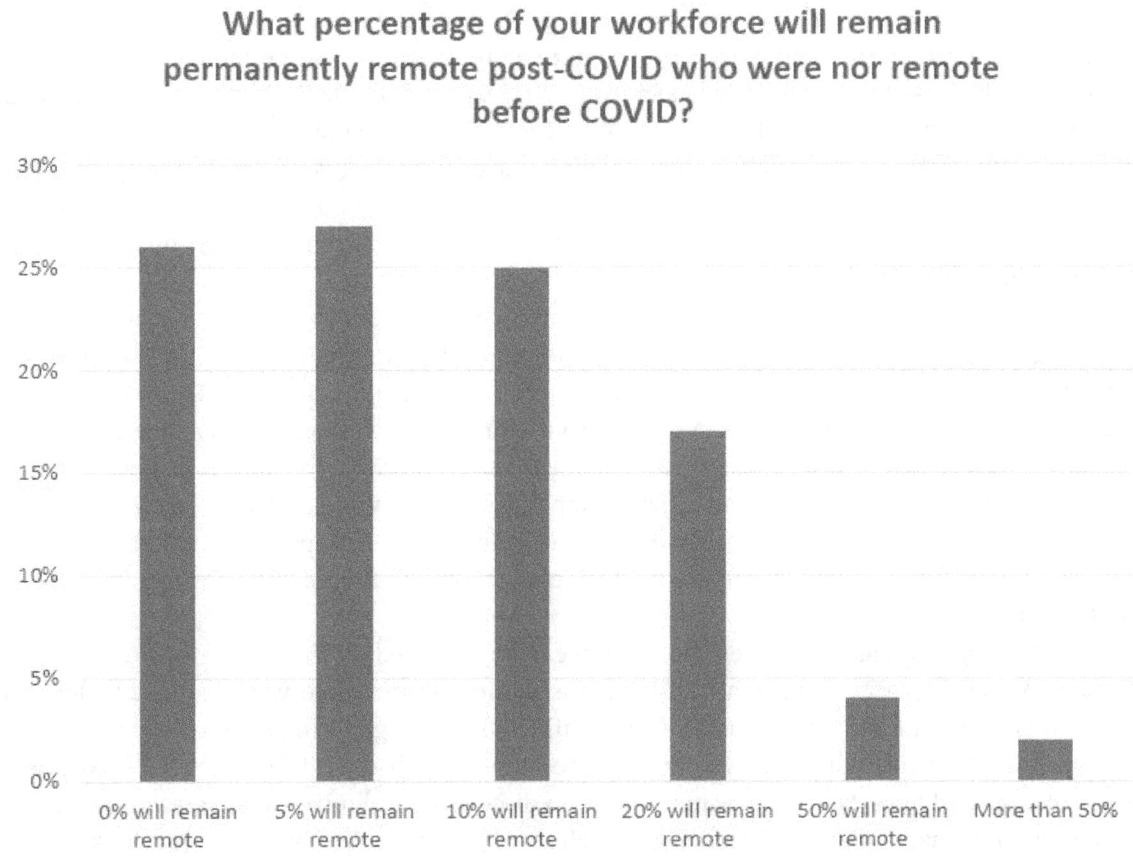

rangement. With the evidence indicating a paradigm shift in employees' expectations, organizations are now (willingly or unwillingly) investing in resources to help employees set up home offices, covering for fixtures, providing computer systems and required applications, and paying for internet and utilities (Stein et al., 2015; Barrero et al., 2021). Figure 2. below provides an overview of the organization's long-term strategy for remote work provision for its employees. According to Figure 2, approximately 75% of employers will continue to offer remote working options. Out of these 75% of companies, 6% will provide extensive work-from-home facilities, with 50-60% of their employees working remotely.

INFLUENCE OF REMOTE WORK ON PRODUCTIVITY LEVELS, EMPLOYEE WELL-BEING AND WORK-LIFE INTEGRATION

Before the COVID-19 crisis, the work was majorly on-site (Karunarathne, 2021). In many industries, workers work remotely from their homes instead of in typical office settings (Ozimek, 2020; Popovici & Popovici, 2020). Due to the massive migration to remote work starting in 2020, businesses are considering hybrid and remote work models (Ozimek, 2020). This shift has allowed professionals and businesses to see the advantages of remote work. Work-life balance (Raghuram et al., 2010; Gilson et al., 2015), collaboration platforms (Gifford, 2022; Butler, 2023), and communication technologies (Sullivan, 2003; Ozimek, 2020; Yang et al., 2022; Dávila Morán, 2023) must be modified for this transition. According to a Gallup survey conducted in June 2022, 8 out of 10 people work remotely or in a hybrid capacity, compared to 2 out of 10 who work exclusively on-site; Future forecasts continue along the same lines (Agrawal, 2023). Most CEOs projected that employees would be on-site 21 to 80% of the time, or one to four days per week (Alexander et al., 2021). (Pereira, 2022). Also, 48% of organizations continue to allow some remote work for their employees, according to FlexJobs' Employee Engagement Report. 26% of respondents questioned about their employer's post-pandemic workplace plans claimed their organization would use a hybrid model, and 22% said they would be allowed to work remotely (Howington, 2022). According to a recent study, being able to work from home has up to 20% happier employees (Robinson, 2022).

A 2020 Deloitte study found that remote work can increase productivity by decreasing travel time, strengthening focus, expanding flexibility, and encouraging innovation; however, remote work could lead to difficulties in cooperation, controlling interruptions, establishing limits, and preventing burnout. Because of this, managing and measuring productivity for remote work demands a change, emphasizing outcomes rather than outputs and humanizing the concept of productivity by considering the workers' needs and well-being (Jensen et al., 2020). Employee productivity and well-being increase with a robust communication system (Papagiannidis & Marikyan, 2020). Companies that convey their rules and procedures in a more detailed, remote-relevant manner and let their employees feel included grow faster (Alexander, 2021).

Work-life integration and employee satisfaction can be impacted differently by remote employment (Bellmann & Hübler, 2021). Mostafa (2021) claims that because remote workers were better able to combine their personal and professional responsibilities, it had a good impact on their psychological health and work-life integration. However, because employees had to deal with increased pressure, stress, isolation, and uncertainty, the same study also discovered a significant adverse effect of remote working on emotional depletion. According to a Harvard Business Review study, remote workers believed they had to be continually accessible to co-workers and managers, undermining their work-life balance and raising their stress levels (Amico, 2023). During the pandemic, remote employees in Latin America reported higher levels of work stress, lower job satisfaction, and less work-life balance than before, according to a study by NCBI (Sandoval-Reyes et al., 2021). The cost of lost production due to poor mental health, especially anxiety, to the global economy may reach $1 trillion annually (World Health Organization, 2022).

Remote employment, however, cannot provide the advantages that employees get from on-site work, such as meeting and learning from new people and emotional and social support (Heydari et al., 2020). In-person work encourages innovation, and the productivity benefits outweigh the advantages of working longer at home for who knows how long. A higher growth rate will shortly outpace the one-time gain from the commute time saved once individuals start working again (Glaeser & Cutler, 2021). Working from home must be sustainable for employees' productivity and preferences and employers' attitudes toward it (Mehdi & Morissette, 2021). Remote working reduces carbon emissions and environmental pollution as transportation decreases (Al-Habaibeh, 2021). According to an OECD survey of thousands of businesses across 25 countries, 90% of workers preferred doing more of their jobs from home in the future, according to the study. The modal choice for working from home is two to three days per week, and managers anticipated that about 60% of their workers would conduct more of their work from home (Criscuolo et al., 2021)

Examples of Companies Offering Fully Remote or Hybrid Work Options After COVID

The global acceptance of remote work has increased as a result of COVID-19. The degree to which employees can work remotely varies considerably between industries. For instance, almost 85% of workers in professional, scientific, and technical services, as well as financial and insurance, may be able to work from home, and only 6% of hospitality and food industry workers can work remotely (Deng et al., 2020). In a report by McKinsey, 87% of employees would take the chance to work more flexibly if their employers offered it. Businesses have realized that a full-time physical presence in the office is optional to achieve outstanding results. Famous firms like Adobe, Spotify, and Salesforce are among those that have shifted to hybrid and remote offices. In reality, more businesses from various sectors are adopting permanent remote workspaces, following in the footsteps of long-time supporters of remote work like Automattic, GitLab, Zapier, and Toptal (Howington, 2022).

3M, SAP, Lyft, Coinbase, Reddit, Spotify, and Hubspot have let employees choose the options they want, being in the office, working from home or hybrid; Atlassian and VISTA have shifted to a completely remote work model (Smith, 2022). A Remote.co (2022) study found that 63% of global employees would "absolutely" hunt for new employment if their current employer would not provide work-from-home opportunities. The significance of work flexibility in today's workforce is demonstrated by the significant propensity of professionals to leave a present position for one that includes remote work. (*Report: 80% Say Salary Is not Keeping up With Inflation*, 2022)

Remote Learning and its Impact on Educational Outcomes and Student Well-Being

The pandemic has accelerated a world in which structural change and labor market disruption are caused by technological breakthroughs like automation and artificial intelligence (AI); this results in an

Figure 3. Global growth of learners registered in online learning
Note. GWood, J. (2022, January 27). These 3 charts show the global growth in online learning. Retrieved June 27, 2023, from https://www.weforum.org/agenda/2022/01/online-learning-courses-reskill-skills-gap/

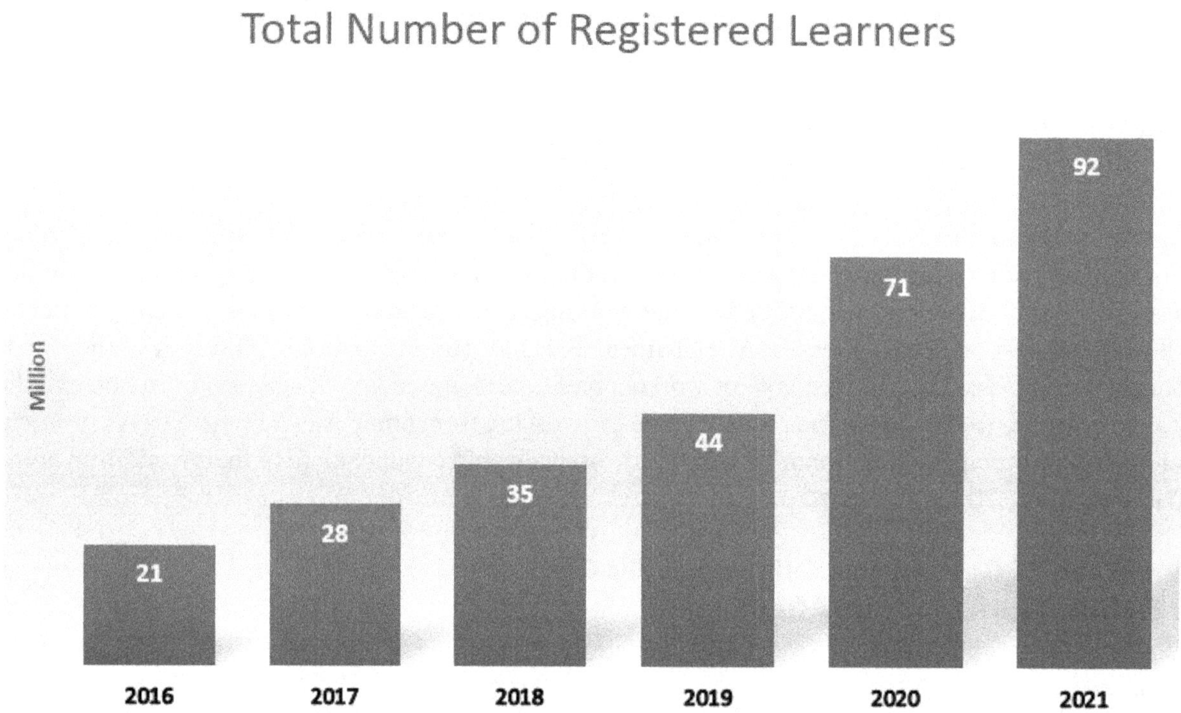

uncertain future for many people regarding their employment (Galanakis, 2021). Post-pandemic many people are enrolling themselves in remote learning to upgrade and prepare themselves for their present role and the dynamic labor market (Marmolejo & Groccia, 2022). People need access to high-quality online education to acquire the skill sets for achieving professional advancement (Littenberg-Tobias & Reich, 2020). Figure 3 illustrates that in 2016, there were 21 million learners enrolled in Coursera; the number almost tripled during COVID-19. Moreover, enrollments further escalated to 92 million in 2021 (Wood, 2022). These increases reflect how widely accepted online learning is becoming, particularly the rise in remote students participating in higher education programs and from underserved or rural areas. Figure 4 illustrates the top 10 countries of the world in terms of the number of enrollments in online courses. USA and India are the top two countries with the highest number of people enrolled in the Coursera online learning platform.

Globally, the COVID-19 pandemic is transforming education; as a result, schools are now compelled to use media and technology to carry on with their instructional programs (Schmidt et al., 2021). The new standard for students of all ages, from elementary school through higher education, is remote learning (Luca et al., 2020). As students and teachers traverse virtual classrooms, video conferencing platforms, and online learning management systems, this has offered challenges and opportunities (Biswas & Nandi, 2020). The benefits of distance learning are distinct and can raise student interest (Frolova, 2020). A flexible timetable that allows students to complete their work at their own pace and on their own time is one of these advantages; Students can now work when they are focused and aware (Turan,

Figure 4. Top ten countries in terms of student enrollment
Note. Impact Report: Serving the world through learning. (2021). In Coursera. Retrieved July 2, 2023, from https://about.coursera.org/press/wp-content/uploads/2021/11/2021-Coursera-Impact-Report.pdf

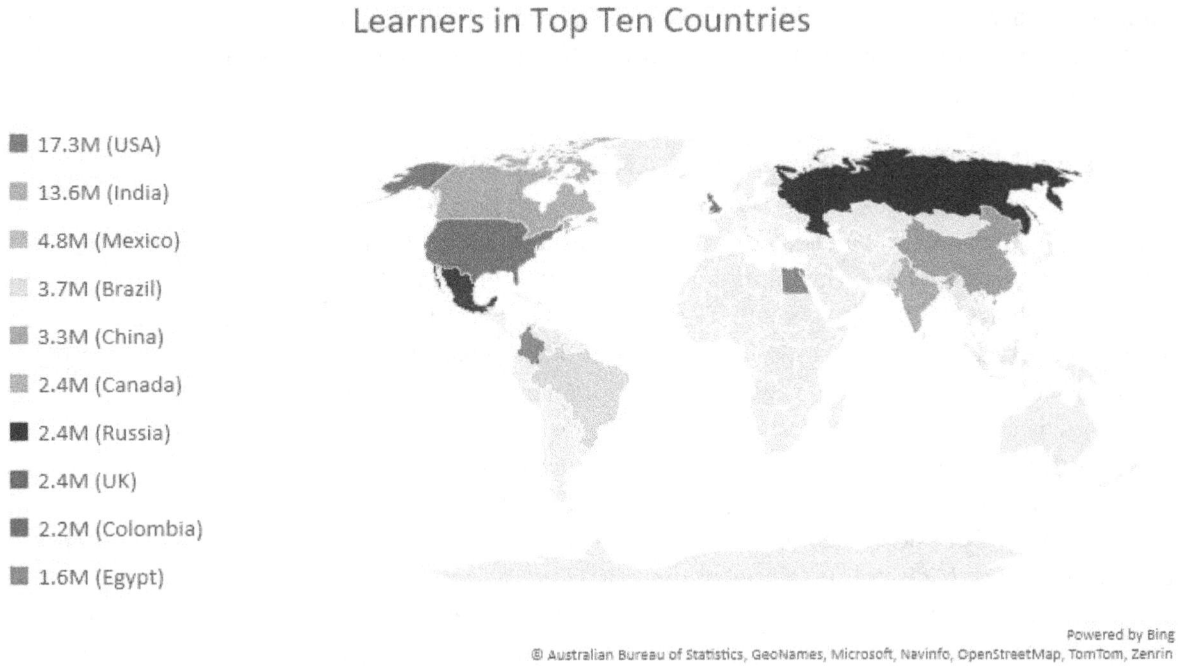

2022). Another benefit of remote learning is having access to online resources (ChimpReports, 2023). Additionally, the design of the learning activities significantly impacts student engagement in a virtual classroom during remote teaching and learning. (Heick, 2021). Strategies like flipping the classroom, breakout room activities and feedback can enhance student engagement in remote learning environments (Venton & Pompano, 2021). Evidence from higher education indicates that prior skills matter because only low-achieving students fared adversely once lectures started to be streamed remotely (Economics Observatory, 2021). Active learning techniques, known to improve engagement, motivation, and learning in conventional classroom experiences, could be enriched using remote learning settings. (Nguyen et al., 2021). Remote learning has had a mixed effect on academic results and student well-being. In an American Psychological Association research, 18% of parents mentioned that greater flexibility in students' schedules is the most significant advantage of remote learning. People have become more resilient during the post-pandemic, reducing the healthcare system's burden. (Zhang, 2022).

On the other hand, Remote learning has also elevated the importance of mental health in the classroom setting (Abramson, 2021). COVID-19 has primarily negative psychological consequences on mental health, involving stress, frustration, boredom, and fear of infection (Brooks et al., 2020). Tension among students was also exacerbated by the evacuation of student residences and the postponement of scheduled activities, including commencement exercises and exchange programs (Lee, 2020). According to a study by Lyubetsky et al. in 2021, abrupt changes in learning environments were a significant source of chronic stress, which increased students' likelihood of experiencing anxiety and depressive symptoms. In recent research on college students, it was shown that participants experienced loneliness and difficulty making friends as a result of remote learning. Some participants described having concentration, time management, self-motivation, and self-directed learning issues (Nandlall et al., 2022). An online survey of Chinese residents revealed that people aged 21 to 40 were more psychologically vulnerable during the COVID outbreak than elderly persons (Ahmed et al., 2020). According to a study on the in-depth experiences of college students, their emotions were like an "emotional rollercoaster," they were accepting of a "new normal," and they were going through "growth under pressure." (Cahapay, 2020).

CHALLENGES IN REMOTE WORK AND LEARNING

Many organizations plan a balanced schedule between remote work and office work (Alexander, 2021). It provides productivity and flexibility and balances the formal and informal organizational structure environment (Jalagat, 2019). Although it offers many benefits, it also poses several challenges, such as cybersecurity risk (Škiljić, 2020), which has given birth to various issues related to personal privacy, account hacking etc. It decreases synchronous communication; face-to-face interaction can never be substituted by any other means because there is a lacuna in communication that is synchronization (Yang, 2019). Further, remote work brings difficulty in concentration in making a healthy work-life balance because of interference between work and personal life (AL-rfou, 2021) as a continuous distraction from the family, a considerable number of digital gadgets can contribute to focus, and the absence of a supervisor needs self-discipline (Karunarathne, 2021).

Furthermore, network or technical issues significantly impact productivity and communication (Ilag, 2021). Insufficient connectivity slows micromanaging as all the communication is online, causing disruptions and difficulties accessing online resources or learning (Deshpande et al., 2016). Moreover, the work-life conflict occurs as boundaries between work and personal life or any surrounding while working remotely is blurred (Lange & Kayser, 2022). The inability to manage the physical separation of the office and home results in anxiety, stress, and difficulty managing a healthy relationship as the home becomes a structured office (Lyubetsky et al. in 2021). Also, with limited supervision, there will be the uncertain possibility of work delays or work completion time, misinterpretation of information and difficulty in managing trust and accountability (Karunarathne, 2021). Nevertheless, a collaborative effort of employees to try to be more productive and exchange ideas (Jalagat, 2019), but in remote working environments, it is not easy to maintain because of time zones, trust-building, spontaneity, physical presence, and technology.

The pandemic has accelerated remote learning, allowing many students and employees to learn modern technologies and concepts to deal with the environment (Biswas & Nandi, 2020). The lack of access to reliable technological resources that many people from low-income families experience contributes to learning setbacks because these platforms need investment in network equipment and technology gadgets (Roy, 2022). Despite the challenges in implementation, several advantages have been acknowledged in the need to shift to remote or online learning, among which stands out is the opportunity for rapid progress in the field of digital education, which, in other circumstances, would take years (Schmidt et al., 2021).

FUTURE DIRECTION FOR REMOTE WORK AND LEARNING

The challenges of remote work and learning are overcome by learning new topologies of networks like artificial intelligence, the Internet of Things and distributed ledger technology (Verma, 2022). Artificial

Intelligence (AI) enables personalized recommendations, automated assessments, and intelligent virtual assistants, improving productivity and knowledge acquisition (Guggenberger et al., 2021). Internet of Things (IoT) devices provide real-time data, enabling seamless connectivity and remote monitoring of equipment and environments (Sharma et al., 2020). Distributed ledger technologies (DLT) ensure secure and transparent record-keeping, facilitating verification of credentials and eliminating fraud in remote work and learning (Fitter et al., 2020). These technologies offer personalized recommendations, real-time connectivity, secure record-keeping, and verification, which can enhance remote work and learning experiences. Furthermore, embracing these advancements, the future of remote work holds immense potential for improved productivity (Glaeser, & Cutler, 2021), seamless collaboration (Jalagat, 2019), and enhanced work-life balance (Gilson et al., 2015). By capitalizing on these technologies and cultivating a culture of continuous growth and adaptability, businesses and individuals can unleash the boundless opportunities of remote work, fueling heightened effectiveness and triumph in the dynamic landscape of the digital era (Elshaiekh, 2018).

The future outcome of remote working will be a hybrid model. Around 55% of executives expect to implement hybrid work arrangements. The hybrid workforce model has various pros and cons (Putri, 2023), but a hybrid workforce is more beneficial for the employees. In a report by McKinsey (2021), employees were asked regarding their priority towards the hybrid model; 87% of employees would like to opt for hybrid work arrangements, and 20-25% of the workers in developed economies could work 3+ weeks remotely. Virtual Reality (VR) and Augmented Reality (AR) adoption in online learning and distant employment are expected to increase. With the help of these technologies, immersive learning opportunities can be improved, and distant meetings and cooperation can be made more attractive (Ramirez, 2022). Project management software and video conferencing are two examples of remote communication solutions that are constantly improving. For remote communication, technologies like Zoom, Microsoft Teams, and Slack have become popular (Slack, 2022). There will be a greater emphasis on cybersecurity and data privacy as remote work and study become part and parcel of life. Investments in strong security measures are required from businesses and educational institutions (CPA, 2019).

Some of the most exciting developments in the field of remote work include personalized learning and skill development (Deloitte, 2020), flexible work policies (PwC, 2021), reskilling and upskilling of individuals (World Economic Forum, 2023), managing mental health and well-being of employees (Buffer, 2021), sustainable remote work practices (Dishman, 2021), and leveraging the world's talent pool (Choudhury, 2021).

CONCLUSION

As a result of the numerous reasons discussed in this study, the evolution of remote work and learning has experienced a dramatic shift. The COVID-19 pandemic compelled organizations and educational institutions to quickly adjust to distant work and learning environments. Geographical constraints were removed by globalization, which made it possible for remote work to become commonplace. Remote work and study are now more accessible and effective than ever, thanks to technological improvements. As businesses and people negotiate the tricky landscape of remote employment, the legal elements of remote work have come into sharper focus. Employers are changing their perspectives and putting less emphasis on office presence while acknowledging the advantages of flexible work arrangements. The impact of remote work on efficiency, employee well-being, and work-life integration brings to light the delicate balance businesses must achieve to maximize these results.

Several leading companies have embraced fully remote or hybrid work options, demonstrating the feasibility and success of these models post-COVID. The innovative business practices and constant technology change backed by AI, VR, and AR have motivated individuals to reskill and upskill to stay competitive. Remote learning has reshaped educational outcomes and student well-being, offering opportunities for personalized learning experiences. However, challenges persist, including issues related to digital equity, cybersecurity, and improved infrastructure. These challenges must be addressed to ensure equitable access to remote work and learning opportunities for all. Instructors have the critical role of enhancing student engagement and learning by designing a creative teaching strategy using various teaching tools and technologies.

Challenges such as communication barriers, isolation, and security concerns have necessitated creative solutions. As we look to the future, remote work and learning will likely continue to evolve. Hybrid models that combine in-person and remote elements may become the norm. Addressing the challenges and leveraging the benefits of remote work and learning will be critical in shaping the future of work and education. In this ever-changing landscape, organizations, educational institutions, and policymakers must adapt and innovate to harness the full potential of remote work and learning, ensuring that they contribute positively to productivity, employee/student well-being, and the overall quality of work and education in the future.

REFERENCES

Abramson, A. (2021). *Capturing the benefits of remote learning*. APA. https://www.apa.org/monitor/2021/09/cover-remote-learning

Agrawal, B. B. W. S. (2023, July 5). *Returning to the Office: The Current, Preferred and Future State of Remote Work*. Gallup.com. https://www.gallup.com/workplace/397751/returning-office-current-preferred-future-state-remote-work.aspx

Ahmed, M. Z., Ahmed, O., Aibao, Z., Hanbin, S., Siyu, L., & Ahmad, A. (2020). Epidemic of COVID-19 in China and associated psychological problems. *Asian Journal of Psychiatry*, *51*, 102092. doi:10.1016/j.ajp.2020.102092 PMID:32315963

Al-Habaibeh, A., Watkins, M., Waried, K., & Javareshk, M. B. (2021). Challenges and opportunities of remotely working from home during Covid-19 pandemic. *Global Transitions*, *3*, 99–108. doi:10.1016/j.glt.2021.11.001 PMID:34870136

Alexander, A., De Smet, A., Langstaff, M., & Ravid, D. (2021). What employees are saying about the future of remote work. McKinsey & Company.

Alexander, A., Mysore, M., Cracknell, R., De Smet, A., Langstaff, M., & Ravid, D. (2021, May 17). *What executives are saying about the future of hybrid work*. McKinsey & Company. https://www.mckinsey.com/capabilities/people-and-organizational-performance/our-insights/what-executives-are-saying-about-the-future-of-hybrid-work

Americans are embracing flexible work—and they want more of it. (2022, June 23). McKinsey & Company. https://www.mckinsey.com/industries/real-estate/our-insights/americans-are-embracing-flexible-work-and-they-want-more-of-it

Amico, L. (2023, May 20). *The Realities of Remote Work.* Harvard Business Review. https://hbr.org/2021/10/the-realities-of-remote-work

Bajpai, P. (2022). Why China Is "The World's Factory". *Investopedia.* https://www.investopedia.com/articles/investing/102214/why-china-worlds-factory.asp#:~:text=In%20addition%20to%20its%20low,duties%2C%20and%20competitive%20currency%20practices

Barrero, J. M., Bloom, N., & Davis, S. J. (2021). Why Working from Home Will Stick. *National Bureau of Economic Research Working Paper Series.* NBER. https://www.nber.org/papers/ w28731

Bellmann, L., & Hübler, O. (2021). Working from home, job satisfaction and work–life balance–robust or heterogeneous links? *International Journal of Manpower, 42*(3), 424–441. doi:10.1108/IJM-10-2019-0458

Biswas, R. A., & Nandi, S. (2020). Teaching in virtual classroom: Challenges and opportunities. *International Journal of Engineering Applied Sciences and Technology, 5*(1), 334–337. doi:10.33564/IJEAST.2020.v05i01.052

Bixenstine, B. A. (2023). Employment Law Implications of a Remote Workplace. *Dispute Resolution Journal, 76*(3).

Bloom, N., Liang, J., Roberts, J., & Ying, Z. J. (2015). Does working from home work? Evidence from a Chinese experiment. *The Quarterly Journal of Economics, 130*(1), 165–218. doi:10.1093/qje/qju032

Brinkley, I., Willmott, B., Beatson, M., & Davies, G. (2020). *Embedding New Ways of Working: Implications for the Post-pandemic Workplace.* CIPD. https://www.cipd.co.uk/knowledge/work/ trends/working-post-pandemic

Brooks, S. K., Webster, R. K., Smith, L. E., Woodland, L., Wessely, S., Greenberg, N., & Rubin, G. J. (2020). The psychological impact of quarantine and how to reduce it: Rapid review of the evidence. *Lancet, 395*(10227), 912–920. doi:10.1016/S0140-6736(20)30460-8 PMID:32112714

Buffer. (2021). *State Of Remote Work 2020.* Buffer. https://buffer.com/state-of-remote-work/2020

Buira, J. (2012). Entre el Mito y la Realidad. Editorial UOC.

Businesswire. (2020). Prodoscore Research from March/April 2020: Productivity Has Increased, Led By Remote Workers. *Business Wire.* https://www.businesswire.com/news/home/20200519005295/en/

Butler, H. (2023). *The History of Remote Work: How it Became What we Know today.* Crossover. https://www.crossover.com/perspective/the-history-of-remote-work

Cahapay, M. B. (2020). Stranded college students amid corona virus disease 2019 pandemic: An existential phenomenology. *Journal of Loss and Trauma, 25*(6-7), 598–604. doi:10.1080/15325024.2020.1770955

CCOHS. (2023, June 13). *Government of Canada Canadian Centre for Occupation Health and Safety.* CCOHS. https://www.ccohs.ca/oshanswers/hsprograms/telework.html

Chalishazar, T. (2022). *Remote Work In IT Industry: Stats, Perks & Best Practices*. Peerbits. https://www.peerbits.com/blog/ultimate-guide-to-remote-work.html#:~:text=Remote%20working%20was%20in%20practice,compared%20to%20the%20office%20working

Chang, K., & Ong, I. (2023, May 31). *Be aware of the compliance risks of a growing remote workforce*. EY. https://www.ey.com/en_sg/you-and-the-taxman/be-aware-of-the-compliance-risks-of-a-growing-remote-workforce

Chávarro, J. M. (2023, February 27). Work-From-Home Regulations Are Coming. Companies Aren't Ready. *MIT Sloan Management Review*. https://sloanreview.mit.edu/article/work-from-home-regulations-are-coming-companies-arent-ready

ChimpReports. (2023). The Impact of Remote Learning on College Student Engagement. *ChimpReports*. https://chimpreports.com/the-impact-of-remote-learning-on-college-student-engagement/

Choudhury, P. (2021, July 7). Our Work-from-Anywhere future. *Harvard Business Review*. https://hbr.org/2020/11/our-work-from-anywhere-future

Church, N. F. (2015). Gauging Perceived Benefits from "Working from Home" as a Job Benefit. *International Journal of Business & Economic Development*, *3*(3), 81–89.

Colquitt, J. A., & George, G. (2011). 'Publishing in AMJ – part 1: Topic choice'. *Academy of Management Journal*, *54*(3), 432–435. doi:10.5465/amj.2011.61965960

Cooper, C. D., & Kurland, N. B. (2002). Telecommuting, Professional Isolation, and Employee Development in Public and Private Organizations. *Journal of Organizational Behavior*, *23*(4), 511–532. doi:10.1002/job.145

CPA. (2019, April 23). *6 cybersecurity tips for organizations with remote workers*. CPA Canada. https://www.cpacanada.ca/en/news/atwork/2019-04-23-remote-cybersecurity

Criscuolo, C., Gal, P., Leidecker, T., Losma, F., & Nicoletti, G. (2021). Telework after COVID-19: survey evidence from managers and workers on implications for productivity and well-being. *Département des affaires économiques de l'OCDE, blog ECOSCOPE, 28.*

Dávila Morán, R.C. (2023). Influence of Remote Work on the Work Stress of Workers in the Context of the COVID-19 Pandemic: A Systematic Review. *Sustainability*, *15,* 12489. . doi:10.3390/su151612489

Delfino, G. F., & van der Kolk, B. (2021). Remote working, management control changes, and employee responses during the COVID-19 crisis. *Accounting, Auditing & Accountability Journal*, *34*(6), 1376–1387. doi:10.1108/AAAJ-06-2020-4657

Deshpande, A., Sharp, H., Barroca, L., & Gregory, P. (2016). *Remote working and collaboration in agile teams*. Agile Research Network.

Dick, E. A., Raithatha, A., Musker, L., Redhead, J., Mehta, A., & Amiras, D. (2020). 'Remote reporting in the COVID-19 era: From pilot study to practice'. *Clinical Radiology*, *75*(9), 710. doi:10.1016/j.crad.2020.06.016 PMID:32654757

Digital.com Staff. (2023). 6 in 10 employers require monitoring software for remote workers. *Digital.com*. https://digital.com/6-in-10-employers-require-monitoring-software-for-remote-workers/

Dishman, L. (2020). Working from 'anywhere' is possible—but not sustainable. *Fast Company*. https://www.fastcompany.com/90545523/working-from-anywhere-is-possible-but-not-sustainable

Donnelly, R., & Johns, J. (2021). Recontextualising remote working and its HRM in the digital economy: An integrated framework for theory and practice. *International Journal of Human Resource Management*, *32*(1), 84–105. doi:10.1080/09585192.2020.1737834

Economics Observatory. (2021, February 8). What is the likely impact of remote learning on educational outcomes? *Economics Observatory*. https://www.economicsobservatory.com/what-likely-impact-remote-learning-educational-outcomes

Eisenhardt, K. M., Graebner, M. E., & Sonenshein, S. (2016). Grand Challenges and Inductive Methods: Rigor without Rigor Mortis. *Academy of Management Journal*, *59*(4), 1113–1123. doi:10.5465/amj.2016.4004

Elshaiekh, N. E. M., Hassan, Y. A. A., & Abdallah, A. A. A. (2018, November). The impacts of remote working on workers performance. In 2018 international Arab conference on information technology (ACIT) (pp. 1-5). IEEE. doi:10.1109/ACIT.2018.8672704

ESDC. (2023, September 12). *Flexible work arrangements for federally regulated employees*. Government of Canada.

Evans, P. (2022). For some employers, remote work is here to stay. *Grand Rapids Business Journal*. https://www.crainsgrandrapids.com/news/real-estate/for-some-employers-remote-work-is-here-to-stay/

Felstead, A. (2022). Psychological and Social Work Factors as Predictors of Mental Distress and Positive Affect: A Prospective, Multilevel Study. *PLoS One*, *11*(3), e0152220. doi:10.1371/journal.pone.0152220

Finkin, M. W. (2017). Chapter 7: Privacy and Autonomy. Emp. Rts. & Emp. Pol'y J., 21, 589.

Fitter, N. T., Raghunath, N., Cha, E., Sanchez, C. A., Takayama, L., & Matarić, M. J. (2020). Are we there yet? Comparing remote learning technologies in the university classroom. *IEEE Robotics and Automation Letters*, *5*(2), 2706–2713. doi:10.1109/LRA.2020.2970939

Frolova, E., Rogach, O., & Ryabova, T. (2020). Benefits and risks of switching to distance learning in a pandemic. *Перспективы Науки и Образования Perspectives of Science and Education*, 79.

Gajendran, R. S., & Harrison, D. A. (2006). *The Good, the Bad, and the Unknown about Telecommuting: Meta-Analysis of Individual Consequences and Mechanisms of Distributed Work*. Academy of Management Annual Meeting Proceedings. https://www.apa.org/pubs/journals/releases/apl-9261524.pdf

Galanakis, C. M., Rizou, M., Aldawoud, T. M., Ucak, I., & Rowan, N. J. (2021). Innovations and technology disruptions in the food sector within the COVID-19 pandemic and post-lockdown era. *Trends in Food Science & Technology*, *110*, 193–200. doi:10.1016/j.tifs.2021.02.002 PMID:36567851

Gartner Survey. (2020). *Gartner CFO Survey Reveals 74% Intend to Shift Some Employees to Remote Work Permanently*. Gartner. https://www.gartner.com/en/newsroom/press-releases/2020-04-03-gartner-cfo-surey-reveals-74-percent-of-organizations-to-shift-some-employees-to-remote-work-permanently2

Gibbs, M., Mengel, F., & Siemroth, C. (2021). Work from home & productivity: Evidence from personnel & analytics data on IT professionals. *University of Chicago, Becker Friedman Institute for Economics Working Paper*, (2021-56).

Gifford, J. (2022). Remote working: Unprecedented increase and a developing research agenda. *Human Resource Development International*, *25*(2), 1–9. doi:10.1080/13678868.2022.2049108

Gifford, J., & Green, M. (2020). *How Could COVID-19 Change the World of Work?* CIPD. www.cipd.co.uk/news-views/changing-work-views/future-work/thought-pieces/covid-19- change-work

Gilson, L., Travis, M., & Maynard, N. C. (2015). Virtual Teams Research: 10 Years, 10 Themes, and 10 Opportunities. *Journal of Management*, *41*(5), 1313–1337. doi:10.1177/0149206314559946

Glaeser, E., & Cutler, D. (2021, September 24). You may get more work done at home. But you'd have better ideas at the office. *The Washington Post*. https://www.washingtonpost.com/outlook/2021/09/24/working-home-productivity-pandemic-remote/

Gong, B., Tobias, P., & Young-Bristol, J. (2023). Leveraging resources to improve supervisors' vision in the remote workplace. *Management Research Review*, *46*(6), 777–789. doi:10.1108/MRR-12-2021-0916

Grant, C. A., Wallace, L. M., & Spurgeon, P. C. (2013). An exploration of the psychological factors affecting remote e-worker's job effectiveness, well-being and work-life balance. *Employee Relations*, *35*(5), 527–546. doi:10.1108/ER-08-2012-0059

Guggenberger, T., Lockl, J., Röglinger, M., Schlatt, V., Sedlmeir, J., Stoetzer, J. C., Urbach, N., & Völter, F. (2021). Emerging digital technologies to combat future crises: Learnings from COVID-19 to be prepared for the future. *International Journal on Management of Innovation & Technology*, *18*(04), 2140002. doi:10.1142/S0219877021400022

GWood. J. (2022, January 27). *These 3 charts show the global growth in online learning*. We Forum. https://www.weforum.org/agenda/2022/01/online-learning-courses-reskill-skills-gap/

Hamingson, N. (2023). Communication Technology and Inclusion Will Shape the Future of Remote Work. *Business News Daily*. https://www.businessnewsdaily.com/8156-future-of-remote-work.html

Hatfield, S. (2021, September 8). *Rethinking the ways we look at productivity in a Work from Anywhere world*. Deloitte United States. https://www2.deloitte.com/us/en/blog/human-capital-blog/2021/remote-work-productivity.html

Heick, T. (2021). 9 Principles Of Student Engagement In A Virtual Classroom. *TeachThought*. https://www.teachthought.com/technology/student-engagement-virtual/

Heydari, M., Xiaohu, Z., Saeidi, M., Lai, K. K., Shang, Y., & Yuxi, Z. (2020). Analysis of the role of social support-cognitive psychology and emotional process approach. *European Journal of Translational Myology*, *30*(3). doi:10.4081/ejtm.2020.8975 PMID:33117505

Horwitz, F. M., Bravington, D., & Silvis, U. (2006). The promise of virtual factors in effectiveness and failure. *Journal of European Industrial Training*, *30*(6), 472–494. doi:10.1108/03090590610688843

Howington, J. (2022, October 20). *Employee Engagement Report: Job Satisfaction and Work Flexibility | FlexJobs*. FlexJobs Employer Blog. https://www.flexjobs.com/employer-blog/employee-engagement-report-job-satisfaction-work-flexibility/

Ilag, B. N. (2021). Tools and technology for effective remote work. *International Journal of Computer Applications*, *174*(21), 13–16. doi:10.5120/ijca2021921109

ILO. (2020). *Teleworking during and after the COVID-19 Pandemic: A Practical Guide*. ILO. https://www.ilo.org/wcmsp5/groups/public/---ed_protect/---protrav/---travail/documents/instructionalmaterial/wcms_751232.pdf

Jalagat, R., & Jalagat, A. (2019). Rationalizing remote working concept and its implications on employee productivity. *Global journal of advanced research*, *6*(3), 95-100.

Jensen, N., Lyons, E., Chebelyon, E., Le Bras, R., & Gomes, C. (2020). Conspicuous monitoring and remote work. *Journal of Economic Behavior & Organization*, *176*, 489–511. doi:10.1016/j.jebo.2020.05.010

Karunarathne, P. (2021). A SWOT Analysis of Remote Working Based on Review of Literature. *International Journal of Business* [IJBTOB]. *Technology and Organizational Behavior*, *1*(4), 253–262. doi:10.52218/ijbtob.v1i4.102

KPMG. (2022, March 9). *Current trends in remote working*. KPMG. https://kpmg.com/xx/en/home/insights/2022/03/insights-on-current-trends-in-remote-working.html

Kraut, R. E. (1989). Telecommuting: The trade-offs of home work. *Journal of Communication*, *39*(3), 19–47. doi:10.1111/j.1460-2466.1989.tb01038.x

Lange, M., & Kayser, I. (2022). The role of self-efficacy, work-related autonomy and work-family conflict on employee's stress level during home-based remote work in Germany. *International Journal of Environmental Research and Public Health*, *19*(9), 4955. doi:10.3390/ijerph19094955 PMID:35564349

Lee, J. (2020). Mental health effects of school closures during COVID-19. *The Lancet. Child & Adolescent Health*, *4*(6), 421. doi:10.1016/S2352-4642(20)30109-7 PMID:32302537

Li, J. C. (2020). Roles of individual perception in technology adoption at organization level: Behavioral model versus toe framework. *Journal of System and Management Sciences*, *10*(3), 97–118.

Littenberg-Tobias, J., & Reich, J. (2020). Evaluating access, quality, and equity in online learning: A case study of a MOOC-based blended professional degree program. *The Internet and Higher Education*, *47*, 100759. doi:10.1016/j.iheduc.2020.100759

Lockee, B. B. (2021). Online education in the post-COVID era. *Nature Electronics*, *4*(1), 5–6. doi:10.103841928-020-00534-0

Lucas, M., Nelson, J., & Sims, D. (2020). *Schools' Responses to COVID-19: Pupil Engagement in Remote Learning*. National Foundation for Educational Research.

Lyubetsky, N., Bendersky, N., Verina, T., Demyanova, L., & Arkhipova, D. (2021). IMPACT of distance learning on student mental health in the COVID-19 pandemic. In *E3S Web of Conferences* (Vol. 273, p. 10036). EDP Sciences. doi:10.1051/e3sconf/202127310036

MacRae, I., & Sawatzky, R. (2020). *Remote Working: Personality and Performance Research Results*. Thomas International.

Marmolejo, F. J., & Groccia, J. E. (2022). Reimagining and redesigning teaching and learning in the post-pandemic world. *New Directions for Teaching and Learning*, *2022*(169), 21–37. doi:10.1002/tl.20480

Maznevski, M. L., & Chudoba, K. M. (2000). Bridging Space over Time: Global Virtual Team Dynamics and Effectiveness. *Organization Science*, *11*(5), 473–492. doi:10.1287/orsc.11.5.473.15200

Mckinsey Global Institute. (2021, February 18). *The future of work after COVID-19*. McKinsey & Company. https://www.mckinsey.com/featured-insights/future-of-work/the-future-of-work-after-covid-19

MehdiT.MorissetteR. (2021). Working from home in Canada: What have we learned so far? In *Statistics Canada*. doi:10.25318/36280001202101000001-eng

Min, S. A., & Kim, B. Y. (2020). Platform leadership and strategy of small and medium enterprises on digital transformation. [IJM]. *International Journal of Management*, *11*(12). doi:10.34218/IJM.11.12.2020.205

MorissetteR.DengZ.MessacarD. (2021). Working from home: Potential implications for public transit and greenhouse gas emissions. In *Statistics Canada*. doi:10.25318/36280001202100400005-eng

Mostafa, B. A. (2021). The Effect of Remote Working on Employees Well-being and Work-Life Integration during Pandemic in Egypt. *International Business Research*, *14*(3), 41. doi:10.5539/ibr.v14n3p41

Nandlall, N., Hawke, L. D., Hayes, E., Darnay, K., Daley, M., Relihan, J., & Henderson, J. (2022). Learning Through a Pandemic: Youth Experiences With Remote Learning During the COVID-19 Pandemic. *SAGE Open*, *12*(3). doi:10.1177/21582440221124122 PMID:36185703

Ng, T. W. H., & Feldman, D. C. (2008). Long Work Hours: A Social Identity Perspective on Meta-Analysis Data. *Journal of Organizational Behavior*, *29*(7), 853–880. doi:10.1002/job.536

Nguyen, T. H., Netto, C. L. M., Wilkins, J. F., Bröker, P., Vargas, E. E., Sealfon, C., Puthipiroj, P., Li, K. S., Bowler, J. E., Hinson, H. R., Pujar, M., & Stein, G. M. (2021). Insights Into Students' Experiences and Perceptions of Remote Learning Methods: From the COVID-19 Pandemic to Best Practice for the Future. *Frontiers in Education*, *6*, 647986. doi:10.3389/feduc.2021.647986

Nickson, D., & Siddons, S. (2004). *Remote Working: Linking People and Organizations*. Routledge London.

OPOCE. (2003, November 18). *EUR-LEX - 32003L0088 - EN*. OPOCE. https://eur-lex.europa.eu/legal-content/EN/TXT/HTML/?uri=CELEX:32003L0088

OzimekA. (2020). The future of remote work. SSRN 3638597.

Papagiannidis, S., & Marikyan, D. (2020). Smart offices: A productivity and well-being perspective. *International Journal of Information Management*, *51*, 102027. doi:10.1016/j.ijinfomgt.2019.10.012

Pasquel Cajas, A. F., Cajas Bravo, V. T., & Dávila Morán, R. C. (2023). Remote Work in Peru during the COVID-19 Pandemic. *Administrative Sciences*, *13*(2), 1–25. doi:10.3390/admsci13020058

Pecujlija, M., & Cosic, D. (2019). Crisis Management: Introducing Companies Organizational Reactivity and Flexibility. New York: Nova (Business Issues, Competition and Entrepreneurship)

Pereira, K. (2022, February 25). *The Future of Work in All Industries is a Hybrid Workforce*. AT&T Business. https://www.business.att.com/learn/research-reports/is-corporate-america-ready-for-the-future-of-work.html

Popovici, V., & Popovici, A. L. (2020). Remote work revolution: Current opportunities and challenges for organizations. *Ovidius Univ. Ann. Econ. Sci. Ser*, *20*, 468–472.

Putri, T., Syafitri, U. D., & Sukmawati, A. (2023). The Role of Human Resource Risk on Employee Performance in The Hybrid Workforce Era. *Jurnal Aplikasi Bisnis dan Manajemen (JABM)*, *9*(2), 386-386.

PwC. (2021, June). *The future of work A journey to 2022*. PwC. https://www.pwc.com/ee/et/publications/pub/future-of-work-report.pdf

Rae, M. (2022). "The right to disconnect": Portugal's new labor legislation for remote workers. In *Sage Business Cases*. SAGE Publications, Ltd. doi:10.4135/9781529600391

Raghuram, S., Tuertscher, P., & Garud, R. (2010). Mapping the Field of Virtual Work: A Cocitation Analysis. *Information Systems Research*, *21*(4), 983–999. doi:10.1287/isre.1080.0227

Ramirez, A. (2022, February 15). Are Virtual Reality And The Metaverse Ready To Support Collaborative Work? *Forbes*. https://www.forbes.com/sites/forbestechcouncil/2022/02/15/are-virtual-reality-and-the-metaverse-ready-to-support-collaborative-work/?sh=2cc9f644716c

Report: 80% Say Salary Isn't Keeping Up With Inflation. (2022, November 22). Remote.co. https://remote.co/report-80-say-salary-isnt-keeping-up-with-inflation/

Reuters. (2021, July 19). *Israeli firm's spyware used to target journalists' cell phones - reports*. Reuters. https://www.reuters.com/technology/israeli-firms-spyware-used-target-journalists-cell-phones-reports-2021-07-19/

Robinson, B. (2022, May 5). Remote Work Increases Employee Happiness By 20%, New Study Finds. *Forbes*. https://www.forbes.com/sites/bryanrobinson/2022/05/05/remote-work-increases-employee-happiness-by-20-new-study-finds/?sh=4f5fe21f3183

Roy, A. K., Breaux, R., Sciberras, E., Patel, P., Ferrara, E., Shroff, D. M., Cash, A. R., Dvorsky, M. R., Langberg, J. M., Quach, J., Melvin, G., Jackson, A., & Becker, S. P. (2022). A preliminary examination of key strategies, challenges, and benefits of remote learning expressed by parents during the COVID-19 pandemic. *School Psychology*, *37*(2), 147–159. doi:10.1037pq0000465 PMID:35266770

Sandoval-Reyes, J., Carlier, S. I., & Oliva, E. J. D. (2021). Remote Work, Work Stress, and Work–Life during Pandemic Times: A Latin America Situation. *International Journal of Environmental Research and Public Health*, *18*(13), 7069. doi:10.3390/ijerph18137069 PMID:34281007

Schmidt, A., Kramer, A. C., Brose, A., Schmiedek, F., & Neubauer, A. B. (2021). Distance learning, parent–child interactions, and affective well-being of parents and children during the COVID-19 pandemic: A daily diary study. *Developmental Psychology*, *57*(10), 1719–1734. doi:10.1037/dev0001232 PMID:34807692

Sharma, M., Singla, M. K., Nijhawan, P., Ganguli, S., & Rajest, S. S. (2020). An application of IOT to develop concept of smart remote monitoring system. *Business Intelligence for Enterprise Internet of Things*, (pp. 233-239).

Škiljić, A. (2020). Cybersecurity and remote working: Croatia's (non-) response to increased cyber threats. *International Cybersecurity Law Review*, *1*(1-2), 51–61. doi:10.136543439-020-00014-3

Slack. (2022, July 29). *The future of remote working: What you need to know*. Slack. https://slack.com/blog/collaboration/future-remote-working-what-to-know

Smith, K. (2013). Here's The Confidential Memo Yahoo Sent Employees About Working From Home. *Business Insider*. https://www.businessinsider.com/yahoo-workingfrom-home-memo-2013-2?r=US&IR=T

Smith, M. (2022, April 13). Twitter, Reddit and 8 other companies offering permanent remote or hybrid work—and hiring right now. *CNBC*. https://www.cnbc.com/2022/04/13/10-companies-that-switched-to-permanent-hybrid-or-remote-work-and-hiring-right-now.html

Stein, M. K., Jensen, T. B., & Hekkala, R. (2015). Comfortably 'Betwixt and Between'?: Delimiting and Blending Space, Time, Tasks and Technology at Work. *Proceedings of the Thirty Sixth International Conference on Information Systems*. IEEE.

Sullivan, C. (2003). What's in a Name? Definitions and Conceptualisations of Teleworking and Homeworking. *New Technology, Work and Employment*, *18*(3), 158–165. doi:10.1111/1468-005X.00118

Sundaram, A. (2020). *Yelp data shows 60% of business closures due to the coronavirus pandemic are now permanent.* CNBC. https://www.cnbc.com/2020/09/16/yelp-data-shows-60percent-of-business-closures-due-to-the-coronavirus-pandemic-are-now-permanent.html

Susilo, D. (2020). Revealing the effect of work-from-home on job performance during the COVID-19 crisis: Empirical evidence from Indonesia. *Journal of Contemporary Issues in Business and Government*, *26*(1), 23–40.

Talent'd by WorldRef. (2023, January 6). *The relationship between globalisation and the rise of remote work*. Linkedin. https://www.linkedin.com/pulse/relationship-between-globalisation-rise-remote-work-

Tenable. (2021, September 22). *Seventy-Four percent of organizations attribute damaging cyberattacks to vulnerabilities in technology put in place during the pandemic, according to global industry study*. Tenable®. https://www.tenable.com/press-releases/seventy-four-percent-of-organizations-attribute-damaging-cyberattacks-to

The European Parliament and The Council of The European Union. (2019, July 11). *DIRECTIVE (EU) 2019/1152 OF THE EUROPEAN PARLIAMENT AND OF THE COUNCIL of 20 June 2019 on transparent and predictable working conditions in the European Union*. Official Journal of the European Union. https://eur-lex.europa.eu/legal-content/EN/TXT/HTML/?uri=CELEX:32019L1152

Turan, Z., Kucuk, S., & Cilligol Karabey, S. (2022). The university students' self-regulated effort, flexibility and satisfaction in distance education. *International Journal of Educational Technology in Higher Education, 19*(1), 35. doi:10.118641239-022-00342-w PMID:35891707

U.S. DEPARTMENT OF LABOR. (2021, January 20). *U.S. Department Of Labor Issues Guidance to Clarify Employers' Obligations To Track Teleworkers' Compensable Hours*. DOL. https://www.dol.gov/newsroom/releases/whd/whd20200824

Useem, J. (2017). When Working From Home Doesn't Work: IBM pioneered telecommuting. Now it wants people back in the office. *The Atlantic*. https://www.theatlantic.com/magazine/archive/2017/11/when-working-from-home-doesnt-work/540660/

Venkatesh, A., & Vitalari, N. P. (1992). An emerging distributed work arrangement: An investigation of computer-based supplemental work at home. *Management Science, 38*(12), 1687–1706. doi:10.1287/mnsc.38.12.1687

Venton, B. J., & Pompano, R. R. (2021). Strategies for enhancing remote student engagement through active learning. *Analytical and Bioanalytical Chemistry, 413*(6), 1507–1512. doi:10.100700216-021-03159-0 PMID:33458779

Verma, S., Sharma, R., Deb, S., & Maitra, D. (2021). Artificial intelligence in marketing: Systematic review and future research direction. *International Journal of Information Management Data Insights, 1*(1), 100002. doi:10.1016/j.jjimei.2020.100002

Virtanen, M., Ferrie, J. E., Singh-Manoux, A., Shipley, M. J., Stansfeld, S. A., Marmot, M. G., Ahola, K., Vahtera, J., & Kivimäki, M. (2011). Long Working Hours and Symptoms of Anxiety and Depression: A 5-year Follow-up of the Whitehall II Study. *Psychological Medicine, 41*(12), 2485–2494. doi:10.1017/S0033291711000171 PMID:21329557

Wang, B., Liu, Y., Qian, J., & Parker, S. K. (2021). Achieving Effective Remote Working During the COVID-19 Pandemic: A Work Design Perspective. *Applied Psychology, 70*(1), 16–59. doi:10.1111/apps.12290 PMID:33230359

Wang, Y., Ariyo, T., Liu, H., & Ma, C. (2022). Does psychosocial support buffer the effect of COVID-19 related stressors on mental health among Chinese during quarantine? *Current Psychology (New Brunswick, N.J.), 41*(10), 7459–7469. doi:10.100712144-021-01663-1 PMID:34075286

Weise, K. (2021). Amazon's profit soars 220 percent as pandemic drives shopping online. *The New York Times*. https://www.nytimes.com/2021/04/29/technology/amazons-profits-triple.html#:~:text=With%20the%20pandemic%20shifting%20sales,the%20same%20period%20last%20year

Wheatley, D., & Gifford, J. (2019). *UK Working Lives: Survey Report 2019*. CIPD Development. http://cipd.co.uk/workinglives

World Economic Forum. (2023, May 1). *The Future of Jobs Report 2020*. WEF. https://www.weforum.org/reports/the-future-of-jobs-report-2020

World Health Organization. (2022). *Mental health at work*. WHO. www.who.int. https://www.who.int/news-room/fact-sheets/detail/mental-health-at-work

Yang, L., Holtz, D., Jaffe, S., Suri, S., Sinha, S., Weston, J., Joyce, C., Shah, N., Sherman, K., Hecht, B., & Teevan, J. (2022). The effects of remote work on collaboration among information workers. *Nature Human Behaviour*, *6*(1), 43–54. doi:10.103841562-021-01196-4 PMID:34504299

Yang, L., Jaffe, S., Holtz, D., Suri, S., Sinha, S., Weston, J., Teevan, J. (2020). How work from home affects collaboration: A large-scale study of information workers in a natural experiment during COVID-19. *arXiv preprint arXiv:2007.15584.*

Zhang, N., Yang, S., & Jia, P. (2022). Cultivating resilience during the COVID-19 pandemic: A socioecological perspective. *Annual Review of Psychology*, *73*(1), 575–598. doi:10.1146/annurev-psych-030221-031857 PMID:34579547

Chapter 13
From Crisis to Opportunity:
How VGI Is Transforming Disaster Response and Recovery Efforts

Munir Ahmad
https://orcid.org/0000-0003-4836-6151
Survey of Pakistan, Pakistan

ABSTRACT

Volunteered geographic information is a crucial tool in disaster response and recovery, transforming data collection and sharing. It has significantly improved disaster management by providing insights into urgent needs, damage estimation, and resource allocation. The distribution of VGI during relief efforts has greatly benefited from social media platforms, supplemented by hashtags and machine learning techniques. Mobile and web-based technologies and community involvement have improved coordination and decision-making. VGI is crucial for monitoring development, evaluating infrastructure, and assisting risk assessment during the recovery phase. It's important to pay attention to issues like data quality, privacy, inclusivity, complexity, obsolescence, appropriateness, accessibility, and technological infrastructure. Future studies should concentrate on automated systems for data validation, resolving privacy and security issues, and encouraging marginalized people to participate.

INTRODUCTION

VGI refers to user-generated digital geographic information, which includes both text and multimedia (See et al., 2016). The production, collection, and dissemination of geographic information are all made possible by the use of the internet and communication technologies. VGI is an essential tool to better comprehend and explore the social, economic, and environmental circumstances of a particular region. There are many sources of VGI, including unstructured social network data platforms with explicit or implicit location information like Twitter, Facebook, and Instagram as well as structured geographical data platforms like OpenStreetMap (OSM). These systems work together to create a vast and varied VGI pool that can be used for many different geographical analyses and applications. VGI is essential in

DOI: 10.4018/978-1-6684-9522-3.ch013

enhancing official data sources since it offers useful data on the state of the impacted populations, the state of the infrastructure, and the state of the roads (Goodchild, 2007; Soden & Palen, 2014).

Over the past few years, there has been a noticeable rise in global crises resulting from climate extremes, natural and human-induced hazards, the ongoing coronavirus pandemic, and various other factors. Communities, infrastructure, agriculture, and the country's economy all suffer greatly from natural disasters. Information gathering about the effects and dangers of natural disasters is essential for reducing and managing vulnerability to catastrophes. This information is mounted on the maps and areas that will encounter natural disasters and those that will be impacted by disasters. Consequently, the significance of maps and spatial data has been widely acknowledged in all four stages of disaster management, namely mitigation, preparedness, response, and recovery (Potts et al., 2013).

During disasters, Governmental organizations have limited resources to quickly gather information and disseminate it to deal with crises. In this situation, volunteering is advantageous for disaster management since volunteers are more likely to take part in different stages of disaster management. People have started using numerous online channels to communicate their ideas, experiences, photographs, and video evidence in recent years due to the popularity and wide adoption of social media platforms (Kankanamge et al., 2020). This has changed the way that geo-data is produced, necessitating the need for researchers to examine and analyze the effects of these data and data practices.

In a study conducted by Kankanamge et al., (2020), real-time Twitter data from the 2010-2011 South East Queensland Floods was employed. The analysis revealed several important findings: first, the use of Twitter emerged as a promising method for gathering citizen knowledge; second, tweets proved helpful in identifying temporal variations in the severity of the disaster; and finally, the spatial analysis of tweets confirmed the efficacy of geographically tagged messages in identifying areas heavily affected by the disaster. Thus, combined results highlighted VGI's potential and usefulness as a source of information for monitoring and evaluating disasters. Another study by Nath et al., (2018) demonstrated the utilization of geotagged social media content from Twitter to support disaster management processes. This study showcased the development of a streamlined map that establishes a connection between volunteers, who are prepared to assist flood victims, and individuals who have expressed their needs for help through social media.

The distinctive characteristics of VGI have shown their value in enhancing processes associated with disasters (Yates & Paquette, 2011). VGI is a vital tool in disaster response and recovery which enables people to provide crucial geospatial data during and after catastrophic events (Vavassori et al., 2022). In terms of disaster awareness, information identification, and information categorization, VGI has become an essential element that traditional approaches cannot match, finally resulting in successful disaster determination.

Additionally, VGI plays an important part in community engagement and resilience building during disaster recovery (B. T. Haworth et al., 2018). People submit data on service availability, housing conditions, and infrastructure repair progress using crowdsourcing platforms and mapping programmes, enabling community involvement in recovery initiatives. By mapping affected areas and superimposing demographic data on top of them, VGI also assists in identifying vulnerable people and prioritizing recovery efforts (CDC, 2015; Dixon et al., 2021).

Although adopting VGI for disaster response and recovery has many benefits, there are still issues that must be resolved. In order to avoid the spread of misleading information and inefficient resource allocation, it is crucial to ensure the authenticity and quality of VGI data (Goodchild & Li, 2012). Major challenges include quality assurance, data validation, and information integration (Azariasgari & Hosseinali, 2023; Xin, 2022). Additionally, when using VGI for disaster management, ethical issues like permission and privacy must be carefully considered (Antoniou, 2017; Blatt, 2015). This calls for the creation and implementation of reliable data collection and distribution practices that protect individual privacy while maximizing the advantages of VGI.

To this effect, the objective of this chapter is to investigate the role of VGI in disaster response and recovery processes. To achieve the objective, the rest of the chapter is organized as follows. Possible roles of VGI in disaster response are endorsed in section 2 whereas VGI's role in disaster recovery is endorsed in section 3. Various challenges are covered in section 4. Section 5 elaborates on how crises can be an opportunity for innovations taking HOTOSM as an example. The chapter's main conclusions are summed up in the last part, along with suggestions for further study.

VGI AND DISASTER RESPONSE

Social media networks are crucial for spreading VGI during catastrophic incidents. The aggregation of pertinent information and its ease of incorporation into disaster management systems are made possible by the usage of hashtags like #Sandy and #NepalEarthquake (Meier, 2015). Analysis of VGI from social media platforms has been useful in determining urgent requirements, evaluating damage, and efficiently allocating resources.

In the context of specific disaster events, several studies have utilized VGI to enhance disaster response and management. Devastating typhoon disasters routinely strike China's southeast coast, causing serious human and financial losses. The government faces a hurdle in compiling accurate statistics about these catastrophes. Yu et al., (2019) employed machine learning techniques such as computational neural network (CNN), to extract typhoon disaster information from social media platforms like Twitter and Weibo. X. Liu et al., (2020) collected and consolidated Weibo platform data and remote sensing images to analyze the service area and identify the most effective accessible path for facility points in responding to earthquake disasters. Similarly, the study (Arapostathis & Karantzia, 2019) showed how well VGI, especially from Twitter, could be integrated to map fire events in Greece. Through the composed efforts of responsible services and the assistance of citizens, a wildfire broke out in the wildland areas of Split, Croatia was countered. The citizens actively participated in firefighting efforts and played a crucial role in promptly sharing valuable disaster-related information through various platforms, including social media (Tavra et al., 2019).

Social media platforms, including Facebook and Twitter, have shown their significant capacity to facilitate communication and coordination among affected people and communities during various types of disasters, be it natural like a hurricane, flood, or earthquake, or a human-induced event like a riot or terrorist attack (Dwarakanath et al., 2021). Dasgupta & Ghosh, (2018) proposed a paradigm for disaster management that makes use of VGI and emphasized the critical role that local volunteers play in providing decision-makers and on-site rescue teams with accurate and timely information during emergency scenarios. Lacasandile et al., (2022) demonstrated a mobile and web-based emergency response system called E-Saklolo, to respond to emergency circumstances (such as medical, fire, rescue, and police) within the community and to lower the number of casualties and fatalities brought on by disasters and emergencies. Chen et al., (2016), implemented a Web GIS application to harvest and utilize geotagged tweets and tested its effectiveness in emergency response with tweets from Hurricane Joaquin in 2015.

Similarly, a web-based GIS platform was developed by Fontes et al., (2017) to combine official data, physical sensor data, and VGI in order to improve disaster response processes in case of emergencies.

Information accessibility plays a key role in crisis response situations. Emergency responders and relief efforts can be efficiently guided by information about the geographic scope, intensity, and socio-economic effects of a disaster occurrence, especially when such data is swiftly shared soon after it is collected (Oddo & Bolten, 2019). Cerutti et al., (2021) concentrated on developing reproducible scientific workflows for disaster response using social media data. Using data from MODIS active fires, qualitative and quantitative evaluation is used to compare the workflows' performance. The results demonstrated how important scientific practices are for improving reproducibility in geospatial analytics. There are many different types of data (such as texts, photographs, audio, and videos) accessible on social media platforms, and together with the enormous volume of information, call for quick and automatic processing in the case of a crisis or emergency. Khatoon et al., (2022) emphasized the need for quick and automatic processing of the diverse types of data available on social media platforms during a crisis or emergency.

Timely and precise access to data regarding the severity and scope of damage resulting from disasters plays a pivotal role in facilitating efficient disaster management (Pi et al., 2020). In a study by Joury et al., (2023) crowdsourcing and community involvement were used to support search and rescue efforts after a devastating earthquake struck southern and central Turkey as well as northern and western Syria. The study focused on three phases of the procedure: emergency response, humanitarian aid response, and methodical response. VGI has significantly contributed to the study of disaster response by offering useful data both before and after a disaster. Its capacity to collect information directly from people who willingly give information about their surroundings has made VGI widely used in disaster management (Kusumo et al., 2017). (Ahmad, 2023a) explored the relationship between community development, citizen diplomacy, and disaster response in the context of VGI.

By employing high-quality VGI data and applying semi-automatic data processing techniques, the development of timely and accurate maps can be facilitated, thereby boosting the effectiveness of crisis management activities (Vavassori et al., 2022). L. Li & Ulaganathan, (2017) aimed to develop a crowd-sourcing mobile application specifically tailored for disaster response that complies with a number of requirements, including user-friendliness, user anonymity, real-time updating and viewing of geographic information, bidirectional communication between users and emergency responders, simplified interface design, and seamless download process. Feng & Sester, (2018) used deep learning techniques to gather high-quality eyewitnesses of rainfall and flooding incidents from social media platforms. The study attempted to extract reliable and informative data by scrutinizing user-generated texts and photographs taken during flooding occurrences in the cities of Paris, London, and Berlin. Similarly, by employing deep learning techniques to analyze helicopter landing spots, (Antoniou & Potsiou, 2020) used end-to-end methodology for the disaster response process. The work trained a deep-learning autoencoder using VGI and satellite imagery.

During catastrophic events, social media platforms are essential for disseminating VGI. Social media networks have provided VGI that has proven useful in identifying immediate needs, assessing damage, and effectively allocating resources. Studies have extracted information on typhoon disasters from social media platforms, mapped fire incidents, and created mobile and web-based emergency response systems using VGI to improve disaster response and management. During many types of disasters, social media platforms like Facebook and Twitter have demonstrated their tremendous capacity to facilitate communication and coordination among affected people and communities. Accessibility to information and the requirement for swift and efficient processing of various kinds of data from social media sites are emphasized.

Effective disaster management depends on timely and accurate access to information on the extent and degree of damage. The creation of timely and accurate maps can be accelerated, and crisis management efforts can be strengthened, by utilizing high-quality VGI data and utilizing semi-automatic data processing techniques. Deep learning algorithms are being used in conjunction with user-friendly crowdsourcing mobile applications to extract accurate and useful data from VGI sources. These developments help in the efficient application of VGI during disaster response operations.

VGI AND DISASTER RECOVERY

VGI continues to be essential to the healing process after the reaction phase. VGI fosters community involvement and resilience by facilitating community engagement in recovery activities (Zook et al., 2010). In tracking recovery progress, VGI has shown VGI has shown its potential in various studies. Yan et al., (2017) presented a VGI-based methodology using Flickr data. Similarly, Lowrie et al., (2022) evaluated the value of using VGI from the Waze platform to report flash floods and assist with the post-disaster recovery process with the case study of Hurricane Harvey. Similarly, in the context of post-disaster recovery evaluation, Kato, (2019) investigated the improvement of Land Cover and Land Use (LCLU) classification using remote sensing images (RS) and OpenStreetMap (OSM) data. The study by Poser & Dransch, (2010a) examined the suitability and appropriateness of utilizing observations from the affected population to quickly estimate flood damage.

Tourism is vulnerable to disaster events. Disasters in tourist areas have long-lasting, major economic effects in addition to physical and human implications. The damaging perception that follows such incidents makes it difficult for the crucial tourism industry to recover. For rebranding initiatives to be successful, it is essential to obtain the most recent data on infrastructure and tourist recovery (Eckle et al., 2017). To plan, monitor, and evaluate recovery in tourist locations, Yan et al., (2020) used public sentiment and perspectives from geotagged social media data to examine the post-disaster recovery process. Using geotagged Flickr images, the study Yan et al., (2017) established a scientific approach and methodologies to track and assess post-disaster tourism recovery. The methodology included crowdsourcing-based qualitative photo analysis, space-time bin-based quantitative photo analysis, and view shed-based data quality enrichment. Similarly, the study Fukui & Ohe, (2019) looked at the function of Twitter in the promotion of tourism, focusing in particular on the process of tourist recovery in a rural area hit by the earthquake and tsunami.

To assess post-disaster recovery, the study by Yingwei et al., (2020) presented a research framework that encompasses three integral components: data acquisition, data quality control, and data mining. This framework is utilized to assess three primary aspects of post-disaster recovery, namely infrastructure status, economic conditions, and safety measures. Social media also plays a significant role in understanding post-disaster dynamics. Oz et al., (2018) explored how people assign blame and accountability on social media in relation to the Flint water crisis, aiming to examine the influence of social media sites on public opinion and determination of responsibility.

Brenner Fernandes, (2019) evaluated the multi-hazard risk conditions in the post-disaster recovery phase of Dominica following the impact of Hurricane Maria using data derived from Unmanned Aerial Vehicles (UAVs) and VGI. In the study by Ghaffarian et al., (2019), training samples are generated automatically using pre-disaster OpenStreetMap building data. The deep learning model is then trained using these samples after co-registering the map with satellite images. This approach enables the automatic updating of building maps in both disaster damage and recovery situations, giving valuable information on the changing state of buildings. The study by Degrossi & Albuquerque, (2014) presented a crowdsourcing-based methodology to collect VGI in the context of flood risk management in Brazil. Similarly, the study Assumpção et al., (2019) presented a methodology to deploy a citizen observatory in the Danube Delta in Romania.

During the post-disaster recovery phase, VGI is essential to the restorative process and community involvement. Numerous studies have shown how useful VGI may be for monitoring recovery efforts and assessing infrastructure, economic situations, and safety precautions. VGI offers insightful information about post-disaster dynamics, public sentiment, and accountability. VGI has been used to update building maps, analyze multi-hazard risk situations, and gather data for citizen observatories and flood risk management. Disasters in tourist destinations have enormous economic repercussions, and successful rebranding projects depend on having access to the most recent information on infrastructure and tourism recovery. In general, VGI helps with effective post-disaster recovery efforts and comprehension of the effects of disasters when paired with social media and cutting-edge technologies.

DISASTER MANAGEMENT PLATFORMS

There are many platforms developed in the context of disaster management. Few were constrained to certain geographical areas such as PetaJakarta.org (Ogie et al., 2019) and some were adopted globally. In this section, globally adopted disaster management platforms such as Ushahidi and HOTOSM are described.

Ushahidi

Ushahidi (Figure 1) is an open-source platform that enables individuals and organizations to create dynamic and interactive maps. It provides a variety of mapping and visualization tools that can be used in conjunction with citizen reporting to produce crisis maps that offer real-time insights (Norheim-Hagtun & Meier, 2010). It is one of the many mapping tools available in the burgeoning subject of crisis mapping, which uses crowdsourcing to create online and interactive maps of areas affected by disasters (Pánek et al., 2017). Ushahidi was first used in the wake of the 2010 Haiti earthquake (Norheim-Hagtun & Meier, 2010) since then it has been used in many disaster events such as for floods in the Czech Republic in 2013 (Pánek et al., 2017).

HOTOSM

Using open mapping activities, the HOT (Humanitarian OpenStreetMap Team) is an international collaborative team dedicated to humanitarian action and community development. They are intended to produce map data that has a significant influence on risk reduction, disaster management, and the achievement of the Sustainable Development Goals (HOTOSM, 2023c). HOTOSM has 452,594 Com-

Figure 1. Ushahidi

munity Mappers (HOTOSM, 2023a). HOTOSM actively engaged in the recent earthquake in Syria and Turkey as well as food in Ecuador (HOTOSM, 2023a) as can be seen in Figure 2.

Figure 2. HOTOSM

CHALLENGES

While VGI has many advantages, there are certain issues that need to be considered as well. In this section, some major VGI-related challenges are described, as summarized and depicted in Figure 3.

Data Quality and Validation

The quality such as accuracy and completeness of VGI and crowdsourced data may vary, necessitating validation and verification procedures to determine its dependability. During disaster response and recovery activities, inaccurate information can make it difficult to allocate resources effectively and make decisions (Ray & Bala, 2020). Poor data quality can also result in the ineffective use of scarce resources and delays in delivering support to the impacted communities. For well-informed decision-making and prompt response actions, accurate and validated data is critical.

To stop the spread of false information and potential data misuse, quality control procedures and data validation methods are crucial. This includes methods of data cleaning, filtering, and cross-validation techniques. Establishing collaborations with academic institutions, organizations, and volunteers may help to ensure data accuracy and reliability in disaster situations. ML techniques can be employed to differentiate between false and actual information as well as to automate the detection and removal of inaccurate information (Ray & Bala, 2020).

Data Security and Privacy

VGI expresses concerns regarding security and privacy. As more members of the community submit data, it becomes increasingly important to safeguard their privacy and obtain their consent (Yingwei et al., 2020). Inadequate data security and privacy controls can result in the disclosure of personal data, weakening confidence and discouraging citizen involvement. If privacy is compromised, VGI's tendency towards opportunism, data-centricity, disruption, and exclusivity will be diminished (B. T. Haworth et al., 2018).

Privacy challenges may reduce people's willingness to provide critical information, impeding the efficiency of disaster response and recovery activities. To maintain data security and privacy, stringent procedures and rules need to be established. To protect sensitive information, data encryption methods, and secure data storage procedures may be implemented (Muthi Reddy et al., 2018). Citizens involved in the VGI collection need to be informed about secure data handling procedures.

Participation and Inclusivity

It can be difficult to ensure that different community members are actively participating in VGI efforts. The inclusiveness of VGI efforts may be constrained by factors such as technological accessibility, literacy levels, linguistic hurdles, and power imbalances within communities (B. T. Haworth et al., 2018). Data that is incomplete or biased may be the consequence of limited involvement and the exclusion of some community members, which may ignore the needs and viewpoints of vulnerable populations (B. T. Haworth, 2018). The accuracy and relevance of VGI data are improved by inclusive involvement, resulting in more efficient decision-making and focused intervention activities.

To close these gaps and guarantee that marginalized perspectives are heard and represented in community-led processes, efforts should be undertaken (Bittner et al., 2016). Outreach campaigns may be organized to raise knowledge of and interest in VGI initiatives, particularly among marginalized communities (B. Haworth et al., 2016). People who might not be technologically savvy or digitally literate should receive training and assistance.

Technological Infrastructure

The full potential of VGI may be hampered by limited access to technology and reliance on social media platforms (L. Li & Ulaganathan, 2017). Some communities can have trouble getting access to and making use of the platforms and tools required for data submission and analysis (Crawford & Finn, 2015). The gathering and use of VGI may be constrained by insufficient technological infrastructure, which would hinder real-time monitoring, data exchange, and decision-making. Critical information collecting may be delayed as a result, and effective reaction team coordination may be hampered.

Overcoming these obstacles can be facilitated by the availability of the necessary infrastructure and making sure everyone has equal access to technology and the Internet, especially in underprivileged areas. Creating user-friendly, multilingual software and platforms that function with a variety of hardware and networks can help to reduce the effects of challenges of limited technological infrastructure.

Specialized Skillset

The absence of digital literacy and the need for certain skill sets from participants make it difficult to use VGI to its full potential in disaster response and recovery activities (L. Li & Ulaganathan, 2017). Individuals may find it difficult to participate successfully in data collection, analysis, and interpretation if they lack the requisite abilities and knowledge (Sboui & Aissi, 2022). The accuracy and usability of the information generated may be hampered by this constraint. The thoroughness and dependability of VGI can be constrained by the absence of specialized knowledge and digital literacy, which can result in the collection of erroneous or incomplete data. Additionally, it might make it more challenging to analyze and interpret data, which would make it harder to gain valuable insights and come to wise conclusions during the response and recovery phases of a disaster.

It is crucial to offer in-depth training and technical help to people and communities engaged in VGI activities in order to solve this dilemma (B. Haworth et al., 2016). Data gathering methods, data analysis methodologies, and digital literacy abilities can all be improved through capacity-building programmes. Additionally, it is important to provide user-friendly tools and platforms while taking into account the varied backgrounds and abilities of potential VGI contributors.

User-Friendliness and Accessibility

The limited usability and accessibility of VGI platforms may prevent their democratization potential from being fully realized (L. Li & Ulaganathan, 2017). It may deter people, especially those with little technological skill, from actively participating in data collecting and sharing procedures if VGI tools and platforms are difficult to use or not intuitive (Radianti & Gjøsæter, 2019). The inclusion and diversity of VGI data may be constrained by a lack of user-friendliness and accessibility, leading to inaccurate or missing information. Additionally, it can prevent the democratization of information and decision-making processes and result in a lack of representation for marginalized people.

VGI platforms should put a strong emphasis on user-friendliness to address these issues, making sure that they are simple to use, intuitive, and need little technical knowledge. Broader participation can be promoted by streamlining data-gathering interfaces and giving clear instructions. Inclusivity can be enhanced by localizing platforms and solutions to support various linguistic and cultural contexts.

Appropriateness

VGI data, which is frequently gathered for a variety of purposes, show varied degrees of precision and detail. While some VGI data could be appropriate for a particular application, it might not be as appropriate for another. This may result in end users using VGI data without thoroughly evaluating whether it is acceptable for their particular needs (Sboui & Aissi, 2022). When making decisions for disaster response and recovery, end users may make mistakes if they rely on VGI data without realizing its appropriateness. The effectiveness of disaster response and recovery procedures can be hampered by the use of improper VGI data.

Establishing reliable methods for assessing and validating the reliability, correctness, and suitability of VGI data for particular applications in disaster response and recovery may help to encounter this challenge. Similarly, increasing awareness among end users about the importance of considering the appropriateness of VGI for their unique requirements. Determining the spatial-semantic similarity between user requirements and available VGI as well as determining whether the VGI is appropriate for a certain use (Sboui & Aissi, 2022) case may also help to mitigate this challenge.

Obsolescence

Another drawback is the possible obsolescence of VGI sources brought on by the quick development of cyberspace, which forces researchers to constantly update their methodologies and adapt them to new and different VGI sources (Yingwei et al., 2020). Inaccurate or inappropriate information may be provided through outdated or outmoded VGI sources, undermining the efficiency of recovery and response to disasters (Ghafoori et al., 2022). It may lead to incorrect resource allocation and a misreading of the situation. Researchers may need to constantly update approaches and adjust to new and different data sources due to the potential obsolescence of VGI sources due to the rapid evolution of cyberspace.

Updated frameworks and procedures to account for new data sources and cutting-edge technologies such as the Ubiquitous-GIS-based approach (Ghafoori et al., 2022) are required. Moreover, to stay current on the newest advancements and implement them into VGI practices, relationships with research institutes, organizations, and technological professionals be encouraged.

Availability of Partial Dataset

Some VGI platforms limit application programming interfaces (APIs) and restrict access to comprehensive datasets (Yingwei et al., 2020) for analysis and decision-making. for analysis and decision-making. Limited access to complete datasets may make it difficult to fully comprehend the crisis scenario, which would reduce the efficacy of response and recovery activities. It might lead to inaccurate judgments and inadequate resource allocation.

To mitigate this challenge, it is required to encourage platforms to offer thorough datasets to enable disaster response and recovery and advocate for open data rules. Creating partnerships and cooperation for data sharing among organizations and stakeholders to guarantee the availability of comprehensive and pertinent datasets will also help.

Data Complexity

With the use of social sensing, anyone can add their data to a wide sensor network, resulting in a low-cost, extensive system that transmits situational awareness data continuously. However, the information obtained by social sensing exhibits certain characteristics that pose challenges. This data is often voluminous, diversified in nature, prone to noise, and might not be entirely reliable in some respects. Additionally, it generally lacks geospatial reference data and is frequently acquired as continuous streams (Z. Li et al., 2019).

Complex and varied VGI data can be difficult to manage and process, which could cause delays and ineffectiveness in decision-making and response activities. The analysis's accuracy and dependability may be impacted by noise and a lack of geographical reference data. To handle the complexity and noise of VGI data, cutting-edge data processing methods and algorithms such as machine learning methods may be employed (Barz et al., 2021). Adding geospatial reference data to the study to improve its accuracy and dependability, such as satellite images or ground truthing will also help.

Figure 3. Challenges of VGI

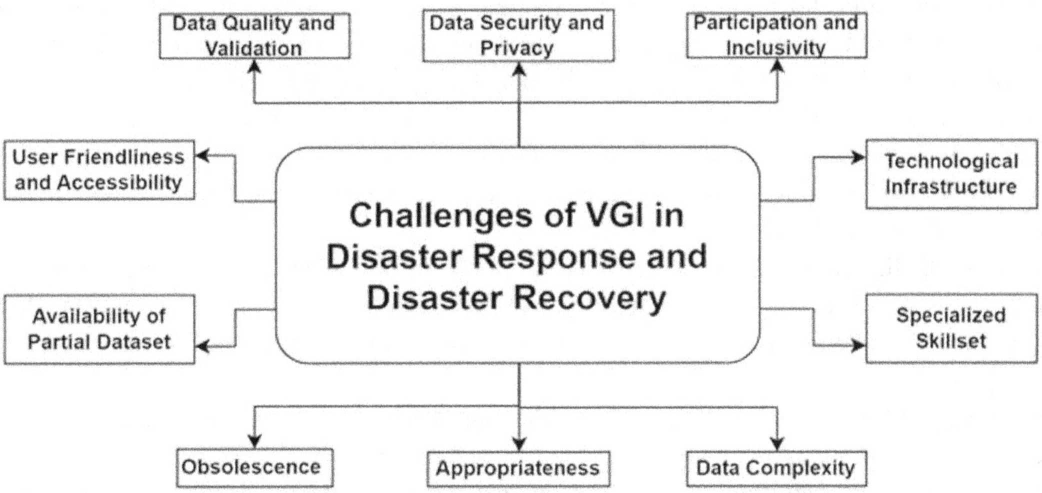

CRISIS AS A CATALYST FOR INNOVATION AND IMPROVEMENT

OpenStreetMap (OSM) has achieved remarkable recognition as one of the most successful VGI endeavors. Functioning as a cooperative platform, it provides a global arena for volunteers from various corners of the world to actively participate in the enrichment of geographic data. It serves as an eminent exemplar of VGI's practical implementation, wherein individuals can generously share their local insights to curate a comprehensive, openly accessible map of the entire world. On this platform, users can supplement and modify map elements, including but not limited to roads, buildings, and noteworthy landmarks.

OSM can assume a central role in advancing sustainable development across diverse sectors, spanning the economy, environment, and society (Ahmad & Ali, 2023). OSM has the potential to enable users to map religious sites, offer information, enhance accessibility, and champion the cause of cultural preservation (Ahmad, 2023b). Even the green space data within OSM holds significant potential for promoting business growth. (Ahmad, 2023c).

The Humanitarian OpenStreetMap Team (HOT) was established following the 2010 Haiti earthquake, with a focus on crisis and disaster mapping using OpenStreetMap. HOTOSM is a prime example of how innovations can be leveraged to benefit from crises and disasters. They have developed the Tasking Manager, a critical tool for coordinating volunteers and organizing groups to map on OpenStreetMap, contributing to a complete and more accurate map of the world. HOT comprised 463,339 community mappers.

The Tasking Manager has listed 2,041 projects on its website (HOTOSM, 2023b). Many of these projects are no longer confined solely to disaster mapping. The Tasking Manager has also been utilized to map missing areas under the overarching initiative known as "MissingMaps". Below are some of the innovative processes that have been implemented through the Tasking Manager to enhance its functionality.

Crisis Response and Mapping: During crises and disasters, there is often an urgent need for up-to-date and accurate maps, as they are crucial for emergency response and recovery efforts. The Tasking Manager can allow volunteers to quickly and collaboratively map affected areas, providing critical information to aid in disaster response. It can thrive during crises as it can address an immediate and pressing need.

Rapid Task Allocation: The Tasking Manager's ability to divide large mapping projects into smaller tasks allows for the rapid allocation of work to volunteers. In times of crisis, this can be essential, as quick responses are required to assess damage, locate resources, and plan recovery efforts. Tasking Manager can streamline task allocation which is especially beneficial during these situations.

Quality Assurance and Data Consistency: Crises demand high-quality and consistent data. The Tasking Manager can help to ensure the quality of mapping by reviewing and validating contributions. During a crisis, the accuracy of mapping data is vital, and the Tasking Manager can enhance data quality which becomes even more valuable.

Community Collaboration: OpenStreetMap, the platform on which the Tasking Manager operates, is community-driven. During crises, communities often come together to address common challenges. Tasking Manager can facilitate community collaboration, where individuals can team up to work on critical mapping projects.

Open Source and Accessibility: The Tasking Manager's open-source nature, with its code accessible on GitHub, makes it a highly adaptable tool. Innovations like Tasking Manager's that are open-source are more likely to evolve and improve over time, as they can be freely accessed and modified by a wide range of contributors. This accessibility can be especially valuable during crises when the need for customization and adaptation is high.

Creative Commons Licensing: The Tasking Manager encourages sharing images and screenshots under a Creative Commons Attribution-Share-like 4.0 International License. This openness allows for broader use and dissemination of mapping data, supporting disaster response and recovery efforts.

CONCLUSION

VGI has become a crucial tool in the response to and recovery from natural disasters. It has revolutionized how data is gathered, examined, and shared before, during, and after disasters. VGI, which consists of user-generated digital geographic data from websites and apps like social media and mapping software, has been shown to improve disaster management initiatives. VGI's use in disaster response has provided insights into urgent requirements, damage estimation, and resource allocation. In addition, during the post-disaster period, VGI has played a crucial role in community participation, fostering resilience, and tracking recovery efforts.

Social media sites have been important distribution points for VGI during disaster relief efforts. To collect pertinent data from social media sites like Twitter, Weibo, and Facebook to identify urgent needs and gauge the disaster's severity, hashtags and machine learning techniques have been very helpful. The advent of mobile and web-based emergency response technologies, along with the involvement of neighborhood volunteers, have enhanced coordination and communication among impacted people and communities. Early access to VGI has aided decision-making, helped with relief efforts, and guided emergency personnel. Information analysis and accessibility during crises have been hastened by the availability of many kinds of data on social media platforms and effective processing tools.

VGI continues to be essential to the restorative process and community involvement during the recovery phase. Studies have shown how valuable VGI is for tracking the status of recovery, assessing infrastructure and economic circumstances, and encouraging tourist rebound. VGI has helped with multi-hazard risk assessment, assisted in the construction of accurate and timely maps, and supported citizen observatories and flood risk management. Insights into public opinion, post-disaster dynamics, and accountability have also been gained from it. VGI has aided in the comprehension of the post-disaster environment and well-informed decision-making for recovery operations by utilizing VGI, remote sensing imagery, and deep learning algorithms.

However, several challenges need to be addressed to fully harness the potential of VGI. It is crucial to ensure data quality and validation to stop the spread of false information and promote informed decision-making. To safeguard individual data and preserve confidence in VGI efforts, privacy, and security issues must be addressed. By removing technological obstacles and guaranteeing equal access to VGI platforms, efforts should be made to increase participation and inclusivity. To enable efficient involvement and data utilization, it is important to give priority to specialized skill sets and the user-friendliness of VGI tools and platforms. In order to reduce the chance of utilizing inaccurate or out-of-date information, consideration should also be made to the suitability of VGI data for certain applications. To solve issues linked to data availability, complexity, and obsolescence, open data policies, collaborative data-sharing efforts, and improvements in data processing techniques are required.

VGI has made a major improvement to the information gathering, processing, and decision-making processes involved in disaster response and recovery. The issues with data quality, privacy, inclusivity, technological infrastructure, specialized skill sets, user-friendliness, data appropriateness, obsolescence, availability, and data complexity must be resolved to fully realize the promise of VGI. By overcoming these obstacles, VGI can keep improving disaster management initiatives and help build communities that are more efficient and resilient.

Further research should focus on the development of automated tools for cross-validation, data cleansing, and filtering. As a result, VGI data will be more trustworthy and accurate, facilitating better resource allocation and decision-making during crisis management. Addressing privacy and security issues related to VGI is also a possible direction of future work. Another direction of future work is to ensure that marginalized communities and individuals have actively participated in improving the inclusion of VGI programs.

REFERENCES

Ahmad, M. (2023a). Connecting People and Places: How Citizen Diplomacy and VGI Are Strengthening Disaster Response and Community Development. In Global Perspectives on the Emerging Trends in Public Diplomacy (pp. 195–226). IGI Global.

Ahmad, M. (2023b). Exploring the Role of OpenStreetMap in Mapping Religious Tourism in Pakistan for Sustainable Development. In *Experiences, Advantages, and Economic Dimensions of Pilgrimage Routes*. IGI Global. doi:10.4018/978-1-6684-9923-8.ch002

Ahmad, M. (2023c). Unleashing Business Potential: Harnessing OpenStreetMap for Intelligent Growth and Sustainability. In *Data-Driven Intelligent Business Sustainability*. IGI Global.

Ahmad, M., & Ali, A. (2023). Mapping the Future of Sustainable Development Through Cloud-Based Solutions: A Case Study of OpenStreetMap. In Promoting Sustainable Management Through Technological Innovation (pp. 153–176). IGI Global. doi:10.4018/978-1-6684-9979-5.ch011

Antoniou, V. (2017). Considerations of Privacy, Ethics and Legal Issues in Volunteered Geographic Information. In Mapping and the Citizen Sensor. doi:10.5334/bbf.f

Antoniou, V., & Potsiou, C. (2020). A deep learning method to accelerate the disaster response process. *Remote Sensing (Basel)*, *12*(3), 544. doi:10.3390/rs12030544

Arapostathis, S. G., & Karantzia, M. (2019). Mapping information of fire events, from VGI source (Twitter), for effective disaster management (in Greece); the fire of north-east Attica, august 2017, (Greece) case study. In Advances in Science, Technology and Innovation. doi:10.1007/978-3-030-01440-7_60

Assumpção, T. H., Mathre, N., Bogatinoska, B., Jonoski, A., Popescu, I., Trifanov, C., & Cimpan, K. (2019). How to monitor the Danube Delta through citizens' campaigns: Sontea-Fortuna case study. In Geophysical Research Abstracts.

Azariasgari, E., & Hosseinali, F. (2023). Evaluating the VGI Users' Level of Expertise. *International Journal of Applied Geospatial Research*, *14*(1), 1–16. doi:10.4018/IJAGR.316770

Barz, B., Schröter, K., Kra, A. C., & Denzler, J. (2021). Finding Relevant Flood Images on Twitter Using Content-Based Filters. Lecture Notes in Computer Science (Including Subseries Lecture Notes in Artificial Intelligence and Lecture Notes in Bioinformatics). 12666 LNCS. doi:10.1007/978-3-030-68780-9_1

Bittner, C., Michel, B., & Turk, C. (2016). Turning the spotlight on the crowd: Examining the participatory ethics and practices of crisis mapping. *ACME, 15*(1).

Blatt, A. J. (2015). The benefits and risks of volunteered geographic information. *Journal of Map & Geography Libraries*, *11*(1), 99–104. doi:10.1080/15420353.2015.1009609

Brenner Fernandes, F. (2019). *Evaluating hurricane recovery in Dominica*. University of Twente.

CDC. (2015). Planning for an Emergency: Strategies for Identifying and Engaging At-Risk Groups. In Center for Disease Control and Prevention.

Cerutti, V., Bellman, C., Both, A., Duckham, M., Jenny, B., Lemmens, R. L. G., & Ostermann, F. O. (2021). Improving the reproducibility of geospatial scientific workflows: the use of geosocial media in facilitating disaster response. In Journal of Spatial Science, 66(3). doi:10.1080/14498596.2019.1654944

Chen, X., Elmes, G., Ye, X., & Chang, J. (2016). Implementing a Real-Time Twitter-Based System for Resource Dispatch in Disaster Management. *GeoJournal*, *81*(6), 863–873. doi:10.100710708-016-9745-8

Crawford, K., & Finn, M. (2015). The limits of crisis data: Analytical and ethical challenges of using social and mobile data to understand disasters. *GeoJournal*, *80*(4), 491–502. doi:10.100710708-014-9597-z

Dasgupta, A., & Ghosh, S. K. (2018). A volunteered geographic information (VGI) framework for disaster management based on mobile services and SDI. In Geospatial Infrastructure, Applications and Technologies: India Case Studies. IEEE. doi:10.1007/978-981-13-2330-0_10

Degrossi, L., & Albuquerque, J. De. (2014). Flood Citizen Observatory: a crowdsourcing-based approach for flood risk management in Brazil. *Agora.Icmc.Usp.Br*, 570–575.

Dixon, B., Johns, R. A., & Fernandez, A. (2021). The role of crowdsourced data, participatory decision-making and mapping of flood related events. *Applied Geography (Sevenoaks, England)*, *128*, 102393. doi:10.1016/j.apgeog.2021.102393

Dwarakanath, L., Kamsin, A., Rasheed, R. A., Anandhan, A., & Shuib, L. (2021). Automated Machine Learning Approaches for Emergency Response and Coordination via Social Media in the Aftermath of a Disaster: A Review. In IEEE Access, 9. doi:10.1109/ACCESS.2021.3074819

Eckle, M., Herfort, B., Yan, Y., Zipf, A., & Kuo, C. L. (2017). Towards using volunteered geographic information to monitor post-disaster recovery in tourist destinations. *Proceedings of the International ISCRAM Conference*. IEEE.

Feng, Y., & Sester, M. (2018). Extraction of pluvial flood relevant volunteered geographic information (VGI) by deep learning from user generated texts and photos. *ISPRS International Journal of Geo-Information*, *7*(2), 39. Advance online publication. doi:10.3390/ijgi7020039

Fontes, D., Fonte, C., & Cardoso, A. (2017). A web GIS-based platform to assist authorities in emergency response using VGI and sensor data. *Proceedings of 2017 4th Experiment at International Conference: Online Experimentation, Exp.at 2017*. IEEE. 10.1109/EXPAT.2017.7984352

Fukui, M., & Ohe, Y. (2019). Assessing the role of social media in tourism recovery in tsunami-hit coastal areas in Tohoku, Japan. *Tourism Economics*. doi:10.1177/1354816618825014

Ghaffarian, S., Kerle, N., Pasolli, E., & Arsanjani, J. J. (2019). Post-disaster building database updating using automated deep learning: An integration of pre-disaster OpenStreetMap and multi-temporal satellite data. *Remote Sensing (Basel)*, *11*(20), 2427. doi:10.3390/rs11202427

Ghafoori, H. R., Sadeghi-Niaraki, A., Alesheikh, A. A., & Choi, S. M. (2022). Ubiquitous GIS based outdoor evacuation assistance: An effective response to earthquake disasters. *International Journal of Disaster Risk Reduction*, *81*, 103232. doi:10.1016/j.ijdrr.2022.103232

Goodchild, M. F. (2007). Citizens as sensors: The world of volunteered geography. In GeoJournal. doi:10.100710708-007-9111-y

Goodchild, M. F., & Li, L. (2012). Assuring the quality of volunteered geographic information. *Spatial Statistics*, *1*, 110–120. doi:10.1016/j.spasta.2012.03.002

Haworth, B., Whittaker, J., & Bruce, E. (2016). Assessing the application and value of participatory mapping for community bushfire preparation. *Applied Geography (Sevenoaks, England)*, *76*, 115–127. Advance online publication. doi:10.1016/j.apgeog.2016.09.019

Haworth, B. T. (2018). Implications of Volunteered Geographic Information for Disaster Management and GIScience: A More Complex World of Volunteered Geography. *Annals of the American Association of Geographers*, *108*(1), 226–240. Advance online publication. doi:10.1080/24694452.2017.1321979

Haworth, B. T., Bruce, E., Whittaker, J., & Read, R. (2018). The good, the bad, and the uncertain: Contributions of volunteered geographic information to community disaster resilience. In Frontiers in Earth Science, 6. doi:10.3389/feart.2018.00183

Joury, E., Eriksson, A., & others. (2023). *Community Engagement and Crowdsourcing for Effective Disaster Response and Rescue Operations During the Earthquake in Syria.*

Kankanamge, N., Yigitcanlar, T., Goonetilleke, A., & Kamruzzaman, M. (2020). Determining disaster severity through social media analysis: Testing the methodology with South East Queensland Flood tweets. *International Journal of Disaster Risk Reduction*, *42*, 101360. doi:10.1016/j.ijdrr.2019.101360

Kato, L. V. (2019). *Integrating openstreetmap data in object based landcover and landuse classification for disaster recovery.* University of Twente.

Khatoon, S., Asif, A., Hasan, M. M., & Alshamari, M. (2022). Social Media-Based Intelligence for Disaster Response and Management in Smart Cities. In Springer Optimization and Its Applications (Vol. 186). Springer. doi:10.1007/978-3-030-84459-2_11

Kusumo, A. N. L., Reckien, D., & Verplanke, J. (2017). Utilising volunteered geographic information to assess resident's flood evacuation shelters. Case study: Jakarta. *Applied Geography (Sevenoaks, England)*, *88*, 174–185. doi:10.1016/j.apgeog.2017.07.002

Lacasandile, A. D., Gunay, K. R., & Bonifacio, C. S. D. (2022). E-Saklolo: A Mobile-based Crowdsourcing Platform for Disaster Risk Management and Emergency Response in the City of Santiago, Isabela Philippines. *Proceedings - 2022 International Conference on Computer Applications Technology, CCAT 2022*. 10.1109/CCAT56798.2022.00012

Li, L., & Ulaganathan, M. N. (2017). Design and development of a crowdsourcing mobile app for disaster response. *International Conference on Geoinformatics, 2017-August*. IEEE. 10.1109/GEOINFORMATICS.2017.8090943

Li, Z., Huang, Q., & Emrich, C. T. (2019). Introduction to social sensing and big data computing for disaster management. In International Journal of Digital Earth, 12(11). doi:10.1080/17538947.2019.1670951

Liu, X., Meng, X., Chen, X., Su, W., Zhang, X., Li, L., & Su, X. (2020). The Research on Assistance Information Acquisition for Earthquake Emergency Response by Aggregating VGI Data and GF-2 Images. *Remote Sensing Technology and Application*, *34*(6), 1286–1295.

Lowrie, C., Kruczkiewicz, A., McClain, S. N., Nielsen, M., & Mason, S. J. (2022). Evaluating the usefulness of VGI from Waze for the reporting of flash floods. *Scientific Reports*, *12*(1), 5268. doi:10.103841598-022-08751-7 PMID:35347160

Meier, P. (2015). Digital humanitarians: How big data is changing the face of humanitarian response. *Digital Humanitarians*. doi:10.1201/b18023

Muthi Reddy, P., Manjula, S. H., & Venugopal, K. R. (2018). Secured Privacy Data using Multi Key Encryption in Cloud Storage. *Proceedings of 5th International Conference on Emerging Applications of Information Technology, EAIT 2018*. IEEE. 10.1109/EAIT.2018.8470399

Nath, R. N., Priya, N., & Robin, C. R. R. (2018). A Social Media Content Based Location and Situation Analysis Model for Disaster Management. In Emergency and Disaster Management. doi:10.4018/978-1-5225-6195-8.ch014

Norheim-Hagtun, I., & Meier, P. (2010). Crowdsourcing for Crisis Mapping in Haiti. *Innovations: Technology, Governance, Globalization*, *5*(4), 81–89. doi:10.1162/INOV_a_00046

Oddo, P. C., & Bolten, J. D. (2019). The Value of Near Real-Time Earth Observations for Improved Flood Disaster Response. *Frontiers in Environmental Science*, *7*, 127. doi:10.3389/fenvs.2019.00127

Ogie, R. I., Clarke, R. J., Forehead, H., & Perez, P. (2019). Crowdsourced social media data for disaster management: Lessons from the PetaJakarta.org project. *Computers, Environment and Urban Systems*, *73*, 108–117. Advance online publication. doi:10.1016/j.compenvurbsys.2018.09.002

Oz, T., Havens, R., & Bisgin, H. (2018). Assessment of Blame and Responsibility through Social Media in Disaster Recovery in the Case of #FlintWaterCrisis. *Frontiers in Communication*, *3*, 45. doi:10.3389/fcomm.2018.00045

Pánek, J., Marek, L., Pászto, V., & Valůch, J. (2017). The Crisis Map of the Czech Republic: The nationwide deployment of an Ushahidi application for disasters. *Disasters*, *41*(4), 649–671. doi:10.1111/disa.12221 PMID:28059447

Pi, Y., Nath, N. D., & Behzadan, A. H. (2020). Convolutional neural networks for object detection in aerial imagery for disaster response and recovery. *Advanced Engineering Informatics*, *43*, 101009. doi:10.1016/j.aei.2019.101009

Poser, K., & Dransch, D. (2010). Volunteered Geographic Information for Disaster Management with Application to Rapid Flood Damage Estimation. *Geomatica*, *64*(1), 89–98.

Potts, K. E., Bennett, R. M., & Rajabifard, A. (2013). Spatially enabled bushfire recovery. *GeoJournal*, *78*(1), 151–163. doi:10.100710708-011-9437-3

Radianti, J., & Gjøsæter, T. (2019). Digital Volunteers in Disaster Response: Accessibility Challenges. Lecture Notes in Computer Science (Including Subseries Lecture Notes in Artificial Intelligence and Lecture Notes in Bioinformatics), 11573 LNCS. doi:10.1007/978-3-030-23563-5_42

Ray, A., & Bala, P. K. (2020). Social media for improved process management in organizations during disasters. *Knowledge and Process Management*, *27*(1), 63–74. doi:10.1002/kpm.1623

Sboui, T., & Aissi, S. (2022). *A Risk-based Approach for Enhancing the Fitness of use of VGI*. IEEE. doi:10.1109/ACCESS.2022.3201022

See, L., Mooney, P., Foody, G., Bastin, L., Comber, A., Estima, J., Fritz, S., Kerle, N., Jiang, B., Laakso, M., Liu, H. Y., Milèinski, G., Nikšieč, M., Painho, M., Podör, A., Olteanu-Raimond, A. M. R., & Rutzinger, M. (2016). Crowdsourcing, citizen science or volunteered geographic information? The current state of crowdsourced geographic information. *ISPRS International Journal of Geo-Information*, *5*(5), 55. doi:10.3390/ijgi5050055

Soden, R., & Palen, L. (2014). *From Crowdsourced Mapping to Community Mapping: The Post-earthquake Work of OpenStreetMap Haiti*. In COOP 2014 - Proceedings of the 11th International Conference on the Design of Cooperative Systems, Nice, France. 10.1007/978-3-319-06498-7_19

TavraM.RacetinI.PerošJ. (2019). Combining social media and authoritative data for crisis mapping: A case study of a wildfire reaching croatian city of split. *International Archives of the Photogrammetry, Remote Sensing and Spatial Information Sciences - ISPRS Archives, 42*(3/W8). doi:10.5194/isprs-archives-XLII-3-W8-415-2019

Vavassori, A., Carrion, D., Zaragozi, B., & Migliaccio, F. (2022). VGI and Satellite Imagery Integration for Crisis Mapping of Flood Events. *ISPRS International Journal of Geo-Information*, *11*(12), 611. doi:10.3390/ijgi11120611

Xin, Y. (2022). Anomaly detection for volunteered geographic information: A case study of Safecast data. *International Journal of Geographical Information Science*, *36*(7), 1423–1442. doi:10.1080/13658816.2021.1981333

Yan, Y., Chen, J., & Wang, Z. (2020). Mining public sentiments and perspectives from geotagged social media data for appraising the post-earthquake recovery of tourism destinations. *Applied Geography (Sevenoaks, England)*, *123*, 102306. doi:10.1016/j.apgeog.2020.102306

Yan, Y., Eckle, M., Kuo, C. L., Herfort, B., Fan, H., & Zipf, A. (2017). Monitoring and assessing post-disaster tourism recovery using geotagged social media data. *ISPRS International Journal of Geo-Information*, *6*(5), 144. doi:10.3390/ijgi6050144

Yates, D., & Paquette, S. (2011). Emergency knowledge management and social media technologies: A case study of the 2010 Haitian earthquake. *International Journal of Information Management*, *31*(1), 6–13. doi:10.1016/j.ijinfomgt.2010.10.001

Yingwei, Y., Dawei, M., & Hongchao, F. (2020). A research framework for the application of volunteered geographic information in post-disaster recovery monitoring. *Tropical Geography*, *40*(2). doi:10.13284/j.cnki.rddl.003239

Yu, J., Zhao, Q., & Chin, C. S. (2019). Extracting typhoon disaster information from VGI based on machine learning. *Journal of Marine Science and Engineering*, *7*(9), 318. doi:10.3390/jmse7090318

Zook, M., Graham, M., Shelton, T., & Gorman, S. (2010). Volunteered Geographic Information and Crowdsourcing Disaster Relief: A Case Study of the Haitian Earthquake. *World Medical & Health Policy*, *2*(2), 6–32. doi:10.2202/1948-4682.1069

Chapter 14
Managing a Breast Cancer Crisis Through Innovation, Community Engagement, and the Expansion of Fisheries Management Education Programs

Darrell Norman Burrell
https://orcid.org/0000-0002-4675-9544
Pellegrino Center for Clinical Bioethics, Georgetown University Medical Center, USA

ABSTRACT

Cancer is a health crisis that has long been plaguing the United States and the world. According to the World Health Organization (WHO), breast cancer is the most common cancer among women worldwide, with nearly 2 million new cases diagnosed in 2018. In the U.S. alone, the American Cancer Society estimates that in 2020, there will be 276,480 new cases of invasive breast cancer and 48,530 deaths from the disease. As a result, breast cancer is a global crisis. Globally, breast cancer is the leading cause of cancer death among women, with an estimated 627,000 deaths in 2018. This chapter will discuss the prevalence of trauma and PTSD among cancer patients and survivors, and the risk factors associated with its development. Additionally, the chapter will discuss the psychological impact of trauma and PTSD on cancer survivors, and the interventions that are available to help manage these issues through a fly-fishing support group for female breast cancer survivors that can be offered as community education programs from state fisheries.

DOI: 10.4018/978-1-6684-9522-3.ch014

INTRODUCTION

Fly fishing is a recreational pursuit and a powerful platform for promoting fisheries management education. Fisheries management involves a complex interplay of ecological, social, and economic factors to ensure the sustainability of aquatic ecosystems and the species they support. Fly fishing is not just a recreational activity but a rich tradition that combines skill, patience, and an appreciation for the environment (Snyder et al., 2016). Over the years, this artful angling technique has garnered a dedicated community of enthusiasts who find solace in the rhythm of casting lines and anticipating a catch (Snyder et al., 2016). Fly fishing can serve as a multifaceted fisheries management education program, engaging participants in ecological awareness, ethical angling practices, resource conservation, and community involvement. State Departments of Fisheries Management have a unique opportunity to contribute significantly to educating community residents about fly fishing and foster the growth of fly-fishing community support groups for cancer survivors. Cancer support groups emerged as innovative responses to the crisis and upheaval caused by a cancer diagnosis, providing individuals with a platform to connect, share experiences, and offer emotional support during their challenging journeys. These groups serve as resilient, patient-driven solutions born from adversity, fostering a sense of community and empowerment amidst the disaster of a cancer diagnosis.

CANCER IS A CRISIS

According to the National Cancer Institute (2020), cancer can cause physical pain and discomfort, fatigue, and a disruption in normal daily activities. In addition, cancer can cause emotional distress, including fear, anxiety, and depression. Cancer patients and survivors are at an increased risk of developing trauma and PTSD due to their experience with the illness and treatment (Pranjic et al., 2016). Additionally, Studies have found that up to 40% of cancer patients and survivors may develop trauma and PTSD (Pranjic et al., 2016). The psychological impact of trauma and PTSD on cancer patients and survivors can be more severe due to the additional physical and cognitive impairments caused by cancer and its treatment (Pranjic et al., 2016). Several risk factors have been identified as contributing to developing trauma and PTSD in cancer survivors (Pranjic et al., 2016). These include the severity of the cancer diagnosis, lifestyle changes due to the illness and treatment, and the psychological impact of the illness (Pranjic et al., 2016; Cordova et al., 2017). Studies have found that PTSD can harm the physical and psychological health of cancer survivors, including increased fatigue, depression, and anxiety (Pranjic et al., 2016; Cordova et al., 2017)

Cancer is a health crisis that has long been plaguing the United States and the world. According to the American Cancer Society (2020), cancer is the second leading cause of death in the United States and is estimated to cause over 600,000 deaths in 2020 alone. Cancer has many symptoms, causes, and treatments and can affect any age, race, or gender. Cancer can have a devastating impact on those affected by it, both physically and emotionally. According to the National Cancer Institute (2020), cancer can cause physical pain and discomfort, fatigue, and a disruption in normal daily activities. In addition, cancer can cause emotional distress, including fear, anxiety, and depression. It can also lead to financial burdens, such as the costs of treatment, lost wages, and other expenses related to managing the illness. Cancer can also significantly impact families (Lu et al., 2023; Meacham Lu et al., 2016). It can cause stress, anxiety, and depression in family members and disrupt everyday family life (Lu et al., 2023; Meacham Lu et al., 2016).

Stress can manifest in physical, mental, and emotional ways and profoundly affect cancer survivors' quality of life (Lu et al., 2023; Meacham Lu et al., 2016). Stress management and reduction are essential aspects of cancer survivorship, as they can help cancer survivors cope with their diagnosis, treatment, and post-treatment life (Lu et al., 2023; Meacham Lu et al., 2016).

Stress is a normal part of life, but it can be overwhelming for cancer survivors. Cancer survivors can experience a wide range of emotions and thoughts, from fear and anxiety to depression and anger, which can become a crisis that is difficult to cope with (Lu et al., 2023; Meacham Lu et al., 2016). Stress can also manifest in physical ways, such as difficulty sleeping, changes in appetite, and increased fatigue (NCCN, 2020).

Stress can also interfere with the treatment process. According to a study by the National Institutes of Health (NIH), cancer survivors who experience high-stress levels may be less likely to adhere to their treatment plan and more likely to experience negative physical and emotional symptoms (NIH, 2019). Furthermore, the NIH study found that high-stress levels can harm the body's natural healing process. This can lead to poorer outcomes and longer recovery times (NIH, 2019).

Stress can also have a crisis impact on the social aspects of life for cancer survivors. According to the National Cancer Institute (NCI), cancer survivors can experience social isolation and stigma due to their diagnosis and treatment (NCI, 2020). This can lead to loneliness and a lack of support, further increasing stress levels.

Cancer is a debilitating and challenging disease to overcome, and the trauma it can cause is often overlooked. Cancer treatment and survivorship can cause trauma and post-traumatic stress disorder (PTSD). The physical and psychological effects of cancer and its treatments can be overwhelming crises, leading to PTSD (Dun et al., 2022). Along with the physical effects of cancer, the treatment and survivorship of cancer can also cause psychological trauma and post-traumatic stress disorder (PTSD). The psychological distress associated with cancer treatment and survivorship is often overlooked and underestimated, yet it can have a long-term effect on a person's quality of life (Dun et al., 2022). Therefore, it is essential to recognize and address this distress and crisis to improve cancer survivors' quality of life (Lu et al., 2023; Meacham Lu et al., 2016).

While medical advances have led to a longer life expectancy for cancer patients, the physical and psychological impact of cancer and its treatment can have long-lasting effects on the survivor's quality of life (Lu et al., 2023; Meacham Lu et al., 2016). One of the most severe psychological impacts of cancer treatment and survivorship is the development of trauma and post-traumatic stress disorder (PTSD). Cancer and its treatments can cause physical and emotional trauma(Lu et al., 2023; Meacham Lu et al., 2016). The physical trauma of cancer can include pain, fatigue, and the side effects of treatments. Emotional trauma can include worry, fear, and anxiety about the diagnosis and the treatment (Son et al., 2020). In addition, there is often a feeling of helplessness, a loss of control, and a lack of support(Son et al., 2020). These can lead to PTSD, especially if the cancer diagnosis is sudden or life-threatening.

The crisis of cancer has proven to be an unexpected crucible for innovation, giving rise to a multitude of transformative breakthroughs in research, treatment, and support. It is within the crucible of this formidable health challenge that cutting-edge therapies, precision medicine, and breakthrough technologies have emerged. Moreover, the cancer experience has spawned innovations in patient advocacy, support networks, and survivorship programs, emphasizing the importance of holistic care. This crisis, while undeniably devastating, has also served as a catalyst for resilience, determination, and the birth of numerous pioneering solutions aimed at alleviating the burden of cancer and improving the lives of those affected by it. In this crucible, the human spirit's capacity to innovate and adapt in the face of adversity shines brightly, offering hope and tangible progress in the ongoing battle against cancer.

PROBLEM STATEMENT

According to the World Health Organization (WHO), breast cancer is the most common cancer among women worldwide, with nearly 2 million new cases diagnosed in 2018 (WHO, 2019). In the U.S. alone, the American Cancer Society estimates that in 2020, there will be 276,480 new cases of invasive breast cancer and 48,530 deaths from the disease (American Cancer Society, 2020). As a result, breast cancer is a global crisis. Globally, breast cancer is the leading cause of cancer death among women, with an estimated 627,000 deaths in 2018 (WHO, 2019). The risk of developing breast cancer increases with age, with about two-thirds of new breast cancers occurring in women over 55 (American Cancer Society, 2020). Globally, the average age at which women are diagnosed with breast cancer is between 55 and 60 (WHO, 2019).

Additionally, the risk of breast cancer increases with lifestyle factors such as alcohol consumption and obesity (American Cancer Society, 2020). The mortality rate from breast cancer has decreased significantly in the U.S. over the past several decades due in part to early detection, improved treatment options, and increased awareness of the disease (American Cancer Society, 2020). However, the mortality rate from breast cancer remains higher in the U.S. than in other developed countries (American Cancer Society, 2020). Globally, the mortality rate from breast cancer has decreased significantly since the 1990s due to improved access to screening, diagnosis, and treatment (WHO, 2019). Although the mortality rate from breast cancer has decreased, the morbidity associated with the disease has not. Breast cancer survivors often face long-term physical, psychological, and financial burdens (American Cancer Society, 2020). This paper will discuss the prevalence of trauma and PTSD among cancer patients and survivors and the risk factors associated with its development. Additionally, the paper will discuss the psychological impact of trauma and PTSD on cancer survivors and the interventions available to help manage these issues through a fly-fishing support group for female breast cancer survivors. This paper will also outline the critical role that state departments of fisheries management can play in partnering with state locations of the American Cancer Society and healthcare organizations to develop fly-fishing support groups for breast cancer survivors.

METHOD

Observation research was the approach used. Observation is a qualitative data collection method comprised of viewing and documenting phenomena in the usual environment (Weston et al., 2021). Viewing and making notes on occurrences in their natural settings are the two main components of the qualitative data collection method known as observation research (Weston et al., 2021). Observational data is documented as field notes (Weston et al., 2021). These notes include specifics regarding the topic of interest's associated setting, participants, and activities (Weston et al., 2021). Field notes can be evaluated independently or with other data types by employing conceptual or theoretical frameworks or determining recurring themes (Weston et al., 2021). Researchers in the field of health services often use observation as a valuable data-gathering tool because it allows them to discover significant components involved in a topic of interest (Weston et al., 2021). This process involves data collection through direct observation of people, their stories, and events that occur in the community. The process involved directly observing program participants of a fly-fishing mental health support group focused on helping female breast cancer survivors manage their cancer diagnosis and treatment crisis. This method also included a review of literature related to how cancer patients experience the diagnosis as a form of triangulation and validation of the observation-based community research activity (Weston et al., 2021). An additional method to triangulate the results was a peer-reviewer independent observation that was separate from what was completed by the primary researcher. This approach aims to document viable and usable solutions that others in global communities can replicate to help those in need, which is the benefit and value of applied community research (Weston et al., 2021). Trends and results are listed in the following paragraphs as direct results and an amalgamation of the literature, observations, and listening to program participants. The process includes observing breast cancer survivors bond through learning about fly fishing.

PREVALENCE OF TRAUMA AND PTSD

Cancer patients and survivors are at an increased risk of developing trauma and PTSD due to their experience with the illness and treatment. Studies have found that cancer patients and survivors often develop trauma and PTSD (Thompson et al., 2011; Son et al., 2020). Additionally, the psychological impact of trauma and PTSD on cancer patients and survivors can be more severe due to the additional physical and cognitive impairments caused by cancer and its treatment (Thompson et al., 2011; Son et al., 2020)

RISK FACTORS

Several risk factors have been identified as contributing to developing trauma and PTSD in cancer survivors. These include the severity of the cancer diagnosis, lifestyle changes due to the illness and treatment, and the psychological impact of the illness (Thompson et al., 2011; Son et al., 2020). For example, one study found that the severity of the cancer diagnosis was the strongest predictor of PTSD, with those diagnosed with more advanced stages of cancer being more likely to develop PTSD (Thompson et al., 2011; Son et al., 2020). Additionally, lifestyle changes due to illness and treatment, such as physical activity, diet, and social activities, can also increase the risk of PTSD in cancer survivors (Thompson et al., 2011; Son et al., 2020). Finally, the psychological impact of the illness, such as fear of recurrence and feelings of guilt, can also increase the risk of PTSD in cancer survivors (Thompson et al., 2011; Son et al., 2020)

PSYCHOLOGICAL IMPACT

The symptoms of PTSD after cancer treatment can vary. It can include a sense of fear, anxiety, and hyperarousal. People may have difficulty sleeping, have flashbacks and nightmares, and experience emotional numbness (Thompson et al., 2011; Son et al., 2020). They may also suffer from physical symptoms, such as an increased heart rate, sweating, and trembling. Some people may also feel angry, irritable, and have difficulty concentrating (Thompson et al., 2011; Son et al., 2020)

The psychological impact of trauma and PTSD on cancer survivors can be significant and can have a long-lasting effect on their quality of life. Studies have found that PTSD can harm cancer survivors' physical and psychological health, including increased fatigue, depression, and anxiety (Thompson et al., 2011; Son et al., 2020). Additionally, PTSD can affect the cancer survivor's ability to engage in activities essential for their well-being, such as physical activity, social activities, and work (Thompson et al., 2011; Son et al., 2020). This can lead to decreased quality of life and an increased risk of recurrence and mortality (Thompson et al., 2011; Son et al., 2020).

INTERVENTIONS

Several interventions are available to help manage the psychological effects of trauma and PTSD in cancer survivors. Cognitive-behavioral therapy (CBT) is an effective intervention for treating PTSD in cancer survivors (Tatrow & Montgomery, 2006). CBT can help cancer survivors identify and address maladaptive thoughts and behaviors contributing to their PTSD and develop coping strategies to manage their symptoms (Tatrow & Montgomery, 2006). Additionally, mindfulness-based interventions effectively treat PTSD in cancer survivors, as they can help reduce stress and improve overall well-being (Tatrow & Montgomery, 2006). Finally, support groups can also benefit cancer survivors, providing a safe space for survivors to discuss their feelings and experiences and share tips for managing their symptoms (Sarason, 2013; Till, 2003; Son et al., 2020).

Cancer survivors are at an increased risk of developing trauma and PTSD due to their experience with the illness and treatment. These issues can significantly negatively impact the survivor's physical and psychological health and overall quality of life (Thompson et al., 2011; Son et al., 2020). However, there are interventions available to help manage the psychological effects of trauma and PTSD in cancer survivors, such as cognitive-behavioral therapy, mindfulness-based interventions, and support groups (Sarason, 2013; Till, 2003; Son et al., 2020; Tatrow & Montgomery, 2006). It is vital for survivors to be aware of their illness's potential psychological impacts and to seek appropriate interventions to help manage their symptoms (Thompson et al., 2011; Son et al., 2020).

OBSERVATION RESEARCH RESULTS FROM FLY-FISHING SUPPORT GROUPS

Key themes include:

Therapeutic Escape and Connection:

Fly fishing allows breast cancer survivors to immerse themselves in the tranquil beauty of natural settings. The rhythmic casting of lines and the sound of flowing water provide a therapeutic escape from the emotional burdens of cancer. Engaging in this shared activity fosters a sense of camaraderie among survivors, allowing them to connect on a deeper level by sharing their stories, challenges, and triumphs.

Physical and Emotional Healing:

The physical act of fly fishing involves gentle movements that can aid post-treatment rehabilitation, promoting an improved range of motion and strength. Furthermore, the meditative aspects of fly fishing encourage mindfulness, reducing stress and anxiety. Breast cancer survivors who participate in fly fishing often report a renewed sense of vitality and a positive shift in their emotional well-being.

Empowerment and Achievement:

Mastering the art of fly fishing instills a sense of accomplishment and empowerment among breast cancer survivors. Learning and practicing the techniques required for successful fly fishing symbolize their resilience and ability to overcome challenges. As survivors achieve proficiency in fly fishing, their confidence grows, enhancing their overall self-esteem.

Building a Supportive Community:

Fly fishing provides breast cancer survivors a platform to unite as a supportive community. Sharing the joys of successful casts, celebrating each catch, and offering encouragement during moments of frustration create a strong bond among survivors. This community becomes a safe space where individuals can express their fears, hopes, and aspirations without judgment.

DISCUSSIONS

It is not uncommon crisis for cancer survivors to feel isolated and disconnected from their peers, especially after treatment has ended. Fortunately, cancer survivors can benefit from social interactions and activities with a support group that can help to connect them with others who have experienced similar challenges. The U.S. organization "Casting for Recovery", uses fly fishing to form a mental health and mindfulness support group for women who are breast cancer survivors. There are chapters of the organization all over the U.S., and women meet together, learn about fly fishing, connect with nature, and experience community and social integration that helps survivors manage the cancer diagnosis, treatment, and recovery crisis.

Socializing with a support group can provide a sense of community, belonging, and connectedness for cancer survivors. It can help reduce feelings of isolation and loneliness, which are common among cancer survivors (Dun et al., 2022). In addition, it can allow cancer survivors to interact with others who have had similar experiences and can relate to their struggles. It can also benefit cancer survivors to share their stories and give advice to one another (Dun et al., 2022).

Social activities with a support group can also help promote self-esteem and self-confidence in cancer survivors. It can allow cancer survivors to talk openly about their experiences and feelings without fear of judgment (Dun et al., 2022). In addition, it can provide a safe space to express their emotions and to feel understood and supported. Social activities with a support group can also build relationships and foster meaningful connections with other survivors.

In addition to social interactions, engaging in activities with a support group can provide cancer survivors with physical and mental benefits. Activities can help reduce stress, improve mood, and increase overall well-being (Dun et al., 2022). It can also provide a distraction from cancer challenges and help reduce feelings of anxiety and depression. Additionally, engaging in activities can help to promote physical activity, which can help to reduce fatigue and improve quality of life (Dun et al., 2022).

Participating in activities with a support group can also provide a sense of purpose and motivation for cancer survivors. It can allow cancer survivors to set and achieve goals, which can help increase self-esteem and self-confidence (Dun et al., 2022). Additionally, it can provide a sense of accomplishment and a sense of pride in their accomplishments.

Social interactions and activities with a support group can benefit cancer survivors. It can help to reduce feelings of isolation and loneliness, promote self-esteem and self-confidence, reduce stress, improve mood, and increase overall well-being. Additionally, it can provide a sense of purpose and motivation and help set and achieve goals. The benefits of socializing and engaging in activities with a support group are numerous and can be invaluable for cancer survivors (Dun et al., 2022).

The value and benefit of the Fly-fishing program as a treatment tool is grounded in a variety of theories. Acceptance and Commitment Therapy (ACT) is a type of psychotherapy that can benefit cancer treatment survivors. ACT is a mindfulness-based approach that emphasizes accepting and committing to the present moment rather than trying to fight or avoid it (Bai et al., 2020; Feros et al., 2013). This approach can help individuals cope with their illness, encouraging them to focus on the present moment and accept their emotions.

The human relations theory, developed by Elton Mayo, proposes that communication and relationships between individuals are essential to improving their overall well-being (Mayo, 1933). This theory suggests that individuals need to feel valued and connected to others to have a sense of purpose and meaning (Mayo, 1933). This theory can benefit cancer treatment survivors by emphasizing the importance of supportive relationships and developing a sense of connection with others.

Sociological theories can also benefit cancer treatment survivors, as they can provide insight into how individuals interact and how society affects their experience of illness. One helpful theory for cancer treatment survivors is the Social Support Theory, which suggests that having supportive relationships with others can positively impact an individual's mental and physical health (Sarason, 2013). This theory emphasizes the importance of having access to social support, as it can provide individuals with emotional and practical assistance, which can benefit their recovery process (Sarason, 2013).

Another sociological theory that can benefit cancer treatment survivors is the Theory of Social Influence, which suggests that individuals are influenced by their social environment (Croyle & Hunt, 1991). This theory suggests that individuals may be more likely to take specific actions if they perceive that others around them are doing the same (Croyle & Hunt, 1991). This theory can benefit cancer treatment survivors as it can help them understand how their social environment may influence their behavior and decisions (Croyle & Hunt, 1991).

INTERPERSONAL RELATIONSHIPS

Interpersonal relationships, support, and friendships can help cancer treatment survivors manage their crises and trauma in various ways (Holt-Lunstad, 2018). These relationships can provide emotional, physical, and informational support to individuals during and after cancer treatment. In addition, these relationships can provide a sense of safety and security, help to reduce stress and improve overall quality of life (Holt-Lunstad, 2018).

There are numerous benefits of having strong friendships, support, and interpersonal relationships for cancer treatment survivors. First, research has shown that having interpersonal relationships can improve physical and psychological health (Holt-Lunstad, 2018; Docherty, 2004; Cain et al., 1986; Jablotschkin, 2022). Studies have found that individuals with strong social relationships have better overall health than those without (Holt-Lunstad, 2018). This can be especially beneficial for cancer treatment survivors dealing with their treatments' physical and psychological side effects. Strong interpersonal relationships can also help reduce stress, improve mood, and provide safety and security (Holt-Lunstad, 2018). This can significantly benefit cancer treatment survivors who may feel overwhelmed and anxious due to their diagnosis and treatments.

In addition to the physical and psychological benefits of interpersonal relationships, they can provide informational support (Holt-Lunstad, 2018). Friends and family can provide helpful advice, information about cancer treatments, resources, and emotional support and understanding. Studies have found that having a solid support network can help individuals cope with the physical and psychological stress of cancer treatments and can provide a sense of comfort and security (Holt-Lunstad, 2018; Docherty, 2004; Cain et al., 1986; Jablotschkin, 2022). Furthermore, having strong interpersonal relationships can help individuals feel more connected to their community and can help them to feel less isolated and alone (Holt-Lunstad, 2018; Docherty, 2004; Cain et al., 1986; Jablotschkin, 2022). This can be especially beneficial for cancer treatment survivors feeling the crisis of being overwhelmed and disconnected from the world.

Local support groups can also be a great source of support for cancer treatment survivors. These groups allow individuals to meet others dealing with similar experiences, share their stories, and support each other (Docherty, 2004; Cain et al., 1986; Jablotschkin, 2022). Many local support groups offer additional resources and services such as workshops, counseling, and social activities (Docherty, 2004; Cain et al., 1986; Jablotschkin, 2022).

EXERCISE

According to the American Cancer Society (ACS), exercise can help to reduce stress levels and improve physical and emotional well-being (ACS, 2020). Exercise can also help to reduce fatigue and improve sleep, which can help to manage stress levels. Stress management and stress reduction are essential aspects of cancer survivorship. Stress can profoundly affect cancer survivors, both physically and emotionally. Fortunately, some strategies can be used to help cancer survivors manage the crisis and reduce their stress levels.

Fly fishing is an angling method using a fly rod, reel, and artificial lures to catch fish. It is distinct from other forms of fishing in that it involves casting rather than trolling or casting with bait (Pagis & Summers-Effler, 2021). Fly fishing is often considered a peaceful and relaxing activity, as it requires little physical exertion and can be done in a quiet, natural setting (Pagis & Summers-Effler, 2021).

Fly fishing has many physical and mental health benefits, including stress reduction, mindfulness, and support for mental health well-being (Pagis & Summers-Effler, 2021). Fly fishing has numerous physical and mental health benefits. It is a form of exercise that can help to reduce stress and improve mental focus (Pagis & Summers-Effler, 2021). Additionally, fly fishing can help improve coordination and balance, as casting the fly rod requires good coordination and balance. Finally, fly fishing can also improve self-esteem, as it is a sport one can practice and improve upon, leading to a greater sense of self-efficacy (Pagis & Summers-Effler, 2021).

Fly fishing can be an excellent tool for stress reduction (Pagis & Summers-Effler, 2021). The physical act of fly fishing can help to reduce stress by providing an outlet for pent-up energy and emotions (Pagis & Summers-Effler, 2021). Additionally, the calming nature of the activity and the peaceful environment it is often practiced can help reduce stress (Pagis & Summers-Effler, 2021). Moreover, the mental focus necessary for fly fishing can help distract from worries and anxieties, providing a welcome respite from stress and worry (Pagis & Summers-Effler, 2021). Fly fishing can also be used as a tool for mindfulness (Pagis & Summers-Effler, 2021). The mental focus and concentration necessary for fly fishing can help bring one into the present moment, allowing one to be mindful and reflective (Pagis & Summers-Effler, 2021).

Additionally, the activity's peaceful nature can help create a calming, meditative atmosphere, allowing one to be mindful and reflective (Pagis & Summers-Effler, 2021). Finally, the physical nature of fly fishing can provide an opportunity to be mindful of one's body and movement, further enhancing the mindfulness experience (Pagis & Summers-Effler, 2021).

Fly fishing can support mental health and well-being (Pagis & Summers-Effler, 2021). Fly fishing can help to reduce stress, increase self-esteem, and promote mindfulness, all of which can help to support mental health and well-being (Pagis & Summers-Effler, 2021). Additionally, fly fishing can be a great way to connect with nature and to spend time in a peaceful, natural setting, which can help to reduce feelings of isolation and loneliness, both of which can harm mental health (Pagis & Summers-Effler, 2021).

Fly fishing is a great activity that can provide numerous physical and mental health benefits. It can be used as a tool for stress reduction, mindfulness, and support for mental health well-being (Pagis & Summers-Effler, 2021). Fly fishing can help to reduce stress, increase self-esteem, improve coordination and balance, and provide an opportunity to be mindful and reflective (Pagis & Summers-Effler, 2021). Additionally, fly fishing can help reduce feelings of isolation and loneliness, which can hurt mental health (Pagis & Summers-Effler, 2021). Finally, fly fishing can be a great way to connect with nature and spend time in a peaceful, natural setting (Pagis & Summers-Effler, 2021).

STORYTELLING

The fly-fishing activity employs storytelling as a critical tool to help treat participants. Storytelling has existed for generations and is an essential part of human culture. Storytelling is an effective tool to inspire, educate, and entertain (Milojević, 2014). In recent years, storytelling has become an essential part of the support group experience for cancer survivors. Support groups allow cancer survivors to share their stories, experiences, and feelings with others who have gone through the same experience. This can help to reduce feelings of isolation and provide a safe place for cancer survivors to express their feelings.

Many people manage crises and navigate the emotions of a crisis through storytelling (Milojević, 2014). Storytelling in support groups is the process of sharing and exchanging stories in an environment of shared understanding and trust (Docherty, 2004; Milojević, 2014). In a support group setting, storytelling can be used to help cancer survivors cope with their diagnosis and the challenges that come along with it (Docherty, 2004; Milojević, 2014This can include sharing stories of how they were first diagnosed, how they dealt with the treatment process, and how they are currently managing their lives post-treatment. Storytelling can also be used to help cancer survivors come to terms with their diagnosis, build resilience, and find hope as they manage their crisis and related trauma (Docherty, 2004; Milojević, 2014

There are many benefits associated with storytelling in support groups for cancer survivors. One of the most important benefits is that it allows cancer survivors to share their stories and experiences with others who have gone through similar experiences (Docherty, 2004). This can reduce feelings of isolation and provide a sense of community and support. Furthermore, storytelling can help cancer survivors to gain insight into their own experiences by hearing stories from others in the group (Docherty, 2004). This can help to provide them with a better understanding of their diagnosis and treatment process, which can help to reduce feelings of distress and increase feelings of hope (Docherty, 2004).

In addition, storytelling can help to reduce stress levels for cancer survivors (Docherty, 2004). This can help to improve mental health and well-being by reducing anxiety and depression (Docherty, 2004).

Storytelling can also help cancer survivors to gain a sense of control over their diagnosis and treatment process, which can help to increase feelings of hope and optimism (Docherty, 2004).

Storytelling can help improve cancer survivors' communication skills as they manage their health crises. By listening to the stories of others in the group, cancer survivors can better understand how to express their feelings and experiences and manage their crises. This can help to build stronger connections with other group members, which can help to reduce feelings of isolation and improve overall mental health and well-being.

Storytelling can help to reduce stress levels for cancer survivors. This can help to improve mental health and well-being by reducing anxiety and depression (Docherty, 2004). Storytelling can also help cancer survivors to gain a sense of control over their diagnosis and treatment process, which can help to increase feelings of hope and optimism (Docherty, 2004). Storytelling can help reduce feelings of isolation, stress levels, and communication skills (Docherty, 2004). This can help to improve mental health and well-being by providing a safe space for cancer survivors to share their stories and experiences with others who have gone through similar experiences. As a result, storytelling can be an effective tool for cancer survivors in support groups and can help improve their overall quality of life and ability to manage their personal crisis with cancer.

CONCLUSION

State Departments of Fisheries Management can serve as a valuable innovative resource for educating community residents about the art and science of fly fishing, especially those recovering from a cancer crisis. These organizations can function as community drivers of change and support. By organizing workshops, seminars, and educational events, they can offer hands-on experience, theoretical knowledge, and practical skills needed to master fly-fishing techniques. These initiatives and innovations can cover various aspects, such as:

Ecology and Conservation: Teaching participants about aquatic ecosystems, fish behavior, and the importance of sustainable fishing practices. Understanding the delicate balance of aquatic environments is essential for preserving natural resources for future generations (Snyder et al., 2016).

Casting Techniques: Providing guidance on casting techniques, tying flies, and selecting appropriate equipment. These skills are fundamental to successful fly fishing and can enhance participants' overall experience.

Ethical Angling: Promoting responsible angling practices, catch-and-release methods, and adherence to fishing regulations. State departments can emphasize the ethical considerations to protect fish populations and ecosystems.

Community Workshops and Events: Organizing community-driven workshops, fishing derbies, and events where fly fishers can come together, share experiences, and learn from each other. These gatherings can strengthen bonds among anglers and create a sense of belonging.

Support for Clubs and Groups: Providing resources, funding, and logistical support to local fly-fishing clubs and groups. State fishery departments can facilitate the formation of these groups, enabling like-minded individuals to collaborate and share their passion.

Access and Infrastructure: Collaborating with local authorities to improve access to fishing locations, maintain fishing infrastructure, and ensure the sustainability of fishing spots. State departments can work to maintain rivers, lakes, and streams, making them welcoming and safe environments for fly fishers.

Tourism and Local Economy: State departments can attract tourists interested in the sport by promoting fly fishing education and community engagement. This influx of visitors can boost local economies through increased tourism spending on accommodations, dining, and other services.

Cultural Preservation: Fly fishing often has deep cultural roots in certain regions. State departments can play a role in preserving and celebrating these cultural traditions by supporting events and activities that showcase the historical and artistic aspects of fly fishing.

Creating communities: State departments can play a significant role in supporting the development of specialized affinity and support groups like those for breast cancer survivors to allow members to bond, learn, grow, and heal through fly-fishing.

RECOMMENDATIONS FOR FUTURE RESEARCH

In light of the emerging role of fly-fishing trips and workshops offered by state departments of fisheries management as a potential stress management and relaxation health intervention for breast cancer survivor support groups, a compelling need exists for comprehensive research to substantiate and enhance our understanding of this innovative approach. To address this gap, there could potential qualitative and quantitative study approaches that could contribute to a deeper exploration of the benefits and effectiveness of utilizing fly fishing in breast cancer survivor support groups.

Qualitative Study Approaches:

- Phenomenological Exploration of Survivor Experiences: A qualitative phenomenological study can delve into the lived experiences of breast cancer survivors who have participated in fly fishing trips and workshops. In-depth interviews or focus groups could capture their perceptions, emotions, and reflections regarding the impact of fly fishing on stress management, relaxation, and overall well-being.
- Narrative Analysis of Transformative Journeys: Conducting narrative analysis on personal narratives shared by breast cancer survivors can uncover the transformative aspects of their journey through fly fishing. Researchers can gain insights into the psychosocial mechanisms at play by analyzing how survivors construct their stories of healing and empowerment.
- Exploration of Group Dynamics and Support: Ethnographic research could be employed to study the dynamics within breast cancer survivor support groups that engage in fly fishing activities. This approach would offer a holistic view of how group interactions, shared experiences, and social support reduce stress and enhance well-being.

Quantitative Study Approaches:

- Randomized Controlled Trials (RCTs): Rigorous RCTs could be designed to assess the impact of fly-fishing interventions on stress and relaxation among breast cancer survivors. Participants could be randomly assigned to either an experimental group engaging in fly fishing activities or a control group receiving conventional support. Validated stress assessment tools and biomarkers could be used to measure outcomes.
- Longitudinal Studies: Longitudinal studies tracking breast cancer survivors' participation in fly fishing workshops over an extended period could provide insights into the sustainability and long-

term effects of the intervention. Surveys and assessments conducted at various time points could reveal trends in stress reduction, relaxation, and overall quality of life.
- Psychophysiological Measures: Employing psychophysiological measures, such as heart rate variability, cortisol levels, and immune markers, could offer objective indicators of stress reduction and relaxation. Comparative studies analyzing these measures before and after fly fishing experiences could provide quantifiable evidence of the intervention's effects.

Mixed-Methods Approaches:

- Triangulation of Data: A mixed-methods approach could combine qualitative and quantitative data to provide a comprehensive understanding of the impact of fly fishing on breast cancer survivors. Qualitative insights could complement quantitative measurements, enriching the interpretation of outcomes and enhancing the validity of the findings.
- Process Evaluation: A mixed-methods design could incorporate process evaluation to investigate how fly-fishing workshops influence stress management and relaxation. Qualitative data could elucidate how specific aspects of the intervention contribute to survivor well-being, guiding the development of future interventions.
- In conclusion, using fly fishing trips and workshops as a stress management and relaxation health intervention for breast cancer survivor support groups presents a fertile ground for future research. By employing the suggested qualitative, quantitative, and mixed-methods study approaches, researchers can deepen our understanding of this innovative intervention's benefits, mechanisms, and effectiveness, ultimately contributing to evidence-based practices that enhance the well-being of breast cancer survivors.

REFERENCES

American Cancer Society. (2020). *Exercise for cancer survivors*. ACS. https://www.cancer.org/treatment/survivorship-during-and-after-treatment/staying-active/exercise.html

Bai, Z., Luo, S., Zhang, L., Wu, S., & Chi, I. (2020). Acceptance and commitment therapy (ACT) to reduce depression: A systematic review and meta-analysis. Journal of affective disorders, 260, 728–737.

Cain, E. N., Kohorn, E. I., Quinlan, D. M., Latimer, K., & Schwartz, P. E. (1986). Psychosocial benefits of a cancer support group. *Cancer*, *57*(1), 183–189. doi:10.1002/1097-0142(19860101)57:1<183::AID-CNCR2820570135>3.0.CO;2-3 PMID:3079660

Cordova, M. J., Riba, M. B., & Spiegel, D. (2017). Post-traumatic stress disorder and cancer. *The Lancet. Psychiatry*, *4*(4), 330–338. doi:10.1016/S2215-0366(17)30014-7 PMID:28109647

Croyle, R. T., & Hunt, J. R. (1991). Coping with health threat: Social influence processes in reactions to medical test results. *Journal of Personality and Social Psychology*, *60*(3), 382–389. doi:10.1037/0022-3514.60.3.382 PMID:2027079

Docherty, A. (2004). Experience, functions, and benefits of a cancer support group. *Patient Education and Counseling*, *55*(1), 87–93. doi:10.1016/j.pec.2003.08.002 PMID:15476994

Dun, L., Xian-Yi, W., & Si-Ting, H. (2022). Effects of Cognitive Training and Social Support on Cancer-Related Fatigue and Quality of Life in Colorectal Cancer Survivors: A Systematic Review and Meta-Analysis. *Integrative Cancer Therapies*, *21*, 15347354221081271. doi:10.1177/15347354221081271 PMID:35225053

Feros, D. L., Lane, L., Ciarrochi, J., & Blackledge, J. T. (2013). Acceptance and Commitment Therapy (ACT) for improving the lives of cancer patients: A preliminary study. *Psycho-Oncology*, *22*(2), 459–464. doi:10.1002/pon.2083 PMID:23382134

Holt-Lunstad, J. (2018). Why social relationships are important for physical health: A systems approach to understanding and modifying risk and protection. *Annual Review of Psychology*, *69*(1), 437–458. doi:10.1146/annurev-psych-122216-011902 PMID:29035688

Jablotschkin, M., Binkowski, L., Markovits Hoopii, R., & Weis, J. (2022). Benefits and challenges of cancer peer support groups: A systematic review of qualitative studies. *European Journal of Cancer Care*, *31*(6), e13700. doi:10.1111/ecc.13700 PMID:36104303

Lu, X., Wu, C., Bai, D., You, Q., Cai, M., Wang, W., Hou, C., & Gao, J. (2023). Relationship between social support and fear of cancer recurrence among Chinese cancer patients: A systematic review and meta-analysis. *Frontiers in Psychiatry*, *14*, 1136013. doi:10.3389/fpsyt.2023.1136013 PMID:36970291

Mayo, E. (1933). *The human problems of an industrial civilization*. Macmillan.

Meacham, E., Orem, J., Nakigudde, G., Zujewski, J. A., & Rao, D. (2016). Exploring stigma as a barrier to cancer service engagement with breast cancer survivors in Kampala, Uganda. *Psycho-Oncology*, *25*(10), 1206–1211. doi:10.1002/pon.4215 PMID:27421234

Milojević, I. (2014). Creating alternative selves: The use of futures discourse in narrative therapy. *Journal of Futures Studies*, *18*(3), 27–40.

Munir, M. (2014). *How to Maintain Interpersonal Relationships*. Very Well Mind. https://www.verywellmind.com/how-to-maintain-interpersonal-relationships-4145371

National Cancer Institute. (2020). *Social and emotional effects of a cancer diagnosis*. NCI. https://www.cancer.gov/about-cancer/coping/emotional-social/social-emotional-effects

National Center for Complementary and Integrative Health. (2020). *Stress management: Using relaxation techniques for stress relief*. NCI. https://nccih.nih.gov/health/stress/relaxation.htm

National Comprehensive Cancer Network. (2020). *Stress management*. NCCN. https://www.nccn.org/patients/resources/life_with_cancer/stress-management.aspx

National Institutes of Health. (2019). *Stress in cancer survivors*. NIH. https://www.ncbi.nlm.nih.gov/pmc/articles/PMC6214096/

Pagis, M., & Summers-Effler, E. (2021, December). Aesthetic engagement. *Sociological Forum*, *36*(S1), 1371–1394. doi:10.1111ocf.12768

Pranjic, N., Bajraktarevic, A., & Ramic, E. (2016). Distress and PTSD in patients with cancer: Cohort study case. *Materia Socio-Medica*, *28*(1), 12. doi:10.5455/msm.2016.28.12-16 PMID:27047260

Sarason, I. G. (Ed.). (2013). *Social support: Theory, research, and applications* (Vol. 24). Springer Science & Business Media.

Snyder, S., Borgelt, B., & Tobey, E. (Eds.). (2016). *Backcasts: A global history of fly fishing and conservation*. University of Chicago Press. doi:10.7208/chicago/9780226366609.001.0001

Son, H. M., Park, E. Y., & Kim, E. J. (2020). Cancer-related fatigue of breast cancer survivors: Qualitative research. *Asian Oncology Nursing*, *20*(4), 141–149. doi:10.5388/aon.2020.20.4.141

Spector, D., Battaglini, C., Alsobrooks, A., Owen, J., & Groff, D. (2012). Do breast cancer survivors increase their physical activity and enhance their health-related quality of life after attending community-based wellness workshops? *Journal of Cancer Education*, *27*(2), 353–361. doi:10.100713187-011-0306-z PMID:22210191

Tatrow, K., & Montgomery, G. H. (2006). Cognitive behavioral therapy techniques for distress and pain in breast cancer patients: a meta-analysis. *Journal of behavioral medicine, 29*, 17–27.

Thompson, S. B., Eccleston, L., & Hickish, T. (2011). *Post-traumatic stress disorder in cancer survivors: Recognising and acknowledging the symptoms.*

Till, J. E. (2003). Evaluation of support groups for women with breast cancer: importance of the navigator role. *Health and quality of life outcomes*, *1*, 1–6.

Weston, L. E., Krein, S. L., & Harrod, M. (2021). Using observation to better understand the healthcare context. *Qualitative Research in Medicine & Healthcare*, *5*(3). doi:10.4081/qrmh.2021.9821 PMID:37441282

WHO. (2019). *Cancer: breast cancer*. WHO. https://www.who.int/cancer/prevention/diagnosis-screening/breast-cancer/en/

Chapter 15
Need to Increase Awareness of NCDs in MICs on the Edge of the Syrian Refugee Crisis

Songul Cinaroglu
https://orcid.org/0000-0001-5699-8402
Hacettepe University, Turkey

Busra Saylan
https://orcid.org/0000-0002-1296-1824
Hacettepe University, Turkey

ABSTRACT

Breast cancer is the most common type of cancer, and the incidence of breast cancer is increasing among women in middle-income countries (MICs). Turkey is one of the MICs and has an emerging economy. Turkey is a major hosting country of refugees, and it is still hosting one million Syrian refugees who are faced with a high risk of noncommunicable diseases. The aim of this study is to point out the current situation and cost of breast cancer in MICs focusing on Turkey and the current refugee flow into this country. This study used a direct examination of the scientific literature and reports. Study results indicate an increasing trend of costs and incidence of breast cancer in MICs and Turkey. Breast cancer is the most common disease among women in Arab world and it is foreseeable that there will be an increase in the number of breast cancer women in the next future in Turkey. To fight against breast cancer in Turkey, health policymakers should enhance public awareness for early diagnosis and treatment, considering the upcoming refugee crisis.

INTRODUCTION

Noncommunicable diseases (NCDs), one of today's biggest health challenges, are emerging as one of the leading causes of death worldwide (WHO, 2018). However, the availability of data on diseases and deaths worldwide also reveals disparities between countries in efforts to combat NCDs (Ezzati et al.,

DOI: 10.4018/978-1-6684-9522-3.ch015

2018). Undoubtedly, low- and middle-income countries (MICs) and their health systems face major challenges in efforts to combat NCDs (Niessen et al., 2018; Islam et al., 2019). NCD deaths remain a major public health problem in all countries, including low- and middle-income countries, with more than three-quarters of these deaths occurring in these countries (WHO, 2022). Learning from the experiences of high-income countries is crucial for MICs to gain insights and develop effective policies and interventions for NCDs (Hearn et al., 2019). Monitoring these interventions at the national level is crucial to reduce the burden and impact of NCDs through feasible and cost-effective interventions and to track global progress and identify challenges (WHO, 2022). The increasing evidence of NCDs' global health significance has prompted WHO member countries to initiate efforts to reduce premature deaths caused by the four major NCDs (cancers, cardiovascular and chronic respiratory diseases, and diabetes in people in the age range 30–69 years) by 25% by 2025 compared to 2010 levels (Ezzati et al., 2018).

While the term NCDs encompasses cardiovascular diseases, diabetes, chronic respiratory diseases, mental illnesses, and injuries, there is a noticeable gap in knowledge and experience regarding cancer (Schrecker, 2020). Cancer types such as breast cancer are among the important non-communicable diseases are the leading causes of death worldwide, and are the most common cancer type among women, especially in developed and developing countries (WHO, 2021). Low and middle-income countries face challenges in dealing with cancer, especially breast cancer, and their health ministries encounter limitations in improving breast cancer outcomes (Elghazawy et al., 2020; Prodhan et al., 2023). Multiple barriers hinder efforts to enhance cancer care outcomes in MICs. These barriers include a lack of scientific and epidemiological data, insufficient information on resource planning for breast cancer control, limited availability of experts and resources, inadequate quality of health statistics data, politicized decision-making processes, and socio-cultural factors that impede effective healthcare delivery (Dankó, 2014; Ginsburg et al., 2018).

Aside from the challenges related to cancer care outcomes, middle-income countries confront significant financial constraints in their efforts to combat cancer effectively (Carrera et al., 2018). Families in MICs often experience significant out-of-pocket (OOP) health expenditures to meet the healthcare needs related to cancer (Ginsburg et al., 2018; O'Neill et al., 2015). Despite breast cancer being a major concern among women in MICs, there has been limited attention given to the OOP costs associated with breast cancer for women and their families (Mustacchi, 2021). OOP payments refer to direct payments made by patients when insurance coverage does not fully cover the cost of healthcare goods and services (Hernández-Vásquez et al., 2020). While the information on OOP health expenditures has been collected in many high-income countries (OECD, 2021), there is a lack of data on OOP expenditures for cancer in MICs like Turkey. Turkey, classified as an upper MIC by the World Bank (World Bank, 2022), has an emerging economy and has witnessed significant improvements in the health status of its population in recent years, thanks to healthcare reform policies such as the Health Transformation Program (HTP) implemented since 2003. The Turkish government has been committed to enhancing the governance and quality of healthcare services and has implemented successful policies for early diagnosis of cancer and other non-communicable diseases (NCDs) such as cardiovascular diseases and diabetes (WHO, 2013; WHO, 2018). However, there is limited information in the literature regarding the current situation and costs of breast cancer in Turkey, especially in the context of the ongoing Syrian refugee crisis.

PROBLEM STATEMENT

Non-communicable diseases are chronic health issues that typically result from a combination of genetic, physiological, environmental, and behavioral factors (Budreviciute et al., 2020). Major types of non-communicable diseases, such as cardiovascular diseases, cancer, chronic respiratory diseases, and diabetes, pose significant global health challenges and disproportionately affect populations in low and middle-income countries (WHO, 2023a). Epidemiological data from low- and middle-income countries indicates an increasing trend in NCDs, contributing to a higher number of deaths in these nations (Ndubuisi, 2021). Despite the recognition of NCDs as a global health challenge, there are limited assessments of how the similarities and differences in the composition of NCDs among low and middle-income countries affect the formulation of health policies and programs in these nations (Ezzati et al., 2018).

Breast cancer, one of the most common types of cancer among NCDs, is the most common worldwide and one of the leading causes of cancer-related deaths in women (Bray et al., 2018). Breast cancer deaths are primarily associated with early mortality, often targeting women under the age of 70 and predominantly occurring in low and middle-income countries. For this reason, it is anticipated that the chronic social disruption resulting from breast cancer could harm low and middle-income countries for future generations (Anderson et al., 2021). Financial resource constraints of low- and middle-income countries limit resource allocations for the control of NCDs such as cancer (Mishra et al., 2021). Therefore, individuals in numerous MICs have to fund their healthcare expenses directly from their own pockets, creating a financial burden on patients with non-communicable diseases and their families (Williams et al., 2018). Considering the limited services and resources available for NCDs in middle-income countries and their effects on service users, our study covers breast cancer and its costs, one of the NCDs, in Turkey, which is under the influence of the Syrian refugee crisis.

PURPOSE STATEMENT

The objective of this book chapter is to compile existing information from the literature regarding the current situation and costs of breast cancer in Turkey, taking into consideration the impact of the Syrian refugee crisis. Therefore, the purpose of this book chapter has been discussed in three steps. Firstly, it will provide an in-depth overview of breast cancer within the realm of NCDs in MICs and the economic implications of this disease. Secondly, it will concentrate on the specific scenario of breast cancer in Turkey, delving into its economic and health-related costs. Lastly, this chapter underscores the pressing need to raise awareness about breast cancer among Syrian refugees residing in Turkey, given their unique healthcare challenges. By accomplishing these objectives, this study aims to illuminate the current landscape of breast cancer in Turkey, shedding light on the economic and health burdens within the context of the Syrian refugee crisis.

Breast Cancer Care in MICs

MICs encompass a diverse range of economies with varying population sizes and income levels. These countries are home to 75% of the world's population and 62% of the world's poor (World Bank, 2023). MICs exhibit differences in social, technological, development, poverty, and health characteristics. While developed countries often observe a higher incidence of prostate and lung cancers in men, and

Figure 1. Average breast cancer incidence and mortality rates by age group and by country income levels (Bellanger M., Zeinomar N., Tehranifar P., Terry MB. (2018). Are global breast cancer incidence and mortality patterns related to country specific economic development and prevention strategies? Journal of Global Oncology, 1-16, pp. 3)

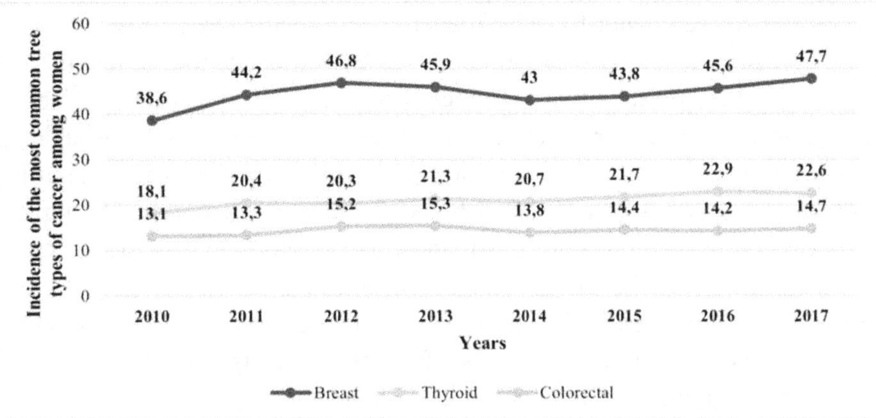

breast and colorectal cancers in women, the pattern is different in MICs. In these countries, prostate, lung, stomach, and liver cancers are more common among men, while breast cancer remains the most prevalent cancer among women (Dare et al., 2021; Pramesh et al., 2022).

Figure 1 presents the incidence rates for all cancers. The data shows that average breast cancer incidence and mortality rates tend to be higher in high-income countries, particularly among individuals aged 75 years and older (Bellanger et al., 2018).

The high incidence of breast cancer in upper-middle-income countries highlights the need for the development of comprehensive programs to combat this disease. Strategies such as assessing the burden of breast cancer, organizing effective programs, providing training, conducting implementation research, advocating for patients, and developing payment policies are crucial in understanding the current situation and addressing breast cancer (IARC, 2023). Despite advancements in cancer care programs, limited resources, challenges in the diagnosis and treatment processes, and a lack of information about breast cancer pose significant barriers in the fight against this disease (Dare et al., 2021; de Sanjose & Tsu, 2019; Shah et al., 2019). To overcome these limitations, it is essential to improve multidisciplinary breast cancer treatment services and foster collaborations with international organizations. The Global Breast Cancer Initiative (GBCI) is one such global summit that aims to address health disparities and develop evidence-based strategies to combat breast cancer in both developed and developing countries. The GBCI provides valuable insights into the current situation of breast cancer and facilitates the development of evidence-based strategies to tackle this disease (WHO, 2023b).

Costs of Breast Cancer in MICs

Most MICs have publicly financed health care systems and health policy makers facing challenges in financing health care services (Jakovljevic et al., 2019). Some costs of health care services like cancer care are much more expensive for some populations than others. Literature suggests that living in Africa and South Asia as compared with living in Europe was associated with greater rates of borrowing or selling to pay for health care. This means that health services are more costly for people living in underdeveloped countries than developed ones. In other words, general health care services and cancer care are more costly for poor populations than rich ones, especially for rural residents, and ensuring the sustainability of the health system is a major concern for developing economies (Strasser et al., 2016).

Patients and families are facing hardship in financing their healthcare needs and the burden of breast cancer has been increasing in recent years among MICs (Bellanger et al., 2018). As a result of this increase health policymakers need to focus on increasing costs of breast cancer. The most important reason for the high costs of cancer care is expensive drugs. The high costs of these drugs are related to numerous factors. First, most cancers are incurable and there is a monopoly in this market. Second drug development costs are high. Many years and millions of dollars are spent on developing cancer drugs. In addition to that, cancer drugs represent, for the most part, a monopoly (Vincent Rajkumar, 2020).

Cancers are a leading cause of death globally, resulting in 10.0 million deaths in 2019. Incidence and mortality rates are rising worldwide, with high-income countries experiencing a higher burden than low- and middle-income countries (LMICs). Cancers have significant economic consequences, impacting productivity, employment, and capital investment. Investing in cancer screening, diagnosis, and treatment could provide substantial health and economic benefits, particularly in LMICs with lower survival rates. The estimated global economic cost of cancers from 2020 to 2050 is substantial, amounting to $25.2 trillion, equivalent to an annual tax of 0.55% on global GDP. The highest economic costs are attributed to tracheal, bronchus, and lung cancer (%15.4), followed by colon and rectal cancer (%10.9), breast cancer (%7.7), liver cancer (%6.5), and leukemia (%6.3) (Chen et al., 2023).

General Picture of Breast Cancer in Turkey

Cancer is a big threat to public health in Turkey and the incidence of all cancers has increased seriously in recent years (Özmen et al., 2019). The infrastructure and expenditures created by the government are not enough for early diagnosis and effective treatment of this disease in Turkey (Gultekin et al., 2018). To create new models in cancer control and to reduce cancer mortality rates, the Ministry of Health (MoH) affiliated Cancer Early Diagnosis Screening and Training Centers (KETEMs) throughout the country these centers improve the awareness of the importance of prevention and early diagnosis of breast cancer in Turkey (MoH, 2022; Özmen et al., 2019). KETEM centers organize cancer screenings in 81 provinces. In recent years, an increase has been observed in the number of KETEM centers in Turkey. Figure 2 shows an increase in the number of KETEM centers in Turkey. It is seen that the number of KETEM centers, which was 132 in 2014, increased to 175 in 2020 (MoH, 2022).

Figure 3 points out the distribution of total cancer incidence (per 100,000 World standard population) by year and sex. It is easy to interpret from this figure that there is a high fluctuating trend for total cancer incidence between 2010 and 2017. Moreover, it can be seen that total cancer incidence is higher among the male population than the female population in Turkey.

Figure 4 shows the incidence of the three most common types of cancer among women from 2010 to 2017 in Turkey. It can be seen that the major cancer type is breast. After breast cancer thyroid and colorectal cancers are common types, respectively. Figure 4 also shows that there is an increasing trend from 2010 to 2017 in different types of cancer incidences.

Literature suggests that an increase in the incidence of breast cancer points out that there is a need to improve awareness of breast cancer, implementing population-based screening programs, and reducing delays are the key strategies to fight against breast cancer in Turkey (Özmen et al., 2019). Additionally, the literature defends the idea that young breast cancer patients have a lower rate of survival than old

Figure 2. Number of MoH affiliated cancer early diagnosis, screening and training centers (KETEM) in Turkey, 2014 to 2020
(Ministry of Health (MoH). (2022). Health Statistics Yearbook-2020)

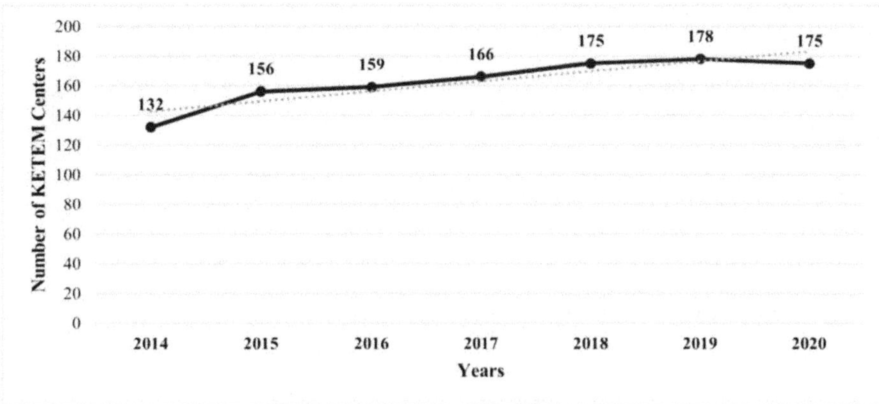

Figure 3. Total cancer incidence by years and sex (per 100.000, world standard population), Turkey, 2010 to 2017
(Ministry of Health (MoH). (2022). Health Statistics Yearbook-2020)

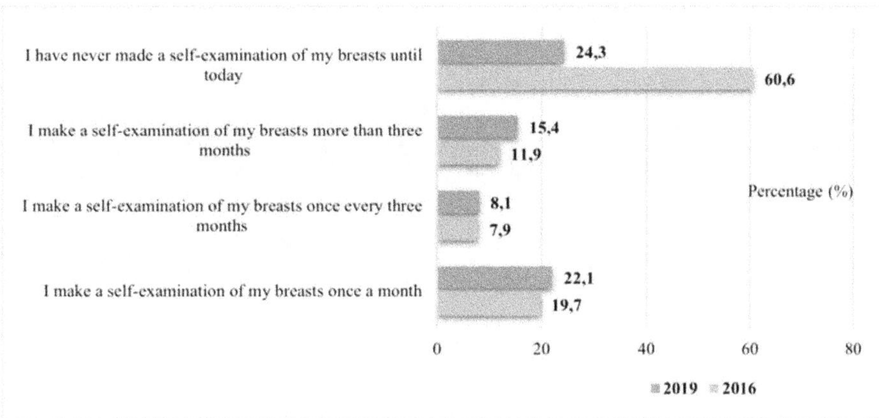

Figure 4. Total cancer incidence in Turkey and the three most common cancer types in women
(Ministry of Health (MoH). (2022). Health Statistics Yearbook-2020)

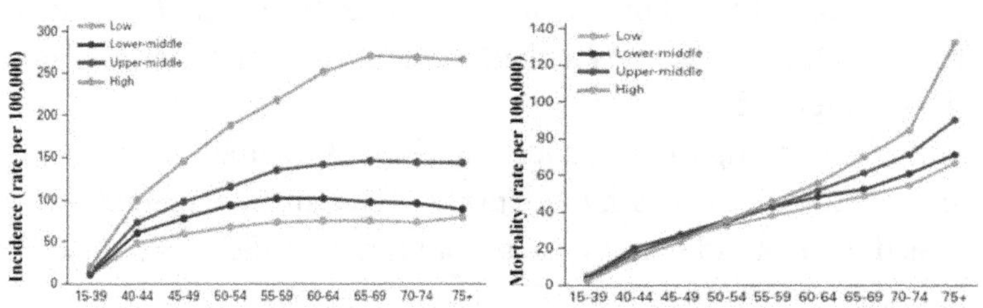

Figure 5. The status of the 15 and over aged individuals regarding making self-examination of breast (%), 2016-2019
(Ministry of Health (MoH). (2022). Health Statistics Yearbook-2020)

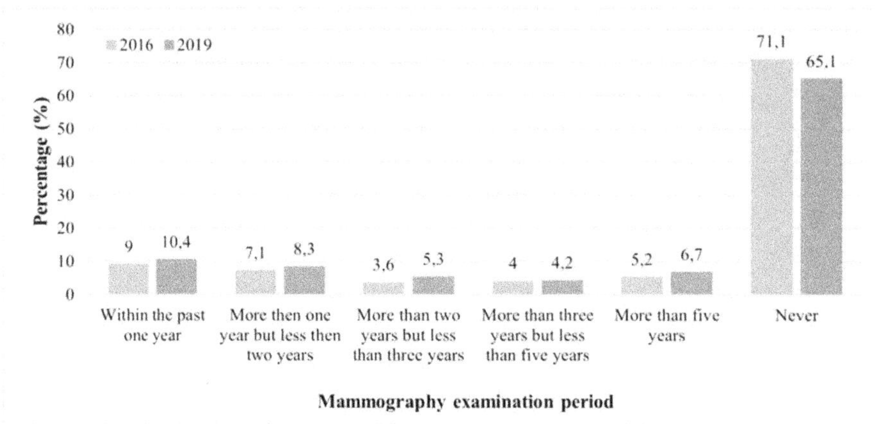

Figure 6. Distribution of the status of 15 and over aged individuals regarding having mammography, 2016-2019
(TurkStat, Health Interview Survey 2019)

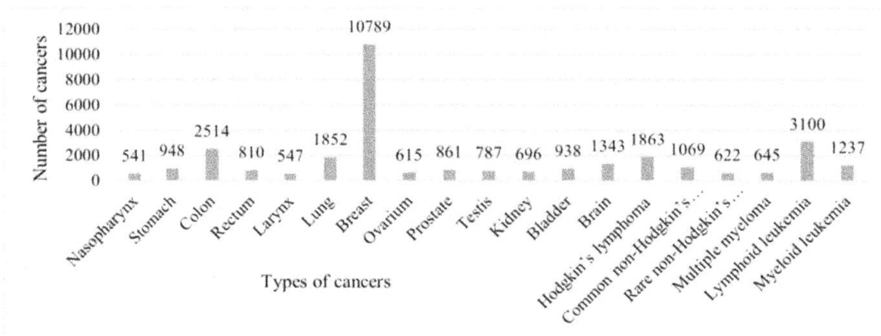

breast cancer patients if they are diagnosed in previous stages. In other words, early diagnosis methods are important for survival. Self-examination is one of the early diagnosis methods of breast cancer. MoH Health Promotion-Turkey research report states that in 2016, 60.6% of women aged 15 and over did not perform breast self-examination at all, and only 11.9% did breast self-examination every 2-3 months. It is stated that in 2019, 24.3% of women aged 15 and over have never done breast self-exams, and only 15.4% do breast self-exams every 2-3 months. Although there has been an increase in the rate of breast self-examination by women aged 15 and over from 2016 to 2019, it is known that this is not yet at the desired level. These results show that there is a need for health promotion programs to encourage self-examination in Turkey (see Figure 5).

For early diagnosis and improving breast cancer survival over time, mammography detection is essential (Kirag & Kızılkaya, 2019). According to TurkStat Health Interview Survey for the year 2019, 65.1% of 15 and over aged women did not have mammography in their lives (see Figure 6).

Cost of Breast Cancer in Turkey

Cancer is a costly disease. Because of the increasing incidence and unawareness of people living in rural parts of the country, there is a need to focus on the costs of breast cancer in Turkey. It is important to remember that in Turkey more than 90% of the population is under the coverage of General Health Insurance and costly cancer disease treatment is provided by the government (SSI, 2020). However, there exists a small number of studies in the literature about the cost-effectiveness of cancer treatment. One of these limited studies emphasizes the cost-effectiveness of gen-expressing profiling in breast cancer care compared with traditional treatment (Özmen et al., 2019). According to the findings of the study conducted by Özmen et al. (2017) to determine the potential cost-effectiveness of a population-based mammography screening program in Turkey for the years 2009-2019, the strategies of the Bahcesehir Mammography Screening Project (BMSP) and the Turkish National Breast Cancer Registry Program (TNBCRP) were compared. Accordingly, it was determined that the BMSP program showed an additional cost of 1,491,727 ₺ compared to the TNBCRP (Özmen et al., 2017) (See Table 1).

Turkey is in the mainland of Anatolia, and it has several neighboring countries from Europe and Asia. Despite Turkey's strong position, the forecast reports maintain that developments are dependent on the maintenance of a stable political and security environment in the country. The possible reasons for political instabilities are anti-government protests and the conflict in close neighboring countries of Turkey, especially in Syria (Tekin, 2015). Syria is one of the LMICs on the Eastern shore of the Mediterranean Sea. In 2014 according to UN statistics, the Syrian population was generally characterized by a young age structure. Unemployment among youth increased between the years 2000 and 2010. Since the outset of the conflict in March 2011, an increasing number of refugees from the Syrian Arab Republic (Syria) came to Turkey and The Republic of Turkey followed an open-door policy for refugees. As a result, the number of Syrians crossing the border into Turkey has dramatically increased. The distribution of socio-demographic characteristics of refugees shows that the gender distribution of Syrians is balanced and 50.90% of them are men and 49.10% of them are women. However, the education levels of Syrian refugees are very low, and a high percentage of Syrians graduated from primary school (26%) and were illiterate (23%) (AFAD, 2017). Syrian women are unaware of breast cancer (Bohsas et al., 2022). In the next section, we focus on the flow of Syrian refugees into Turkey and point out the need to control NCDs and breast cancer among them.

Table 1. Cancer costs in Turkey (2009-2019)

Costs	BMSP	TNBCRP
Cost of screening including false positives	1.875.260 ₺	0
Cost of diagnosis and treatment	1.392.228 ₺	1.716.107 ₺
Cost due to work loss	322.214 ₺	383.818 ₺
Total Cost	3.579.499 ₺	2.087.772 ₺
BMSP: Bahçeşehir Mammography Screening Project; TNBCRP: Turkish National Breast Cancer Registry Program; ₺: Turkish Liras		

Reference: Özmen et. all. (2017). Cost-effectiveness of breast cancer screening in Turkey, a developing country: Results from Bahçeşehir Mammography Screening Project. European Journal of Breast Health, 13(3), 117.

Flows of Syrian Refugees Into Turkey and Their Health Status

Political instabilities and military confrontation are the main reasons for the refugee crisis in the Middle East especially in Syria. The number of people affected by international conflict in the Syrian Arab Republic (Syria) is continuing to increase (UN, 2020). According to the United Nations High Commissioner of Refugees (UNHCR), over 3 million fled to Syria's immediate neighbors Turkey, Lebanon, Jordan, and Iraq for the years between 2011-2013 (UNHCR, 2014). Since the civil war in Syria that started in March 2011, the Republic of Turkey has followed an open-door policy for Syrian refugees, and the number of Syrians crossing the border into Turkey has increased significantly. Despite Europe's response to the refugee crisis has been limited, most of the Syrian refugees are hosted by Middle East countries. Turkey is the largest host of refugees. Most of the Syrian refugees in Turkey came from the region close to the Syrian-Turkish border which is also the region's intense conflict. According to the UNHCR statistics, mobility trends of Syrian refugees show that 2 million Syrians registered by UNHCR in Egypt, Iraq, Jordan, and Lebanon. Moreover, 3.5 million Syrians are registered by the Government of Turkey, additionally, more than 41.742 Syrian refugees are registered in North Africa (UNHCR, 2023). Figure 7 highlights the increasing trend of registered Syrian refugees from 2013 to 2022.

AFAD (Prime Ministry Disaster & Emergency Management Authority) is a national disaster and emergency management authority that successfully coordinated Turkey's response to several devastating earthquakes and floods among others and helped survivors get their lives. AFAD completed successful missions to improve humanitarian assistance in nearly 50 countries around the globe. The agency runs a network of several refugee camps to provide access to housing, healthcare, and educational support (AFAD, 2017). Figure 8 shows cities a large number of refugees are living in Turkey. These cities are located on the Syrian border of Turkey, as shown in red color on Turkey's map. The high number of refugees are living in Şanlıurfa, Gaziantep, and Kilis for the year 2017, respectively.

Turkey hosts a large number of refugees in the region. Due to this high number, of health problems of refugees, have a potential risk factor for Turkey, thus continuous monitoring of Syrian refugees' access to health services is critically important. Figure 9 presents percentages of Syrian refugees' access to medication by considering gender distribution (Syrians living in camps and non-camp settings are

Figure 7. Trend of registered Syrian refugees
(UNHCR (2023) Trend of Registered Syrian Refugees)

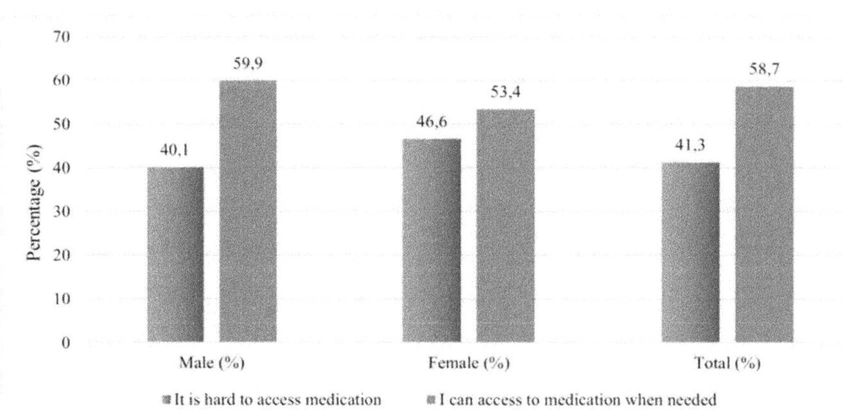

Figure 8. Number of refugees living in the camps
(AFAD Republic of Turkey Prime Ministry Disaster and Emergency Management Presidency, Syrian Refugees in Turkey, 2017, Field survey on demographic on demographic view, living conditions and future expectations of Syrians in Turkey)

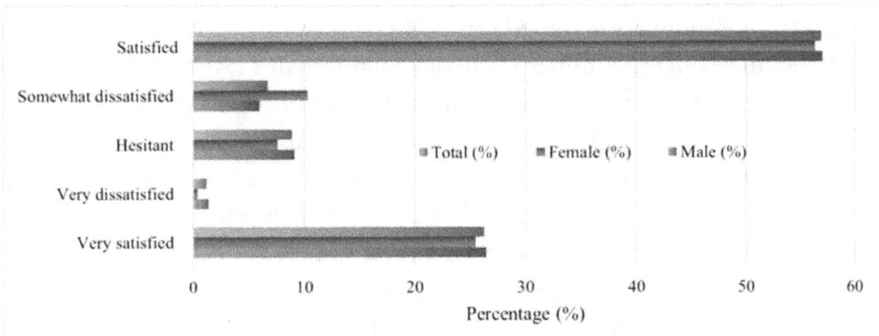

Figure 9. Access of Syrians to medications, 2017
(AFAD Republic of Turkey Prime Ministry Disaster and Emergency Management Presidency, Syrian Refugees in Turkey, 2017, Field survey on demographic on demographic view, living conditions and future expectations of Syrians in Turkey)

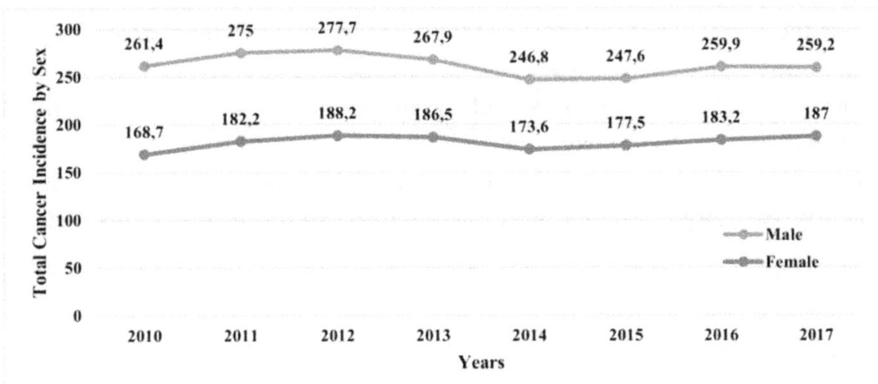

Figure 10. Satisfaction rates of Syrians with regard to the health services they enjoyed in Turkey, 2017
(AFAD Republic of Turkey Prime Ministry Disaster and Emergency Management Presidency, Syrian Refugees in Turkey, 2017, Field survey on demographic on demographic view, living conditions and future expectations of Syrians in Turkey)

included in the percentages). Considering the gender distribution of Syrian refugees' access to medicine, it is seen that 59.9% of men and 53.4% of women can access medicine when they need it (AFAD, 2017).

Figure 10 shows that satisfaction rates of Syrians concerning health services they enjoyed in Turkey show that a high majority of them are satisfied (56.90%) with health services. Moreover, the percentage of satisfaction with health services is higher for males than females (AFAD, 2017).

In Turkey, MoH has implemented a detailed survey to examine the health status of Syrian refugees in collaboration with AFAD and WHO named: "*Health Status Survey of Syrian Refugees Living in Turkey: Noncommunicable Disease Risk Factor Surveillance among Syrian Refugees*" (AFAD, 2016). This survey includes five major risk factors classified as follows: daily cigarette smoking, consuming less than 5 portions per day of fruit and /or vegetables, failing to meet physical activity recommendations, being overweight or obese, and having high blood pressure. These risk factors are showing the overall risk for NCDs. Table 2 indicates that 58.7% of Syrian refugees aged 18-69 were at high risk (with 3-5 risk factors). Moreover, having 3-5 risk factors were more common among men (61.3%) than women (56.1%). It is noticeable that a remarkable percentage of men (81.7%) and women (87.1%) aged 45-69 years have more than 3 risk factors (AFAD, 2016).

Due to this increased health problems of refugees are a potential risk factor for public health in Turkey. Chronic bronchitis, diabetes, and hypertension are diseases refugees face. Because of the high potential of disease increases, there is a need to take early action to combat diseases that refugees face. To draw attention to this situation WHO made a call to assist the Government in Turkey in sustaining a high level of health care services for the host and Syrian refugee population. In addition to that, Turkey has provided technical assistance to health sector partners in a range of public health issues, including communicable disease control, detection, and response (WHO, 2020). Women's health is essential in terms of reproductive capacity, maternal morbidity, and the future health status of the community. In

Table 2. Summary of combined risk factors

Age group (years)	n	% with 0 risk factors	95% C.I.	% with 1-2 risk factors	95% C.I.	% with 3-5 risk factors	95% C.I.
Men							
18-44	273	0.3	-0.2-0.7	45.1	39.0-51.2	45.7	48.6-60.8
45-69	141	0.8	-0.8-2.4	17.5	10.7-24.2	81.7	74.9-88.6
18-69	414	0.4	-0.2-0.9	38.3	33.3-43.3	61.3	56.3-66.3
Women							
18-44	440	0.24	-0.2-0.7	53.7	49.0-58.3	46.1	41.5-50.7
45-69	184	-	-	12.9	7.9-17.8	87.1	82.2-92.1
18-69	624	0.19	-0.2-0.5	43.8	39.8-47.8	56.1	52.1-60.1
Total							
18-44	713	0.3	-0.1-0.6	49.4	45.6-53.3	50.3	46.5-54.1
45-69	325	0.4	-0.4-1.2	15.13	11.0-19.3	84.5	80.3-88.7
18-69	1038	0.3	0.0-0.6	41.1	37.9-44.3	58.7	55.5-61.8

Reference: AFAD Republic of Turkey Prime Ministry Disaster and Emergency Management Presidency, 2016, Health Status Survey of Syrian Refugees in Turkey.

this regard, the following section gives a brief overview of Syrian refugee women's health status by focusing on cancers.

The Need to Increase Awareness of NCDs and Breast Cancer Among Syrian Refugees

Despite the number of refugee camps that have existed for many years, little information is available on cancer and other chronic diseases in this context. With a poor understanding of the cancer burden in refugee populations in LMICs, UNHCR reports that little additional cancer-related information is available. In other words, underreporting of cancer will likely remain a problem, especially in the absence of screening and detection programs (Walker et al., 2022).

Cervical cancer screening is an essential part of women's routine health care and it is associated with reduced incidence and mortality from the disease. According to the AFAD study results about cervical cancer screening of Syrian women's shows of all adult women aged 18-69 years, 7.2% had a screening for cervical cancer in the year 2016. Accordingly, it shows the age groups and cervical cancer screening percentages among Syrian women. refugee women, It is noteworthy that a low percentage (8%) of young women aged 30-44 have cervical cancer screening (AFAD, 2017). Improvements in the number of cervical cancer screenings are critical for cervical health which provides major public health advances in the 20th century (Small Jr et al., 2017).

In addition to the prevalence of NCDs, breast cancer is an increasing threat to MICs. Previous literature suggests that in Syria for the years 2009 and 2011, breast cancer accounted for 222 (33.1%) of 670 approved applications. In Syria average cost per cancer treatment was $3978 in 2010, and $4981

Figure 11. Types of cancer and the total number of cancer cases, 2012-2015
(Göktaş B, Yılmaz S, Gönenç İM, Akbulut Y, SözüerA. (2018). Cancer Incidence Among Syrian Refugees in Turkey, 2012–2015. International Migration & Integration. 19:253-258)

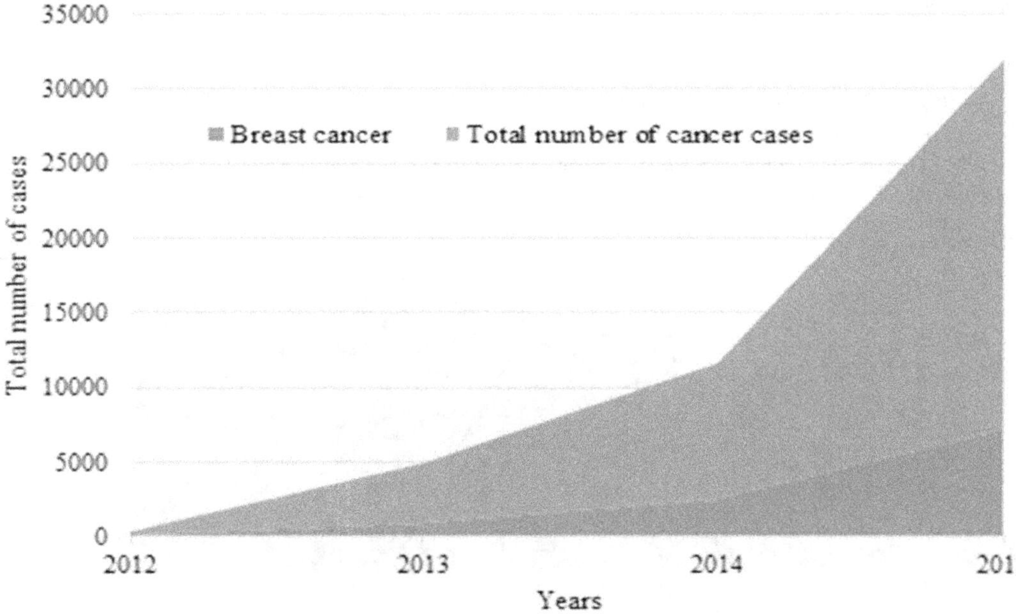

Table 3. Cancer types and incidence among Syrian refugees according to age groups, 2012-2015

Type of cancer	Age groups		
	0-18 years	19-64 years	65 and over
Nasopharynx	9	506	26
Stomach	1	824	123
Colon	6	2212	296
Rectum	7	653	150
Larynx	2	361	184
Lung	12	1293	547
Breast	4	9977	808
Ovarium	10	580	25
Prostate	2	327	532
Testis	37	741	9
Kidney	356	313	27
Bladder	14	617	307
Brain	593	699	51
Hodgkin's lymphoma	487	1341	35
Common non-Hodgkin's lymphoma	169	771	129
Rare non-Hodgkin's lymphoma	238	355	29
Multiple myeloma	-	482	163
Lymphoid leukemia	2586	459	55
Myeloid leukemia	230	953	54
Others	1966	3902	598
Total number of cancer cases	6729	27366	4148

Reference: Göktaş B, Yılmaz S, Gönenç İM, Akbulut Y, Sözüer A. (2018). Cancer Incidence Among Syrian Refugees in Turkey, 2012–2015. International Migration & Integration. 19:253-258.

Figure 12. Changes in the number of breast cancer and total number of cancer cases among Syrian refugees between the years 2012 and 2015
(Göktaş B, Yılmaz S, Gönenç İM, Akbulut Y, Sözüer A. (2018). Cancer Incidence Among Syrian Refugees in Turkey, 2012–2015. International Migration & Integration. 19:253-258)

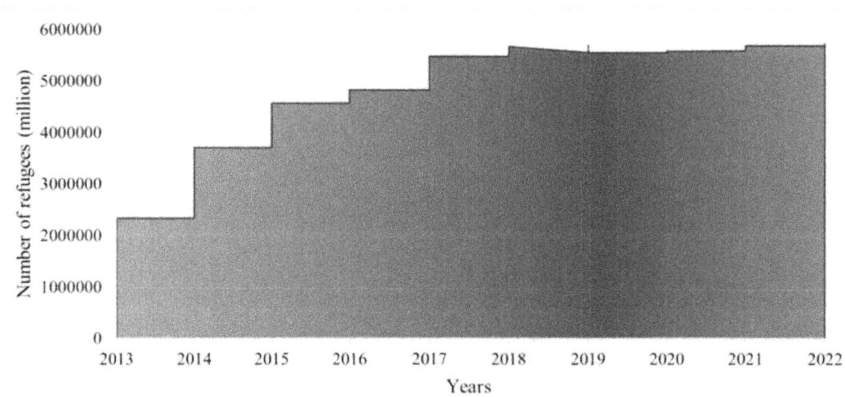

in 2011 (Spiegel et al., 2014). Lack of breast cancer awareness, inaccessibility of health care screening, unaffordable treatment, and competing health care needs such as communicable diseases are important risk factors for breast cancer in these societies. The current emphasis on breast cancer is on creating breast cancer awareness among the public and utilizing media which is the main source of information for public health (Spiegel et al., 2014). Göktaş et al. (2018) conducted a retrospective study of 38.243 refugees with cancer by obtaining data from MoH, Institution of Public Hospitals in Turkey from 2012 to 2015. Figure 11 shows that, the number of breast cancer cases is high among Syrian refugees with a total number of 10789 cases (Göktaş et al., 2018).

Table 3 highlights cancer types and incidence among Syrian refugees according to age groups between the years 2012 and 2015. It is seen that the number of breast cancer cases is high among Syrian refugees between the 19-64 years of age group (Göktaş et al., 2018).

Figure 12 indicates an increasing trend of breast cancer cases and the total number of cancer cases among Syrian refugees in Turkey from 2012 to 2015. There has been a remarkable increase in breast cancer and the total number of cancer cases among Syrian refugees between the years 2012-2015 (Göktaş et al., 2018). The incidence of breast cancer will continue to rise disproportionately in LMICs, and demographic changes and age-related problems among older refugees lead to problems in delivering sustainable cancer services. This increasing trend will continue in the next future regarding cancer care in host countries (Alawa et al., 2020). Early diagnosis and treatment of breast cancer are important to improve the health status of women citizens and refugee people. Moreover, improving health and education services for refugees is a key issue to fight against the increase in cancer cases.

DISCUSSION

This study provides a review of the increasing incidence of breast cancer in MICs by specifically focusing on Turkey, in the age of the Syrian refugee crisis. The reason for a close look at breast cancer is that it is the most common type of cancer and the incidence of breast cancer is increasing among women in MICs. Turkey is one of the MICs and has an emerging economy. Nowadays, Turkey's socio-economic dynamics are threatened by political instabilities in the region. One of the major reasons for these instabilities is the refugee crisis. Turkey is a major hosting country of refugees and it is still hosting one million Syrian people and Syrian refugees are faced with high risk of NCDs. This study points out the current situation and cost of breast cancer in MICs by focusing on Turkey and the current refugee flow into this country.

The scarcity of financial resources is the major limitation to combat with social and health outcomes of high refugee flows for policymakers in MICs. MICs are facing difficulties in managing their poor populations' health needs. This socio-political crisis will affect primary cancer prevention by affecting personal lifestyle choices, environmental risk factors, and public policy on cancer prevention (Kerschbaum & Nüssler, 2019). On the other hand, despite MICs having low financial resources compared with high-income countries, the burden of diseases increasing in these countries. Cancer is one of the most common NCDs among women in developed and developing countries. However, diagnosis and treatment of cancer in refugees are neglected in MICs. Literature suggests that cancer in refugees causes a substantial burden on the health system of host countries (Abdul-Khalek et al., 2020) and breast cancer is the most prevalent cancer type in the Arab World among females (Hashim et al., 2018). In Turkey, a remarkable increase in breast cancer cases among Syrian refugees between the years 2012 and 2015 necessitates further policy actions to better monitor and control women's health in Turkey (Göktaş et al., 2018).

The 1951 Refugee Convention states that refugees can access only health services equivalent to that of the host population. Priorities for UNHCR are immunization, nutritional support, control of communicable diseases, and epidemics. Cancer, cardiovascular, and chronic diseases have become the priority of both developed and developing countries (World Bank, 2020). Despite the high percentage (56.90%) of Syrian refugees who are satisfied with health services in Turkey (AFAD, 2017), there is a long way to go in to fight against chronic diseases and cancer among refugees.

In light of an increasing trend in breast cancer cases in MICs, policymakers should improve the number of early and advanced stages at diagnosis. Because early detection and cure are cost-effective ways of treating breast cancer and overcoming a high number of cancer cases. Additionally, well-performed breast self-examinations with a physician who could interpret the women's findings were critical for the success of early diagnosis of breast cancer. In this regard, effective planning of physicians and nursing personnel is critical to enhancing women's awareness of NCDs and breast cancer. Collaborations with international health and humanitarian aid organizations, such as WHO will provide many lights to improve the number of health personnel and quality of cancer care outcomes. A deep understanding of societal dynamics in the region and continuous monitoring of Syrian refugees' health outcomes is highly recommended.

CONCLUSION

The mounting cases of non-communicable diseases (NCDs) and the escalating incidence of breast cancer within the Syrian refugee population in Turkey highlight a pressing public health concern. It is evident that the prevalence of breast cancer among Syrian refugee women in Turkey is on the rise, signaling the urgent need for proactive measures. Cancer, particularly in its advanced stages, imposes a substantial economic burden on both individuals and the healthcare system. While the cost of treating breast cancer is relatively lower in the early stages of the disease in Turkey, the financial strain intensifies as the cancer progresses. In light of these challenges, it is imperative to formulate comprehensive policies that prioritize early detection, continuous monitoring, and effective treatment strategies for cancer patients, especially within the Syrian refugee community. Initiatives aimed at bolstering early diagnosis and treatment, such as the establishment of more accessible diagnostic centers, the promotion of self-examination, and the implementation of mammography screening programs, are of paramount importance. Collaboration with international health organizations can further enhance the resources and expertise available for tackling breast cancer within this vulnerable population.

Additionally, raising awareness about breast cancer through targeted education programs tailored to the needs of refugees is indispensable. To curb the rising incidence of breast cancer and its associated burden, Turkey must invest in the expansion of nationwide cancer screening and prevention programs. This endeavor is particularly crucial given Turkey's proximity to the ongoing refugee crisis, as it ensures that healthcare resources are optimized and made available to those who need them the most. In this context, policymakers can take important steps toward mitigating the impact of breast cancer on Syrian refugees and the broader population by adopting a multifaceted approach that includes early detection, accessibility to treatment, international cooperation, and community education.

REFERENCES

Abdul-Khalek, R. A., Guo, P., Sharp, F., Gheorghe, A., Shamieh, O., Kutluk, T., Fouad, F., Coutts, A., Aggarwal, A., Mukherji, D., Abu-Sittah, G., Chalkidou, K., & Sullivan, R. (2020). The economic burden of cancer care for Syrian refugees: A population-based modelling study. *The Lancet. Oncology*, *21*(5), 637–644. doi:10.1016/S1470-2045(20)30067-X PMID:32359488

AFAD (Republic of Turkey Prime Ministry Disaster and Emergency Management Presidency). (2016). *Health status survey of Syrian refugees in Turkey*. Halk Sağlığı Kurumu.

AFAD (Republic of Turkey Prime Ministry Disaster and Emergency Management Presidency). (2017). *Field survey on demographic view, living conditions and future expectations of Syrians in Turkey*. Prime Ministry Disaster and Emergency Management Presidency.

Alawa, J., Hamade, O., Alayleh, A., Fayad, L., & Khoshnood, K. (2020). Cancer awareness and barriers to medical treatment among Syrian refugees and Lebanese citizens in Lebanon. *Journal of Cancer Education*, *35*(4), 709–717. doi:10.100713187-019-01516-3 PMID:30924080

Anderson, B. O., Ilbawi, A. M., Fidarova, E., Weiderpass, E., Stevens, L., Abdel-Wahab, M., & Mikkelsen, B. (2021). The global breast cancer initiative: A strategic collaboration to strengthen health care for non-communicable diseases. *The Lancet Oncology*, *22*(5), 578–581. doi:10.1016/S1470-2045(21)00071-1 PMID:33691141

Bellanger, M., Zeinomar, N., Tehranifar, P., & Terry, M. B. (2018). Are global breast cancer incidence and mortality patterns related to country-specific economic development and prevention strategies? *Journal of Global Oncology*, *4*(4), 1–16. doi:10.1200/JGO.17.00207 PMID:30085889

Bohsas, H., Swed, S., Alibrahim, H., Sawaf, B., & Elsayed, M. (2022). Assessment awareness of breast cancer signs, risk factors, and barriers: An online cross-sectional study in Syria. *International Journal of Medical Students*, *10*, S178.

Bray, F., Ferlay, J., Soerjomataram, I., Siegel, R. L., Torre, L. A., & Jemal, A. (2018). Global cancer statistics 2018: GLOBOCAN estimates of incidence and mortality worldwide for 36 cancers in 185 countries. *CA: a Cancer Journal for Clinicians*, *68*(6), 394–424. doi:10.3322/caac.21492 PMID:30207593

Budreviciute, A., Damiati, S., Sabir, D. K., Onder, K., Schuller-Goetzburg, P., Plakys, G., Katileviciute, A., Khoja, S., & Kodzius, R. (2020). Management and prevention strategies for non-communicable diseases (NCDs) and their risk factors. *Frontiers in Public Health*, *8*, 1–11. doi:10.3389/fpubh.2020.574111 PMID:33324597

Carrera, P. M., Kantarjian, H. M., & Blinder, V. S. (2018). The Financial burden and distress of patients with cancer: Understanding and stepping-up action on the financial toxicity of cancer treatment. *CA: a Cancer Journal for Clinicians*, *68*(2), 153–165. doi:10.3322/caac.21443 PMID:29338071

Chen, S., Cao, Z., Prettner, K., Kuhn, M., Yang, J., Jiao, L., Wang, Z., Li, W., Geldsetzer, P., Bärnighausen, T., Bloom, D. E., & Wang, C. (2023). Estimates and projections of the global economic cost of 29 cancers in 204 countries and territories from 2020 to 2050. *JAMA Oncology*, *9*(4), 465–472. doi:10.1001/jamaoncol.2022.7826 PMID:36821107

Dankó, D. (2014). Health technology assessment in middle-income countries: Recommendations for a balanced assessment system. *Journal of Market Access & Health Policy*, *2*(1), 23181. doi:10.3402/jmahp.v2.23181 PMID:27226832

Dare, A. J., Knapp, G. C., Romanoff, A., Olasehinde, O., Famurewa, O. C., Komolafe, A. O., Olatoke, S., Katung, A., Alatise, O. I., & Kingham, T. P. (2021). High-burden cancers in middle-income countries: A review of prevention and early detection strategies targeting at-risk populationsprevention and early detection of cancers in MICs. *Cancer Prevention Research (Philadelphia, Pa.)*, *14*(12), 1061–1074. doi:10.1158/1940-6207.CAPR-20-0571 PMID:34507972

de Sanjose, S., & Tsu, V. D. (2019). Prevention of cervical and breast cancer mortality in low-and middle-income countries: A window of opportunity. *International Journal of Women's Health*, *11*, 381–386. doi:10.2147/IJWH.S197115 PMID:31308762

Elghazawy, H., Bakkach, J., Zaghloul, M. S., Abusanad, A., Hussein, M. M., Alorabi, M., eldin, N. B., Helal, T., Zaghloul, T. M., Venkatesulu, B. P., Elghazaly, H., & Al-Sukhun, S. (2020). Implementation of breast cancer continuum of care in low-and middle-income countries during the COVID-19 pandemic. *Future Oncology (London, England)*, *16*(31), 2551–2567. doi:10.2217/fon-2020-0574 PMID:32715776

Ezzati, M., Pearson-Stuttard, J., Bennett, J. E., & Mathers, C. D. (2018). Acting on non-communicable diseases in low-and middle-income tropical countries. *Nature*, *559*(7715), 507–516. doi:10.103841586-018-0306-9 PMID:30046068

Ginsburg, O., Rositch, A., Conteh, L., Mutebi, M., Paskett, E., & Subramanian, S. (2018). Breast cancer disparities among women in low-and middle-income countries. *Current Breast Cancer Reports*, *10*(3), 179–186. doi:10.100712609-018-0286-7

Göktaş, B., Yılmaz, S., Gönenç, İ. M., Akbulut, Y., & Sözüer, A. (2018). Cancer incidence among Syrian refugees in Turkey, 2012–2015. *Journal of International Migration and Integration*, *19*(2), 253–258. doi:10.100712134-018-0549-1

Gultekin, M., Ozturk, C., Karaca, S., Boztaş, G., Turan, S. H., Dundar, S., Hacikamiloglu, E., Araz, L., Murtuza, K., & Keskinkilic, B. (2018). Centralization of mammography reporting with mobile trucks: Turkish experience. *Preventive Medicine Reports*, *10*, 317–322. doi:10.1016/j.pmedr.2018.04.008 PMID:29868386

Hashim, M. J., Al-Shamsi, F. A., Al-Marzooqi, N. A., Al-Qasemi, S. S., Mokdad, A. H., & Khan, G. (2018). Burden of breast cancer in the arab world: Findings from global burden of disease, 2016. *Journal of Epidemiology and Global Health*, *8*(1-2), 54–58. doi:10.2991/j.jegh.2018.09.003 PMID:30859788

Hearn, J., Ssinabulya, I., Schwartz, J. I., Akiteng, A. R., Ross, H. J., & Cafazzo, J. A. (2019). Self-management of non-communicable diseases in low-and middle-income countries: A scoping review. *PLoS One*, *14*(7), e0219141. doi:10.1371/journal.pone.0219141 PMID:31269070

Hernández-Vásquez, A., Rojas-Roque, C., Vargas-Fernández, R., & Rosselli, D. (2020). Measuring out-of-pocket payment, catastrophic health expenditure and the related socioeconomic inequality in Peru: A comparison between 2008 and 2017. *Journal of Preventive Medicine and Public Health*, *53*(4), 266–274. doi:10.3961/jpmph.20.035 PMID:32752596

IARC (International Agency for Research on Cancer). (2023). *Population Fact Sheets:Income Levels*. IARC. https://gco.iarc.fr/today/fact-sheets-populations

Islam, S. M. S., Tabassum, R., Liu, Y., Chen, S., Redfern, J., Kim, S. Y., Ball, K., Maddison, R., & Chow, C. K. (2019). The role of social media in preventing and managing non-communicable diseases in low-and-middle income countries: Hope or hype? *Health Policy and Technology*, *8*(1), 96–101. doi:10.1016/j.hlpt.2019.01.001

Jakovljevic, M., Jakab, M., Gerdtham, U., McDaid, D., Ogura, S., Varavikova, E., Merrick, J., Adany, R., Okunade, A., & Getzen, T. E. (2019). Comparative financing analysis and political economy of noncommunicable diseases. *Journal of Medical Economics*, *22*(8), 722–727. doi:10.1080/13696998.2019.1600523 PMID:30913928

Kerschbaum, E., & Nüssler, V. (2019). Cancer prevention with nutrition and lifestyle. *Visceral Medicine*, *35*(4), 204–209. doi:10.1159/000501776 PMID:31602380

Kirag, N., & Kızılkaya, M. (2019). Application of the champion health belief model to determine beliefs and behaviors of Turkish women academicians regarding breast cancer screening: A cross sectional descriptive study. *BMC Women's Health*, *19*(1), 1–10. doi:10.118612905-019-0828-9 PMID:31694619

MoH (Ministry of Health). (2022). *Health Statistics Year Book-2020*. Republic of Türkiye Ministry of Health General Directorate of Health Information Systems Republic of Türkiye Ministry of Health General Directorate of Health Information Systems.

Mustacchi, G. (2021). Cost/benefit evaluations in low-middle/upper-middle income countries: Biases about "out of pocket money". *Current Medical Research and Opinion*, *7*(5), 819–820. doi:10.1080/03007995.2021.1893674 PMID:33617396

Ndubuisi, N. E. (2021). Noncommunicable diseases prevention in low-and middle-income countries: An overview of health in all policies (HiAP). *INQUIRY: The Journal of Health Care Organization, Provision, and Financing*, *58*, 1–6. PMID:34420412

Niessen, L. W., Mohan, D., Akuoku, J. K., Mirelman, A. J., Ahmed, S., Koehlmoos, T. P., Trujillo, A., Khan, J., & Peters, D. H. (2018). Tackling socioeconomic inequalities and non-communicable diseases in low-income and middle-income countries under the sustainable development agenda. *Lancet*, *391*(10134), 2036–2046. doi:10.1016/S0140-6736(18)30482-3 PMID:29627160

O'Neill, K. M., Mandigo, M., Pyda, J., Nazaire, Y., Greenberg, S. L., Gillies, R., & Damuse, R. (2015). Out-of-pocket expenses incurred by patients obtaining free breast cancer care in Haiti: A pilot study. *Surgery*, *158*(3), 747–755. doi:10.1016/j.surg.2015.04.040 PMID:26150200

OECD. (2021). *Health at a Glance 2021*. Organisation for Economic Cooperation and Development. https://www.oecd-ilibrary.org/sites/ae3016b9-en/index.html?itemId=/content/publication/ae3016b9-en

Özmen, V., Gürdal, S. Ö., Cabioğlu, N., Özcinar, B., Özaydın, A. N., Kayhan, A., Aribal, E., Sahin, C., Saip, P., & Alagöz, O. (2017). Cost-effectiveness of breast cancer screening in Turkey, a developing country: Results from Bahçeşehir Mammography Screening Project. *European Journal of Breast Health*, *13*(3), 117–122. doi:10.5152/ejbh.2017.3528 PMID:28894850

Özmen, V., Özmen, T., & Doğru, V. (2019). Breast cancer in Turkey; an analysis of 20.000 patients with breast cancer. *European Journal of Breast Health, 15*(3), 141–146. doi:10.5152/ejbh.2019.4890 PMID:31312788

Pramesh, C., Badwe, R. A., Bhoo-Pathy, N., Booth, C. M., Chinnaswamy, G., Dare, A. J., & Gospodarowicz, M. (2022). Priorities for cancer research in low-and middle-income countries: A global perspective. *Nature Medicine, 28*(4), 649–657. doi:10.103841591-022-01738-x PMID:35440716

Prodhan, A. S. U., Islam, D. Z., Khandker, S. S., Jamiruddin, M. R., Abdullah, A., Godman, B., & Adnan, N. (2023). Breast cancer management in the era of Covid-19; key issues, contemporary strategies, and future implications. *Breast Cancer: Targets and Therapy*, 51-89.

Schrecker, T. (2020). Globalization and health: Political grand challenges. *Review of International Political Economy, 27*(1), 26–47. doi:10.1080/09692290.2019.1607768

Shah, S. C., Kayamba, V., Peek, R. M. Jr, & Heimburger, D. (2019). Cancer control in low-and middle-income countries: Is it time to consider screening? *Journal of Global Oncology, 5*(5), 1–8. doi:10.1200/JGO.18.00200 PMID:30908147

Small, W. Jr, Bacon, M. A., Bajaj, A., Chuang, L. T., Fisher, B. J., Harkenrider, M. M., & Viswanathan, A. N. (2017). Cervical cancer: A global health crisis. *Cancer, 123*(13), 2404–2412. doi:10.1002/cncr.30667 PMID:28464289

Spiegel, P., Khalifa, A., & Mateen, F. J. (2014). Cancer in refugees in Jordan and Syria between 2009 and 2012: Challenges and the way forward in humanitarian emergencies. *The Lancet. Oncology, 15*(7), e290–e297. doi:10.1016/S1470-2045(14)70067-1 PMID:24872112

SSI (Turkish Social Security Institution). (2020). *Strategic plan (2019–2023)*. Republic of Turkey Ministry of Health Strasser.

Tekin, E. (2015). The impacts of political and economic uncertainties on the tourism industry in Turkey. *Mediterranean Journal of Social Sciences, 6*(2 S5), 265.

TurkStat. (2019). *Türkiye health survey-2019.* TurkStat. https://data.tuik.gov.tr/Bulten/Index?p=Turkiye-Saglik-Arastirmasi-2019-33661

UN. (2020). *Refugees.* UN. https://www.unhcr. org/refugees.html?gclid=CjwKCAjwqJ_1BRBZEiwAv73uwH-g8pVAEhyeyYc8ARjr R5JLE4Qn4K1XVdsHRVEqXVtbPhwVscnR9xoCdtwQAvD_BwE

UNHCR (United Nations High Commissioner for Refugees). (2014). *Syria regional refugee response.* UNHCR. http://data.unhcr.org/syrianrefugees/regional.php

UNHCR (United Nations High Commissioner for Refugees). (2023). *Trend of registered Syrian refugees.* UNHCR. https://data.unhcr.org/en/situations/syria

Vincent Rajkumar, S. (2020). The high cost of prescription drugs: Causes and solutions. *Blood Cancer Journal, 10*(6), 1–5. doi:10.103841408-020-0338-x PMID:32576816

Walker, P. F., Settgast, A., & DeSilva, M. B. (2022). Cancer screening in refugees and immigrants: A global perspective. *The American Journal of Tropical Medicine and Hygiene*, *106*(6), 1593–1600. doi:10.4269/ajtmh.21-0692 PMID:35533696

WHO. (2013). *Turkey, country cooperation strategy at a glance*. WHO. https://www.who.int/country-focus/cooperation_strategy/ccsbrief_tur_en.pdf

WHO. (2018). *Noncommunicable Diseases country profiles 2018*. WHO. https://www.who.int/publications/i/item/9789241514620

WHO. (2020). *The World Bank in Turkey country snapshot: an overview of the World Bank's work in Turkey*. WHO. https://thedocs.worldbank.org/en/doc/1818015 87125378913-0080022020/original/TurkeySnapshotApr2020.pdf

WHO. (2021). *Breast cancer: prevention and control*. WHO. https://www. who.int/news-room/fact-sheets/detail/breast-cancer

WHO. (2022). *Noncommunicable diseases: progress monitor 2022*. WHO. https://www.who.int/publications/i/item/9789240047761

WHO. (2023a). *Noncommunicable diseases*. WHO. https://www.who.int/news-room/fact-sheets/detail/noncommunicable-diseases#:~:text=Noncommunicable%20diseases%20(NCDs)%20kill%2041,%2D%20and%20middle%2Dincome%20countries

WHO. (2023b). *Global breast cancer initiative implementation framework: assessing, strengthening and scaling up of services for the early detection and management of breast cancer*. Geneva: World Health Organization. https://www.who.int/initiatives/global-breast-cancer-initiative

Williams, J., Allen, L., Wickramasinghe, K., Mikkelsen, B., Roberts, N., & Townsend, N. (2018). A systematic review of associations between non-communicable diseases and socioeconomic status within low-and lower-middle-income countries. *Journal of Global Health*, *8*(2), 020409. doi:10.7189/jogh.08.020409 PMID:30140435

World Bank. (2020). *How tackling the world's deadliest diseases can boost a healthy workforce and economic growth*. World Bank. https://www.worldbank.org/en/news/immersive-story/2020/02/06/tackling-worlds-deadliest-diseases-can-boost-healthy-workforce-and-economic-growth

World Bank. (2022). *World Bank country and lending groups* World Bank. https://datahelpdesk.worldbank.org/knowledgebase/articles/906519-world-bank-country-and-lending-groups

World Bank. (2023). *Middle-Income countries: overview*. World Bank. https://www.worldbank.org/en/country/mic/overview

Compilation of References

Abd Elrahman, A. S., & Asaad, M. (2021). Urban design & urban planning: A critical analysis to the theoretical relationship gap. *Ain Shams Engineering Journal, 12*(1), 1163–1173. doi:10.1016/j.asej.2020.04.020

Abdeen, F. N., Fernando, T., Kulatunga, U., Hettige, S., & Ranasinghe, A. (2021). Challenges in Multi-agency collaboration in disaster management: A Sri Lankan perspective. *International Journal of Disaster Risk Reduction, 62*, 102399. doi:10.1016/j.ijdrr.2021.102399

Abdul-Khalek, R. A., Guo, P., Sharp, F., Gheorghe, A., Shamieh, O., Kutluk, T., Fouad, F., Coutts, A., Aggarwal, A., Mukherji, D., Abu-Sittah, G., Chalkidou, K., & Sullivan, R. (2020). The economic burden of cancer care for Syrian refugees: A population-based modelling study. *The Lancet. Oncology, 21*(5), 637–644. doi:10.1016/S1470-2045(20)30067-X PMID:32359488

About Us. (2022). American Telemedicine Association. https://www.americantelemed.org/about-us/

Abramson, A. (2021). *Capturing the benefits of remote learning*. APA. https://www.apa.org/monitor/2021/09/cover-remote-learning

Adbulrauf, A. L., & Fombad, M. C. (2017). Personal Data Protection in Nigeria: Reflections on Opportunities, Options and Challenges to Legal Reforms. *The Liverpool Law Review, 38*(2), 105–135. doi:10.100710991-016-9189-8

Adedoyin, O. B., & Soykan, E. (2020). COVID-19 pandemic and online learning: The challenges and opportunities. *Interactive Learning Environments*, 1–13. doi:10.1080/10494820.2020

Adu, K., & Ngulube, P. (2016). Preserving the digital heritage of public institutions in Ghana in the wake of electronic government. *Library Hi Tech, 34*(4), 748–763. doi:10.1108/LHT-07-2016-0077

AFAD (Republic of Turkey Prime Ministry Disaster and Emergency Management Presidency). (2016). *Health status survey of Syrian refugees in Turkey*. Halk Sağlığı Kurumu.

AFAD (Republic of Turkey Prime Ministry Disaster and Emergency Management Presidency). (2017). *Field survey on demographic view, living conditions and future expectations of Syrians in Turkey*. Prime Ministry Disaster and Emergency Management Presidency.

Agency for Healthcare Research and Quality. (2018, June). *Access and Disparities in Access to Health Care*. AHRQ. https://www.ahrq.gov/research/findings/nhqrdr/nhqdr15/access.html

Agrawal, B. B. W. S. (2023, July 5). *Returning to the Office: The Current, Preferred and Future State of Remote Work*. Gallup.com. https://www.gallup.com/workplace/397751/returning-office-current-preferred-future-state-remote-work.aspx

Ahmad, M. (2023a). Connecting People and Places: How Citizen Diplomacy and VGI Are Strengthening Disaster Response and Community Development. In Global Perspectives on the Emerging Trends in Public Diplomacy (pp. 195–226). IGI Global.

Ahmad, M., & Ali, A. (2023). Mapping the Future of Sustainable Development Through Cloud-Based Solutions: A Case Study of OpenStreetMap. In Promoting Sustainable Management Through Technological Innovation (pp. 153–176). IGI Global. doi:10.4018/978-1-6684-9979-5.ch011

Ahmad, M. (2023b). Exploring the Role of OpenStreetMap in Mapping Religious Tourism in Pakistan for Sustainable Development. In *Experiences, Advantages, and Economic Dimensions of Pilgrimage Routes*. IGI Global. doi:10.4018/978-1-6684-9923-8.ch002

Ahmad, M. (2023c). Unleashing Business Potential: Harnessing OpenStreetMap for Intelligent Growth and Sustainability. In *Data-Driven Intelligent Business Sustainability*. IGI Global.

Ahmed, M. Z., Ahmed, O., Aibao, Z., Hanbin, S., Siyu, L., & Ahmad, A. (2020). Epidemic of COVID-19 in China and associated psychological problems. *Asian Journal of Psychiatry*, *51*, 102092. doi:10.1016/j.ajp.2020.102092 PMID:32315963

Ahmed, S. M., Ahmed, S., & Mayo, R. (2020). African American's perceptions of COVID-19 exposure risks, testing, and willingness to participate in biomedical research: A United States cross-sectional survey. *Journal of Health Disparities Research and Practice*, *13*(5), 1–12.

Akandere, G., & Zerenler, M. (2022). Doğu Avrupa ülkelerinin çevresel ve ekonomik performansının bütünleşik CRITIC-TOPSIS yöntemiyle değerlendirilmesi. *Selçuk Üniversitesi Sosyal Bilimler Meslek Yüksekokulu Dergisi, 25*(Özel Sayı), 524-535. doi:10.29249/selcuksbmyd.1156615

Akbulut, O. Y. (2019). CRITIC ve EDAS yöntemleri ile İş Bankası'nın 2009-2018 yılları arasındaki performansının analizi. *Ekonomi Politika ve Finans Araştırmaları Dergisi*, *4*(2), 249–263. doi:10.30784/epfad.594762

Akiki, T. J., Averill, C. L., & Abdallah, C. G. (2017). A network-based neurobiological model of PTSD: Evidence from structural and functional neuroimaging studies. *Current Psychiatry Reports*, *19*(11), 1–10. doi:10.100711920-017-0840-4 PMID:28924828

Akkuş, B., & İzci, N. A. (2018). Sistem yaklaşımı, kavramları ve yönetim. *Recep Tayyip Erdoğan University Journal of Social Sciences, 4*(7), 223-237. https://dergipark.org.tr/en/pub/rteusbe/issue/34053/370196

Aktan, C. C., & Börü, D. (2006). Corporate Social Responsibility, Corporate Culture, Organizations, Rules and Institutions (Editor; Coşkun Can Aktan). CMB Publication No: 195. CMB.

Al Jowf, G. I., Ahmed, Z. T., Reijnders, R. A., de Nijs, L., & Eijssen, L. M. (2023). To Predict, Prevent, and Manage Post-Traumatic Stress Disorder (PTSD): A Review of Pathophysiology, Treatment, and Biomarkers. *International Journal of Molecular Sciences*, *24*(6), 5238. doi:10.3390/ijms24065238 PMID:36982313

Al Ridhawi, I., Otoum, S., Aloqaily, M., Jararweh, Y., & Baker, T. (2020). Providing secure and reliable communication for next-generation networks in smart cities. *Sustainable Cities and Society*, *56*, 102080. doi:10.1016/j.scs.2020.102080

AlamS. (2017, January). Impact of Blue Ocean Strategy on Organizational Performance: A Literature Review Toward Implementation Logic. SSRN. doi:10.9790/487X-1901030119

Alawa, J., Hamade, O., Alayleh, A., Fayad, L., & Khoshnood, K. (2020). Cancer awareness and barriers to medical treatment among Syrian refugees and Lebanese citizens in Lebanon. *Journal of Cancer Education*, *35*(4), 709–717. doi:10.100713187-019-01516-3 PMID:30924080

Albahri, A. S., Hamid, R. A., Albahri, O. S., & Zaidan, A. A. (2021). Detection-based prioritisation: Framework of multi-laboratory characteristics for asymptomatic COVID-19 carriers based on integrated Entropy–TOPSIS methods. *Artificial Intelligence in Medicine*, *111*, 101983. doi:10.1016/j.artmed.2020.101983 PMID:33461683

Albert-Henry, T. (2018, August 2). *3 significant ethical issues medical school does not prepare you for. American Medical Association.* AMA. https://www.ama-assn.org/education/accelerating-change-medical-education/3-big-ethical-issues-medical-school-doesn-t-prepare

Alexander, A., De Smet, A., Langstaff, M., & Ravid, D. (2021). What employees are saying about the future of remote work. McKinsey & Company.

Alexander, A., Mysore, M., Cracknell, R., De Smet, A., Langstaff, M., & Ravid, D. (2021, May 17). *What executives are saying about the future of hybrid work*. McKinsey & Company. https://www.mckinsey.com/capabilities/people-and-organizational-performance/our-insights/what-executives-are-saying-about-the-future-of-hybrid-work

Al-Gasawneh, J. A., AlZubi, K. N., Anuar, M. M., & Padlee, S. F. ul-Haque, A., & Saputra, J. (2022, January 12). *Marketing Performance Sustainability in the Jordanian Hospitality Industry: The Roles of Customer Relationship Management and Service Quality*. ProQuest. https://www.proquest.com/central/docview/2621383917/fulltextPDF/33C795C2AD3243F7PQ/2?accountid=14244

Al-Habaibeh, A., Watkins, M., Waried, K., & Javareshk, M. B. (2021). Challenges and opportunities of remotely working from home during Covid-19 pandemic. *Global Transitions*, *3*, 99–108. doi:10.1016/j.glt.2021.11.001 PMID:34870136

Alkan, N., & Kahraman, C. (2021). Evaluation of government strategies against COVID-19 pandemic using q-rung orthopair fuzzy TOPSIS method. *Applied Soft Computing*, *110*, 107653. doi:10.1016/j.asoc.2021.107653 PMID:34226821

Allam, Z., & Jones, D. S. (2021). Future (post-COVID) digital, smart, and sustainable cities in the wake of 6G: Digital twins, immersive realities, and new urban economies. *Land use policy*, *101*, 105201. American Diabetes Association (ADA) Diabetes Technology Working Group. *Diabetes Care*, *43*(1), 250–260.

Allard, I. N. (2011). Examining the relationship between organizational culture and performance: Moderators of the culture gap. *Dissertation Abstracts International Section A*, *71*, 3329.

Alper, D. (2011). Patent Degerlemesi ve Reel Opsiyonlar/Patent Valuation and Real Options. *Business and Economics Research Journal*, *2*(1), 153.

Alsan, M., & Wanamaker, M. (2018). Tuskegee and the Health of Black Men. *The Quarterly Journal of Economics*, *133*(1), 407–455. doi:10.1093/qje/qjx029 PMID:30505005

Al-Sharif, R., & Pokharel, S. (2022). Smart city dimensions and associated risks: Review of the literature. *Sustainable Cities and Society*, *77*, 103542. doi:10.1016/j.scs.2021.103542

Alshrari, A. S., Hudu, S. A., Imran, M., Asdaq, S. M. B., Ali, A. M., & Rabbani, S. I. (2022). Innovations and development of COVID-19 vaccines: A patent review. *Journal of Infection and Public Health*, *15*(1), 123–131. doi:10.1016/j.jiph.2021.10.021 PMID:34742639

Altuntas, F., & Gok, M. S. (2021). The effect of COVID-19 pandemic on domestic tourism: A DEMATEL method analysis on quarantine decisions. *International Journal of Hospitality Management*, *92*, 102719. doi:10.1016/j.ijhm.2020.102719 PMID:33519015

Altuntas, S., Erdogan, Z., & Dereli, T. (2020). A clustering-based approach for the evaluation of candidate emerging technologies. *Scientometrics*, *124*(2), 1157–1177. doi:10.100711192-020-03535-0

American Cancer Society. (2020). *Exercise for cancer survivors.* ACS. https://www.cancer.org/treatment/survivorship-during-and-after-treatment/staying-active/exercise.html

American College of Obstetricians and Gynecologists Committee on Ethics. (2007). *Ethical Decision Making in Obstetrics and Gynecology.* (ACOG Committee Opinion Number 390). ACOG. https://www.acog.org/from_home/publications/ethics/co390.pdf

American Medical Association. (2011). Opinion 2.30 – Information from Unethical Experiments. *Code of Medical Ethics.* AMA. https://www.ama-assn.org/ama/pub/physician-resources/medical-ethics/code-medical-ethics/opinion230.page?

American Medical Association. (2018). Sexual harassment in medicine: An analysis of surveys, A.M.A. policies, and best practices. AMA. https://www.ama-assn.org/system/files/2019-03/sexual-harassment-medicine.pdf

American Medical Association. (n.d.). *Ethics Timeline: 1941 to 1980.* AMA. https://www.ama-assn.org/ama/pub/physician-resources/medical-ethics/code-medical-ethics/history-ama-ethics/ethics-timeline-1941-1980.page?

American Nurses Association. (2001). *Code of Ethics for Nurses.* ANA. http://nursingworld.org/MainMenuCategories/EthicsStandards/CodeofEthicsforNurses.aspx

American Psychiatric Association. (2013). *Diagnostic and statistical manual of mental disorders* (5th ed.). APA.

American Society of Plastic Surgeons. (2020). *Plastic Surgery Statistics Report 2020.* ASPS National Clearinghouse of Plastic Surgery Procedural Statistics. https://www.plasticsurgery.org/documents/News/Statistics/2020/plastic-surgery-statistics-full-report-2020.pdf

Americans are embracing flexible work—and they want more of it. (2022, June 23). McKinsey & Company. https://www.mckinsey.com/industries/real-estate/our-insights/americans-are-embracing-flexible-work-and-they-want-more-of-it

Amico, L. (2023, May 20). *The Realities of Remote Work.* Harvard Business Review. https://hbr.org/2021/10/the-realities-of-remote-work

Anderson, B. O., Ilbawi, A. M., Fidarova, E., Weiderpass, E., Stevens, L., Abdel-Wahab, M., & Mikkelsen, B. (2021). The global breast cancer initiative: A strategic collaboration to strengthen health care for non-communicable diseases. *The Lancet Oncology, 22*(5), 578–581. doi:10.1016/S1470-2045(21)00071-1 PMID:33691141

Anderson, D. L. (2019). *Organization development: The process of leading organizational change.* Sage Publications.

Anderson, T. (2011). *The theory and practice of online learning* (2nd ed.). AU Press.

Anders, R., Willemin-Petignat, L., Rolli Salathé, C., Samson, A. C., & Putois, B. (2022). Profiling police forces against stress: Risk and protective factors for post-traumatic stress disorder and burnout in police officers. *International Journal of Environmental Research and Public Health, 19*(15), 9218. doi:10.3390/ijerph19159218 PMID:35954576

Ansari, A. (2020). Prevalence of sexual harassment in medical education: A systematic review. *Journal of Medical Education and Curricular Development, 7*(1), 1–7.

Antoniou, V. (2017). Considerations of Privacy, Ethics and Legal Issues in Volunteered Geographic Information. In Mapping and the Citizen Sensor. doi:10.5334/bbf.f

Antoniou, V., & Potsiou, C. (2020). A deep learning method to accelerate the disaster response process. *Remote Sensing (Basel), 12*(3), 544. doi:10.3390/rs12030544

Arapostathis, S. G., & Karantzia, M. (2019). Mapping information of fire events, from VGI source (Twitter), for effective disaster management (in Greece); the fire of north-east Attica, august 2017, (Greece) case study. In Advances in Science, Technology and Innovation. doi:10.1007/978-3-030-01440-7_60

Argyris, C. (1983). Action science and intervention. *The Journal of Applied Behavioral Science, 19*(2), 115–135. doi:10.1177/002188638301900204

Asogwa, E. B., Ezeani, N. C., & Asogwa, N. M. (2021). Status of electronic records management (e-RM) in African university libraries: Experience from Nigerian universities. Status of e-RM in African university libraries. *Library Management, 42*(8/9), 515–530. doi:10.1108/LM-04-2021-0036

Assumpção, T. H., Mathre, N., Bogatinoska, B., Jonoski, A., Popescu, I., Trifanov, C., & Cimpan, K. (2019). How to monitor the Danube Delta through citizens' campaigns: Sontea-Fortuna case study. In Geophysical Research Abstracts.

Attaran, M. (2022). Blockchain technology in healthcare: Challenges and opportunities. *International Journal of Healthcare Management, 15*(1), 70–83. doi:10.1080/20479700.2020.1843887

Attard, C., & Holmes, K. (2020). "It gives you that sense of hope": An exploration of technology use to mediate student engagement with mathematics. *Heliyon, 6*(1), e02945. doi:10.1016/j.heliyon.2019.e02945 PMID:31922039

Aydın, G. Z. (2021). Evaluation of regional health services in Turkey using CRITIC based TOPSIS methods. *Uluslararası Sağlık Yönetimi ve Stratejileri Araştırma Dergisi, 7*(2), 412-433. https://dergipark.org.tr/en/pub/usaysad/issue/64697/988692

Ayoung, D. A., Boatbil, S. C., & Baada, N. F. (2016). Disaster preparedness libraries Insights from polytechnic librarians in Ghana. *Information Development, 32*(5), 1296–1305. doi:10.1177/0266666915588794

Azariasgari, E., & Hosseinali, F. (2023). Evaluating the VGI Users' Level of Expertise. *International Journal of Applied Geospatial Research, 14*(1), 1–16. doi:10.4018/IJAGR.316770

B., M. (2020, July 24). *Why is it so hard to find a black therapist?* TODAY.com. https://www.today.com/tmrw/why-it-so-hard-find-black-therapist-t187608

Babatunde, M., & Ighravwe, D. (2019). A CRITIC-TOPSIS framework for hybrid renewable energy systems evaluation under techno-economic requirements. *Journal of Project Management, 4*(2), 109–126. doi:10.5267/j.jpm.2018.12.001

Bachmann, P., & Frutos-Bencze, D. (2022). R&D and innovation efforts during the COVID-19 pandemic: The role of universities. *Journal of Innovation & Knowledge, 7*(4), 100238. doi:10.1016/j.jik.2022.100238

Bai, Z., Luo, S., Zhang, L., Wu, S., & Chi, I. (2020). Acceptance and commitment therapy (ACT) to reduce depression: A systematic review and meta-analysis. Journal of affective disorders, 260, 728–737.

Bajpai, P. (2022). Why China Is "The World's Factory". *Investopedia.* https://www.investopedia.com/articles/investing/102214/why-china-worlds-factory.asp#:~:text=In%20addition%20to%20its%20low,duties%2C%20and%20competitive%20currency%20practices

Baker, R., Caplan, A., Emanuel, L. L., & Latham, S. R. (1997). Crisis, Ethics, and the American Medical Association 1847 and 1997. *JAMA, 278*(2), 163-164. doi:10.1001/jama.278.2.163

Balcik, B., & Beamon,, B. (2008). *Facility Location In Humanitarian Relief.*

Balogun, T., & Kalusopa, T. (2021). A framework for digital preservation of Indigenous knowledge system (IKS) in repositories in South Africa. *Records Management Journal, 31*(2), 176–196. doi:10.1108/RMJ-12-2020-0042

Bandura, A. (1977). *Social learning theory.* Prentice-Hall.

Barbarosoğlu, G., Özdamar, L., & Çevik, A. (2002). An Interactive Approach For Hierarchical Analysis Of Helicopter Logistics In Disaster Relief Operations. *European Journal of Operational Research, 140*(1), 118–133. doi:10.1016/S0377-2217(01)00222-3

Barbazza, A., Collan, M., Fedrizzi, M., & Luukka, P. (2014). Consensus modeling in multiple criteria multi-expert real options-based valuation of patents. *In Intelligent Systems' 2014: Proceedings of the 7th IEEE International Conference Intelligent Systems IS'2014*. Springer International Publishing.10.1007/978-3-319-11313-5_25

Barker, K. H. (1997). The Business of Government and the Future of Government *Archives. The American Archivist*, *60*(2), 234–252. doi:10.17723/aarc.60.2.p728118660482531

Barrero, J. M., Bloom, N., & Davis, S. J. (2021). Why Working from Home Will Stick. *National Bureau of Economic Research Working Paper Series*. NBER. https://www.nber.org/papers/ w28731

Barz, B., Schröter, K., Kra, A. C., & Denzler, J. (2021). Finding Relevant Flood Images on Twitter Using Content-Based Filters. Lecture Notes in Computer Science (Including Subseries Lecture Notes in Artificial Intelligence and Lecture Notes in Bioinformatics). 12666 LNCS. doi:10.1007/978-3-030-68780-9_1

Bauer, G. F., Hämmig, O., Schaufeli, W. B., & Taris, T. W. (2014). A critical review of the job demands-resources model: Implications for improving work and health. *Bridging occupational, organizational and public health: A transdisciplinary approach*, 43-68.

Becker, A. M., & Knoop, A. A. (2019). Digital Health Technologies: An Overview and Considerations for Policymakers. *Journal of Medical Internet Research*, *21*(3), e11453. doi:10.2196/11453

Beckhard, R., & Harris, R. T. (1987). *Organizational transitions: Managing complex change*. Addison-Wesley.

Beemsterboer, P. (2010). *Ethics and Law in Dental Hygiene* (2nd ed.). Saunders Elsevier.

Bellanger, M., Zeinomar, N., Tehranifar, P., & Terry, M. B. (2018). Are global breast cancer incidence and mortality patterns related to country-specific economic development and prevention strategies? *Journal of Global Oncology*, *4*(4), 1–16. doi:10.1200/JGO.17.00207 PMID:30085889

Bellmann, L., & Hübler, O. (2021). Working from home, job satisfaction and work–life balance–robust or heterogeneous links? *International Journal of Manpower*, *42*(3), 424–441. doi:10.1108/IJM-10-2019-0458

Benis, A., Tamburis, O., Chronaki, C., & Moen, A. (2021). One digital health: A unified framework for future health ecosystems. *Journal of Medical Internet Research*, *23*(2), e22189. doi:10.2196/22189 PMID:33492240

Berkowitz, E. N. (2022). *Essentials of Health Care Marketing* (5th ed.). Jones & Bartlett Learning.

Bhadra, D., Dhar, N. R., & Salam, M. A. (2022). Sensitivity analysis of the integrated AHP-TOPSIS and CRITIC-TOPSIS method for selection of the natural fiber. *Materials Today: Proceedings*, *56*, 2618–2629. doi:10.1016/j.matpr.2021.09.178

Bhopal, R. (2008). Ethical issues in health research on ethnic minority populations: Focusing on inclusion and exclusion. The Association of Research Ethics Committees. *Research Ethics*, *4*(1), 15–19. https://journals.sagepub.com/doi/pdf/10.1177/174701610800400104. doi:10.1177/174701610800400104

Biasetti, P., & de Mori, B. (2021). The Ethical Matrix as a Tool for Decision-Making Process in Conservation. *Frontiers in Environmental Science*, *9*, 584636. doi:10.3389/fenvs.2021.584636

Biggs, J. S., Willcocks, A., Burger, M., & Makeham, M. A. (2019). Digital health benefits evaluation frameworks: building the evidence to support Australia's National Digital Health Strategy. *Medical Journal of Australia*, *210*, S9-S11.

Binder, R. (2018). *Sexual harassment in medical schools: The challenge of covert retaliation as a barrier to reporting.* L.W.W. https://journals.lww.com/academicmedicine/Fulltext/2018/12000/Sexual_Harassment_in_Medical_Schools__The.17.aspx

Biswas, R. A., & Nandi, S. (2020). Teaching in virtual classroom: Challenges and opportunities. *International Journal of Engineering Applied Sciences and Technology*, *5*(1), 334–337. doi:10.33564/IJEAST.2020.v05i01.052

Bittner, C., Michel, B., & Turk, C. (2016). Turning the spotlight on the crowd: Examining the participatory ethics and practices of crisis mapping. *ACME, 15*(1).

Bixenstine, B. A. (2023). Employment Law Implications of a Remote Workplace. *Dispute Resolution Journal, 76*(3).

Blatt, A. J. (2015). The benefits and risks of volunteered geographic information. *Journal of Map & Geography Libraries*, *11*(1), 99–104. doi:10.1080/15420353.2015.1009609

Bloom, N., Davis, S. J., & Zhestkova, Y. (2021, May). Covid-19 shifted patent applications toward technologies that support working from home. *AEA Papers and Proceedings. American Economic Association*, *111*, 263–266. doi:10.1257/pandp.20211057

Bloom, N., Liang, J., Roberts, J., & Ying, Z. J. (2015). Does working from home work? Evidence from a Chinese experiment. *The Quarterly Journal of Economics*, *130*(1), 165–218. doi:10.1093/qje/qju032

Blume, A. W. (2016). Advances in Substance Abuse Prevention and Treatment Interventions Among Racial, Ethnic, and Sexual Minority Populations. *Alcohol Research : Current Reviews*, *38*(1), 47–54. PMID:27159811

Bohsas, H., Swed, S., Alibrahim, H., Sawaf, B., & Elsayed, M. (2022). Assessment awareness of breast cancer signs, risk factors, and barriers: An online cross-sectional study in Syria. *International Journal of Medical Students*, *10*, S178.

Bowker, L., & Villamizar, C. (2017). Embedding a records manager as a strategy for helping to positively influence an organization's records management culture. Embedding a records manager. *Records Management Journal*, *27*(1), 57–68. doi:10.1108/RMJ-02-2016-0005

Bozkurt, A., & Sharma, R. C. (2020). Emergency remote teaching in a time of global crisis due to Coronavirus pandemic. *Asian Journal of Distance Education*, *15*(1), 1–6.

Brandon, D., Isaac, L., & LaVeist, T. (2005). The Legacy of Tuskegee and Trust in Medical Care: Is Tuskegee Responsible for Race Differences in Mistrust of Medical Care? - Research - Hopkins Center for Health Disparities Solutions. *Journal of the National Medical Association*, *97*(7). https://www.jhsph.edu/healthdisparities/Research/the_legacy_of_tuskegee_and_trust_in_medical_care_is_tuskegee_responsible_for_race_differences_in_mistrust_of_medical_care.html PMID:16080664

Brandt, A. (1978). Racism and Research: The Case of the Tuskegee Syphilis Study. *The Hastings Center Report*, *8*(6), 21–29. doi:10.2307/3561468 PMID:721302

Bransford, J., Brown, A., & Cocking, R. (1999). *How people learn: Brain, mind experience and school.* National Academy Press/National Research Council., Retrieved from https://www.colorado.edu/MCDB/LearningBiology/readings/Howpeople-learn.pdf

Bray, F., Ferlay, J., Soerjomataram, I., Siegel, R. L., Torre, L. A., & Jemal, A. (2018). Global cancer statistics 2018: GLOBOCAN estimates of incidence and mortality worldwide for 36 cancers in 185 countries. *CA: a Cancer Journal for Clinicians*, *68*(6), 394–424. doi:10.3322/caac.21492 PMID:30207593

Brenner Fernandes, F. (2019). *Evaluating hurricane recovery in Dominica*. University of Twente.

Brinkley, I., Willmott, B., Beatson, M., & Davies, G. (2020). *Embedding New Ways of Working: Implications for the Post-pandemic Workplace*. CIPD. https://www.cipd.co.uk/knowledge/work/ trends/working-post-pandemic

Brookings Institution. (2020). *Police use of force: What the data say*. Brookings Institution. https://www.brookings.edu/research/police-use-of-force-what-the-data-say/

Brooks, S. K., Webster, R. K., Smith, L. E., Woodland, L., Wessely, S., Greenberg, N., & Rubin, G. J. (2020). The psychological impact of quarantine and how to reduce it: Rapid review of the evidence. *Lancet*, *395*(10227), 912–920. doi:10.1016/S0140-6736(20)30460-8 PMID:32112714

Brown, N. T., Snethen, J. A., & Greenberg, C. S. (2021). When pandemics collide: the impact of COVID-19 on childhood obesity. *J Pediatr Nursing, 56*, 90–98. [PMC free article] [PubMed] [Google Scholar]

Budreviciute, A., Damiati, S., Sabir, D. K., Onder, K., Schuller-Goetzburg, P., Plakys, G., Katileviciute, A., Khoja, S., & Kodzius, R. (2020). Management and prevention strategies for non-communicable diseases (NCDs) and their risk factors. *Frontiers in Public Health*, *8*, 1–11. doi:10.3389/fpubh.2020.574111 PMID:33324597

Buffer. (2021). *State Of Remote Work 2020*. Buffer. https://buffer.com/state-of-remote-work/2020

Buira, J. (2012). Entre el Mito y la Realidad. Editorial UOC.

Bulğurcu, B. (2019). Çok nitelikli fayda teorisi ile CRITIC yöntem entegrasyonu: Akıllı teknoloji tercih örneği. *OPUS Journal of Society Research*, *13*(19), 1930–1957. doi:10.26466/opus.584123

Bumrungrad International Hospital. (2022). *Bumrungrad International Hospital*. Bumrungrad International Hospital. https://www.bumrungrad.com/en/medical-travel

Burchell, B., Miller, J., Brewin, C., Soffia, M., & Wang, S. (2023). The association between job quality and the incidence of PTSD amongst police personnel. *Policing. Journal of Policy Practice*, 17.

Burke, W. W. (2018). Organization change: Theory & practice. *Sage (Atlanta, Ga.).*

Burrell, D. N., Bhargava, N., Kemp, R. E., & Vemuganti, D. (2018). Public health and safety leadership challenges around law enforcement ethics and whistleblowing in the age of the# Black Lives Matter movement. *International Journal of Latest Research in Humanities and Social Science*, *2*, 1–12.

Burrell, D. N., Burton, S. L., & McGrath, G. E. (2023). Racially Motivated Police Brutality Is a Community Public Health Issue in the United States. [IJHSTM]. *International Journal of Health Systems and Translational Medicine*, *3*(1), 1–15. doi:10.4018/IJHSTM.315296

Businesswire. (2020). Prodoscore Research from March/April 2020: Productivity Has Increased, Led By Remote Workers. *Business Wire*. https://www.businesswire.com/news/home/20200519005295/en/

Butler, H. (2023). *The History of Remote Work: How it Became What we Know today*. Crossover. https://www.crossover.com/perspective/the-history-of-remote-work

Cahapay, M. B. (2020). Stranded college students amid corona virus disease 2019 pandemic: An existential phenomenology. *Journal of Loss and Trauma*, *25*(6-7), 598–604. doi:10.1080/15325024.2020.1770955

Cain, E. N., Kohorn, E. I., Quinlan, D. M., Latimer, K., & Schwartz, P. E. (1986). Psychosocial benefits of a cancer support group. *Cancer*, *57*(1), 183–189. doi:10.1002/1097-0142(19860101)57:1<183::AID-CNCR2820570135>3.0.CO;2-3 PMID:3079660

Carrasco, M. (2021, September 1). *Colleges Seek Virtual Mental Health Services*. Inside Higher Ed. https://www.insidehighered.com/news/2021/09/20/colleges-expand-mental-health-services-students

Carrera, P. M., Kantarjian, H. M., & Blinder, V. S. (2018). The Financial burden and distress of patients with cancer: Understanding and stepping-up action on the financial toxicity of cancer treatment. *CA: a Cancer Journal for Clinicians*, *68*(2), 153–165. doi:10.3322/caac.21443 PMID:29338071

Carroll, A. B. (1991). *The Corporate Social Responsibility Pyramid: Towards the Moral Governance of Organizational Stakeholders*. Business Horizons. http: www.cbe.wwu.edu/dunn/ Reprint.pyramidofcsr.pdf

Carroll, W. R. (2009). Organizational culture, HRM and firm performance: Examining relationships using the competing values framework in call centres. *Dissertation Abstracts International Section A*, *70*, 932.

CCOHS. (2023, June 13). *Government of Canada Canadian Centre for Occupation Health and Safety.* CCOHS. https://www.ccohs.ca/oshanswers/hsprograms/telework.html

CDC. (2011, June 15). The Tuskegee Timeline. *U.S. Public Health Service Syphilis Study at Tuskegee*. CDC. https://www.cdc.gov/tuskegee/timeline.htm

CDC. (2015). Planning for an Emergency: Strategies for Identifying and Engaging At-Risk Groups. In Center for Disease Control and Prevention.

Ceeney, N. (2008). The Role of a 21st-Century National Archive- The Relevance of the Jenkinsonian Tradition, and a Re-definition for the Information Society. *Journal of the Society of Archivists*, *29*(1), 57–71. doi:10.1080/00379810802499868

Centers for Disease Control and Prevention. (2015). *Health care access disparities: Delaying or skipping care due to cost.* CDC. https://www.cdc.gov/health disparities/health careaccess/delaying-skipping-care-due-cost.htm

Centers for Disease Control and Prevention. (2019). *Health, United States, 2018: With Special Feature on Aging*. CDC. https://www.cdc.gov/nchs/data/hus/hus18.pdf

Centers for Disease Control and Prevention. (2020). Health disparities and inequalities. CDC. https://www.cdc.gov/minorityhealth/healthdisparities/index.html

Centers for Disease Control and Prevention. (2022, July 12). *Prioritizing Minority Mental Health*. Centers for Disease Control and Prevention. https://www.cdc.gov/healthequity/features/minority-mental-health/index.html

Centers for Medicare and Medicaid Services. (2018). *National health expenditure projections 2017-2026*. CMS. https://www.cms.gov/research-statistics-data-and-systems/statistics-trends-and-reports/nationalhealthexpenddata/nhe-projections.html

Cerutti, V., Bellman, C., Both, A., Duckham, M., Jenny, B., Lemmens, R. L. G., & Ostermann, F. O. (2021). Improving the reproducibility of geospatial scientific workflows: the use of geosocial media in facilitating disaster response. In Journal of Spatial Science, 66(3). doi:10.1080/14498596.2019.1654944

Chalishazar, T. (2022). *Remote Work In IT Industry: Stats, Perks & Best Practices*. Peerbits. https://www.peerbits.com/blog/ultimate-guide-to-remote-work.html#:~:text=Remote%20working%20was%20in%20practice,compared%20to%20the%20office%20working

Chambers, E., & Boulton, M. (2011). Intervention action research as a knowledge practice. *Educational Action Research*, *19*(3), 371–387.

Chang, K., & Ong, I. (2023, May 31). *Be aware of the compliance risks of a growing remote workforce*. EY. https://www.ey.com/en_sg/you-and-the-taxman/be-aware-of-the-compliance-risks-of-a-growing-remote-workforce

Chávarro, J. M. (2023, February 27). Work-From-Home Regulations Are Coming. Companies Aren't Ready. *MIT Sloan Management Review*. https://sloanreview.mit.edu/article/work-from-home-regulations-are-coming-companies-arent-ready

Chen, S., Cao, Z., Prettner, K., Kuhn, M., Yang, J., Jiao, L., Wang, Z., Li, W., Geldsetzer, P., Bärnighausen, T., Bloom, D. E., & Wang, C. (2023). Estimates and projections of the global economic cost of 29 cancers in 204 countries and territories from 2020 to 2050. *JAMA Oncology, 9*(4), 465–472. doi:10.1001/jamaoncol.2022.7826 PMID:36821107

Chen, X., Elmes, G., Ye, X., & Chang, J. (2016). Implementing a Real-Time Twitter-Based System for Resource Dispatch in Disaster Management. *GeoJournal, 81*(6), 863–873. doi:10.100710708-016-9745-8

Chen, X., Orom, H., Hay, J. L., Waters, E. A., Schofield, E., Li, Y., & Kiviniemi, M. T. (2019). Differences in rural and urban health information access and use. *The Journal of Rural Health, 35*(3), 405–417. doi:10.1111/jrh.12335 PMID:30444935

Cheung-Judge, M., & Holbeche, L. (2021). *Organization development: A practitioner's guide for O.D. and H.R* (3rd ed.). Kogan Page.

ChimpReports. (2023). The Impact of Remote Learning on College Student Engagement. *ChimpReports*. https://chimpreports.com/the-impact-of-remote-learning-on-college-student-engagement/

Choudhury, P. (2021, July 7). Our Work-from-Anywhere future. *Harvard Business Review*. https://hbr.org/2020/11/our-work-from-anywhere-future

Christian, L. (2020). 3 ways to build a more equitable industry with purpose-driven marketing. Future of Marketing. *Think with Google*. https://www.thinkwithgoogle.com/future-of-marketing/management-and-culture/diversity-and-inclusion/social-impact/

Church, N. F. (2015). Gauging Perceived Benefits from "Working from Home" as a Job Benefit. *International Journal of Business & Economic Development, 3*(3), 81–89.

Clark, L. T., Watkins, L., Piña, I. L., Elmer, M., Akinboboye, O., Gorham, M., & Regnante, J. M. (2019). Increasing Diversity in Clinical Trials: Overcoming Critical Barriers. *Current Problems in Cardiology, 44*(5), 148–172. doi:10.1016/j.cpcardiol.2018.11.002 PMID:30545650

Cloud Hospital. (2022, May 13). *Plastic surgery market real facts you need to know.* ICloudHospital. https://icloudhospital.com/articles/inside-thailand%27s-plastic-surgery-market-real-facts-you-need-to-know

Cohen, E. (2014). Medical Tourism in Thailand. *AU-GSB e-JOURNAL, 1*(1). Retrieved from Medical Tourism in Thailand: http://www.assumptionjournal.au.edu/index.php/AU-GSB/article/view/381

Colby, S. L., & Ortman, J. M. (2015, March). *Projections of the Size and Composition of the U.S. Population: 2014 to 2060 Population Estimates and Projections*. Census. https://www.census.gov/content/dam/Census/library/publications/2015/demo/p25-1143.pdf

Collan, M., Fedrizzi, M., & Luukka, P. (2013). A multi-expert system for ranking patents: An approach based on fuzzy pay-off distributions and a TOPSIS–AHP framework. *Expert Systems with Applications, 40*(12), 4749–4759. doi:10.1016/j.eswa.2013.02.012

Collingwood, J. (2022, January 4). *ITIJ*. Retrieved from Quality Healthcare with easy access in Thailand: https://www.itij.com/latest/long-read/quality-healthcare-easy-access-thailand

Collins, K. (2020). Sexual harassment in medical education and healthcare workplaces. *Nursing Forum, 55*(4), 573–580.

Colquitt, J. A., & George, G. (2011). 'Publishing in AMJ – part 1: Topic choice'. *Academy of Management Journal, 54*(3), 432–435. doi:10.5465/amj.2011.61965960

Cooper, N. (2022). *World's Best Hospitals.* Newsweek. https://www.newsweek.com/best-hospitals-2021/thailand

Cooper, C. D., & Kurland, N. B. (2002). Telecommuting, Professional Isolation, and Employee Development in Public and Private Organizations. *Journal of Organizational Behavior*, *23*(4), 511–532. doi:10.1002/job.145

Cooper, J. (1999). Ethical Issues and Their Practical Application in a Psychological Autopsy Study of Suicide. *Journal of Clinical Nursing*, *8*(4), 467–475. doi:10.1046/j.1365-2702.1999.00276.x PMID:10624264

Cordova, M. J., Riba, M. B., & Spiegel, D. (2017). Post-traumatic stress disorder and cancer. *The Lancet. Psychiatry*, *4*(4), 330–338. doi:10.1016/S2215-0366(17)30014-7 PMID:28109647

Corrado, E. M., & Moulaison, H. L. (2014). *Digital preservation for libraries, Archives and Museums*. Rowman & Littlefield.

Cousins, J. B. (2011). Intervention action research: A methodology for developing, enacting, and evaluating interventions. *New Directions for Evaluation*, *2011*(130), 7–20.

CPA. (2019, April 23). *6 cybersecurity tips for organizations with remote workers*. CPA Canada. https://www.cpacanada.ca/en/news/atwork/2019-04-23-remote-cybersecurity

Craig, K. J. T., Fusco, N., Gunnarsdottir, T., Chamberland, L., Snowdon, J. L., & Kassler, W. J. (2021). Leveraging Data and Digital Health Technologies to Assess and Impact Social Determinants of Health (SDoH): A State-of-the-Art Literature Review. *Online Journal of Public Health Informatics*, *13*(3). doi:10.5210/ojphi.v13i3.11081 PMID:35082976

Crawford, K., & Finn, M. (2015). The limits of crisis data: Analytical and ethical challenges of using social and mobile data to understand disasters. *GeoJournal*, *80*(4), 491–502. doi:10.100710708-014-9597-z

Criscuolo, C., Gal, P., Leidecker, T., Losma, F., & Nicoletti, G. (2021). Telework after COVID-19: survey evidence from managers and workers on implications for productivity and well-being. *Département des affaires économiques de l'OCDE, blog ECOSCOPE, 28.*

Croyle, R. T., & Hunt, J. R. (1991). Coping with health threat: Social influence processes in reactions to medical test results. *Journal of Personality and Social Psychology*, *60*(3), 382–389. doi:10.1037/0022-3514.60.3.382 PMID:2027079

Dai, H., Milkman, K. L., & Riis, J. (2014). The fresh start effect: Temporal landmarks motivate aspirational behavior. *Management Science*, *60*(10), 2563–2582. doi:10.1287/mnsc.2014.1901

Dalen, J. E., & Alpert, J. S. (2018, July 15). Medical Tourists: Incoming and Outgoing. *The American Journal of Medicine*, *132*(1), 9–10. doi:10.1016/j.amjmed.2018.06.022 PMID:30016635

Daniels, N. (1996). *Justice and Justification. Reflective Equilibrium in Theory and Practice*. Cambridge University Press. doi:10.1017/CBO9780511624988

Dankó, D. (2014). Health technology assessment in middle-income countries: Recommendations for a balanced assessment system. *Journal of Market Access & Health Policy*, *2*(1), 23181. doi:10.3402/jmahp.v2.23181 PMID:27226832

Dare, A. J., Knapp, G. C., Romanoff, A., Olasehinde, O., Famurewa, O. C., Komolafe, A. O., Olatoke, S., Katung, A., Alatise, O. I., & Kingham, T. P. (2021). High-burden cancers in middle-income countries: A review of prevention and early detection strategies targeting at-risk populationsprevention and early detection of cancers in MICs. *Cancer Prevention Research (Philadelphia, Pa.)*, *14*(12), 1061–1074. doi:10.1158/1940-6207.CAPR-20-0571 PMID:34507972

Dasgupta, A., & Ghosh, S. K. (2018). A volunteered geographic information (VGI) framework for disaster management based on mobile services and SDI. In Geospatial Infrastructure, Applications and Technologies: India Case Studies. IEEE. doi:10.1007/978-981-13-2330-0_10

Dávila Morán, R.C. (2023). Influence of Remote Work on the Work Stress of Workers in the Context of the COVID-19 Pandemic: A Systematic Review. *Sustainability*, *15*, 12489. . doi:10.3390/su151612489

Dawes, D. E. (2019). The Future of Health Equity in America: Addressing the Multiple, Intersecting Determinants of Health. *Ethnicity & Disease*, *29*(Suppl 2), 343–344. doi:10.18865/ed.29.S2.343 PMID:31308602

de Araujo Andrade, T., Nascimento, J. A. C. Junior, Santos, A. M., Borges, L. P., Quintans-Junior, L. J., Walker, C. I. B., Frank, L. A., & Serafini, M. R. (2021). Technological scenario for masks in patent database during Covid-19 pandemic. *AAPS PharmSciTech*, *22*(2), 1–22. doi:10.120812249-021-01918-x PMID:33575845

De Jonge, J., & Kompier, M. A. (1997). A critical examination of the demand-control-support model from a work psychological perspective. *International Journal of Stress Management*, *4*(4), 235–258. doi:10.1023/B:IJSM.0000008152.85798.90

de Sanjose, S., & Tsu, V. D. (2019). Prevention of cervical and breast cancer mortality in low-and middle-income countries: A window of opportunity. *International Journal of Women's Health*, *11*, 381–386. doi:10.2147/IJWH.S197115 PMID:31308762

Dean, B. (2021, October 10). *Social Network Usage & Growth Statistics: How Many People Use Social Media in 2022?* Bancklinko. https://backlinko.com/social-media-users

Degrossi, L., & Albuquerque, J. De. (2014). Flood Citizen Observatory: a crowdsourcing-based approach for flood risk management in Brazil. *Agora.Icmc.Usp.Br*, 570–575.

Delaney, B., & De Jong, A. (2015). Media Archives and Digital Preservation Overcoming Cultural Barriers. *New Review of Information Networking*, *20*(1-2), 73–89. doi:10.1080/13614576.2015.1112626

Delfino, G. F., & van der Kolk, B. (2021). Remote working, management control changes, and employee responses during the COVID-19 crisis. *Accounting, Auditing & Accountability Journal*, *34*(6), 1376–1387. doi:10.1108/AAAJ-06-2020-4657

Demerouti, E., Bakker, A. B., Nachreiner, F., & Schaufeli, W. B. (2001). The job demands-resources model of burnout. *The Journal of Applied Psychology*, *86*(3), 499–512. doi:10.1037/0021-9010.86.3.499 PMID:11419809

Deniz, N. (2020). Teknoloji yönetiminde MOORA ve ARAS çok ölçütlü karar verme teknikleri ile patent değerleme. *Dumlupınar Üniversitesi Sosyal Bilimler Dergisi*, (64), 191-207. https://dergipark.org.tr/tr/pub/dpusbe/issue/53850/684050>

Deshpande, A., Sharp, H., Barroca, L., & Gregory, P. (2016). *Remote working and collaboration in agile teams*. Agile Research Network.

Devettere, R. (2010). *Practical Decision Making in Health Care Ethics: Cases and Concepts* (3rd ed.). Georgetown University Press.

Dhara, A., Kaur, G., Kishan, P. M., Majumder, A., & Yadav, R. (2022). An efficient decision support system for selecting very light business jet using CRITIC-TOPSIS method. *Aircraft Engineering and Aerospace Technology*, *94*(3), 458–472. doi:10.1108/AEAT-04-2021-0135

Dick, E. A., Raithatha, A., Musker, L., Redhead, J., Mehta, A., & Amiras, D. (2020). 'Remote reporting in the COVID-19 era: From pilot study to practice'. *Clinical Radiology*, *75*(9), 710. doi:10.1016/j.crad.2020.06.016 PMID:32654757

Digital.com Staff. (2023). 6 in 10 employers require monitoring software for remote workers. *Digital.com*. https://digital.com/6-in-10-employers-require-monitoring-software-for-remote-workers/

Dikopoulou, A., & Mihiotis, A. (2012). The contribution of records management to good governance. *The TQM Journal*, *24*(2), 123–141. doi:10.1108/17542731211215071

Dinh-Le, C., Chuang, R., Chokshi, S., & Mann, D. (2019). Wearable health technology and electronic health record integration: A scoping review and future directions. *JMIR mHealth and uHealth, 7*(9), e12861. doi:10.2196/12861 PMID:31512582

Dishman, L. (2020). Working from 'anywhere' is possible—but not sustainable. *Fast Company*. https://www.fastcompany.com/90545523/working-from-anywhere-is-possible-but-not-sustainable

Dixon, B., Johns, R. A., & Fernandez, A. (2021). The role of crowdsourced data, participatory decision-making and mapping of flood related events. *Applied Geography (Sevenoaks, England), 128*, 102393. doi:10.1016/j.apgeog.2021.102393

Dobbin, F., & Kalev, A. (2019). The promise and peril of sexual harassment programs. *Proceedings of the National Academy of Sciences, 116*(25), 12255–12260. 10.1073/pnas.1818477116

Docherty, A. (2004). Experience, functions, and benefits of a cancer support group. *Patient Education and Counseling, 55*(1), 87–93. doi:10.1016/j.pec.2003.08.002 PMID:15476994

Donnelly, R., & Johns, J. (2021). Recontextualising remote working and its HRM in the digital economy: An integrated framework for theory and practice. *International Journal of Human Resource Management, 32*(1), 84–105. doi:10.1080/09585192.2020.1737834

Do, Q. N., Mishra, N., Wulandhari, N. B. I., Ramudhin, A., Sivarajah, U., & Milligan, G. (2021). Supply chain agility responding to unprecedented changes: Empirical evidence from the UK food supply chain during COVID-19 crisis. *Supply Chain Management, 26*(6), 737–752. doi:10.1108/SCM-09-2020-0470

Downs, J. (2012). *Sick From Freedom: African-American Illness and Suffering During the Civil War and Reconstruction*. Oxford University Press. doi:10.1093/acprof:osobl/9780199758722.001.0001

Dube, K., & Nhamo, G. (2020). Evidence and impact of climate change on South African national parks. [Elsevier]. *Environmental Development*, 33.

Dube, K., Nhamo, G., & Chikodzi, D. (2021). Rising Sea level and its implications on coastal tourism development in Cape Town, South Africa. *Journal of Outdoor Recreation and Tourism, 33*, 33. doi:10.1016/j.jort.2020.100346

Dun, L., Xian-Yi, W., & Si-Ting, H. (2022). Effects of Cognitive Training and Social Support on Cancer-Related Fatigue and Quality of Life in Colorectal Cancer Survivors: A Systematic Review and Meta-Analysis. *Integrative Cancer Therapies, 21*, 15347354221081271. doi:10.1177/15347354221081271 PMID:35225053

Dunton, G. F., Do, B., & Wang, S. D. (2020). Early effects of the COVID-19 pandemic on physical activity and sedentary behavior in children living in the U.S. *BMC Public Health, 20*, 1351.

Durant, R. W., Wenzel, J. A., Scarinci, I. C., Paterniti, D. A., Fouad, M. N., Hurd, T. C., & Martin, M. Y. (2014). Perspectives on Barriers and Facilitators to Minority Recruitment for Clinical Trials Among Cancer Center Leaders, Investigators, Research Staff, and Referring Clinicians: Enhancing Minority Participation in Clinical Trials (EMPaCT). *Cancer, 120 Suppl 7*(0 7), 1097–1105. doi:10.1002/cncr.28574

Durmuşoğlu, A., & Durmuşoğlu, Z. D. U. (2022). Remembering medical ventilators and masks in the days of covıd-19: Patenting in the last decade in respiratory technologies. *IEEE Transactions on Engineering Management*, 1–15. doi:10.1109/TEM.2022.3151636

Dwarakanath, L., Kamsin, A., Rasheed, R. A., Anandhan, A., & Shuib, L. (2021). Automated Machine Learning Approaches for Emergency Response and Coordination via Social Media in the Aftermath of a Disaster: A Review. In IEEE Access, 9. doi:10.1109/ACCESS.2021.3074819

Earp, B. J., & Payton, C. F. (2001). Data Protection in the University Setting: Employee Perceptions of Student Privacy. *Proceedings of the 34th Hawaii International Conference on System Sciences*. IEEE 10.1109/HICSS.2001.927152

Easwaramoorthy, M., & Zarinpoush, F. (2006). *Interviewing For Research*. Imagine Canada.

Ebi, O. A. (2021). *Post–1996 Service delivery in South Africa: Constitutional and Social Contract perspectives*. [PhD Thesis, University of the Western Cape].

Eckle, M., Herfort, B., Yan, Y., Zipf, A., & Kuo, C. L. (2017). Towards using volunteered geographic information to monitor post-disaster recovery in tourist destinations. *Proceedings of the International ISCRAM Conference*. IEEE.

Economics Observatory. (2021, February 8). What is the likely impact of remote learning on educational outcomes? *Economics Observatory*. https://www.economicsobservatory.com/what-likely-impact-remote-learning-educational-outcomes

Edgelow, M., Legassick, K., Novecosky, J., & Fecica, A. (2023). Return to work experiences of Ontario public safety personnel with work-related psychological injuries. *Journal of Occupational Rehabilitation*, 1–12. doi:10.100710926-023-10114-6 PMID:37022655

Eisenhardt, K. M., Graebner, M. E., & Sonenshein, S. (2016). Grand Challenges and Inductive Methods: Rigor without Rigor Mortis. *Academy of Management Journal*, *59*(4), 1113–1123. doi:10.5465/amj.2016.4004

Elghazawy, H., Bakkach, J., Zaghloul, M. S., Abusanad, A., Hussein, M. M., Alorabi, M., eldin, N. B., Helal, T., Zaghloul, T. M., Venkatesulu, B. P., Elghazaly, H., & Al-Sukhun, S. (2020). Implementation of breast cancer continuum of care in low-and middle-income countries during the COVID-19 pandemic. *Future Oncology (London, England)*, *16*(31), 2551–2567. doi:10.2217/fon-2020-0574 PMID:32715776

Elliott, D. (16 Feb 2021). *In Tuskegee, Painful History Shadows Efforts to Vaccinate African Americans*. NPR. https://www.npr.org/2021/02/16/967011614/in-tuskegee-painful-history-shadows-efforts-to-vaccinate-african-americans

Elmqvist, T., Andersson, E., Frantzeskaki, N., McPhearson, T., Olsson, P., Gaffney, O., Takeuchi, K., & Folke, C. (2019). Sustainability and resilience for transformation in the urban century. *Nature Sustainability*, *2*(4), 267–273. doi:10.103841893-019-0250-1

Elshaiekh, N. E. M., Hassan, Y. A. A., & Abdallah, A. A. A. (2018, November). The impacts of remote working on workers performance. In 2018 international Arab conference on information technology (ACIT) (pp. 1-5). IEEE. doi:10.1109/ACIT.2018.8672704

Erdogan, Z., Altuntas, S., & Dereli, T. (2022). Predicting patent quality based on machine learning approach. *IEEE Transactions on Engineering Management*, 1–14. doi:10.1109/TEM.2022.3207376

Erkılıç, C. E. (2021). Hastane hizmetleri sektörünün CRITIC temelli TOPSIS yöntemi ile finansal performansının değerlendirilmesi, *Pamukkale Üniversitesi Sosyal Bilimler Enstitüsü Dergisi. Sayı*, *46*, 63–84. doi:10.30794/pausbed.865686

Ernst, H. (1998). Patent portfolios for strategic R&D planning. *Journal of Engineering and Technology Management*, *15*(4), 279–308. doi:10.1016/S0923-4748(98)00018-6

Ertemel, A. V., Menekse, A., & Camgoz Akdag, H. (2023). Smartphone addiction assessment using pythagorean Fuzzy CRITIC-TOPSIS. *Sustainability (Basel)*, *15*(5), 3955. doi:10.3390u15053955

ESDC. (2023, September 12). *Flexible work arrangements for federally regulated employees*. Government of Canada.

Eshuis, L. V., van Gelderen, M. J., van Zuiden, M., Nijdam, M. J., Vermetten, E., Olff, M., & Bakker, A. (2021). Efficacy of immersive PTSD treatments: A systematic review of virtual and augmented reality exposure therapy and a meta-analysis of virtual reality exposure therapy. *Journal of Psychiatric Research*, *143*, 516–527. doi:10.1016/j.jpsychires.2020.11.030 PMID:33248674

Evans, P. (2022). For some employers, remote work is here to stay. *Grand Rapids Business Journal.* https://www.crainsgrandrapids.com/news/real-estate/for-some-employers-remote-work-is-here-to-stay/

Express Healthcare. (2010). *Healthcare and Marketing or Healthcare Marketing?: Consumerism driving a change to result in healthcare marketing.* ProQuest. https://www.proquest.com/docview/217541725/fulltext/8C6DE098C0A74B1DPQ/1?accountid=14244

Ezzati, M., Pearson-Stuttard, J., Bennett, J. E., & Mathers, C. D. (2018). Acting on non-communicable diseases in low- and middle-income tropical countries. *Nature*, *559*(7715), 507–516. doi:10.103841586-018-0306-9 PMID:30046068

Fabiano, P. M., Perkins, H. W., Berkowitz, A., Linkenbach, J., & Stark, C. (2003). Engaging men as social justice allies in ending violence against women: Evidence for a social norms approach. *Journal of American College Health*, *52*(3), 105–112. doi:10.1080/07448480309595732 PMID:14992295

Fabunmi, A.; Paris, M & Fabunmi, M (2006). Digitization of Library Resources: Challenges and Implications for Policy and Planning. *International Journal of African & African American Studies, 5*(2) 23 – 36.

Fairfield, J. (2021, October 17). Thailand's healthcare system ranked among best in the world. *Asean Now.* https://aseannow.com/topic/1235740-thailands-healthcare-system-ranked-among-best-in-the-world/

Falciola, L., & Barbieri, M. (2022). Searching and analyzing patent-relevant Covid-19 information. *World Patent Information*, *68*, 102094. doi:10.1016/j.wpi.2022.102094

Fan, K., & Zhao, Y. (2022). Mobile health technology: A novel tool in chronic disease management. *Intelligent Medicine*, *2*(1), 41–47. doi:10.1016/j.imed.2021.06.003

Fan, S., Liu, G., Tu, Y., Zhu, J., Zhang, P., & Tian, Z. (2023). Improved multi-criteria decision making method integrating machine learning for patent competitive potential Evaluation: A case study in water pollution abatement technology. *Journal of Cleaner Production*, *403*, 136896. doi:10.1016/j.jclepro.2023.136896

Fan, W., Xu, Z., Wu, B., He, Y., & Zhang, Z. (2022). Structural multi-objective topology optimization and application based on the criteria importance through intercriteria correlation method. *Engineering Optimization*, *54*(5), 830–846. doi:10.1080/0305215X.2021.1901087

Farr, D. E., Brandt, H. M., Comer, K. D., Jackson, D. D., Pandya, K., Friedman, D. B., Ureda, J. R., Williams, D. G., Scott, D. B., Green, W., & Hébert, J. R. (2015). Cancer Research Participation Beliefs and Behaviors of a Southern Black Population: A Quantitative Analysis of the Role of Structural Factors in Cancer Research Participation. *Journal of Cancer Education*, *30*(3), 522–529. doi:10.100713187-014-0749-0 PMID:25385692

Faust, K. L., & Ven, T. V. (2014). Policing disaster: An analytical review of the literature on policing, disaster, and post-traumatic stress disorder. *Sociology Compass*, *8*(6), 614–626. doi:10.1111oc4.12160

Felstead, A. (2022). Psychological and Social Work Factors as Predictors of Mental Distress and Positive Affect: A Prospective, Multilevel Study. *PLoS One*, *11*(3), e0152220. doi:10.1371/journal.pone.0152220

Feng, Y., & Sester, M. (2018). Extraction of pluvial flood relevant volunteered geographic information (VGI) by deep learning from user generated texts and photos. *ISPRS International Journal of Geo-Information*, *7*(2), 39. Advance online publication. doi:10.3390/ijgi7020039

Fenwick, K. M., Dyer, K. E., Klap, R., Oishi, K., Moreau, J. L., Yano, E. M., Bean-Mayberry, B., Sadler, A. G., & Hamilton, A. B. (2022). Expert recommendations for designing reporting systems to address patient-perpetrated sexual harassment in healthcare settings. *Journal of General Internal Medicine*, *37*(14), 3723–3730. doi:10.100711606-022-07467-8 PMID:35266124

Fernandez, M. A., & Short, M. (2014). Wounded Warriors with PTSD: A compilation of best practices and technology in treatment. *The Professional Counselor*, *4*(2), 114–121. doi:10.15241/maf.4.2.114

Feros, D. L., Lane, L., Ciarrochi, J., & Blackledge, J. T. (2013). Acceptance and Commitment Therapy (ACT) for improving the lives of cancer patients: A preliminary study. *Psycho-Oncology*, *22*(2), 459–464. doi:10.1002/pon.2083 PMID:23382134

Ferri, F., Grifoni, P., & Guzzo, T. (2020). Online learning and emergency remote teaching: Opportunities and challenges in emergency situations. *Societies (Basel, Switzerland)*, *10*(4), 1–18. doi:10.3390oc10040086

Finch, S. (2014). Thailand top destination for medical tourists. *Canadian Medical Association Journal*, *186*(1), E1–E2. doi:10.1503/cmaj.109-4655 PMID:24246587

Finkin, M. W. (2017). Chapter 7: Privacy and Autonomy. Emp. Rts. & Emp. Pol'y J., 21, 589.

Fitter, N. T., Raghunath, N., Cha, E., Sanchez, C. A., Takayama, L., & Matarić, M. J. (2020). Are we there yet? Comparing remote learning technologies in the university classroom. *IEEE Robotics and Automation Letters*, *5*(2), 2706–2713. doi:10.1109/LRA.2020.2970939

Flannery, R. B. Jr, & Greenhalgh, T. (2018). Coroners and PTSD: Treatment Implications. *The Psychiatric Quarterly*, *89*(4), 765–770. doi:10.100711126-018-9580-9 PMID:29651735

Fontes, D., Fonte, C., & Cardoso, A. (2017). A web GIS-based platform to assist authorities in emergency response using VGI and sensor data. *Proceedings of 2017 4th Experiment at International Conference: Online Experimentation, Exp.at 2017*. IEEE. 10.1109/EXPAT.2017.7984352

Fortune Business Insights. (2020). *Medical Tourism Market Size, Share & COVID-19 Impact Analysis, By Service (Medical et al., and Alternative Treatment), By Service Providers (Public and Private), and Regional Forecasts, 2021-2028*. Fortune Business Insights.

Frakt, A., & Pizer, S. (2018). The U.S. healthcare cost crisis: What might be done? *The New England Journal of Medicine*, *378*(2), 159–162. doi:10.1056/NEJMp1714269

Frolova, E., Rogach, O., & Ryabova, T. (2020). Benefits and risks of switching to distance learning in a pandemic. *Перспективы Науки и Образования Perspectives of Science and Education*, 79.

Frost, R. (2005). *Corporate Social Responsibility and Globalization: Re-evaluation*. A World connected. http://www.aworldconnected.org/article.php/524

Fukui, M., & Ohe, Y. (2019). Assessing the role of social media in tourism recovery in tsunami-hit coastal areas in Tohoku, Japan. *Tourism Economics*. doi:10.1177/1354816618825014

Gabard, D. L., & Martin, M. W. (2011). *Physical Therapy Ethics*. F.A. Davis Company.

Gajendran, R. S., & Harrison, D. A. (2006). *The Good, the Bad, and the Unknown about Telecommuting: Meta-Analysis of Individual Consequences and Mechanisms of Distributed Work*. Academy of Management Annual Meeting Proceedings. https://www.apa.org/pubs/journals/releases/apl-9261524.pdf

Galanakis, C. M., Rizou, M., Aldawoud, T. M., Ucak, I., & Rowan, N. J. (2021). Innovations and technology disruptions in the food sector within the COVID-19 pandemic and post-lockdown era. *Trends in Food Science & Technology*, *110*, 193–200. doi:10.1016/j.tifs.2021.02.002 PMID:36567851

Gardiner, P. (2016). Sexual harassment in healthcare: Prevalence, prevention, and response. *Nursing Standard*, *30*(31), 8–13.

Gardner, S., & Johnson, P. R. (2001). Sexual harassment in healthcare: Strategies for employers. *Hospital Topics*, *79*(4), 5–11. http://libproxy.lib.unc.edu/login?url=https://www.proquest.com/scholarly-journals/sexual-harassment-healthcare-strategies-employers/docview/214588405/se-2. doi:10.1080/00185860109597912 PMID:11942090

Garrison, D. R., & Shale, D. (1990). *Education at a distance: From issues to practice*. Robert E. Krieger.

Gartner Survey. (2020). *Gartner CFO Survey Reveals 74% Intend to Shift Some Employees to Remote Work Permanently*. Gartner. https://www.gartner.com/en/newsroom/press-releases/2020-04-03-gartner-cfo-surey-reveals-74-percent-of-organizations-to-shift-some-employees-to-remote-work-permanently2

Garza, M. A., Quinn, S. C., Li, Y., Assini-Meytin, L., Casper, E. T., Fryer, C. S., & Thomas, S. B. (2017). The influence of race and ethnicity on becoming a human subject: Factors associated with participation in research. Contemporary clinical trials communications, 7, 57–63. doi:10.1016/j.conctc.2017.05.009

Gasser, U., Ienca, M., Scheibner, J., Sleigh, J., & Vayena, E. (2020). Digital tools against COVID-19: taxonomy, ethical challenges, and navigation aid. *The Lancet. Digital Health*, *2*(8), e425–e434. PMID:32835200

Gathara, D., Serrem, K., Kigen, S., Nyandigisi, A., & Snow, R. W. (2016). Mobile phone-based infectious disease surveillance system, Kenya. *Emerging Infectious Diseases*, *22*(4), 715–721. doi:10.3201/eid2204.150842

Gaur, S., Dosapati, S., & Tawalare, A. (2023). Stakeholder assessment in construction projects using a CRITIC-TOPSIS approach. *Built Environment Project and Asset Management*, *13*(2), 217–237. doi:10.1108/BEPAM-10-2021-0122

Gersons, B. P. (1989). Patterns of PTSD among police officers following shooting incidents: A two-dimensional model and treatment implications. *Journal of Traumatic Stress*, *2*, 247–257.

Ghaffarian, S., Kerle, N., Pasolli, E., & Arsanjani, J. J. (2019). Post-disaster building database updating using automated deep learning: An integration of pre-disaster OpenStreetMap and multi-temporal satellite data. *Remote Sensing (Basel)*, *11*(20), 2427. doi:10.3390/rs11202427

Ghafoori, H. R., Sadeghi-Niaraki, A., Alesheikh, A. A., & Choi, S. M. (2022). Ubiquitous GIS based outdoor evacuation assistance: An effective response to earthquake disasters. *International Journal of Disaster Risk Reduction*, *81*, 103232. doi:10.1016/j.ijdrr.2022.103232

Gibbs, M., Mengel, F., & Siemroth, C. (2021). Work from home & productivity: Evidence from personnel & analytics data on IT professionals. *University of Chicago, Becker Friedman Institute for Economics Working Paper*, (2021-56).

Gifford, J., & Green, M. (2020). *How Could COVID-19 Change the World of Work?* CIPD. www.cipd.co.uk/news-views/changing-work-views/future-work/thought-pieces/covid-19- change-work

Gifford, J. (2022). Remote working: Unprecedented increase and a developing research agenda. *Human Resource Development International*, *25*(2), 1–9. doi:10.1080/13678868.2022.2049108

Gilbert-Ouimet, M., Trudel, X., Brisson, C., Milot, A., & Vézina, M. (2014). Adverse effects of psychosocial work factors on blood pressure: Systematic review of studies on demand-control-support and effort-reward imbalance models. *Scandinavian Journal of Work, Environment & Health*, *40*(2), 109–132. doi:10.5271jweh.3390 PMID:24108310

Gilson, L., Travis, M., & Maynard, N. C. (2015). Virtual Teams Research: 10 Years, 10 Themes, and 10 Opportunities. *Journal of Management, 41*(5), 1313–1337. doi:10.1177/0149206314559946

Ginsburg, O., Rositch, A., Conteh, L., Mutebi, M., Paskett, E., & Subramanian, S. (2018). Breast cancer disparities among women in low-and middle-income countries. *Current Breast Cancer Reports, 10*(3), 179–186. doi:10.100712609-018-0286-7

Glaeser, E., & Cutler, D. (2021, September 24). You may get more work done at home. But you'd have better ideas at the office. *The Washington Post*. https://www.washingtonpost.com/outlook/2021/09/24/working-home-productivity-pandemic-remote/

Göktaş, B., Yılmaz, S., Gönenç, İ. M., Akbulut, Y., & Sözüer, A. (2018). Cancer incidence among Syrian refugees in Turkey, 2012–2015. *Journal of International Migration and Integration, 19*(2), 253–258. doi:10.100712134-018-0549-1

Gong, B., Tobias, P., & Young-Bristol, J. (2023). Leveraging resources to improve supervisors' vision in the remote workplace. *Management Research Review, 46*(6), 777–789. doi:10.1108/MRR-12-2021-0916

Goodchild, M. F. (2007). Citizens as sensors: The world of volunteered geography. In GeoJournal. doi:10.100710708-007-9111-y

Goodchild, M. F., & Li, L. (2012). Assuring the quality of volunteered geographic information. *Spatial Statistics, 1*, 110–120. doi:10.1016/j.spasta.2012.03.002

Grant, C. A., Wallace, L. M., & Spurgeon, P. C. (2013). An exploration of the psychological factors affecting remote e-worker's job effectiveness, well-being and work-life balance. *Employee Relations, 35*(5), 527–546. doi:10.1108/ER-08-2012-0059

Green, B. (2004). Post-traumatic stress disorder in UK police officers. *Current Medical Research and Opinion, 20*(1), 101–105. doi:10.1185/030079903125002748 PMID:14741078

Greenfield, B., & Jensen, G. M. (2010). Beyond a code of ethics: Phenomenological ethics for everyday practice. *Physiotherapy Research International, 15*(2), 88–95. doi:10.1002/pri.481 PMID:20564757

Grimaldi, M., Cricelli, L., Di Giovanni, M., & Rogo, F. (2015). The patent portfolio value analysis: A new framework to leverage patent information for strategic technology planning. *Technological Forecasting and Social Change, 94*, 286–302. doi:10.1016/j.techfore.2014.10.013

Guderian, C. C., Bican, P. M., Riar, F. J., & Chattopadhyay, S. (2021). Innovation management in crisis: Patent analytics as a response to the COVID-19 pandemic. *R & D Management, 51*(2), 223–239. doi:10.1111/radm.12447

Guggenberger, T., Lockl, J., Röglinger, M., Schlatt, V., Sedlmeir, J., Stoetzer, J. C., Urbach, N., & Völter, F. (2021). Emerging digital technologies to combat future crises: Learnings from COVID-19 to be prepared for the future. *International Journal on Management of Innovation & Technology, 18*(04), 2140002. doi:10.1142/S0219877021400022

Gultekin, M., Ozturk, C., Karaca, S., Boztaş, G., Turan, S. H., Dundar, S., Hacikamiloglu, E., Araz, L., Murtuza, K., & Keskinkilic, B. (2018). Centralization of mammography reporting with mobile trucks: Turkish experience. *Preventive Medicine Reports, 10*, 317–322. doi:10.1016/j.pmedr.2018.04.008 PMID:29868386

Gupta, S., Vijayvargy, L., & Gupta, K. (2021). Assessment of stress level in urban area's during COVID-19 outbreak using CRİTİC and TOPSIS: A case of Indian cities. *Journal of Statistics and Management Systems, 24*(2), 411–433. doi:10.1080/09720510.2021.1879470

Gurrala, K. R., Helmy, M., & Ndiaye, M. (2022, March). *Edible packaging selection employing Hybrid CRITIC and TOPSIS Method.* 2022 International Conference on Decision Aid Sciences and Applications (DASA), Chiangrai, Thailand. 10.1109/DASA54658.2022.9765061

GWood. J. (2022, January 27). *These 3 charts show the global growth in online learning*. We Forum. https://www.weforum.org/agenda/2022/01/online-learning-courses-reskill-skills-gap/

H.R. 1647 - 117th Congress (2021-2022): TREATS Act. (2021, May 18). https://www.congress.gov/bill/117th-congress/house-bill/1647

H.R. 4040 - 117th Congress (2021-2022): Advancing Telehealth Beyond COVID–19 Act of 2021. (2022, July 28). https://www.congress.gov/bill/117th-congress/house-bill/4040

Haleem, A., Javaid, M., Singh, R. P., & Suman, R. (2021). Telemedicine for healthcare: Capabilities, features, barriers, and applications. *Sensors International.*

Haley, S. J., Southwick, L. E., Parikh, N. S., Rivera, J., Farrar-Edwards, D., & Boden-Albala, B. (2017). Barriers and strategies for recruiting racial and ethnic minorities: Perspectives from neurological clinical research coordinators. *Journal of Racial and Ethnic Health Disparities*, *4*(6), 1225–1236. doi:10.100740615-016-0332-y PMID:28176157

Hamel, L. M., Penner, L. A., Albrecht, T. L., Heath, E., Gwede, C. K., & Eggly, S. (2016). Barriers to clinical trial enrollment in racial and ethnic minority patients with cancer. *Cancer control. Cancer Control*, *23*(4), 327–337. doi:10.1177/107327481602300404 PMID:27842322

Hamingson, N. (2023). Communication Technology and Inclusion Will Shape the Future of Remote Work. *Business News Daily*. https://www.businessnewsdaily.com/8156-future-of-remote-work.html

Hashim, M. J., Al-Shamsi, F. A., Al-Marzooqi, N. A., Al-Qasemi, S. S., Mokdad, A. H., & Khan, G. (2018). Burden of breast cancer in the arab world: Findings from global burden of disease, 2016. *Journal of Epidemiology and Global Health*, *8*(1-2), 54–58. doi:10.2991/j.jegh.2018.09.003 PMID:30859788

Hatfield, S. (2021, September 8). *Rethinking the ways we look at productivity in a Work from Anywhere world.* Deloitte United States. https://www2.deloitte.com/us/en/blog/human-capital-blog/2021/remote-work-productivity.html

Haworth, B. T., Bruce, E., Whittaker, J., & Read, R. (2018). The good, the bad, and the uncertain: Contributions of volunteered geographic information to community disaster resilience. In Frontiers in Earth Science, 6. doi:10.3389/feart.2018.00183

Haworth, B. T. (2018). Implications of Volunteered Geographic Information for Disaster Management and GIScience: A More Complex World of Volunteered Geography. *Annals of the American Association of Geographers*, *108*(1), 226–240. Advance online publication. doi:10.1080/24694452.2017.1321979

Haworth, B., Whittaker, J., & Bruce, E. (2016). Assessing the application and value of participatory mapping for community bushfire preparation. *Applied Geography (Sevenoaks, England)*, *76*, 115–127. Advance online publication. doi:10.1016/j.apgeog.2016.09.019

Haykır, E. (2011). Entelektüel sermayenin önemi. sınıflandırılması ve ölçme yöntemleri: kuramsal bir çerçeve, *Sosyal bilimler dergisi.* (1) 86-99. https://dergipark.org.tr/tr/pub/iusosbil/issue/9498/118670

Headley, M. (2020). Creating a culture that puts an end to sexual harassment in healthcare. *Medical Environment Update, 30*(3), 6–8. http://libproxy.lib.unc.edu/login?url=https://www.proquest.com/trade-journals/creating-culture-that-puts-end-sexual-harassment/docview/2355327831/se-2

Health Tourism. (n.d.). Medical Tourism in the USA. *Health Tourism.* https://www.health-tourism.com/medical-tourism/usa-research/#:~:text=Reasons%20Why%20American%20Patients%20are%20Traveling%20Abroad%20for,6%20Researching%20medical%20tourism%20for%20USA%20patients%20

Health Tourism. (n.d.). *Medical Tourism to Thailand*. Health Tourism. https://www.health-tourism.com/medical-tourism-thailand/

Hearn, J., Ssinabulya, I., Schwartz, J. I., Akiteng, A. R., Ross, H. J., & Cafazzo, J. A. (2019). Self-management of non-communicable diseases in low-and middle-income countries: A scoping review. *PLoS One*, *14*(7), e0219141. doi:10.1371/journal.pone.0219141 PMID:31269070

Heick, T. (2021). 9 Principles Of Student Engagement In A Virtual Classroom. *TeachThought*. https://www.teachthought.com/technology/student-engagement-virtual/

Heintzelman, C. (2003). The Tuskegee Syphilis Study and Its Implications for the 21st Century. *The New Social Worker*. https://www.socialworker.com/tuskegee.htm

Hemmings, A. (2006). *Great ethical divides: Bridging the gap between institutional review boards and researchers*. Ethical Researcher.

Hernández-Vásquez, A., Rojas-Roque, C., Vargas-Fernández, R., & Rosselli, D. (2020). Measuring out-of-pocket payment, catastrophic health expenditure and the related socioeconomic inequality in Peru: A comparison between 2008 and 2017. *Journal of Preventive Medicine and Public Health*, *53*(4), 266–274. doi:10.3961/jpmph.20.035 PMID:32752596

Heydari, M., Xiaohu, Z., Saeidi, M., Lai, K. K., Shang, Y., & Yuxi, Z. (2020). Analysis of the role of social support-cognitive psychology and emotional process approach. *European Journal of Translational Myology*, *30*(3). doi:10.4081/ejtm.2020.8975 PMID:33117505

Higgs, M., & Rowland, D. (2008). *The change handbook: The definitive resource on today's best methods for engaging whole systems*. Berrett-Koehler.

Hodges, C., Moore, S., Lockee, B., Trust, T., & Bond, A. (2020). The difference between emergency remote teaching and online learning. *EDUCAUSE Review*. https://er.educause.edu/articles/2020/3/the-difference-between-emergency-remote-teaching-and-online-learning

Hoffman, K., Burroughs, E., Brown, C., & Smith, M. (2020). Telehealth: A solution to the mental health crisis caused by COVID-19. *Journal of Mental Health (Abingdon, England)*, *4*(3), 119–124.

Hoffman, M. T., Rick, F., Rohde, R. F., & Gillso, L. (2019). *Rethinking Catastrophe? Historical trajectories and modeled future vegetation change in Southern Africa*. Anthropocene.

Holmberg, B. (1989). *Theory and practice of distance education*. Routledge.

Holt-Lunstad, J. (2018). Why social relationships are important for physical health: A systems approach to understanding and modifying risk and protection. *Annual Review of Psychology*, *69*(1), 437–458. doi:10.1146/annurev-psych-122216-011902 PMID:29035688

Horwitz, F. M., Bravington, D., & Silvis, U. (2006). The promise of virtual factors in effectiveness and failure. *Journal of European Industrial Training*, *30*(6), 472–494. doi:10.1108/03090590610688843

Howington, J. (2022, October 20). *Employee Engagement Report: Job Satisfaction and Work Flexibility | FlexJobs*. FlexJobs Employer Blog. https://www.flexjobs.com/employer-blog/employee-engagement-report-job-satisfaction-work-flexibility/

Huang, J. (2020). Successes and Challenges: Online Teaching and Learning of Chemistry in Higher Education in China in the Time of COVID-19. *Journal of Chemical Education*, *97*(9), 2810–2814. doi:10.1021/acs.jchemed.0c00671

Huang, J. Y. (2016). Patent portfolio analysis of the cloud computing industry. *Journal of Engineering and Technology Management*, *39*, 45–64. doi:10.1016/j.jengtecman.2016.01.002

Huang, L. C., & Lıu, C. W. (2018). Patent quality evaluation with entropy weight method and improved TOPSIS: The case of geriatric technology. *2018 International Conference on Management Science and Engineering (ICMSE),* (pp. 156-164). IEEE. 10.1109/ICMSE.2018.8745300

Humphreys, C., McCarthy, G., Dowling, M., Kertesz, M., & Tropea, R. (2014). Improving the Archiving of Records in the Out-of-Home Care Sector. *Australian Social Work, 67*(4), 509–524. doi:10.1080/0312407X.2013.856453

IARC (International Agency for Research on Cancer). (2023). *Population Fact Sheets:Income Levels.* IARC. https://gco.iarc.fr/today/fact-sheets-populations

Ighravwe, D., & Babatunde, M. (2018). Selection of a mini-grid business model for developing countries using CRITIC-TOPSIS with interval type-2 fuzzy sets. *Decision Science Letters, 7*(4), 427–442. doi:10.5267/j.dsl.2018.1.004

Ilag, B. N. (2021). Tools and technology for effective remote work. *International Journal of Computer Applications, 174*(21), 13–16. doi:10.5120/ijca2021921109

ILO. (2020). *Teleworking during and after the COVID-19 Pandemic: A Practical Guide.* ILO. https://www.ilo.org/wcmsp5/groups/public/---ed_protect/---protrav/---travail/documents/instructionalmaterial/wcms_751232.pdf

Imran, M., Kumar Arora, M., Asdaq, S. M. B., Khan, S. A., Alaqel, S. I., Alshammari, M. K., Alshehri, M. M., Alshrari, A. S., Ali, A. M., Al-shammeri, A. M., Alhazmi, B. D., Harshan, A. A., & Alam, M. T. (2021). Discovery, development, and patent trends on molnupiravir: A prospective oral treatment for COVID-19. *Molecules (Basel, Switzerland), 26*(19), 5795. doi:10.3390/molecules26195795 PMID:34641339

International Healthcare Research Center (IHRC). (2017). *Medical Tourism: Global Trends & Statistics.* IHRC. https://ihrc.org/medical-tourism-global-trends-statistics/

Işık, Ö. (2019). Türkiye'de hayat dışı sigorta sektörünün finansal performansının CRITIC tabanlı TOPSIS ve MULTIMOORA yöntemiyle değerlendirilmesi. *Business & Management Studies: An International Journal, 7*(1), 542–562. doi:10.15295/bmij.v7i1.1090

Islam, S. M. S., Tabassum, R., Liu, Y., Chen, S., Redfern, J., Kim, S. Y., Ball, K., Maddison, R., & Chow, C. K. (2019). The role of social media in preventing and managing non-communicable diseases in low-and-middle income countries: Hope or hype? *Health Policy and Technology, 8*(1), 96–101. doi:10.1016/j.hlpt.2019.01.001

Ismagilova, E., Hughes, L., Rana, N. P., & Dwivedi, Y. K. (2020). Security, privacy, and risks within smart cities: Literature review and development of a smart city interaction framework. *Information Systems Frontiers,* 1–22. PMID:32837262

Jaber, N., Al-Remawi, M., Al-Akayleh, F., Al-Muhtaseb, N., Al-Adham, I. S., & Collier, P. J. (2022). A review of the antiviral activity of Chitosan, including patented applications and its potential use against COVID-19. *Journal of Applied Microbiology, 132*(1), 41–58. https://dergipark.org.tr/tr/pub/dpusbe/issue/53850/684050. doi:10.1111/jam.15202 PMID:34218488

Jablotschkin, M., Binkowski, L., Markovits Hoopii, R., & Weis, J. (2022). Benefits and challenges of cancer peer support groups: A systematic review of qualitative studies. *European Journal of Cancer Care, 31*(6), e13700. doi:10.1111/ecc.13700 PMID:36104303

Jacobs, R., Mannion, R., Davies, H. O., Harrison, S., Konteh, F., & Walshe, K. (2013). The relationship between organizational culture and performance in acute hospitals. *Social Science & Medicine, 76,* 76115–76125. doi:10.1016/j.socscimed.2012.10.014 PMID:23159305

Jagsi, R., Griffith, K. A., Jones, R., Perumalswami, C. R., Ubel, P., & Stewart, A. (2016). Sexual Harassment and Discrimination Experiences of Academic Medical Faculty. *Journal of the American Medical Association, 315*(19), 2120. doi:10.1001/jama.2016.2188 PMID:27187307

Jakovljevic, M., Jakab, M., Gerdtham, U., McDaid, D., Ogura, S., Varavikova, E., Merrick, J., Adany, R., Okunade, A., & Getzen, T. E. (2019). Comparative financing analysis and political economy of noncommunicable diseases. *Journal of Medical Economics, 22*(8), 722–727. doi:10.1080/13696998.2019.1600523 PMID:30913928

Jalagat, R., & Jalagat, A. (2019). Rationalizing remote working concept and its implications on employee productivity. *Global journal of advanced research, 6*(3), 95-100.

James, K. (2021, April 8). Bystander training: The best defense against sexual harassment. *The Energy Law Blog.* https://www.theenergylawblog.com/2021/04/articles/business/employment-law/bystander-training-the-best-defense-against-sexual-harassment/ doi:10.7326/M18-2047

Jamieson, D. W., & Milbrandt, J. M. (2018). Peter B. Vaill: A life in the art of managing and leading change. The Palgrave Handbook of Organizational Change Thinkers, 1, 26. doi:10.1007/978-3-319-49820-1_60-2

JD Power. (2022). *J.D. Power 2022 U.S. Telehealth Satisfaction Study*. J.D. Power. https://www.jdpower.com/sites/default/files/file/2022-09/2022132%20U.S.%20Telehealth.pdf

Jeffery, K. A., & Bauer, C. F. (2020). Students' responses to emergency remote online teaching reveal critical factors for all teaching. *Journal of Chemical Education, 97*(9), 2472–2485. doi:10.1021/acs.jchemed.0c00736

Jensen, N., Lyons, E., Chebelyon, E., Le Bras, R., & Gomes, C. (2020). Conspicuous monitoring and remote work. *Journal of Economic Behavior & Organization, 176*, 489–511. doi:10.1016/j.jebo.2020.05.010

Jeong, S., Kim, S., & Kim, J. (2020). City data hub: Implementation of standard-based smart city data platform for interoperability. *Sensors (Basel), 20*(23), 7000. doi:10.339020237000 PMID:33297506

Jethro, D. (2021). Ash: Memorializing the 2021 University of Cape Town Library Fire. *The Journal of Objects. Art and Belief., 17*(5), 671–677.

Johnson, C. E. (2022). *Organizational ethics: a practical approach* (5th ed.). SAGE.

Jonassen, D. (1992). Designing hypertext for learning. In E. Scanlon & T. O'Shea (Eds.), *New directions in educational technology* (pp. 123–130). Springer-Verlag. doi:10.1007/978-3-642-77750-9_10

Jones, J. H. (1993). *Bad blood: The Tuskegee syphilis experiment.* The Free Press.

Jonsen, A., Siegler, M., & Winslade, W. (2002). Clinical ethics: a practice approach to ethical decisions in clinical medicine, (5th ed.) Columbus, OH: McGraw-Hill/ Appleton & Lange.

Jotisakulratana, M., Koomgun, N., Virojrid, R., & Udomsaph, B. (2013). Applying International Patent Classification (IPC) to strategic planning processes of an R&D organization: The case of NECTEC, Thailand. *In 2013 Proceedings of PICMET'13: Technology Management in the IT-Driven Services (PICME*T). IEEE.

Joury, E., Eriksson, A., & others. (2023). *Community Engagement and Crowdsourcing for Effective Disaster Response and Rescue Operations During the Earthquake in Syria.*

Kaiser Family Foundation. (2018). *2018 employer health benefits survey.* KFF. https://www.kff.org/report-section/ehbs-2018-section-two-trends-in-employer-sponsored-insurance/

Kalıp, N. G., Erzurumlu, Y. Ö., & Gün, N. A. (2022). Qualitative and quantitative patent valuation methods: A systematic literature review. *World Patent Information, 69*, 102111. doi:10.1016/j.wpi.2022.102111

Kalvakolanu, S., Sama, H. R., Mathew, M., & Somasekhar, D. (2022). Measuring job satisfaction levels of airport employees using entropy, critic and TOPSIS methods. *International Journal of Business Excellence, 27*(1), 1–22. doi:10.1504/IJBEX.2022.123031

Kampmeier, R. H. (1972). The Tuskegee study of untreated Syphilis. *Southern Medical Journal, 65*(10), 1247–1251. doi:10.1097/00007611-197210000-00016 PMID:5074095

Kampmeier, R. H. (1974). Final report on the Tuskegee syphilis study. *Southern Medical Journal, 67*(11), 1349–1353. doi:10.1097/00007611-197411000-00019 PMID:4610772

Kamruzzaman, M. M., Yan, B., Sarker, M. N. I., Alruwaili, O., Wu, M., & Alrashdi, I. (2022). Blockchain and fog computing in IoT-driven healthcare services for smart cities. *Journal of Healthcare Engineering, 2022*, 2022. doi:10.1155/2022/9957888 PMID:35126961

Kankanamge, N., Yigitcanlar, T., Goonetilleke, A., & Kamruzzaman, M. (2020). Determining disaster severity through social media analysis: Testing the methodology with South East Queensland Flood tweets. *International Journal of Disaster Risk Reduction, 42*, 101360. doi:10.1016/j.ijdrr.2019.101360

Karia, R. (2020). *COVID-19 and its modes of transmission.* NIH.

Karrouri, R., Hammani, Z., Benjelloun, R., & Otheman, Y. (2021). Major depressive disorder: Validated treatments and future challenges. *World Journal of Clinical Cases, 9*(31), 9350–9367. doi:10.12998/wjcc.v9.i31.9350 PMID:34877271

Karunarathne, P. (2021). A SWOT Analysis of Remote Working Based on Review of Literature. *International Journal of Business* [IJBTOB]. *Technology and Organizational Behavior, 1*(4), 253–262. doi:10.52218/ijbtob.v1i4.102

Kato, L. V. (2019). *Integrating openstreetmap data in object based landcover and landuse classification for disaster recovery.* University of Twente.

Katuu, S., & Van der Walt, T. (2016). Assessing the legislative and regulatory framework supporting the management of records in South Africa's public health sectors. *South African Journal of Information Management, 18*(1), a686. doi:10.4102ajim.v18i1.686

Kazan, H., & Ozdemir, O. (2014). Financial performance assessment of large scale conglomerates via TOPSIS and CRITIC methods. *International Journal of Management and Sustainability, 3*(4), 203–224. doi:10.18488/journal.11/2014.3.4/11.4.203.224

Keestra, S., Rodgers, F., Osborne, R., & Wimmer, S. (2022). University patenting and licensing practices in the United Kingdom during the first year of the COVID-19 pandemic. *Global Public Health: An International Journal for Research, Policy and Practice, 17*(5), 641–651. doi:10.1080/17441692.2022.2049842 PMID:35298347

Kerschbaum, E., & Nüssler, V. (2019). Cancer prevention with nutrition and lifestyle. *Visceral Medicine, 35*(4), 204–209. doi:10.1159/000501776 PMID:31602380

Khan, M. A., & Afzal, H. (2011). High level of education builds up a strong relationship between organizational culture and organizational performance in Pakistan. *International Journal of Human Resource Management, 22*(7), 1387–1400. doi:10.1080/09585192.2011.561955

Khan, U. N., & Akhter, S. (2017). Right to Information as an Instrumental Force of Good Governance in South Asia. *A Research Journal of South Asian Studies. South Asian Studies, 32*(1), 151–160.

Khatoon, S., Asif, A., Hasan, M. M., & Alshamari, M. (2022). Social Media-Based Intelligence for Disaster Response and Management in Smart Cities. In Springer Optimization and Its Applications (Vol. 186). Springer. doi:10.1007/978-3-030-84459-2_11

Khumalo, B. N., & Baloyi, C. (2017). The possible benefits of Freedom of Information laws to the records management landscape in the ESARBICA region. *Information Development*, 1–15.

Kim, W. C., & Mauborgne, R. (2005). *Blue Ocean Strategy.* Arthur McKeown. https://arthurmckeown.typepad.com/files/blue-ocean-strategy---wikipedia.pdf

Kim, G., & Bae, J. (2017). A novel approach to forecast promising technology through patent analysis. *Technological Forecasting and Social Change*, *117*, 228–237. doi:10.1016/j.techfore.2016.11.023

Kirag, N., & Kızılkaya, M. (2019). Application of the champion health belief model to determine beliefs and behaviors of Turkish women academicians regarding breast cancer screening: A cross sectional descriptive study. *BMC Women's Health*, *19*(1), 1–10. doi:10.118612905-019-0828-9 PMID:31694619

Kirkwood, C. (2021). *The Fire Disaster in the University of Cape Town's Jagger Library, and its consequences*. HDL. https://hdl.handle.net/10520/ejc-cabo_v2021_n1_a5

Kirsch, L. (2004). Action research: A participatory approach for organizational development. *Human Resource Development International*, *7*(3), 383–395.

Kothgassner, O. D., Goreis, A., Kafka, J. X., Van Eickels, R. L., Plener, P. L., & Felnhofer, A. (2019). Virtual reality exposure therapy for post-traumatic stress disorder (PTSD): A meta-analysis. *European Journal of Psychotraumatology*, *10*(1), 1654782. doi:10.1080/20008198.2019.1654782 PMID:31489138

Kotrba, L. M., Gillespie, M. A., Schmidt, A. M., Smerek, R. E., Ritchie, S. A., & Denison, D. R. (2012). Do consistent corporate cultures have better business performance? Exploring the interaction effects. *Human Relations*, *65*(2), 241–262. doi:10.1177/0018726711426352

Kotter, J. (1996). *Leading change*. Harvard Business School Press.

Kovács, G., & Spens, K. M. (2007). Humanitarian Logistics in Disaster Relief Operations. *International Journal of Physical Distribution & Logistics Management, 37*(2), 99–114.

Kovács, G., & Spens, K. M. (2009). Identifying Challenges in Humanitarian Logistics. *International Journal of Physical Distribution & Logistics Management*, *39*(6), 506–528. doi:10.1108/09600030910985848

KPMG. (2022, March 9). *Current trends in remote working*. KPMG. https://kpmg.com/xx/en/home/insights/2022/03/insights-on-current-trends-in-remote-working.html

Kraut, R. E. (1989). Telecommuting: The trade-offs of home work. *Journal of Communication*, *39*(3), 19–47. doi:10.1111/j.1460-2466.1989.tb01038.x

Kumar, A., & Kumar, K. (2020). Digital health and urban sustainability: The emerging trends and opportunities. *Sustainability*, *12*(18), 7520.

Kusumo, A. N. L., Reckien, D., & Verplanke, J. (2017). Utilising volunteered geographic information to assess resident's flood evacuation shelters. Case study: Jakarta. *Applied Geography (Sevenoaks, England)*, *88*, 174–185. doi:10.1016/j.apgeog.2017.07.002

Kutty, A. A., Abdella, G. M., Kucukvar, M., Onat, N. C., & Bulu, M. (2020). A system thinking approach for harmonizing smart and sustainable city initiatives with United Nations sustainable development goals. *Sustainable Development (Bradford)*, *28*(5), 1347–1365. doi:10.1002d.2088

Lacasandile, A. D., Gunay, K. R., & Bonifacio, C. S. D. (2022). E-Saklolo: A Mobile-based Crowdsourcing Platform for Disaster Risk Management and Emergency Response in the City of Santiago, Isabela Philippines. *Proceedings - 2022 International Conference on Computer Applications Technology, CCAT 2022*. 10.1109/CCAT56798.2022.00012

Lancsar, E., & Louviere, J. (2008). *Conducting Discrete Choice Experiments to Inform Healthcare Decision Making.* SpringerLink. https://link-springer-com.libproxy.lib.unc.edu/article/10.2165/00019053-200826080-00004

Lane, A. J., & Skirboll, S. (2020). Digital Health Incentives: An Analysis of Current Federal and State Policies. *Health Affairs*, *39*(3), 472–479. doi:10.1377/hlthaff.2019.00633

Langarizadeh, M., Tabatabaei, M. S., Tavakol, K., Naghipour, M., Rostami, A., & Moghbeli, F. (2017). Telemental Health Care, an Effective Alternative to Conventional Mental Care: A Systematic Review. *Acta Informatica Medica*, *25*(4), 240–246. doi:10.5455/aim.2017.25.240-246 PMID:29284913

Lange, M., & Kayser, I. (2022). The role of self-efficacy, work-related autonomy and work-family conflict on employee's stress level during home-based remote work in Germany. *International Journal of Environmental Research and Public Health*, *19*(9), 4955. doi:10.3390/ijerph19094955 PMID:35564349

Lee, J. (2020). Mental health effects of school closures during COVID-19. *The Lancet. Child & Adolescent Health*, *4*(6), 421. doi:10.1016/S2352-4642(20)30109-7 PMID:32302537

Lee, S. J., & Yu, K. (2004). Corporate culture and organizational performance. *Journal of Managerial Psychology*, *19*(4), 340–359. doi:10.1108/02683940410537927

Lee, S., Yoon, B., Lee, C., & Park, J. (2009). Business planning based on technological capabilities: Patent analysis for technology-driven roadmapping. *Technological Forecasting and Social Change*, *76*(6), 769–786. doi:10.1016/j.techfore.2009.01.003

Lees, T., Elliott, J. L., Gunning, S., Newton, P. J., Rai, T., & Lal, S. (2019). A systematic review of the current evidence regarding interventions for anxiety, PTSD, sleepiness, and fatigue in the law enforcement workplace. *Industrial Health*, *57*(6), 655–667. doi:10.2486/indhealth.2018-0088 PMID:30760652

Lei, Q., Liu, C., Xie, W., & Bao, X. (2021). A TOPSIS-Based Model for Evaluating the Performance of the Intellectual Property Value Strategies of Science and Technology Enterprises. *Discrete Dynamics in Nature and Society*, *2021*, 1–6. doi:10.1155/2021/4745702

Lerner, B. H. (2004). Sins of omission—Cancer research without informed consent. *The New England Journal of Medicine*, *351*(7), 628–630. doi:10.1056/NEJMp048108 PMID:15306661

Li, Z., Huang, Q., & Emrich, C. T. (2019). Introduction to social sensing and big data computing for disaster management. In International Journal of Digital Earth, 12(11). doi:10.1080/17538947.2019.1670951

Liang, S. Y., & Escobar, M. J. (2020). Digital Health in Urban Settings: Opportunities and Challenges. *Journal of Medical Internet Research*, *22*(4), e16356. doi:10.2196/16356 PMID:32347802

Li, J. C. (2020). Roles of individual perception in technology adoption at organization level: Behavioral model versus toe framework. *Journal of System and Management Sciences*, *10*(3), 97–118.

Li, L., & Ulaganathan, M. N. (2017). Design and development of a crowdsourcing mobile app for disaster response. *International Conference on Geoinformatics, 2017-August*. IEEE. 10.1109/GEOINFORMATICS.2017.8090943

Lim, B. (1995). Examining the organizational culture and organizational performance link. *Leadership and Organization Development Journal*, *16*(5), 16–21. doi:10.1108/01437739510088491

Lindsey, M. A., Joe, S., Nebbitt, V., & Thurlow, M. L. (2017). Help-Seeking Behaviors and Mental Health Service Utilization Among African American College Students. *Journal of College Student Development*, *58*(2), 133–149. doi:10.1353/csd.2017.0013

Lin, Y., Alshehri, Y., Alnazzawi, N., Abid, M., Khan, S. A., Jabeen, F., & Elwarfalli, I. (2023). Social media analytics and their applications to evaluate an activity in online health interventions using CRITIC and TOPSIS techniques. *Soft Computing*, 1–13. doi:10.100700500-023-08004-3 PMID:37362268

LiQ.YinX.YinW.DongX.LiQ. (2023). Evaluating human-computer interaction education based on active learning methods using the CRITIC and TOPSIS approach. Research Square, 10.21203/rs.3.rs-2490226/v1

Littenberg-Tobias, J., & Reich, J. (2020). Evaluating access, quality, and equity in online learning: A case study of a MOOC-based blended professional degree program. *The Internet and Higher Education*, *47*, 100759. doi:10.1016/j.iheduc.2020.100759

Liu, P., Zhang, Y., Wang, Y., & Zou, X. (2020). Mental health and psychological distress among the general population during the COVID-19 pandemic: A systematic review. *International Journal of Environmental Research and Public Health*, *17*(13), 4813. PMID:32635450

Liu, X., Meng, X., Chen, X., Su, W., Zhang, X., Li, L., & Su, X. (2020). The Research on Assistance Information Acquisition for Earthquake Emergency Response by Aggregating VGI Data and GF-2 Images. *Remote Sensing Technology and Application*, *34*(6), 1286–1295.

Liu, Y., & Liu, J. (2019). Digital health and urban sustainability: A review of recent trends. *Telemedicine Journal and e-Health*, *25*(2), 145–151.

Liu, Y., & Yang, R. (2023). Independent innovation capacity of chinese high-tech ındustries Using CRITIC and TOPSIS Methods. *Journal of Engineering Science & Technology Review*, *16*(1), 18–25. doi:10.25103/jestr.161.03

Li, X., Wang, K., Liu, L., Xin, J., Yang, H., & Gao, C. (2011). Application of the entropy weight and TOPSIS method in safety evaluation of coal mines. *Procedia Engineering*, *26*, 2085–2091. doi:10.1016/j.proeng.2011.11.2410

Li, Y., Wei, M., Liu, L., Yu, B., Dong, Z., & Xue, Q. (2021). Evaluation of the effectiveness of VOC-contaminated soil preparation based on AHP-CRITIC-TOPSIS model. *Chemosphere*, *271*, 129571. doi:10.1016/j.chemosphere.2021.129571 PMID:33460903

Lockee, B. B. (2021). Online education in the post-COVID era. *Nature Electronics*, *4*(1), 5–6. doi:10.103841928-020-00534-0

Longenecker, J. T., Gebregziabher, M., Park, E. R., Shih, T., & Karter, A. J. (2017). Digital health interventions for chronic disease management: A systematic review. *Journal of Medical Internet Research*, *19*(7). Advance online publication. doi:10.2196/jmir.7153

Lowrie, C., Kruczkiewicz, A., McClain, S. N., Nielsen, M., & Mason, S. J. (2022). Evaluating the usefulness of VGI from Waze for the reporting of flash floods. *Scientific Reports*, *12*(1), 5268. doi:10.103841598-022-08751-7 PMID:35347160

Lucas, J. W., & Villarroel, M. A. (2021). Telemedicine use among adults: United States. NCHS Data Brief, no 445. Hyattsville, MD: National Center for Health Statistics. https://dx.doi.org/ doi:10.15620/cdc:121435

Lucas, M., Nelson, J., & Sims, D. (2020). *Schools' Responses to COVID-19: Pupil Engagement in Remote Learning*. National Foundation for Educational Research.

Lucas, T., Weidner, N., & Janisse, J. (2012). Where does work stress come from? A generalizability analysis of stress in police officers. *Psychology & Health*, *27*(12), 1426–1447. doi:10.1080/08870446.2012.687738 PMID:22612444

Luker, T. (2017). Decolonising Archives: Indigenous Challenges to Records Keeping in 'Reconciling' Settler Colonial State. *Australian Feminist Studies, 32*(91-92), 91–92. doi:10.1080/08164649.2017.1357011

Luukka, P. (2020). N—ary norm operators and TOPSIS. In *2020 IEEE International Conference on Fuzzy Systems (FUZZ-IEEE)*. IEEE. 10.1109/FUZZ48607.2020.9177580

Luukka, P., & Collan, M. (2016). Histogram ranking with generalised similarity-based TOPSIS applied to patent ranking. *Journal of Engineering and Technology Management, 25*(4), 437–448. doi:10.1504/IJOR.2016.075290

Lu, X., Wu, C., Bai, D., You, Q., Cai, M., Wang, W., Hou, C., & Gao, J. (2023). Relationship between social support and fear of cancer recurrence among Chinese cancer patients: A systematic review and meta-analysis. *Frontiers in Psychiatry, 14*, 1136013. doi:10.3389/fpsyt.2023.1136013 PMID:36970291

Lyubetsky, N., Bendersky, N., Verina, T., Demyanova, L., & Arkhipova, D. (2021). IMPACT of distance learning on student mental health in the COVID-19 pandemic. In *E3S Web of Conferences* (Vol. 273, p. 10036). EDP Sciences. doi:10.1051/e3sconf/202127310036

Macklin, D. S., Smith, L. A., & Dollard, M. F. (2006). Public and private sector work stress: Workers compensation, levels of distress and job satisfaction, and the demand-control-support model. *Australian Journal of Psychology, 58*(3), 130–143. doi:10.1080/00049530600940190

MacMillan, C. (2021). *Why Telehealth for Mental Health Care is Working*. Yale Medicine. https://www.yalemedicine.org/news/telehealth-for-mental-health

MacRae, I., & Sawatzky, R. (2020). *Remote Working: Personality and Performance Research Results*. Thomas International.

Maharjan, B., & Bhandari, S. (2020). Role of digital health in urban sustainability: A systematic review. *International Journal of Environmental Research and Public Health, 17*(5), 1486. PMID:32106591

Majumder, P., Biswas, P., & Majumder, S. (2020). Application of new TOPSIS approach to identify the most significant risk factor and continuous monitoring of death of COVID-19. *Electronic Journal of General Medicine, 17*(6), em234. doi:10.29333/ejgm/7904

Makwae, N. E. (2021). Legal frameworks for personnel records management in support of accountability in devolved governments: A case of Garissa County Government. Personnel records management. *Records Management Journal, 31*(2), 109–133. doi:10.1108/RMJ-05-2019-0024

Malan, L. (2005). Intergovernmental relations and co-operative government in South Africa: the ten–year review. *Politeia, 41*(2).

Mandal, J., Acharya, S., & Parija, S. C. (2011). Ethics in human research. *Tropical Parasitology, 1*(1), 2–3. doi:10.4103/2229-5070.129140 PMID:23509672

Mardani, A., Saraji, M. K., Mishra, A. R., & Rani, P. (2020). A novel extended approach under hesitant fuzzy sets to design a framework for assessing the key challenges of digital health interventions adoption during the COVID-19 outbreak. *Applied Soft Computing, 96*, 106613. doi:10.1016/j.asoc.2020.106613 PMID:32834799

Marks, J. D., & Augenstein, J. (2022). *Health Highlights: Telehealth Policies in the Omnibus FY 2022 Spending Bill.* Manatt Health. https://www.manatt.com/insights/newsletters/health-highlights/telehealth-policies-in-the-omnibus-fy-2022spendin#:~:text=Providers%20will%20not%20be%20required,the%20case%20of%20hospice%20patients

Marmolejo, F. J., & Groccia, J. E. (2022). Reimagining and redesigning teaching and learning in the post-pandemic world. *New Directions for Teaching and Learning, 2022*(169), 21–37. doi:10.1002/tl.20480

Martin, M. A., Swider, S. M., Olinger, T., Avery, E., Lynas, C. M., Carlson, K., & Rothschild, S. K. (2011). Recruitment of Mexican American adults for an intensive diabetes intervention trial. *Ethnicity & Disease*, *21*(1), 7–12. PMID:21462723

Marutha, S. N., & Ngulube, P. (2012). Electronic records management in the public health sector of the Limpopo province in South Africa. *Journal of the South African Society of Archivists*, *45*, 39–67.

Mathew, B. (2021, February 12). *Healthcare Report*. Retrieved from Impact of Social Media on Healthcare Marketing: https://healthcare.report/articles/impact-of-social-media-on-healthcare-marketing

Matlala, E. M., Ncubem, R. T., & Parbanath, S. (2022). The State of digital records preservation in South Africa's public sector in the 21st Century: A literature review. *Records Management Journal*, *32*(2), 198–212. doi:10.1108/RMJ-02-2021-0004

Mayo Foundation for Medical Education and Research. (2017, October 13). *Generalized anxiety disorder*. Mayo Clinic. https://www.mayoclinic.org/diseases-conditions/generalized-anxiety-disorder/symptoms-causes/syc-20360803

Mayo Foundation for Medical Education and Research. (2018, January 6). *Autism spectrum disorder*. Mayo Clinic. https://www.mayoclinic.org/diseases-conditions/autism-spectrum-disorder/symptoms-causes/syc-20352928

Mayo Foundation for Medical Education and Research. (2019, June 22). *Adult attention-deficit/hyperactivity disorder (ADHD)*. Mayo Clinic. https://www.mayoclinic.org/diseases-conditions/adult-adhd/symptoms-causes/syc-20350878

Mayo Foundation for Medical Education and Research. (2021, February 16). *Bipolar disorder*. Mayo Clinic. https://www.mayoclinic.org/diseases-conditions/bipolar-disorder/symptoms-causes/syc-20355955

Mayo Foundation for Medical Education and Research. (2022, October 14). *Depression (major depressive disorder)*. Mayo Clinic. https://www.mayoclinic.org/diseases-conditions/depression/symptoms-causes/syc-20356007

Mayo, E. (1933). *The human problems of an industrial civilization*. Macmillan.

Maznevski, M. L., & Chudoba, K. M. (2000). Bridging Space over Time: Global Virtual Team Dynamics and Effectiveness. *Organization Science*, *11*(5), 473–492. doi:10.1287/orsc.11.5.473.15200

McDonald, A. D., Sasangohar, F., Jatav, A., & Rao, A. H. (2019). Continuous monitoring and detection of post-traumatic stress disorder (PTSD) triggers among veterans: A supervised machine learning approach. *IISE Transactions on Healthcare Systems Engineering*, *9*(3), 201–211. doi:10.1080/24725579.2019.1583703

Mckinsey Global Institute. (2021, February 18). *The future of work after COVID-19*. McKinsey & Company. https://www.mckinsey.com/featured-insights/future-of-work/the-future-of-work-after-covid-19

McNeil, D. (2010, October 1). U.S. Apologizes for Syphilis Tests in Guatemala. *New York Times*. https://www.nytimes.com/2010/10/02/health/research/02infect.html

Meacham, E., Orem, J., Nakigudde, G., Zujewski, J. A., & Rao, D. (2016). Exploring stigma as a barrier to cancer service engagement with breast cancer survivors in Kampala, Uganda. *Psycho-Oncology*, *25*(10), 1206–1211. doi:10.1002/pon.4215 PMID:27421234

MehdiT.MorissetteR. (2021). Working from home in Canada: What have we learned so far? In *Statistics Canada*. doi:10.25318/36280001202101000001-eng

Meier, P. (2015). Digital humanitarians: How big data is changing the face of humanitarian response. *Digital Humanitarians*. doi:10.1201/b18023

Mentis, A. F. A., Lee, D., & Roussos, P. (2023). Applications of artificial intelligence− machine learning for detection of stress: A critical overview. *Molecular Psychiatry*, 1–13. doi:10.103841380-023-02047-6 PMID:37020048

Mikulak, A. (Ed.). (2022, February 22). *Women's experiences of sexual assault and harassment linked with high blood pressure*. National Institute of Mental Health. https://www.nimh.nih.gov/news/science-news/2022/womens-experiences-of-sexual-assault-and-harassment-linked-with-high-blood-pressure

Miles, A., & Mezzich, J. E. (2011). Advancing global communication and research for personalized healthcare. *International Journal of Person Centered Medicine*, *1*(1), 1–5. doi:10.5750/ijpcm.v1i1.10

Milojević, I. (2014). Creating alternative selves: The use of futures discourse in narrative therapy. *Journal of Futures Studies*, *18*(3), 27–40.

Min, S. A., & Kim, B. Y. (2020). Platform leadership and strategy of small and medium enterprises on digital transformation. [IJM]. *International Journal of Management*, *11*(12). doi:10.34218/IJM.11.12.2020.205

Mnjama, N. (2005). Archival landscape in Eastern and Southern Africa. *Library Management*, *26*(8/9), 457–470. doi:10.1108/01435120510631747

MoH (Ministry of Health). (2022). *Health Statistics Year Book-2020.* Republic of Türkiye Ministry of Health General Directorate of Health Information Systems Republic of Türkiye Ministry of Health General Directorate of Health Information Systems.

Mohamadghasemi, A., Hadi-Vencheh, A., & Hosseinzadeh Lotfi, F. (2020). The multiobjective stochastic CRITIC–TOPSIS approach for solving the shipboard crane selection problem. *International Journal of Intelligent Systems*, *35*(10), 1570–1598. doi:10.1002/int.22265

Mohammed, M. A., Abdulkareem, K. H., Al-Waisy, A. S., Mostafa, S. A., Al-Fahdawi, S., Dinar, A. M., Alhakami, W., Baz, A., Al-Mhiqani, M. N., Alhakami, H., Arbaiy, N., Maashi, M. S., Mutlag, A. A., García-Zapirain, B., & Torre Díez, I. D. L. T. D. L. (2020). Benchmarking methodology for selection of optimal COVID-19 diagnostic model based on entropy and TOPSIS methods. *IEEE Access : Practical Innovations, Open Solutions*, *8*, 99115–99131. doi:10.1109/ACCESS.2020.2995597

Mohmmed, A. O., Khidhir, B. A., Nazeer, A., & Vijayan, V. J. (2020). Emergency remote teaching during Coronavirus pandemic: The current trend and future directive at Middle East College Oman. *Innovative Infrastructure Solutions*, *5*(3), 1–11. doi:10.100741062-020-00326-7

Moon, M. R., & Khin-Maung-Gyi, F. (2009). The history and role of institutional review boards. *The Virtual Mentor*, *11*(4), 311–321. PMID:23195065

Moore, M. (1989). Three types of interaction. *American Journal of Distance Education*, *3*(2), 1–6. doi:10.1080/08923648909526659

Moore, M., & Kearsley, G. (1996). *Distance education: A systems view*. Wadsworth Publishing Company.

MorissetteR.DengZ.MessacarD. (2021). Working from home: Potential implications for public transit and greenhouse gas emissions. In *Statistics Canada*. doi:10.25318/36280001202100400005-eng

Mostafa, B. A. (2021). The Effect of Remote Working on Employees Well-being and Work-Life Integration during Pandemic in Egypt. *International Business Research*, *14*(3), 41. doi:10.5539/ibr.v14n3p41

Mouritsen, J., & Koleva, G. (2005). Packing and unpacking knowledge: Patents and intellectual capital. *Journal of Intellectual Capital*, *6*(3), 308–321. doi:10.1108/14691930510611076

Muchefa, L., & Chigodora, T. (2016). A historical account of backlog challenges at National Archives of Zimbabwe and the Access Implications. *ESARBICA Journal*, *35*, 112–119.

Mudzaki, F. (2017). Establishing a lasting solution to collection development policy: Challenges for audiovisual archives to enhance access in Zimbabwe. *ESARBICA Journal*, *36*, 94–107.

Mukundan, R., Jain, K., & Pathari, V. (2019). A model for measuring and ranking a firm's patent portfolio. *Technology Analysis and Strategic Management*, *31*(9), 1029–1047. doi:10.1080/09537325.2019.1583327

Mullon, A. P., & Ngoepe, M. (2019). An integrated framework to elevate information governance to a national level in South Africa. *Records Management Journal*, *29*(1/2), 103–116. doi:10.1108/RMJ-09-2018-0030

Munir, M. (2014). *How to Maintain Interpersonal Relationships.* Very Well Mind. https://www.verywellmind.com/how-to-maintain-interpersonal-relationships-4145371

Munro, E., Holmes, L., & Ward, H. (2005). Researching vulnerable groups: Ethical issues and the effective conduct of research in local authorities. *British Journal of Social Work*, *35*(7), 1023–1024. doi:10.1093/bjsw/bch220

Mustacchi, G. (2021). Cost/benefit evaluations in low-middle/upper-middle income countries: Biases about "out of pocket money". *Current Medical Research and Opinion*, *7*(5), 819–820. doi:10.1080/03007995.2021.1893674 PMID:33617396

Muthi Reddy, P., Manjula, S. H., & Venugopal, K. R. (2018). Secured Privacy Data using Multi Key Encryption in Cloud Storage. *Proceedings of 5th International Conference on Emerging Applications of Information Technology, EAIT 2018.* IEEE. 10.1109/EAIT.2018.8470399

Nadeau, K. (2021, February). *New data show that the majority of U.S. medical students are women.* MLO. https://www.mlo-online.com/21206907.

Nandlall, N., Hawke, L. D., Hayes, E., Darnay, K., Daley, M., Relihan, J., & Henderson, J. (2022). Learning Through a Pandemic: Youth Experiences With Remote Learning During the COVID-19 Pandemic. *SAGE Open*, *12*(3). doi:10.1177/21582440221124122 PMID:36185703

Nath, R. N., Priya, N., & Robin, C. R. R. (2018). A Social Media Content Based Location and Situation Analysis Model for Disaster Management. In Emergency and Disaster Management. doi:10.4018/978-1-5225-6195-8.ch014

National Cancer Institute. (2020). *Social and emotional effects of a cancer diagnosis.* NCI. https://www.cancer.gov/about-cancer/coping/emotional-social/social-emotional-effects

National Center for Biotechnology Information (NCBI). (2017). *Medical Tourism: An Overview.* NCBI. https://www.ncbi.nlm.nih.gov/pmc/articles/PMC5546406/

National Center for Complementary and Integrative Health. (2020). *Stress management: Using relaxation techniques for stress relief.* NCI. https://nccih.nih.gov/health/stress/relaxation.htm

National Commission for the Protection of Human Subjects of Biomedical and Behavioural Research. (1979). *The Belmont report.* NCPHSBBR.

National Comprehensive Cancer Network. (2020). *Stress management.* NCCN. https://www.nccn.org/patients/resources/life_with_cancer/stress-management.aspx

National Institutes of Health. (2008). Protecting Human Research Participants. Retrieved from http://phrp.nihtraining.com/index.php

National Institutes of Health. (2019). *Stress in cancer survivors.* NIH. https://www.ncbi.nlm.nih.gov/pmc/articles/PMC6214096/

Ndubuisi, N. E. (2021). Noncommunicable diseases prevention in low-and middle-income countries: An overview of health in all policies (HiAP). *INQUIRY: The Journal of Health Care Organization, Provision, and Financing*, *58*, 1–6. PMID:34420412

Ndugga, N., Hill, L., Artiga, S., & Haldar, S. (14 July 2022). *Latest Data on COVID-19 Vaccinations by Race/Ethnicity*. KFF. https://www.kff.org/coronavirus-covid-19/issue-brief/latest-data-on-covid-19-vaccinations-by-race-ethnicity/

Nel, D. & Masilela, L., (2020), Open Governance for Improved Service Delivery Innovation in South Africa. *International Journal of eBusiness and eGovernment Studies, 12*(1), 33-47. 10.34111/ijebeg.20201210333

Nelson, D. L., & Quick, J. C. (2008). Understanding Organizational Behavior. Mason, OH: Centage Learning.

Nengomasha, T. C., & Nyanga, H. E. (2012). Managing semi-current records: A case for records centers for the public service of Namibia. *Journal for Studies in Humanities and Social Sciences, 1*(2).

Ng, T. W. H., & Feldman, D. C. (2008). Long Work Hours: A Social Identity Perspective on Meta-Analysis Data. *Journal of Organizational Behavior*, *29*(7), 853–880. doi:10.1002/job.536

Ngulube, P., & Tafor, V. F. (2006). The Management of Public records and archives in the member countries of ESARBICA. *Journal of the Society of Archivists*, *27*(1), 57–58. doi:10.1080/00039810600691288

Nguyen, A., & Yuvejwattana, S. (2022, May 19). *Thailand to Promote Medical Tourism in Post-Covid Era, PM Says.* Bloomberg. https://www.bloomberg.com/news/articles/2022-05-19/thailand-to-promote-medical-tourism-in-post-covid-era-pm-says

Nguyen, T. H., Bui, T. T. T., Nguyen, A. T. T., Pham, T. H., Ngo, T. H., Bui, T. T., & Hong, N. X. (2019). Prevalence of sexual harassment among medical students in Vietnam: A cross-sectional survey. *BMC Medical Education*, *19*(1), 1–9. PMID:30606170

Nguyen, T. H., Netto, C. L. M., Wilkins, J. F., Bröker, P., Vargas, E. E., Sealfon, C., Puthipiroj, P., Li, K. S., Bowler, J. E., Hinson, H. R., Pujar, M., & Stein, G. M. (2021). Insights Into Students' Experiences and Perceptions of Remote Learning Methods: From the COVID-19 Pandemic to Best Practice for the Future. *Frontiers in Education*, *6*, 647986. doi:10.3389/feduc.2021.647986

Nichols, M. (2011). Ethical decision making. *CME Resource*, *3707*, 1–40.

Nichols, M., & Leonard, J. M. (2011). Medical ethics for physicians. *CME Resource*, *4717*, 1–26.

Nickson, D., & Siddons, S. (2004). *Remote Working: Linking People and Organizations*. Routledge London.

Niessen, L. W., Mohan, D., Akuoku, J. K., Mirelman, A. J., Ahmed, S., Koehlmoos, T. P., Trujillo, A., Khan, J., & Peters, D. H. (2018). Tackling socioeconomic inequalities and non-communicable diseases in low-income and middle-income countries under the sustainable development agenda. *Lancet*, *391*(10134), 2036–2046. doi:10.1016/S0140-6736(18)30482-3 PMID:29627160

Nieuwenhuijsen, M. J. (2020). Urban and transport planning pathways to carbon neutral, liveable and healthy cities; A review of the current evidence. *Environment International*, *140*, 105661. doi:10.1016/j.envint.2020.105661 PMID:32307209

Nievas, V. (2015). Post-traumatic stress disorder and police officers. *Australian Police Journal*, *69*(4).

Noree, T., Hanefeld, J., & Smith, R. (2015). Medical tourism in Thailand: A cross-sectional study. *Bulletin of the World Health Organization*, *94*(1), 30–36. doi:10.2471/BLT.14.152165 PMID:26769994

Norheim-Hagtun, I., & Meier, P. (2010). Crowdsourcing for Crisis Mapping in Haiti. *Innovations: Technology, Governance, Globalization*, *5*(4), 81–89. doi:10.1162/INOV_a_00046

Notaro, E., Pascoe, V. L., Hippe, D. S., Lachance, K., Shinohara, M. M., & DeNiro, K. L. (2021). Prevalence of sexual harassment and sexual assault from patient to provider among women in dermatology and across specialties. *International Journal of Women's Dermatology, 7*(3), 270–275. doi:10.1016/j.ijwd.2020.10.006 PMID:34222582

O'Neill, K. M., Mandigo, M., Pyda, J., Nazaire, Y., Greenberg, S. L., Gillies, R., & Damuse, R. (2015). Out-of-pocket expenses incurred by patients obtaining free breast cancer care in Haiti: A pilot study. *Surgery, 158*(3), 747–755. doi:10.1016/j.surg.2015.04.040 PMID:26150200

O'Reilly, C. I. III, Caldwell, D. F., Chatman, J. A., & Doerr, B. (2014). The promise and problems of organizational culture: CEO personality, culture, and firm performance. *Group & Organization Management, 39*(6), 595–625. doi:10.1177/1059601114550713

Oddo, P. C., & Bolten, J. D. (2019). The Value of Near Real-Time Earth Observations for Improved Flood Disaster Response. *Frontiers in Environmental Science, 7*, 127. doi:10.3389/fenvs.2019.00127

Odongo, O. J. (2018). Achieving information safety in a disaster environment: The way forward for Africa. *Regional Journal of Information and Knowledge Management, 3*(1), 15–29.

OECD. (2017). *Medical tourism: A global overview*. OECD. https://www.oecd-ilibrary.org/docserver/9789264270770-en.pdf?expires=1594850587&id=id&accname=guest&checksum=9C9F4DD4DE2C2A4E4F4BD3266D86F10F

OECD. (2021). *Health at a Glance 2021*. Organisation for Economic Cooperation and Development. https://www.oecd-ilibrary.org/sites/ae3016b9-en/index.html?itemId=/content/publication/ae3016b9-en

Ogbomo, O.M, Ejedafiru, F.E & Olukotun, V (2023). Human Factors affecting the preservation of serial materials: A case study of Federal university libraries in north-central Nigeria. *Regional Journal of Information and Knowledge Management, 8*(1)

Ogbomo, O. B., Ejedafiru, F. E., & Olukotun, V. (2023). Human Factors Affecting the Preservation of Series Materials: A Case Study of Federal University Libraries in North Central Nigeria. *Management, 8*(1), 1–10.

Ogie, R. I., Clarke, R. J., Forehead, H., & Perez, P. (2019). Crowdsourced social media data for disaster management: Lessons from the PetaJakarta.org project. *Computers, Environment and Urban Systems, 73*, 108–117. Advance online publication. doi:10.1016/j.compenvurbsys.2018.09.002

Oh, S. S., Galanter, J., Thakur, N., Pino-Yanes, M., Barcelo, N. E., White, M. J., de Bruin, D. M., Greenblatt, R. M., Bibbins-Domingo, K., Wu, A. H. B., Borrell, L. N., Gunter, C., Powe, N. R., & Burchard, E. G. (2015). Diversity in clinical and biomedical research: A promise yet to be fulfilled. *PLoS Medicine, 12*(12), e1001918. doi:10.1371/journal.pmed.1001918 PMID:26671224

Okoro, H. M. (2011). The relationship between organizational culture and performance: Merger in the Nigerian banking industry. [Dissertation, University of Phoenix].

Olu, O., Muneene, D., Bataringaya, J. E., Nahimana, M. R., Ba, H., Turgeon, Y., Karamagi, H. C., & Dovlo, D. (2019). How can digital health technologies contribute to the sustainable attainment of universal health coverage in Africa? A perspective. *Frontiers in Public Health, 7*, 341. doi:10.3389/fpubh.2019.00341 PMID:31803706

Onocak, D. (2023). BİST'te İşlem gören konaklama işletmelerinin finansal performanslarının CRITIC ağırlıklandırmalı TOPSIS yöntemine göre değerlendirilmesi. *Muhasebe ve Finansman Dergisi*, (97), 79–98. doi:10.25095/mufad.1177612

OPOCE. (2003, November 18). *EUR-LEX - 32003L0088 - EN*. OPOCE. https://eur-lex.europa.eu/legal-content/EN/TXT/HTML/?uri=CELEX:32003L0088

Owen Jarus. (2020, March 20). *20 of the worst epidemics and pandemics in history*. Live Science. https://www.livescience.com/worst-epidemics-and-pandemics-in-history.html

OzimekA. (2020). The future of remote work. SSRN 3638597.

Özmen, V., Gürdal, S. Ö., Cabioğlu, N., Özcinar, B., Özaydın, A. N., Kayhan, A., Aribal, E., Sahin, C., Saip, P., & Alagöz, O. (2017). Cost-effectiveness of breast cancer screening in Turkey, a developing country: Results from Bahçeşehir Mammography Screening Project. *European Journal of Breast Health*, *13*(3), 117–122. doi:10.5152/ejbh.2017.3528 PMID:28894850

Özmen, V., Özmen, T., & Doğru, V. (2019). Breast cancer in Turkey; an analysis of 20.000 patients with breast cancer. *European Journal of Breast Health*, *15*(3), 141–146. doi:10.5152/ejbh.2019.4890 PMID:31312788

Oz, T., Havens, R., & Bisgin, H. (2018). Assessment of Blame and Responsibility through Social Media in Disaster Recovery in the Case of #FlintWaterCrisis. *Frontiers in Communication*, *3*, 45. doi:10.3389/fcomm.2018.00045

Oztekin, A. (2017, May 2). *Creating a marketing strategy in the healthcare industry: a holistic data analytic approach*. ProQuest. https://www-proquest-com.libproxy.lib.unc.edu/docview/2112472733?pq-origsite=summon

Page-Reeves, J., Marin, A., Bleecker, M., Moffett, M. L., DeerInWater, K., EchoHawk, S., & Medin, D. (2017). From Community Data to Research Archive. *Gateways : International Journal of Community Research & Engagement*, *10*, 282–297. doi:10.5130/ijcre.v10i1.4947

Pagis, M., & Summers-Effler, E. (2021, December). Aesthetic engagement. *Sociological Forum*, *36*(S1), 1371–1394. doi:10.1111ocf.12768

Pánek, J., Marek, L., Pászto, V., & Valůch, J. (2017). The Crisis Map of the Czech Republic: The nationwide deployment of an Ushahidi application for disasters. *Disasters*, *41*(4), 649–671. doi:10.1111/disa.12221 PMID:28059447

Papagiannidis, S., & Marikyan, D. (2020). Smart offices: A productivity and well-being perspective. *International Journal of Information Management*, *51*, 102027. doi:10.1016/j.ijinfomgt.2019.10.012

Pappas, S. (2021, November 1). *Effective therapy with black women*. Monitor on Psychology. https://www.apa.org/monitor/2021/11/ce-therapy-black-women

Parker, K. A. (2016). *A paradigm of police stress from the lens of retired police officers: A phenomenological study. (Order No. 3718153)*. Available from ProQuest Dissertations & Theses Global.

Pasquel Cajas, A. F., Cajas Bravo, V. T., & Dávila Morán, R. C. (2023). Remote Work in Peru during the COVID-19 Pandemic. *Administrative Sciences*, *13*(2), 1–25. doi:10.3390/admsci13020058

Pecujlija, M., & Cosic, D. (2019). Crisis Management: Introducing Companies Organizational Reactivity and Flexibility. New York: Nova (Business Issues, Competition and Entrepreneurship)

Peeples, L. (2020). *What the data say about police brutality and racial bias—and which reforms might work.*

Pereira, K. (2022, February 25). *The Future of Work in All Industries is a Hybrid Workforce*. AT&T Business. https://www.business.att.com/learn/research-reports/is-corporate-america-ready-for-the-future-of-work.html

Perrin, A., & Anderson, M. (2021). *Digital divide persists even as Americans with lower incomes make gains in tech adoption*. Pew Research Center. https://www.pewresearch.org/fact-tank/2021/01/28/digital-divide-persists-even-as-americans-with-lower-incomes-make-gains-in-tech-adoption/

Perry, A., & Wisnom, D. III. (2004). *The DNA of Brands The Rules for Creating Unique and Durable Brands* (Z. Yılmaz, Trans.). MediaCat Books.

Petty, M. M., Beadles, N. A., Lowery, C. M., Chapman, D. F., & Connell, D. W. (1995). Relationship between organizational culture and organizational performance. *Psychological Reports*, *76*(2), 483–492. doi:10.2466/pr0.1995.76.2.483 PMID:8559874

Phillips, M. D., & Naval War College. (2020). *The Ethics of Emerging Technologies in the Diagnosis and Treatment of PTSD among Service Members*. Naval War College.

Phillips, S. P., & Schneider, M. S. (1993). Sexual harassment of female doctors by patients. *The New England Journal of Medicine*, *329*(26), 1936–1939. doi:10.1056/NEJM199312233292607 PMID:8247058

Phinney, D. (2022). *Duke Health Telehealth Past, Present, and Future*. Duke Health.

Pickens, W. J. (2011). *Critical incidents in law enforcement: A phenomenological analysis of coping with traumatic stress. (Order No. 3448468)*. Available from ProQuest Dissertations & Theses Global.

Piret, J., & Boivin, G. (2021). Pandemics throughout history. *Frontiers in Microbiology*, *11*, 631736. doi:10.3389/fmicb.2020.631736 PMID:33584597

Pi, Y., Nath, N. D., & Behzadan, A. H. (2020). Convolutional neural networks for object detection in aerial imagery for disaster response and recovery. *Advanced Engineering Informatics*, *43*, 101009. doi:10.1016/j.aei.2019.101009

Polite, B. N., Adams-Campbell, L. L., Brawley, O. W., Bickell, N., Carethers, J. M., Flowers, C. R., Foti, M., Gomez, S. L., Griggs, J. J., Lathan, C. S., Li, C. I., Lichtenfeld, J. L., McCaskill-Stevens, W., & Paskett, E. D. (2017). Charting the future of cancer health disparities research: A position statement from the American Association for Cancer Research, the American Cancer Society, the American Society of Clinical Oncology, and the National Cancer Institute. *CA: a Cancer Journal for Clinicians*, *67*(5), 353–361. doi:10.3322/caac.21404 PMID:28738442

Polkowski, T., & Cho, J. (n.d.). *Medical Tourism in Thailand: A Multi-Billion-Dollar Blue Ocean*. Blue Ocean Strategy. https://www.blueoceanstrategy.com/blog/medical-tourism-in-thailand-multi-billion-dollar-blue-ocean/

Popovici, V., & Popovici, A. L. (2020). Remote work revolution: Current opportunities and challenges for organizations. *Ovidius Univ. Ann. Econ. Sci. Ser*, *20*, 468–472.

Poser, K., & Dransch, D. (2010). Volunteered Geographic Information for Disaster Management with Application to Rapid Flood Damage Estimation. *Geomatica*, *64*(1), 89–98.

Potts, K. E., Bennett, R. M., & Rajabifard, A. (2013). Spatially enabled bushfire recovery. *GeoJournal*, *78*(1), 151–163. doi:10.100710708-011-9437-3

Praharaj, S. (2021). Area-based urban renewal approach for smart cities development in India: Challenges of inclusion and sustainability. *Urban Planning*, *6*(4), 202–215. doi:10.17645/up.v6i4.4484

Pramesh, C., Badwe, R. A., Bhoo-Pathy, N., Booth, C. M., Chinnaswamy, G., Dare, A. J., & Gospodarowicz, M. (2022). Priorities for cancer research in low-and middle-income countries: A global perspective. *Nature Medicine*, *28*(4), 649–657. doi:10.103841591-022-01738-x PMID:35440716

Pranjic, N., Bajraktarevic, A., & Ramic, E. (2016). Distress and PTSD in patients with cancer: Cohort study case. *Materia Socio-Medica*, *28*(1), 12. doi:10.5455/msm.2016.28.12-16 PMID:27047260

Prodhan, A. S. U., Islam, D. Z., Khandker, S. S., Jamiruddin, M. R., Abdullah, A., Godman, B., & Adnan, N. (2023). Breast cancer management in the era of Covid-19; key issues, contemporary strategies, and future implications. *Breast Cancer: Targets and Therapy*, 51-89.

Purcarea, V. L. (2019). The impact of marketing strategies in healthcare systems. *Journal of Medicine and Life*, *12*(2), 93–96. doi:10.25122/jml-2019-1003 PMID:31406509

Purnell, L. (2005). *The Purnell Model for Cultural Competence*. ProQuest. https://www.proquest.com/docview/220301419?pq-origsite=gscholar&fromopenview=true

Putri, T., Syafitri, U. D., & Sukmawati, A. (2023). The Role of Human Resource Risk on Employee Performance in The Hybrid Workforce Era. *Jurnal Aplikasi Bisnis dan Manajemen (JABM), 9*(2), 386-386.

PwC. (2021, June). *The future of work A journey to 2022*. PwC. https://www.pwc.com/ee/et/publications/pub/future-of-work-report.pdf

Qiu, W., Rutherford, S., Mao, A., & Chu, C. (2017). The pandemic and its impacts. *Health, Culture and Society (Pittsburgh, Pa.)*, *9*, 1–11. doi:10.5195/HCS.2017.221

Queirós, C., Passos, F., Bártolo, A., Marques, A. J., Da Silva, C. F., & Pereira, A. (2020). Burnout and stress measurement in police officers: Literature review and a study with the operational police stress questionnaire. *Frontiers in Psychology*, *11*, 587. doi:10.3389/fpsyg.2020.00587 PMID:32457673

Quinn, S. C. (2004). Ethics in Public Health Research. *American Journal of Public Health*, *94*(6), 918–922. doi:10.2105/AJPH.94.6.918 PMID:15249289

Radianti, J., & Gjøsæter, T. (2019). Digital Volunteers in Disaster Response: Accessibility Challenges. Lecture Notes in Computer Science (Including Subseries Lecture Notes in Artificial Intelligence and Lecture Notes in Bioinformatics), 11573 LNCS. doi:10.1007/978-3-030-23563-5_42

Rae, M. (2022). "The right to disconnect": Portugal's new labor legislation for remote workers. In *Sage Business Cases*. SAGE Publications, Ltd. doi:10.4135/9781529600391

Raghuram, S., Tuertscher, P., & Garud, R. (2010). Mapping the Field of Virtual Work: A Cocitation Analysis. *Information Systems Research*, *21*(4), 983–999. doi:10.1287/isre.1080.0227

Ramamoorthy, A., Pacanowski, M. A., Bull, J., & Zhang, L. (2015). Racial/ethnic differences in drug disposition and response: A review of recently approved drugs. *Clinical Pharmacology and Therapeutics*, *97*(3), 263–273. doi:10.1002/cpt.61 PMID:25669658

Ramirez, A. (2022, February 15). Are Virtual Reality And The Metaverse Ready To Support Collaborative Work? *Forbes*. https://www.forbes.com/sites/forbestechcouncil/2022/02/15/are-virtual-reality-and-the-metaverse-ready-to-support-collaborative-work/?sh=2cc9f644716c

Rao, P. M., & Deebak, B. D. (2022). Security and privacy issues in smart cities/industries: Technologies, applications, and challenges. *Journal of Ambient Intelligence and Humanized Computing*, 1–37.

Rawls, J. (1999). *A theory of justice* (revised ed.). Harvard University. doi:10.4159/9780674042582

Ray, A., & Bala, P. K. (2020). Social media for improved process management in organizations during disasters. *Knowledge and Process Management*, *27*(1), 63–74. doi:10.1002/kpm.1623

Reine, R. (2019). Archivists and Time: Conceptions of Time and Long-Term Information Preservation among Archivists. *Journal of Contemporary Archival Studies*, *6*(6).

Reinicke, K. (2022). *Men after #MeToo: Being an ally in the fight against sexual harassment*. Springer Nature Switzerland.

Report: 80% Say Salary Isn't Keeping Up With Inflation. (2022, November 22). Remote.co. https://remote.co/report-80-say-salary-isnt-keeping-up-with-inflation/

Rest, J. (1979). *Development in judging moral issues*. University of Minnesota Press.

Reuters. (2021, July 19). *Israeli firm's spyware used to target journalists' cell phones - reports*. Reuters. https://www.reuters.com/technology/israeli-firms-spyware-used-target-journalists-cell-phones-reports-2021-07-19/

Robbins, S. P., & Judge, T. A. (2015). *Organizational Behavior.* Pearson Education, Inc.

Robinson, B. (2022, May 5). Remote Work Increases Employee Happiness By 20%, New Study Finds. *Forbes*. https://www.forbes.com/sites/bryanrobinson/2022/05/05/remote-work-increases-employee-happiness-by-20-new-study-finds/?sh=4f5fe21f3183

Robinson, R. K., Geralyn, M. F., Tinney, C. H., Crow, S. M., & Hartman, S. J. (2005). Sexual harassment in the workplace: Guidelines for educating healthcare managers. *Journal of health and human services administration*. https://pubmed.ncbi.nlm.nih.gov/16318016/

Robinson, T. N., Banda, J. A., Hale, L., Lu, A. S., Fleming-Milici, F., & Calvert, S. L. (2017). Screen media exposure and obesity in children and adolescents. *Pediatrics*.

Rogers, E. M. (1995). *Diffusion of innovations* (4th ed.). Free Press.

Rogosnitzky, M., Berkowitz, E. & Jadad, A. R. (2020). Delivering benefits at speed through real-world repurposing of off-patent drugs: the COVID-19 pandemic as a case in point. *JMIR Public Health and Surveillance*, *6*(2) e19199. doi:10.2196/19199

Rohmah, A. A., Rachmawati, R., & Mei, E. T. W. (2023). Smart City Achievement Through Implementation of Digital Health Services in Handling COVID-19 Indonesia. *Smart Cities*, *6*(1), 639–651. doi:10.3390martcities6010030

Rosemond, K. V. (2018). *Post-traumatic stress disorder in public safety workers: Cultural aspects and implications for effective treatment. (Order No. 10285161)*. Available from ProQuest Dissertations & Theses Global.

Rostamzadeh, R., Ghorabaee, M. K., Govindan, K., Esmaeili, A., & Nobar, H. B. K. (2018). Evaluation of sustainable supply chain risk management using an integrated fuzzy TOPSIS-CRITIC approach. *Journal of Cleaner Production*, *175*, 651–669. doi:10.1016/j.jclepro.2017.12.071

Roy, A. K., Breaux, R., Sciberras, E., Patel, P., Ferrara, E., Shroff, D. M., Cash, A. R., Dvorsky, M. R., Langberg, J. M., Quach, J., Melvin, G., Jackson, A., & Becker, S. P. (2022). A preliminary examination of key strategies, challenges, and benefits of remote learning expressed by parents during the COVID-19 pandemic. *School Psychology*, *37*(2), 147–159. doi:10.1037pq0000465 PMID:35266770

Rubbio, I., Bruccoleri, M., Pietrosi, A., & Ragonese, B. (2020). Digital health technology enhances resilient behaviour: Evidence from the ward. *International Journal of Operations & Production Management*, *40*(1), 34–67. doi:10.1108/IJOPM-02-2018-0057

Ryan Chance, R. K. (2015). Where there is fire, there is politics: Ungovernability and Material Life in Urban South Africa. *Cultural Anthropology*, *30*(3), 394–423. doi:10.14506/ca30.3.03

S.2061 - 117th Congress (2021-2022): Telemental Health Care Access Act of 2021. (2021, June 15). https://www.congress.gov/bill/117th-congress/senate-bill/2061

Sahai, S., Ciby, M. A., & Kahwaji, A. T. (2020). Workplace isolation: A systematic review and synthesis. [IJM]. *International Journal of Management*, *11*(12), 2745–2758.

SAMHSA. (2020). *National Guidelines for Behavioral Health Crisis Care*. SAMHSA. https://www.samhsa.gov/sites/default/files/national-guidelines-for-behavioral-health-crisis-care-02242020.pdf

SAMHSA. (n.d.). Double jeopardy: Covid-19 and behavioral health disparities for black and Latino Communities in the U.S. *SAMHSA.gov*. https://www.samhsa.gov/sites/default/files/covid19-behavioral-health-disparities-black-latino-communities.pdf

Sammut-Bonnici, T., & Galea, D. (2015). Pest analysis. Wiley Encyclopedia of Management, 1–1. https://doi.org/doi:10.1002/9781118785317.weom120113

Sandoval-Reyes, J., Carlier, S. I., & Oliva, E. J. D. (2021). Remote Work, Work Stress, and Work–Life during Pandemic Times: A Latin America Situation. *International Journal of Environmental Research and Public Health*, *18*(13), 7069. doi:10.3390/ijerph18137069 PMID:34281007

Sarason, I. G. (Ed.). (2013). *Social support: Theory, research, and applications* (Vol. 24). Springer Science & Business Media.

Saravanakumar, K., Robinson, Y., Madhu, P., & Manoj, M. (2022). Selection of oil and best bio-diesel blend based on performance and emission characteristics of IC engine: An integrated CRITIC-TOPSIS Approac. *Journal of Scientific and Industrial Research*, *81*(12), 1342–1352. doi:10.56042/jsir.v81i12.47120

Saultz, J. W., Jones, S. M., McDaniel, S. H., Bagley, B., McCormally, T., Marker, J. E., Weida, J. A., & Green, L. A. (2015). A new foundation for the delivery and financing of American health care. *Family Medicine*, *47*(8), 612–619. PMID:26382119

Saunders-Hastings, P. R., & Krewski, D. (2016). Reviewing the history of pandemic influenza: Understanding patterns of emergence and transmission. *Pathogens (Basel, Switzerland)*, *5*(4), 66. doi:10.3390/pathogens5040066 PMID:27929449

Saxena, P., Kumar, V., & Ram, M. (2022). A novel CRITIC-TOPSIS approach for optimal selection of software reliability growth model (SRGM). *Quality and Reliability Engineering International, 38*(5), 2501-2520. doi:10.1002/qre.3087

Sboui, T., & Aissi, S. (2022). *A Risk-based Approach for Enhancing the Fitness of use of VGI*. IEEE. doi:10.1109/ACCESS.2022.3201022

Scharff, D. P., Mathews, K. J., Jackson, P., Hoffsuemmer, J., Martin, E., & Edwards, D. (2010). More than Tuskegee: Understanding mistrust about research participation. *Journal of Health Care for the Poor and Underserved*, *21*(3), 879–897. doi:10.1353/hpu.0.0323 PMID:20693733

Schaufeli, W. B. (2017). Applying the job demands-resources model: A 'how to' guide to measuring and tackling work engagement and burnout. *Organizational Dynamics*, *46*(2), 120–132. doi:10.1016/j.orgdyn.2017.04.008

Schmidt, A., Kramer, A. C., Brose, A., Schmiedek, F., & Neubauer, A. B. (2021). Distance learning, parent–child interactions, and affective well-being of parents and children during the COVID-19 pandemic: A daily diary study. *Developmental Psychology*, *57*(10), 1719–1734. doi:10.1037/dev0001232 PMID:34807692

Scholl, R. W. (1981). An analysis of macro models of organizations: The goal and political models. *Administration & Society*, *13*(3), 271–298. doi:10.1177/009539978101300303

Schrecker, T. (2020). Globalization and health: Political grand challenges. *Review of International Political Economy*, *27*(1), 26–47. doi:10.1080/09692290.2019.1607768

Scott, B. K., Miller, G. T., Fonda, S. J., Yeaw, R. E., Gaudaen, J. C., Pavliscsak, H. H., Quinn, M. T., & Pamplin, J. C. (2020). Advanced digital health technologies for COVID-19 and future emergencies. *Telemedicine Journal and e-Health*, *26*(10), 1226–1233. doi:10.1089/tmj.2020.0140 PMID:32456560

See, L., Mooney, P., Foody, G., Bastin, L., Comber, A., Estima, J., Fritz, S., Kerle, N., Jiang, B., Laakso, M., Liu, H. Y., Milèinski, G., Nikšieč, M., Painho, M., Podör, A., Olteanu-Raimond, A. M. R., & Rutzinger, M. (2016). Crowdsourcing, citizen science or volunteered geographic information? The current state of crowdsourced geographic information. *ISPRS International Journal of Geo-Information, 5*(5), 55. doi:10.3390/ijgi5050055

Shah, S. C., Kayamba, V., Peek, R. M. Jr, & Heimburger, D. (2019). Cancer control in low-and middle-income countries: Is it time to consider screening? *Journal of Global Oncology, 5*(5), 1–8. doi:10.1200/JGO.18.00200 PMID:30908147

Shank, G. (1993). Abductive multiloguing: The semiotic dynamics of navigating the Net. *The Arachnet Electronic Journal of Virtual Culture, 1*(1). http://serials.infomotions.com/aejvc/aejvc-v1n01-shank-abductive.txt

Shan, R., Sarkar, S., & Martin, S. S. (2019). Digital health technology and mobile devices for the management of diabetes mellitus: State of the art. *Diabetologia, 62*(6), 877–887. doi:10.100700125-019-4864-7 PMID:30963188

Sharma, M., Singla, M. K., Nijhawan, P., Ganguli, S., & Rajest, S. S. (2020). An application of IOT to develop concept of smart remote monitoring system. *Business Intelligence for Enterprise Internet of Things*, (pp. 233-239).

Shea, T., & De Cieri, H. (2011). *Workplace stress evaluation tools: A snapshot review.* ISCRR & Monash University.

Shields, J., Pechek, A. A., Brinck, E. A., & Sprong, M. E. (2020). Strategies for improving employment outcomes of veterans diagnosed with post-traumatic stress disorder (PTSD). *Rehabil Prof, 28*, 225–244.

Shore, N., Brazauskas, R., Drew, E., Wong, K. A., Moy, L., Corage Baden, A., & Seifer, S.D. (2010). Understanding Community-Based Processes for Research Ethics Review: A National Study. *Am J Public Health*, AJPH.2010.194340. doi:<p> doi:10.2105/AJPH.2010.194340</p>

Sieck, C. J., Sheon, A., Ancker, J. S., Castek, J., Callahan, B., & Siefer, A. (2021). Digital inclusion as a social determinant of health. *NPJ Digital Medicine, 4*(1), 52. doi:10.103841746-021-00413-8 PMID:33731887

Škiljić, A. (2020). Cybersecurity and remote working: Croatia's (non-) response to increased cyber threats. *International Cybersecurity Law Review, 1*(1-2), 51–61. doi:10.136543439-020-00014-3

Skloot, R. (2010). *The Immortal Life of Henrietta Lacks.* Crown Publishers.

Slack. (2022, July 29). *The future of remote working: What you need to know.* Slack. https://slack.com/blog/collaboration/future-remote-working-what-to-know

Slavicek, G., & Forsdahl, G. (2009). Ethics and regulatory aspects in medical research. *International Journal of Stomatology & Occlusion Medicine, 2*(1), 45–49. doi:10.100712548-009-0007-y

Slebi-Acevedo, C. J., Pascual-Muñoz, P., Lastra-González, P., & Castro-Fresno, D. (2019). Multi-response optimization of porous asphalt mixtures reinforced with aramid and polyolefin fibers employing the CRITIC-TOPSIS based on Taguchi methodology. *Materials (Basel), 12*(22), 3789. doi:10.3390/ma12223789 PMID:31752227

Small, W. Jr, Bacon, M. A., Bajaj, A., Chuang, L. T., Fisher, B. J., Harkenrider, M. M., & Viswanathan, A. N. (2017). Cervical cancer: A global health crisis. *Cancer, 123*(13), 2404–2412. doi:10.1002/cncr.30667 PMID:28464289

Smedley, B. D., Stith, A. Y., & Nelson, A. R. (2003). *Unequal Treatment: Confronting Racial and Ethnic Disparities in Health Care.* National Academy of Sciences.

Smith, D.G., Johnson W.B. (2017). Lots of men are gender-equality allies in private. Why not in public? *Harward Business Review.*

Smith, K. (2013). Here's The Confidential Memo Yahoo Sent Employees About Working From Home. *Business Insider.* https://www.businessinsider.com/yahoo-workingfrom-home-memo-2013-2?r=US&IR=T

Smith, M. (2022, April 13). Twitter, Reddit and 8 other companies offering permanent remote or hybrid work—and hiring right now. *CNBC*. https://www.cnbc.com/2022/04/13/10-companies-that-switched-to-permanent-hybrid-or-remote-work-and-hiring-right-now.html

Snyder, S., Borgelt, B., & Tobey, E. (Eds.). (2016). *Backcasts: A global history of fly fishing and conservation*. University of Chicago Press. doi:10.7208/chicago/9780226366609.001.0001

Soden, R., & Palen, L. (2014). *From Crowdsourced Mapping to Community Mapping: The Post-earthquake Work of OpenStreetMap Haiti*. In COOP 2014 - Proceedings of the 11th International Conference on the Design of Cooperative Systems, Nice, France. 10.1007/978-3-319-06498-7_19

Sommers, B., Collins, S., Gunja, M., & Beutel, S. (2012). Rising insured rates, but persistent uninsurance among working-age adults in a weakened economy: Evidence from the Commonwealth Fund Biennial Health Insurance Survey, 2010. *Health Affairs*, *31*(6), 1188–1198. 10.1377/hlthaff.2011.1176

Son, H. M., Park, E. Y., & Kim, E. J. (2020). Cancer-related fatigue of breast cancer survivors: Qualitative research. *Asian Oncology Nursing*, *20*(4), 141–149. doi:10.5388/aon.2020.20.4.141

Soomro, & Yanos, P. T. (2019). Predictors of Mental Health Stigma among Police Officers: the Role of Trauma and PTSD. *Journal of Police and Criminal Psychology, 34*(2), 175–183. https://doi.org/ doi:10.1007/s11896-018-9285-x

Spector, D., Battaglini, C., Alsobrooks, A., Owen, J., & Groff, D. (2012). Do breast cancer survivors increase their physical activity and enhance their health-related quality of life after attending community-based wellness workshops? *Journal of Cancer Education*, *27*(2), 353–361. doi:10.100713187-011-0306-z PMID:22210191

Spiegel, P., Khalifa, A., & Mateen, F. J. (2014). Cancer in refugees in Jordan and Syria between 2009 and 2012: Challenges and the way forward in humanitarian emergencies. *The Lancet. Oncology*, *15*(7), e290–e297. doi:10.1016/S1470-2045(14)70067-1 PMID:24872112

SSI (Turkish Social Security Institution). (2020). *Strategic plan (2019–2023)*. Republic of Turkey Ministry of Health Strasser.

Stakeholder Letter Urging Senate to Take Action This Fall on Telehealth. (2022). American Telemedicine Association. https://www.americantelemed.org/wp-content/uploads/2022/09/Telehealth-Stakeholder-Letter-to-Senate-FINAL.pdf

Stanojković, J., & Radovanović, M. (2017). Selection of solid carbide end mill for machining aluminum 6082-T6 using CRITIC and TOPSIS methods. *Journal of Production Engineering*, *20*(1), 133–136. doi:10.24867/JPE-2017-01-133

Stebbing, J., & Bower, M. (2004). Lessons for HIV from Tuskegee. *Journal of HIV Therapy*, *9*(3), 50–52. PMID:15534560

Stein, M. K., Jensen, T. B., & Hekkala, R. (2015). Comfortably 'Betwixt and Between'?: Delimiting and Blending Space, Time, Tasks and Technology at Work. *Proceedings of the Thirty Sixth International Conference on Information Systems*. IEEE.

Stelnicki, A. M., Jamshidi, L., Fletcher, A. J., & Carleton, R. N. (2021). Evaluation of before operational stress: A program to support mental health and proactive psychological protection in public safety personnel. *Frontiers in Psychology*, *12*, 3218. doi:10.3389/fpsyg.2021.511755 PMID:34484013

Stone, J. (2002). Race and healthcare disparities: Overcoming vulnerability. *Theoretical Medicine and Bioethics*, *23*(6), 499–518. doi:10.1023/A:1021524431845 PMID:12546167

Stone, L., Phillips, C., & Douglas, K. A. (2019). Sexual assault and harassment of doctors, by doctors: A qualitative study. *Medical Education*, *53*(8), 833–843. doi:10.1111/medu.13912 PMID:31144346

Storz, U. (2022). The COVID-19 vaccine patent race. *Nature Biotechnology*, *40*(7), 1001–1004. doi:10.103841587-022-01376-1 PMID:35831656

Sullivan, C. (2003). What's in a Name? Definitions and Conceptualisations of Teleworking and Homeworking. *New Technology, Work and Employment*, *18*(3), 158–165. doi:10.1111/1468-005X.00118

Sundaram, A. (2020). *Yelp data shows 60% of business closures due to the coronavirus pandemic are now permanent.* CNBC. https://www.cnbc.com/2020/09/16/yelp-data-shows-60percent-of-business-closures-due-to-the-coronavirus-pandemic-are-now-permanent.html

Susilo, D. (2020). Revealing the effect of work-from-home on job performance during the COVID-19 crisis: Empirical evidence from Indonesia. *Journal of Contemporary Issues in Business and Government*, *26*(1), 23–40.

Sutton, L. B., Erlen, J. A., Glad, J. M., & Siminoff, L. A. (2003). Recruiting vulnerable populations for research: Revisiting the ethical issues. *Journal of Professional Nursing*, *19*(2), 106–112. doi:10.1053/jpnu.2003.16 PMID:12748936

Swanson, G. M., & Ward, A. J. (1995). Recruiting minorities into clinical trials toward a participant-friendly system. *Journal of the National Cancer Institute*, *87*(23), 1747–1759. doi:10.1093/jnci/87.23.1747 PMID:7473831

Swartz, P., Da Veiga, A., & Martins, N. (2021). Validating an information privacy governance questionnaire to measure the perceptions of employees. *Information and Computer Security*, *29*(5), 761–789. doi:10.1108/ICS-08-2020-0135

Sweeney, B. (2022). *Digital Marketing Quickstart Guide*. ClydeBank Media, LLC.

Sweeney, B. (2022). *Digital Marketing; Quickstart Guide*. ClydeBank Media.

Swisher, L. L., & Davis, C. M. (2005). The realm-individual-process-situation (RIPS) model of ethical decision-making. *HPA Resource*, *5*(3), 1–8.

Talent'd by WorldRef. (2023, January 6). *The relationship between globalisation and the rise of remote work*. Linkedin. https://www.linkedin.com/pulse/relationship-between-globalisation-rise-remote-work-

Tan, S. Y., & Taeihagh, A. (2020). Smart city governance in developing countries: A systematic literature review. *sustainability, 12*(3), 899.

Tandon, S., Kumar, V., & Singh, V. B. (2022). *An empirical analysis of code smells using CRITIC-TOPSIS method.* 2022 12th International Conference on Cloud Computing, Data Science & Engineering (Confluence), Noida, India. 10.1109/Confluence52989.2022.9734202

Tatrow, K., & Montgomery, G. H. (2006). Cognitive behavioral therapy techniques for distress and pain in breast cancer patients: a meta-analysis. *Journal of behavioral medicine, 29*, 17–27.

TavraM.RacetinI.PerošJ. (2019). Combining social media and authoritative data for crisis mapping: A case study of a wildfire reaching croatian city of split. *International Archives of the Photogrammetry, Remote Sensing and Spatial Information Sciences - ISPRS Archives, 42*(3/W8). doi:10.5194/isprs-archives-XLII-3-W8-415-2019

Taylor, J., & Gibson, K. L. (2017). Digitization, digital interaction, and social media: Embedded barriers to democratic heritage. *International Journal of Heritage Studies*, *23*(5), 408–420. doi:10.1080/13527258.2016.1171245

Tekin, E. (2015). The impacts of political and economic uncertainties on the tourism industry in Turkey. *Mediterranean Journal of Social Sciences, 6*(2 S5), 265.

Tenable. (2021, September 22). *Seventy-Four percent of organizations attribute damaging cyberattacks to vulnerabilities in technology put in place during the pandemic, according to global industry study*. Tenable®. https://www.tenable.com/press-releases/seventy-four-percent-of-organizations-attribute-damaging-cyberattacks-to

Thakkar, P. & Paliwal, M. S. (2021). *Ghole, selection of power generation technology using a combination of CRITIC and TOPSIS*. 2021 IEEE 2nd International Conference On Electrical Power and Energy Systems (ICEPES), Bhopal, India. . doi:10.1109/ICEPES52894.2021.9699756

The European Parliament and The Council of The European Union. (2019, July 11). *DIRECTIVE (EU) 2019/1152 OF THE EUROPEAN PARLIAMENT AND OF THE COUNCIL of 20 June 2019 on transparent and predictable working conditions in the European Union*. Official Journal of the European Union. https://eur-lex.europa.eu/legal-content/EN/TXT/HTML/?uri=CELEX:32019L1152

Thomas, A., & Kopczak, L. R. (2007). Life-saving supply chains: Challenges and the path forward. In *Building supply chain excellence in emerging economies* (pp. 93–111). Springer US. doi:10.1007/978-0-387-38429-0_4

Thompson, S. B., Eccleston, L., & Hickish, T. (2011). *Post-traumatic stress disorder in cancer survivors: Recognising and acknowledging the symptoms.*

Till, J. E. (2003). Evaluation of support groups for women with breast cancer: importance of the navigator role. *Health and quality of life outcomes*, *1*, 1–6.

Tomasini, R., & Van Wassenhove, L. N. (2009). From preparedness to partnerships: Case study research on humanitarian logistics. *International Transactions in Operational Research*, *16*(5), 549–559. doi:10.1111/j.1475-3995.2009.00697.x

Torke, A. M., Corbie-Smith, G. M., & Branch, W. T. (2004). African American patients ‘ perspectives on medical decision-making. *Archives of Internal Medicine*, *164*(5), 525–530. doi:10.1001/archinte.164.5.525 PMID:15006829

Treichler, C. (2022). The Top 6 Online Mental Health & Therapy On-Demand Services of 2022. *Online Doctor.* https://www.onlinedoctor.com/best-online-mental-health-therapy-on-demand-services/

Tripathi, A. D., Mishra, R., Maurya, K. K., Singh, R. B., & Wilson, D. W. (2019). Estimates for world population and global food availability for global health. In *The role of functional food security in global health* (pp. 3–24). Academic Press. doi:10.1016/B978-0-12-813148-0.00001-3

Trivellas, P., Reklitis, P., & Platis, C. (2013). The effect of job-related stress on employees' satisfaction: A survey in health care. *Procedia: Social and Behavioral Sciences*, *73*, 718–726. doi:10.1016/j.sbspro.2013.02.110

Troxel, A. B., Asch, D. A., Vijayaraghavan, M., & Burdick, T. E. (2017). Policy approaches to promote digital health: A review. *Health Affairs*, *36*(7), 1201–1208. PMID:28679806

Tsai, T., & Harasym, P. (2010). A medical ethical reasoning model and its contribution to medical education. *Medical Education*, *44*(9), 864–873. doi:10.1111/j.1365-2923.2010.03722.x PMID:20716096

Tseng, Y. J., & Shih, Y. L. (2020). Developing epidemic forecasting models to assist disease surveillance for influenza with electronic health records. *International Journal of Computers and Applications*, *42*(6), 616–621. doi:10.1080/1206212X.2019.1633762

TSS Ad Hoc Advisory Panel. (1973). *Final Report of the Tuskegee Syphilis Study Ad Hoc Advisory Panel*. USF. https://www.research.usf.edu/cs/library/docs/finalreport-tuskegeestudyadvisorypanel.pdf

Turan, Z., Kucuk, S., & Cilligol Karabey, S. (2022). The university students' self-regulated effort, flexibility and satisfaction in distance education. *International Journal of Educational Technology in Higher Education*, *19*(1), 35. doi:10.118641239-022-00342-w PMID:35891707

TurkStat. (2019). *Türkiye health survey-2019.* TurkStat. https://data.tuik.gov.tr/Bulten/Index?p=Turkiye-Saglik-Arastirmasi-2019-33661

Tuskegee Syphilis Study Legacy Committee. (1996). Final Report of the Tuskegee Syphilis Study Legacy Committee I www.hsl.virginia.edu. *University of Virginia Health Systems, Claude Moore Health Sciences Library*. US Able Net. http://transcoder.usablenet.com/tt/www.hsl.virginia.edu/historical/medical_history/bad_blood/report.cfm

Tuskegee University National Center for Bioethics in Research and Health Care. (n.d.). *About the USPHS Syphilis Study*. Tuskegee University. https://www.tuskegee.edu/about_us/centers_of_excellence/bioethics_center/about_the_usphs_syphilis_study.aspx

Tymchuk, A. (1981). Ethical decision making and psychological treatment. *Journal of Psychiatric Treatment and Evaluation*, *3*(6), 507–513. PMID:11651663

U.S. Bureau of Labor Statistics. (2020, September 3). *High deductible health plans and health savings account*. U.S. Bureau of Labor Statistics. https://www.bls.gov/ncs/ebs/factsheet/high-deductible-health-plans-and-health-savings-accounts.htm

U.S. Department of Health and Human Services. (2021). *Telehealth for Providers: What You Need to Know*. CMS. https://www.cms.gov/files/document/telehealth-toolkit-providers.pdf

U.S. Department of Justice. (2017). Police-community relations. US DoJ. https://www.justice.gov/ag/page/file/906896/download

U.S. Department of Justice. (2020). Report to the nation on police use of force. US DoJ. https://www.justice.gov/opa/report-nation-police-use-force

U.S. DEPARTMENT OF LABOR. (2021, January 20). *U.S. Department Of Labor Issues Guidance to Clarify Employers' Obligations To Track Teleworkers' Compensable Hours*. DOL. https://www.dol.gov/newsroom/releases/whd/whd20200824

Ulusoy, H., Swigart, V., & Erdemir, F. (2011). Think globally, act locally: Understanding sexual harassment from a cross-cultural perspective. *Medical Education*, *45*(6), 603–612. doi:10.1111/j.1365-2923.2010.03918.x PMID:21501219

UN. (2020). *Refugees*. UN. https://www.unhcr. org/refugees.html?gclid=CjwKCAjwqJ_1BRBZEiwAv73uwH-g8pVAEhyeyYc8ARjr R5JLE4Qn4K1XVdsHRVEqXVtbPhwVscnR9xoCdtwQAvD_BwE

UNESCO. (2020). *Education: From disruption to recovery*. UNESCO. https://en.unesco.org/covid19/educationresponse

UNESCO. (2021). *Education: From disruption to recovery*. UNESCO. https://en.unesco.org/covid19/educationresponse #durationschoolclosures.

UNHCR (United Nations High Commissioner for Refugees). (2014). *Syria regional refugee response*. UNHCR. http://data.unhcr.org/syrianrefugees/regional.php

UNHCR (United Nations High Commissioner for Refugees). (2023). *Trend of registered Syrian refugees*. UNHCR. https://data.unhcr.org/en/situations/syria

Useem, J. (2017). When Working From Home Doesn't Work: IBM pioneered telecommuting. Now it wants people back in the office. *The Atlantic*. https://www.theatlantic.com/magazine/archive/2017/11/when-working-from-home-doesnt-work/540660/

van der Meer, C. A., Bakker, A., Smit, A. S., van Buschbach, S., den Dekker, M., Westerveld, G. J., & Olff, M. (2017). Gender and age differences in trauma and PTSD among Dutch treatment-seeking police officers. *The Journal of Nervous and Mental Disease*, *205*(2), 87–92. doi:10.1097/NMD.0000000000000562 PMID:27434192

Van Wassenhove, L. N. (2006). Blackett Memorial Lecture. Humanitarian Aid Logistics: Supply Chain Management in Hih Gear. *The Journal of the Operational Research Society*, *57*(5), 475–489. doi:10.1057/palgrave.jors.2602125

Vavassori, A., Carrion, D., Zaragozi, B., & Migliaccio, F. (2022). VGI and Satellite Imagery Integration for Crisis Mapping of Flood Events. *ISPRS International Journal of Geo-Information, 11*(12), 611. doi:10.3390/ijgi11120611

Velasquez, M., Andre, C., Shanks, T., & Meyer, M. (n.d.). *Thinking ethically: A framework for moral decision-making.* SCU. https://www.scu.edu/ethics/publications/iie/v7n1/thinking.html

Venkatesh, A., & Vitalari, N. P. (1992). An emerging distributed work arrangement: An investigation of computer-based supplemental work at home. *Management Science, 38*(12), 1687–1706. doi:10.1287/mnsc.38.12.1687

Venson, L. S., Ngoepe, M., & Ngulube, P. (2014). The role of public archives in national development in selected countries in the East and Southern Africa Regional Branch of the International Council on Archives region. *Innovation, 48*, 43–63.

Venton, B. J., & Pompano, R. R. (2021). Strategies for enhancing remote student engagement through active learning. *Analytical and Bioanalytical Chemistry, 413*(6), 1507–1512. doi:10.100700216-021-03159-0 PMID:33458779

Verma, S., Sharma, R., Deb, S., & Maitra, D. (2021). Artificial intelligence in marketing: Systematic review and future research direction. *International Journal of Information Management Data Insights, 1*(1), 100002. doi:10.1016/j.jjimei.2020.100002

Vig, K. D., Mason, J. E., Carleton, R. N., Asmundson, G. J. G., Anderson, G. S., & Groll, D. (2020). Mental health and social support among public safety personnel. *Occupational Medicine, 70*(6), 427–433. doi:10.1093/occmed/kqaa129 PMID:32705138

Vincent Rajkumar, S. (2020). The high cost of prescription drugs: Causes and solutions. *Blood Cancer Journal, 10*(6), 1–5. doi:10.103841408-020-0338-x PMID:32576816

Viner, R. M., Russell, S. J., Croker, H., Packer, J., Ward, J., Stansfeld, C., Mytton, O., Bonell, C., & Booy, R. (2020). Review School closure and management practices during coronavirus outbreaks including COVID-19: A rapid systematic review. *The Lancet. Child & Adolescent Health, 2019*(20), 1–8. doi:10.1016/S2352-4642(20)30095-X PMID:32272089

Violanti, J. M., Ma, C. C., Mnatsakanova, A., Fekedulegn, D., Hartley, T. A., Gu, J. K., & Andrew, M. E. (2018). Associations between police work stressors and post-traumatic stress disorder symptoms: Examining the moderating effects of coping. *Journal of Police and criminal psychology, 33*, 271–282.

Virtanen, M., Ferrie, J. E., Singh-Manoux, A., Shipley, M. J., Stansfeld, S. A., Marmot, M. G., Ahola, K., Vahtera, J., & Kivimäki, M. (2011). Long Working Hours and Symptoms of Anxiety and Depression: A 5-year Follow-up of the Whitehall II Study. *Psychological Medicine, 41*(12), 2485–2494. doi:10.1017/S0033291711000171 PMID:21329557

Von Robertson, R., & Chaney, C. D. (2019). *Police use of excessive force against African Americans: Historical antecedents and community perceptions.* Rowman & Littlefield.

Walker, P. F., Settgast, A., & DeSilva, M. B. (2022). Cancer screening in refugees and immigrants: A global perspective. *The American Journal of Tropical Medicine and Hygiene, 106*(6), 1593–1600. doi:10.4269/ajtmh.21-0692 PMID:35533696

Walsh, B. (2020). COVID-19: The history of pandemics. *BBC Future.* https://www.bbc.com/future/article/20200325-COVID-19-the-history-of-pandemics

Wamukoya, J., & Mutula, S. (2009). Public Sector Information management in East and Southern Africa: Implications for FOI, democracy, and integrity in government. *International Journal of Information Management, 29*(5), 331–341.

Wang, B., & Hsieh, C. H. (2015). Measuring the value of patents with fuzzy multiple criteria decision making: Insight into the practices of the Industrial Technology Research Institute. *Technological Forecasting and Social Change, 92*, 263–275. doi:10.1016/j.techfore.2014.09.015

Wang, B., Liu, Y., Qian, J., & Parker, S. K. (2021). Achieving Effective Remote Working During the COVID-19 Pandemic: A Work Design Perspective. *Applied Psychology*, *70*(1), 16–59. doi:10.1111/apps.12290 PMID:33230359

Wang, C., Wang, L., Gu, T., Yin, J., & Hao, E. (2023). CRITIC-TOPSIS-Based evaluation of smart community safety: A case study of Shenzhen, China. *Buildings*, *13*(2), 476. doi:10.3390/buildings13020476

Wang, S. J., Edelman, E. J., & Park, E. R. (2018). Digital health interventions: A review of the literature. *Journal of the American Medical Informatics Association : JAMIA*, *25*(1), 1–10. doi:10.1093/jamia/ocy003

Wangutusi, J. (2009). *Assessing the Impact of Institutional E-Readiness for Provision of Archival Information to Researchers: The Case of Kenya National Archives and Documentation Service.*

Wang, Y., Ariyo, T., Liu, H., & Ma, C. (2022). Does psychosocial support buffer the effect of COVID-19 related stressors on mental health among Chinese during quarantine? *Current Psychology (New Brunswick, N.J.)*, *41*(10), 7459–7469. doi:10.100712144-021-01663-1 PMID:34075286

Wartick, S.L. & ve Cochran, P.L. (2013). The Evolution of the Corporate Social Performance Model. *The Academy of Management Review, 10.*

Washington, H. (2006). *Medical Apartheid: The Dark History of Medical Experimentation on Black Americans from Colonial Times to the Present*. First Anchor Books.

Weathers, F. W., Newman, E., Blake, D. D., Nagy, L. M., Schnurr, P. P., Kaloupek, D. G., & Keane, T. M. (2004). *Clinician-administered PTSD scale:(CAPS)*. Western Psychological Services.

Webber-Ritchey, K. J., & Lane-Cordova, A. D. (2021). Health disparities and COVID-19 pandemic: Increasing clinical research participation among African Americans. *Journal of Health Disparities Research and Practice*, *14*(2), 5.

Wedge, D. (July 9, 2020). *Strategies Based on COVID-19 Patient Characteristics could improve outcomes, reduce hospital strain, research suggests - hospital data confirming the higher disease burden on patients who face social adversities also under possible care strategies*. Health City. https://healthcity.bmc.org/research/covid-19-patient-characteristics-could-inform-tailored-strategies

Weiling, S., & Hao, Y. X. Z. (2018). The Patent portfolios value evaluation based on the TOPSIS-Entropy method. *In 2018 Portland International Conference on Management of Engineering and Technology (PICMET)*. IEEE. 10.23919/PICMET.2018.8481868

Weise, K. (2021). Amazon's profit soars 220 percent as pandemic drives shopping online. *The New York Times*. https://www.nytimes.com/2021/04/29/technology/amazons-profits-triple.html#:~:text=With%20the%20pandemic%20shifting%20sales,the%20same%20period%20last%20year

Weston, L. E., Krein, S. L., & Harrod, M. (2021). Using observation to better understand the healthcare context. *Qualitative Research in Medicine & Healthcare*, *5*(3). doi:10.4081/qrmh.2021.9821 PMID:37441282

Wheatley, D., & Gifford, J. (2019). *UK Working Lives: Survey Report 2019*. CIPD Development. http://cipd.co.uk/workinglives

White, C. (2019). *Three ways to create a work culture that brings out the best in employees*. T.E.D. Talk. https://www.ted.com/talks/chris_white_3_ways_to_create_a_work_culture_that_brings_out_the_best_in_employees

Whitelaw, S., Pellegrini, D. M., Mamas, M. A., Cowie, M., & Van Spall, H. G. (2021). Barriers and facilitators of the uptake of digital health technology in cardiovascular care: A systematic scoping review. *European Heart Journal. Digital Health*, *2*(1), 62–74. doi:10.1093/ehjdh/ztab005 PMID:34048508

WHO. (2013). *Turkey, country cooperation strategy at a glance*. WHO. https://www.who.int/countryfocus/cooperation_strategy/ccsbrief_tur_en.pdf

WHO. (2018). *Noncommunicable Diseases country profiles 2018*. WHO. https://www.who.int/publications/i/item/9789241514620

WHO. (2019). *Cancer: breast cancer*. WHO. https://www.who.int/cancer/prevention/diagnosis-screening/breast-cancer/en/

WHO. (2020). *The World Bank in Turkey country snapshot: an overview of the World Bank's work in Turkey*. WHO. https://thedocs.worldbank.org/en/doc/1818015 87125378913-0080022020/original/TurkeySnapshotApr2020.pdf

WHO. (2021). *Breast cancer: prevention and control*. WHO. https://www. who.int/news-room/fact-sheets/detail/breast-cancer

WHO. (2022). *Noncommunicable diseases: progress monitor 2022*. WHO. https://www.who.int/publications/i/item/9789240047761

WHO. (2023a). *Noncommunicable diseases*. WHO. https://www.who.int/news-room/fact-sheets/detail/noncommunicable-diseases#:~:text=Noncommunicable%20diseases%20(NCDs)%20kill%2041,%2D%20and%20middle%2Dincome%20 countries

WHO. (2023b). *Global breast cancer initiative implementation framework: assessing, strengthening and scaling up of services for the early detection and management of breast cancer*. Geneva: World Health Organization. https://www.who.int/initiatives/global-breast-cancer-initiative

Wicklund, E. (2020). *Guidelines for Marketing a Practice's New Telehealth Platform*. mHealth Intelligence. https://mhealthintelligence.com/news/guidelines-for-marketing-a-practices-new-telehealth-platform

Wicklund, E. (2020, November 25). *Guidelines for marketing a practice's new telehealth platform*. Mental Health Intelligence. https://mhealthintelligence.com/news/guidelines-for-marketing-a-practices-new-telehealth-platform

Williams, J., Allen, L., Wickramasinghe, K., Mikkelsen, B., Roberts, N., & Townsend, N. (2018). A systematic review of associations between non-communicable diseases and socioeconomic status within low-and lower-middle-income countries. *Journal of Global Health*, *8*(2), 020409. doi:10.7189/jogh.08.020409 PMID:30140435

WIPO. (2022), *World Intellectual Property Report 2022*. WIPO. https://www.wipo.int/edocs/pubdocs/en/wipo-pub-944-2022-en-world-intellectual-property-report-2022-the-direction-of-innovation.pdf (accessed 27 January 2023)

World Bank. (2020). *How tackling the world's deadliest diseases can boost a healthy workforce and economic growth*. World Bank. https://www.worldbank.org/en/news/immersive-story/2020/02/06/tackling-worlds-deadliest-diseases-can-boost-healthy-workforce-and-economic-growth

World Bank. (2022). *World Bank country and lending groups* World Bank. https://datahelpdesk.worldbank.org/knowledgebase/articles/906519-world-bank-country-and-lending-groups

World Bank. (2023). *Middle-Income countries: overview*. World Bank. https://www.worldbank.org/en/country/mic/overview

World Economic Forum. (2023, May 1). *The Future of Jobs Report 2020*. WEF. https://www.weforum.org/reports/the-future-of-jobs-report-2020

World Health Organization. (2000). [*Health Systems: Improving Performance*. Geneva.]. *World Health Report*, 2000.

World Health Organization. (2021). *Global expenditure on health: Public spending on the rise?* World Health Organization.

World Health Organization. (2022). *Mental health at work.* WHO. www.who.int. https://www.who.int/news-room/fact-sheets/detail/mental-health-at-work

World Tourism Organization (WTO). (2017). *Medical Tourism: Trends and Implications.* WTO. https://www.e-unwto.org/doi/pdf/10.18111/9789284419133

Wu, H., Liu, S., Wang, J., & Yang, T. (2020). Construction safety risk assessment of bridges in the marine environment based on CRITIC and TOPSIS models. *Journal of Coastal Research, 108*(SI), 206-210. doi:10.2112/JCR-SI108-040.1

Xin, Y. (2022). Anomaly detection for volunteered geographic information: A case study of Safecast data. *International Journal of Geographical Information Science*, *36*(7), 1423–1442. doi:10.1080/13658816.2021.1981333

Xu, Y., Siyi, C., & Mengyang, P. (2020). Dynamic radiator threat assessment based on CRITIC-TOPSIS. [in Chinese]. *Journal of Beijing University of Aeronautics and Astronautics*, *46*(11), 2168–2175. doi:10.13700/j.bh.1001-5965.2019.0585

Yancy, C. W. (2020). COVID-19 and African Americans. *Journal of the American Medical Association*, *323*(19), 1891–1892. doi:10.1001/jama.2020.6548 PMID:32293639

Yang, L., Jaffe, S., Holtz, D., Suri, S., Sinha, S., Weston, J., Teevan, J. (2020). How work from home affects collaboration: A large-scale study of information workers in a natural experiment during COVID-19. *arXiv preprint arXiv:2007.15584.*

Yang, Y., & Cornelious, L. (2003, November). *Ensuring the quality of online education instruction.* Paper presented at Mid-South Educational Research Association Conference, Biloxi, MS.

Yang, Y., Li, C., Xue, W., & Kang, S. (2019, April). Economic benefit evaluation analysis for distributed energy generation projects based on CRITIC-TOPSIS model. In IOP Conference Series: Earth and Environmental Science, 252(3), 032059, IOP Publishing. doi:10.1088/1755-1315/252/3/032059

Yang, L., Holtz, D., Jaffe, S., Suri, S., Sinha, S., Weston, J., Joyce, C., Shah, N., Sherman, K., Hecht, B., & Teevan, J. (2022). The effects of remote work on collaboration among information workers. *Nature Human Behaviour*, *6*(1), 43–54. doi:10.103841562-021-01196-4 PMID:34504299

Yan, Y., Chen, J., & Wang, Z. (2020). Mining public sentiments and perspectives from geotagged social media data for appraising the post-earthquake recovery of tourism destinations. *Applied Geography (Sevenoaks, England)*, *123*, 102306. doi:10.1016/j.apgeog.2020.102306

Yan, Y., Eckle, M., Kuo, C. L., Herfort, B., Fan, H., & Zipf, A. (2017). Monitoring and assessing post-disaster tourism recovery using geotagged social media data. *ISPRS International Journal of Geo-Information*, *6*(5), 144. doi:10.3390/ijgi6050144

Yates, D., & Paquette, S. (2011). Emergency knowledge management and social media technologies: A case study of the 2010 Haitian earthquake. *International Journal of Information Management*, *31*(1), 6–13. doi:10.1016/j.ijinfomgt.2010.10.001

Yavuz, N., & Baki, B. (2019). Patent değerlerinin çok kriterli karar verme yöntemleri ile sıralanması: Otomotiv sektöründe bir uygulama, *Karadeniz Teknik Üniversitesi Sosyal Bilimler Enstitüsü Sosyal Bilimler Dergisi*, *9*(17) 27-52. <https://dergipark.org.tr/tr/pub/sbed/issue/46469/448470>

Yearby, R. (2018). Racial disparities in health status and access to healthcare: The continuation of inequality in the United States due to structural racism. *American Journal of Economics and Sociology*, *77*(3-4), 1113–1152. doi:10.1111/ajes.12230

Yenisu, E., Şahin, F., & Öztekkeli, H. (2019). Yönetim düşüncesinin evriminde sistem kuramının etkileri: Kavramsal bir çözümleme. *Akademi Sosyal Bilimler Dergisi*, *6*(18), 514-527. https://dergipark.org.tr/en/pub/asbider/issue/48571/616909

Yigitcanlar, T., Kankanamge, N., Regona, M., Ruiz Maldonado, A., Rowan, B., Ryu, A., Desouza, K. C., Corchado, J. M., Mehmood, R., & Li, R. Y. M. (2020). Artificial intelligence technologies and related urban planning and development concepts: How are they perceived and utilized in Australia? *Journal of Open Innovation*, *6*(4), 187. doi:10.3390/joitmc6040187

Yingwei, Y., Dawei, M., & Hongchao, F. (2020). A research framework for the application of volunteered geographic information in post-disaster recovery monitoring. *Tropical Geography*, *40*(2). doi:10.13284/j.cnki.rddl.003239

Yin, J., Wang, J., Wang, C., Wang, L., & Chang, Z. (2023). CRITIC-TOPSIS based evaluation of smart community governance: A case study in China. *Sustainability (Basel)*, *15*(3), 1923. doi:10.3390u15031923

Yuan, X., & Song, W. (2022). Evaluating technology innovation capabilities of companies based on Entropy-TOPSIS: The case of solar cell companies. *Information Technology and Management*, *23*(2), 65–76. doi:10.100710799-021-00344-6

Yuan, Y. (2023). Decision support system for evaluating English media analytics and the role of visualization in online business development using CRITIC and TOPSIS approaches. *Soft Computing*, 1–15. doi:10.100700500-023-08094-z

Yu, H., Gao, Y., Yang, L., Liu, F., Gao, X., & Tan, Q. (2023). Knowledge reasoning of transmission line component detection using CRITIC and TOPSIS approaches. *Soft Computing*, *27*(2), 991–1004. doi:10.100700500-022-07540-8

Yu, J., Zhao, Q., & Chin, C. S. (2019). Extracting typhoon disaster information from VGI based on machine learning. *Journal of Marine Science and Engineering*, *7*(9), 318. doi:10.3390/jmse7090318

Zebley, K. (2022). *Comments on the CY2023 Physician Fee Schedule proposed rule (CMS-1700-P)*. American Telemedicine Association. https://www.americantelemed.org/wp-content/uploads/2022/08/CY23-PFS-Comments_ATA_FINAL.pdf

Zebley, K. (2022). *Updates on the ATA and ATA Action's Policy and Advocacy Work*. American Telemedicine Association.

Zhang, N., Yang, S., & Jia, P. (2022). Cultivating resilience during the COVID-19 pandemic: A socioecological perspective. *Annual Review of Psychology*, *73*(1), 575–598. doi:10.1146/annurev-psych-030221-031857 PMID:34579547

Zhang, W., Bo, Z. H. A. O., Yashuo, L. I., Liming, Z. H. O. U., Kang, N. I. U., Jıang, H., & Guangrui, L. I. (2022). Construction of spare parts importance evaluation for cross-region harvester based on CRITIC and TOPSIS method. *INMATEH - Agricultural Engineering*, *68*(3), 798–808. doi:10.35633/inmateh-68-79

Zhang, W., Wang, Y., Yang, L., & Wang, C. (2020). Suspending classes without stopping learning: China's education emergency management policy in the COVID-19 outbreak. *Journal of Risk and Financial Management*, *13*(3), 55. doi:10.3390/jrfm13030055

Zhao, X., Zhang, X., & Emmanuel, A. (2022). Research and demonstration of technology opportunity identification model based on text classification and core patents. *Computers & Industrial Engineering*, *171*, 108403. doi:10.1016/j.cie.2022.108403

Zhuang, W., Fan, Z., Chu, Y., Wang, H., Yang,Y., Wu, L., Sun, N., Sun, G., Shen, Y., Lin, X., Guo, G., & Xi, S. (2020). Chinese patent medicines in the treatment of coronavirus disease 2019 (COVID-19) in China. *Frontiers in Pharmacology*, *11*(2020). doi:10.3389/fphar.2020.01066

Zook, M., Graham, M., Shelton, T., & Gorman, S. (2010). Volunteered Geographic Information and Crowdsourcing Disaster Relief: A Case Study of the Haitian Earthquake. *World Medical & Health Policy*, *2*(2), 6–32. doi:10.2202/1948-4682.1069

Zulqarnain, R. M., Siddique, I., Jarad, F., Ali, R., & Abdeljawad, T. (2021). Development of TOPSIS technique under pythagorean fuzzy hypersoft environment based on correlation coefficient and its application towards the selection of antivirus mask in COVID-19 pandemic. *Complexity*, *2021*, 1–27. doi:10.1155/2021/6634991

About the Contributors

Saeed Siyal is a Research Fellow at School of Economics and Management, Beijing University of Chemical Technology. He has more than 10 years of teaching and research experience nationally in different universities in Pakistan and China. He has published in well-reputed peer-reviewed and impact factor research journals. Recently his research has been accepted in the European Academy of Management Annual Conference (EURAM), British Academy of Management Annual Conference (BAM) and 3rd international conference on environmental research and public health (an MDPI conference). He is a member of "Association for Psychological Science (APS)" and "The Society of Digital Information and Wireless Communications (SDIWC)". His current research interests include HRM, Management, organizational behavior, and leadership,.

***

Munir Ahmad has a PhD in Computer Science with over 23 years of extensive experience in Spatial Data Production, Management, Processing, Visualization, and Quality Control. A seasoned professional with extensive knowledge in the field, having served as a trainer for the latest spatial technologies. With a passion for research and over 25 publications in the same field, I am dedicated to advancing the industry and spreading knowledge through my expertise and experience. #SpatialData #GIS #GeoTech"

Usha Ajithkumar Malayankandy is Professor & Head, Department of Education, SASTRA University, Tamil Nadu, India. Her research interests are in the areas of ICT based innovative practices in education, teaching pedagogy, human rights, child rights, TVET and curriculum design and development. She is committed to promoting a culture of excellence, ethics, and engagement in her work

Fatma Altuntas is an Assistant Professor at Istanbul Topkapi University, Faculty of Economics, Administrative and Social Sciences. She received a Ph.D. degree from the Department of Business Administration, Gebze Technical University, Her current research interests include Data Mining, Innovation, and Technology Management. Her research appeared in SSCI index journals such as International Journal of Hospitality Management, Cluster Computing, and Kybernetes.

María Báez is an organizational leadership psychologist, consultant, and coach. She is the founder-CEO of MBaez Consulting Llc, an organization specializing in organizational diagnostic and change management. She also provides leadership development and growth training, such as mindful leadership applied to diversity, inclusion, equity, ethics, organizational readiness, and emotional intelligence. She has a Bachelor of Industrial Engineering, a Master of Operations Management, and a second Master of Business Administration with a concentration in Human Resources. Her first book, written in English and Spanish, What is happening to me? What do I do? It has changed the lives of many girls around the world. After facing a difficult transition with language, gender, and racial discrimination, she overcame the challenges to become an expert in corporate human resources, immigration policies/practices/procedures, and organizational leadership psychology. Some of her work and certifications include the Mindful Leader Talk Podcast, Certified Workplace Mindfulness Facilitator, Mindfulness-Based Stress Reduction, New York City and New York State M/WBE, Certified Success Principles Trainer, Strategic Intervention Trainer, and Visiting Scholar at the Rutgers Center for Minority Serving Institutions, the visiting scholars' program of the Samuel DeWitt Proctor Institute for Leadership, Equity, and Justice. Maria's diverse background should be of great value to organizations that realize that business, technology, and education have client engagements and operations that are highly global, international, and culturally diverse.

Darrell Norman Burrell is visiting scholar at Pellegrino Center for Clinical Bioethics at Georgetown University Medical Center and the Samuel DeWitt Proctor Institute for Leadership, Equity, and Justice at Rutgers University. Dr. Burrell has two doctorate degrees and five graduate degrees. Dr. Burrell received his first doctoral degree in Health Education from A.T. Still University in 2010. Dr. Burrell has a 2nd doctorate, a Doctor of Philosophy (Ph.D.) in Cybersecurity Leadership and Organizational Behavior at Capitol Technology University, Laurel, MD. He also has a 3rd Doctorate in Business Administration from Capitol Technology University. Dr. Burrell completed a Master of Arts in Interfaith Action at Claremont Lincoln University as a Global Peacemaker Fellow in 2016. He has an EdS (Education Specialist Post Master's Terminal Degree) in Higher Education Administration from The George Washington. He has two graduate degrees, one in Human Resources Management/Development and another in Organizational Management from National Louis University. Dr. Burrell has a graduate degree in Sales and Marketing Management from Prescott College. He has over 20 years of management, teaching, and training experience in academia, government, and private industry.

Nazlı Gülfem Gidener received her B.S. degree in Management from Bilkent University and her M.Sc. And PhD degrees from Dokuz Eylül Maritime Faculty. She has been conducting her academic research and lecturing activies at Dokuz Eylül University Maritime Faculty for over ten years. Her research interests are services marketing, business to business marketing, supply chain management and logistics.

Nisa Chand is an Assistant Professor in the Leadership Department at the University Canada West. She holds a Ph.D. in Human Resources Management from Cardiff University, UK. She earned her Master's degree in Management from Bristol University, UK. Dr. Chand is a chartered Professional in HR and has Obtained CPHR designation from Canada and SHRM-SCP from the USA. She teaches Organizational Behaviour, and CPHR courses at University Canada West. Besides her teaching career, Dr. Chand has also worked in several managerial roles within and outside of academia. Dr. Chand has recently edited her book 'International Human Resources', 2023 with Tophat Publishers, Toronto.

Songul Cinaroglu is an Associate Professor in the Department of Health Care Management at Hacettepe University, Turkey. She is a former visiting researcher at the Karlsruhe Institute of Technology (KIT)-Steinbuch Center for Computing (SCC)-Germany, the University of Hamburg-Center for Health

Economics (HCHE)-Germany, The University of Michigan-USA and the University of Alabama-USA. Her main research interest is health economics, policy, and outcomes research.

Margie Crowe is a retired United States Air Force lieutenant colonel, leadership & DEI consultant, published writer, higher education director and professor with broad experience in government and civilian programs, strategic planning, as well as published works focused on leadership practices affecting policies and programs in social justice, anti-racism, and DEI. She has consulted for the military, law enforcement, and private sector, as well as presented at academic and professional conferences on topics related to leadership, DEI, and digital equity and literacy. Margie holds a BA in political science, MS in international relations/national security, MA in special education, a postgraduate degree and a doctorate degree in educational leadership, and a training certificate in racial equity literacy facilitation.

Marlena Daryousef holds an MBA and Doctor of Management degree from Colorado Technical University with over ten years of business development and consulting across multiple business verticals. Marlena has a proven track record of helping both startups and established businesses improve their business optimization, stakeholder engagement, quality and risk management processes, and problem-solving.

Nazlı Gülfem Gidener received her B.S. degree in Management from Bilkent University and her M.Sc. And PhD degrees from Dokuz Eylül Maritime Faculty. She has been conducting her academic research and lecturing activies at Dokuz Eylül University Maritime Faculty for over ten years. Her research interests are services marketing, business to business marketing, supply chain management and logistics.

Allison Huff is an assistant professor in UArizona's Department of Family & Community Medicine, and focuses on technology to address complex disorders, particularly focusing on how technology impacts SDOH. Previously, she was a behavioral health clinician working with individuals with serious mental illnesses and substance use disorders. Dr. Huff is PI and Co-I on several NSF, HRSA, and industry sponsored grants and leads clinical trials and research programs. She also is a mentor for several underserved pre-professional health and pre-med students each summer and through the academic year. Dr. Huff's Doctor of Health Education is from A.T. Still University, her Master of Education in Instructional Technology is from University of Oklahoma, and her Bachelor's in Psychology is from University of West Florida.

Aleha Ingle is a highly experienced professional with a passion for developing and improving workplace culture. Aleha's career journey began with the United States Air Force where she gained valuable experience in key leadership skills. Beyond her professional accomplishments, Aleha is known for her thirst for knowledge. While in the Air Force, she managed to complete 6 Associate's degrees, 2 Bachelor's degrees, and 3 Master's degrees, all focusing on the concepts of leadership, management, and culture. Throughout her 21-year career, Aleha has demonstrated a keen ability to identify areas for improvement in workplace culture and implement effective strategies to bring about positive change. She is highly skilled in identifying major pain points that include failing processes and toxic managers and has a proven track record of success in creating positive, productive work environments. She brings a wealth of experience to any team and is an extremely valuable asset to any organization seeking to create a positive, productive work environment.

Laura A. Jones is a recognized risk management visionary and strategist known for her thought leadership. With a risk and quality systems management background, she blends niche skills that underscore program development and sustainability. She has designed and implemented risk management programs from concept to global execution for organizations across multiple industries in the areas of governance, risk, compliance, and quality systems management. With a broad range of experiences, she expertly integrates quality assurance principles and systems-thinking approaches with leading practices to optimize business processes. She has received industry-level awards for establishing best-in-class practices. Dr. Jones earned a Ph.D. in Product Management from Capital Technology University, M.S. in Quality Systems Management, B.S. in Management Studies, and a graduate certificate in Cybersecurity Policy. She completed executive education programs at Harvard Kennedy School (Leadership Decision Making), Carnegie Mellon University's Heinz College of Information Systems and Public Policy (Chief Risk Officer Program), and the University of California Berkeley's Haas School of Business (Artificial Intelligence: Business Strategies and Applications). Dr. Jones has earned several professional certifications in the areas of risk management, information systems, information technology, governance, and project management. Dr. Jones previously served as the Associate Dean of Student Academic Affairs for the National Graduate School of Quality Management. She is an Adjunct Professor at Capitol Technology University and an Adjunct Instructor at Carnegie Mellon University's Heinz College of Information Systems and Public Policy.

Judith-Jolie Mairs-Levy is an an accomplished professional with expertise in a mélange of disciplines, and wears many hats: She is a Cross-Cultural Epidemiologist, Integrative Public Health Scientist and Wellness Practitioner and Research Analyst, Health Sciences Expert, Medical Anthropologist and Technologist, Certified National Crisis Counsellor, Medical Writer, Doctoral Chair & Faculty, as well as a Cybersecurity and Health and Telehealth Educator. As such, she has developed and facilitated courses on related topics at the undergraduate and graduate levels. Dr. Mairs has published articles in several medical and public health related journals, and also serves as reviewer and editor for several medical and business management journals. She is incredibly involved in her community and carves time out from her busy schedule for volunteering to improve her community. She is committed to advancing diversity, equity, inclusion, and belonging (DEI&B), and is an executive board member for several organizational committees. Recently, Dr. Mairs was also appointed Commissioner by the Mayor, and now serves on the Montgomery County' Senior Citizens Council Commission. She also serves on the Montgomery County' City of Rockville's Community Caregiver Grant Program Application Review Panel. Such diverse combination of skills set and experience, affords her a unique and multi-faceted understanding of the management and daily operations of traditional health care as well as tele-health, hospital systems and related budget and finance, community grassroots programs geared towards prevention, and improvement in health and living conditions, successful and sustainable construction, LEED + Lean health infrastructure, health insurance system and operations, the need for cultural competency, sensitivity and diversity in health care and other settings, health care reform, and comparative healthcare systems. At St. Christopher's Children's Hospital in Philadelphia, she collaborated with Dr. Judith McColgan (M.D.) on the development of a critical curriculum for medical pediatric residents, geared to improving their knowledge, attitudes and how to detect, suspect, and report cases of child abuse, as they deliver care. She was integral to several successful grant proposals for implementation of community child-abuse outreach, and others for health and wellness programs. Dr. Mairs was a critical member of the National Dissemination Task Force on Best Practices for individuals living with HIV/AIDs; a multi-sited, HRSA-funded project with the Einstein School of Medicine and one of the Nation's 'Special Projects of National Significance' (SPNS). She is currently involved with a similar initiative with the City of Philadelphia, Department of Public Health. She was also instrumental in the implementation of the first mobile Syringe Exchange Program in New Jersey at the University of Medicine and Dentistry of New Jersey (UMDNJ); related logistical development of brochures for the Camden Syringe Access Program Blood Borne Pathogens Exposure Control Plan Template; and in 2007, she collaborated with The Department of Human Services (Division of Addiction Services) to develop the New Jersey Drug and Alcohol Abuse Treatment. Dr. Mairs is a recognized expert in a plethora of disciplines and fields of study and practice that explore topics including but not limited to HIV/AIDS, Alzheimer's, Autism, built environments and food security, the challenges of the marginalized and underserved, disease prevention and health literacy; access to care; community-based research; and social determinants of health. Her research interests are positioned within a framework of health promotion and disease prevention, wholistic care, health equity and cultural competency, education and employment opportunities for the poor, social justice, and global and population health. She was recently in Nairobi, Kenya where she was invited by a sustainability company that will be providing electricity, better sanitation, clean and safer drinking water, sustainable Agri-farming and employment opportunities, and not in the least, telemedicine/telehealth, to remote villages such as Kisumu, (dubbed the "Forgotten Mile"), where Dr. Mairs presented on telehealth at the company's opening event on March 1, 2023. Dr. Mairs is a graduate of the Universities of Toronto and York in Toronto, Canada, and Drexel, Benedictine, and A.T. Still School of Osteopathic Medicine, Dentistry & Health Sciences in the USA. Her professional qualifications include a Doctorate in Public Health Education and Research, a MPH with concentrations in Epidemiology and Health Promotion, and Disaster Preparedness and Mitigation, a combined double major honors degree in Medical Anthropology and Health Sciences, and a B.Sc. in Abnormal Psychology. Dr. Mairs is of Canadian citizenship, and currently resides in the state of Maryland, within the Washington, DC metropolitan area.

Grace McGrath is a class of 2020 graduate of the University at Albany. They were a Business Major and Education Minor. Throughout their three undergrad years, they learned so much through various internships, jobs, and outside community engagement. After college, they accepted a position at the Office of the Commissioner of Higher Education in Helena, Montana, as an AmeriCorps VISTA. Now, they currently work at Marymount University as a Graduate Admissions Coordinator. They also attend graduate school at Marymount University, pursuing their master's degree in Forensic and Legal Psychology. In their downtime, they do freelance copywriting and volunteer work. After getting their master's degree, they want to pursue being a federal higher education policy advisor focused on victims' advocacy.

Quatavia McLester is a PhD candidate in the Business and Industrial/Organizational Psychology program at The Chicago School of Professional Psychology – Washington, D.C. She holds a Master of Science in Industrial/Organizational Psychology from Austin Peay State University. She holds a Bachelor of Science in Psychology and a minor in Applied Statistics and Data Analysis from Kennesaw State University. She is currently serving as a Board Certified Behavior Analyst for a mental healthcare service provider. Her research interests include processes and outcomes of organizational development and change at the individual, group, and systems levels within the healthcare field, the effects of destructive leadership within organizations, and the use of healthcare technology in the mental healthcare space.

Nkholedzeni Sidney Netshakhuma is currently the Postdoctoral Research Fellowship with the University of Cape Town, Centre for African Studies effective from January 2023. His research interest includes Records Management, Archives management and Heritage management, and Political and liberation movements archives. He has published more than 60 articles and book chapters. He currently served as a Deputy Chairperson of the South Africa Higher Education Records and Archives Management Forum. He reviewed more than 60 research articles and book chapters. He obtained Ph.D. Information Science, Masters of Information Science, Post Diploma in Archival Studies, BTECH (Archival Studies at the University of South Africa (UNISA), BPHIL (Information Science at the University of Stellenbosch), BA (History and Political Studies at the University of Venda.

Elizabeth I. Omotoye, a clinical research coordinator at Advocate Health, is presently enrolled in her second year of study for a Ph.D. in business with a concentration in healthcare at the University of the Cumberlands. Omotoye graduated with a bachelor's degree in microbiology from Bowen University in Nigeria and a master's degree in public health from Louisiana State University Shreveport. Her interest is deeply rooted in elevating healthcare for underserved communities.

William Quisenberry resides in Lexington, KY, and has a diverse background that includes studying and practicing within the field of business administration, coordinating implementation projects for Fortune 500 clients, managing and overseeing vendors/suppliers, operations management, project management, marketing, research analysis, consulting, and teaching at the collegiate level. Dr. Quisenberry has collaborated and worked on projects with a variety of major organizations in the marketplace that include: Lexmark International, Halliburton, Branch Banking and Trust, The U.S. Department of Veterans Affairs, Wal-Mart, The U.S. Army Corps of Engineers, Accenture, IBM, Best Buy, Lockheed Martin, John Hancock Financial, and the World Trade Center Association. Dr. Quisenberry holds a Bachelor of Business Administration (BBA) degree in Finance, a BBA in Marketing, as well as a Master of Business Administration degree from Sullivan University's Graduate School of Business, and a Post-Graduate Certification in Forensic Accounting from Davenport University. He also possesses a Doctor of Business Administration (DBA) degree with a specialization in Leadership from Walden University.

Kevin Richardson currently serves as an Associate Professor of Business & Technology at Edward Waters University. He is a Certified Diversity Professional and a Certified Trainer. Dr. Richardson has two doctoral degrees and three graduate degrees. In 2016, he received his first doctorate degree in Operations and Quality Management Systems from The National Graduate School (Washington, DC). In 2021, Dr. Richardson received a Philosophy of Doctorate (Ph.D.) in Technology Management of Information Systems from Capitol Technology University (Laurel, MD). He completed a Master of Science in Natural Resources Economics and Corporate Sustainability at Virginia Tech University (Blacksburg, VA). Dr. Richardson has a graduate degree in Information Systems Engineering Management from Harrisburg Science & Technology University (Harrisburg, PA), and his third master's degree in Counseling Psychology from Springfield College (Charleston, SC). Dr. Richardson has over 25 years of management, teaching, and training trainer experience in academia, government, and private industries. His university teaching experience included teaching at Edward Waters University, Bethune Cookman University, Allen University, The National Graduate School of Quality Management, and Morris College.

Busra Saylan completed her master's degree from Hacettepe University, Faculty of Economics and Administrative Sciences, Department of Health Management. Her thesis is "Comparison of Health Professionals' Attitudes Towards Integrated Health Campuses (City Hospitals)" on city hospitals, which is one of the most up-to-date health policies in Turkey. She is currently pursuing a Ph.D. education at Hacettepe University. Her main research interests are big data, health informatics, and data analytics in integrated health campuses and health services.

Delores Springs served in healthcare, human services, and nonprofit leadership for over twenty years. Dr. Springs' compassion and drive for perfection are her strongest attributes. She specializes in designing competence building strategies and solutions in nonprofit, healthcare, government, academic, for-profit, and human service-oriented sectors. Dr. Springs has a doctorate in Strategic Leadership with a concentration in Strategic Foresight, a master's degree in Human Services and Executive leadership, and a bachelor's degree in Psychology. Along with her educational background, she holds specializes in Business and Leadership, Healthcare Organization Operations, Building Foundations in Global Markets, and in other areas that include Lean Six Sigma, Diversity & Inclusion, Project Management, and other certifications in business and leadership.

Kiran Thakur, CPHR, SHRP-SCP, is an Assistant Professor at University Canada West. She has over 12 years of teaching experience in higher education in Human Resource Management and Organization Behavior. Born and raised in India, Kiran received her Bachelor's in Science and Bachelor of Education from Himachal Pradesh University, Master's of Business Administration from Sikkim Manipal University and Ph.D. from I.K.G. Punjab Technical University, India. Dr. Kiran is an active researcher with publications in reputed academic journals. She has also participated in and presented her work at various international conferences. Her research interests are Work-Life Balance, Spirituality at the Workplace, employee engagement, leadership, Digital HR and Sustainability. In addition to her scholarly activities, Kiran is also regarded as a passionate and engaging teacher who encourages students to think critically and creatively. Kiran believes in creating a conducive learning environment where students feel free to share their experiences and thoughts to reflect upon the topic of discussion and can learn through active participation and peer learning. When not teaching or researching, Kiran enjoys exploring courses on Coursera, cooking, and spending time with family.

Kiana Zanganeh has significant research interests in women's health, health disparities, healthcare management, public health, management consulting, and medicine. She currently is a first year medical student at Lake Erie College of Osteopathic Medicine - Bradenton. She completed a Master of Science degree in Healthcare Management from the Florida Institute of Technology in December 2021 and completed her undergraduate degree in Biomedical Science in May 2020 from the Florida Institute of Technology where she was a student athlete.

Index

I

L

M

N

O

P

R

S

T

U

V

W

www.ingramcontent.com/pod-product-compliance
Lightning Source LLC
LaVergne TN
LVHW060420300926
849162LV00006B/1483